V&R

Novum Testamentum et Orbis Antiquus

Series Archaeologica 8a

In collaboration with the foundation "Bibel und Orient" of the University of Fribourg/Switzerland
Edited by Martin Ebner (Bonn), Peter Lampe (Heidelberg), Stefan Schreiber (Augsburg),
and Jürgen Zangenberg (Leiden)

Khirbet Qumrân and Aïn Feshkha

IV A

Qumran Cave 11Q
Archaeology and New Scroll Fragments

Edited by

Jean-Baptiste Humbert o.p. (EBAF)

Editor of the Excavations by Roland de Vaux at Qumran

Marcello Fidanzio (ISCAB FTL)

Director of the Qumran Caves Publication Project

École biblique et archéologique française de Jérusalem

Istituto di Cultura e Archeologia delle Terre Bibliche - Facoltà di Teologia di Lugano

VANDENHOECK & RUPRECHT GÖTTINGEN

Bibliographic information published by the Deutsche Nationalbibliothek
The Deutsche Nationalbibliothek lists this publication in the Deutsche Nationalbibliografie;
detailed bibliographic data available online: http://dnb.d-nb.de.

Typesetting: Luigi Caiafa
Printed and bound: Hubert & Co. BuchPartner, Göttingen
Printed in the EU

Vandenhoeck & Ruprecht Publishers | www.vandenhoeck-ruprecht-verlage.com
ISSN 1420-4622
ISBN 978-3-525-56469-1

Qumran Cave 11Q, March 2017 (Photo by Giorgio Skory)

Contents

Foreword – *Florentino García Martínez* xi

Contributors xiii
Abbreviations xv
Lists of Figures, Plates, and Tables xvii

Introduction – *Marcello Fidanzio* 1

Chapter One
Archival Sources and First Publications on the Excavations of Cave 11Q
Marcello Fidanzio (ed.) 11

Chapter Two
La grotte 11Q : morphologie, investigation, mobilier et function
Jean-Baptiste Humbert 45
Appendix A
La grotte 11Q : cadre géologique
Gérard Massonnat 67
Appendix B
Notes from the 2017 Excavation of Cave 11Q
Marcello Fidanzio, Marco De Pietri, Alessandro Maifredi, and Benedetta Torrini 71

Chapter Three
Description de la poterie recueillie dans la grotte 11Q
Jean-Baptiste Humbert, Marius Burdajewicz, and Frédéric Guyot 87

Chapter Four
Textiles and Strings from Cave 11Q
Naama Sukenik, Orit Shamir, Mireille Bélis, and Mauro Rottoli 97
Appendix A
Linen Textile Gr11Q75: A Scroll Wrapper from Cave 11Q
Marcello Fidanzio and Naama Sukenik 119
Appendix B
Analysis of the Blue Color from Textile Gr11Q31a
Naama Sukenik, Alexander Varvak, Zohar Amar, and Iluz David 123

Chapter Five
Organic Materials from Cave 11Q
A. Leather, Basketry, Ropes, Wood and Seeds
Joan E. Taylor and Naama Sukenik 125
B. Gr11Q9/1 and 2
Joan E. Taylor 135
Appendix
The Radiocarbon Dating of String from Gr11Q9/1 and 2
Johannes van der Plicht 143

Chapter Six
The Radiocarbon Dates of Samples from Qumran Cave 11Q
Joan E. Taylor, Johannes van der Plicht, Kaare Lund Rasmussen, Naama Sukenik, Orit Shamir, and Mireille Bélis 147

Chapter Seven
Metal and Stone Artefacts
Dennis Mizzi and Annalisa Faggi 157

Chapter Eight
The Preservation and Digitization of the Manuscripts Attributed to Cave 11Q
Pnina Shor, Oren Ableman, Orit Rosengarten, Beatriz Riestra, Helena Libman, Tanya Bitler, Tanya Treiger, Ashlyn Oprescu ... 177
Appendix
Manuscripts from Cave 11Q: Photo Collections by Hunzinger and Allegro
Marcello Fidanzio (ed.) 191

Chapter Nine
The Retrieval of Unknown Manuscript Fragments from Cave 11Q
Marcello Fidanzio 199

Chapter Ten
Nouveaux menus fragments de la Grotte 11Q (P1344, P1345 et P1038B)
Émile Puech 203

Chapter Eleven
Preliminary Publication of Cave 11Q Fragments from Box 1032A
Oren Ableman 231
Appendix
Nouveaux menus fragments de la Grotte 11Q (boîte 1032A/1)
Émile Puech 245

Chapter Twelve
Revisiting the Manuscripts and Fragments from Qumran Cave 11Q
Eibert Tigchelaar 249

Bibliography 263
Index of Materials from Cave 11Q 281
Index of Modern Authors 285
Index of Sites and Place Names 287

Foreword

Florentino García Martínez

When I was in Jerusalem finalizing the preparation of the publication of the Dutch share of manuscripts from Cave 11Q (published in 1998, DJD 23), I asked Jean-Baptiste Humbert, the archaeologist in charge of Roland de Vaux's excavations at Qumran, if it could be possible to include in the volume the final report on the archeological excavation of the cave prepared by de Vaux. I was assuming that de Vaux has, in fact, completed such a report, because he wrote in 1962, referring to Cave 11Q: "Le rapport détaillé sur la fouille que nous avons faite après cette découverte aura sa place normale en tête de la publication des textes qui proviennent de cette grotte" (DJD 3, 4 n.2). Obviously a "rapport détaillé" would have been more than the two pages de Vaux dedicated to Cave 11Q in the "rapport préliminaire" on the Revue Biblique (*RB* 63 [1956] 573-4). However, Humbert told me that there was no such final report ready for publication, and that due to other commitments it would take a long time to prepare such a document. To avoid delaying any further the already long overdue publication of the texts, I decided to go ahead with the issuing of a volume that did not include the promised publication of the cave excavation.

In retrospect, I think it was a good decision, which somehow has helped to shape the content of this book, making it possible to showcase the progress achieved in archeology and in the analysis of the different materials sourced from Cave 11Q over the past fifty years.

De Vaux's excavation was followed several years later, in 1988, by the excavation carried out by Joseph Patrich, and more recently, in 2017, by a new excavation carried out by Marcello Fidanzio and Dan Bahat. Both excavations have been duly published and their main results are summarized in this volume, complementing and adding new elements to de Vaux's excavation. In this way, this book not only offers the reader all the extant materials on de Vaux's excavation (forming in this way a "rapport détaillé" of the 1956 excavation), but also all the relevant archaeological data and analysis which may lead to an understanding of the cave in the Qumran period as a repository for manuscripts rather than as a sectarian residence as assumed by de Vaux (DJD 3, 34; ADSS, 51), and asserted by me based on his authority (STDJ 90, 206-8).

Due to the substantial progress made on the study of the textiles and organic materials, new dating obtained by radiocarbon analysis, and the digitization and systematic imaging of scroll fragments with new techniques, this book also offers to the reader a plethora of new insights that were not possible either in de Vaux's time or at the time of the preparation of DJD 23.

The study of the textiles includes those found in de Vaux's excavation, and also those found in the excavations by Patrich and Fidanzio; all of them are examined by digital optical microscope (Dino-Lite). The blue color from one of them has been identified as Indigo and Indurubin using a High Performance Liquid Chromatography method – techniques only recently available. New radiocarbon dating of linen textiles from Cave 11Q, including the wrapper of the Temple Scroll in the Schøyen Collection (run at the Center for Isotope Research, Groningen University in 2015 and 2016) shows that, though the textiles correlate with the occupation of Qumran, they were manufactured over an extended period of time, which would counteract the interpretation of Cave 11Q being exclusively a "young cave" as indicated by the paleography of the manuscripts.

The analysis of the organic materials performed in 2004 with new radiocarbon dating revealed that Cave 11Q was visited several times: a wooden object, clearly man-made, was tested twice, and dated to some time around the 10th century CE, and as such aligned with the date provided by a piece of cotton from Cave 11Q. Two items identified in de Vaux's excavation as possibly made of leather with a cord are now interpreted as "knot amulets" involving animal body parts: the radiocarbon dating carried out in 2015 and 2016 placed its deposition in Cave 11Q in the 18th or 19th century. This clearly show that Cave 11Q was accessible and was occasionally visited after the deposition of the manuscripts.

The digitization and systematic imaging of the scroll fragments began in 2011. The uploading of the multispectral images obtained to the Leon Levy Dead Sea Scrolls Digital Library, together with new photographic tools that make it possible to read the text on different layers of wads of fragments, have enabled the inclusion in this volume of new fragments from Cave 11Q not published in DJD 23, and have led to the correction of some of the readings of the DJD edition based on the PAM photographs available at that time.

The new minute leather and tiny papyri fragments published here by Emile Puech were discovered in 2015 by, respectively, Mireille Bélis, when studying the textiles from Cave 11Q, and by Mauro Rottoli when examining a box of organic material selected by Oren Ableman. The new leather fragments published by Ableman are a selection of the materials found in box 1032A with debris from Cave 11Q. In 1996, E. Tigchelaar examined this and other boxes with materials from Cave 11Q (*RdQ* 18/70 [1998] 326-7 n.5) containing, among other things, hundreds of tiny unphotographed fragments; Tigchelaar selected the fragments and the wads on which writing was visible to the naked eye to undergo infra-red photography, and these photographs are included in DJD 23. The ongoing project of the Israel Antiquities Authority (IAA) to catalog and process all these fragments has allowed Ableman to examine some of the them with a Dino-Lite digital microscope and put them in a new plate where the images have been captured with the multispectral imaging system. A few have been selected for publication here.

Eibert Tigchelaar offers in this volume an evaluation of all manuscripts material attributed, rightly or wrongly, to Cave 11Q, concluding that out of all the fragments that have already been published after DJD 23, only one can be assigned to Cave 11Q with certainty – the Vatican Paleo-Hebrew fragment published by Giancarlo Lacerenza, which belongs to 11Q22. After reviewing the major publications of Cave 11Q manuscripts, Tigchelaar corrects some occasionally erroneous assignations to manuscripts or placements of fragments appearing in DJD 23 and enhances several readings of that publication thanks to the high-quality IAA photographs now available. He also contributes to the publication of new fragments. Of the remaining as yet unpublished fragments of 11Q19, the Temple Scroll, published by Yigael Yadin, Tigchelaar, in an Appendix to his contribution, offers readings of the new plates of the "Cigar Box" and of both the photographs taken by Ira Rabin in 2000 from "LXII (15)" as well as the new IAA plates X78-X79.

This volume clearly improves our understanding of Cave 11Q in relation to what was possible with the summary reports on the archaeology published by de Vaux, but it also enhances our knowledge of the texts found in the Cave. Of course, we will never know what de Vaux would have told us in a final report. Nevertheless, one thing is entirely clear: the way archaeology is done these days and the way in which the results of the excavations are presented are very different than in de Vaux's time. The editing of the texts also differs. The availability of new technologies has modified the way we look at the remains uncovered and also how we present them. The new imaging and digitizing of the scroll fragments have enhanced the possibility of editing them correctly. But one element that the present volume makes fully clear is that today, presenting archaeology and texts is a large, collaborative exercise: no less than 30 different authors from several institutions in various countries have contributed the chapters of the book, all for the benefit of the reader.

Contributors

Oren Ableman, *Israel Antiquities Authority*
Zohar Amar, *Bar-Ilan University*
Mireille Bélis, *chercheur associé École Biblique et Archéologique Française*
Tanya Bitler, *Israel Antiquities Authority*
Marius Burdajewicz, *University of Warsaw*
Iluz David, *Bar-Ilan University*
Marco De Pietri, *research fellow Istituto di Cultura e Archeologia delle Terre Bibliche – Facoltà di Teologia di Lugano*
Annalisa Faggi, *indipendent scholar*
Marcello Fidanzio, *Istituto di Cultura e Archeologia delle Terre Bibliche – Facoltà di Teologia di Lugano*
Florentino García Martínez, *KU Leuven and University of Groningen*
Frédéric Guyot, *Institut Français d'Archeologie Orientale*
Jean-Baptiste Humbert, *École Biblique et Archéologique Française*
Helena Libman, *Israel Antiquities Authority*
Alessandro Maifredi, *Centro Studi Sotterranei*
Gérard Massonnat, *chercheur associé École Biblique et Archéologique Française*
Dennis Mizzi, *University of Malta*
Ashlyn Oprescu, *Israel Antiquities Authority*
Johannes van der Plicht, *University of Groningen*
Émile Puech, *Centre National de la Recherche Scientifique and École Biblique et Archéologique Française*
Kaare Lund Rasmussen, *University of Southern Denmark*
Beatriz Riestra, *Israel Antiquities Authority*
Orit Rosengarten, *Israel Antiquities Authority*
Mauro Rottoli, *Musei Civici di Como and Università degli Studi di Trento*
Orit Shamir, *Israel Antiquities Authority*
Pnina Shor, *Israel Antiquities Authority*
Naama Sukenik, *Israel Antiquities Authority*
Joan E.Taylor, *King's College London*
Eibert Tigchelaar, *KU Leuven*
Benedetta Torrini, *research fellow Istituto di Cultura e Archeologia delle Terre Bibliche – Facoltà di Teologia di Lugano*
Tanya Treiger, *Israel Antiquities Authority*
Alexander Varvak, *Bar-Ilan University*

Abbreviations

ANGSBA	Annual of the Nelson Glueck School of Biblical Archaeology
ANYAS	Annals of the New York Academy of Sciences
AASOR	Annual of the American Schools of Oriental Research
ATN	*Archaeological Textiles Newsletter*
ATS	Ancient Textiles Series
ATR	*Archaeological Textiles Review*
BAIAS	Bulletin of the Anglo-Israel Archaeological Society
BASOR	*Bulletin of the American Schools of Oriental Research*
BETL	Bibliotheca Ephemeridum Theologicarum Lovaniensium
BKAT	Biblischer Kommentar Altes Testament
CAL News	*Comprehensive Aramaic Lexicon Newsletter*
COMSt Bull	*Comparative Oriental Manuscript Studies Bulletin*
CRFJ	Centre de recherche français à Jérusalem
CSCO	Corpus Scriptorum Christianorum Orientalium
DHA	*Dyes in History and Archaeology*
DJD	Discoveries in the Judean Desert
DSD	*Dead Sea Discoveries*
EI	*Eretz Israel*
HA-ESI	*Hadashot Arkheologiyot - Excavations and Surveys in Israel*
HBM	Hebrew Bible Monographs
HdO	Handbook of Oriental Studies
Hen	*Henoch*
HSS	Harvard Semitic Studies
HUCA	*Hebrew Union College Annual*
IAA Reports	Israel Antiquities Authority Reports
ICOM-CC	International Council of Museums - Committee for Conservation
IEJ	*Israel Exploration Journal*
ISCAB.SA	Istituto di Cultura e Archeologia delle Terre Bibliche. Serie Archeologica
JASR	*Journal of Archaeological Science: Reports*
JEMAHS	*Journal of Eastern Mediterranean Archaeology and Heritage Studies*
JRASS	Journal of Roman Archaeology. Supplementary Series

JSJ	*Journal for the Study of Judaism*
JSJSup	Journal for the Study of Judaism. Supplement Series
JSRS	*Judea and Samaria Research Studies*
LSS	Levant Supplementary Series
LSTS	Library of Second Temple Studies
MdB	*Le Monde de la Bible*
MSSMNIA	Monograph Series of the Sonia and Marco Nadler Institute of Archaeology
NIM B	*Nuclear Instruments and Methods in Physics Research Section B Beam Interactions with Materials and Atoms*
NTOA.SA	Novum Testamentum et Orbis Antiquus. Series Archaeologica
OIP	Oriental Institute Publications
PACT	Journal of the European Study Group on Physical, Chemical and Mathematical Techniques Applied to Archaeology
PEQ	*Palestine Exploration Quarterly*
PMB	Publications of Museum of the Bible
RB	*Revue Biblique*
RdQ	*Revue de Qumrân*
SBL RBS	Society of Biblical Literature. Resources for Biblical Studies
SBT	Studies in Biblical Theology
STDJ	Studies on the Texts of the Desert of Judah
RTLu	*Rivista Teologica di Lugano*
VHA	*Vegetation History and Archaeobotany*
VT	*Vetus Testamentum*
VTSup	Vetus Testamentum Supplements

Lists of Figures, Plates, and Tables

List of Figures

Introduction
Map of the area, satellite image: Khirbet Qumran, Cave 1Q, and Cave 11Q ..... p. 2
March 1956: De Vaux, Rousée and Delprat outside Cave 11Q ..... p. 3
The Palestine Archaeological Museum / Rockefeller Museum ..... p. 3
De Vaux's field notes: Plan of Cave 5Q ..... p. 6
DJD 6 (pp. 18-19): Pottery from Cave 4Q ..... p. 6

Chapter One
The field notes and the excavation diary ..... p. 12
The excavation diary, 21/2 - 24/2/1956 ..... p. 13
The excavation diary, 25/2 - 29/2/1956 ..... p. 13
The excavation diary, 1/3 - 13/3/1956 ..... p. 14
The excavation diary, 13/3 - 14/3/1956 ..... p. 14
The excavation diary, 14/3 - 22/3/1956 ..... p. 15
The field notes ..... p. 15
The inventory, hardbound book, 72 ..... p. 20
The inventory, hardbound book, 73 ..... p. 20
The inventory, hardbound book, 74 ..... p. 21
The inventory, hardbound book, 75 ..... p. 21
Patrich's plan and cross-section ..... p. 24
De Vaux's photo album, 553 ..... p. 25
De Vaux's photo album, 554 ..... p. 26
De Vaux's photo album, 555 ..... p. 26
De Vaux's photo album, 556 ..... p. 27
De Vaux's photo album, 557 ..... p. 27
De Vaux's photo album, 558 ..... p. 28
De Vaux's photo album, 560 ..... p. 28
Location of Cave 11Q: Towards the North (de Vaux 15.026) ..... p. 29
Location of Cave 11Q: Towards the North (de Vaux 15.020) ..... p. 29
Location of Cave 11Q: Closer view (de Vaux 15.021) ..... p. 30
Cave 11Q (de Vaux 14.401) ..... p. 30

Cave 11Q: Towards the North (de Vaux 15.023) ... p. 31
Cave 11Q: Towards the North-West (de Vaux 15.022) ... p. 31
Entrance to Cave 11Q (de Vaux 14.402) ... p. 32
Inside Cave 11Q: view from the entrance (de Vaux 14.403) ... p. 32
Cave 11Q: view from the entrance towards the South-East (PAM 42.104) ... p. 33
Cave 11Q: towards the North (PAM 42.103) ... p. 33
Mattock Gr11Q6 (PAM 42.451) ... p. 34
Mattock Gr11Q6 (PAM 42.449) ... p. 34
Metal and stone artefacts from Cave 11Q (PAM 43.734) ... p. 35
Pottery from Cave 11Q (PAM 43.736) ... p. 35
Cave 11Q: View from inside towards the entrance (de Vaux 15.028) ... p. 36
Cave 11Q: View from the entrance, towards the South-East (de Vaux 15.027) ... p. 36
Sifting of the soil outside Cave 11Q (de Vaux 15.024) ... p. 37
Delprat and Starcky in the entrance chamber (S. Weiss) ... p. 38
Rousée and Delprat in the entrance chamber (S. Weiss) ... p. 38
Rousée at the entrance of the cave (S. Weiss) ... p. 39
Cave 11Q: The entrance (EBAF Archive) ... p. 39
The cliff above Cave 11Q (EBAF Archive) ... p. 40
Starcky in the entrance chamber (EBAF Archive) ... p. 41
Rousée, de Vaux, Delprat, and Bedouin workers at Cave 11Q (EBAF Archive) ... p. 41
Rousée and de Vaux at Cave 11Q, towards the excavation camp (EBAF Archive) ... p. 42
The excavation camp (EBAF Archive) ... p. 42
The entrance of Cave 11Q (Estate John Allegro) ... p. 43
John and Joan Allegro at the entrance of Cave 11Q (Estate John Allegro) ... p. 44
The entrance of Cave 11Q towards the Dead Sea (Estate John Allegro) ... p. 44

Chapter Two
Location of Caves 1Q, 2Q, and 11Q ... p. 46
General view of the cliff of Qumran, with the location of Cave 11Q ... p. 47
Entrance of Cave 11Q: Present time ... p. 47
Cave 11Q: Chamber (b) after looting ... p. 48
Entrance of Cave 11Q ... p. 49
Plan and section of Cave 11Q ... p. 50
Cave 11Q: Masonry, South of chamber (b), towards chamber (d), 1956 ... p. 51
Cave 11Q: The entrance area after the unblocking of the opening ... p. 53
Cave 11Q: Debris after the unblocking of the entrance ... p. 53
View of the entrance to Cave 11Q, from outside, 1956 ... p. 54
View of the entrance to Cave 11Q, from inside, 1956 ... p. 54
Cave 11Q: Chamber (b), 1956 ... p. 55
Cave 11Q: The “entrance” of the “inner chamber” from chamber (b) ... p. 56
Cave 11Q: General view of chamber (c): the “inner chamber” ... p. 56
Cave 11Q: View of the chamber (b) from chamber (c) ... p. 58
Cave 11Q: Lower part of the sediment in chamber (b), blown-up detail ... p. 58
Cave 11Q: Interpretation of the stratigraphy of the sediment in chamber (b) ... p. 58
Reconstruction of the stratigraphy at the entrance of Cave 11Q ... p. 60

Cave 11Q: The excavators at the entrance of chamber (c), 1956 ..... p. 60
Interpretation of the stratigraphy at the entrance of Cave 11Q, blown-up detail ..... p. 61
Cave 11Q: Remains of the partition between chamber (b) and (c), 1956 blown-up detail ..... p. 64

Chapter Two. Appendix A
Entrance of Cave 11Q: Geology ..... p. 68
Limestone to the North of the entrance of Cave 11Q ..... p. 68
The cliff: Geology ..... p. 69
Fracture at the entrance of Cave 11Q ..... p. 69
Fracture on the ceiling at the entrance of Cave 11Q ..... p. 70
Karstique canal inside Cave 11Q ..... p. 70
Natural "pillar" dividing the entrance chamber from the inner chamber ..... p. 70

Chapter Two. Appendix B
Cave 11Q: Plan ..... p. 72
Cave 11Q: Entrance area. Blocks A and B ..... p. 74
Cave 11Q: Entrance area. Aerial photo, with detail of the cliff ..... p. 74
Cave 11Q: Entrance area, from above the cave ..... p. 75
Area above Cave 11Q ..... p. 75
Cave 11Q: Section. Way in for flowing of the water..... p. 76
Area around Cave 11Q: Digital Terrain Model ..... p. 76
Area around Cave 11Q: Digital Terrain Model showing the basin and the water flow ..... p. 76
Cave 11Q: Accumulation of fine material behind Block A ..... p. 77
Cave 11Q: Breach behind Block A, 3D rendering ..... p. 77
Traces of sediment still visible along the eastern side, inside Cave 11Q ..... p. 78
Cave 11Q: 2 March 1956 ..... p. 79
Cave 11Q: Accumulation of soil along the western side, inside the entrance chamber ..... p. 80
Cave 11Q: Sounding in Operation B ..... p. 80
Cave 11Q: Sounding in Operation B, western section ..... p. 81
Cave 11Q: So-called "arch" ..... p. 82
Cave 11Q: So-called "pillar" ..... p. 83
Cave 11Q: Wedge behind the "arch", left of the "pillar" ..... p. 83
Stone structures (A-C) inside Cave 11Q: 3 March 1956 ..... p. 84
Cave 11Q: Dry-stone wall, 1956 ..... p. 84
Cave 11Q: Sketch of the passage and the upper chamber ..... p. 85
Cave 11Q: The upper chamber, South to North. ..... p. 85
Cave 11Q: The upper chamber, North to South ..... p. 86

Chapter Four
Textile Gr11Q36, warp-faced weaving (Dino-Lite) ..... p. 100
Textile Gr11Q80, balanced weaving (Dino-Lite) ..... p. 100
Textile Gr11Q29, basket weaving ..... p. 100
Textile Gr11Q50, half-basket weaving ..... p. 100
Textile Gr11Q76 with no identical width threads (Dino-Lite) ..... p. 100
Textile Gr11Q33, repp starting border (Dino-Lite) ..... p. 100

Textile Gr11Q39 with closing cord (Dino-Lite) ..... p. 101
Textile Gr11Q121 with crowded selvedge (Dino-Lite) ..... p. 101
Textile Gr11Q78 with reinforced selvedge (Dino-Lite) ..... p. 101
Textile Gr11Q26, rolled and whipped hem ..... p. 102
Textile Gr11Q75, single thread sewn hem (Dino-Lite) ..... p. 102
Textile Gr11Q58 with patch ..... p. 102
Textile Gr11Q132 with darning (Dino-Lite) ..... p. 103
Textile Gr11Q124 with knot (Dino-Lite) ..... p. 103
Textile Gr11Q31 with blue decoration ..... p. 104
Textile Gr11Q107 with blue decoration (Dino-Lite) ..... p. 104
Textile Gr11Q75 ..... p. 105
Detail of textile Gr11Q75 with weaving faults (Dino-Lite) ..... p. 114
Textile fragment adherent to a scroll fragment ..... p. 115
Detail of textile Gr11Q46b with tied corner (Dino-Lite) ..... p. 116

Chapter Four. Appendix A
Textile Gr11Q75 ..... p. 120
Gr11Q75 (Dino-Lite) ..... p. 120
Gr11Q75: Knot (Dino-Lite) ..... p. 121
Gr11Q75: String (Dino-Lite) ..... p. 121
Gr11Q75: Final part of the string ..... p. 121
Gr11Q75: String function and diameter measure ..... p. 121
Gr11Q75: The system of scroll wrapping ..... p. 122
DJD 1 (Plate I): Remains of a scroll in its linen wrapper ..... p. 122

Chapter Five A
Sandal 96-9105 from the Cave of the Letters ..... p. 126
Two sandals of the Early Roman period from the Dead Sea area ..... p. 126
Basket from the Cave of the Letters ..... p. 127

Chapter Five B
De Vaux's inventory: Card Gr11Q9 ..... p. 136
Gr11Q9/1: Back and front showing string puncturing artefact and knots ..... p. 137
Gr11Q9/1: X-Ray ..... p. 137
Gr11Q9/1: CT scans of object ..... p. 138
Gr11Q9/1: Magnification showing congealed substance or connecting tube between string knots ..... p. 138
Gr11Q9/2: Magnification showing layers of organic material ..... p. 139
Detail of photograph showing an item found during 11Q excavations, similar in shape to Gr11Q9/1 ... p. 141

Chapter Eight
11Q4 Ezek, PAM 43.742 ..... p. 178
Removal of pressure sensitive tape from a fragment ..... p. 179
11Q5 Ps^a, Plate 975 ..... p. 180
11Q1 paleoLev^a, Plate 1039/1 ..... p. 180

11Q11 apocrPs, Plate 61 .... p. 181
11Q10 tgJob, Plates 631-624-634 .... p. 181
11Q17 ShirShabb, Plate 609 .... p. 182
11Q18 NJ, Plate 570 .... p. 182
11Q14 Sefer ha-Milhamah, Plate 607/1 .... p. 182
11Q20 T[b], Plate 580 .... p. 183
11Q7 Ps[c], Plate 606/1 .... p. 184
11Q13 Melch, Plate 579 .... p. 184
Unidentified scrolls fragments from Cave 11Q in Box 1032A .... p. 185
Textile still attached to 11Q24, P567-Fg010-R -D20052014-color .... p. 185
PAM negatives with fragments from various manuscripts, PAM 44.114, PAM 42.177 .... p. 186
DJD 23, Plate XXXV, a virtual plate with fragments of the same manuscripts from different Plates and PAMs .... p. 186
The MegaVision Imaging System .... p. 186
Plate 697 .... p. 189

Chapter Eight. Appendix
Manuscripts from Cave 11Q: 5/09/1957, photos by John Marco Allegro .... pp. 192-195
Manuscripts from Cave 11Q: 5/09/1957, photos by Claus-Hunno Hunzinger .... pp. 196-197

Chapter Nine
The cigar box "Grotte 11Q du 4/3" .... p. 200
A few of the tiny leather fragments retrieved in the cigar box "Grotte 11Q du 4/3" .... p. 200
The tiny papyrus fragments stored in box 1038B .... p. 201
The tiny fragments stored in box 1032A .... p. 202

Chapter Ten
P1344 - Fragm. 9 = 11Q22 8 .... p. 205
P1344 - Fragm. 12 = 11Q1 - 11QpaléoLv (frg.) .... p. 209
P1345 - Fragm. 44 .... p. 210
P1345 - Fragm. 7 = 11Q2 10 - 11QLv[b] 10 .... p. 210
P1345 - Fragms. 34A = 11Q2 11 - 11QLv[b] 11, Lv 18,11; 34B = 11Q23 4 - 11QcryptLv[f] 4 .... p. 211
P1345 - Fragm. 36 = 11Q2 12(?) - 11QLv[b] 12(?) .... p. 212
P1344 - Fragm. 1 = 11Q14 5 - 11QSefer ha-Milḥamah 5 .... p. 212
P1344 - Fragm. 2 = 11QRT[a] - 11Q19 .... p. 213
P1344 - Fragm. 3 (= 11Q7 - 11QPs[c]) .... p. 213
P1344 - Fragm. 4 .... p. 214
P1344 - Fragm. 5 .... p. 214
P1344 - Fragm. 7 = 11Q20 44 - 11QT[b] 44 .... p. 214
P1344 - Fragm. 8 .... p. 215
P1344 - Fragm. 10 .... p. 216
P1344 - Fragm. 11 .... p. 216
P1345 - Fragm. 6 .... p. 216
P1345 - Fragm. 8 (= 11Q20 - RT[b]) .... p. 217
P1345 - Fragm. 9 .... p. 217

P1345 - Fragm. 14 = 11Q20 45 - 11QRT[b] 45 .... p. 217
P1345 - Fragm. 17 (= 11Q20 - 11QRT[b]) .... p. 218
P1345 - Fragm. 20 .... p. 218
P1345 - Fragm. 24 = 11Q20 46 - 11QRT[b] 46 - XIV 17-18 .... p. 218
P1345 - Fragm. 28 .... p. 219
P1345 - Fragm. 32 .... p. 219
P1345 - Fragm. 33 .... p. 220
P1345 - Fragm. 38 .... p. 220
P1345 - Fragm. 43 .... p. 221
P1345 - Fragm. 49 .... p. 221
P1345 - Fragm. 51 .... p. 221
P1345 - Fragm. 54 .... p. 221
P1345 - Fragm. 58 = 11Q6/7 - 11QPs[b/c](?) .... p. 222
P1038B - Fragm. 3 = 11QpapLv 14,25-27 .... p. 224
P1038B - Fragm. 5 = 11Q28 3 - 11QpapJg 12,6-7 (?) .... p. 226
P1038B - Fragm. 9 = 11Q28 4 - 11QpapJg 13,23-24 (?) .... p. 226
P1038B - Fragm. 4 = 11Q28 5 - 11QpapJg 16,4-5 .... p. 226
P1038B - Fragm. 6 = 11Q28 6 - 11QpapJg 18,5 (?) .... p. 228
P1038B - Fragm. 7 = 11Q28 7 - 11QpapJg 18,27 .... p. 228
P1038B - Fragm. 8 = 11Q28 8 - 11QpapJg (?) ou 11QpapLv (?) .... p. 228

Chapter Eleven

The box 1032A .... p. 232
1032A Fragm.1 .... p. 234
1032A Fragm. 5 .... p. 234
1032A Fragm. 8 – 11Q8, Ps 37:3-4 .... p. 236
1032A Fragm. 8, tilted view .... p. 236
11Q8 Fragm. 5, Ps 36:13-37:4 (5?) .... p. 236
1032A Fragm. 24 – 11Q11(?) .... p. 237
1032A Fragm. 37 .... p. 238
1032A Fragm. 41 – Lev 13:51-52, 11Q2 (?) .... p. 238
1032A Fragm. 47 – 11Q17 .... p. 239
1032A Fragm. 48 .... p. 240
1032A Fragm. 55 – Deut 19:5 (?), 11Q3 (?) .... p. 241
1032A Fragm. 62 – Jubilees 5:19 (?), 11Q12 (?) .... p. 241
1032A Fragm. 68 – 11Q21, Temple Scroll 22:13-14 .... p. 242
1032A Fragm. 81 – 11Q5, Ps 147:1-2 .... p. 242

Chapter Twelve

The LII Photograph .... p. 260
IAA PX78-X79 frags. 4, 8, and 9 joined .... p. 260

List of Plates

Chapter Three
Jar and lid "Kando" .... p. 93
Roman pottery from Cave 11Q .... p. 94
Iron Age pottery from Cave 11Q .... p. 95
Chalcolithic pottery from Cave 11Q .... p. 96

Chapter Seven
Gr11Q2 Knife blade .... p. 159
Gr11Q3 Loop attachment (?) .... p. 162
Gr11Q4 File/Chisel .... p. 164
Gr11Q6 Mattock .... p. 166
Gr11Q6 Mattock .... p. 167
Gr11Q10 Awl/Punch (?) .... p. 170
Gr11Q11 Key .... p. 172
Gr11Q12 Bead .... p. 174

Chapter Ten
Box P1344 .... p. 204
Box P1345 .... p. 204
Box P1038B .... p. 225

Chapter Eleven
Fragments from Box 1032A/1 .... p. 233

List of Tables

Introduction
Items registration systems .... p. 10

Chapter Four
Diagram of the material fibers in Cave 11Q textiles .... p. 99
Linen textiles from Cave 11Q .... pp. 106-111
Cotton textiles from Cave 11Q .... p. 112
Strings from Cave 11Q .... p. 112

Chapter Five A
List of organic objects from Cave 11Q .... p. 130

Chapter Five B
Radiocarbon Results of Gr11Q9/1 and 2 .... p. 139

Chapter Five B. Appendix

Calibration curve showing averaged results on Gr11Q9/1 and Gr11Q9/2 linen thread .... p. 145
Calibration curve for results of re-testing Gr11Q-9/1 .... p. 145

Chapter Six

Calibration curve for 11Q linen string, Gr11Q198 .... p. 150
The Radiocarbon Dates of Samples from Qumran Cave 11Q .... p. 151
Calibration curve for 11Q linen, Gr11Q119 .... p. 152
Calibration curve for 11Q linen, Gr11Q132 .... p. 152
Calibration curve for 11Q linen, Gr11Q107 .... p. 152
Calibration curve for 11Q linen, Gr11Q76 .... p. 152
Calibration curve for 11Q linen Gr11Q101 .... p. 152
Calibration curve for Christmas Cave linen, IAA 585785 .... p. 152
Calibration curve for the Temple Scroll Wrapper (MS 5095/1) .... p. 152

Introduction

Marcello FIDANZIO

Cave 11Q was discovered in early 1956. It is the only cave that has remained unpublished out of all those excavated under the direction of Roland de Vaux in the vicinity of Qumran. This volume presents the final report on the excavations of the Cave, bringing to completion the first publication about the caves of the Qumran area. At the same time, this is also the first volume in what is a larger initiative (the Qumran Caves Publication Project) concerned with the comprehensive publication of the material and documentation relating to the de Vaux excavations at the caves of Qumran. Storerooms and archives still contain such a quantity of unpublished material and documentation as to justify an operation on this scale.

During the work on the archaeological material from Cave 11Q carried out for this volume, many tiny fragments of manuscripts were found in the storerooms; these fragments, most of which were collected during the 1956 excavation, had not been known so far. These, too, are published in the volume, which as such presents the final report on the 11Q excavations as well as the edition of these new fragments, followed by a reevaluation of the entire set of texts found within the cave. The purpose of this volume is to make these data available and to allow such data to be studied. The legacy of those who led the way will thus enable others to porsue the work.

History of the research – Situated at x: 243652.818; y: 629357.345; z: -282.992 (entrance point according to the Israeli Grid),[1] Cave 11Q is located around 1.5 km north of Khirbet Qumran and 500 m north of Cave 1Q. The cave was designated as 11Q, since it was the eleventh cave in which manuscripts had been discovered in the twentieth century.[2] The Bedouins, who were at the forefront of the main discoveries at Qumran, were the first to enter the cave, and they looted it in early 1956. Having received the news, Gerald Lankester Harding and Roland de Vaux decided to excavate it during the fifth and final excavation of excavations at Khirbet Qumran, already scheduled for the month of February. The excavations were carried out on behalf of the Department of Antiquities of Jordan (DAJ), the École Biblique et Archéologique Française (EBAF) and the Palestine Archaeological Museum (PAM). Several years later, in 1988, the cave was excavated again by Joseph Patrich on behalf of the Hebrew University of Jerusalem and

1. Survey by Gabriel Levi, Mabat 3D Technologies, March 2017.

2. In Cave 10Q only a fragment of inscribed pottery was found, with two Hebrew letters. M. Baillet, "Textes des grottes 2Q, 3Q, 6Q, 7Q à 10Q," in Id., J.T. Milik, and R. de Vaux, *Les 'petites grottes' de Qumrân: Exploration de la falaise. Les grottes 2Q, 3Q, 5Q, 6Q, 7Q à 10Q. Le rouleau de cuivre* (DJD 3; Oxford: Clarendon, 1962), 45-164, on p. 164.

Fig. 1. Map of the area (satellite image, QGIS): Khirbet Qumran (=KhQ), Cave 1Q, and Cave 11Q

the University of Texas;[3] and most recently, an excavation was carried out in 2017 by the present author and Dan Bahat, on behalf of the Istituto di Cultura e Archeologia delle Terre Bibliche of the Facoltà di Teologia di Lugano (ISCAB FTL) and the Università della Svizzera Italiana.

Figs. 2-3. March 1956: de Vaux, Rousée and Delprat outside Cave 11Q (color slides EBAF)

The results of the first excavation were presented by de Vaux in a brief preliminary report published in 1956.[4] In the same year, the Suez Crisis brought about the first changes to the organization of the works on Qumran: Harding had to leave his position as director of the DAJ, and the entire responsibility was assumed by de Vaux, who actually had already taken on a central role in the Qumran excavations and publications.[5] The editorial project envisaged the publication of the manuscripts together with their archaeological context. The of results the excavation would be published in the first part of the volume (or of the first of the volumes) on the manuscripts found in a given cave:[6] accordingly, the first volume in the Discoveries in the Judean Desert (DJD) series, 1955, presents the archaeology of Cave 1Q; the same for Murabba'at (DJD 2, 1961), and the so-called 'petites grottes' (DJD 3, 1963). The chapter on the archaeology of Cave 4Q was published posthumously, in DJD 6 in 1977, though it had been written by de Vaux back in 1964 or 1965.[7]

Fig. 4. The Palestine Archaeological Museum / Rockefeller Museum, where the materials from Qumran were stored

3. A small area at the entrance of the cave was checked later, in 1991, on behalf of the University of Haifa.

4. R. de Vaux, "Fouilles de Khirbet Qumrân: rapport préliminaire sur les 3e, 4e, et 5e campagnes," *RB* 63 (1956) 533-77, on pp. 573-4.

5. On this passage and its consequences, see W.W. Fields, *The Dead Sea Scrolls: A Full History: Vol. 1: 1947-1960* (Leiden: Brill, 2009); M. Fidanzio, "L'agenda di Qumran," in G. Paximadi and M. Fidanzio (ed.), *TerraSancta II: Ricerche storiche ed archeologiche: Atti dei convegni 2012-2014* (ISCAB.SA 2; Lugano/Siena: Eupress FTL/Cantagalli 2017) 151-67, on pp. 155-8.

6. Cfr. G.L. Harding, "Foreword," in D. Barthélemy, D. and J.T. Milik, *Qumran Cave 1* (DJD 1; Oxford: Clarendon, 1955) v. In DJD 3 de Vaux wrote about Cave 11Q: "Le rapport détaillé sur la fouille que nous avons faite après cette découverte aura sa place normale en tête de la publication des textes qui proviennent de cette grotte." R. de Vaux, "Archéologie," in Baillet, Milik, and de Vaux, *Les 'petites grottes' de Qumrân*, 3-50, on p. 4, n. 2

7. P. Benoit, "Préface," in R. de Vaux and J.T. Milik, *Qumrân Grotte 4.II: I. Archéologie. II. Tefillin, Mezuzot et Targums (4Q128-4Q157)* (DJD 6; Oxford: Clarendon, 1977) v-vi, on p. vi.

Starting in 1967, work on the archaeology of Qumran came to a halt: after the Six-Day War, the EBAF archaeologists did not return to the Rockefeller, where the excavated materials were stored, until much later;[8] in addition, de Vaux died unexpectedly in 1971, and the whole operation was put on hold. Reports (albeit rather limited in some cases) had been published on Caves 1Q-10Q and the other caves in the Qumran area in which archaeological material had been found, while a final report on Cave 11Q was missing, as was a volume on the archaeology of the settlement.[9]

When, in 1986-87, the EBAF decided to resume the publication of the Qumran excavations, the appointed team found itself facing a major, wide-ranging task: they chose the Khirbeh as their starting point, whereas the caves remained in the background.

Patrich worked at Cave 11Q in 1988, as part of a broader program of new explorations of the area around Qumran, which led to the excavation of new caves and to a new investigation of some of those already excavated. The excavation of Cave 11Q produced no significant results, and was briefly presented in an article summarizing Patrich's work at the Qumran caves.[10]

In 2014, an international conference entirely dedicated to the Qumran caves was organized by the ISCAB FTL and the EBAF.[11] The conference laid the groundwork for the project of a final report on the caves in the Qumran area excavated by de Vaux. The Qumran Caves Publication Project (QCPP) was launched in 2015 by the EBAF and the ISCAB FTL, and it is directed by the present author under the scientific supervision of Jean-Baptiste Humbert, who is in charge of the publication of the de Vaux's excavations at Qumran.[12]

During the preparation of this volume, a further excavation was carried out in Cave 11Q in March 2017 for documentation and verifications needed for the final report. The report on this excavation was published in the same year[13].

Qumran Caves Publication Project – A brief overview of the existing publications, the documentation stored in the archives and the material from the excavations, allows for some considerations on the current situation and on the need for a new publication program on the entirety of the caves investigated by de Vaux.

In terms of the publications, examining DJD volumes 1, 3 and 6, we find that the reports on the archaeology of the caves are very concise, and their length is commensurate with the quantity and state of preservation of the manuscripts discovered in a given cave. Accordingly, the chapters devoted to the archaeology of Caves 1Q and 4Q occupy between 30 and 40 pages each, and also set out plans and sections, whereas the volume on the so-called 'petites grottes'[14]

8. The circumstances are explained in J.-B. Humbert and E. Villeneuve, *L'affaire Qumrân: Les découvertes de la mer Morte* (Découvertes Gallimard 498; Paris: Gallimard, 2006), 37; K. Galor and J. Zangenberg, "Qumran Archaeology in Search of a Consensus," in K. Galor, J.-B. Humbert, and J. Zangenberg (ed.), *Qumran: The Site of the Dead Sea Scrolls: Archaeological Interpretations and Debates* (STDJ 57; Leiden: Brill, 2006) 1-15, on p. 2; J.-B. Humbert, "Introduction," in Id., A. Chambon, and J. Młynarczyk, *Khirbet Qumrân et 'Aïn Feshkha: Vol. IIIA: L'archéologie de Qumrân: Reconsidération de l'interprétation. Les installations périphériques de Khirbet Qumrân. Qumran Terracotta Oil Lamps* (NTOA.SA 5A; Göttingen: Vandenhoeck & Ruprecht, 2016) 13-21, on p.13.

9. Harding, "Foreword"; R. de Vaux, *Archaeology and the Dead Sea Scrolls* (The Schweich Lectures 1959; London: Oxford University Press for the British Academy, 1973), ix.

10. J. Patrich, "Khirbet Qumran in the Light of New Archaeological Explorations in the Qumran Caves," in M.O. Wise et al. (ed.), *Methods of Investigation of the Dead Sea Scrolls and the Khirbet Qumran Site: Present Realities and Future Prospects* (ANYAS 722; New York: New York Academy of Sciences, 1994) 73-95, on pp. 77, 90.

11. M. Fidanzio (ed.), *The Caves of Qumran: Proceedings of the International Conference, Lugano 2014* (STDJ 118; Leiden: Brill, 2016).

12. The work is supervised by an Advisory Board chaired by the director of the EBAF and the rector of the FTL, and composed of: George Brooke, Florentino García Martínez, Adrian Schenker, Francis Schimdt, Pnina Shor, Emanuel Tov and Jürgen Zangenberg.

13. M. Fidanzio et al., "Campagna di scavi ISCAB-FTL e USI alla grotta 11Q di Qumran, marzo 2017," *RTLu* 22 (2017) 437-66.

14. The definition of 'petites grottes' is not based on the morphology of the caves or the set of materials, but on the content of manuscripts. "Le troisième volume des Discoveries in the Judaean Desert est consacré aux 'petites grottes' de Qumran. Nous avons ainsi désigné les grottes de la région de Qumran qui ont livré un lot de manuscrits moins important que les 'grandes grottes' 1Q, 4Q, 11Q." R. de Vaux,

summarizes the archaeology of 46 caves over just 34 pages, with no plans or sections. On the morphology of the 'petites grottes', there is just a brief description, followed by a discussion on whether the cave may have been inhabited – a question associated with the understanding of the function of the caves as proposed by de Vaux, in the relation to his general interpretation of Qumran.

In all the publications, considerable space is devoted these to pottery: a detailed analysis of these chapters revealed a certain amount of room for improvement. The first volume (DJD 1) presents a typological study of jars and lids: comparing it with de Vaux's inventory (kept in the EBAF archives), we can point out a few discrepancies between the description of a given object and its typological identification.[15] In addition, the photographs of the pottery published in the same volume do not indicate which object they refer to, and comparing them with the inventory it is clear that, in some instances, the published photographs feature objects that are not described, whereas there are no photographs of a number of objects that are described: what is provided is just a general photographic illustration of the repertoire rather than a documentation of the individual objects that are described.[16] Moreover, a new analysis of the objects highlighted the need to improve some of the drawings.

With the exception of the textiles from Cave 1Q, published in DJD 1,[17] the other archaeological materials found in the caves are only briefly described and/or illustrated with a small photograph. Today, much of these items are considered worthy of greater scrutiny and may offer useful information for a better understanding of the material culture of the caves. These observations are not intended to present a superficial, after-the-event critique of the work done by de Vaux and the group led by him;[18] rather, the aim is to highlight the opportunity of continuing with the work.

In the archives, there is a wealth of documentation produced during the excavations: excavation diaries, inventories of materials, plans and photographs. In these archival sources, we came upon valuable information still unpublished: for instance, in the EBAF archives there is a plan of Cave 3Q drawn in 1952 by Henry de Contenson (the EBAF fellow archaeologist who had discovered and excavated it) which is not included in the volume about the 'petites grottes'. The plan clearly shows the findspots of the manuscript fragments, the Copper Scroll and the other materials. Referring to another of the 'petites grottes', Cave 5Q, we find in de Vaux's field notes a plan with measurements down to the centimeter. As such, absence of data in the publications does not necessarily indicate a lack of documentation. Some of the excavation diaries were published later on,[19] but others remained unpublished until now, such as those referring to Caves 7Q-9Q.

Moving on to the materials, let us firstly consider the pottery, the most extensively published class of apart from manuscripts. The quantity of pottery kept in the storerooms is in some cases far greater than what has been inventoried so far.[20] As for Cave 2Q, we have three items in the inventory, but in the storerooms, we actually found 23; for Cave 3Q, we have 29 items in the inventory, but, in the storerooms, there are around 100, including vessels with a complete profile. These items are always diagnostic: the team led by de Vaux, after an initial on-site selection, brought to Jerusalem a certain number of ceramics that were restored and partially inventoried. The publications offer a selection of materials based on typology. In

"Preface," in Baillet, Milik, and de Vaux, " *Les 'petites grottes' de Qumrân*," v.

15. See M. Fidanzio and J.-B. Humbert, "Finds from the Qumran Caves: Roland de Vaux's Inventory of the Excavations (1949-1956)," in Fidanzio, *The Caves of Qumran*, 263-332, on p. 265, n. 14.

16. Fidanzio and Humbert, "Finds from the Qumran Caves," 276, n. a.

17. G.M. Crowfoot, "The Linen Textiles," in D. Barthélemy and J.T. Milik, *Qumran Cave 1* (DJD 1; Oxford: Clarendon, 1955) 18-38.

18. De Vaux's work was worthwhile, and became the basis for Paul W. Lapp's volume entitled *Palestinian Ceramic Chronology 200 B.C.-A.D. 70* (New Haven: American Schools of Oriental Research, 1961), one of the prominent publications on pottery at that time.

19. J.-B. Humbert and A. Chambon (ed.), *Fouilles de Khirbet Qumrân et de 'Aïn Feshkha: Vol. I: Album de photographies. Répertoire du fonds photographique. Synthèse des notes de chantier du Père Roland de Vaux OP* (NTOA.SA 1; Fribourg/Göttingen: Éditions Universitaires/Vandenhoeck & Ruprecht, 1994).

20. A similar situation exists for the pottery and other classes of materials from the Khirbeh and from 'Ain Feshkha. See R. Donceel, "Reprise des travaux de publication des fouilles au Khirbet Qumrân," *RB* 99 (1992), 561-2.

the storerooms and laboratories, there are also other classes of material, about which information had been only partially published (as in the case of the textiles), or merely mentioned and not otherwise studied, as in the case of other organic materials or metals. Therefore, there is a clear need to revisit all of the material and to publish it in its entirety. De Vaux himself provided an example in this sense: if we analyze his inventory and compare it with the publications, we can see that he worked on the pottery typology twice – once when putting together the inventory, and again for the publications in DJD 3 and 6. For the publications, de Vaux re-examined all of the materials, not just those inventoried, but also those which were stored and labeled generically as "tesson." In the case of Cave 4Q, the last cave published by de Vaux, DJD 6 presents five such items that were stored but not inventoried, out of a total of 25 published items: a more in-depth understanding of the repertoire led de Vaux to document and publish uninventoried materials, which could be useful to gain a more comprehensive knowledge.[21]

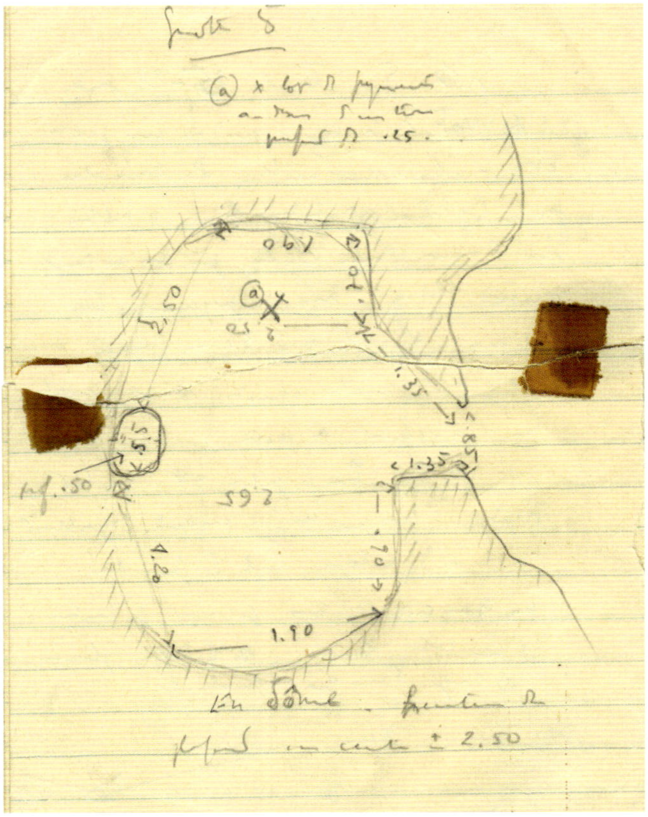

Fig. 5. De Vaux's field notes: plan of Cave 5Q

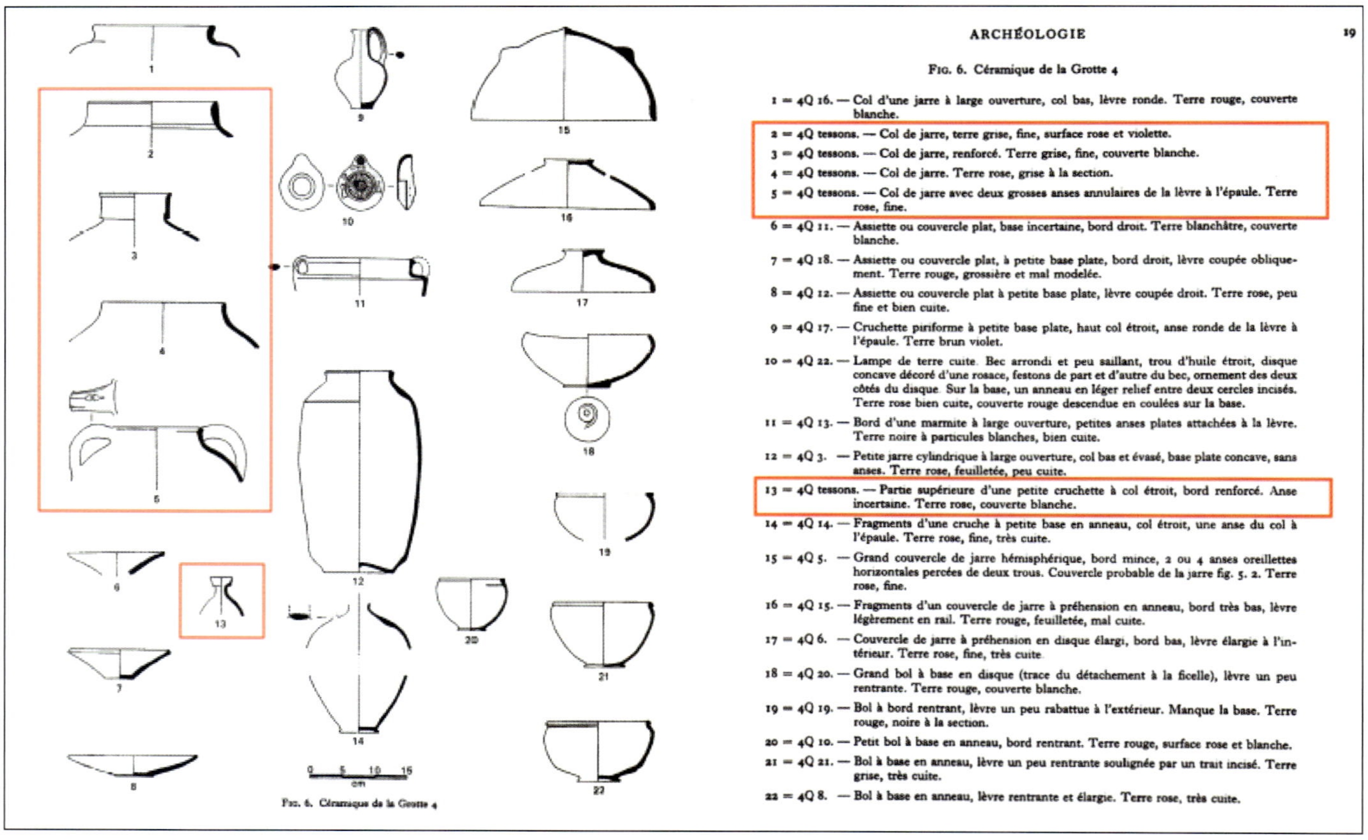

ARCHÉOLOGIE 19

Fig. 6. Céramique de la Grotte 4

1 = 4Q 16. — Col d'une jarre à large ouverture, col bas, lèvre ronde. Terre rouge, couverte blanche.

2 = 4Q tessons. — Col de jarre, terre grise, fine, surface rose et violette.

3 = 4Q tessons. — Col de jarre, renforcé. Terre grise, fine, couverte blanche.

4 = 4Q tessons. — Col de jarre. Terre rose, grise à la section.

5 = 4Q tessons. — Col de jarre avec deux grosses anses annulaires de la lèvre à l'épaule. Terre rose, fine.

6 = 4Q 11. — Assiette ou couvercle plat, base incertaine, bord droit. Terre blanchâtre, couverte blanche.

7 = 4Q 18. — Assiette ou couvercle plat, à petite base plate, bord droit, lèvre coupée obliquement. Terre rouge, grossière et mal modelée.

8 = 4Q 12. — Assiette ou couvercle plat à petite base plate, lèvre coupée droit. Terre rose, peu fine et bien cuite.

9 = 4Q 17. — Cruchette piriforme à petite base plate, haut col étroit, anse ronde de la lèvre à l'épaule. Terre brun violet.

10 = 4Q 22. — Lampe de terre cuite. Bec arrondi et peu saillant, trou d'huile étroit, disque concave décoré d'une rosace, festons de part et d'autre du bec, ornement des deux côtés du disque. Sur la base, un anneau en léger relief entre deux cercles incisés. Terre rose bien cuite, couverte rouge descendue en coulées sur la base.

11 = 4Q 13. — Bord d'une marmite à large ouverture, petites anses plates attachées à la lèvre. Terre noire à particules blanches, bien cuite.

12 = 4Q 3. — Petite jarre cylindrique à large ouverture, col bas et évasé, base plate concave, sans anses. Terre rose, feuilletée, peu cuite.

13 = 4Q tessons. — Partie supérieure d'une petite cruchette à col étroit, bord renforcé. Anse incertaine. Terre rose, couverte blanche.

14 = 4Q 14. — Fragments d'une cruche à petite base en anneau, col étroit, une anse du col à l'épaule. Terre rose, fine, très cuite.

15 = 4Q 5. — Grand couvercle de jarre hémisphérique, bord mince, 2 ou 4 anses oreillettes horizontales percées de deux trous. Couvercle probable de la jarre fig. 5. 2. Terre rose, fine.

16 = 4Q 15. — Fragments d'un couvercle de jarre à préhension en anneau, bord très bas, lèvre légèrement en rail. Terre rouge, feuilletée, mal cuite.

17 = 4Q 6. — Couvercle de jarre à préhension en disque élargi, bord bas, lèvre élargie à l'intérieur. Terre rose, fine, très cuite.

18 = 4Q 20. — Grand bol à base en disque (trace du détachement à la ficelle), lèvre un peu rentrante. Terre rouge, couverte blanche.

19 = 4Q 19. — Bol à bord rentrant, lèvre un peu rabattue à l'extérieur. Manque la base. Terre rouge, noire à la section.

20 = 4Q 10. — Petit bol à base en anneau, bord rentrant. Terre rouge, surface rose et blanche.

21 = 4Q 21. — Bol à base en anneau, lèvre un peu rentrante soulignée par un trait incisé. Terre grise, très cuite.

22 = 4Q 8. — Bol à base en anneau, lèvre rentrante et élargie. Terre rose, très cuite.

Fig. 6. DJD 6, Pottery from Cave 4Q (on pp.18-19)

21. See Fidanzio and Humbert, "Finds from the Qumran Caves," 280.

Today, given our better knowledge of the region, the wide interest on Qumran, and the debates on interpretation, it is necessary to make all of the material available. This is the priority for the QCPP, which envisages the publication of three or four volumes on the caves.[22]

The present volume – When working on unpublished materials and documentation relating to Qumran, it is essential to take account of the delays in publication, which in the past led to so many problems. This situation influenced the scheduling of our works: we decided to begin with the unpublished Cave 11Q, with the aim of giving priority to the publication of the data. It would certainly have been better to proceed with a study encompassing the material from all the caves, but this would have meant that the first volume would only have been issued some years later; this would in turn have exposed the publication to the risk of new interruptions, as had occurred in the past. Further investigations and laboratory analyses of the material from Cave 11Q would have been possible, and in certain cases opportune. Sometimes we have to recognize the truth of the saying "le mieux est l'ennemi du bien" (seeking the best is the enemy of the good), and the many shortcomings of which the editors of this volume are aware should not impede progress – what is important is to publish the data as soon as possible. Further study will be carried out in the future. In terms of the caves as a whole, in subsequent volumes more space will be devoted to comparative analyses and historical overviews of the periods in which human activity left its traces in the caves of the Qumran area.

The work on Cave 11Q did not come out of the blue with the launch of the QCPP: working on the Khirbeh, Humbert had also paid attention to the material of the caves. Mireille Bélis, appointed by the EBAF to study the textiles of Qumran, presented some textiles from Cave 11Q in preliminary publications[23] and later continued her work on these materials; Orit Shamir and Naama Sukenik (Israel Antiquities Authority – IAA) studied Cave 11Q textiles stored in the IAA's organic materials laboratory[24] and Sukenik published the scroll wrapper attributed to the Temple Scroll, which is currently in the Schøyen Collection;[25] a few organic materials from Cave 11Q had been subjected to archaeometric analysis,[26] and Joan Taylor received authorization from the EBAF to analyze and study a further number of organic materials. Our criterion was not to start the work anew, but to facilitate the completion of the ongoing studies. The genesis of this volume explains why certain materials were subject to analysis to a greater extent than others, depending on the work that was already under way.

Shortly after the beginning of the work, the discovery of new manuscript fragments from Cave 11Q led to the addition of new chapters on the texts. We also decided to integrate into the volume materials and data (some of them unpublished) from the subsequent excavations at Cave 11Q: Patrich; Fidanzio and Bahat

In April 2017, a workshop gathered all the contributors to discuss the content of the single chapters and the publication as a whole.[27] In the volume different interpretations of the data are provided, reflecting sometimes divergent interpretations of the Qumran phenomenon. As long as the data are made available,

22. A joint project aims to provide documentation about materials and archives scattered across museums and private collections in different parts of the world. The Network for Dispersed Qumran Caves Artefacts and Archives (Leverhulme Trust) comprises Joan Taylor, Dennis Mizzi and the present author.

23. M. Bélis, "Des Textiles: Catalogues et Commentaires," in J.-B. Humbert and J. Gunneweg (ed.), *Khirbet Qumrân et 'Aïn Feshkha: Vol. II:* Études d'anthropologie, de physique et de chimie (NTOA.SA 3; Fribourg/Göttingen: Éditions Universitaires/Vandenhoeck & Ruprecht, 2003) 207-76; Id., "The Unpublished Textiles from the Qumran Caves," in Fidanzio, *The Caves of Qumran,* 123-36.

24. Both a part of the textiles from the de Vaux excavation and those from the Patrich excavation. On the Qumran textiles, see their article: O. Shamir, and N. Sukenik, "Qumran Textiles and the Garments of Qumran's Inhabitants," *DSD* 18 (2011) 206-25.

25. N. Sukenik, "The Temple Scroll Wrapper from Cave 11: MS 5095/2, MS 5095/4, MS 5095/1," in T. Elgvin, K. Davis, and M. Langlois (ed.), *Gleanings from the Caves: Dead Sea Scrolls and Artefacts from the Schøyen Collection* (LSTS 71; London: Bloomsbury T&T Clark, 2016) 339-50.

26. K.L. Rasmussen et al., "Cleaning and Radiocarbon Dating of Material from Khirbet Qumran," in J. Gunneweg, C. Greenblatt, and A. Adriaens (ed.), *Bio- and Material Cultures at Qumran: Papers from a COST Action G8 Working Group Meeting held in Jerusalem, Israel on 22-23 May 2005* (Stuttgart: Fraunhofer IRB Verlag, 2006) 139-64, on pp. 149-52.

27. Alongside the authors, the workshop also benefitted from the presence of George Brooke, Peter Dubovsky, Jodi Magness, and Jürgen Zangenberg, who were invited to respond to the papers and who offered valuable input.

the debate on the interpretation stimulates research itself and is appreciated by the editors as enriching the work.

Plan of the volume – Publishing a report on an excavation carried out 60 years before, by archaeologists who are no longer alive, raises a methodological question. As a first step, we decided to proceed with an edition of the documentation held in the archives (excavation diary, photographic album, inventory of materials), and of the first publications. This was then followed by an analysis of the sources aiming to retrace the progress of the excavation and to propose, as far as possible, an archaeological synthesis. Some topics were then reconsidered in light of the results of the 2017 excavation.

The inventory of the materials and their study are then presented according to the different classes of material (pottery, textiles, other organic materials, metals), and these are followed by the results of some radiocarbon dating analysis. As a whole, this section of the volume offers information on the chronology, typology and function of individual items, and puts forward ideas on the reconstitution of the assemblages related to the different periods. There follows a chapter dedicated to the conservation and digitization of the scrolls, focusing readers' attention on the manuscripts as artefacts.

The next section is devoted to hitherto-unknown manuscript fragments – the circumstances of the retrieval are clarified, and two chapters present proposals for identification. Lastly, a reevaluation of the entire set of manuscripts attributed to Cave 11Q, makes it possible to update our overall understanding and to outline a profile of the cave through the prism of the texts.

Main results – The archaeology of Cave 11Q has to face, first and foremost, the problem of a context disturbed by the intervention of the Bedouins, who were the first to discover the cave and looted it. Moreover, those who try to reconstruct de Vaux's unpublished excavation have access only to the rather laconic documentation of the 1950s. The reconstruction of the contexts remains the subject of speculation. A consensus has been reached among the authors of this volume on the fact that de Vaux, in his preliminary report,[28] presented a stratigraphy reconstructed on the basis of the materials discovered within the cave. The materials often came from a context which have been interferred with. We must therefore acknowledge the limitations of our potential for understanding and accept the considerable space left for the interpretation of the available data.

Access to the cave: Cave 11Q was the last to be discovered; the blocked entrance had impeded its discovery during the 1952 exploration of the area, and indeed it was not uncovered until 1956. The material found inside the cave had been dated to between the Chalcolithic period and the Roman period – the latter contemporaneous to the main occupation of the settlement at Qumran. These data, combined with an interpretation of the cave as a hiding place for the Scrolls,[29] led to the widespread assumption that the cave had remained closed from the time of the deposition of the manuscripts or the abandonment of the cave, until its discovery in the 1950s. But the study and radiocarbon analysis of some organic materials reveal traces of human activity within the cave around the 10th century CE and possibly even in the 18th or 19th century. As such, after the deposition of the manuscripts, there were other accesses to the cave on the part of someone with no interest in the scrolls, given that a large number of manuscripts were left inside the cave. Questions arise about the closure of the cave in a subsequent period. A study conducted in the area of the entrance indicated the possibility that natural phenomena may have contributed to the access being blocked, as it was the case when it was discovered in the 1950s.

Among the material, the most significant assemblage is associated with the deposition of the scrolls and their conservation: a leather tab and thongs from scroll ties, textiles, pottery, alongside the manuscripts themselves. Remains of textiles have been found still attached to fragments of manuscripts from Cave 11Q. The tab and the thongs found in Cave 11Q are similar to those still attached to other scrolls. A lid found during the excavations and the jar and lid on display in Kando's shop in Bethlehem (these, too, allegedly

28. De Vaux, "Fouilles de Khirbet Qumrân."

29. The function of the cave as a hiding place for scrolls was not proposed by de Vaux. He considered Cave 11Q to have been a dwelling place for people associated with the community residing in the settlement or living in tents nearby; the manuscripts discovered in Cave 11Q would have been texts for use by the inhabitants of Cave 11Q, who left them there upon the arrival of the Romans. See DJD 3, p. 34.

from Cave 11Q) may have contained scrolls closed with tabs and thongs, wrapped in textiles.[30]

The presence of manuscripts, pottery and textiles (most of them supposedly connected with the scrolls' preservation), and the limited number of miscellaneous artefacts, make it possible to relate Cave 11Q with many others in the Qumran area in which manuscripts were found or that yielded a similar repertoire, even in the absence of manuscripts at the time of the discovery in the mid-twentieth century. Equally, it is possible to highlight the singularity of the Qumran phenomenon with respect to other discoveries in the Judaean Desert. This situation is illustrated in various chapters on the archaeological material within the volume, and in the reevaluation of the content of the manuscripts, offering an interesting parallel between the results of the study of the archaeology and the study of the texts.[31]

This volume presents fragments of manuscripts from de Vaux's excavation of the cave; some of these fragments have been matched with the manuscripts acquired from the Bedouins, confirming the provenance of the latter from Cave 11Q.

The analysis of the textiles from Cave 11Q has shed light on the various types of scroll wrappers: along with the scroll wrapper attributed to the Temple Scroll, published by Sukenik for the Schøyen Collection,[32] there is possibly another type represented by Gr11Q75 textile, found in de Vaux's excavations and published in this volume.

The radiocarbon analysis conducted on a few pieces of linen indicate that the linen was manufactured at different times over an extended period, with the possibility that these fabrics were produced between the 4th century BCE and the 3rd century CE. These data open the way to further investigations into the use of linen textiles, their relationship to the manuscripts and the contribution that they can make to the dating of the deposition of the scrolls in the caves.

30. An evidence to this link is provided by Cave 1Q: a decomposed manuscript is still preserved in its scroll wrapper and a fragment of rim is attached to the textile. A photograph of materials found in Cave GQ12 (discovered in the exploration of March 1952) shows the bottom of a jar with linen textiles inside.

31. On this topic see also Fidanzio, *The Caves of Qumran*.

32. Sukenik, "Temple Scroll Wrapper."

A peculiar feature of Cave 11Q, with respect to other Qumran caves, is the presence of a small assemblage of metal artefacts, which are here interpreted as a tool kit. This possible tool kit may have been hidden together with the manuscripts or at some other time. Here, too, we have an element that allows us to reflect on the nature of the deposition (or depositions) of material within the cave. These discussions relate to the function of the cave: the volume does not address the issue directly, but all the contributors agree on the need to abandon the idea of the dwelling function proposed by de Vaux.[33] This point has already been made in various previous studies,[34] and it is confirmed by the archaeological analysis of Cave 11Q presented in this volume.

Some materials point to human activity within the cave at different times, and the documentation is provided here. It will be possible to carry out a more in-depth investigation on other periods after the study of the materials found in the other caves in the area.

Storerooms and registration system – The materials excavated by de Vaux in Cave 11Q are stored in various storerooms and laboratories. Initially, they had all been taken to the Rockefeller Museum, but some were then transferred to the IAA's organic materials laboratory for conservation purposes. The manuscripts are now at the IAA's Dead Sea Scrolls Conservation Laboratory, whereas the mattock is on show at the Shrine of the Book. The materials excavated by Patrich are stored in the storerooms of the Hebrew University of Jerusalem (pottery) and in the IAA's organic materials laboratory (textiles). The materials

33. De Vaux, "Archéologie," 34. See also F. García Martínez, "Cave 11 in Context," in C. Hempel (ed.), *The Dead Sea Scrolls: Texts and Context* (STDJ 90; Leiden: Brill, 2010) 199-209, on pp. 206-8.

34. J. Patrich, "Did Extra-Mural Dwelling Quarters exist at Qumran?," in L.H. Schiffman, E.Tov, and J.C. VanderKam (ed.), *The Dead Sea Scrolls Fifty Years after their Discovery: Proceedings of the Jerusalem Congress, July 20–25, 1997* (Jerusalem: Israel Exploration Society/Shrine of the Book, 2000) 720–27; M. Broshi and H. Eshel, "Residential Caves at Qumran," *DSD* 6 (1999) 328-48, on p. 332; D. Stökl Ben Ezra, "Old Caves and Young Caves: A Statistical Reevaluation of a Qumran Consensus," *DSD* 14 (2007) 313-33, on p. 322, n. 31; Id., "Further Reflections on Caves 1 and 11: A Response to Florentino García Martínez," in Hempel, *The Dead Sea Scrolls*, 211-23, on p. 220; J.E. Taylor, *The Essenes, the Scrolls, and the Dead Sea* (Oxford: Oxford University Press, 2012), 279, n. 30; D. Mizzi, "Miscellaneous Artefacts from the Qumran Caves: An Exploration of Their Significance," in Fidanzio, *The Caves of Qumran*, 137-60, on pp. 144-53.

excavated by Fidanzio and Bahat are stored in the IAA organic materials laboratory.

The materials from the de Vaux excavation are registered using different systems: de Vaux's own inventory, limited to 13 objects; the inventory prepared by Bélis, covering a part of the textiles and other organic material; and the IAA inventory of textiles and organic material (which overlaps to some extent with Bélis' inventory). The manuscripts have their own system, established in the years after their discovery. For the final report, we decided to label all objects except for the manuscripts from the 1956 excavation using a single system, the same adopted by de Vaux for some other caves. Over the course of the explorations and excavations, de Vaux modified the registration system mainly to meet the requirements generated by the discoveries.[35] For Cave 11Q, the objects were labeled with 11Q followed by the object number.[36] This system is problematic in that it overlaps perfectly with that used for the designation of the manuscripts. Thus, for example, 11Q1 may refer to both PaleoLev[a] and to a pottery lid.[37] For this reason, we decided to follow the system used by de Vaux for the caves from 4Q to 10Q, in which all materials except the manuscripts) are labeled as follows: Gr (= Caves) N (= number of the cave) Q (= Qumran) N (=number of the object).[38] The prefix Gr enables the differentiation between the manuscripts and all other archaeological material. According to this system, the aforementioned pottery lid, for instance, is labeled Gr11Q1. The index of the materials from Cave 11Q at the end of this volume indicates the correspondences between this system and the systems used by Bélis and the IAA. The materials found in Patrich's excavations are labeled P11Q N (= number of the object), whereas those from Fidanzio and Bahat's excavation are labeled FB11Q N (= number of the object).

De Vaux 1956	Manuscripts	11Q N
	Other materials	Gr11Q N
Patrich 1988, 1991		P11Q N
Fidanzio-Bahat 2017		FB11Q N

Acknowledgments – In conclusion, it gives me great pleasure to thank those who in various ways have made this publication possible: the Qumran Caves Publication Project originated by Jean-Baptiste Humbert, who wanted to re-open the caves dossier and supported those who had already worked on this topic; Marcel Sigrist, director of the EBAF when the project began, worked to establish an institutional collaboration between the EBAF and the FTL; and his successor, Jean Jacques Pérennès, channeled his energies to allow the work to continue, in a profound synergy with the rector of the FTL, René Roux. A a word of thanks goes to Giorgio Paximadi, president of the ISCAB FTL, who accompanied the various phases of the project. Joseph Patrich, HUJI, kindly allowed us access to the materials collected in his excavation at Cave 11Q; Marco De Pietri, ISCAB FTL research fellow, and Benedetta Torrini, ISCAB FTL research fellow , have spent countless hours working with me for this publication, Antonio Tombolini, FTL, and Maura Sala contributed to the editing of the volume; Alegre Savariego, curator of Rockefeller collections national treasures IAA, facilitated the research through her great willingness to support the work at the storerooms of the Rockefeller Museum; Jean-Michel de Tarragon, in charge of the photo collection at EBAF, provided valuable assistance in researching the photographs of de Vaux's excavations; Elena Rigaud, former archivist at EBAF, did a remarkable work of reorganizing the documentation; Jürgen Zangenberg, co-editor of the NTOA series, helped us throughout the project, ever-ready to understand and facilitate any issues that arose.

The publication of this volume would not have been possible without the support of a number of different institutions and individuals: the Direction Générale de la Coopération Internationale du Ministère des Affaires Étrangères (France), the Divisione della Cultura e degli Studi Universitari del Dipartimento dell'Educazione, della Cultura e dello Sport (Canton Ticino CH), the Chiara Lupinacci Foundation, the Italian speaking Section of Swiss Lieutenancy of the Equestrian Order of the Holy Sepulchre of Jerusalem, the Dead Sea Scrolls Foundation, and Umberto Giovine.

35. See M. Fidanzio, "Which Cave Does This Pottery Come From? The Information Written on the Pottery Found in the Qumran Caves (R. de Vaux Excavations 1949–1956)" *RB* 122 (2015) 128-31.

36. See M. Fidanzio (ed.), "Archival Sources and First Publications on the Excavations of Cave 11Q," in this volume; Fidanzio and Humbert, "Finds from the Qumran Caves," 270-7.

37. This problem arose in the publication of the pottery bearing inscriptions, A. Lemaire, "Inscriptions du Khirbeh, des grottes et de 'Aïn Feshkha," in Humbert and Gunneweg, *Khirbet Qumrân et 'Aïn Feshkha,* 341-88, on pp. 373-7.

38. This system returns to the proposal put forward in Fidanzio and Humbert, "Finds from the Qumran Caves," 271, n. 32.

Chapter One

Archival Sources and First Publications on the Excavations of Cave 11Q

Marcello Fidanzio (ed.)

Cave 11Q was discovered and first excavated over 60 years ago. The passage of time and the death of the excavators now raise the fundamental question of how to publish the final report.

As a first step, the editors of this volume choose to make available all the written and photographic sources stored at the École Biblique et Archéologique Française (EBAF).These comprise different types of documents: personal notes, more formal notes, single photographs, photographs organised into albums with captions, and two copies of the inventory of materials. Publishing these documents and images – mostly intended for internal use – has the limitation of presenting the material out of its context, since we do not have the additional knowledge of those who produced it. For instance, in a previous study, it had been possible to reconstruct the relationship across the two copies of the inventory (in a card index and in a hardbound book, see below). The card index is the primary inventory, from which the hardbound book is derived, and comparing the two made it possible to identify and correct a few inconsistencies contained in the hardbound book.[1] Some other facts are still unclear, such as the find-dates of some artefacts, recorded differently in the excavation diary and the inventory,[2] or the physical absence, both in the inventory and in the storerooms, of a number of seemingly important items mentioned in the excavation diary or in de Vaux's published preliminary report.[3]

In this chapter, the archival sources are accompanied by explanatory footnotes and comments providing information inferred from other documents stored at EBAF and at the St. Étienne Dominican Convent in Jerusalem. All known documents and images concerning Cave 11Q stored in the EBAF archives are published here. Nevertheless, it is possible that other texts, drawings or photographs may be lost, or that in the future some additional material may be retrieved in Jerusalem, Amman, or elsewhere.

The preliminary report and a number of other texts published by the excavators, or by people familiar with the excavation, are also reproduced in this

1. Studying this material has also enabled the clarification of a number of marginal details that had remained enigmatic in the official publication in DJD. See M. Fidanzio and J.-B. Humbert, "Finds from the Qumran Caves: Roland de Vaux's Inventory of the Excavations (1949-1956)," in M. Fidanzio (ed.), *The Caves of Qumran: Proceedings of the International Conference, Lugano 2014* (STDJ 118; Leiden: Brill, 2016) 263-332, on pp. 278-280.

2. See D. Mizzi and A. Faggi, "Metal and Stone Artefacts," in this volume.

3. See below the notes to the inventory.

chapter. It includes the brief report published on Patrich's excavations, which also provides the first plan of the cave.

1. Archival Sources on Roland de Vaux's Excavation of Cave 11Q (1956)

1.1 *Excavation Diary and Field Notes*

Among the documentation on Qumran stored in the EBAF archives, two notebooks contain handwritten notes taken by Roland de Vaux during the excavation of Cave 11Q (Fig. 1).

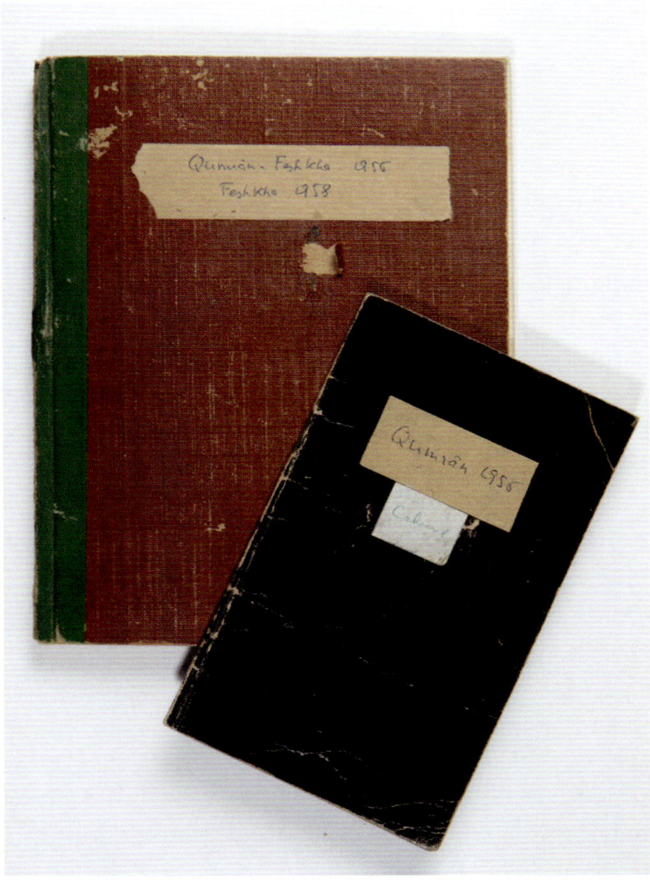

Fig. 1. The notebooks: the field notes (front) and the excavation diary (back). Photo Giorgio Skory[4]

One of these is a hardbound notebook (16 × 20 cm), catalogued in the EBAF inventory as number 7. The first page (a sort of handwritten frontispiece) bears the title, "Khirbet Qumran 1956." This is the excavation diary and contains concise notes about the work done, updated in all probability at the end of each day. Early on in the diary, among the notes we find the names of some of the team members and special visitors.[5] Everyone is presented with their own title (P., Abbé, Dr.), and de Vaux introduces himself in third person and with his title, later proceeding in first person plural: "20/2 Les PP: de Vaux, Rousée, l'Abbé Delprat partent l'après-midi. Nous trouvons la route…" Given this formal tone, this text appears to have been possibly intended for other audiences as well.

The other record is a paperback notebook (10 × 16 cm), catalogued as number 8. It is part of a series of smaller notebooks, which de Vaux probably carried in his pocket during excavations. This notebook contains de Vaux's field notes. It is less accurate, having large parts of strikethrough text and corrections, with the central pages torn out. Sometimes, however, more precise information is to be found here than in the excavation diary.[6] The notes are ordered with reference to the different areas excavated in 1956, with one or two pages given over to each area. Each note is introduced by the date on which it was written. In the case of Cave 11Q, we find only one long note – a sort of summary of what had happened until then, compiled on 3 March, a week after excavation work began on the cave.

In contrast to his notes on the excavation of the Khirbeh, de Vaux did not subsequently prepare a typed excavation diary on the caves.[7] De Vaux's records on

4. All figures are courtesy of EBAF, except of Fig. 1, Giorgio Skory, and Figs 42-46, Estate John Allegro.

5. The two master builders, Ibrahim and Azmi, with de Vaux, Rousée, and Delprat. A few days later, Kurth and Nobs came from Jericho to study the skeletons found in the tombs. Elsewhere, the text is less accurate: the coming of the architect Charles Couäsnon (EBAF), which is recorded in the *Chronique du Couvent de Saint Etienne* and confirmed by notes as "verification de plan" in the excavation diary on the days after his arrival, is not mentioned; Gerald Lankester Harding is referred to, without a title, only when he brought the electrical generator to facilitate the excavation inside the cave.

6. For instance, in the field notes there are measurements taken at the entrance of the cave ("porte"), after having removed the blockage. These dimensions are not present in the excavation diary.

7. About the transcription of the Khirbet Qumran excavations diary see J-B. Humbert, "Introduction," in J-B. Humbert and A. Chambon (ed.), *The Excavations of Khirbet Qumran and 'Aïn Feshkha: Synthesis of Roland de Vaux's Field Notes* (NTOA.SA 1B; trans. and rev. S.J. Pfann; Fribourg/Göttingen: Éditions Universitaires/Vandenhoeck & Ruprecht, 2003), xiii-xiv; S.J. Pfann, "Preface to the English Edition," in Humbert

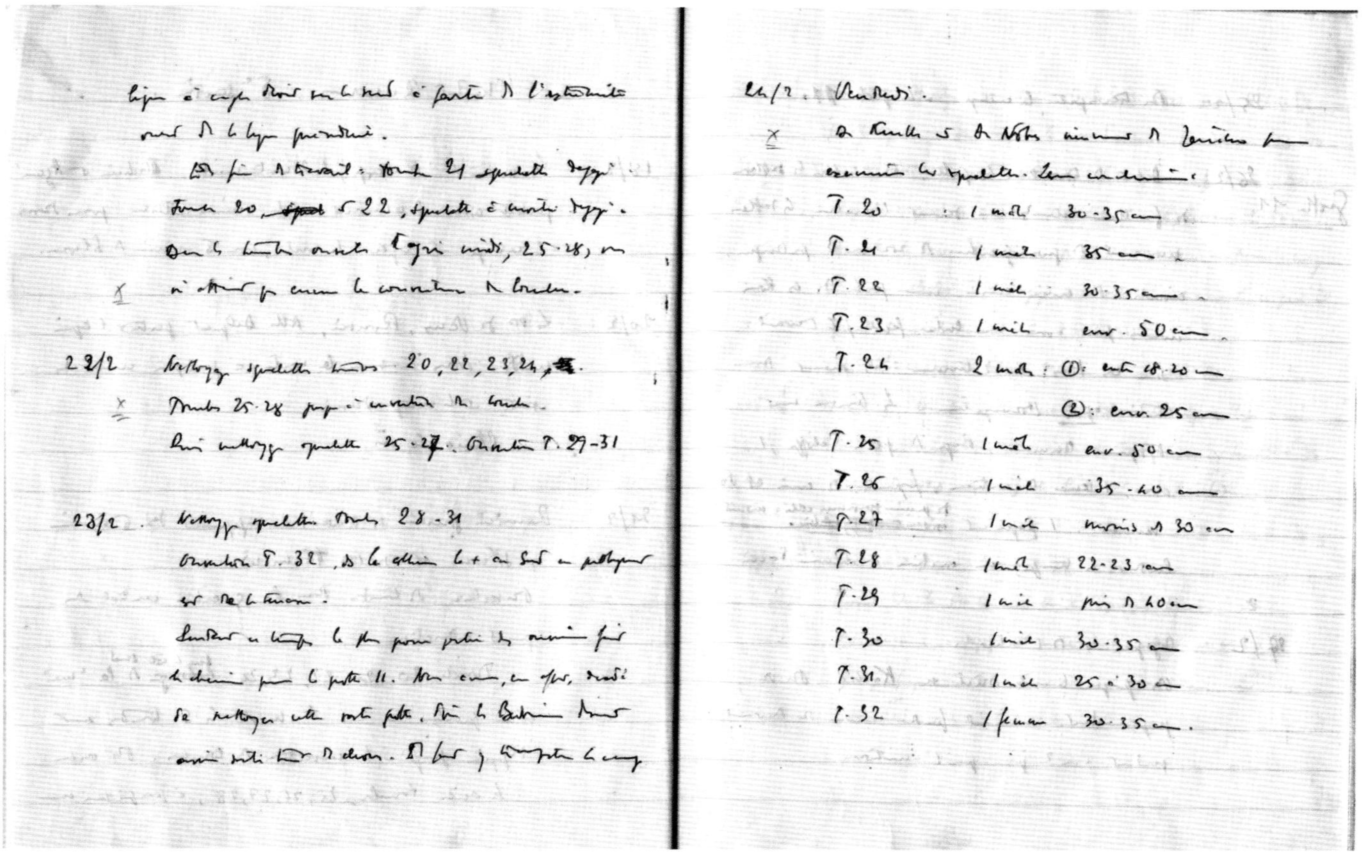

Fig. 2. The excavation diary, 21/2 - 24/2/1956 (notes about Cave 11Q on 23/2)

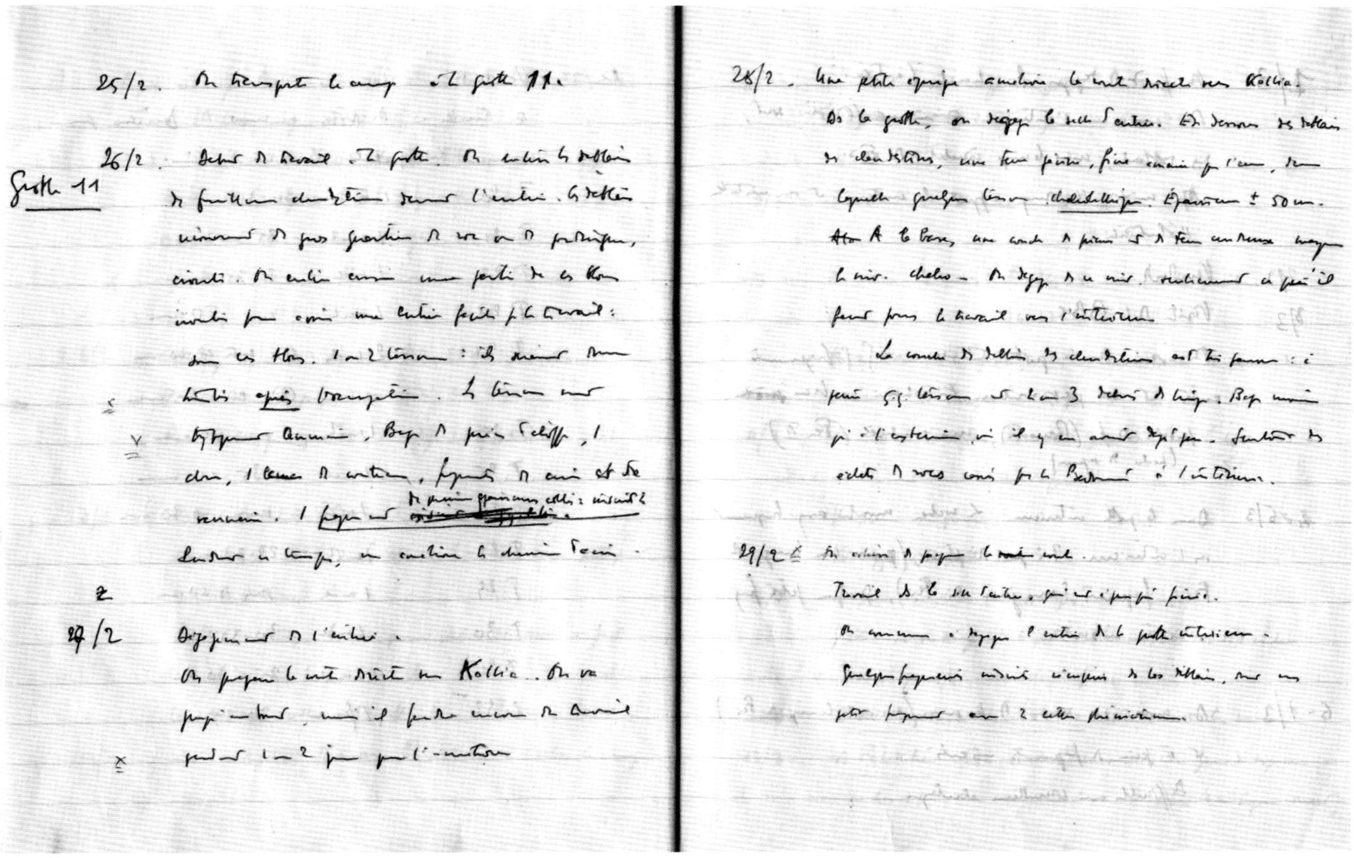

Fig. 3. The excavation diary, 25/2 - 29/2/1956

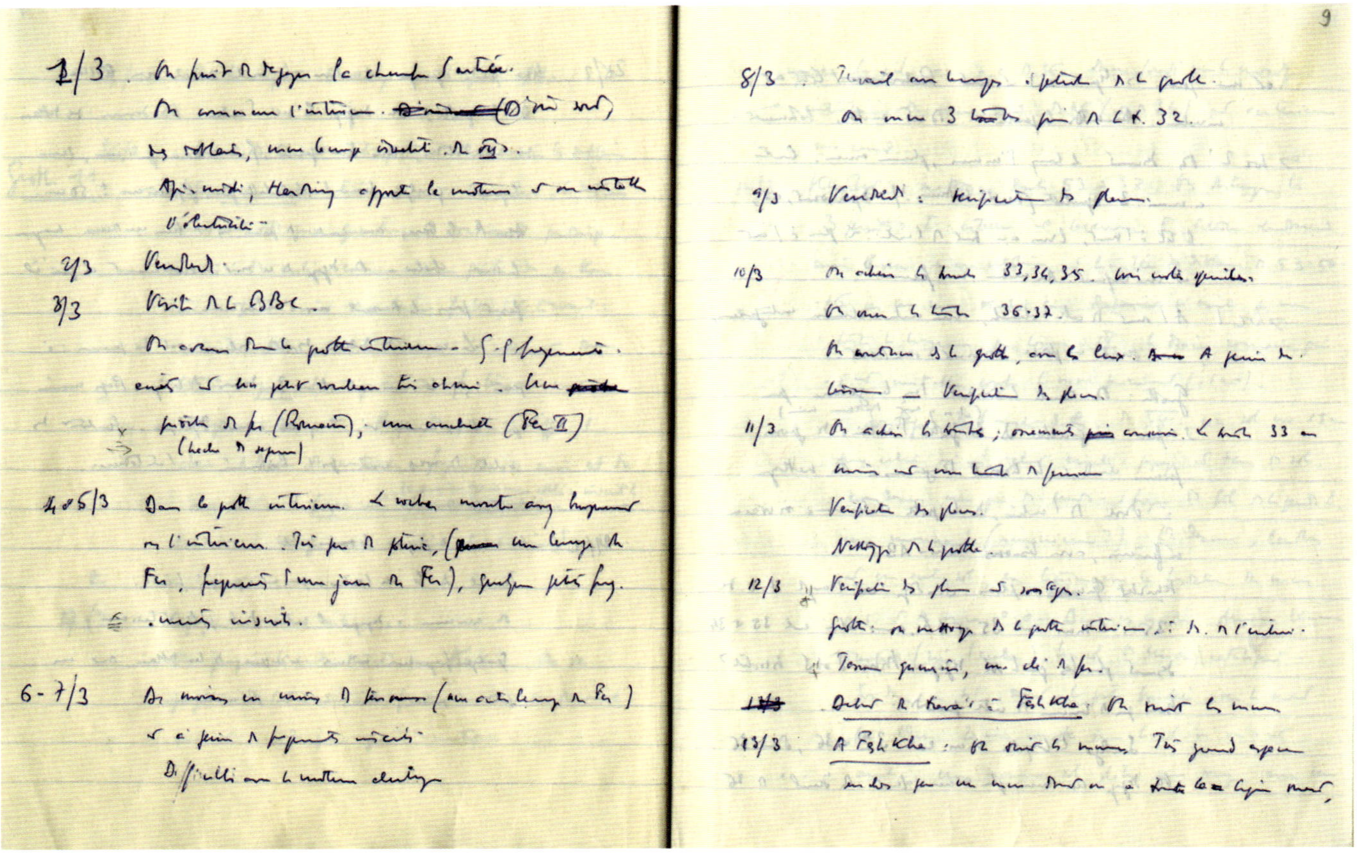

Fig. 4. The excavation diary, 1/3 - 13/3/1956

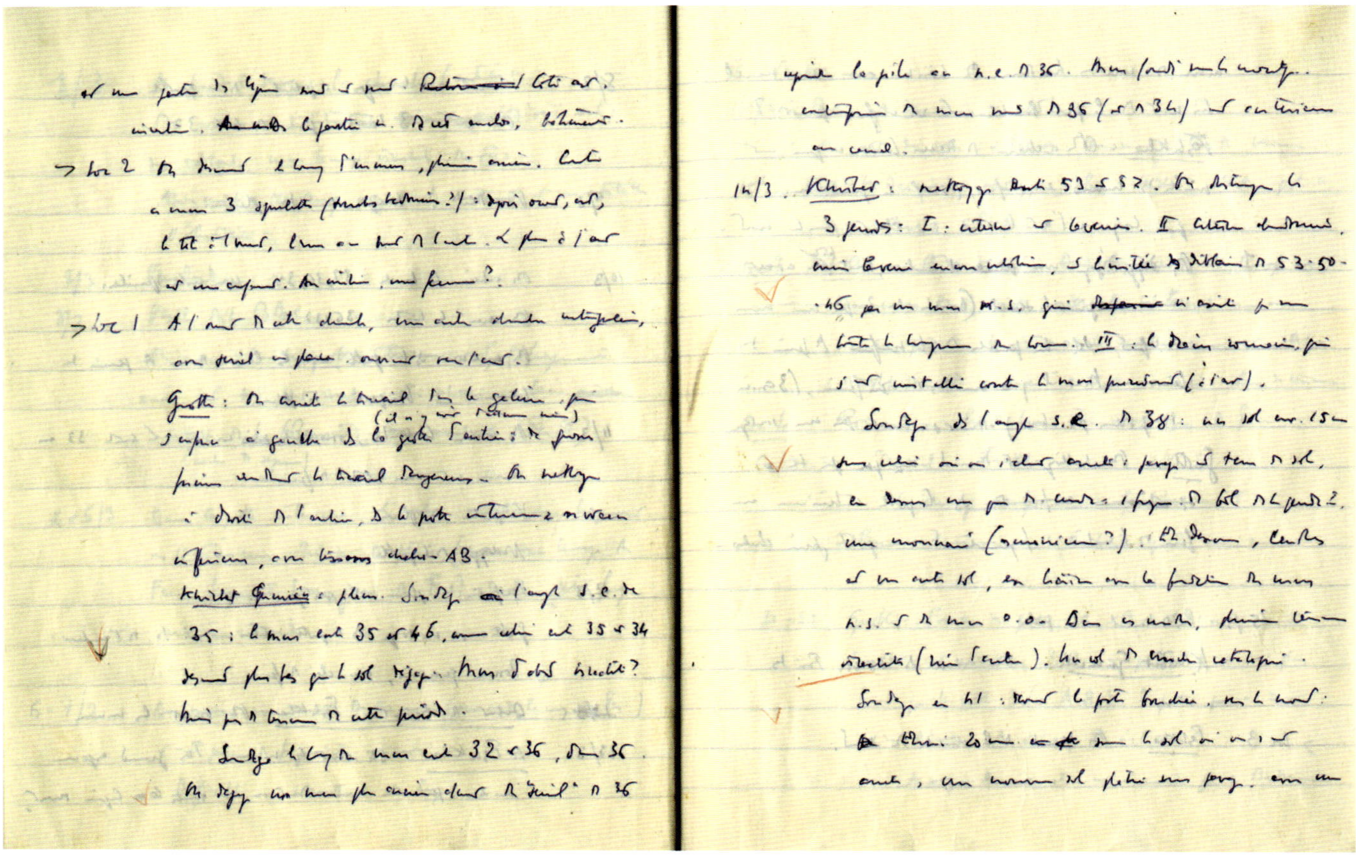

Fig. 5. The excavation diary, 13/3 - 14/3/1956 (notes about Cave 11Q on 13/3)

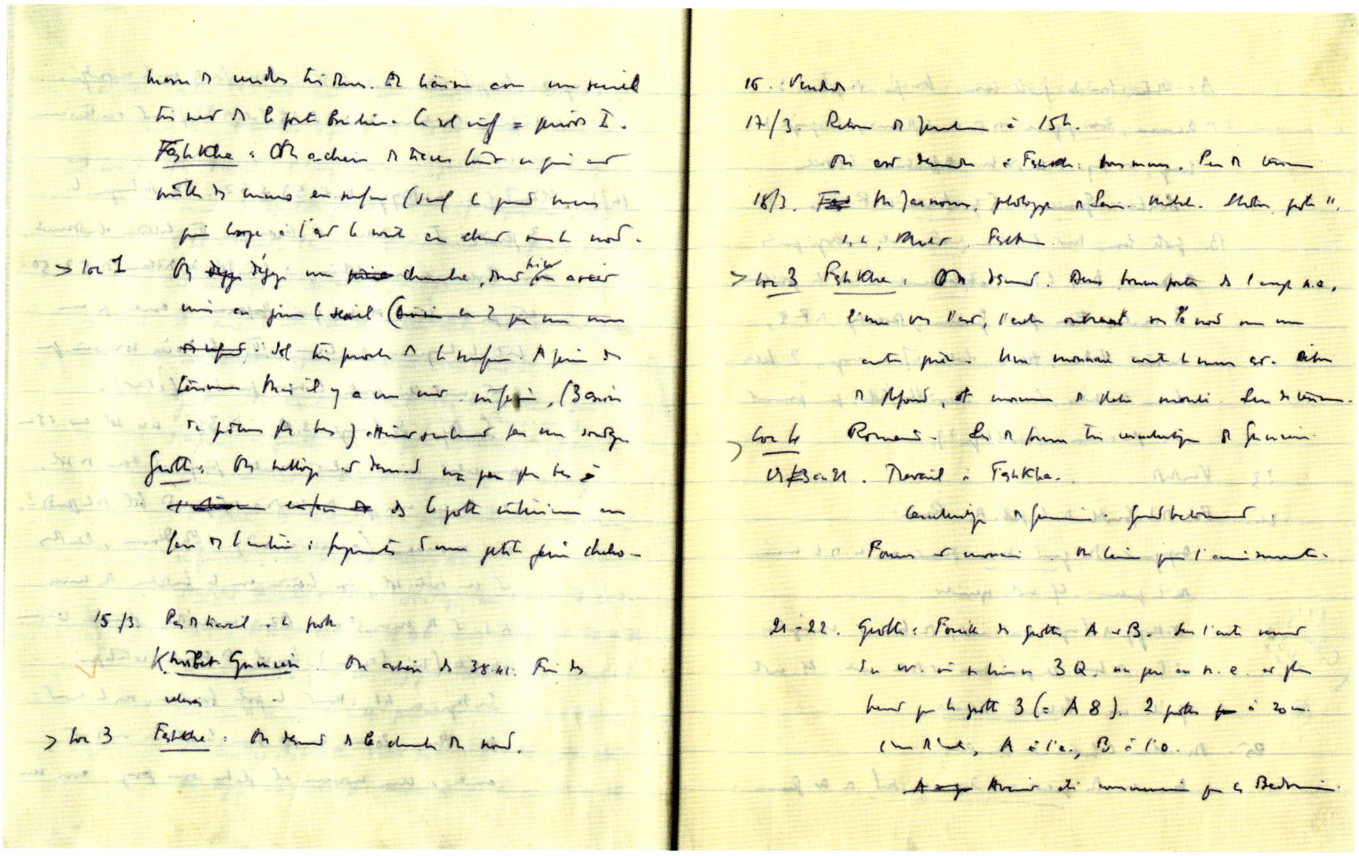

Fig. 6. The excavation diary, 14/3 - 22/3/1956 (notes about Cave 11Q on 14-15/3)

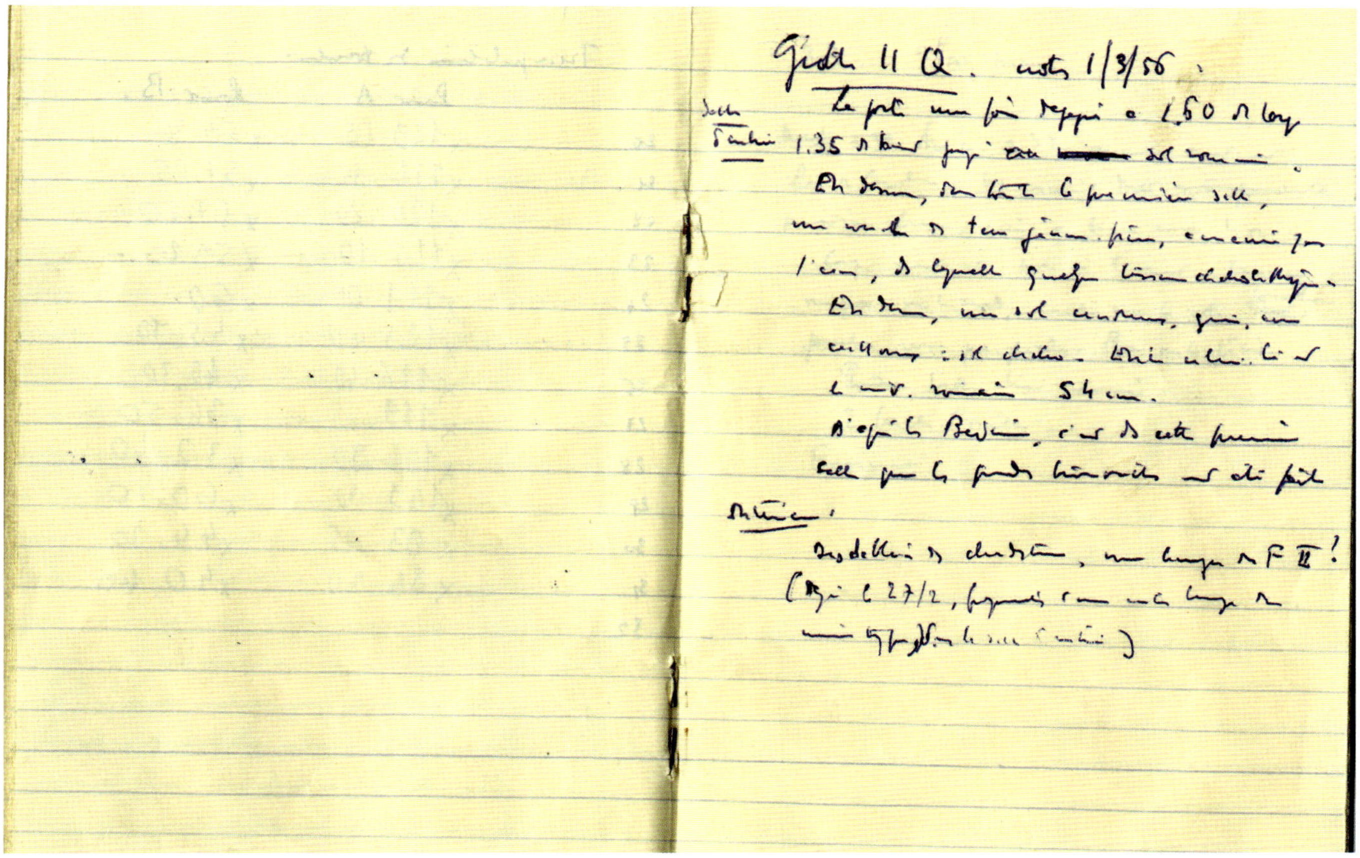

Fig. 7. The field notes

Cave 11Q were published in 1994[8]. Rather than being a literal transcription, the two sources were integrated into a single text, with sentences re-phrased, in line with the curators' intention of turning some notes into a proper French text, in order to facilitate the reader's understanding. The list of the finds, which follows the text, is not in the original manuscripts, and was prepared by the editors of the 1994 volume, on the basis of the inventory of materials (see below 1.2), to fit in with the standard followed for the Khirbeh. The English translation by Stephen Pfann – revised from the original text and often quoted in scientific texts ever since –, for Cave 11Q relies on the formulations of the text published in French.[9] A comparison with the original manuscripts reveals a number of issues both in the French and the English editions. Due to these issues and the objective difficulty of reading the manuscripts, we have decided to publish here a photographic reproduction of the sources, followed by a literal transcription of the French text, and a revision of the English translation.

1.1.1 *Transcriptions*[10]

EXCAVATION DIARY

23/2 [...]
Pendant ce temps la plus grand partie des ouvriers fait | le chemin pour la grotte 11. Nous avons, en plus, décidé | de nettoyer cette vaste grotte. D'ici les Bedouins disent | avoir sorti tant de choses. Il faut y transporter le camp.

24/2 [...]

25/2 On transporte le camp à la grotte 11.

26/2 (Grotte 11) Début du travail à la grotte. On enlève les déblais | des fouilleurs clandestins devant l'entrée. Les déblais | recouvrent de gros quartiers de roc ou de poudingue, | écroulés.
On enlève aussi une partie de ces blocs | écroulés pour avoir une entrée facile p [i.e. pour] le travail : | dans ces blocs. 1 ou 2 tessons : ils seraient donc | tombés après l'occupation. Les tessons sont | typiquement Qumrân. Bcp [i.e. beaucoup] des pièces de chiffon, 1 | clou, 1 lame de couteau, fragments de cuir et de | vannerie. 1 fragment de plusieurs épaisseurs collées : inscrits ? | Pendant ce temps, on améliore le chemin d'accès.

27/2 Dégagement de l'entrée.
On prépare la route directe vers Kalhia.. On va | jusqu'au bout, mais il faudra encore du travail | pendant 1 ou 2 jours pour l'ouverture

----

28/2 Une petite équipe améliore la route directe vers Kalhia. | Ds [i.e. dans] la grotte, on dégage la salle d'entrée. En-dessous des déblais | des clandestins, une terre jaune, fine amenée par l'eau, dans | laquelle quelques tessons chalcolithiques. Épaisseur +/- 50 cm. | À la base, une couche de pierres et de terre cendreuse marque | le niv. [i.e. niveau] chalco [i.e. chalcolithique]. On dégage de ce niv. [i.e. niveau] seulement ce qu'il | faut pour le travail vers l'intérieur.
La couche de déblais des clandestins est très pauvre : à | peine q.q [i.e. quelques] tessons et 2 ou 3 débris de linge. Bcp [i.e. beaucoup] moins | qu'à l'extérieur, où il y en avait déjà peu. Surtout des | éclats de rocs cassés par les Bédouins à l'intérieur.

29/2 On achève de préparer la route.
Travail ds [i.e. dans] la salle d'entrée, qui est à peu près finie.
On commence à dégager l'entrée de la grotte intérieure. Quelques fragments inscrits récupérés dans les déblais, dont un | petit fragment avec 2 lettres phéniciennes.

1/3 On finit de dégager la chambre d'entrée.
On commence l'intérieur. D'où sort, | des déblais, une lampe israélite. du VIIe.
Après-midi, Harding apporte le moteur et on installe | l'électricité.

---

and Chambon, *Excavations of Khirbet Qumran*, xvi-xvii.

8. J.-B. Humbert and A. Chambon (ed.), *Fouilles de Khirbet Qumrân et de 'Aïn Feshkha: Vol. I: Album de photographies. Répertoire du fonds photographique. Synthèse des notes de chantier du Père Roland de Vaux OP* (NTOA.SA 1; Fribourg/Göttingen: Éditions Universitaires/Vandenhoeck & Ruprecht, 1994), 344.

9. Humbert and Chambon, *Excavations of Khirbet Qumran*, 67-8.

10. Text compiled by Jean-Baptiste Humbert and Marcello Fidanzio, with the collaboration of Jean-Michel de Tarragon and Marco De Pietri.

2/3 Vendredi

3/3 Visite de la BBC.
On avance dans la grotte intérieure. Q.q [i.e. quelques] fragments | écrits et un petit rouleau très abîmé. Une | pioche de fer (Romaine) [*below the line*] (hache de sapeur) ; une cruchette (Fer II)

4 et 5/3 Dans la grotte intérieure. Le rocher monte assez brusquement | vs [i.e. vers] l'intérieur. Très peu de poterie, (une lampe du | Fer, fragments d'une jarre du Fer), quelques petits frag. | .ments inscrits.

6-7/3 De moins en moins de tessons (une autre lampe du Fer) | et à peine de fragments inscrits
Difficultés avec le moteur électrique

8/3 Travail aux lampes à pétrole ds [i.e. dans] la grotte. On ouvre 3 tombes puis de la T.32.

9/3 Vendredi : vérification des plans.

10/3 On achève les tombes 33, 34, 35. Voir notes spéciales.
On ouvre les tombes 36-37.
On continue ds [i.e. dans] la grotte, avec les lux. À peine de | tessons. Vérification des plans.

11/3 On achève les tombes ; ossements conservés. La tombe 33 au | moins est une tombe de femme
Vérification des plans.
Nettoyage de la grotte.

12/3 Vérification des plans et sondages.
Grotte : on nettoye dans la grotte intérieure. à dr. [i.e. droite] de l'entrée. | Tessons qumrân, une clé de fer. Début du travail à Feshkha. On suit les murs.

13/3 À Feshkha : On suit les murs. [...]

[...]
Grotte : On arrête le travail dans la galerie, qui | s'enfonce à gauche ds [i.e. dans] la grotte d'entrée [*above the line*] (il n'y avait d'ailleurs rien) : de grosses | pierres rendent le travail dangereux. On nettoye | à droite de l'entrée, ds [i.e. dans] la grotte intérieure : niveau | inférieur, avec tessons chalco [i.e. chalcolithique] - AB [i.e. Ancien Bronze].

Khirbet Qumrân : plans. [...]

14/3 Khirbet : nettoyage [...]

[...]
Grotte : On nettoye et descend un peu plus bas | ds [i.e. dans] la grotte intérieure en face de l'entrée : fragments d'une petite jarre chalco [i.e. chalcolithique].

15/3 Pas de travail à la grotte

FIELD NOTES

Grotte 11Q. notes 1/3/56.

Salle d'entrée La porte une fois dégagée a 1,60 de large | 1,35 de haut jusqu'au sol romain. | En dessous, dans toute la première salle, | une couche de terre jaune, fine, amenée par | l'eau, ds [i.e. dans] laquelle quelques tessons chalcolithiques. | En dessous, un sol cendreux, gris, avec | cailloux : sol chalco. [i.e. chalcolithique] Entre celui ci et | le niv. romain 54 cm.
D'après les Bédouins, c'est ds [i.e. dans] cette première | salle que les grandes trouvailles ont été faites.

Interieur :
Dans déblais des clandestins, une lampe du F II ? | (déjà le 27/2, fragments comme la lampe du même type dans le sol d'entrée)

1.1.2 *Translation*[11]

EXCAVATION DIARY

23/2 [...]
During this time the greater part of the workers make the path for cave 11. In addition, we have decided to clean out this vast cave. From here the Bedouins say they have released many things. It is necessary to move the camp there.

24/2 [...]

25/2 We move the camp to cave 11.

11. Translation by Joan Taylor.

26/2 (Cave 11) Beginning of work at the cave. We remove the debris of clandestine diggers in front of the entrance. The debris covers large pieces of rock or pudding stone, collapsed. We remove also a portion of these collapsed blocks in order to have an easy entry for the work: in these blocks. 1 or 2 sherds: therefore they would have fallen after the occupation. The sherds are typically Qumran. Many pieces of textile, 1 nail, 1 knife blade, fragments of leather and basketry. 1 fragment of several thicknesses glued: written? Meanwhile, we improve the access path.

27/2 Clearance of the entrance. We prepare the direct route towards Kalhia. We go to the end, but it will still need to take 1 or 2 days' more work before opening.

28/2 A small team improves the direct route towards Kalhia. In the cave, we clear the entrance chamber. Below the debris of the clandestine [diggers], a yellow, fine, earth, brought by water, in which, some Chalcolithic sherds. Thickness +/- 50 cm. At the base, a layer of stones and ashy earth marks the Chalcolithic level. We remove from this level only what is needed for the work towards the interior.
The layer of debris of the clandestine [diggers] is very poor: hardly any sherds and 2 or 3 bits of cloth. Much less than outside, where there were a few already. Mainly some splinters of rocks broken by the Bedouins inside.

29/2 We complete the preparation of the route.
Work in the entrance chamber, which is almost finished.
We start to clear the entrance of the inner cave.
Some inscribed fragments recovered in the debris, one of which is a small fragment with 2 Phoenician letters.

1/3 We finish clearing the entrance chamber.
We start the interior. From which there comes, out of the debris, an Israelite lamp. of the VIIth [century]. In the afternoon, Harding brings the engine and we install the electricity.

2/3 Friday

3/3 Visit of the BBC.
We advance into the inner cave. Some written fragments, and a small scroll, very damaged. An iron mattock (Roman) [*below the line*: (sapper's axe)]. A juglet (Iron II)

4 and 5/3 In the inner cave. The rock climbs quite abruptly towards the inside. Very little pottery (a lamp from [the] Iron [age], fragments of a jar from [the] Iron [age]), some small written fragments.

6-7/3 Fewer and fewer sherds (another lamp from [the] Iron [age]) and hardly any written fragments. Difficulties with the electric motor.

8/3 Working with oil lamps in the cave. We open three tombs after T.32.

9/3 Friday: verification of plans.

10/3 We complete the tombs 33, 34, 35. See special notes.
We open tombs 36-37. We continue in the cave, with the lamps. Hardly any sherds. Verification of plans.

11/3 We complete the tombs; bones conserved. Tomb 33 at least is a woman's tomb Verification of plans. Cleaning of the cave.

12/3 Verification of plans and soundings. Cave: we clean in the inner cave. To the right of the entry. Qumran sherds, an iron key.
Beginning of work at Feshkha. We follow the walls.

13/3 At Feshkha: we follow the walls.

[...]

Cave: we stop the work in the gallery, which sinks to the left in the entrance cave [*above the line*: (there was nothing else)]: large stones make the work dangerous. We clean to the right of the entry, in the inner cave: lower level, with Chalcolithic – Early Bronze sherds. Khirbet Qumran: plans. [...]

14/3 Khirbet: cleaning [...]

Cave: we clean and descend a little lower in the inner cave facing the entrance: fragments of a small Chalcolithic jar.

15/3 No work at the cave

FIELD NOTES

Cave 11Q. Notes 1/3/56

Entrance chamber. The doorway, once cleared, is 1.60 meters wide, 1.35 meters high, to the Roman floor. Below, throughout the first chamber, a layer of yellow, fine, earth, brought by water, in which some Chalcolithic sherds. Below, an ashy soil, grey, with pebbles: Chalcolithic soil. Between this one and the Roman level 54 cm. According to the Bedouins, it is in this first chamber that the great finds have been made.

Interior:
In the debris of the clandestine [diggers], a lamp from Iron II? (already on 27/2, fragments like the lamp of the same type in the soil of the entrance)

1.1.3 *Notes*

a. In the excavation diary, the entries are taken daily, except for two instances: 4-5 and 6-7 March, when an entry spans two days. During these days, de Vaux went to Jerusalem, back and forth, several times.[12]

b. The 1956 excavation started on 18 February and ended on 28 March. It had already been planned when, in February, de Vaux got to know about the discovery of a new cave in which manuscripts had been found. The excavation started with some tombs, then the camp was moved near Cave 11Q.

c. On some days, other works were carried out while excavating the cave: on 28 February, the field notes record the triangulation of tombs previously excavated. Later, from 8 to 11 March, tombs 33-37 were excavated. On 6 March, Charles Coüasnon arrived at Qumran[13], and from 9 to 13 March de Vaux notes "verification of plans" (most probably, these are the plans of the *Khirbeh*), in parallel with the excavation at the cave.[14] After the work on the tombs was concluded, excavations started at 'Ain Feshkha on 12 March. On 13-14 March the work on Cave 11Q was completed; in the meantime, plan drawings and some soundings were carried out at Khirbet Qumran, while excavations proceeded at 'Ain Feshkha.

d. During the excavation at Cave 11Q, de Vaux faced a dispute with John Allegro, culminating in a letter of renunciation which appeared in the London Times on 16 March.[15]

e. The excavation diary registers work in Cave 11Q until 14 March. However, the photographs by Sabine Weiss (below) taken on 21 March show further work in the cave, perhaps without any significant results. See also the article by Patrick Skehan (below) about his visit on 18 March.

1.2 *Inventory*

As mentioned at the beginning of the chapter, two copies of the inventory are stored in the EBAF archives: a card index and a hardbound book. For the finds from Cave 11Q they yeld the information is the same. The inventory data are: inventory number, description, often a drawing,[16] class of material, dimensions, date and findspot. Since the card index has already been made available in a previous publication,[17] and there are also many cards reproduced in various chapters on the finds of this volume, we publish here the hardbound book's pages on Cave 11Q, Figs 8-11.

12. The *Chronique du Couvent de Saint Étienne* (EBAF archives), on Saturday 3 March, states: "Les Pères de Qumrân reviennent pour deux jours." Monday 5 March: "Les PP de Vaux et Rousée repartent pour Qumrân." The *Comptes-Rendus du Séances du Conseil* (EBAF archives) present a statement by the council held on Sunday 4 March, in which de Vaux was a registered participant. De Vaux left again for Qumran on 5 March, and came back to Jerusalem on 6 March; the *Chronique du Couvent* of Tuesday 6 March states: "Le P de Vaux revient le soir faire réparer un moteur de génératrice électrique." During those days, de Vaux wrote to Allegro twice (EBAF archives): the first letter is dated 4 March, on the occasion of a "short visit to Jerusalem;" the second letter, dated 6 March, replies to a letter by Allegro, sent on 3 March, and refers to a return "to Jerusalem for a few hours for a conference at the Palestine Museum." The *Chronique du Couvent* of Wednesday 7 March states: "Le P de Vaux chante la messe de St Thomas. Les séminaristes des Pères Lazaristes y assistent au complet. Après la messe ils sont reçus en salle commune. [...] Le P de Vaux, reparti ce matin pour Qumrân avec le moteur réparé, revient ce soir. Le moteur est de nouveau en panne." The *Chronique du Couvent* Thursday 8 March remarks that "Le P. de Vaux repart avec son moteur enfin remis en état."

13. Chronique du Couvent de Saint Étienne (EBAF archives),

14. See R. de Vaux, "Fouilles de Khirbet Qumrân: rapport préliminaire sur les 3e, 4e, et 5e campagnes," RB 63 (1956) 533-77, on p. 534.

15. See W.W. Fields, *The Dead Sea Scrolls: A Full History. Vol. 1: 1947-1960* (Leiden: Brill, 2009), 303-27.

16. In the card index small photographs of the objects are added, taken from PAM photographs reproduced in this chapter, Figs 32-3.

17. Fidanzio and Humbert, "Finds from the Qumran Caves."

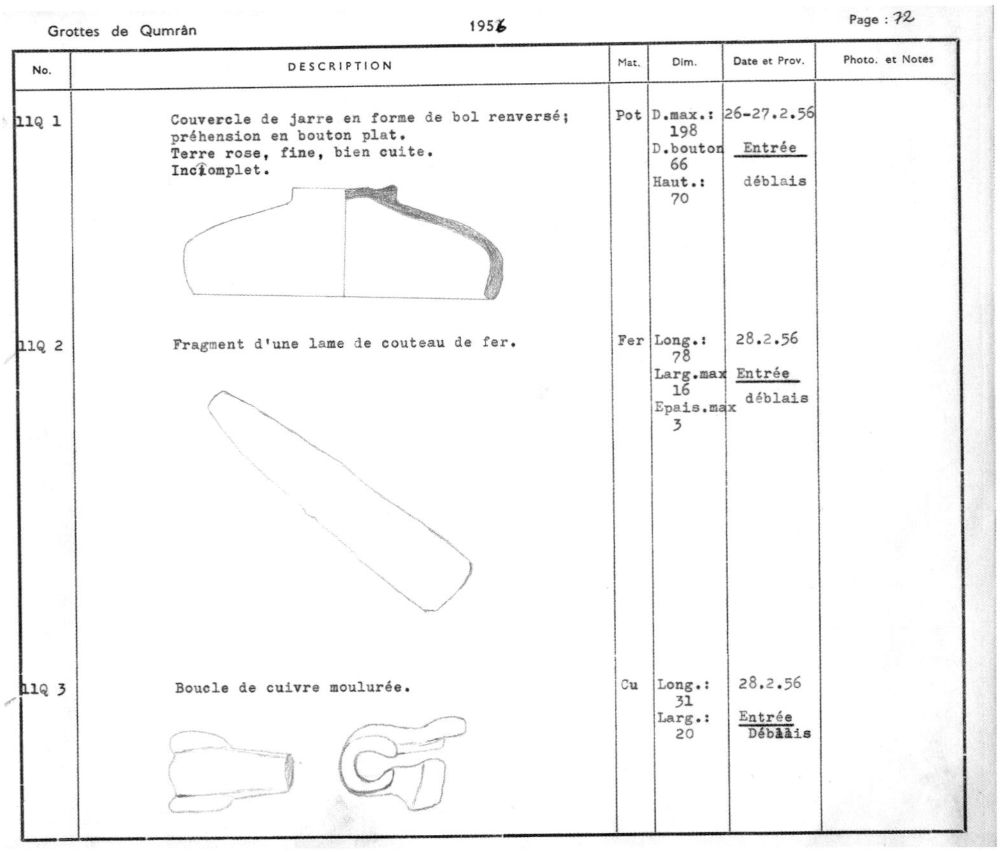

Grottes de Qumrân 1956 Page : 72

No.	DESCRIPTION	Mat.	Dim.	Date et Prov.	Photo. et Notes
11Q 1	Couvercle de jarre en forme de bol renversé; préhension en bouton plat. Terre rose, fine, bien cuite. Incomplet.	Pot	D.max.: 198 D.bouton 66 Haut.: 70	26-27.2.56 Entrée déblais	
11Q 2	Fragment d'une lame de couteau de fer.	Fer	Long.: 78 Larg.max 16 Epais.max 3	28.2.56 Entrée déblais	
11Q 3	Boucle de cuivre moulurée.	Cu	Long.: 31 Larg.: 20	28.2.56 Entrée Déblais	

Fig. 8. The inventory, hardbound Book, 72

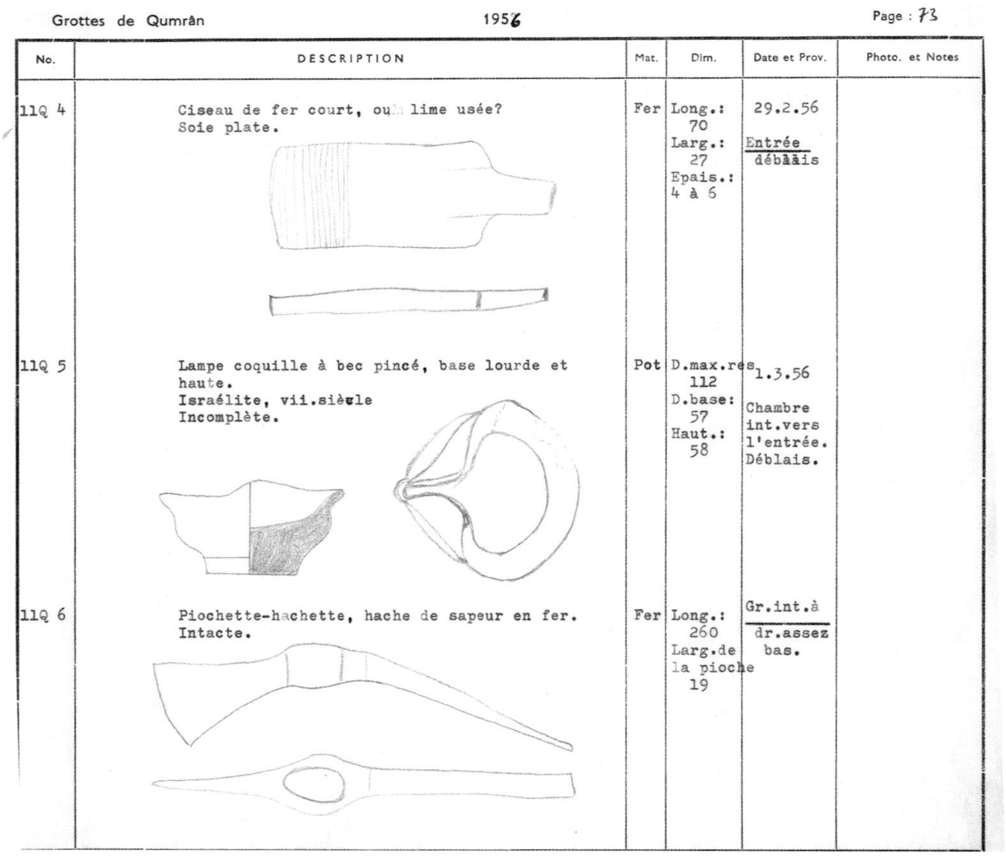

Grottes de Qumrân 1956 Page : 73

No.	DESCRIPTION	Mat.	Dim.	Date et Prov.	Photo. et Notes
11Q 4	Ciseau de fer court, ou lime usée? Soie plate.	Fer	Long.: 70 Larg.: 27 Epais.: 4 à 6	29.2.56 Entrée déblais	
11Q 5	Lampe coquille à bec pincé, base lourde et haute. Israélite, vii.siècle Incomplète.	Pot	D.max.res 112 D.base: 57 Haut.: 58	1.3.56 Chambre int.vers l'entrée. Déblais.	
11Q 6	Piochette-hachette, hache de sapeur en fer. Intacte.	Fer	Long.: 260 Larg.de la pioche 19	Gr.int.à dr.assez bas.	

Fig. 9. The inventory, hardbound Book, 73

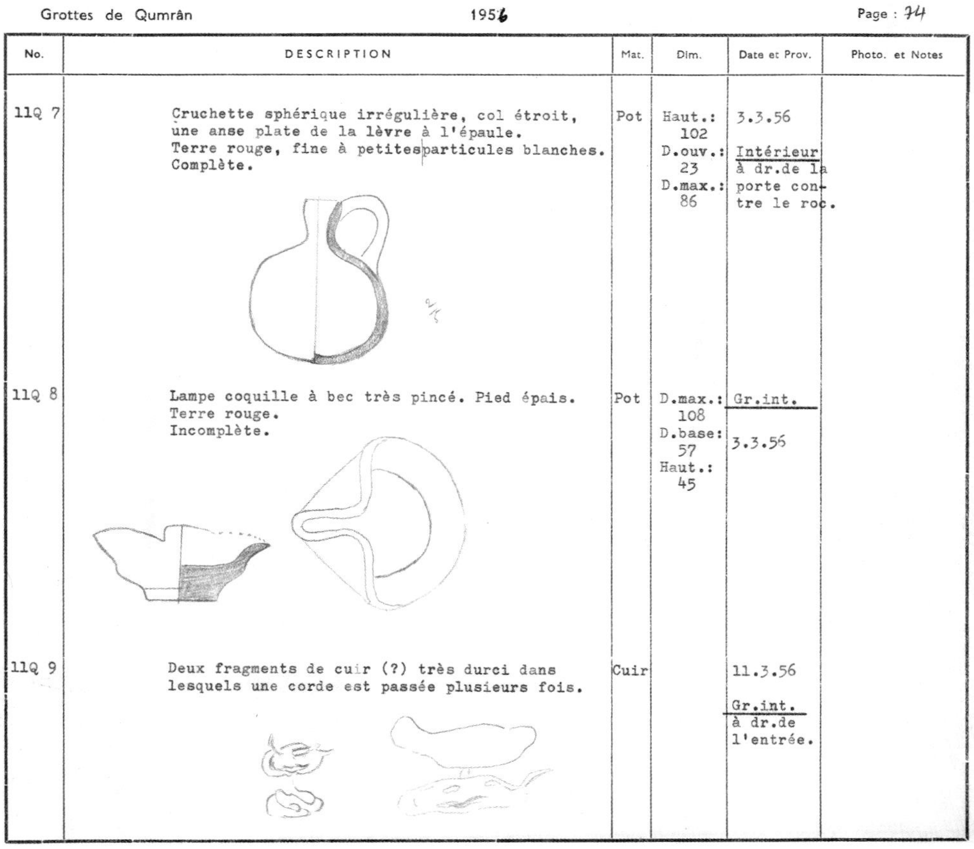

Grottes de Qumrân 1956 Page : 74

No.	DESCRIPTION	Mat.	Dim.	Date et Prov.	Photo. et Notes
11Q 7	Cruchette sphérique irrégulière, col étroit, une anse plate de la lèvre à l'épaule. Terre rouge, fine à petites particules blanches. Complète.	Pot	Haut.: 102 D.ouv.: 23 D.max.: 86	3.3.56 Intérieur à dr.de la porte contre le roc.	
11Q 8	Lampe coquille à bec très pincé. Pied épais. Terre rouge. Incomplète.	Pot	D.max.: 108 D.base: 57 Haut.: 45	Gr.int. 3.3.56	
11Q 9	Deux fragments de cuir (?) très durci dans lesquels une corde est passée plusieurs fois.	Cuir		11.3.56 Gr.int. à dr.de l'entrée.	

Fig. 10. The inventory, hardbound Book, 74

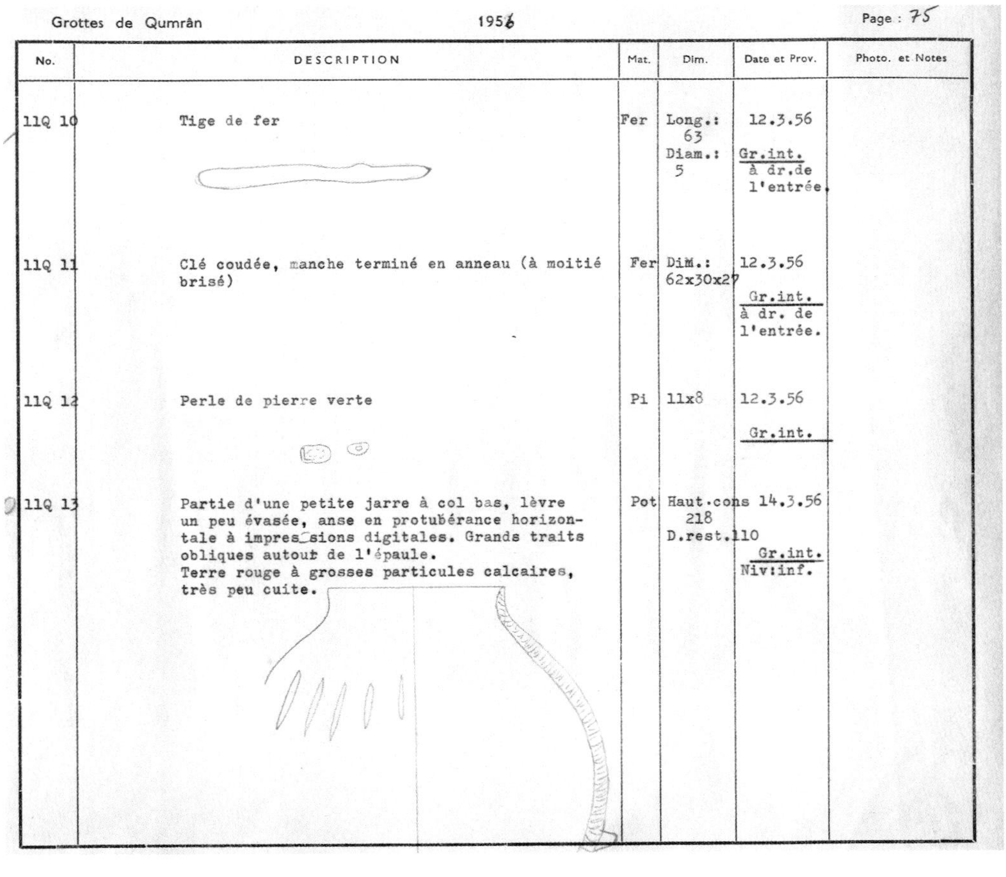

Grottes de Qumrân 1956 Page : 75

No.	DESCRIPTION	Mat.	Dim.	Date et Prov.	Photo. et Notes
11Q 10	Tige de fer	Fer	Long.: 63 Diam.: 5	12.3.56 Gr.int. à dr.de l'entrée.	
11Q 11	Clé coudée, manche terminé en anneau (à moitié brisé)	Fer	Dim.: 62x30x27	12.3.56 Gr.int. à dr. de l'entrée.	
11Q 12	Perle de pierre verte	Pi	11x8	12.3.56 Gr.int.	
11Q 13	Partie d'une petite jarre à col bas, lèvre un peu évasée, anse en protubérance horizontale à impressions digitales. Grands traits obliques autour de l'épaule. Terre rouge à grosses particules calcaires, très peu cuite.	Pot	Haut.cons 218 D.rest.110	14.3.56 Gr.int. Niv:inf.	

Fig. 11. The inventory, hardbound Book, 75

1.2.1 *Notes*

a. In the inventory, we find neither any manuscript fragments nor any textiles. They are nevertheless both mentioned in the excavation diary and in the preliminary report. Some classes of materials (coins, textiles) were entrusted to other scholars and inventoried separately.[18]

b. The inventory does not include any basketry, ropes, or sherds of Iron II jars, although they are kept in storerooms and mentioned in the excavation diary and the preliminary report. Other objects found in Cave 11Q are preserved in storerooms (a leather tab from a scroll, small wooden objects, seeds), but are not mentioned in written sources.

c. The catalogue and the preliminary report mention two Iron II lamps. The excavation diary records a third lamp (though some problems arise in comparing the diary to the inventory also concerning the find-date of the second lamp), while the field notes mention fragments of a further lamp. The storerooms hold only two lamps from Cave 11Q.

d. In the preliminary report, two lids and a juglet, in connection to the main occupation of Khirbet Qumran, are mentioned.[19] Their absence both in the inventory and the storerooms is surprising, considering the common interest for the period when the deposition of the manuscripts took place. This is even more crucial, since the only remaining pottery find assigned to the Roman period is the lid Gr11Q1.

18. As regards textiles, this occurred for Cave 1Q and Murabba'at caves only, due to the death of Grace M. Crowfoot. The remaining textiles stayed stored until the 90s. See M. Bélis, "Des Textiles: Catalogues et Commentaires," in J.-B. Humbert and J. Gunneweg (ed.), *Khirbet Qumrân et 'Aïn Feshkha: Vol. II: Études d'anthropologie, de physique et de chimie* (NTOA.SA 3; Fribourg/Göttingen: Éditions Universitaires/Vandenhoeck & Ruprecht, 2003) 207-76; Id., "The Unpublished Textiles from the Qumran Caves," in Fidanzio, *The Caves of Qumran*, 123-36. The same happened for the coins from Khirbet Qumran inventoried by Augustus Spijkerman. See B. Callegher, "The Coins of Khirbet Qumran from the Digs of Roland de Vaux: Returning to Henri Seyrig and Augustus Spijkerman," in M. Fidanzio (ed.), *The Caves of Qumran: Proceedings of the International Conference, Lugano 2014* (STDJ 118; Leiden: Brill, 2016) 221-237.

19. De Vaux, "Fouilles de Khirbet Qumrân," 574.

2. Preliminary Report and Other Published Texts

R. de Vaux, "Fouilles de Khirbet Qumrân : rapport préliminaire sur les 3e, 4e, et 5e campagnes," *RB* 63 (1956) 533-77, on pp. 573-4.

[Page 573] Peu avant l'ouverture de notre campagne de 1956, nous avons appris que les Bédouins avaient découvert, dans la région de Qumrân, une nouvelle grotte contenant des manuscrits. Le Musée Archéologique de Palestine s'emploie à rassembler les éléments de cette trouvaille, qui est importante, mais nous ne pouvons considérer ici que notre travail de fouille.

La grotte a été repérée par nous et, étant la onzième grotte où des documents écrits ont été trouvés, elle a reçu l'indicatif 11Q. Elle se trouve à presque 2 km au nord du Khirbet, un peu au sud de la Grotte 3, où nous avions découvert les rouleaux de cuivre en 1952. Elle comprend une première chambre circulaire, à l'arrière de laquelle s'ouvre une grande chambre dont le sol rocheux monte rapidement. Celle-ci était remplie de guano de chauves-souris, qui a rendu le travail fort pénible. Nous avons vidé entièrement ces deux chambres.

[Page 574] La chambre antérieure a été la plus habitée. On distingue trois périodes d'occupation. Au-dessus du sol vierge, une couche contient des tessons chalcolithiques de facture très grossière ; la seule pièce vraiment caractéristique est une petite jarre incomplète à col bas, avec anse horizontale à impressions digitales et de grands traits obliques incisés autour du col. Cette couche est surmontée d'un dépôt naturel de terre jaune, puis d'une couche israélite, avec des fragments de jarres, deux lampes à bec pincé et à base épaisse, une cruchette sphérique : l'ensemble date du VIIe siècle avant notre ère. Il y a enfin une couche contemporaine de l'occupation de Khirbet Qumrân. Elle contenait quelques objets de fer, une piochette, un ciseau (ou une lime), un couteau, et peu de poterie ; mais les formes sont bien caractéristiques et ont leurs parallèles au Khirbet et dans les autres grottes, en particulier une cruchette et deux couvercles en forme de bol renversé. Dans cette couche ont été recueillis des débris de linge et de vannerie, des bouts de cordes et quelques fragments inscrits sur peau, dont plusieurs en caractères paléo-hébreux.

Si pauvres qu'ils soient, ces fragments écrits compléteront utilement ce qu'on espère récupérer des Bédouins. L'histoire de la grotte est intéressante en elle-même. Son occupation à l'époque israélite s'accorde avec les observations faites au Khirbet et avec des trouvailles isolées venant d'autres grottes. Nous avions déjà eu, lors de notre exploration de 1952, quelques indices d'une occupation de cette région à l'époque chalcolithique ; ils sont maintenant plus nets. Les trois périodes chalcolithique, israélite tardive et romaine paraissent être les seules où ce coin du désert ait été un peu habité.

R. de Vaux, "Archéologie," in M. Baillet, J.T. Milik, and R. de Vaux, *Les 'petites grottes' de Qumrân : Exploration de la falaise. Les grottes 2Q, 3Q, 5Q, 6Q, 7Q à 10Q. Le rouleau de cuivre* (DJD 3; Oxford: Clarendon, 1962) 3-36, on pp. 4, 34.

[Page 4] Nous savions bien que nous n'avions pas épuise toutes les possibilités et, de fait, les Bedouins ont trouvé après nous, en septembre 1952, un trou rocheux qui contenait des fragments, la grotte 6Q et en janvier 1956 une grotte dont l'entrée était bouchée et dont ils ont tiré un important lot de manuscrits, la grotte 11Q. [Cf. provisoirement Revue Biblique, lxiii, 1956, p. 573. Le rapport détaillé sur la fouille que nous avons faite après cette découverte aura sa place normale en tête de la publication des textes qui proviennent de cette grotte.]

[...]

[Page 34] Si l'on considère seulement les grottes qui contenaient des documents écrits, la présence de ceux-ci s'explique de différentes façons. Ces textes peuvent être ceux qu'un membre ou un petit groupe de la communauté avaient à leur usage et qu'ils ont abandonnés dans la grotte qu'ils habitaient (grottes 5Q, 7 à 9Q, 11Q) ou qu'ils ont entreposes ou caches, avec leur vaisselle, dans une cavité voisine de leur lieu de campement (grottes 2Q, 3Q, 6Q).

R. de Vaux, *Archaeology and the Dead Sea Scrolls* (The Schweich Lectures 1959; London: Oxford University Press for the British Academy, 1973), 51, 56-57.

[Page 51] In 1956, a little to the south of Cave 3Q, they [i.e. the Bedouins] opened up a cave (Cave 11Q), the entrance of which had become blocked, and took an important group of manuscripts from it. It was excavated by the three institutions working at Khirbet Qumran at the time [...]. This cave had been inhabited in the Chalcolithic period, in Iron Age II, and finally at the same period as Khirbet Qumran, as the pottery found there (but rare elsewhere) attests.

[...]

[Page 56] The natural cavities in the rock cliffs, on the other hand, vary greatly in character. There are caves with wide mouths and high roofs which still serve, on occasion, as shelters for shepherds and their flocks, as well as others which [Page 57] would once have been habitable although they have subsequently been damaged by falls of rock. Caves 3Q and 11Q are cases in point.

G.L. Harding, "Recent Discoveries in Jordan," *PEQ* 90 (1958) 7-18, on p. 17.

Early in 1956 the Bedouins found another cave containing manuscripts, a little to the north of Cave 1, and only a few yards from where we pitched our camp when in 1952 we examined some 50 caves in the vicinity. The cave is situated some 50 feet up the scarp, and the entrance had collapsed anciently, leaving only a very small hole to give access to the interior, which was why we had missed it. Cave hunting is now the chief occupation of the Ta'amireh, and many of them devote their whole time to it, so they have ample leisure in which to examine every little nook and cranny. I think that not more than one in every ten of the cracks and hole into which they insert themselves produces anything at all, and only about one in twenty yields any inscribed material, and then usually in small quantity. But in this case their luck was in, and I was brought some truly magnificent pieces of scrolls, the best in conditions that we have seen since Cave 1, though they were not in jars.

P.W. Skehan, *ASOR Newsletter* 5, Jerusalem 15 June 1956.

The American School chose Sunday, March 18, for an all-day picnic in that area. We quite easily reached not only the Essene settlement itself, but also the "built spring" farther south at Ein Feshkha. [...] The most novel feature of the day, however, was to find the excavation tents of Père de Vaux, G. L. Harding and their staff, pitched neither at the settlement (near which they examined a number of burials and isolated structures, again this season), nor at Ein Feshkha (which yielded traces of an occupation contemporary with Qumran, sufficiently large in scope to call for fuller excavation in future winter seasons), but almost a kilometer north of Cave 1. Just to the north [...] there looks out over an irregular shelf, neither so high on the cliff-face as Cave 1, nor so low as the marly stratum occupied by the Qumran settlement, a newly rediscovered cave which had been plugged at the opening with fairly enormous masses of rock. The Bedouin reclaimed this in February from centuries of occupation by bats; these had left it filled with guano almost to the roof. What the Bedouin found is, in detail a story for the future; but it was enough to set the archaeologists digging again, until Père de Vaux, in some indignation at coming upon a seemingly Chalcolithic level amid the dust and acrid fumes of the cave, offered to leave that part of the operation for his visitors to undertake.

J.A. Fitzmyer, *Responses to 101 Questions on the Dead Sea Scrolls* (New York: Paulist, 1992), 5.

The small Cave 6 was found by Bedouins, as was Cave 11. In the latter case, the Bedouins noticed a bat fly into a crevice of the cliffs a little south of Cave 3, which they then opened and proceeded to clean out completely, recovering many valuable texts from the guano-filled cave. Archaeologists, however, did eventually retrieve a few fragments from Cave 11, which served again to verify the texts subsequently bought from the Bedouins as actually derived from that cave.

3. Report on Joseph Patrich's Excavations of Cave 11Q (1988, 1991)

J. Patrich, "Khirbet Qumran in the Light of New Archaeological Explorations in the Qumran Caves," in M.O. Wise et al. (ed.), *Methods of Investigation of the Dead Sea Scrolls and the Khirbet Qumran Site: Present Realities and Future Prospects* (ANYAS 722; New York: New York Academy of Sciences, 1994) 73-95, on pp. 77, 82, 90.

[Page 77] Cave 11Q. The cave was nor excavated or recorded by the 1952 expedition. In 1956 the Taamire Bedouin found here several large documents, including a Psalms Scroll, an Aramaic paraphrase of Job, and presumably the Temple Scroll as well. As a consequence it was entirely cleaned out by de Vaux, who was working then at Khirbet Qumran. The finds included a small pick, a chisel, and a knife, all of iron. The amount of pottery was small, but typical of Qumran, including a jar and two lids; there were in addition pieces of linen, basketry, ropes, and several inscribed parchments.

Starting our dig, a 20m long conveyer was installed in the cave, half inside and half outside, conveying the dirt and stones down the terrace that was [Page 90] formed in front of the cave by the dump of the previous dig. No layer that could be attributed to the Qumran period was found. Only four tiny Roman potsherds were retrieved by us from the dump heaped inside the cave, and two pieces of cloth were found in the innermost crevice.

It is clear that the scrolls were found by the Bedouin in the uppermost level, or in the north crevice. The crevice to the right of the entrance, cleared by us, was full of sterile aeolian sand.

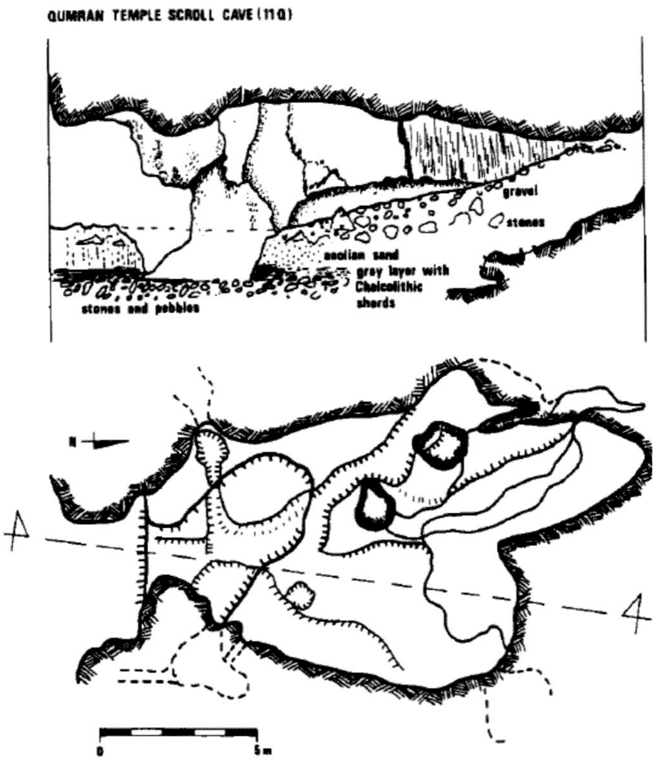

Fig. 12. Patrich's plan and cross-section (Patrich, "Khirbet Qumran," 82, Fig. 5)

4. Photographs

4.1 *De Vaux's Album*

In the Qumran archive of the EBAF, there is a multivolume photographic album. Each photograph carries a caption, and they are almost thematically organized. The photographs on Cave 11Q originate from different sources: eleven photographs documenting the excavation, taken by de Vaux ("Leica": serial numbers 15.020-024, 15.026-028; "9x12": serial numbers 14.401-403), and five PAM photographs (two of the cave, PAM 42.103-104; four of the artefacts, PAM 42.449-451, 43.734). De Vaux listed his photographs ("Leica" and "9x12" referring to the cameras used) in a notebook recording the dates when the photographs were taken and a caption. These dates are not in the album, but given the interest in documentation from the excavation, they have been inserted after the original captions of the photographs.

Fig. 13. De Vaux's photo album, 553

Fig. 14. De Vaux's photo album, 554

Fig. 15. De Vaux's photo album, 555

Fig. 16. De Vaux's photo album, 556

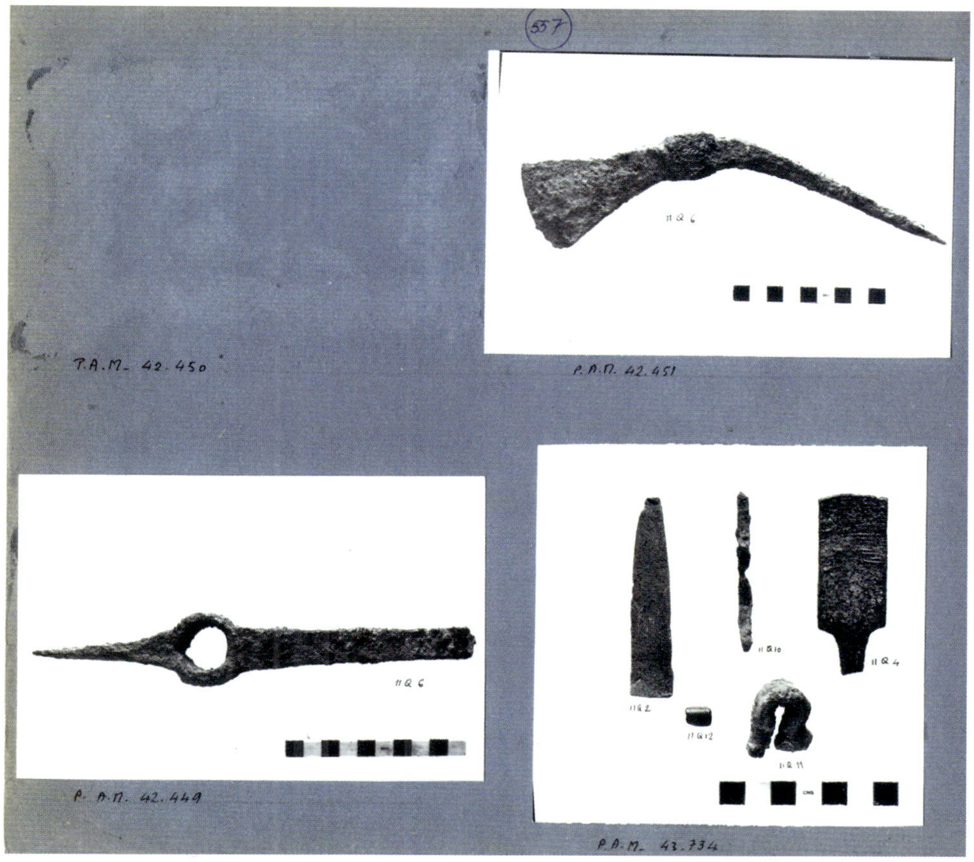

Fig. 17. De Vaux's photo album, 557

Fig. 18. De Vaux's photo album, 558

Fig. 19. De Vaux's photo album, 560

Fig. 20. 15.026 Situation de la Grotte 11. Vers le Nord [1-3 March 1956]

Fig. 21. 15.020 Situation de la Grotte 11. Vers le Nord [1-3 March 1956]

Fig. 22. 15.021 Situation de la Grotte 11. De plus près [1-3 March 1956]

Fig. 23. 14.401 Grotte 11Q [3 March 1956]

Fig. 24. 15.023 Grotte 11. Vers le Nord [1-3 March 1956]

Fig. 25. 15.022 Grotte 11. Vers le Nord.Ouest [1-3 March 1956]

Fig. 26. 14.402 Entrée de la Grotte 11Q [3 March 1956]

Fig. 27. 14.403 Intérieur de la Grotte 11Q. Pris de l'entrée [3 March 1956]

Fig. 28. PAM 42.104 Grotte 11Q. De l'entrée vers le S.E. [1-3 March 1956]

Fig. 29. PAM 42.103 Grotte 11Q vers le Nord [1-3 March 1956]

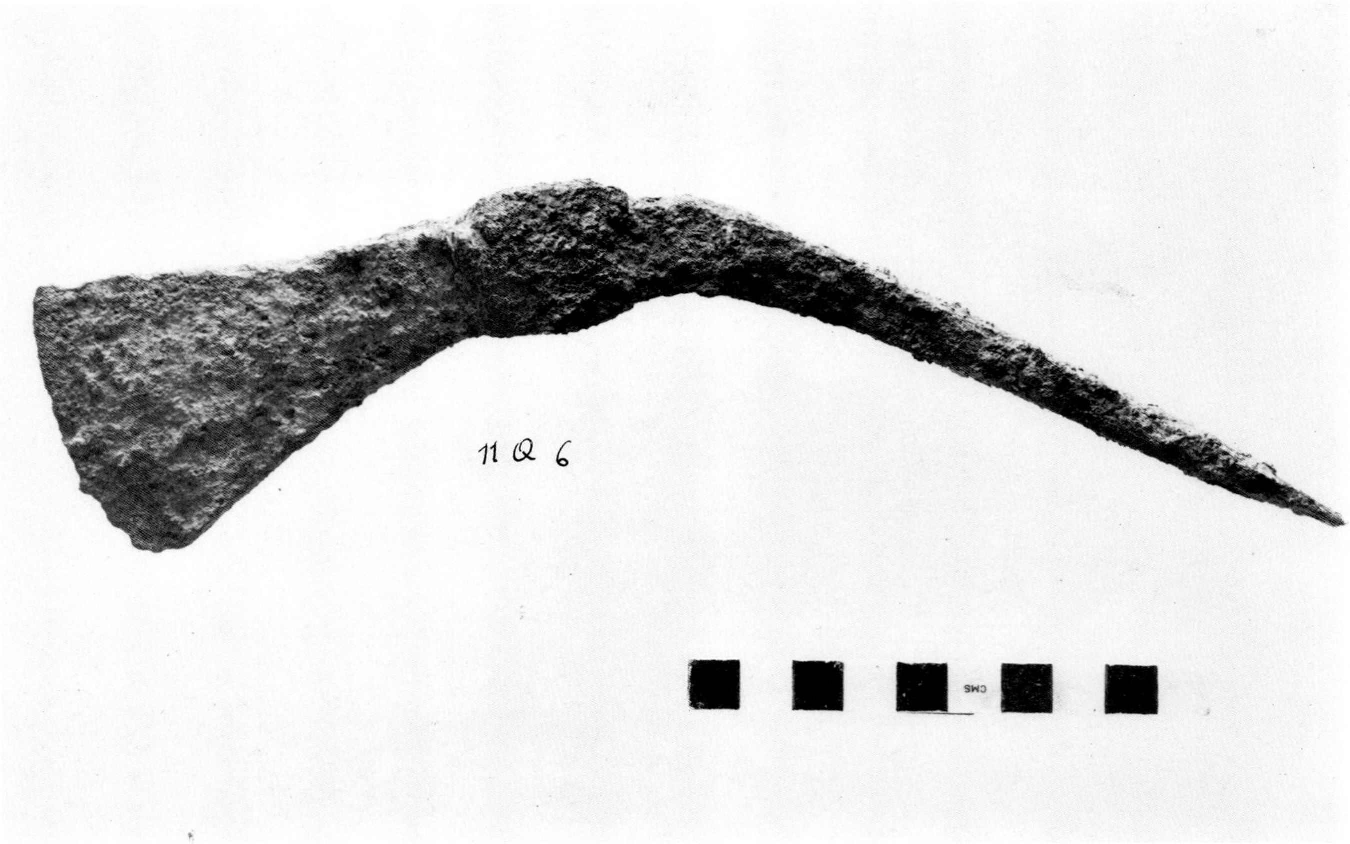

Fig. 30. PAM 42.451 [Mattock]

Fig. 31. PAM 42.449 [Mattock]

Fig. 32. PAM 43.734 [Metals and stone artefacts]

Fig. 33. PAM 43.736 Grotte 11 [Pottery]

Fig. 34. 15.028 Grotte 11. De l'intérieur vers l'entrée. Vers le S.E. [1-3 March 1956]

Fig. 35. 15.027 Vue de l'entrée de la Grotte 11. Vers le S.E. [1-3 March 1956]

Fig. 36. 15.024 Triage dans la terre à l'extérieur de la Gr. 11 [1-3 March 1956]

4.2 *Sabine Weiss*

A series of photographs was taken by Sabine Weiss. The *Chronique du Couvent de Saint Étienne* carries the following entry for 21 March: "Le P Prieur va à Qumrân avec l'Abbé Starcky et M. et Mme Weiss, deux reporters photographes de l'agence Rapho, recommandés par le P Louvel, et qui viennent effectuer un reportage sur Qumrân, mais aussi sur Jérusalem et le couvent de St Etienne. Le P de Vaux fouille de nouvelles grottes." Weiss took artistic photographs, nevertheless some of them document to some extent the situation a week after the last notes on the cave in the excavation diary.

Fig. 37. Delprat and Starcky in the entrance chamber (Photo Sabine Weiss)

Fig. 38. Rousée and Delprat in the entrance chamber (Photo Sabine Weiss)

Fig. 39. Rousée at the entrance (Photo Sabine Weiss)

4.3 *More Photographs in EBAF Archives*

EBAF archives hold more color photographs; technically, they look as if they were taken under different conditions.[20]

As regards photo 42, the excavation in the entrance chamber seems to have reached an advanced stage, similar to the one portrayed in photographs by Weiss.

Fig. 40. Cave 11Q: the entrance (color slides EBAF)

20. I thank the photographer Giorgio Skory for this technical note.

Fig. 41. The cliff above Cave 11Q (color slides EBAF)

Fig. 42. Starcky in the entrance chamber (color slides EBAF)

Fig. 43. Rousée, de Vaux, Delprat, and Bedouin workers at Cave 11Q (color slides EBAF)

Fig. 44. Rousée and de Vaux at Cave 11Q, towards the excavation camp (color slides EBAF)

Fig. 45. The excavation camp (color slides EBAF)

4.4 *John Marco Allegro*

Some photographs of Cave 11Q are in John Marco Allegro's collection. They show 11Q after de Vaux' excavation.[21]

Fig. 46. The entrance of Cave 11Q (Estate John Allegro)

21. Courtesy Estate John Allegro. Allegro's photographs were made available thanks to Judith Anne Brown and the Network for Dispersed Qumran Caves Artefacts and Archives.

Figs. 47-48. John and Joan Allegro at the entrance of Cave 11Q (Estate John Allegro)

Fig. 49. The entrance of Cave 11Q towards the Dead Sea (Estate John Allegro)

Chapter Two

La grotte 11Q : morphologie, investigation, mobilier et fonction

Jean-Baptiste HUMBERT

La grotte 11Q est la seule que de Vaux n'eut pas le temps de publier. Les autres l'ont été, mais avec la sobriété dont il était coutumier, qui manifeste son souci de concision, allant droit au but, quand pour lui l'essentiel suffisait. Il serait étonné de voir qu'aujourd'hui nous en fassions un volume dont rien ne s'apparente à sa manière, mais le temps a passé. Pour lui, les grottes furent un chaînon décisif de son interprétation, où des asiles ont un jour été convertis par accident en chambres fortes pour manuscrits.

Le laconisme de ses notes montre assez qu'il y a vu des faits, dissimuler les manuscrits qui seuls comptaient, des actions plus que les lieux. Il avait vu et le peu a suffi. Quelques mots sous sa plume rappellent sans commentaire son idée que 11Q avait été habitée. Les preuves étaient faibles. De passer outre avantageait la version essénienne.

La fouille passée, de Vaux n'y est pas revenu. Il était inutile d'insister, le sauvetage était fait et le site épuisé. Le contexte archéologique saccagé l'aura découragé : descendre dans le pillage du bédouin pour ramasser des miettes négligées, s'il en eut le scrupule la tâche ne l'a pas autrement mobilisé. Il est vrai qu'en même temps il surveillait la fouille des tombes du cimetière dont il attendait beaucoup ; il vaquait d'un chantier à l'autre et l'un l'a mieux retenu que l'autre.

Comme souvent dans l'étude archéologique de Qumrân, une distance s'accroît avec le temps, et le sujet que nous abordons s'est transformé, ou déformé. Aujourd'hui nos questions ne sont plus celles que de Vaux s'étaient posées. Notre enquête tient plus d'une exégèse des documents que d'une entreprise achéologique. Nous publions autrement que de Vaux l'aurait fait.

La moindre trace, le plus ténu des indices, de préférence sujets à controverse, sont maintenant passés au crible pour, dans une entreprise presque désespérée, récupérer ce que la fouille n'a pas retenu.

Si la publication exhaustive est un dû, n'oublions pas que maints détails de l'histoire sont effacés et que le luxe de l'examen est probablement vain. Ayant revisité l'endroit, nous peinons à retrouver ce que de Vaux aurait vu et décrit.

À partir d'un site dévasté, d'archives lacunaires, de ce que chacun peut apprendre en déchiffrant les fac-similés des documents originaux que le présent volume nous offre, le doute s'insinue et nous gagne de croire que nous apporterions du nouveau. Telle fut la fouille hier, tel est ce que l'on peut retrouver aujourd'hui. Que le lecteur prenne ce qu'il pourra, nous nous satisferions qu'il en profite.

1. Description de la grotte 11Q

Fig. 1. Localisation des grottes 1Q, 2Q, 11Q

1.1. *Situation* (Fig. 1)

La cavité 11Q s'ouvre dans le plus bas ressaut de la falaise, à 1500 m environ au nord de Qumrân. Elle ouvre au sud-est, surplombe d'une vingtaine de mètres en pente douce le cheminement à une distance de 150 mètres au pied de la falaise (Fig. 2). Elle est la dernière cachette découverte par les bédouins, ignorée des explorations de la falaise dans les années cinquante et des fouilleurs de 3Q : elle n'était pas visible puisque dissimulée avec efficacité. Il faut souligner le paradoxe qu'à l'origine la plus exposée donc la plus vulnérable de la série, elle fut l'ultime découverte.

L'anfractuosité n'est pas l'issue d'un système hydrologique. Elle résulte de la dissolution d'une strate dans l'un des paliers inférieurs dans l'abrupt de la falaise. Les bancs calcaires se sont dissociés, facilitant un évidement horizontal, éboulé par endroits. Le plafond de la grotte est une dalle d'un seul tenant, basculée vers le sud. La couche calcaire dissoute par l'érosion a laissé un vide à peu près uniforme de deux mètres de hauteur. Entre les éboulements de l'aplomb, au long du banc rocheux et sur plus d'une centaine de mètres vers le nord, se succèdent des anfractuosités et des abris sous roche, dont les grottes A et B, 3Q et la grotte 24 de J. Patrich ; 11Q est l'abri le plus méridional. En contrehaut du banc, d'importants conglomérats de poudingue éclaté, se sont disloqués au pied du ressaut. La cavité s'ouvre alors entre des éboulis. La grotte elle-même est un creux en arrière des éboulements.

1.2 *Les lieux ont été bouleversés*

La caverne, aujourd'hui accessible et béante, est facile à observer (Fig. 3). Cependant elle ne livre plus rien de l'espace qu'elle avait au premier siècle. Pour restituer son aspect au moment de la fouille, nous n'avons que les notes succinctes que de Vaux a rédigées dans la Revue biblique,[1] dans le Journal de la fouille, et des photographies toujours prises avec économie. Les sols n'ont pas été décapés comme dans la fouille régulière de la *khirbeh*. Rappelons que les sédiments archéologiques avaient été bouleversés avant l'arrivée des archéologues. Depuis 1956, la surface de la caverne a été retournée à répétition par des fouilleurs plus ou moins autorisés, qui ont surcreusé les sols et curé les crevasses : nulle part le sol supérieur ancien ne subsiste. Les restes de maçonneries ont été démolis. En conséquence, il nous est presque impossible de dresser une élévation précise de l'espace au premier siècle, puisque la référence nécessaire à la confection d'une coupe s'appuie sur des niveaux en place. Hors des fouilles régulières, la recherche de manuscrits s'est apparentée à une vaine course

1. R. de Vaux, « Fouilles de Khirbet Qumrân, Rapport préliminaire sur les 3e, 4e et 5e campagnes », *RB* 63 (1956) 533-77, p. 573-4.

Fig. 2. Panorama de la falaise de Qumrân avec la localisation de la grotte 11Q

Fig. 3. L'entrée de la grotte 11Q aujourd'hui

Fig. 4. La salle (b) après vandalisme

au trésor : il suffisait de savoir que les manuscrits n'avaient jamais été ni enfouis ni enterrés, puisque les entrées des cachettes avaient été scellées. Les rouleaux avaient été « déposés » pour être repris. Il était strictement inutile de creuser. Le contexte archéologique de la grotte a été complètement détruit sans raison. Ne restent que l'enveloppe géologique puis terre et blocs en désordre (Fig. 4).

1.3 *Le porche d'entrée*

L'entrée reconnue de 11Q s'ouvre au sud-est. Aujourd'hui elle est béante et de passage aisé, bien visible depuis le bas de la falaise (Fig. 5). Pourtant dans l'Antiquité, il est douteux que les visiteurs aient connu une telle ouverture. Dans son Journal, de Vaux donne un aperçu des travaux dont l'essentiel concerne le dégagement de l'entrée.

L'accès antique était moins large et en tout cas surbaissé (voir *infra*). Le blocage a vraisemblablement été construit par ceux qui, ayant caché des manuscrits, ont pris le temps d'obturer l'accès car son orientation le rendait visible du pied de la falaise. Après avoir déposé des biens précieux, il était sage d'en dissimuler l'entrée.

1.4 *La distribution des salles* (Fig. 6)

De Vaux a distingué les espaces et les a nommés de façon pragmatique sans toujours éviter l'équivoque que suscite l'emploi du mot « entrée » pour désigner différents endroits. Nous les avons marqués par des lettres pour faciliter la description. L'« entrée » (a) est le porche qui introduit sous la roche. La « salle d'entrée » (b) est la partie antérieure de la cavité ouverte sur la pente. La « grotte intérieure » (c) se prolonge à droite de la salle d'entrée ; le passage entre (b) et (c) concerne « l'entrée de la grotte intérieure » (l) ; de Vaux avait soupçonné que la caverne aurait abrité des reclus. Dans la grotte intérieure, le vide (d) s'ouvre à gauche comme aussi depuis la salle d'entrée (b), en transition avec la salle (c) ; mais comme l'accès entre (b) et (d) est plus facile depuis la salle (b) et malaisé entre (c) et (d), et puisqu'on tient debout dans la salle (d), nous considérons cette dernière comme la seconde chambre de la grotte intérieure. Le passage entre (d) et (f) est étroit et surbaissé, c'est pourquoi de Vaux a vu dans la salle (b) le début d'un corridor sans issue qui s'amenuise en étroiture (f-g) fort basse de plafond au long du côté sud. De Vaux l'appelle « la galerie à gauche ». Elle est encombrée de gros cailloux, on n'y progresse d'abord courbé, puis à

Fig. 5. À l'approche de l'entrée de la caverne

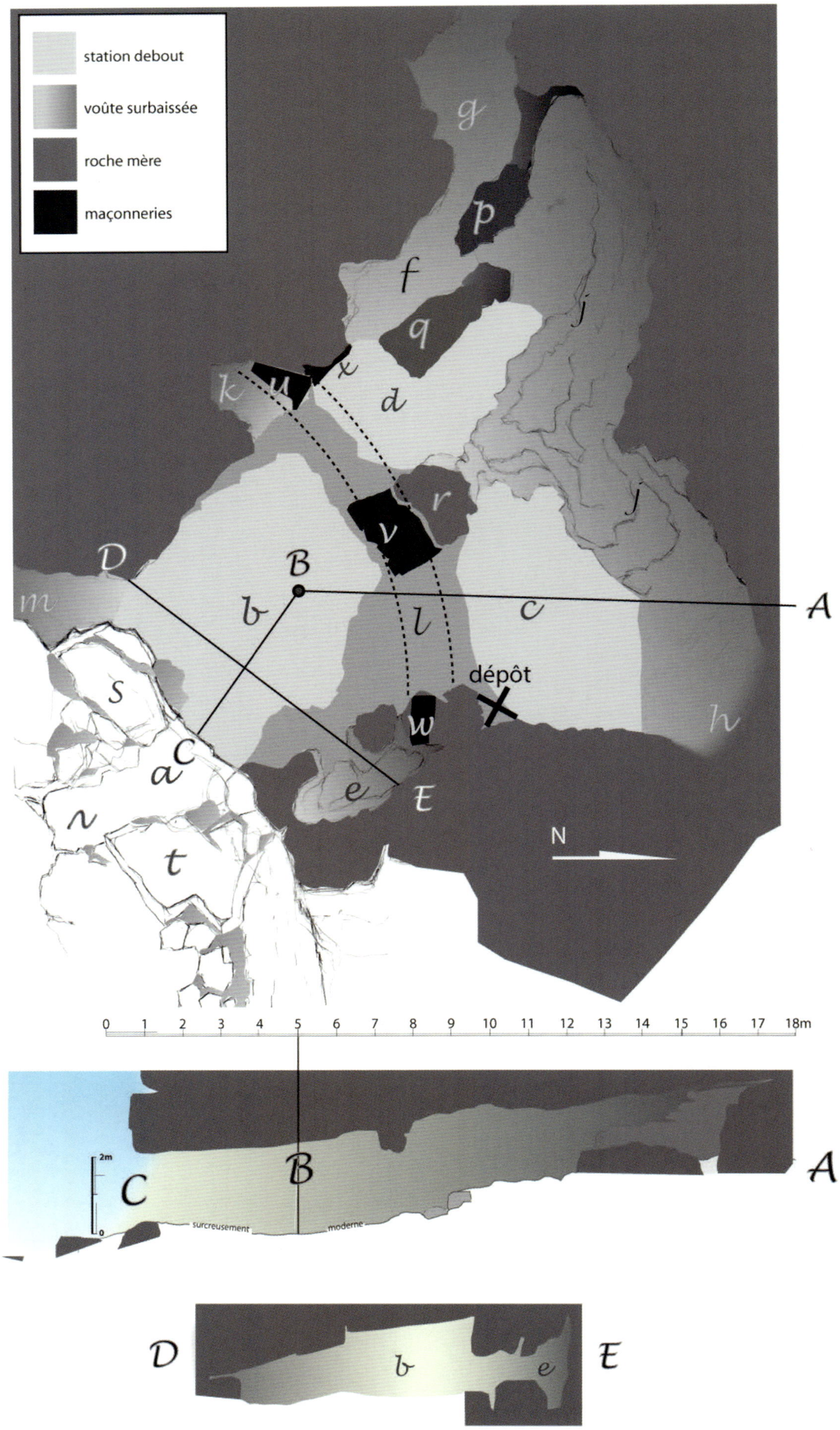

Fig. 6. Relevé et coupe de la cavité

genoux. Le plafond s'abaisse sans s'interrompre à la rencontre d'une couche de terre. Compartimenté par les reliefs accusés des plafonds hauts ou bas, où la hauteur détermine les trois « salles », l'ensemble de la cavité s'organise autour d'un témoin géologique en forme de pilier (r).

Comme les sols ont été profondément et irrégulièrement excavés, il serait hasardeux aujourd'hui de restituer en élévation des circulations originales, conjecturées. Le niveau de la couche romaine est signalé sous le porche que de Vaux donne à 1,35 m sous la voûte toujours en place. Nous avons alors la certitude que les auteurs de la cache pouvaient à peine tenir debout dans la salle d'entrée (b). À l'époque géologique, lors de la dislocation de la falaise, une large portion du plafond (l) s'était affaissée entre (b) et (c). Il fallait alors se courber sous le plafond bas en (l) pour passer de (b) en (c), sur un sol montant ; au contraire, pour passer de (b) en (d) le sol descend. La différence de niveau entre (c) et (d) est sensible et seul le plafond plat leur confère une sorte d'unité. La salle (d) est encombrée d'un gros quartier (q) détaché du plafond avant l'époque historique car profondément enfoncé dans la caillasse. Si l'espace de la salle (c) est plus vaste que celui de la salle (b), l'endroit où l'on peut tenir debout est réduit par le sol montant fortement et la banquette (j) surélevée en équerre, large et impropre à la déambulation : pour une circulation romaine, la hauteur sous plafond dut dépendre de l'épaisseur de la couche d'alluvions aujourd'hui disparue. C'est dans cette salle que les manuscrits avaient été déposés.

Le passage malaisé de la salle (c) à la salle (d) s'ouvre par un ressaut peu praticable. La salle (d) est exiguë et son sol est encombré aujourd'hui des blocs que les fouilleurs ont déplacés avec peine du diverticule (f) pour observer l'élargissement (g), dans lequel on hésite à s'engager tant il est bas. Un parement de pierre plus profond (x), visible sur les photographies (Fig. 7), atteste qu'un sol plus bas y avait été aménagé, que nous rattacherons à l'occupation chalcolithique. Sa position recoupant l'alignement de la cloison marque un passage de (b) en (d). À l'époque de Qumrân, seules les salles (b) et (c) étaient de plain-pied, praticables sans effort, et c'est là qu'il faut replacer l'épisode du pillage bédouin.

Fig. 7. Accroche de maçonnerie (u) dans l'anfractuosité et parement inférieur maçonné (x), au sud de la salle (b), vers la salle (d)

La caverne primitive n'avait probablement pas la configuration qu'on lui voit aujourd'hui. Au fond de la salle (c), la limite orientale n'est ici qu'un talus de terre meuble à main droite au point (h) où le plafond rocheux s'interrompt en surplomb. Plus au nord en façade de la falaise et dans la fracture horizontale du banc rocheux, une crevasse en puits et en contre-haut correspond *grosso modo* au fond (h) de la cavité 11Q ; nous avions fait l'hypothèse qu'elle avait pu constituer une seconde entrée. Elle semblait avoir été l'objet d'un dégagement récent ; le fond de l'anfractuosité montrait l'état d'un travail interrompu : les fouilleurs, de Vaux ou des clandestins ou encore des explorations postérieures, en avaient abandonné le dégagement. L'endroit, reconsidéré en mars 2017, n'a pu être un passage. Un espace contigu, vidé par un phénomène de suffosion, a cependant été accessible depuis la grotte, et la reculée était idéale ; la cavité s'ouvre dans l'éboulis instable, mal colmaté au bord vertical du banc rocheux (voir le compte-rendu en annexe). Le creux ne semble pas avoir été connu de ceux qui avaient caché les rouleaux, à moins qu'ils l'aient considéré peu fiable : il n'a pas servi.

2. Le déroulement de la fouille

De Vaux a mené l'investigation comme les bédouins l'avaient faite, de l'extérieur vers l'intérieur. L'option d'une approche différée de la cavité profonde indique que la salle d'entrée n'était guère praticable.

2.1 *Les travaux à l'entrée*

Nous ne savons pas quelle était la disposition archéologique, en avant de l'entrée, qui avait attiré l'attention des bédouins. En 1956, ils avaient acquis dix ans d'expérience assidue et une compétence pour apprécier la configuration du rocher et des éboulis, et il est fort possible qu'ils y aient reconnu un blocage construit. Un trou plus ancien était-il visible ? La cache aurait été visitée au Moyen Âge s'il est vrai que des tissus de cette époque y ont été recueillis il y a peu. Une dizaine de chiffons, à défaut de toute autre trouvaille, témoigneraient d'un passage furtif et non pas d'une occupation. Plus encore, qui dans ces époques de la plus faible habitation autour de le mer Morte, serait venu pratiquer un simple trou que l'exploration de 1952 n'aurait pas remarqué ? La grotte est restée ignorée jusqu'en 1956. Les fragments de textiles ont été testés au C^{14} ; pour autant que nous jugions ces tests utiles malgré le biais qui peut les affecter, il reste sage de ne pas leur accorder un crédit qui inventerait une chronologie : une marge aléatoire ne peut être évitée quand les échantillons ont pu être contaminés lors des manipulations maladroites et qu'ils peuvent provenir des vêtements en lambeaux des ouvriers. Tout fouilleur expérimenté suspecte que, dans les conditions où l'on sait que la fouille fut conduite, rien n'évite que des objets modernes s'y soient égarés ; les ouvriers de de Vaux portaient des habits déchirés. Même si on parvenait à confirmer l'exactitude des résultats, des fragments hétérogènes à la série des toiles ne devraient pas servir, dans un dossier déjà si complexe, à ajouter à Qumrân des supputations inutiles.

Nombre d'indices montrent que l'entrée avait été camouflée dans l'Antiquité. Un foyer, à la limite de l'abri pour éviter l'enfumage, atteste l'habitation chalcolithique. La fermeture de l'ouverture primitive est plus tardive dans laquelle les bédouins avaient dû pratiquer ou élargir un trou. « On enlève les déblais des fouilleurs clandestins devant l'entrée. Les déblais recouvrent de gros quartiers de roc ou de poudingue écroulés ».[2] Une telle quantité de grosses pierres aurait-elle roulé d'en haut, où aucun éboulis géologique meuble ne se voit, et par un hasard extraordinaire pour obturer précisément l'entrée de la cavité ? Elles n'ont pas été déplacées sous l'effet d'un tremblement de terre, comme le montre leur position au pied même de l'aplomb rocheux : une secousse sismique aurait dispersé les roches détachées sur la forte pente sans causer l'entassement que l'on restitue. Il faut y voir la preuve que la grotte a été scellée de main d'homme. Une observation attentive du blocage aurait distingué l'empilement construit d'un éboulement naturel « On enlève aussi une partie de ces blocs écroulés pour améliorer l'entrée et faciliter le travail ».[3] Qu'il ait fallu deux journées d'ouvrier (les 26 et 27 février 56) pour élargir l'ouverture est vraisemblable, puisque seuls deux hommes pouvaient se tenir dans l'étroit espace entre les deux rochers qui encadrent l'entrée. Les photographies (Figs. 8 et 9) montrent le long tas de pierres étalées de main d'homme, de couleur plus claire, encore indemnes de l'altération solaire. De Vaux n'a pas cherché à restituer l'ouverture primitive : il a élargi un passage qu'il voulait praticable (Figs. 10 et 11) et dont il donne les dimensions : 1,35 m en hauteur et 1,60 m de largeur (1 mars 56), ce qui n'apporte rien à la restitution de la morphologie primitive de la cavité. Sa béance (a) s'est aggravée depuis (Fig. 3).

2. Journal de fouille, le 26/2/56.

3. Journal de fouille, le 26/2/56.

Fig. 8. Secteur de l'entrée après déblocage de l'ouverture

Fig. 9. Déblai de couleur claire après l'ouverture de l'entrée

Fig. 10. Vue de l'entrée de la caverne à la fin des fouilles

Fig. 11. Vue de l'entrée de l'intérieur de la caverne

Fig. 12. La salle (b) à la fin des fouilles

2.2 *L'investigation dans les salles*

Les cailloux erratiques et les amas de guano ont été évacués suivant la progression du travail. De Vaux a dégagé la salle d'entrée (b) en deux jours, les 28 et 29 février 56. La photographie (Fig. 12) donne une idée du volume évacué par les fouilleurs, toutefois sans atteindre le rocher ; le sol exposé n'est pas un niveau archéologique mais l'arrêt du dégagement ; au nord-est, un vestige du sédiment atteint presque un mètre d'épaisseur qui nous servira de témoin. Le Journal ne dit rien de la fouille que les photographies montrent étendue ; il est possible qu'une espèce de tranchée dans l'axe ait été pratiquée pour gagner la grotte intérieure. De Vaux n'a pas jugé utile d'y discerner la couche qu'il suppose romaine sur toute la surface disponible, parce qu'il considérait que le sédiment saccagé ne contenait rien « que quelques tessons et deux ou trois débris de linge ».[4] Son intérêt et ses forces étaient conjugués pour la récupération de manuscrits. Cependant nous devons tenir compte de la répétition dans le Journal du mot « déblais ». Les déblais sont à l'entrée en (a), puis dans la salle d'entrée (b), enfin dans la grotte intérieure (c) ; nous en concluons que les clandestins avaient partout ravagé des sédiments que de Vaux a tamisés. Presque rien n'a été trouvé en place, de Vaux a récupéré ce que les bédouins avaient négligé. D'après la photographie nous estimons le niveau du sol dit romain à peu près au sommet du témoin qui porte une portion du mur (w) aujourd'hui démontée.

Le Journal ne décrit presque rien du travail dans la « grotte intérieure », la salle (c) (Figs. 13 et 14) ; nous apprenons que le contexte bouleversé n'a pas mérité la consignation d'une observation détaillée. À plus forte raison quand de Vaux a noté la version des bédouins que la cachette était en (b) et non en (c) : « c'est dans cette première salle que les grandes trouvailles ont été faites ».[5] Nous pouvons en douter. Le travail « dans la grotte intérieure » aura été pourtant mené avec ténacité : commencé le 1 mars, poursuivi du 3 au 6 ; repris le 8, puis du 10 au 14 ; soit dix jours en tout. L'insistance à dégager le fond venait de ce que les rares objets découverts en étaient sortis : flacon,[6]

4. Journal de fouille, le 28/2/56.

5. Notes de chantier, le 1/3/56.

6. L'habitude de l'archéologie palestinienne a traduit en « cruchette » l'anglais *juglet*. Nous résistons à l'emprunt puisque cruchette n'est pas reçu en français. Le mot juste serait

Fig. 13. L'« entrée » de la « grotte intérieure » depuis la salle (b)

Fig. 14. Vue panoramique de la salle (c), la « grotte intérieure »

lampe du Fer, petite jarre chalcolithique, clé en fer. De Vaux cherchait des manuscrits ; il note le 29 fevrier il note « quelques fragments inscrits récupérés dans les déblais », les 4 et 5 mars « quelques petits fragments inscrits », les 6 et 7 mars « à peine de fragments inscrits ». La position des fragments aurait dû le convaincre que les jarres avaient été déposées en cet endroit précis, les fragments s'étant détachés lors de la manipulation du dépôt. Dans cette salle intérieure, l'éclairage naturel était assez faible pour que le recours à un générateur électrique parût souhaitable. L'obscurité n'était pas complète mais les gros blocs de rocher qui séparaient de la salle (b) faisaient écran. Un appoint était nécessaire. Notons pourtant que les trouvailles ont été faites dans les déblais bédouins et plutôt au début de mars, sauf la clé recueillie le 12 mars, et la petite jarre chalcolithique le 13 mars parce que plus profonde et éventuellement en place.

Les bédouins ont peut-être tenté de dégager la galerie (f) qui s'enfile à gauche de la salle (d), De Vaux a vite aussi abandonné le projet de l'explorer : « Le travail est dangereux [...] On arrête le travail dans la galerie qui s'enfonce à gauche dans la grotte d'entrée [...] il n'y avait d'ailleurs rien »[7] (Fig. 4, le carré noir, au centre, indique l'ouverture de la galerie). La difficulté venait de ce qu'il était dangereux de déplacer de lourds blocs dans un espace trop bas de plafond. Il était improbable que le pierrier fût artificiel, les auteurs de la cache n'auraient pas enfoui des jarres sous des pierres.

Cependant, avant notre reconsidération des lieux en 2015, Patrich a évacué, de l'ensemble de la cavité, un important volume de terre et de pierres qu'il est difficile d'estimer. Un tapis roulant lui a facilité l'opération. Son commentaire est laconique.[8] Le sol a été abaissé. Il a retrouvé quelques tessons chalcolithiques en élargissant la tranchée de de Vaux. Le croquis qu'il en donne p. 82 permet de localiser son sondage jusqu'au rocher dans la salle (b) par un affaissement dans le sol actuel (Fig. 15, le déblai à droite du personnage). D'autres fouilleurs clandestins ont dû creuser dans les trois salles en aggravant le dommage : les maçonneries n'avaient pas subsisté, Patrich ne les a pas vues en place.[9] Des pillards modernes auront naïvement estimé que murs et murettes scellaient des cachettes. Aujourd'hui, il faut considérer que l'endroit a été vandalisé.

2.3 *Stratigraphie*

Au cours des investigations successives, le sédiment archéologique a été en grande partie anéanti. Pour restituer une stratification et l'articulation des occupations en suivant les notes que de Vaux a laissées, l'aide des photographies est décisive. Tout d'abord, il convient de tenir compte de l'évolution naturelle de la cavité avant de dresser l'histoire des interventions humaines qui l'ont modifiée.

La falaise est abrupte avec de hauts ressauts et des failles ; le ruissellement y est violent précipitant les matériaux mobiles. Dans une fracture du banc supérieur (fig. 5), repérée en façade à droite au sommet de l'entrée et qui rejoint le diverticule (e), les infiltrations ont été fortes. Un vestige du sédiment, épargné par la fouille à droite dans la salle d'entrée (b), illustre un pendage des alluvions vers le sud (fig. 16). Des boues liquides se seraient écoulées à l'entrée de la cavité, « ... une terre jaune, fine amenée (sic) par l'eau »,[10] telle une déjection en minces couches répétées. Cependant, le géologue G. Massonnat préfère y voir un dépôt éolien. Les deux processus ont pu alterner. Le pendage des couches minces s'infléchirait vers l'intérieur de la cavité selon la direction du vent et l'apport des eaux, ce que nous ne pouvons plus vérifier.

Sur l'agrandissement d'une photographie, le témoin offre de voir une accumulation en deux éléments distincts (Fig. 16). Le témoin n'est pas complet sur le cliché puisque la fouille l'a écrêté ; nous commençons

cruchon, petite cruche qui, munie d'une base, se pose : sa fonction ne convient guère car le cruchon est une vaisselle de boisson. Dans les descriptions typologiques, les lexiques de l'archéologie anglaise, très pauvres de vocabulaire, ne retiennent que la morphologie, *grosso modo : jar* (vase fermé) et *bowl* (vase ouvert). Nous tentons au contraire à privilégier la fonction des vases et non leur forme ; le petit vase de 11Q doit être nommé « flacon » puisque son goulot étroit en fait un verseur qui retient le liquide. Il est ici associé aux lampes coquilles, et put fort bien contenir l'huile destinée à l'éclairage.

7. Journal de fouille, le 13/3/56.

8. J. Patrich, «Khirbet Qumran in the Light of New Archaeological Explorations in the Qumran Caves», in M.O. Wise et al. (ed.), *Methods of Investigation of the Dead Sea Scrolls and the Khirbet Qumran Site: Present Realities and Future Prospects* (ANYAS 722; New York: New York Academy of Sciences, 1994) 73-95. Nous le remercions pour la permission d'examiner et de dessiner les tessons qu'il avait gardés.

9. Communication orale.

10. Journal de fouille, le 28/2/56.

Fig. 15. Vue de la salle (b) en contrebas de la salle (c)

Fig. 16. Base du témoin du comblement dans la salle (b) (extrait agrandi)

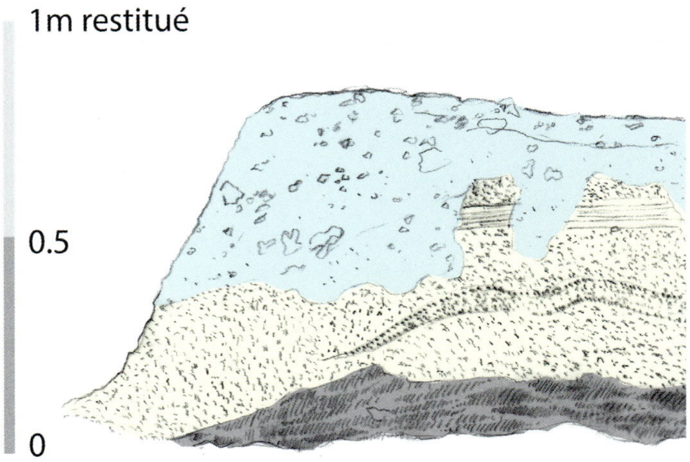

Fig. 17. Interprétation de la stratification du témoin dans la salle (b)

à soupçonner que le comblement de la salle d'entrée (b) était épais.

Nous voyons (1) une couche basse, d'un matériau fin, éventuellement limoneux ou éolien, surmontée d'une couche (2) détritique, granuleuse et contenant de petits cailloux. Les couches témoignent de deux périodes différentes, discontinues. Il faut donc restituer *a priori* un comblement à surface uniforme et admettre que le bas de l'ouverture antique, sous la voûte, était contenu par une barre géologique qui a retenu le dépôt ; au contraire de la grotte profonde, moins sujette à la force du vent ou trop élevée pour être atteinte par les limons.

Au cours de la fouille, le déblaiement pour gagner la hauteur requise au passage fut l'occasion d'un sondage dans l'entrée, jusqu'au rocher atteint à plus de 50 cm de profondeur (Fig. 17). De Vaux a tranché dans les couches et établi une stratigraphie sommaire qu'il aura attribuée à l'ensemble de la cavité. Il en a donné lui-même une description schématique que nous croyons exacte, même incomplète. Gardons à l'esprit qu'il a sondé au plus épais du comblement et la figure 20 en montre la coupe. Il est probable que la nappe répandue ait été arrêtée par le sol montant à l'entrée de la salle (c) plus profonde.

De Vaux a décrit la stratification selon trois « occupations » : il faut préciser ce qu'il entendait par ce terme, quelques commentateurs en ayant outrepassé le sens. Par « occupation », il entend ici des « présence humaine » sans plus ; il a encore utilisé le terme « niveau » dans la même acception que « traces » ; quand il mentionne le « niveau du Fer », il ne s'appuie que sur le maigre mobilier identifié. Il ne peut s'agir en aucun cas du constat d'un sol repéré en plan ou d'une lecture stratigraphique en coupe, mais d'un passage humain.

Il a constaté dans la salle d'entrée (b) que la couche la plus épaisse était une accumulation de terre jaune « limoneuse » aux rares tessons chalcolithiques, constituant le seul repère en position stratigraphique. Le sédiment archéologique paraît désordonné, en tout cas dispersé. La base du dépôt est marquée par une couche caillouteuse avec diffusion de cendre, posée à même le roc (28 février), manifestation de la plus ancienne occupation. S'agit-il des cendres d'un foyer ou de traces de décomposition de matières organiques par combustion lente ? La présence de matières organiques suppose une intervention humaine qu'attesteraient les tessons. En dépit du manque de précision quant à la position des poteries, il est probable que l'apport géologique de la masse jaune a scellé la couche qui contient la cendre ; un foyer est plausible à l'aplomb du porche à ouverture plus grande qu'au premier siècle. À haute époque, l'entrée était donc exposée, et les occupants du IVe millénaire, l'ayant vue, l'avaient élue et fréquentée comme un refuge ou un relai, et de préférence dans la salle (b).

Le niveau romain que de Vaux cherchait à restituer s'est montré insaisissable sous le sol bouleversé par les clandestins : il l'a placé par déduction, et sans plus argumenter, au haut de la couche jaune dans le sondage à l'entrée. Au-dessous du « sol romain, [...] une couche de terre jaune, en-dessous, un sol cendreux [...]. Entre celui-ci et le niv. romain 54 cm ».[11] Or le 28 février, il en avait déjà mesuré l'épaisseur : « une terre jaune, fine amenée par l'eau, dans laquelle quelques tessons chalcolithiques. Épaisseur +/- 50 cm ».[12] Situons donc son sol romain à plus de 0,50 m au-dessus du seuil rocheux. Le témoin stratigraphique montrait les deux couches 1 (jaune) et 2 (bleu) et le sol romain serait interstitiel (Fig. 18) ; la photographie, dans la mesure où nous y lisons une stratification, ne montre pas de sol, mais il faut rappeler que l'endroit n'était pas habité et qu'une surface non piétinée n'est pas décelable. La couche basse 1 (jaune) est un dépôt dont le sommet marque un changement vers un climat plus humide, avec reprise d'une érosion accrue au cours des deux millénaires postérieurs à l'occupation romaine ; le matériau véhiculé fut alors plus grossier et contient des petits cailloux. Selon la proposition de de Vaux, l'entrée aurait eu à l'époque une hauteur de 1,35 m, et la couche 2 (bleue) serait post-Qumrân.

Dans la *grotte intérieure*, la salle (c), dans et sous les déblais bédouins, une couche en partie arrachée, dont l'épaisseur n'est pas donnée parce que bouleversée, a fourni l'essentiel des trouvailles de 11Q, fragments inscrits, outils de fer et poterie. La remarque contredit l'affirmation des bédouins, que « c'est dans la première salle que les grandes trouvailles ont été faites ».[13] Les ouvriers chargés de collecter les fragments de cuir auraient-ils été gênés par l'obscurité puisqu'un générateur a fourni un éclairage (au 1 mars) qui, défaillant, a été remplacé par

11. Notes de chantier, le 1/3/56.

12. Journal de fouille, le 28/2/56.

13. Notes de chantier, le 1/3/56.

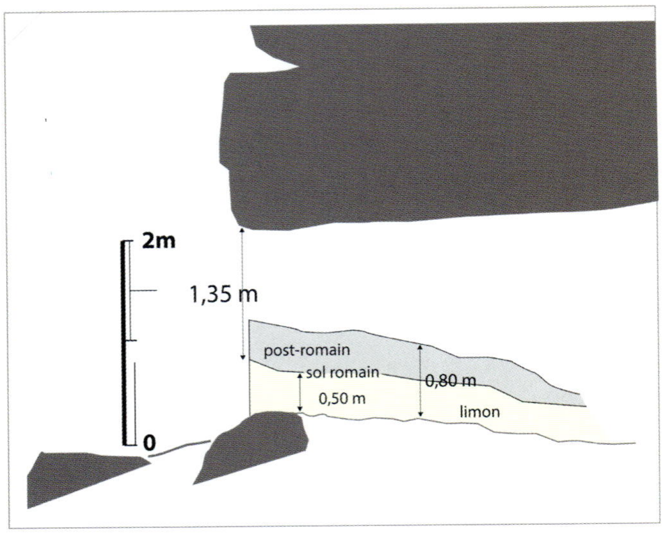

Fig. 18. Reconstitution de la stratification du sondage à l'entrée

des lampes à pétrole (au 8 mars) ? L'investigation a été concentrée dans la profondeur de la salle (c).

De Vaux mentionne sans l'avoir repérée une occupation du Fer simple témoin d'une fréquentation aux VII-VIe s. avec des lampes de l'époque retrouvées « dans les déblais ». L'archéologue a échoué à la situer dans la stratification. Les six siècles qui séparent les deux visites des périodes du Fer et romaine n'auraient-ils produit qu'une maigre couche qui les aurait confondues ? Les deux occupations, indistinctes en élévation, ont-elles alors été recouvertes par une accumulation naturelle pendant les deux millénaires qui nous séparent de Qumrân ? De Vaux n'a pas conclu parce que la couche 2 avait été détruite par les clandestins.

La stratigraphie reste une approximation parce que les bouleversements modernes ont empêché toute référence quant à la position des trouvailles. La séquence de de Vaux fut établie *a posteriori*. Confronté au désordre et pressé par le temps, il a localisé le mobilier quand c'était possible, et n'a livré que des indications. Dans les fiches d'enregistrement, selon une logique acceptable, il s'est s'appuyé sur la typologie pour réattribuer aux périodes qu'il avait définies les objets issus des déblais ou du tamisage. On peut reconstituer une succession des couches selon de Vaux.

1 - *Un massif d'érosion* - La surface lors de l'entrée des clandestins n'est pas définie et il ignore la forme du dépôt des deux derniers millénaires (nous verrons *infra* que la restitution est envisageable). Cependant le niveau put y atteindre une assez grande épaisseur et occuper la majeure partie de la salle d'entrée (b). L'apport des deux derniers millénaires aurait gagné jusqu'aux jarres cachées dans la salle (c) et en enfouir au moins la partie basse. On expliquerait par là les « déblais » de la salle (c) puisque les bédouins auraient dû les dégager.

2 - *Un « sol romain »* - Juste au-dessus de la couche 1, plus récente, le « sol romain » a été associé aux rares tessons que de Vaux assigne, avec raison, au corpus de Qumrân, et éventuellement la jarre Kando 393 complète, si l'on considère comme acquis son attribution à 11Q. Les fragments de manuscrits sont issus du même contexte que celui d'où sont sorties les poteries. Cependant il n'est pas possible de préciser l'endroit exact des trouvailles : le passage vers la salle profonde (c) avait été bouleversé par les pillards qui avaient emporté les jarres et abandonné des miettes. La photographie célèbre de S. Weiss est une mise en scène, la fouille achevée (Fig. 19). Quoi qu'il soit, ce que de Vaux a récupéré l'a été dans des couches supérieures.

Fig. 19. Mise en scène de fouilleurs à l'entrée de la salle (c), cliché Sabine Weiss avec permission de l'auteur

3 - *Une trace du Fer tardif* - La fréquentation de l'époque du Fer n'a pas laissé d'autres traces décelables que des tessons, aucun sol n'a été détecté. De Vaux recueille deux lampes typiques du VII-VIe s., des fragments de deux jarres et un flacon. Leur abandon dans la cavité est plus ancien de six siècles que la fin de Qumrân et les deux niveaux de circulation étaient confondus, sinon proches.

4 - *Une installation chalcolithique* - Sous le niveau de l'ambulation « romaine », la couche de terre jaune de moins de 50 cm d'épaisseur résulte de l'apport d'érosion des trois millénaires avant le tournant de l'ère ; elle scelle l'installation « chalcolithique » : couche cendreuse avec des cailloux et des tessons chalcolithiques, qui repose sur un rocher vierge.

2.4 *Tentative de réinterprétation*

Une alternative est possible qui aurait l'avantage de la simplicité. Un cliché de l'époque, (Fig. 20), de piètre qualité, améliore cependant le champ de l'investigation. Il donne la chance d'observer une stratification litée, plus complète en vis-à-vis du témoin que nous avons d'abord commenté. Il s'agit de la coupe sud du sondage que de Vaux a pratiqué à l'entrée. Le photographe qui voulait fixer sur la pellicule l'entrée de la grotte vue de l'intérieur a élargi son champ jusqu'au bord du sondage. Les couches y ont été moins perturbées par les clandestins parce, sous le porche, elles étaient moins prometteuses de trouvailles, et le sédiment semble intact. L'interprétation par de Vaux des couches supérieures et de la position du mobilier est remise en question.

Nous la lisons à partir du bas :

I. couche noircie, de cailloux mêlés de cendres (chalcolithique),
II. couche grise, limon ou apport éolien (1),
III. couche blanchâtre, apport granuleux (2),
IV. couche détritique qui atteint la voûte à l'entrée. Le litage horizontal se poursuit sans accident à l'aplomb de l'ouverture : l'avant du porche comblé a contenu les sédiments. L'horizontalité milite plutôt en faveur d'une décantation. Cette partie de la grotte a pu être inondée à répétition, à haute époque.

En dépit du mauvais état du cliché, la figure 20 suscite un commentaire qui peut s'inscrire en faux contre l'altitude du niveau romain, que de Vaux avait accepté, pour la placer au sommet du comblement. Deux pierres insérées entre la voûte et le remplissage, scellent l'orifice peuvent être la base ou partie du pierrier qui colmatait l'ouverture. La position des pierres ne laisse pas d'étonner : malgré l'écrasement en deux dimensions de la photographie, les pierres semblent bien s'appuyer à la couche IV, et lui seraient donc postérieures. Nous concevons avec peine que des pierres aient pu glisser

Fig. 20. La coupe sud du sondage de Vaux à l'entrée, interprétation de la stratification, (extrait agrandi)

sous l'encorbellement dans une position qui réclame une intervention humaine. Alors, si les deux pierres sont le vestige de la fermeture de la grotte, les auteurs de la cache auront pénétré la grotte en rampant dans une ouverture fort basse. En sortant ils l'auront scellée. L'important amoncellement de pierres, que nous avons décrit devant l'entrée, trahit le soin que les auteurs de la cache auront mis pour protéger leur bien.

Nous en tirerons qu'ils étaient entrés dans une salle (b) sans pouvoir s'y tenir debout et qu'en revanche, la grotte intérieure (c) offrait un espace retiré, plus vaste et plus discret que ne le montre aujourd'hui la béance de la caverne (Fig. 13). Le bilan que l'on tire de tout cela est que la cavité était au premier siècle d'accès médiocre, de pénétration malaisée, impropre à l'habitation et qu'en revanche, elle présentait les conditions requises pour une cachette.

3. Les différents mobiliers et leur contexte

La pauvreté du mobilier et son caractère fragmentaire confirment la fréquentation accidentelle des lieux. En démontant le blocage dans l'entrée, les fouilleurs ont recueilli de menus objets : « Dans ces blocs, un ou deux tessons : ils seraient donc tombés après (souligné) l'occupation. Les tessons sont typiquement Qumrân. Beaucoup de pièces de chiffon, un clou, une lame de couteau, fragments de cuir et de vannerie. Un fragment de plusieurs épaisseurs collées : inscrits ? ».[14] L'assemblage renvoie à un contexte qumrânien. Lorsque de Vaux parle de « l'occupation » il entend la référence historique de Qumrân. Les trouvailles n'étaient en l'état ni de dépôt ni d'abandon : nous y verrions plutôt la collecte d'objets mélangés et fragmentaires, contenu renversé d'un panier de bédouins lors du franchissement du trou étroit pratiqué pour se hisser hors la cavité. Les interstices entre les pierres seront restés vides : les objets ayant glissé n'étaient pas facilement récupérables, en tout cas leur intérêt n'a pas entraîné le démontage d'un tas de pierres considérable. Dans l'hypothèse que les tessons seraient antérieurs au tas de pierres, il est peu probable que les acteurs de la cache y aient brisé de la poterie avant d'accumuler les blocs. En revanche, dans l'hypothèse du panier bédouin renversé, nous ne voyons pas que des bédouins aient cru bon d'emporter « des tessons ». À moins que le vase emporté n'ait été complet, recueilli, puis cassé, enfin abandonné car sans plus aucune valeur. On penserait volontiers, mais en vain, que le vase était la marmite dont Patrich a sauvé un fragment. De Vaux n'a pas conservé les tessons perdus dans le blocage et tout ceci n'est que pure supposition.

Le sédiment de la grotte 11Q était stratifié avant la découverte. Les bédouins l'ont inversé et la fouille a touché le sédiment « de plus ou moins 50 cm »[15] sous le porche (a), préservé de la pioche bédouine avant déblocage de l'entrée. Dans la salle (b) il faut admettre qu'il n'y a pas eu de trouvailles en position stratifiée, sauf les quelques tessons chalcolithiques dans le limon. Ne sont récupérés dans les déblais, le 28 février, que des lambeaux de textiles négligés par les pillards : les chiffons ont été abandonnés comme ceux tombés dans le blocage. L'exception d'une lampe du Fer (Journal le 1 mars) sortie des déblais n'atteste pas, de fait, un niveau dans la salle (b) à l'époque du Fer. On se demandera d'où provenaient les déblais. Les clandestins savaient que les jarres à manuscrits n'étaient pas enterrées mais resserrées dans un angle discret. Il vaut mieux comprendre que les déblais dans la salle « b » proviennent de la salle (c), tirés selon la pente ; ils ont été accumulés par les bédouins qui cherchaient un passage vers (c). La lampe du Fer a dû être extraite, par eux, de la grotte intérieure (c) comme les chiffons avec les déblais : une autre lampe du Fer identique a été recueillie dans la salle (c) et il y a peu de raison de les séparer.

La note de de Vaux : « d'après les bédouins, c'est dans la première salle que les grandes trouvailles ont été faites »[16] soulève un doute : elle laisse entendre qu'à cause des déblais, les « trouvailles » auraient été proches de l'entrée. Nous sommes enclins à ne pas croire les bédouins. Il est douteux que les jarres aient été déposées dans la salle d'entrée (b) plutôt que dans l'endroit plus profond de la salle (c). L'essentiel du mobilier retrouvé par les fouilleurs s'y trouvait concentré : dans la « grotte intérieure » (c), immédiatement à droite après le passage (l) entre (b) et (c), hors de la vue d'un visiteur non averti. Les bédouins auront apporté les jarres dans la salle « b » moins basse et mieux éclairée pour en examiner le contenu. Dans leur manipulation, les jarres auront été cassées, quelques fragments de toiles y auront été éparpillés et abandonnés.

14. Journal de fouille, le 26/2/56.

15. Journal de fouille, le 28/2/56.

16. Notes de chantier, le 1/3/56.

L'investigation fut poursuivie le 3 mars dans la salle (c), « ... on avance dans la grotte intérieure ». Les fouilleurs auront d'abord tamisé les déblais et creusé plus bas « à droite de l'entrée » de la salle (c) (le 12 mars) ; là seulement gisaient les quelques objets : une pointe de fer, une hache de sapeur et une clé en fer. Les poteries de l'époque du Fer témoignent d'une visite ponctuelle dans une époque plus reculée : les parties supérieures d'une jarre de stockage et d'une jarre « bocal », deux lampes « coquille » un flacon à huile pour les lampes trahissent une simple halte dans la fin du VII^{e}s. Ces objets étaient mêlés aux trouvailles romaines : un couvercle de jarre à manuscrits, la jarre Kando 393 (?), et son couvercle (?) si leur association était montrée, « un petit rouleau très abîmé » (le 3 mars), des fragments de peau (le 29 février et les 3-4-5 mars), et d'où les fouilleurs ont encore tiré quelques « tessons qumrâniens » (le 12 mars) non conservés.

De Vaux ne doute pas qu'il a touché ici la couche nommée par déduction le « sol romain » (le 1 mars). Le contexte est mélangé. Il s'impose que la salle (c) a été l'endroit choisi pour cacher les manuscrits : à l'emplacement du creusement dans le sol, en bas à gauche de la photographie (Fig. 14). Nous ne pouvons affirmer que les deux lots, les manuscrits et le matériel métallique, ont été déposés en même temps ; en effet rien ne le prouve, le transport et la mise à l'abri de jarres ne requéraient pas d'outils de ce genre. Si les deux lots étaient séparés, il faudrait envisager que les pièces de fer ont été abandonnées avant la cache des manuscrits scellée par le blocage de l'entrée. Les objets métalliques appartiennent à la période romaine, et leur présence suggère que leur propriétaire, connaissant l'endroit, aurait guidé les auteurs de la cache. Ou bien un fuyard aurait pensé récupérer ses outils auxquels il était attaché ; en particulier la petite clé, qui est celle d'un coffre.

De la poterie chalcolithique a été recueillie dans les salles (b) et (c), principalement des vases de stockage : on aurait entreposé ici des denrées alimentaires dans un habitat épisodique (voir *infra*). Le mobilier est fragmentaire et la fouille complète du site n'en aurait pas changé le profil typologique d'un niveau dispersé. Le vase le plus complet est une petite jarre dont le fond manque, recueilli dans la salle (c) ; deux cols à lèvre denticulée de jarres globulaires à fond plat et deux différents bords de jarres *holemouth* restituent un volume de stockage convenable ; il est possible que l'une de ces dernières ait servi de marmite. De rares tessons épars proviennent de poteries à large courbure, à paroi épaisse de plus d'un centimètre. Ils attestent la présence d'un réservoir d'eau ou d'un silo à grain. Enfin, il faut insister sur le fait qu'il s'agit de poteries incomplètes. Le mobilier a été brisé et dispersé : dans la période chalcolithique, les restes de l'installation avaient été déjà déclassés. Elle fut de courte durée.

4. Occupation et fonction

Nous sommes tributaires des remarques de de Vaux dans le Journal pour restituer les traces des occupations humaines. La plus vaste des caches à manuscrits, 11Q, ne présente aucun caractère d'habitat au temps de Qumrân. Les sols éventuels ont disparu car les surfaces de circulation épisodique des deux périodes n'ont pas été durcies. Une nouvelle expertise n'est plus possible. En revanche aucun aménagement, même en fondation, n'affecte le porche d'entrée alors qu'un habitat à long terme au tournant de l'ère n'aurait pas manqué d'en fermer l'accès pour se protéger des animaux ou se prémunir des vents froids de l'hiver. Les traces les plus sensibles sont chalcolithiques. Au siècle de Qumrân, on ne conçoit pas des reclus dans une cavité non aménagée ; mis à part les objets de la cachette, rien d'un autre mobilier ; aucun déchet, aucun autre dépôt ne témoigne d'une présence humaine. Les alentours en avant de l'entrée sont stériles et le chemin tracé qui y mène est moderne.

Il faut objecter à ce constat négatif que des maçonneries évidentes séparent la salle d'entrée (b) de la grotte intérieure (c). Nous les attribuons à la période chalcolithique. On pouvait se tenir dans la salle (b) pendant le jour, et les salles (c) et (d), plus obscures, pouvaient servir pour entreposer ou se protéger durant la nuit. La partition ancienne de l'espace n'est pas l'ouvrage de bergers plus ou moins modernes : une telle construction aurait été conçue pour une fréquentation répétée, ce qui n'est pas le cas puisqu'ici ni traces de feux ni déchets de bergerie n'ont été détectés dans un espace qui avait été scellé dans l'Antiquité. Dans la grotte 24 de Patrich,[17] à 50 m au nord de 11Q, une couche de fumier, datée au C^{14} de l'époque de Qumrân, atteste que des abris ont été occupés le long du banc rocheux ; ce n'est pas le cas de 11Q. Nous en concluons que la cache des manuscrits achevée, une habitation se serait

17. Patrich, «Khirbet Qumran», 90.

maintenue dans ce secteur. Les maçonneries dans la grotte sont anciennes. De Vaux ne les a pas couchées sur un plan, les fouilleurs ne les ont ni décrites ni commentées. Elles auront conforté de Vaux dans le classement de 11Q parmi les cavités habitables, et renforcé son idée de troglodytes à Qumrân.

D'après les photographies, nous restituons trois éléments construits (u), (v), (w) (Fig. 6), auxquels il faut ajouter un blocage-parement évident (x) sur le côté gauche où s'engage la galerie (d). Les différents éléments sont de même facture, ils sont de la même main et contemporains. La maçonnerie (v) contre le pilier naturel (r) était mieux conservée, érigée avec soin, sans assises, les blocs imbriqués les uns dans les autres pour une meilleure solidité. Elle a tenu par appui au rocher. L'hypothèse qu'elle aurait soutenu la voûte ne peut être retenue. Même à haute époque, les constructeurs savaient bien qu'un mur en pierres sèches ne résiste pas à la pression éventuelle d'une masse rocheuse instable. Les photographies montrent un reste de maçonnerie dans l'anfractuosité (k) : le creux du rocher va en s'amincissant et la construction put accrocher la cloison (u-v) à la paroi sud, fermant la salle (d) en rejoignant le pilier (r). Une partie de la cloison (u-v) a pu s'effondrer, comme en témoigne l'amas de pierres constaté en cet endroit ; de Vaux a noté des blocs cassés gisant sur le sol de la salle (b) : « surtout des éclats de rocs cassés par les Bédouins ».[18] Si la cloison (u-v) a existé, son effondrement aura causé l'amas de pierres qui obstruait l'entrée de la salle (d), et que les bédouins auront dégagé brutalement en cassant quelques blocs. À main droite, la salle (b) devait être séparée de la salle (c). Un assez gros rocher, encore en place ou déplacé de peu, gêne le passage vers la salle « c » ; une photographie montre le bloc, au moment de la fouille, surmonté d'une maçonnerie (w) de plusieurs pierres (Fig. 21). Le bloc, comme un montant de porte posé de chant, prolongeait la cloison (w), isolant (b) de (c), à l'endroit de « l'entrée de la salle intérieure ». Nous voyons dans l'arrangement les trois éléments résiduels d'une séparation en dur entre les deux cavités (b) et (c). Ici encore, les parties non appuyées de la cloison en pierres sèches se sont effondrées.

Il semble que la maçonnerie (v) contre le pilier (r) ne s'enfonce pas plus bas que l'occupation correspondant au « sol romain ». D'après les photographies, la maçonnerie (v) reposait sur le rocher qu'aujourd'hui nous vérifions en sursaut : le sol d'occupation

Fig. 21. Vestiges construits de la cloison séparant les salles (b) et (c) (extrait agrandi)

chalcolithique devait s'étendre plus bas sans rejoindre la base de la maçonnerie (v).

Il est raisonnable d'attribuer à l'époque chalcolithique les cloisonnements de pierre qui partagent l'espace en deux parties bien distinctes. La salle d'entrée (b) ouverte sur la campagne joue le rôle habituel de la cour où l'on vit en profitant de la lumière et où le foyer est entretenu. La porte perçait la cloison (v-w) pour communiquer avec la partie intérieure (c), profonde et obscure, lieu de stockage des outils et des denrées ; la salle (d), a été aménagée avec au moins un parement (x) qui rectifie la paroi au sud ; l'endroit le plus reculé de l'installation put être plus réservé. Un dossier des aménagements de grottes de la même époque est aujourd'hui assez bien documenté.[19] Avec vraisemblance, l'argument de la poterie nous aide à attribuer la partition de l'espace au IVe millénaire. Nous avons dit que le mobilier chalcolithique désignait un stockage et que des poteries accusaient de trop grandes dimensions pour rappeler la précarité d'une simple halte. Un tel mobilier, lourd, difficile à transporter, trahit une installation saisonnière, avec une certaine fréquence. Monter des murs de bonne façon correspond à une installation voulue à long terme. L'eau était disponible. Certes la région est aride

18. Journal de fouille, le 28/2/56.

19. Un exemple parmi d'autres : Y. Govrin, «Horvat Hor: A Dwelling Cave from the Chalcolithic Period in the Northern Negev», *JIPS* 20 (1987) 119-27 n'est qu'une indication : replacer la grotte 11Q dans une étude d'ensemble de l'époque chalcolithique déborde notre sujet.

mais après les pluies, des flaques d'eau demeurent au pied de la cascade du wadi Qumrân et quelques ruissellements pérennes dans la palmeraie de 'Aïn Feshkha étaient potables. 11Q a été une habitation, mais chalcolithique, sans autre postérité.

Enfin, les lampes « coquille » et les fragments de jarres dont un « bocal » de la période finale du Fer judéen attestent que des individus y ont bivouaqué. Une halte de l'âge du Fer peut surprendre en cet endroit écarté, si proche de la forteresse de la même époque qui gît sous l'établissement qumrânien. Plusieurs grottes dans les environs ont livré quelques tessons du Fer. Un refuge dans une époque troublée est une éventualité. L'unique tesson du Fer recueilli par de Vaux dans 9Q a soulevé la question de la date des grottes artificielles : sa présence, bien qu'aberrante, fit supposer que les chambres auraient été creusées dans la terrasse marneuse dès le VII^e^s. av. J.-C. Dans l'hypothèse contraire d'un creusement plus tardif, nous comprenons difficilement qu'un tesson du Fer y ait été déposé, et par qui l'aurait-il été ? Nous avons proposé que ces cavités n'avaient pas été des cellules isolées les unes des autres, en décalque des grottes, mais un refuge de chambres reliées entre elles et effondrées.[20] Un seul tesson du Fer est un indice faible, cependant nous ne pouvons écarter l'hypothèse de refuges souterrains du VII^e^s. L'installation de l'époque du Fer dans le secteur aurait alors été plus développée qu'on ne l'a cru.

Ce long développement n'aura d'utilité que de brider d'autres interprétations plus ou moins fantaisistes, en tout cas superflues, lorsque d'un point de vue strictement archéologique le bilan de 11Q est décevant. Et le lien entre la cache et les manuscrits censés en provenir est distendu. En bref, 11Q a été une cavité visitée à différentes époques parce qu'elle était visible du pied de la falaise et accessible. Assez grande, elle a abrité un habitat saisonnier chalcolithique, n'a été qu'une halte au VII^e^s. av. J.-C., avant d'être enfin élue et scellée pour cacher des manuscrits. Oubliée jusqu'en 1956, elle a alors été saccagée par des bédouins, et de Vaux en a sauvé ce qu'il a pu.

20. J.-B. Humbert, « Cacher et se cacher à Qumrân : grottes et refuges. Morphologie, fonctions, anthropologie », in M. Fidanzio (ed.), *The Caves of Qumran: Proceedings of the International Conference, Lugano 2014* (STDJ 118; Leiden: Brill, 2016) 34-63, p. 58.

Chapter Two

Appendix A

La grotte 11Q: cadre géologique

Gérard MASSONNAT

La grotte 11 de Qumran est située dans la formation Bina d'âge Turonien du Crétacé supérieur, dans la partie sommitale des calcaires Kj du *Judea Group* du Cénomanien-Turonien (de -100 à -90 millions d'années environ).

La formation constitue la base des falaises qui forment la bordure occidentale de la mer Morte, sous les calcaires Ks sénoniens qui composent l'essentiel des reliefs.

Le pied des falaises est recouvert d'éboulis calcaires non consolidés, tandis que la base des falaises est drapée d'éboulis de même composition mais consolidés (Fig. 1).

Les calcaires sont affectés par une fracturation intense, organisée selon deux directions principales N 30° et N 120°, ainsi que l'illustrent les mesures réalisées sur une dalle située immédiatement au nord de l'entrée de la cavité (Fig. 2).

Le fond de la grotte est plat, et les figures de dissolution karstique, observables au sein de la cavité, témoignent toutes d'écoulements aquifères majoritairement horizontaux au cours de la phase de karstogenèse à l'origine de la grotte. Latéralement dans la falaise, d'autres cavités situées au même niveau confirment ces observations et suggèrent l'existence d'un niveau de base piézométrique proche du plancher de la grotte à l'époque de sa genèse. Il est facile d'imaginer une telle configuration en bordure du lac Lisan, de façon contemporaine des derniers dépôts des marnes pléistocènes (Fig. 3).

La cavité s'ouvre sur une fracture verticale d'orientation N 150°, conjuguée au plafond avec une fracture N 30° (Figs. 4-5).

Le pendage stratigraphique des calcaires crétacés est subhorizontal, et les plans de stratification sont préférentiellement utilisés pour le développement des dissolutions karstiques ; c'est le cas notamment des parois nord et ouest sur lesquelles les dissolutions ont largement entamé les volumes sur le plancher de la cavité.

Certains des conduits karstiques sont emplis soit de *terra rossa* (c'est le cas du fond de la cavité, sur sa paroi nord), soit d'éboulis consolidés comme à l'entrée de la grotte coté nord (Fig. 6).

La cavité est séparée en deux chambres par un pilier naturel vierge de toute karstification (Fig. 7).

Fig. 1. Entrée de la Grotte 11Q. A : Calcaire crétacé ; B : Eboulis consolidés

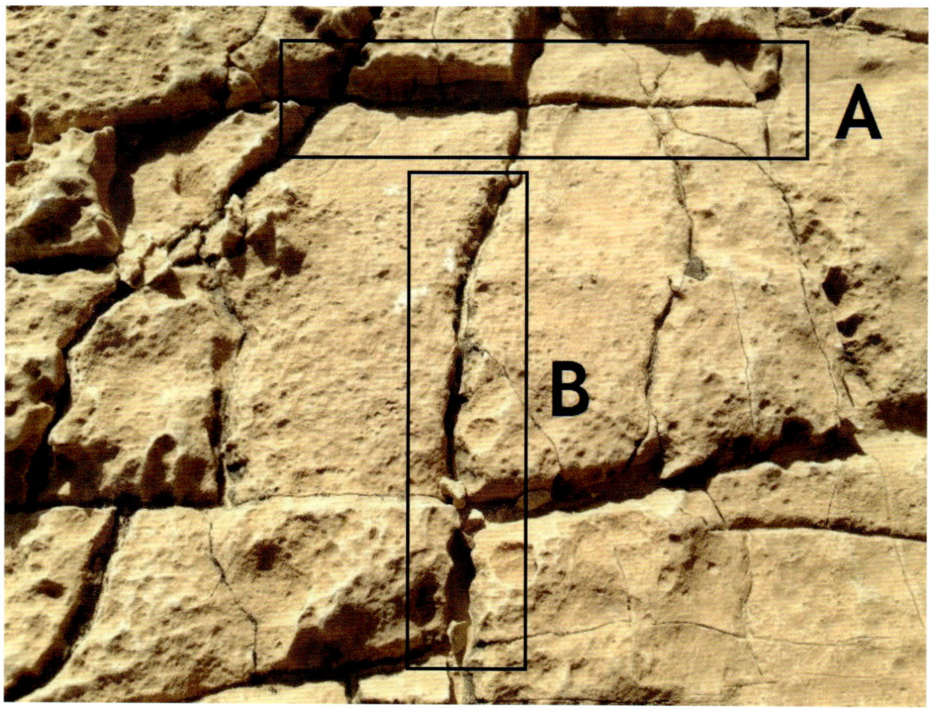

Fig. 2. Calcaires au nord de l'entrée de la Grotte 11Q. A : Fracture de direction N 30° ; B : Fracture de direction N 120°

Fig. 3. La falaise. Paléo niveau de base hydraulique

Fig. 4. A : Fracture N 150° qui détermine l'entrée de la cavité

Fig. 5. A : fracture N 30° au plafond à l'entrée de la cavité

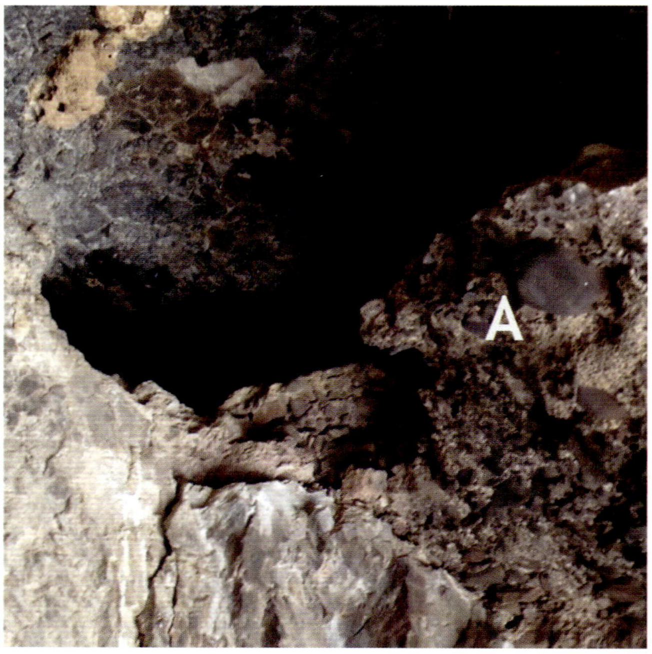

Fig. 6. A : Conduit karstique partiellement comblé par des éboulis de pente consolidés

Fig. 7. Pilier naturel qui sépare la chambre d'entrée de la chambre du fond

Chapter Two
Appendix B

Notes from 2017 Excavation of Cave 11Q

Marcello FIDANZIO, Marco DE PIETRI,
Alessandro MAIFREDI, and Benedetta TORRINI

From 8 to 19 March 2017, an excavation was carried out at Cave 11Q under the direction of Marcello Fidanzio and Dan Bahat, on behalf of the Istituto di Cultura e Archeologia delle Terre Bibliche - Facoltà di Teologia di Lugano (ISCAB-FTL) and the Università della Svizzera Italiana (USI). The results were presented in the excavation report.[1] In this appendix we set out some notes to the descriptions of morphology and stratigraphy proposed above by Jean-Baptiste Humbert, and include some considerations on the interpretation of certain issues.

The notes follow the various areas of the cave. Point 1 focuses on the area of the entrance, with a discussion on the blockage which inhibited the cave's discovery until 1956. Point 2 discusses the sediment inside the cave, traces of which are still noticeable. Point 3 presents the stratigraphic sounding carried out in the entrance chamber in order to document part of the lower levels. Point 4 deals with current stability conditions of the cave. It also draws attention to details that may explain the presence of drystone walls documented in a few photographs of the 1956 excavation. Finally, point 5 comprises a description of a so far unknown upper chamber, discovered during the 2017 excavation.

Findings recovered in the 2017 excavation, namely organic material, were entrusted to the specialists appointed for the publication of Cave 11Q materials, and have been included in the following chapters of this volume.

A 3D scan of Cave 11Q was realized at the end of the excavation. Data were processed by Gilad Lidor and Francesco Pusterla (USI) to achieve the plan (Fig. 1) and the section of the cave (Fig. 6).

1. Entrance

Cave 11Q is the largest of the natural caves yielding manuscripts found in the 20th century (plan, Fig. 1); it is easy to access, visible even at a distance. However, it was the very last to be discovered, in 1956.[2] The

1. M. Fidanzio et al., "Campagna di scavi ISCAB-FTL e USI alla grotta 11Q di Qumran, marzo 2017," *RTLu* 22 (2017) 437-66. See also: J.-B. Humbert, "La grotte 11Q: morphologie, investigation, mobilier et fonction," in this volume, 52.

2. This occurrence is even odder, if we consider that in 1952, after the discovery of Cave 2Q, a large exploration of the area in the vicinity of Qumran took place (10th-29th March 1952). The expedition camp was located beneath Cave 1Q; after a few days, Cave 3Q was discovered, less than a kilometer north of Cave 1Q and 300 meters north of Cave 11Q. The team led by Henry de Contenson (fellow archaeologist at the EBAF) walked every day nearby Cave 11Q to reach

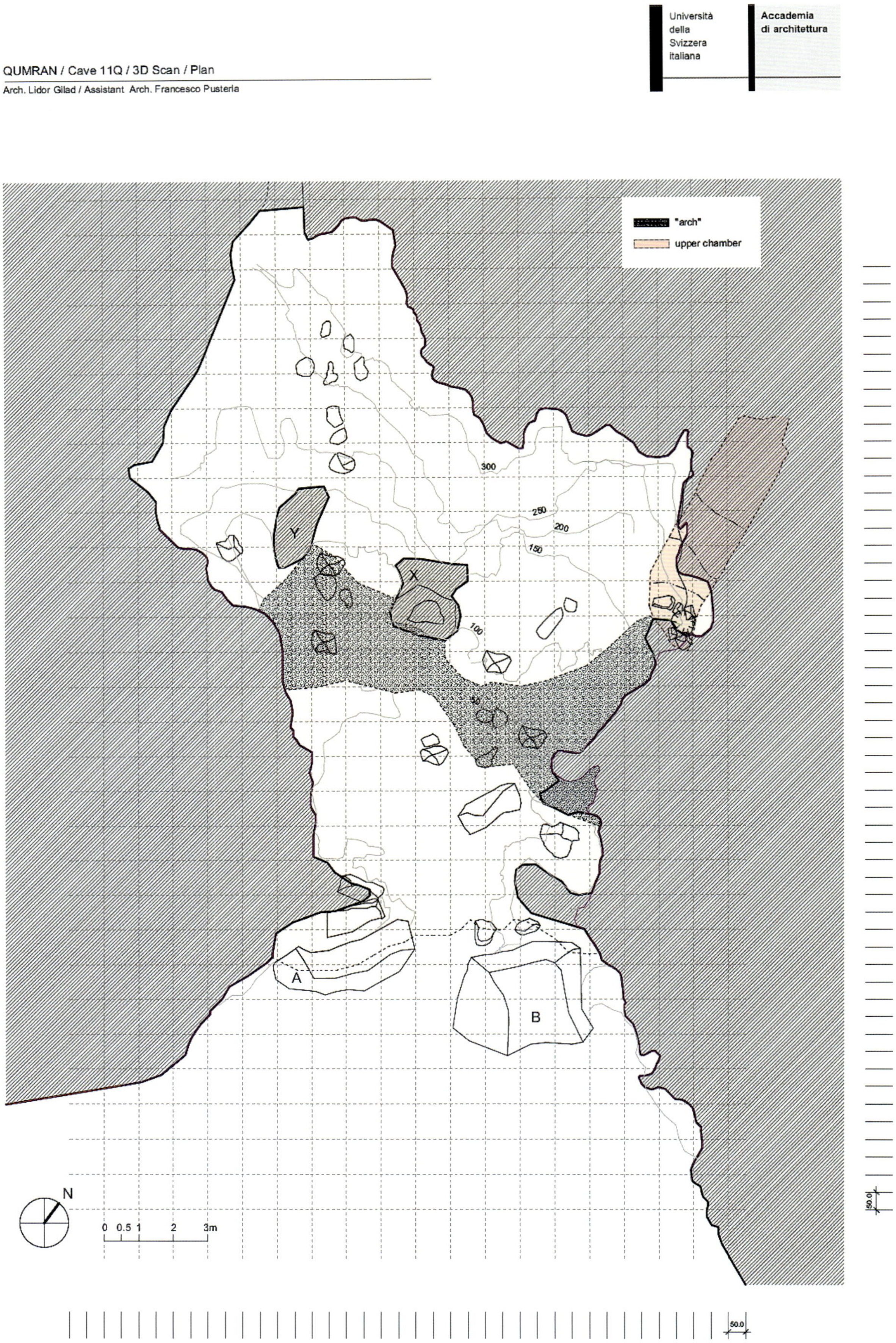

Fig. 1. Cave 11Q. Plan (survey by Gabriel Levi, Mabat 3D Technologies, and Alessandro Maifredi; rendering by Lidor Gilad and Francesco Pusterla)

excavators wrote that the entrance to the cave was blocked at the time of discovery.[3] It has been often assumed that Cave 11Q had remained closed from antiquity until re-opened by the Bedouins in 1956. However, recent studies of the materials found in Cave 11Q attest it was accessed during the Middle Ages and again during the 18th or 19th century.[4] In past debates, the closure was often linked to the deposition of the manuscripts, as a safety measure to hide them. Nevertheless, considering the later frequentations of the cave, at times without any peculiar interest in manuscripts,[5] why was the cave found blocked in 1956? Was the blockage due to natural phenomena or to human intervention?

At the beginning of the excavation in February 1956, de Vaux wrote in the excavation diary that his team had widened the entrance to ease the work inside the cave.[6] Unfortunately, no photograph documents the situation before the beginning of the works at the entrance, and all our attempts of reconstruction rely on the limited information available in the written sources and on the geo-morphological analysis of the area conducted during the 2017 excavation.

As regards the geo-morphological condition, two large blocks of conglomerate lie in front of the entrance of Cave 11Q (labelled A and B in Figs 1-4). Block A to the west collapsed from the ceiling above the entrance; block B to the east originated from the cliff-side orthogonal to the entrance. Photographs (Figs 3-4) and the plan (Fig. 1) show the eastern block lying farther away (about 1 m) from the entrance.

The area above the cave is naturally shaped as a catchment basin (*impluvium*): there are signs of overflow from the slope directly above the entrance of the cave (Fig. 5). The overflow runs forward down the valley along the rocky cliffs and the slope below. At the entrance of Cave 11Q, the advanced position of block B causes some of the water to be redirected towards the cave (see section, Fig. 6). Thanks to aerial images it was possible to reconstruct a three-dimensional Digital Terrain Model (DTM), using Structure From Motions (SFM) software. From this model, the water flow lines were determined using calculation algorithms. Later, we achieved a delimitation of the river basin which covers an area of about 3000 m^2 (Figs. 7-8) including Cave 11Q. This condition led to the accumulation of heterogeneous sediment at the entrace. It is still visible between block A, along its inner side, and the entrance: here lies an accumulation of fine material, covered by a conglomerate slab (Fig. 9). Above the cave, in the middle of the basin, there are some blocks quite similar to those involved in the closure of the entrance. Behind block A, a long, narrow breach runs from the ceiling to the bottom of the sediment (Fig. 9): before the discovery in 1956, the situation of the whole area of the entrance may have been quite similar to the one preserved in this spot (Fig. 10). Therefore, the blockage of the entrance of Cave 11Q can be explained by natural processes.[7]

Cave 3Q, never noticing the former, while in the meantime six more teams were exploring the same area.

3. R. de Vaux, "Archéologie," in M. Baillet, J.T. Milik, and R. de Vaux, *Les 'petites grottes' de Qumrân: Exploration de la falaise. Les grottes 2Q, 3Q, 5Q, 6Q, 7Q à 10Q. Le rouleau de cuivre* (DJD 3; Oxford: Clarendon, 1962) 3-36, on p. 4; Id., *Archaeology and the Dead Sea Scrolls* (The Schweich Lectures 1959; London: Oxford University Press for the British Academy, 1973), 51; G.L. Harding, "Recent Discoveries in Jordan," PEQ 90 (1958) 7-18, on p. 17 briefly describes the situation: "The entrance had collapsed in ancient times, leaving only a very small hole to give access to the inside, which was why we had missed it". J.A. Fitzmyer, *Responses to 101 Questions on the Dead Sea Scrolls* (New York: Paulist, 1992), 5 tells about how the Bedouins noticed the cave: "The Bedouins noticed a bat fly into a crevice of the cliffs a little south of Cave 3, which they then opened."

4. K.L. Rasmussen et al., "Cleaning and Radiocarbon Dating of Material from Khirbet Qumran," in J. Gunneweg, C. Greenblatt, and A. Adriaens (ed.), *Bio- and Material Cultures at Qumran: Papers from a COST Action G8 Working Group Meeting Held in Jerusalem, Israel on 22-23 May 2005* (Stuttgart: Fraunhofer IRB, 2006) 139-64, on pp. 149-52; O. Shamir et al., "Textiles and Cords from Qumran Cave 11," in this volume; J.E. Taylor, "Organic Items from Cave 11Q: B. 11Q-9/1 and 9/2," in this volume.

5. This assumption can be argued from the number of scrolls found in the cave in 1956.

6. Excavation diary, 26 February 1956.

7. This geo-morphological analysis does not exclude the possibility that human interventions contributed to the sealing of the cave, although no clear evidence, nor any specific record in de Vaux's Excavation diary stands for that.

Fig. 2. Entrance area. Blocks A and B (Photo by Giorgio Skory)

Fig. 3. Entrance area. Aerial photo, with detail of the cliff (Photo by Giorgio Skory)

Fig. 4. Entrance area. To be noted the distance between Blocks A and B (Photo by Marcello Fidanzio)

Fig. 5. Area above Cave 11Q (Photo by Giorgio Skory)

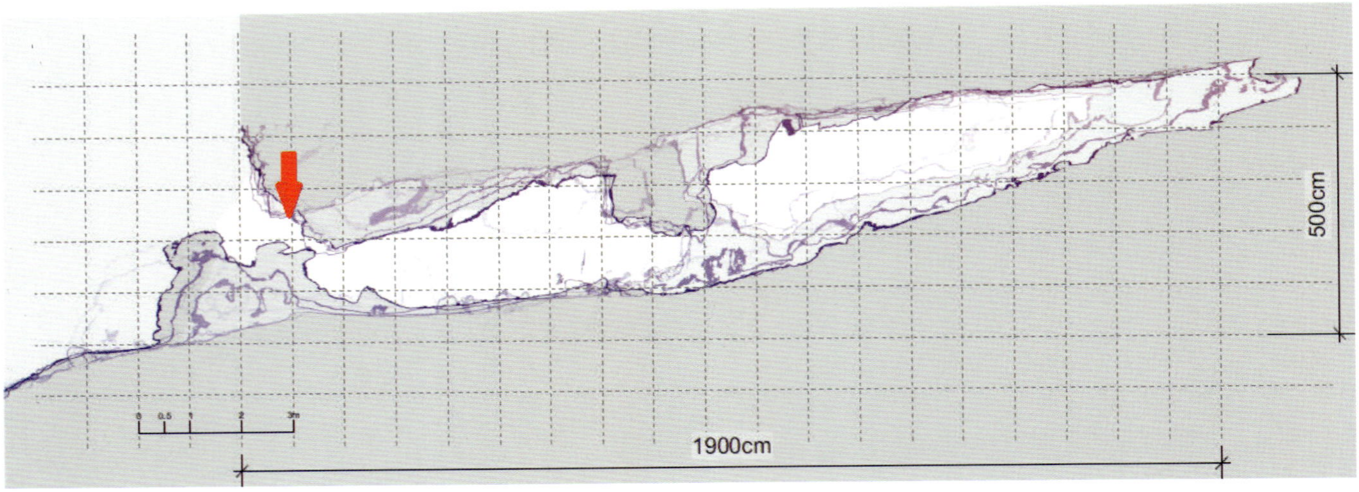

Fig. 6. Cave 11Q. Section (survey by Gabriel Levi, Mabat 3D Technologies, and Alessandro Maifredi; rendering by Lidor Gilad and Francesco Pusterla). Way in for flowing of the water

Fig. 7. Area around Cave 11Q. Digital Terrain Model (by Alessandro Maifredi)

Fig. 8. Area around Cave 11Q. Digital Terrain Model showing the basin and the water flow (by Alessandro Maifredi)

Fig. 9. Accumulation of fine material behind Block A (Photo by Alessandro Maifredi)

Fig. 10. Breach behind Block A (3D rendering by Alessandro Maifredi)

Fig. 11. Traces of sediment still visible along the eastern side of the cave (Photo by Marcello Fidanzio)

2. Sediment

As noticed above, blocks A and B convey part of the water flow into the cave. At the same time, the blocks hold back the sediment brought in by water.[8] Wind is another factor behind the sediment accumulation.[9]

Clear traces of sediment are still visible inside the cave, mainly along the eastern side (Fig. 11). These traces are at the same level of the soil mound documented in the photographs of 1956 excavation (Fig. 12). De Vaux measured the distance between the surface of the soil and the upper limit of the cave's entrance ("la porte") as 1.35 m high.[10] This measure is coherent with the level of the sediment still visible along the eastern side of the cave. The sediment encumbered a large area in the entrance chamber; the lowest spot may have been at the center of the chamber: here, during the 2017 excavation, we found a huge amount of gastropods shells, accounting for the presence of stagnant water.

3. Stratigraphy

Inside the entrance chamber, an accumulation of soil lay along the western side, maybe resulting from previous archaeological excavations (Fig. 13); here, we established our excavation area (defined as Operation B), divided into two squares (1.80 × 1.80m, each).

After a first cleaning, we found an upper layer characterized by grey sand [SU 201],[11] followed by a deposit of sterile yellow material [SU 202], which covered a layer of darker and more compact soil (probably the

8. Describing the uppermost layer in the entrance chamber, de Vaux wrote: "terre jaune, fine amenée par l'eau." Excavation diary, 28 February; Field notes, 1 March.

9. "Sterile aeolian sand" was identified by Patrich in a crevice to north-east of the entrance. J. Patrich, "Khirbet Qumran in the Light of New Archaeological Explorations in the Qumran Caves," in M.O. Wise et al. (ed.), *Methods of Investigation of the Dead Sea Scrolls and the Khirbet Qumran Site: Present Realities and Future Prospects* (ANYAS 722; New York: New York Academy of Sciences, 1994) 73-95, on p. 90.

10. Field notes, 1 March 1956.

11. In this layer, we retrieved some scattered materials (not *in situ*), mainly concentrated in the northern square: fragments of linen textile (FB11Q1 and FB11Q2), fruits of *Balanites Aegyptiaca* and *Ziziphus spina-Christi* (FB11Q3 and FB11Q4), two small wooden objects (FB11Q5), and fragments of ovine bones (FB11Q6 = B201.F21).

Fig. 12. Cave 11Q. 2 March 1956 (EBAF Archive)

first reliable context, the surface of [SU 203], quoted below).

To verify the possible presence of unexcavated layers, a sounding was opened in the central square of the excavation area (Fig. 14). Measuring initially 1.80×0.90 m, the sounding was then extended southwards to form a trench of 1.80 m per side, thus achieving a more extensive investigation. Once the sounding was completed, a well-preserved stratigraphic sequence was clearly visible on the western section of the trench (Fig. 15). A layer of yellow soil of about 0.50m in depth ([SU 203], Fig. 15, A) covers a layer of grey soil with blackish inclusions, gravel and stones ([SU 204=205], Fig. 15, B). Underneath it lies a greyish layer of clay, eroded at some points and filled with gravel ([SU 206], Fig. 15, C).

It is noteworthy to compare the western section of the sounding with the notes left by de Vaux in his documentation, about the stratigraphy of the entrance chamber:

Excavation diary, 28 February 1956: "En-dessous des déblais des clandestins, une terre jaune, fine amenée par l'eau, dans laquelle quelques tessons chalcolithiques. Épaisseur +/- 50 cm. À la base, une couche de pierres et de terre cendreuse marque le niveau chalcolithique".

Field notes, 1 March 1956: "Salle d'entrée : la porte une fois dégagée a 1,60 de large 1,35 de haut jusqu'au sol romain. En-dessous, dans toute la première salle, une couche de terre jaune, fine, amenée par l'eau, dans laquelle quelques tessons chalcolithiques. En-dessous, un sol cendreux, gris, avec cailloux : sol chalcolithique. Entre celui-ci et le niveau romain 54 cm."

In the documentation of the 1956 excavation there are no sections nor photographs showing what is described. The stratigraphy retrieved and documented in the western section of the sounding achieved in 2017 season appears similar to the one described by de Vaux.

Moreover, it needs to be pointed out that the exposed stratigraphy lacks the upper portion of the yellow layer, and all that used to lie upon it, since it had already been removed by previous excavations and frequentation of the site.

Fig. 13. Accumulation of soil along the western side, inside the entrance chamber (Photo by Marco De Pietri)

Fig. 14. Sounding in Operation B (Photo by Giorgio Skory)

Fig. 15. Sounding in Operation B, western section (Photo by Giorgio Skory)

4. Current Stability Conditions of the Cave

The cave's ceiling is composed of a limestone sub-horizontal stratum. In the middle of the cave, in the zone between the inner and outer part, there is another rock layer, partially detached from the ceiling and forming a sort of "arch" spanning through the cave's width (Fig. 16). This "arch" seems to be somehow sustained by a central rock, a "pillar", connecting the ceiling to the ground. Actually, this "pillar" is not aligned with the axis of the "arch" (Fig. 1, X and Fig. 17).

The cave also features by several sub-vertical faults, running northwest to southeast and crossing the cave from opposite directions. This phenomenon causes the formation of rock wedges that detach from the core, as it can be observed in a remarkable wedge behind the "arch", to the left of the "pillar" (Fig. 1, Y and Fig. 18). A fallen conglomerate slab is also visible to the right of entrance hall.

This situation may explain the funcion of some stone structures documented in the photographs of 1956 excavation: a thick dry-stone wall along the axis of the "pillar" (Fig. 19, B) and more stone structures at the shoulders of the "arch" (Fig. 19, A,C). They had already been dismantled at the time of Patrich's first excavation, in 1988.[12] What was the function of these structures? When were they built? We notice that de Vaux never mentions them, neither in the preliminary report, nor in the Excavation diary. Given that the aforementioned structures could have been major traces of human activity inside the cave, and de Vaux's interpretation of Cave 11Q as a dwelling place,[13] the lack of this information looks noteworthy. Comparing different photographs of 1956 excavation (Figs 19-20), it is possible to observe that the left portion of the wall along the axis of the "pillar" had been rebuilt during the excavation.

Fig. 16. So-called "arch" (Photo by Alessandro Maifredi)

12. Oral communication by Joseph Patrich, September 2015.

13. De Vaux, "Archéologie," 34; Id., *Archaeology*, 57.

Fig. 17. So-called "pillar" (Photo by Alessandro Maifredi)

Fig. 18. Wedge behind the "arch", left of the "pillar" (Photo by Giorgio Skory)

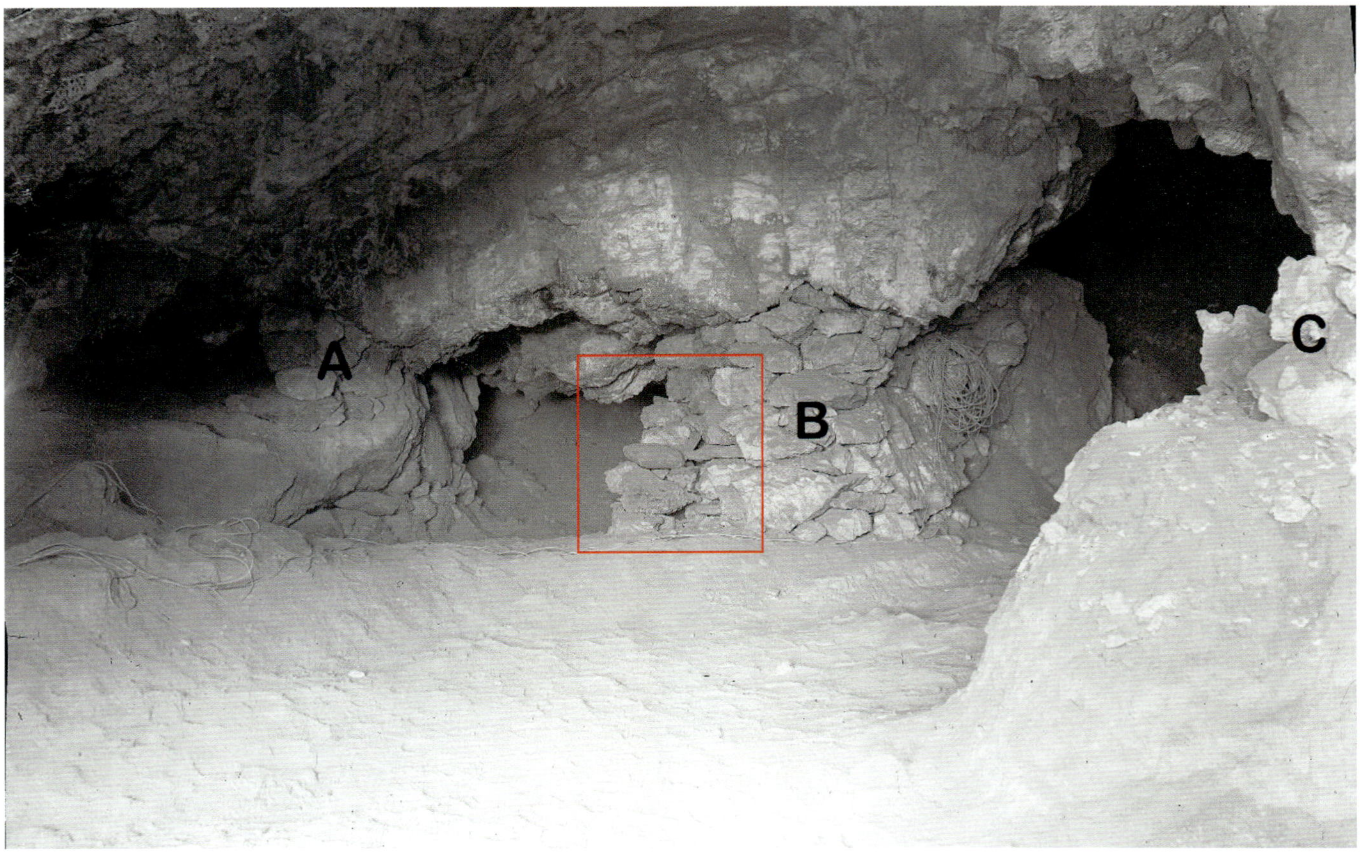

Fig. 19. Stone structures (A-C). 3 March 1956 (EBAF Archive)

Fig. 20. Dry-stone wall. Photo taken on the last days of 1956 excavation (EBAF Archive)

We can therefore suggest that excavators in 1956, possibly aware of the fragile stability of the cave and subsequent danger, may have erected supporting walls for the "pillar" and other hazardous spots; hence the stone structures can be explained as safety measures built during that excavation, a practice still in use in excavations of caves in the region.

5. The Upper Chamber

The speleological investigation performed in March 2017 by Alessandro Maifredi led to the discovery of an upper chamber never documented before. In the northern corner of the cave a narrow vertical passage, 2.5 m in length (Fig. 21), was discovered after removing some fallen stones that were obstructing the way. This passage leads to an upper chamber (figs 22-23): the room, rectangular in plan (Fig. 1), measures about 2 × 6 m. Its height reaches 3.5 m at the entry point, decreasing to 1.2 m at the deep end of the chamber (North). The western side is made of limestone (Fig. 22, A), while the remaining sides and the ceiling are composed of conglomerates. The ground is composed of materials resulting from crumbling conglomerates.

A surface analysis in the upper chamber provided no evidence of human activity. Due to safety reasons (the presence of large boulders in a precarious position), no further analysis has been undertaken.

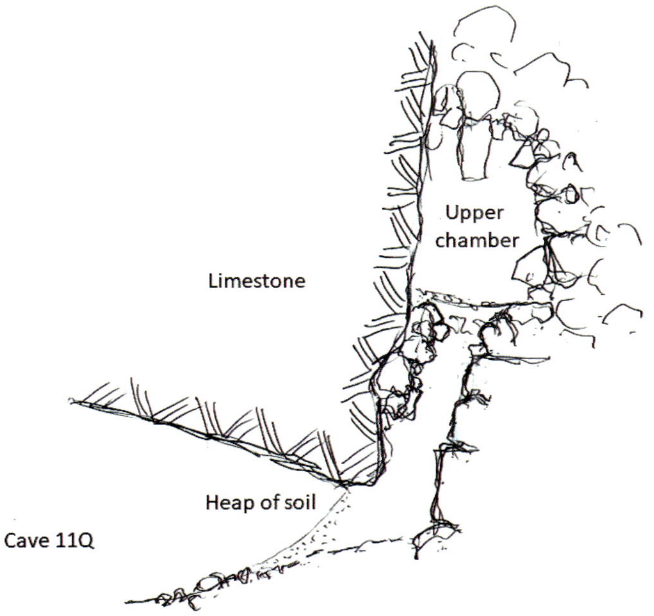

Fig. 21. Sketch of the passage and the upper chamber (Drawn by Jean-Baptiste Humbert)

Fig. 22. The upper chamber, South to North. A = western limestone side (Photo by Giorgio Skory)

Fig. 23. The upper chamber, North to South (Photo by Giorgio Skory)

Chapter Three

Description de la poterie recueillie dans la grotte 11Q

Jean-Baptiste HUMBERT, Marius BURDAJEWICZ, and Frédéric GUYOT

1. La poterie romaine de la grotte 11Q (Pl. 1-2)

Jean-Baptiste Humbert

La composition des caches n'est pas sûre quand la provenance des poteries ne l'est guère. La reconstitution du mobilier de la grotte 11Q est un bon exemple de recomposition. Ce que nous savons des jarres de 11Q est un acquis fort modeste. En revanche, la grotte a fourni de nombreux textiles dont nous savons que certains ont enveloppé des rouleaux. Il y a un paradoxe dans la répartition jarres-textiles. Que sait-on enfin de l'importance du dépôt ? De Vaux a décidé de fouiller la grotte parce que « ... les bédouins disent avoir sorti beaucoup de choses » (Journal, le 23 février 56) et « c'est dans cette première salle que les grandes trouvailles ont été faites » (Notes, le 1 mars 56), mais où sont-elles ? Serait-ce simple vantardise de leur part, ou ont-ils dispersé les trouvailles ? Comment peut-on reformuler avec assurance un lien entre les textiles ramassés dans la fouille, les rouleaux, et les poteries attribués à la grotte 11Q ? L'inventaire des textiles fera le tri entre cordons, ficelles, sacs, enveloppes ou housses : il compte au moins 190 entrées.[1] Il sera loisible d'en comparer la liste à celle des rouleaux désignés 11Q, dont un seul recueilli par les fouilleurs, « au moins un petit rouleau très abîmé » (Journal, le 3 mars 56), et de confronter la liste avec la rareté des poteries restituées, sans prétendre au succès à cause des aléas de la collecte. Des poteries ou des fragments de poteries récupérés, de Vaux a sauvé un couvercle de jarre tubulaire retrouvé « dans les déblais ». Il n'a pas conservé quelques « tessons qumrâniens » (Journal le 12 mars 56), peu nombreux et sans forme. Patrich n'a rien ajouté qui modifie la donne. Il demeure que le nombre des toiles récupérées témoigne d'un vrai dépôt, et la jarre Kando 393, l'une des plus volumineuses de la série, vraisemblablement sortie de 11Q bien qu'issue du marché, put contenir de nombreux rouleaux.

On attendait deux jarres, puisque le rapport de l'exploration de la grotte avait mentionné deux couvercles.[2] Il fallut renoncer à la seconde, puisque l'enregistrement ne signale qu'un couvercle. En fait les fragments éparpillés par les bédouins avaient laissé croire à deux objets distincts qui, une fois recollés, en ont reconstitué un seul. Dans le déroulement de la fouille, le lien avec les manuscrits n'est plus manifesté que par un couvercle et des fragments d'étoffes.

1. Voir N. Sukenik et al., «The Textiles and the Strings from 11Q», dans ce volume.

2. R. de Vaux, « Fouilles de Khirbet Qumrân : Rapport préliminaire sur les 3e, 4e, et 5e campagnes », *RB* 63 (1956) 533-77, p. 574.

Le seul exemplaire de jarre attesté par son couvercle « in situ » a disparu ; aurait-il été cassé à haute époque ou du fait de la fouille sauvage ? Il serait surprenant qu'une poterie intacte ait laissé s'échapper, au cours du pillage, le « petit rouleau très abîmé » signalé dans le Journal (3 mars 56). Il y a de fortes chances pour que la jarre et son couvercle aient été cassés, éventuellement par des bédouins pressés, et le moment de son déplacement nous est inconnu. Les toiles auraient-elles été arrachées, abandonnées sur place, et le contenant emporté avec le reste du contenu ? Si l'on envisage que des qumrâniens sont venus rechercher leur bien, nous ne voyons pas qu'il aient ouvert sacs et étuis sur place pour n'emporter que des rouleaux nus dans une jarre sans couvercle. Des textiles abandonnés ne se seraient pas conservés pendant 2000 ans. Un scénario plus vraisemblable est que des bédouins auraient emporté l'objet qui nous manque ; et qu'en ont-ils fait ? Cassée, elle aura été jetée ; entière, elle aura été vendue. On a évoqué l'éventualité qu'elle soit aux mains de Georges Roux[3] avec qui le lien est rompu sans qu'il ait fourni des indications utiles. Parmi celles qui ont été achetées et qui composent le corpus des « jarres à manuscrits » , personne ne saurait aujourd'hui l'identifier. Le lien entre leur provenance et leur acquisition sur le marché est perdu. Reconnaissons que le nombre exact et le type des poteries entreposées dans la grotte ne sont pas connus.

Gr11Q1

Description : couvercle de jarre à manuscrits, type bol renversé en forme complète. Extérieur : beige ; intérieur : orangé. Pâte : fine, homogène, rouge brique. Dégraissant : assez nombreux grains fins et moyens, rares moyens blancs calcaire. Cuisson : assez bien cuit.

P11Q1

Description : fragment de panse de marmite à paroi fine. Extérieur : brun rouge, intérieur : brun rouge brûlé. Pâte : fine. Légèrement fissurée.

La grotte 11Q aura livré la jarre Kando 393 et son couvercle : en toute rigueur scientifique, sa provenance et celle de son couvercle supposé ne sont pas démontrées. De quelle grotte vient-elle ? Il y a probabilité. Les antiquaires de Bethléem, qui n'en sont pas les découvreurs mais les acquéreurs, ne sont pas en mesure d'assurer son origine exacte : ils l'ont acquise des bédouins. Acceptons l'éventualité que la jarre Kando 393 et son couvercle viennent de 11Q. Pourtant jarre et couvercle ont des origines différentes car leurs pâtes ne sont pas identiques, et le couvercle semble trop grand pour s'adapter harmonieusement à l'épaule. *A contrario*, rien n'indique que les usagers des poteries aient respecté la chaîne de fabrication originale des potiers. Si l'on acceptait l'association jarre-couvercle, le couple résulterait d'un rapprochement de convenance et indiquerait l'utilisation de seconde main.

La jarre Kando 393 s'insère, selon la typologie, dans la série des « jarres à manuscrits » et ne s'en écarte que par sa grande taille. Il est difficile de concevoir que, dans un tel contenant, on n'ait déposé que quelques rouleaux. Nous supposons qu'au moins deux jarres ont été déposées dans 11Q. Peut-on soupçonner que deux jarres aient contenu des lots qu'il ne fallait pas mélanger ? Leur contenance était amplement suffisante aux trente rouleaux escomptés que 11Q aurait livrés.

Avec une grande ouverture et sans anses, coiffée de son couvercle-entonnoir, « l'individu Kando » a reçu l'étiquette de « jarre à manuscrit » . Elle ne s'insère pas en variante dans le type tubulaire, mais se range parmi les exemplaires les plus pansus de la série. Elle serait plutôt une forme mixte, proche des exemples à couvercle lacé. Ses parallèles, quant à la forme, sont la GQ 29-8, à peine plus réduite en taille ; puis KhQ1401, inscrite, du locus 84 nous la rapprochons encore des Gr7Q5 à plus large ouverture.

Jarre Kando 393

Jarre ventrue à base annulaire ; lourdement restaurée. Extérieur : rouge-beige ; intérieur : rouge. Pâte fine, homogène. Dégraissant : grains moyens blancs, clairsemés.

Couvercle Kando

Couvercle de jarre type entonoir renversé ; intact. Extérieur : rouge-brun ; intérieur : rose-brun. Sans cassure, description de la pâte impossible.

3. Voir une description dans E. Puech, « Notes en marge de 11QpaléoLévitique. Le fragment L, des fragments inédits et une jarre de la grotte 11 », *RB* 96 (1989) 161-83, p. 181-2, et Pl. III.

2. La poterie de l'époque du Fer (Pl. 3)

Marius Burdajewicz

Le mobilier de l'époque du Fer issu de 11Q est peu nombreux et fragmentaire. Son intérêt est donc limité et rien ne le rattache à un événement historique. Les formes reconstituées appartiennent à la vaisselle commune et leur chronologie demeure approximative. Témoin d'une simple halte ou d'un refuge épisodique, le lot doit être regardé dans un lien avec le site sous-jacent à l'établissement de Qumrân. D'autres anfractuosités dans la bordure occidentale de la mer Morte ont fourni quelque vaisselle de la même période. L'occupation à partir de 700 av. J.-C. y fut très précaire. L'ensemble des données à venir peut gagner en cohérence. La chronologie n'y gagnera rien. L'affermissement du royaune de Juda en sera précisé.

2.1 *Jarre « bocal », sans col*

Les jarres sans col appartiennent à la grande famille bien attestée dans la Palestine du Fer II, dont on retiendra plusieurs variantes. Les formes complètes connues par ailleurs ont un corps cylindrique et le fond arrondi[4]. Le diamètre de l'ouverture oscille entre 18 et 14 cm.

Gr11Q15

Jarre à large bord replié à l'intérieur et pincé, horizontal, le pli externe, à bourrelet saillant. Extérieur : rouge-orangé ; intérieur : rouge brique. Pâte fine, bien malaxée, homogène ; dégraissant ; nombreux grains fins et serrés, calcaire blanc. Cuisson : bien cuit.

Le type semble plutôt rare. Les exemplaires proviennent de contextes des VIIIe et VIIe s. de Ramat Rahel, niveau V[5], ou des VIIe-VIe s. de Gezer[6]. À Jérusalem, le type est déja connu au VIIIe s.[7], mieux attesté dans la phase « 8 », VIIe - VIe s.[8]

Parallèles

Khirbet Qumrân : 4706 (Loc 72), 4901 (Tr. Est), 3104 (Tr. Ouest) ;[9] Tell el-Jurn (Tel Goren) V, 650/630 – 582/1 av. J.-C. ;[10] Jérusalem *colline sud-est* ;[11] *Quartier Juif*, niveau 7 ;[12] Vallée du Tyropoeon, niveau XI du VIIIe s. ;[13] Ramat Rahel V ;[14] Tell el-Ful, niveaux pré-IIIA et IIIB ;[15] Tell el-Naṣbeh ;[16] Tell Mashash (Masos) ;[17] Gezer VA ;[18] Megiddo, niveaux IV-I.[19]

---

4. Cf. Y. Aharoni, *Excavations at Ramat Rahel: Seasons 1961 and 1962* (Serie Archeologica 6; Rome: Centro di Studi Semitici, 1964).

5. Aharoni, *Excavations at Ramat Rahel*, Fig. 12 : *8*.

6. S. Gitin, *Gezer III: A Ceramic Typology of the Late Iron II, Persian and Hellenistic Periods at Tell Gezer* (ANGSBA 3; Jerusalem: Hebrew Union College, 1990), 130-1, type 10B.

7. D. Ben-Ami, «The Iron Age Pottery», in Id., *Jerusalem: Excavations in the Tyropoeon Valley (Giv'ati Parking Lot): Vol. 1* (IAA Reports 52, Jerusalem: Israel Antiquities Authority, 2013) 63-82, p. 74-77.

8. H.J. Franken, «The Twelve Pottery Classes», in Id. and M.L. Steiner, *Excavations in Jerusalem 1961-1967: Vol. 2: The Iron Age Extramural Quarter on the South-East Hill* (Oxford: Oxford University Press, 1990) 99-121, Figs 6-44.

9. M. Burdajewicz, *L'Age du Fer à Qumrân* – à paraître.

10. I. Yezerski, «Pottery of Stratum V», in E. Stern, *En-Gedi Excavations I: Final report* (1961-1965) (Jerusalem: Hebrew University, 2007) 86-129, Pl. 8 : 13-9.

11. Franken and Steiner, *Excavations in Jerusalem 1961-1967*, Fig. 6 : 42 : 31.

12. De Groot, A., G. Hillel, and I. Yezerski, «Iron Age II Pottery», in H. Geva (ed.), *Jewish Quarter Excavations in the Old City of Jerusalem Conducted by Nahman Avigad, 1969-1982: Vol. 2: The Finds from Areas A, W and X-2: Final Report* (Jerusalem: Israel Exploration Society, 2003) 1-49, Pl. 1 : 10 : 11-13.

13. Ben-Ami, *Jerusalem: Excavations in the Tyropoeon Valley,* Figs 3.4 : 2 et 3.5 : 8.

14. Aharoni, *Excavations at Ramat Rahel*, Fig. 12 : *8*.

15. N.L. Lapp, *The Third Campaign at Tell el-Ful: The Excavations of 1964* (AASOR 45; Cambridge, MA: American Schools of Oriental Research, 1981), Pl. 49 : 3, 15-16.

16. J.C. Wampler, «Three Cistern Groups from Tell el-Naṣbeh», *BASOR* 92 (1941) 25-43, Pl. 26 : 436, Fig. 4 : X175.

17. O. Zimhoni, «The Pottery», in V. Fritz. and A. Kempinski, *Ergebnisse der Ausgrabungen auf der Hirbet el-Msas (Tel Masos) 1972-1975* (Wiesbaden: Harrassowitz, 1983) 127-130, Pl. 166 : 5.

18. Gitin, *Gezer III*, 130-2, Pl. 26 : 30 ; 45 : 8.

19. R.S. Lamon and G.A. Shipton, *Megiddo I: Seasons of 1925-34: Strata I-V* (OIP 42; Chicago: University of Chicago Press, 1939), Pl. 11, 54.

2.2 *Jarre avec col*

La grotte 11Q n'a livré que les fragments de deux jarres dont les cols manquent. De deux types différents, elles se rangent néanmoins dans les formes de contenants les plus répandues en Judée, avec un col haut. L'une (Gr11Q14) retient l'attention par sa petite taille ; elle appartient au tpe à épaule tombante et arrondie. La seconde possède un épaule plus haute et à carène marquée, plus fréquente sur la côte.

Gr11Q14

Grand fragment de la panse d'une jarre. Extérieur : rouge clair ; intérieur : brun-rouge

Pâte identique à 11Q15 : fine, bien malaxée, homogène ; Dégraissant : nombreux grains fins et serrés, calcaire blanc. Cuisson : assez bien cuit.

Gr11Q42

Epaule d'une jarre. Extérieur : rouge clair ; intérieur : rouge-brun. Pâte fine, homogène, légèrement poreuse. A section rouge clair côté externe et gris noir côté interne. Dégraissant grains moyens calcaire blanc clairsemés et rares très fins blancs. Cuisson : bien cuit.

Parallèles

Jérusalem, *Ophel* ;[20] Tell el-Jurn (Tel Goren) V ;[21] Tell el-Nasbeh, Citernes 370 et 304 ;[22] Arad VII et V ;[23] Tell ʿIra VII et VI ;[24] Beersheva II ;[25] Tell Masos, de la fin du VIIe au début du VIe s. ;[26] Qadesh Barnéa, niveau 2.[27]

2.3 *Lampes « coquille »*

Les deux lampes, Gr11Q8 et Gr11Q5, sont du type commun, dit « coquille » . Elles sont assez difficiles à dater parce que la forme dérive d'un type plus ancien sans base et que seule varie la hauteur de la base en disque. Les bases gagneraient en hauteur avec le temps jusqu'à la fin du VIIe s. Les variantes trahissent une chronologie entre VIIIe et VIIe s.[28] La lampe Gr11Q5 a une base haute et massive comme celles de Tell el-Ful, IIIB.[29] La lampe Gr11Q8, qui selon nous serait un peu plus récente que les autres, possède un pied plus bas, avec l'élégance de forme et de proportions du type ancien, au début du VIIIe s. Elle peut être encore de la fin de VIIe ou du début du VIe s., parce qu'aux VIII/VIIe s. les deux types furent contemporains.

Parallèles

Grottes : GQ 39-6 (grotte GQ 39) ;[30] Cave of the Pool ;[31] Khirbet Qumrân : 3348 (Loc 46) et 4414 (Loc 87) ;[32] Tell el-Jurn (Tel Goren) V ;[33] Jérusalem,

20. E. Mazar and B. Mazar, *Excavations in the South of the Temple Mount: The Ophel of Biblical* Jerusalem (Qedem 29; Jerusalem: The Hebrew University, 1989), Pl. 27 : 5.
21. Yezerski, «Pottery of Stratum V», Pl. 9 : 5-10.
22. Wampler, «Three Cistern Groups from Tell el-Naṣbeh», Figs 2 : X4, X88 ; 7 : X1, X2.
23. Z. Herzog et al., «The Israelite Fortress at Arad», *BASOR* 254 (1984) 1-34, Figs 25 : 15 ; 29 : 11.
24. L. Freud, "Pottery. 2. Iron Age," in I. Beit-Arieh (ed.), *Tel ʿIra: A Stronghold in the Biblical Negev* (MSSMNIA 15; Tel Aviv: Emery and Claire Yass Publications in Archaeology, 1999) 189-289, niveau VII = Fig. 6.75 : 1 ; niveau VI = Figs 6.62 : 19 ; 6.91 : 13 ; 6.69 : 14 ; 6.10 : 6.
25. Y. Aharoni (ed.), *Beer-Sheba I: Excavations at Tel Beer-Sheba: 1969-1971 Seasons* (Publications of the Institute of Archaeology 2; Tel Aviv: Tel Aviv University, Institute of Archaeology, 1973), Pl. 73 : 4.
26. Zimhoni, «The Pottery», Pl. 166 : 11, 14.
27. H. Bernick-Greenberg, «The Ceramic Assemblages and the Wheel-Made Pottery Typology», in R. Cohen and H. Bernick-Greenberg, *Excavations at Kadesh Barnea (Tell el-Qudeirat) 1976-1982* (IAA Reports 34; Jerusalem: Israel Antiquities Authority, 2007) 131-85, Pl. 11.77 : 2.
28. A. Mazar and N. Panitz-Cohen, *Timnah (Tel Batash) II: The Finds from the First Millenium BCE* (Qedem 42; Jerusalem: Hebrew University, 2001), 133.
29. Lapp, *The Third Campaign at Tell el-Ful*, Pl. 71 : 4, 7-13.
30. R. de Vaux, « Archéologie », in M. Baillet, J.T. Milik and R. de Vaux, *Les 'petites grottes' de Qumrân : Exploration de la falaise. Les grottes 2Q, 3Q, 5Q, 6Q, 7Q à 10Q. Le rouleau de cuivre* (DJD 3 ; Oxford : Clarendon, 1962) 3-36, p. 12, Fig. 5 : 3, Pl. VII ; Burdajewicz, *L'Age du Fer à Qumrân.*
31. N. Avigad, «Expedition A - Nahal David», *IEJ* 12 (1962) 169-83, p. 174, Fig. 4.
32. Burdajewicz, *L'Age du Fer à Qumrân (à praitre).*
33. Yezerski, «Pottery of Stratum V», Pl. 11 : 6-11.

niveau 9 ;[34] Ramat Rahel V ;[35] Lakish II ;[36] Timnah (Tel Batash) II ;[37] Arad VI ;[38] Tell Mashash (Masos) ;[39] ʻAïn Qudeirât (Qadesh-Barnea) Niveau 2.[40]

2.4 *Flacon*

Les publications décrivent habituellement ces petits vases à col étroit comme des « cruchettes » ou « puisettes », mais la cruche, et son dérivé cruchette sont des vases qui servent la boisson, ou comme des vases à onguent ou parfum, ce qui ne convient ni dans un cas ni dans l'autre. Le flacon Gr11Q7, de petite dimension, avec un col très étroit pour verser parcimonieusement, est parfaiement adapté à contenit l'uile pour les lampes. Nous pouvons croire que le flacon accompagnait les deux lampes retrouvées au même endroit.

Gr11Q7

Objet perdu. Flacon, corps sphérique, anse à section ronde, de fabrication grossière. « Terre rouge, fine à petites particules blanches » (catalogue des fouilles)

3. Le mobilier chalcolithique (Pl. 4)

Frédéric Guyot

Les cultures ghassoulienne et chalcolithique dans le bassin de la mer Morte sont bien attestées, et fouillées depuis longtemps. La documentation est connue et accessible. Il n'est pas étonnant de les retrouver dans des abris de la région de Qumrân en face du site majeur de Teleilat Ghassoul. La palmeraie qui prospérait dans ce secteur a pu attirer des chasseurs. La vaisselle recueillie est des plus communes.

Toutes les poteries sont chalcolithiques d'après leurs formes et leurs matériaux (fabrique, dégraissants, cuisson). Elles datent plus précisément du chalcolithique final (ou Ghassoulien), soit dernier quart du 5e millénaire. Contemporaines du mobilier des fouilles de Beersheva, Ghassoul et les grottes d'Umm Qatafa.[41]

Les pâtes - On distingue deux groupes de production : A et B. Les deux productions ne présentent aucun traitement de surface, un seul exemple d'engobe, pas de brunissage. Simple lissage à main humide ; l'emploi de barbotine durant le lissage est difficile à préciser.

A - Argile à dégraissants minéraux, calcite broyée et ajout d'élément siliceux. Ensemble homogène (sable fin <1 mm, éruptif ?).

B - Fabrique plus grossière contenant un grand nombre d'éléments clastiques (silex + calcaire), sans doute naturellement présents dans l'argile : argiles peu propices à la production de la poterie. Peu cuites ; elle s'effritent. Ce qui ne signifie pas que les potiers étaient moins qualifiés. Plutôt moins d'investissement.

Gr11Q13

Pot à col pourvu d'anses oreillettes horizontales à impressions digitées (commun). Les incisions obliques sur l'épaule sont moins attestées. Fabrique A.

Gr11Q16 et Gr11Q49

Jarres de stockage à décor digité sur la lèvre. Pâte épaisse courante dans la période. Fabrique B.

34. De Groot, Hillel, and Yezerski, «Iron Age II Pottery», Pls 1.6 : 8 ; 1.14 : 21.

35. Aharoni, *Excavations at Ramat Rahel*, Figs 11 : 36-38 ; 27 : 8 ; 28 : 50.

36. O. Zimhoni, «The Pottery of Levels III and II», in D. Ussishkin, *The Renewed Archaeological Excavations at Lachish (1973-1994): Vol. 4* (MSSMNIA 22; Tel Aviv: Emery and Claire Yass Publications in Archaeology, 2004) 1789-899, Figs 26.54 : 17, 26.55 : 18-20.

37. Mazar and Panitz-Cohen, *Timnah*, Type L3, p. 133-4.

38. Herzog et al., «The Israelite Fortress at Arad», Figs 18 : 13 ; 22 : 17 ; 25 : 14 ; 29 : 10.

39. Zimhoni, «The Pottery», Pl. 166 : 16-19.

40. Bernick-Greenberg, «The Ceramic Assemblages», Pls 11.78 : 12 ; 11.83 : 7 ; 11.115 : 17.

41. J. Perrot, «Umm Qatafa and Umm Qala'a: Two 'Ghassulian' caves in the desert of Judea», *EI* (1992) 100-11 ; C. Commenge-Pellerin, *La poterie d'Abou Matar et de l'Ouadi Zoumeili (Beersheva) au IVe millénaire avant l'ère chrétienne* (Cahiers du CRFJ 3 ; Paris : Association Paléorient, 1987) ; Id., *La poterie de Safadi (Beersheva) au IVe millénaire avant l'ère chrétienne* (Cahiers du CRFJ 5 ; Paris : Association Paléorient, 1990).

Gr11Q17 et Gr11Q18

Jarres sans col dites *holemouth*. Ont pu servir de petit contenant ou de vase de cuisson, mais le manque de fond ne permet pas de préciser.

Traces de lissage sous le bord et sur la paroi interne. Formes courantes, pas de diagnostique. Fabrique A.

Gr11Q38

Fond de jarre à paroi épaisse. Probablement forme fermée. Fabrique A.

P11Q2

Fabrique A. Tesson de grand vase de stockage. Extérieur : engobe brun.

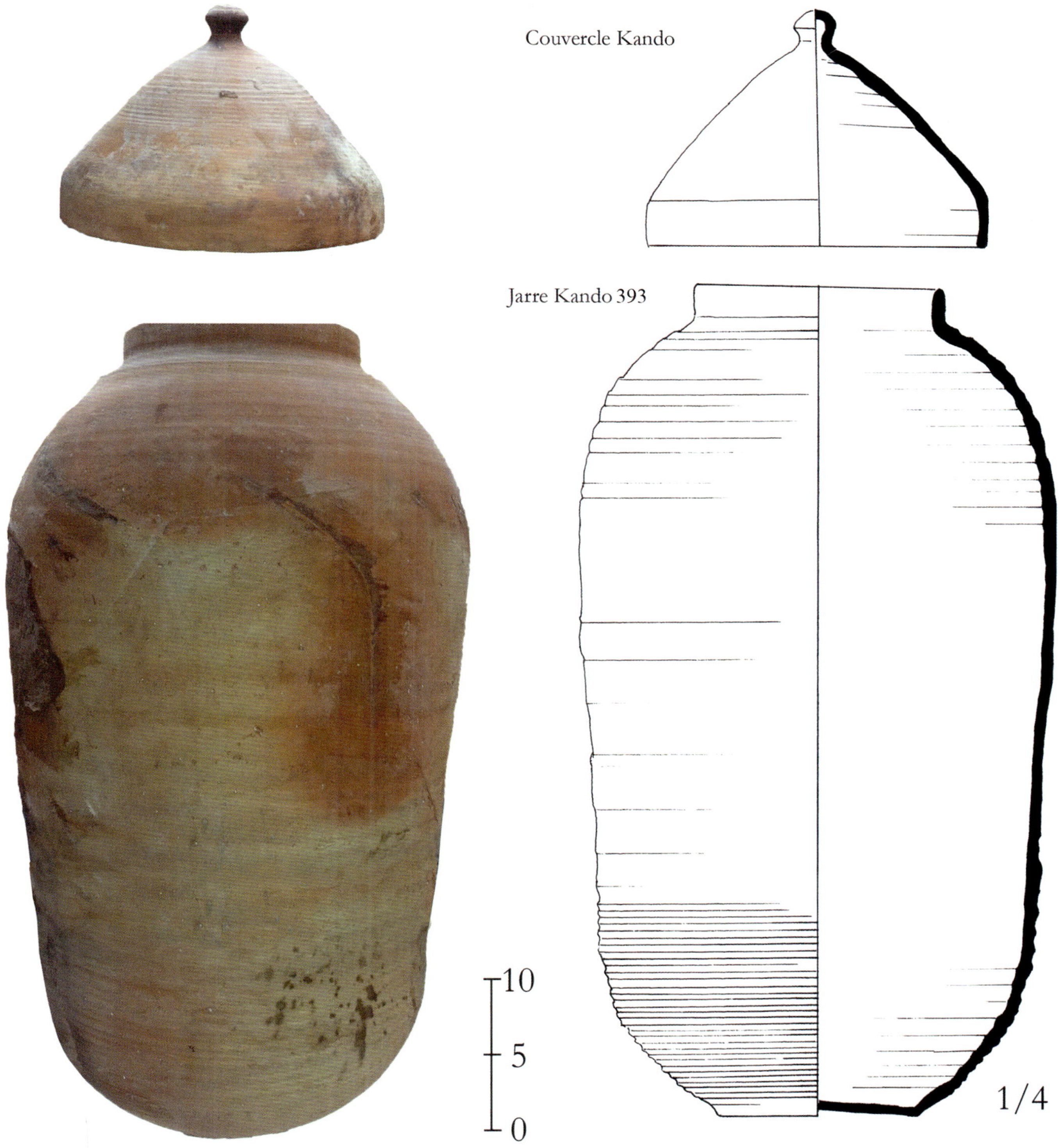

Planche 1. Jarre et couvercle Kando

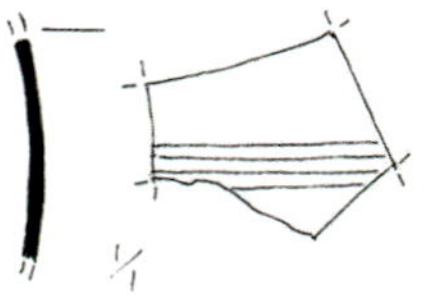

1/1

P 11Q 1

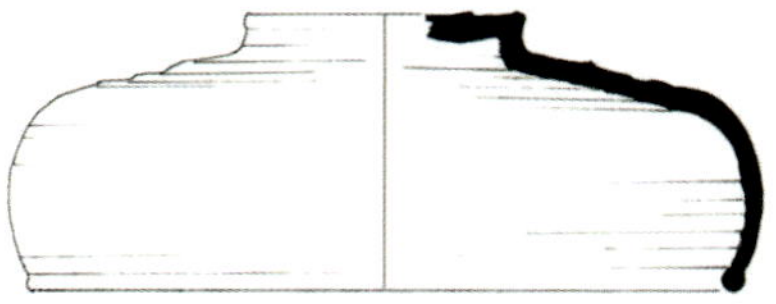

Gr11Q 1

1/4

0 5 10

Planche 2. Poterie romaine de la grotte 11Q

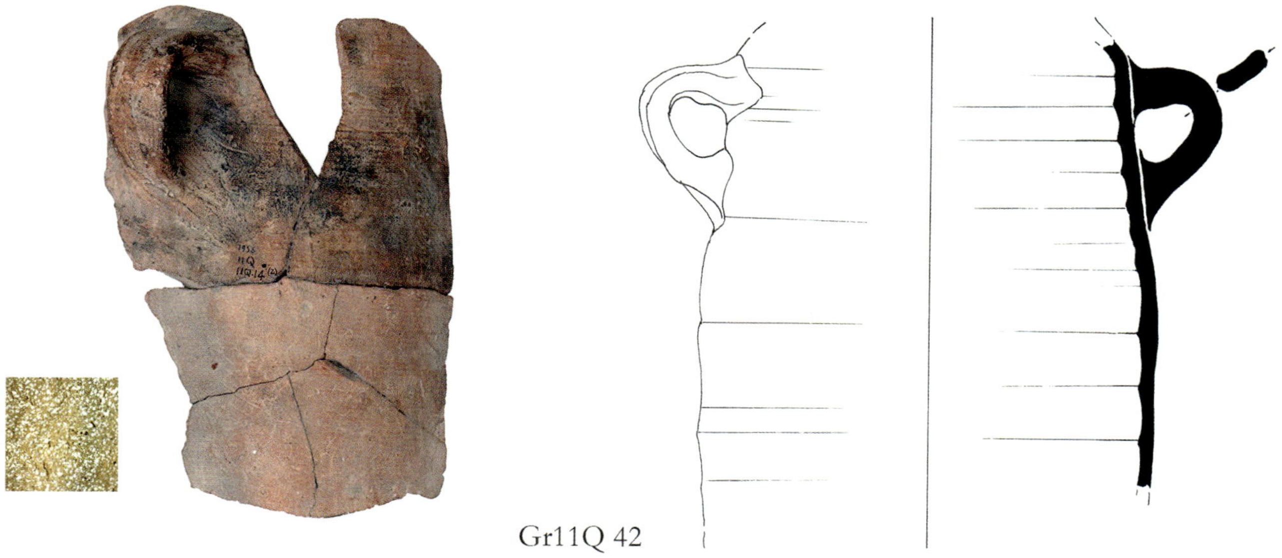

Gr11Q 42

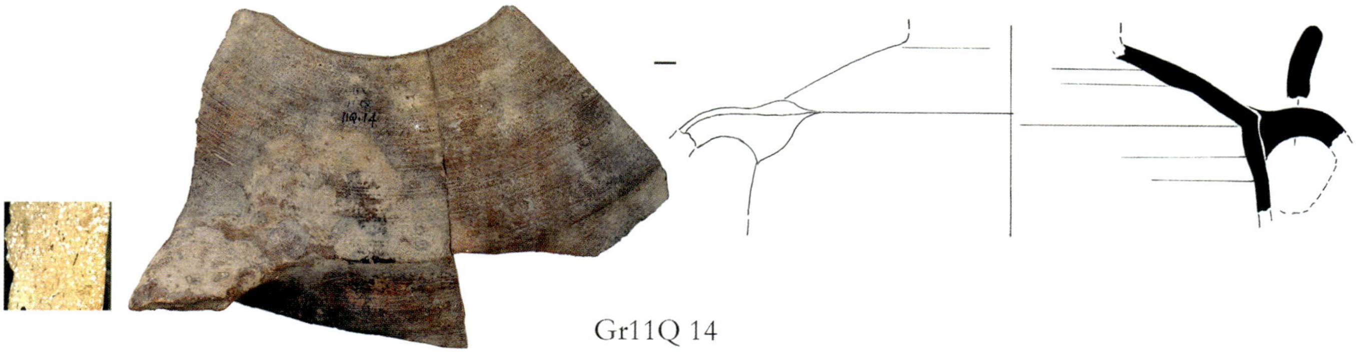

Gr11Q 14

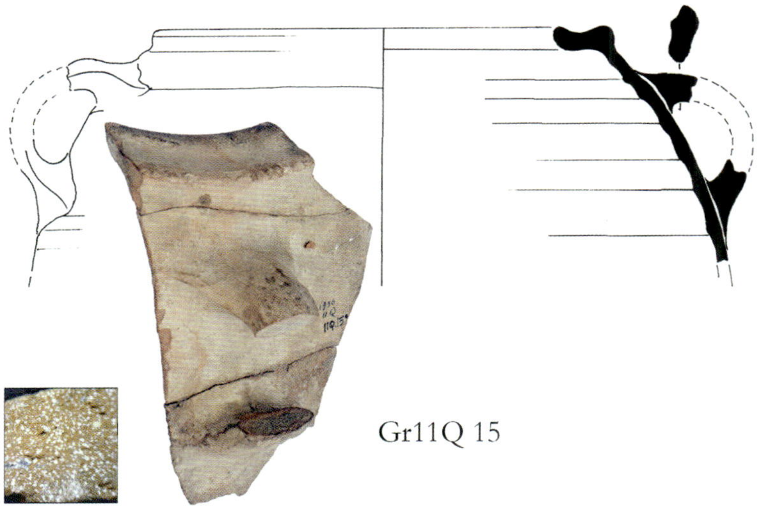

Gr11Q 15

Gr11Q 7

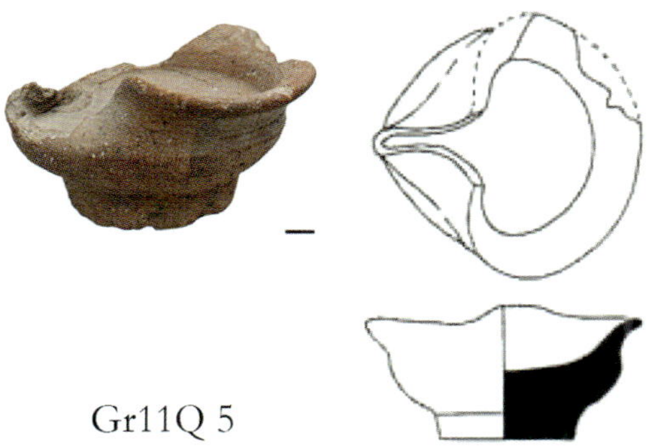

Gr11Q 5

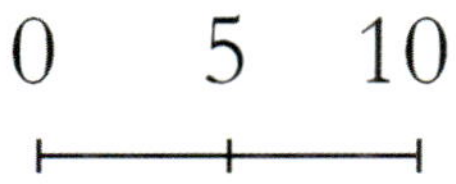

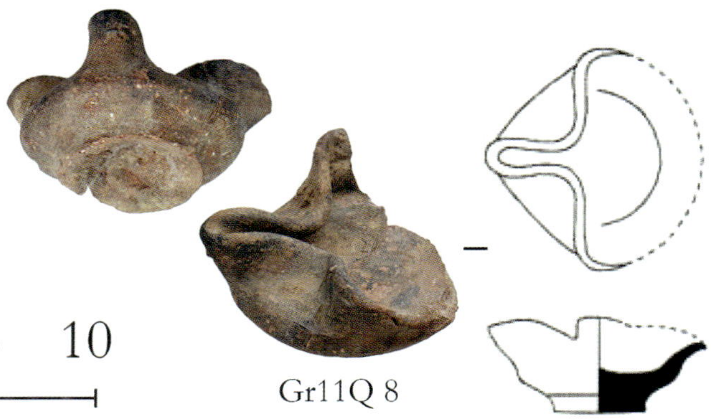

Gr11Q 8

Planche 3. Poterie de l'Âge du Fer de la grotte 11Q

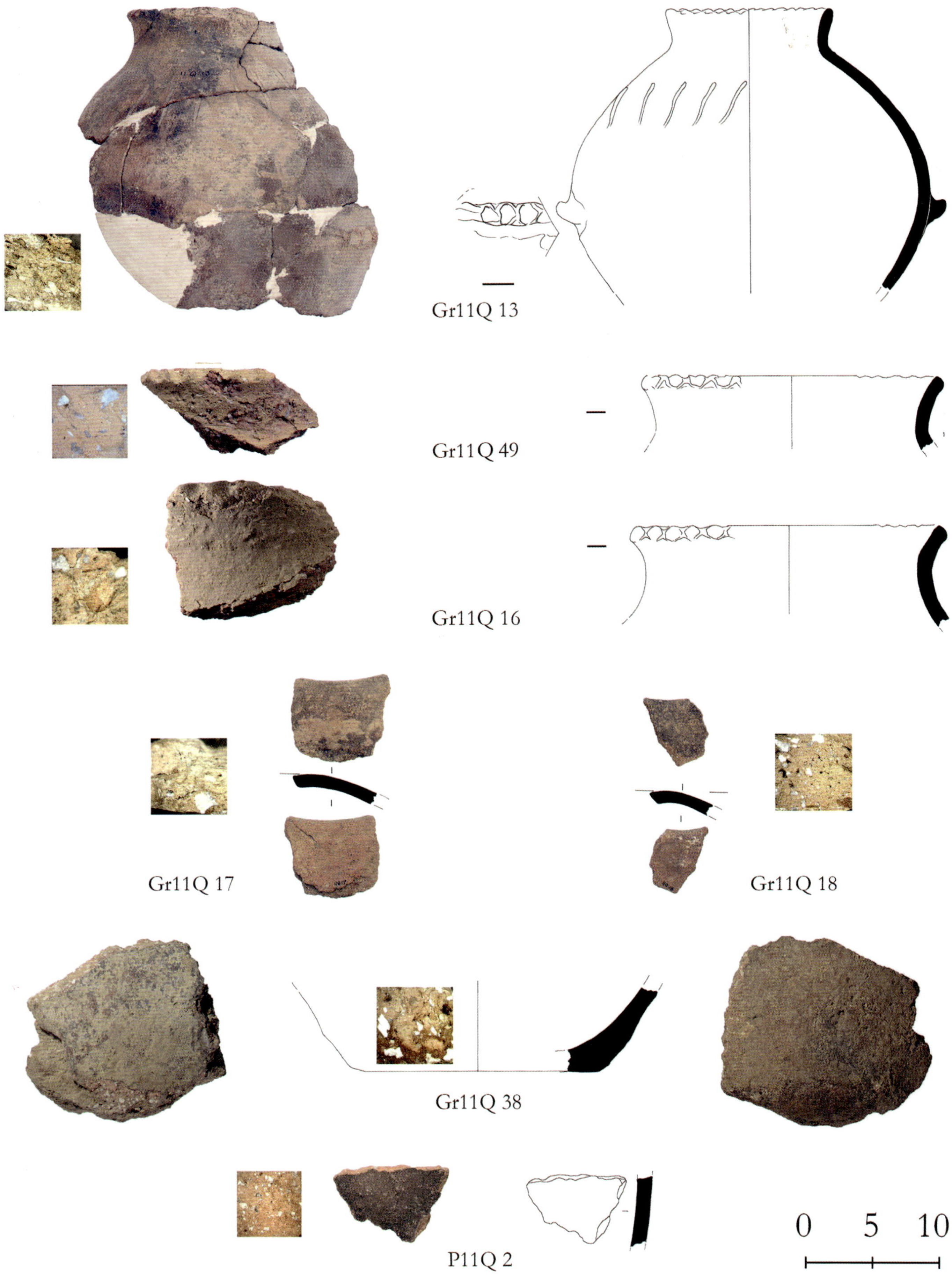

Planche 4. Poterie de l'époque chalcolithique de la grotte 11Q

Chapter Four

Textiles and Strings from Cave 11Q

Naama SUKENIK, Orit SHAMIR, Mireille BÉLIS, and Mauro ROTTOLI

Qumran cave 11Q yielded the biggest assemblage of textiles and strings found in the caves of the Qumran area. Some textiles have been published or mentioned in several publications: Bélis' contribution dealing with 130 textiles, including some from Cave 11Q;[1] Sukenik's publication of the Temple Scroll wrapper stored in the Schøyen Collection and purchased from the Kando family,[2] and other studies about Qumran textiles.[3]

In this paper, a comprehensive research is presented for the first time, carried out on the 205 textiles and strings known to us from Cave 11Q. All the textiles were examined by digital optical microscope (Dino-Lite); the analysis took into account a variety of parameters including: materials identification, spin directions, weaving techniques, number of threads per cm, density, edges, patching, sewing, decoration, and special features. This helps us understand the function and the origin of these textiles and gives us new insights about Cave 11Q. Textiles provide us insights about the people who used them, their social and economic status, and the differences and variations compared to other Roman and Hellenistic sites which yielded textiles. Moreover, as it might be expected, textiles from Cave 11Q can be compared to textiles from Cave 1Q already published by Grace M. Crowfoot, which is considered the pioneering contribution dealing with Qumran textiles.[4]

1. The Artefacts

1.1 *Finds and Their Condition*

205 textiles and strings from Cave 11Q are stored today at the storeroom of organic material (National Treasures) of the Israel Antiquities Authority (IAA). Textile preservation was carried out in the organic

1. M. Bélis, "Des Textiles: Catalogues et Commentaires," in J.-B. Humbert and J. Gunneweg (ed.), *Khirbet Qumrân et 'Aïn Feshkha: Vol. II: Études d'anthropologie, de physique et de chimie* (NTOA.SA 3; Fribourg/Göttingen: Éditions Universitaires/Vandenhoeck & Ruprecht, 2003) 207-76.
2. N. Sukenik, "The Temple Scroll Wrapper from Cave 11: MS 5095/2, MS 5095/4, MS 5095/1," in T. Elgvin, K. Davis, and M. Langlois (ed.), *Gleanings from the Caves: Dead Sea Scrolls and Artefacts from the Schøyen Collection* (LSTS 71; London: Bloomsbury T&T Clark, 2016) 339-50.
3. O. Shamir and N. Sukenik, "Qumran Textiles and the Garments of Qumran's Inhabitants," *DSD* 18 (2011) 206-25; M. Bélis, "The Unpublished Textiles from the Qumran Caves," in M. Fidanzio (ed.), *The Caves of Qumran: Proceedings of the International Conference, Lugano 2014* (STDJ 118; Leiden: Brill, 2016) 123-36.
4. G.M. Crowfoot, "The Linen Textiles," in D. Barthélemy and J.T. Milik, *Qumran Cave 1* (DJD 1; Oxford: Clarendon, 1955) 18-38.

material conservation laboratory of the IAA. Most of them were found by Roland de Vaux in 1956,[5] including textiles adhering to scrolls;[6] eight fragments were collected by Joseph Patrich in 1988,[7] and two more fragments by Marcello Fidanzio in the 2017 excavation.[8] One more textile, identified as a wrapper of the Temple Scroll, is kept in the Schøyen collection.[9] No complete textiles were found, most of them are only fragments; some textiles present cutting signs, probably done in recent times by looters. Some textiles were dirty because of soil, but animals droppings were not found[10].

1.2 *Material*

92 percent (172 items) of the textiles are made of linen (see Fig. A), a fiber derived from the stalks of the flax plant *Linum usitatissimum*, characterized by a strong flexible fiber reaching up to a length of 50-120cm. Linen thread has been used since the Neolithic Age and became a popular raw material in the textile industry throughout Levant and worldwide.[11] It was also used in the Roman period for various purposes such as garment,[12] loincloth, socks,[13] shrouds,[14] simple sacks,[15] kerchiefs and other bands.[16] Linen was also found to be the sole raw material in Cave 1Q.[17]

Six percent (11 items, see Table 2) of the textiles, which were collected by de Vaux's and Patrich's excavations, are made of cotton: they are similar to cotton textiles found in other Judean caves, and probably date to the Medieval period.[18] First evidence of cotton textiles from Israel were dated to Byzantine period as import product,[19] but the cotton became popular raw material only from the 9th century CE onwards.[20] Three textiles made from synthetic fibers are dated to recent times and are not included in the catalogue. In this paper, we focus on the linen textiles which, according to the radiocarbon analysis, date to the Hellenistic and Roman period. The dates indicate that the linen textiles from Cave 11Q were manufactured at different times stretching from the second century B.C. until the second century C.E.

5. R. de Vaux, "Fouilles de Khirbet Qumrân: rapport préliminaire sur les 3e, 4e, et 5e campagnes," *RB* 63 (1956) 533-77, on pp. 573-4.

6. Some of the textiles (items nos 154-62 in Table 1) were found with the scroll fragments in the Dead Sea Scrolls conservation laboratory (IAA). Some of them are still adhering to the parchment.

7. J. Patrich, "Khirbet Qumran in the Light of New Archaeological Explorations in the Qumran Caves," in M.O. Wise et al. (ed.), *Methods of Investigation of the Dead Sea Scrolls and the Khirbet Qumran Site: Present Realities and Future Prospects* (ANYAS 722; New York: New York Academy of Sciences, 1994) 73-95, on p. 40; O. Shamir and T. Schick "Chalcolithic to Medieval Textiles from the Judean Desert Caves Survey," in O. Peleg-Barkat et al. (ed.), *Between the Sea and Desert: On Kings, Nomads, Cities and Monks. Essays in Honor of Joseph Patrich* (Tzemach: Kinneret Institute for Galilean Archaeology, forthcoming). Items nos 163-70 in Table 1.

8. Items nos 154-55 in Table 1.

9. Sukenik, "Temple Scroll Wrapper."

10. In order to better analyze the production techniques all artefacts were cleaned by R. Vinitsky and V. Nosikovsky at the organic materials conservation laboratory (IAA).

11. R.J. Forbes, *Studies in Ancient Technology: Vol. 5* (Leiden: Brill, 1956), 27; D. Zohary, M. Hopf, and E. Weiss, *Domestication of Plants in the Old World* (Oxford: Oxford University Press, 42013), 103-6.

12. Y. Yadin, *The Finds from the Bar Kokhba Period in the Cave of Letters* (Jerusalem: Israel Exploration Society, 1963), 256.

13. A. Sheffer and H. Granger-Taylor, "Textiles from Masada: A Preliminary Selection," in J. Aviram, G. Foerster, and E. Netzer (ed.), *Masada IV: The Yigael Yadin Excavations 1963-1965: Final Reports* (Jerusalem: Israel Exploration Society/ Hebrew University, 1994) 149-256, on pp. 221-2.

14. O. Shamir, "A Burial Textile from the First Century CE in Jerusalem Compared to Roman Textiles in the Land of Israel and the Turin Shroud," *SHS Web of Conferences 15* (2015), https://doi.org/10.1051/shsconf/20151500010.

15. Yadin, *Finds from the Bar Kokhba Period*, 259-61.

16. Yadin, *Finds from the Bar Kokhba Period*, 261-7. The use of linen was discussed in Shamir and Sukenik, "Qumran Textiles."

17. Crowfoot, "Linen Textiles."

18. Other textiles from Qumran were identified as cotton, see: Crowfoot, "Linen Textiles," nos 11-12.

19. Cotton was imported to Palestine during the Byzantine period but still in small quantities: few textiles were found in 'En Boqeq, Nessana and Rogem Zafir: O. Shamir, "Textile Trade to Palestine in the Roman Period," in K. Droß-Krüpe and M.-L. Nosch (ed.), *Textiles, Trade and Theories from the Ancient Near East to the Mediterranean* (Münster: Ugarit-Verlag, 2016) 231-45, on p. 235 and references therein.

20. O. Shamir and A. Baginski, "Textile Hoard from Jericho Cave 38 in the Qarantal Cliff," in O. Guri-Rimon (ed.), *Hoards and Genizot as Chapters in History* (Haifa: Hecht Museum, University of Haifa, 2013) 77*-87*; O. Shamir and A. Baginski, "The Later Textiles, Basketry and Cordage from Caves in the Judean Desert," *'Atiqot* 14 (1993) 241-55.

and generally they would correlate with the time of the Qumran settlement.[21]

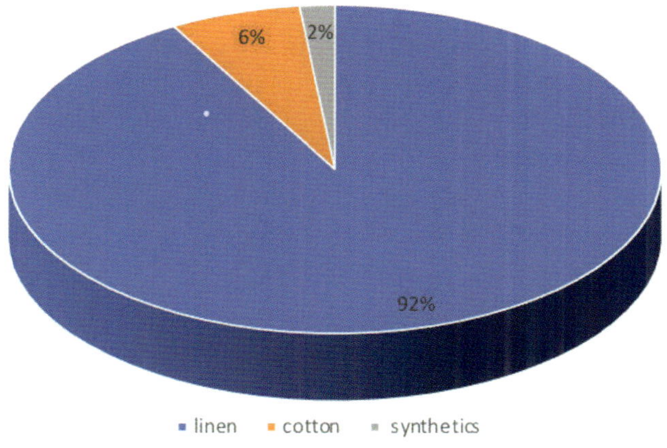

Fig. A Diagram of the material fibers in Cave 11Q textiles

1.3 *Spinning and Weaving*

All the linen threads have been spun in the S direction in the warp as in the weft, which is a common practice in ancient Israel and follows the natural spin direction of flax fibers.[22] The spinning tightness in most cases spans between 26°- 45° angle, and all of them appear as single yarns, not plied nor spliced. All textiles are made in plain weave-tabby and its variations include warp-faced (where the warp threads are higher than the wefts; e.g. textile Gr11Q36, Fig. 1), and the ones made in balanced weaving (where the thread count of the warp threads per cm - tpc - is the same of the weft) were observed in the linen textiles (textile Gr11Q80, Fig. 2). Those weaving techniques are the most simple ones, and were common for linen textiles found at other sites, including Masada,[23] the Cave of the Letters,[24] Mo'a,[25] and more. Only one textile was made by basket weave (extended tabby) (Gr11Q29, Fig. 3), where two threads are taken instead of one in both warp and weft; another textile (Gr11Q50, Fig. 4) was made by half-basket, where only one system is paired. Although those techniques are typical mainly to sacks which need stronger textile,[26] item Gr11Q29 shows a blue decoration (see Fig. 3) which implies other purposes.

According to spinning tightness and threads' density, there are clear differences in the quality of the weaving. The finest cloth is a tightly-spun, evenly woven fabric with a high number of thin threads per cm (count of 24 warps and 16 wefts per cm as for Gr11Q59b); the more coarse and uneven the yarn, the lower the count (8 x 8 tpc, Gr11Q189). The threads' density does not achieve the quality of the Chalcolithic textiles from the Judean Desert, which reach ca. 46 warp threads per cm and 30 weft threads per cm and are much thinner and more delicate.[27] There are differences among the textiles as far as the thickness of the threads is concerned: In some textiles, the threads are narrower than in others, which is consistent with Crowfoot's report on the textiles found in Cave 1Q.[28] Furthermore, in some cases, the thickness of the threads is not uniform even within the same textile (e.g. Gr11Q76, Fig. 5), attesting for the quality of the textiles.

1.4 *Edges*

The edges preserved in a few textiles from Cave 11Q are similar to those of other linen textiles from the Roman period in the region, and there were no special efforts other than those to reinforce the edges in order to prevent their raveling. Three textiles have starting border, which aims to anchor the main warp to the cloth beam[29] and to help in the spacing and ordering of the warps, overcoming the tendency to crowding. The starting border is composed of plied threads made of a few strands giving strength and decorative effect, while the main weave begins directly after the starting border. Textile Gr11Q33 has repp starting border

21. See Taylor et al., "The Radiocarbon Dates of Samples from Qumran Cave 11Q," in this volume; M. Müller et al., "Identification of Ancient Textile Fibres from Khirbet Qumran Caves Using Synchrotron Radiation Microbeam Diffraction," *Spectrochimica Acta Part B: Atomic Spectroscopy* 59/10-11 (2004) 1669-74.
22. O. Shamir and S.A. Rosen, "Early Bronze Age Textiles from the Ramon I Rock Shelter in the Central Negev," *IEJ* 65 (2015) 129-39, on p. 136.
23. Sheffer and Granger-Taylor, "Textiles from Masada," 163.
24. Yadin, *Finds from the Bar Kokhba Period*, 252-3.
25. Shamir, "Textiles, Basketry, Cordage and Whorls from Mo'a (Moje Awad)," *'Atiqot* 50 (2005) 99-152, on p. 104.
26. Yadin, *Finds from the Bar Kokhba Period*, 254.
27. O. Shamir, "Textiles from the Chalcolithic Period, Early and Middle Bronze Age in the Southern Levant - The Continuation of Splicing," *ATR* 57 (2015) 12-25, on p. 18.
28. Crowfoot, "Linen Textiles," 19, 31-32, Fig. 8.
29. J.P. Wild, *Textiles in Archaeology* (Princes Risborough/Aylesbury/Bucks, UK: Shire, 1988), 46.

Fig. 1. Textile Gr11Q36, warp-faced weaving (Photo by Naama Sukenik by Dino-Lite)

Fig. 2. Textile Gr11Q80, balanced weaving (Photo by Naama Sukenik by Dino-Lite)

Fig. 3. Textile Gr11Q29, basket weaving (Photo by Clara Amit, courtesy IAA)

Fig. 4. Textile Gr11Q50, half-basket weaving (Photo by Clara Amit, courtesy IAA)

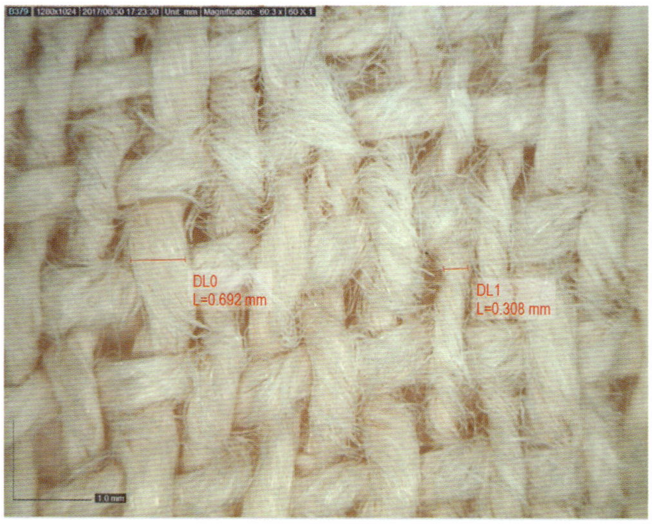

Fig. 5. Textile Gr11Q76 with nonidentical width threads (Photo by Naama Sukenik by Dino-Lite)

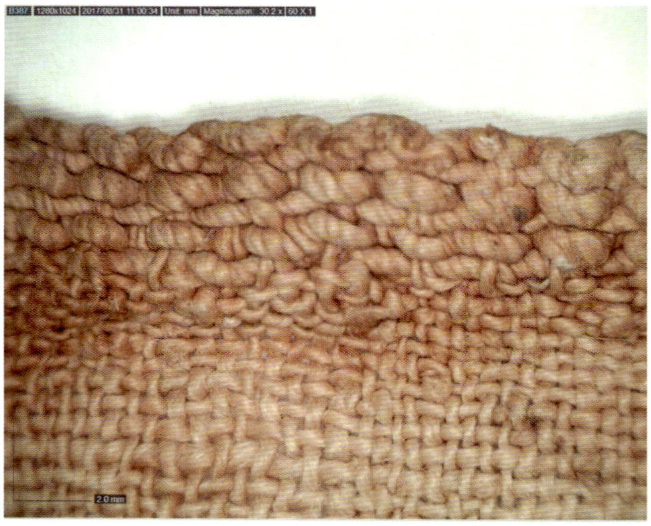

Fig. 6. Textile Gr11Q33, repp starting border (Photo by Naama Sukenik by Dino-Lite)

made of 6 S2Z threads (Fig. 6) similar to what was also found in Cave 1Q.[30] Other textiles with starting border are Gr11Q74 made of 4 S2Z threads and Gr11Q95 which was made in a similar way.

One of the textiles (Gr11Q39, Fig. 7) shows closing cord. These cords are made by twisting together the length of warp threads left bare when weaving is finished and serve to prevent unravelling,[31] likewise the textiles found in Cave 1Q.[32] Seven textiles have plain selvedges with no special strengthening which was regarded by linen weavers as adequate, while wool weavers usually took further precautions.[33]

In few fragments, a crowded selvedge was observed where the warps near the selvedge are crowded (e.g. Gr11Q101, Gr11Q121, Fig. 8); although, reinforced selvedge was found only on one textile (Gr11Q78, Fig. 9) consisting of four strands, each of double threads.

31 textiles bear hems. Hem is a finished edge formed by folding back or rolling a raw edge and stitching it in place.[34]

In most cases in Cave 11Q, textiles were rolled and whipped (Fig. 10) as also found in Cave 1Q.[35] The edges were either sewn with a single thread (e.g. Gr11Q75, Fig. 11), double threads (e.g. Gr11Q41) or whipped around with two-ply threads (e.g. Gr11Q26).

Hems are actually an important feature occurring after cutting the fabric, which sometimes indicates secondary use (see below). It is important to note that the sewing of the edges is usually non-uniform and irregular, except for a few textiles like the

Fig. 7. Textile Gr11Q39 with closing cord (Photo by Naama Sukenik by Dino-Lite)

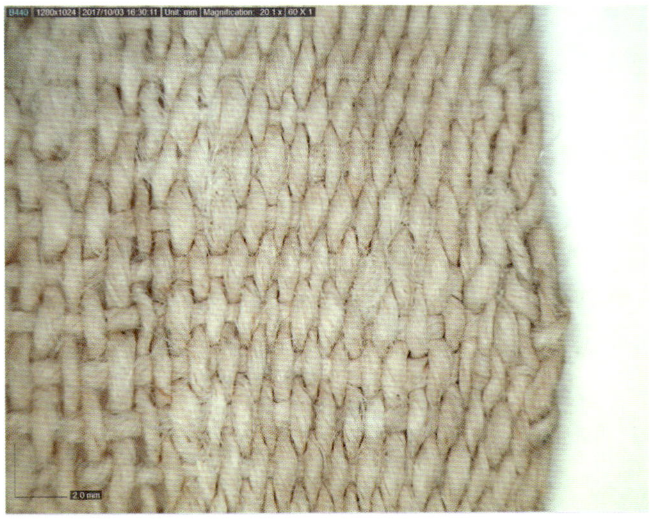

Fig. 8. Textile Gr11Q121 with crowded selvedge (Photo by Naama Sukenik by Dino-Lite)

Fig. 9. Textile Gr11Q78 with reinforced selvedge (Photo by Naama Sukenik by Dino-Lite)

30. Crowfoot, "Linen Textiles," 19.

31. H. Granger-Taylor, "Weaving Clothes to Shape in the Ancient World: The Tunic and Toga of the Arringatore," *Textile History* 13 (1982) 13-25, on p. 5.

32. Crowfoot, "Linen Textiles," 21-2. See also textiles nos. 5, 28, 30, 45, 46.

33. Wild, *Textiles in Archaeology*, 46.

34. A. Morrell, *The ATN Guide to Structural Sewing: Terms and Techniques* (Manchester: Manchester Polytechnic, 1990), 5.

35. Crowfoot, "Linen Textiles," 21, Fig. 9.1.

Fig. 10. Textile Gr11Q26, rolled and whipped hem (Photo by Clara Amit, courtesy IAA)

Fig. 11. Textile Gr11Q75, single thread sewn hem (Photo by Naama Sukenik by Dino-Lite)

wrapper of the Temple Scroll which seems to have been carefully sewn.[36]

Six textiles display different hems made by folded and sewn edge, thus we can assume that some of them were used as patches (like Gr11Q58, see Fig. 12).

36. Sukenik, "Temple Scroll Wrapper," 341-2.

Fig. 12. Textile Gr11Q58 with patch (Photo by Clara Amit, courtesy IAA)

1.5 *Sewing, Mending and Patches*

In antiquity, garments and other clothes were too valuable to be hastily discarded, therefore the careful patching and repair of textiles were common practices. The Romans were known to use shears, needles and thread for cutting and sewing. At the same time, evidence of repairs such as darning and patches is relatively rare at Qumran.[37] In our assemblage, seven textiles were patched (see Table 1)[38] to cover tears or worn out areas. Patching is carried out with great care, and the sewing of edges is usually uniform.

Darning is yet another way of repairing a fabric and was usually executed with great skill and less frequency. One textile (Gr11Q132, Fig. 13) shows darning, which is very rare in the region during the Roman Period and was found only in one imported wool textile wrapper at Masada.[39] The mending at Qumran uses two sewing threads. Darning was known in the Eastern Mediterranean region, and certainly had a long history in Egypt e.g. at the

37. Crowfoot, "Linen Textiles," 19. This darning is made in a different technique.

38. Textiles Gr11Q31a, Gr11Q36b, Gr11Q58a, Gr11Q63, Gr11Q68, Gr11Q85, Gr11Q113. Three more textiles (Gr11Q81, Gr11Q102, Gr11Q114) with sewn edge were probably used also as patches.

39. Sheffer and Granger-Taylor, "Textiles from Masada," 223-6.

Fig. 13. Textile Gr11Q132 with darning (Photo by Naama Sukenik by Dino-Lite)

cemeteries of el-Deir,[40] Berenike,[41] Krokodilopolis,[42] and Mons Claudianus.[43] This practice is later featured in the sewing, and radiocarbon analysis indicated that our textile dates between 55-125 CE, hence later than the other linen textiles from 11Q.[44]

Sewing at Qumran was used for two purposes: stitching patches and reinforcing edges. As mentioned before, the edges were cut, rolled and whipped with single, double plied threads. The quality of the sewing varies and the stitches are sometimes irregular, attesting to an unskilled or careless hand.

Some textiles present little knots used to join two threads together (e.g. Gr11Q26, Gr11Q124, Fig. 14). It was observed on well-made dense fabrics with a high number of yarns per cm without weaving mistakes. This phenomenon is not attested at any other site such as Masada or Nabatean sites along the Spice Routes. It is hard to know if it is an indication of the quality of textiles, or a mere production technique, or evidence of an inferior technical ability.

Fig. 14. Textile Gr11Q124 with knot (Photo by Naama Sukenik by Dino-Lite)

1.6 *Decoration*

Decoration is very rare in the assemblage of 11Q textiles. Blue decoration appears with some variations in a few fragments. This practice to decorate scroll wrappers was mentioned in the Mishna: "Scroll wrappers, whether figures are portrayed on them or not, are susceptible to uncleanness."[45]

Five textiles are decorated with blue narrow bands or stripes: two blue threads were found in two different textiles (Gr11Q31a, Fig. 15 and Gr11Q36a), one with a single blue thread (on a patch, Gr11Q36c), one with three faded blue threads (Gr11Q107, Fig. 16), and another (Gr11Q29) with paired blue threads in basket weave (Fig. 3). Additionally, one string made of blue threads was found separately (Gr11Q32). Similar decoration with blue bands was found on a scroll wrapper from Cave 1Q, creating three rectangular patterns, one

40. F. Letellier-Willemin, "The Long and Narrow Sleeved Tunic of the Mummy W14 of El Deir," in A. de Moor, C. Fluck, and P. Linscheid (ed.), *Textiles, Tools and Techniques of the 1st Millennium AD from Egypt and Neighbouring Countries: Proceedings of the 8th Conference of the Research Group 'Textiles from the Nile Valley': Antwerp, 4th-6th October 2013* (Tielt: Lannoo Publishers, 2015) 26-37, on pp. 32-3.

41. J.P. Wild and F. Wild, "Berenike and Textile Trade on the Indian Ocean," in K. Droß-Krüpe (ed.), *Textile Trade and Distribution in Antiquity* (Wiesbaden: Harrassowitz, 2014) 91-110, on p. 13.

42. P. Linscheid and C. Fluck, "Textiles from Krokodilopolis and Herakleopolis Magna in the Museum für Spätantike und Byzantinische Kunst, Berlin," *ATN* 21 (1995) 15-7, on p. 17.

43. U. Mannering, "The Roman Tradition of Weaving and Sewing: A Guide to Function?" *ATN* 30 (2000) 10-6, on p. 12.

44. Taylor et al., "Radiocarbon Dates."

45. Mishna Kelim 28, 4.

inside the other.[46] This unique geometric pattern in blue dye is not attested at the other sites and, according to Crowfoot, 22 textiles used as a scroll wrapper were decorated.[47] The same decoration was also found in Cave 4Q.[48] This pattern was discussed by Crowfoot, who noted that it is unique, difficult to make, and could represent the ground plan of some religious building.[49] Yigael Yadin noticed that this design corresponds with the plan of the Temple described in the Temple Scroll;[50] nevertheless, in the Temple Scroll wrapper this decoration is lacking, making it hard to accept this hypothesis.[51]

Be that as it may, we suggest that our textiles have the same design as those found in Cave 1Q, but only tiny fragments were preserved. It should be emphasized that the blue decorations in Qumran textiles are very narrow using only 1-3 threads, as opposed to other textiles in the Roman Period usually decorated with a wide blue band such as at 'En Rahel, where the band is ca. 12 cm wide.[52] Analysis of the blue color by HPLC-DAD from textile Gr11Q31 (see Fig. 15) indicate the presence of Indigotin from a plant source, probably woad (*Isatis tinctoria L.*), which was well-known in the Roman period.[53] According to microscope examination, we can determine that the fibers were dyed before spinning and weaving. The Temple Scroll wrapper is the only one from Cave 11Q decorated with selfbands – a group of weft threads in a single shed. Two textiles from Cave 1Q (nos 7 and 58) are also decorated with selfbands.[54]

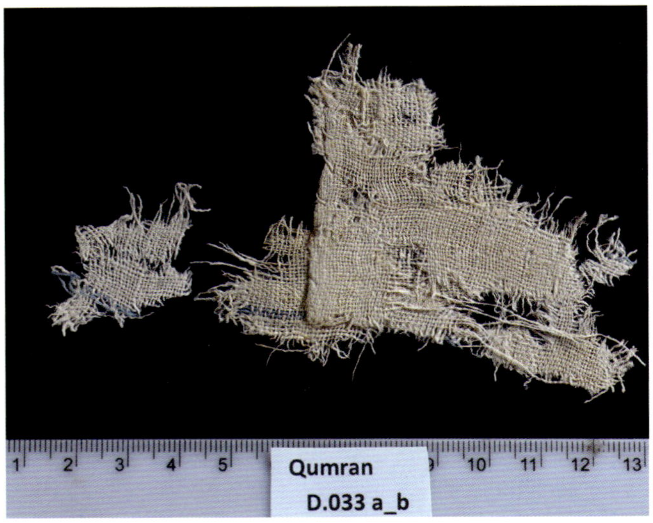

Fig. 15. Textile Gr11Q31 with blue decoration (Photo by Clara Amit, courtesy IAA)

Fig. 16. Textile Gr11Q107 with blue decoration (Photo by Naama Sukenik by Dino-Lite)

1.7 *Strings and Cords*

In our assemblage, there is a large amount of strings (22), probably related to the textiles. All the strings are made by linen in various techniques, but most of them are in Z-spun and S-plied, made of 2-6 strings (see Table 2). The width of the strings spans between 0.1-0.25 cm. Although only three strings are still tied to the textiles (Gr11Q75, Gr11Q79, Gr11Q99), we can assume that the other strings, or at least some of them, were tied to textiles and were used in the same way as the cord in textile Gr11Q75 (Fig. 17). It measures about 50 cm, 1.2 mm in diameter and was probably wrapped around a cylindrical object (see Appendix A below). Two more fragments of

46. Crowfoot, "Linen Textiles," 20.

47. Crowfoot, "Linen Textiles," 19, 24-5.

48. Textile no. 464131 (unpublished).

49. Crowfoot, "Linen Textiles," 25.

50. Yadin, "Temple Scroll," 138.

51. Sukenik, "Temple Scroll Wrapper."

52. Shamir, "Textiles, Basketry, and Cordage from 'En Rahel," *'Atiqot* 38 (1999) 91-124, on p. 92, Fig. 4.

53. See Appendix B. For more details about Indigotin see: N. Sukenik et al., "A Re-Evaluation of the Textile Dyes in the Cave of Letters," in J. Ortiz et al. (ed.), *Textiles, Basketry and Dyes in the Ancient Mediterranean World: Proceedings of the Vth International Symposium on Textiles and Dyes in the Ancient Mediterranean World (Montserrat, 19-22 March, 2014)* (Purpureae Vestes V: Textiles and Dyes in Antiquity; Valencia: Universitat de València, 2016) 263-73, on pp. 267-8.

54. Crowfoot, "Linen Textiles."

Fig. 17. Textile Gr11Q75 (Photo by Clara Amit courtesy IAA)

textiles are tied on their corner to strings (Gr11Q79 and Gr11Q46b). One string (Gr11Q66a) has a knot at the end, and it may also have been tied to textile. One string has a blue color (Gr11Q32), probably indicating the importance of the object.

2. Catalogue

Table 1-3 lists the assemblage of textiles, cords and strings which were found in Cave 11Q according to a variety of technical features, including fiber material, measurement, number of threads per cm, spin direction,[55] weaving technique, and density of weave. Additionally, we looked at weaving faults, color, and sewing. The small size and state of preservation of some textile fragments made it difficult or impossible to identify weaves, designs, fiber types, and other technical aspects. In these cases, data were not presented.

3. Discussion

3.1 *Dating*

We can date the textiles from Cave 11Q mainly to the Hellenistic, Roman, and the Medieval period. As for the linen textiles, most if not all of them date to Hellenistic and Roman periods (radiocarbon analysis[56] and technical features) like the linen textiles from Cave 1Q.[57] The high percentage of linen textiles (92% see Fig. A) attests to the main human activity in the cave during this period. If the linen textiles were used to wrap a scroll or to pad a jar containing scrolls (see below), these data can account for the time when the scrolls were deposited in the cave. We must remember that textiles usually have a 'shelf-life' relatively shorter than leather and scrolls.[58]

As for the cotton textiles (about 6% of the assemblage), never found in Hellenistic and Roman periods in Judaea, we have already stated that they were mainly used during the Medieval period. In any case, the radiocarbon analysis confirms this dating[59]. Thus, we can assume that during the Medieval period people entered the cave.[60]

3.2 *Origin of the Textiles*

According to technical aspects, we can assume that the assemblage of the textiles from Cave 11Q indicates rather local production from Israel than imported textiles. As stated by Crowfoot about Cave 1Q textiles,[61] the threads are not very fine like in Egyptian textiles, and the count of the threads is low if compared to the Egyptian specimens, where warp threads usually predominate. Moreover, all or most of the fabrics from Qumran were probably made by the warp-weighted loom, which was not used in Egypt, except for a few specific cases. The flax was grown in Israel as agriculture crop. Flax could

55. It is not always possible, especially in linen textiles, to determine which is the warp and which the weft in a fragment of textile if none of the edges is preserved.

56. See Taylor et al., "Radiocarbon Dates."

57. J.E. Taylor et al., "Qumran Textiles in the Palestine Exploration Fund, London: Radiocarbon Dating Results," *PEQ* 137 (2005) 159-67; Crowfoot, "Linen Textiles," 27.

58. Yadin, *Finds from the Bar Kokhba Period*, 171; see also Taylor et al., "Radiocarbon Dates."

59. K.L. Rasmussen et al., "Cleaning and Radiocarbon Dating of Material from Khirbet Qumran," in J. Gunneweg, C. Greenblatt, and A. Adriaens (ed.), *Bio- and Material Cultures at Qumran: Papers from a COST Action G8 Working Group Meeting Held in Jerusalem, Israel on 22-23 May 2005* (Stuttgart: Fraunhofer IRB, 2006) 139-64, on pp. 149-52.

60. A wooden artifact from the same cave dates to the 10th century, which suggests human activity in the cave in the Abbasid/Fatimid Periods. See Rasmussen et al., "Cleaning and Radiocarbon Dating," 150-2.

61. Crowfoot, "Linen Textiles," 22.

Tab. 1. Linen Textiles from Cave 11Q

	Inventory No.	Other No.	Size		Spinning direction		Spinning tightness		TPC		Weaving technique	D	Color		COMMENTS
			WA (cm)	WE (cm)	WA	WE	WA	WE	WA	WE			WA	WE	
1	Gr11Q26	D028	13	13	S	S	M	M	14	14	BAL	M	W	W	Bleached. One edge rolled and whipped with 2-plied threads. The fabric knotted at one end.
2	Gr11Q27	D029	21	2.5	S	S	M	M	14	8	T	D	U	U	Two identical fragments knotted together. Cut strip.
3	Gr11Q28	D030	12	4	S	S	M	M	12	8	T	L	W	W	Two identical fragments knotted together.
4	Gr11Q29	D031	4	1	S	S	M	M	2x2	6x2	T	M	U	U, BL	Basket weave, decorated with blue band, consists of 4x2 threads.
5	Gr11Q31a	D033a	9	6	S	S	M	M	16	14	T	M	W	W, BL	Bleached. Decorated with two blue threads. Patched with DO33b.
6	Gr11Q31b	D033b	2	3	S	S	M	M	16	14	T	M	W	W	Bleached
7	Gr11Q32	D034	5.5	3	S	S	M	M	14	8	T	M	W	W	
8	Gr11Q33	D035	9	6	S	S	M	M	15	13	T	D	U	U	Starting border made of 6 S2Z threads. Weaving faults.
9	Gr11Q34	D038	4.5	1,6	S	S	M	M	10	10	BAL	M	U	U	
10	Gr11Q36a	D036a	36	33.5	S	S	M	M	20	12	T	M	U	U	Plain selvedge, edge rolled and whipped with double threads, two patches D036b, D036c. Remains of faded blue bands.
11	Gr11Q36b	D036b	14	14.2	S	S	M	M	14	11	T	M	U	U	A patch on D036a.
12	Gr11Q36c	D036c	4.5	1.2	S	S	M	M			T	M	W	W	Bleached. A patch on D036a. Remains of faded blue threads at the edge.
13	Gr11Q37	D039	6	3	S	S	M	M	12	12	BAL	M	W	W	Bleached.
14	Gr11Q39	D041	9	21	S	S	M	M	12	12	BAL	L	U	U	Closing cord.
15	Gr11Q40a	D042a	3.5	1.7	S	S	M	M	12	12	BAL	L	W	W	
16	Gr11Q40b	D042b	1.7	1.5	S	S	M	M	12	12	BAL	L	U	U	
17	Gr11Q41	D043	17	22	S	S	M	M	14	14	BAL	M	U	U	One edge rolled and whipped with double threads.
18	Gr11Q44	D046	8	12.5	S	S	M	M	16	12	T	D	U	U	
19	Gr11Q45	D066	4.2	1.2	S	S	M	M	14	14	BAL	M	W	W	Bleached. One edge rolled and whipped with double threads.
20	Gr11Q46a	D079a	15	5	S	S	M	M	14	9	T	M			One edge rolled and whipped with single thread.

21	Gr11Q46b	D079b	19	10	S	S	M	M	15	11	T	M			The fabric knotted at one corner and tied with string.
22	Gr11Q47b	D080a2	9.5	1.5	S	S	M	M	24	16	T	D	W	W	
23	Gr11Q48	D081	13	5	S	S	M	M	12	12	BAL	L	W	W	Bleached.
24	Gr11Q50	D084	3	1	S	S	M	M			Half basket	M	U	U	
25	Gr11Q51	D086	15	13	S	S	M	M	15	12	T	M	W	W	Bleached.
26	Gr11Q52	D087	20	9	S	S	M	M	12	12	BAL	M	U	U	
27	Gr11Q53	D088	2	3	S	S	M	L	18	18	BAL	D	W	W	Bleached. Remains of sewing. Very delicate textile.
28	Gr11Q54	D089	7.5	4.5	S	S	M	M	15	10	T	M	W	W	
29	Gr11Q55	D090	9	11	S	S	M	M	12	12	BAL	M	W	W	Bleached. One edge rolled and whipped with double threads.
30	Gr11Q56	D091	3	2	S	S	M	M	16	16	BAL	D	U	U	Remains of rolled and whipped hem with 2 threads.
31	Gr11Q58a	D093a	12	9.5	S	S	M	M	20	12	T	M	W	W	Bleached. There is a patch.
32	Gr11Q58b	D093b	7	5	S	S	M	M	12	12	BAL	M	W	W	Bleached. A patch on D093a.
33	Gr11Q59a1	D094A	16	12	S	S	M	M	14	12	BAL	M	W	W	
34	Gr11Q59b	D094B	1.8	1	S	S	M	M	24	16	T	D	W	W	
35	Gr11Q60	D095	12	7	S	S	M	M	14	12	T	D	W	W	Bleached. One edge rolled and whipped with 2-plied threads.
36	Gr11Q61	D096	6	6	S	S	M	M	12	12	BAL	M	U	U	
37	Gr11Q63	D098	27	11	S	S	M	M	14	14	BAL	L	W	W	Bleached. A patch. Edges are folded and sewn. Remains of the main textiles.
38	Gr11Q64a	D114a	15	6	S	S	M	M	16	12	T	D	U	U	Weaving faults.
39	Gr11Q67	D117	15	3.5	S	S	M	M	12	10	T	M	W	W	Bleached. One edge rolled and whipped with a single thread.
40	Gr11Q68	D119	3	3	S	S	M	M	14	14	BAL	M	W	W	Bleached. Remains of stitching threads for a patch.
41	Gr11Q70	D121	15	1.3	S	S	M	M	12	12	BAL	M	W	W	Bleached. Folded edge, sewn.
42	Gr11Q71	D122	14	1.5	S	S	M	M	18	10	T	M	U	U	
43	Gr11Q72	D123	9	1	S	S	M	M	16	12	T	D	W	W	Bleached. Plain selvedge.
44	Gr11Q73	D124	7	1	S	S	M	M	12	10	T	D	W	W	Bleached. One edge rolled and whipped with 2-plied threads.
45	Gr11Q74	D125	9	8.6	S	S	M	M	16	12	T	D	W	W	Bleached. Two fragments: one with starting border made of 4 (S2Z) threads, the other with plain selvedge.

46	Gr11Q75	D053	26	33.5	S	S	M	M	14	14	BAL	M	U	U	Three edges rolled and whipped with a single thread, knotted at a corner by a string.
47	Gr11Q76	577220	1.5	4	S	S	M	M	14	8	T	M	W	W	Bleached. Bright white.
48	Gr11Q77	577221	4.5	4.5	S	S	M	M	15	10	WA.F	D	W	W	Bleached. Plain selvedge.
49	Gr11Q78	577222	3	10.5	S	S	M	M	16	10	T	D	W	W	Bleached. Reinforced selvedge.
50	Gr11Q79	577223	9	7	S	S	M	M	16	10	T	D	W	W	Bleached. Cut textile.
51	Gr11Q80	577224	7	7.5	S	S	M	M	14	12	T	M	W	W	Bleached
52	Gr11Q81	577225	7	5.5	S	S	M	M	14	14	BAL	M	W	W	Bleached. Patch? Sewn with linen threads.
53	Gr11Q82	577226	6.5	5.5	S	S	M	M	12	12	BAL	M	W	W	Bleached.
54	Gr11Q83	577227	13.5	1.5	S	S	M	M	18	10	WA.F	D	W	W	Bleached. Bright white.
55	Gr11Q84	577228	5	6	S	S	M	M	14	12	T	M	W	W	Bleached. One edge rolled and whipped with Z-plied threads.
56	Gr11Q85	577229	5.5	3	S	S	M	M	14	11	T	M	W	W	Bleached. Patch sewn in linen threads (double threads).
57	Gr11Q86	577230	6	3	S	S	M	M	13	11	T	D	W	W	Bleached. One stitch.
58	Gr11Q87	577231	6	3.5	S	S	M	M	15	11	T	D	W	W	Bleached.
59	Gr11Q88	577232	11.5	3	S	S	M	M	10	10	BAL	M	W	W	Bleached. One edge rolled and whipped with one thread.
60	Gr11Q89	577233	8	8	S	S	M	M	12	10	T	M	W	W	Bleached. Folded edge, sewn.
61	Gr11Q90	577234	9	6	S	S	M	M	16	11	T	M	W	W	
62	Gr11Q91	577235	11	6.6	S	S	M	M	12	10	T	M	W	W	Bleached. Folded edge not sewn.
63	Gr11Q92	577236	7.5	12	S	S	M	M	13	11	T	M	W	W	Bleached.
64	Gr11Q93	577237	5.5	8	S	S	M	M	13	10	T	M	W	W	Bleached.
65	Gr11Q94	577238	7	11	S	S	M	M	11	11	BAL	M	W	W	Bleached. One edge rolled and whipped with 2-plied threads S2Z.
66	Gr11Q95	577239	12	6	S	S	M	M	12	10	T	M	U	U	Starting border made of plied threads.
67	Gr11Q96	577240	5	12	S	S	M	M	14	12	T	M	W	W	Bleached.
68	Gr11Q97	577241	10	8.5	S	S	M	M	16	12	T	D	U	U	
69	Gr11Q98	577242	12	11.5	S	S	M	M	14	10	T	M	W	W	Bleached. One edge rolled and whipped with 2 plied threads.
70	Gr11Q99	577243	6	7	S	S	M	M	11	11	BAL	M	W	W	Bleached. Compound selvedge consists of four compounds each of double threads.
71	Gr11Q100	577244	2	5.5	S	S	M	M	12	12	BAL	M	W	W	Bleached. One edge rolled and whipped with one thread.
72	Gr11Q101	577245	7	3.8	S	S	M	M	12	12	BAL	D	W	W	Bleached. Plain selvedge.
73	Gr11Q102	577246	9	4	S	S	M	M	14	10	T	L	W	W	Bleached. Two textiles sewn together (patches?).
74	Gr11Q103	577247	8	4	S	S	M	M	15	11	T	M	U	U	

75	Gr11Q104	577248	9	6	S	S	M	M	15	9	WA.F	D	W	W	Bleached. Simple selvedge.
76	Gr11Q105	577249	7.5	14	S	S			11	10	BAL	M	W	W	Bleached. Bright white.
77	Gr11Q106	577251	3	3	S	S	M	M	12	10	T	M	U	U	
78	Gr11Q107	577252	6	4	S	S	M	M	14	12	T	M	W	W	Bleached. Blue decoration (faded) of line made of three threads (c14).
79	Gr11Q108	577253	2.5	4.5	S	S	M	M	13	9	T	M	W	W	Bleached. Rolled and whipped with 2-plied threads 2SZ.
80	Gr11Q109	577254	6	4.5	S	S	M	M	12	12	BAL	M	W	W	Bleached. One edge rolled and whipped with one thread.
81	Gr11Q110	577255	5.5	4.5	S	S	M	M	14	12	T	M	U	U	
82	Gr11Q111	577256	10	10	S	S	M	N	14	10	T	D	W	W	Bleached. One edge rolled and whipped with two threads not plied.
83	Gr11Q112	577257	5	11	S	S	M	M	14	10	T	D	W	W	Bleached.
84	Gr11Q113	577258	8.5	4.5	S	S	M	M	14	12	T	M	W	W	Bleached. Edge of textile with two sewn hems and two patches.
85	Gr11Q114	577259	5	4.5	S	S	M	M	15	11	T	M	W	W	Bleached. Three textiles sewn in linen threads (patches?).
86	Gr11Q115	577260	6	6	S	S	M	M	13	11	T	L	W	W	Bleached.
87	Gr11Q116	577261	8.5	8	S	S	M	M	12	9	T	M	W	W	Bleached. Two edges of textiles with two sewn hems with one thread. One side rolled and sewn, the other side folded and sewn.
88	Gr11Q117	577262	10.7	7.5	S	S	M	M	12	10	T	M	W	W	Bleached? Grey color.
89	Gr11Q118	577263	11.5	7	S	S	M	M	14	14	BAL	M	U	U	One edge rolled and whipped with two threads.
90	Gr11Q119	577264	12.5	10	S	S	M	M	16	10	T	M	W	W	Bleached. Grey stain.
91	Gr11Q120	577265	12.5	10.5	S	S	M	L	12	12	BAL	M	W	W	Bleached.
92	Gr11Q121	577280	18	2	S	S	M	T	18	10	WA.F	D	W	W	Bleached. Plain selvedge. One edge rolled and whipped.
93	Gr11Q122	577281	18.5	6.5	S	S	M	M	10	8	T	L	W	W	Bleached.
94	Gr11Q123	577282	12	10	S	S	M	M	10	10	BAL	M	W	W	Bleached. Folded edge, sewn.
95	Gr11Q124	577284	20.5	10	S	S	M	M	12	8	T	M	W	W	Bleached. Knots in the threads.
96	Gr11Q125	577285	11.5	12	S	S	M	M	12	10	T	L	W	W	Bleached. Knot in the threads.
97	Gr11Q126	577286	16.5	9	S	S	M	M	11	9	T	M	W	W	Bleached. Cut textile.
98	Gr11Q127	577287	15	13.5	S	S	M	M	10	10	BAL	M	W	W	Bleached. One edge rolled and whipped with one thread.
99	Gr11Q128	577288	9	3	S	S	M	M	13	10	T	L	U	U	
100	Gr11Q129	577289	22.5	20	S	S	M	M	12	10	T	M	W	W	Bleached.
101	Gr11Q130	577290	33.5	10	S	S	M	M	18	12	T	D	W	W	Bleached. Plain selvedge.

102	Gr11Q131	577291	9.5	27	S	S	M	M	14	10	T	M	W	W	Bleached.
103	Gr11Q132	577293	21.5	9	S	S	M	M	16	10	WA.F	M	U	U	Darning.
104	Gr11Q133	814794	3	1.5	S	S	M	M			T	L	W	W	Bleached. Small fragment.
105	Gr11Q134	814795	5.2	2	S	S	M	M	14	12	T	M	W	W	Bleached.
106	Gr11Q135	814796	5.3	3.6	S	S	M	M	14	14	BAL	M	W	W	Bleached.
107	Gr11Q136	814798	2	4	S	S	M	M	14	14	BAL	D	W	W	Bleached.
108	Gr11Q137	814800	4	3	S	S	M	M	12	12	BAL	M	W	W	Bleached.
109	Gr11Q138	814801	4.25	3.65	S	S	M	M	14	14	BAL	M	W	W	Bleached.
110	Gr11Q139	814802	2.4	2.2	S	S	M	M	14	14	BAL	M	W	W	Bleached. One stitch with plied threads (Z).
111	Gr11Q140	814805	6.2	3	S	S	M	M	14	14	BAL	M	W	W	Bleached.
112	Gr11Q141	814806	3	5.5	S	S	M	M	14	12	T	M	W	W	Bleached.
113	Gr11Q142	814808	5.2	4	S	S	M	M	14	12	T	M	W	W	Bleached.
114	Gr11Q143	814809	6	2.8	S	S	M	M	14	14	BAL	D	W	W	Bleached.
115	Gr11Q144	814811	4.8	1.6	S	S	M	M	10	10	BAL	M	W	W	Bleached. Two fragments.
116	Gr11Q145	814812	5	4	S	S	M	M	14	10	T	M	W	W	Bleached. Two fragments.
117	Gr11Q146	814813	7	4	S	S	M	M	14	12	T	D	W	W	Bleached.
118	Gr11Q147	814814	1.8	6	S	S	M	M	12	12	BAL	M	W	W	Bleached. Two fragments.
119	Gr11Q148	814815	5.6	8.4	S	S	M	M	14	12	T	M	W	W	Bleached.
120	Gr11Q149	814816	6	6	S	S	M	M	18	16	T	D	W	W	Bleached.
121	Gr11Q150	814817	7.4	3	S	S	M	M	16	14	T	M	W	W	Bleached. Two fragments.
122	Gr11Q151	814818	4.65	4	S	S	M	M	16	12	T	M	U	U	Three fragments.
123	Gr11Q152	814819	5.6	4.3	S	S	M	M	14	12	T	M	W	W	Bleached.
124	Gr11Q153	814820	5.3	5	S	S	M	M	12	12	BAL	M	W	W	Bleached.
125	Gr11Q154	814821	4.75	7	S	S	M	M	16	14	T	M	W	W	Bleached.
126	Gr11Q155	814822	9.4	3	S	S	M	M	14	14	BAL	M	W	W	Bleached. Three fragments.
127	Gr11Q156	814823	8.6	4	S	S	M	M	20	12	WA.F	D	W	W	Bleached.
128	Gr11Q157	814824	12.5	7	S	S	M	M	14	14	BAL	L	W	W	Bleached. Two fragments.
129	Gr11Q158	814825	7.7	4	S	S	M	M	16	12	T	M	W	W	Bleached.
130	Gr11Q159	814826	7	4	S	S	M	M	14	12	T	M	W	W	Bleached.
131	Gr11Q160	814828	4.3	6	S	S	M	M	12	10	T	M	W	W	Bleached. One edge rolled and whipped with two threads.
132	Gr11Q161	814829	2.7	7.3	S	S	M	M	14	10	T	M	W	W	Bleached.
133	Gr11Q162	814830	4.3	5	S	S	M	M	12	12	BAL	M	W	W	Bleached.
134	Gr11Q163	814836	4	4	S	S	M	M	12	10	T	M	W	W	
135	Gr11Q164	814841	4.5	9.3	S	S	M	M	16	10	T	M	W	W	Bleached.
136	Gr11Q165	814842	7.4	3	S	S	M	M	12	12	BAL	M	W	W	Bleached.
137	Gr11Q166	814843	6	4.2	S	S	M	M	14	14	BAL	M	W	W	Bleached.
138	Gr11Q167	814844	5	6.5	S	S	M	M	12	10	T	L	W	W	Bleached.
139	Gr11Q168	814845	9	7	S	S	M	M	14	12	T	M	W	W	Bleached.
140	Gr11Q169	814846	5.8	5.7	S	S	M	M	18	10	WA.F	D	W	W	Bleached.
141	Gr11Q170	814847	5	4	S	S	M	M	16	12	T	M	W	W	Bleached.

142	Gr11Q171	814848	9	7	S	S	M	M	14	14	BAL	L	W	W	Bleached. Very fragile.
143	Gr11Q172	814849	9	9.7	S	S	M	M	14	12	T	M	W	W	Bleached.
144	Gr11Q173	814850	7	4.5	S	S	M	M	12	12	BAL	M	W	W	Bleached. Two fragments.
145	Gr11Q174	814851	4.2	10	S	S	M	M	14	10	T	M	W	W	Bleached.
146	Gr11Q175	814853	4	5	S	S	M	M	12	12	T	M	W	W	Bleached. Another small fragment with one edge rolled and whipped.
147	Gr11Q176	814854	3.7	3.5	S	S	M	M	12	12	BAL	D	W	W	Bleached.
148	Gr11Q177	814856	3	1.65	S	S	M	M			T	M	W	W	Bleached. Small fragment with one stitch.
149	Gr11Q178	814858	3.65	3	S	S	M	M	14	12	T	M	W	W	Bleached.
150	Gr11Q179	814859	22	1.8	S	S	M	M	10	10	BAL	M	W	W	Bleached. Long cord knotted to the edge of the textile S3z (3z).
151	Gr11Q180	816288	4.5	1	S	S	M	M					W	W	Bleached. One edge rolled and whipped with 3 threads and faded blue.
152	Gr11Q181	55	2.5	1.5	S	S	M	M	14	14	T	M	U	U	
153	Gr11Q182	567	1.2	1	S	S	M	M			T	D	U	U	The source of this fragment is uncertain
154	Gr11Q183	988			S	S	M	M			T	M	U	U	9 larger fragments and others smaller.
155	Gr11Q184	1030A1	3	3	S	S	M	M	16	20	T	M	U	U	
156	Gr11Q185	1030A2	3	3	S	S	M	M	16	18	T	M	U	U	
157	Gr11Q186	1030A5	3.5	3	S	S	M	M	14	14	T	M	U	U	One edge rolled and whipped.
158	Gr11Q187	1030A6	3.5	3	S	S	M	M	20	14	T	M	U	U	
159	Gr11Q188	1032A	ca. 6	ca. 6	S	S	M	M	16	14	T	M	U	U	3 larger fragments and 2 others smaller.
160	Gr11Q189	1034A-2	3.5	1.5	S	S	M	L	8	8	T	L	U	U	Textile strictly adhering to the parchment.
161	Gr11Q195	D054	16	4	S	S	M	M	14	10	T	D	U	U	Any small fragments.
162	Gr11Q196	D083	9	4.5	S	S	M	M	12	8	T	L	U	U	
163	P11Q3	B2 no. 1	6	3.3	S	S	M	M	13	13	BAL	D	U	U	
164	P11Q4	B2 no. 2	6.5	5	S	S	M	M	9	9	BAL	D	U	U	
165	P11Q5	B2 no. 3	7.5	6	S	S	M	M	38	17	WA.F	D	U	U	
166	P11Q6	B2 no. 4	1.3	1	S	S	M	M	12	12	BAL	M	U	U	
167	P11Q7	B2 no. 5	2.5	2	S	S	M	M	12	10	T	M	U	U	
168	P11Q8	B2 no. 6	1.2	1	S	S	M	M	13	10	T	D	U	U	
169	P11Q9	B2 no. 7	1.8	1.2	S	S	M	M			T	D	U	U	
170	P11Q10	B1 no. 1	3.3	1.4	S	S	M	M	12	12	BAL	D	W	W	Bleached.
171	FB11Q1	B201.F1	6.3	2	S	S	M	M	20	20	BAL	M	U	U	
172	FB11Q2	B201.F23	1	1.4	S	S	M	M			T	M	U	U	

Tab. 2. Cotton textiles from Cave 11Q

	Inventory No.	Other No.	Size		spinning direction		spinning tightness		TPC		Weaving Technique	D	Color		Comments
			WA (cm)	WE (cm)	WA	WE	WA	WE	WA	WE			WA	WE	
1	Gr11Q30	D032	3,5	1,1	Z	Z	M	M	12	12	BAL	D	W, BL	W, BL	
2	Gr11Q35	D037	11	9,7		-	-	-	-	-	-	-	U	U	Fibers.
3	Gr11Q47a	D080a1	15	1	Z	Z	M	M	20	20	BAL	D	W	W	
4	Gr11Q57	D092	1	7	Z	Z	M	M	10	14	T	D	U	U	
5	Gr11Q62	D097	4	2.5	Z	Z	M	M	20	16	T	D	W	W	
6	Gr11Q65	D115	6	2	Z	Z	M	M	12	12	BAL	D	W	W	Fringes on warp threads.
7	Gr11Q69	D120	2	4	Z	Z	M	M	16	14	T	D	W	W	
8	Gr11Q190	577292	3	4	Z	Z	M	M	12	12	BAL	D	C	C	Selvedge and stitch.
9	Gr11Q191	814827	2.9	2.6	Z	Z	M	M	14	14	BAL	D	C	C	Two fragments.
10	Gr11Q192	814807	5.4	3.4	Z	Z	M	M	10	12	BAL	D	W	W	Fringes on warp threads.
11	P11Q11	B1 no. 2	3.5	3.3	Z	Z	M	M	27	21	T	D	U	U	Very thin threads. Recent?

Tab. 3. Strings from Cave 11Q

	Inventory No.	Other No.	Material	Size			COMMENTS
				L (cm)	Ø (cm)		
1	Gr11Q25	D027	linen			S	C. 8 threads are knotted to a throng. See Taylor and Sukenik in this volume.
2	Gr11Q32	D034	undet.			S??	Blue threads.
3	Gr11Q43	D045	undet.	10	0.5	S2z	Knot at one end.
4	Gr11Q59a2	D094a2	(sample)	10	0.25	Z2s(4s)	Carbonate concretions.
5	Gr11Q64b	D114b	linen	3.5	0.1	Z2s	
6	Gr11Q66a	D116A	linen	10	0.4	Z2s(4s)	
7	Gr11Q66b	D116B	undet.	6	0.2	S2z	Fibres not well separated.
8	Gr11Q66c	D116C	linen	12	0.1	S2z	Fibres not well separated.
9	Gr11Q66d	D116D	linen	7	0.2	S2z	Fibres not well separated.
10	Gr11Q66e	D116E	undet.	16.5	0.25	S3z(4s)	Knot at one end, the other end is problematic.
11	Gr11Q66f	D116F	linen	5	0.5	S2z	Fibres not well separated.
12	Gr11Q66g	D116G	linen	9	0.3	S2z	Fibres not well separated.
13	Gr11Q66h	D116H	linen	15	0.25	S2z(6S)	Fibres not well separated.
14	Gr11Q66i	D116I	(sample)	21	0.2	S6s	
15	Gr11Q66j	D116J	linen	4	0.5	S2z	Fibres not well separated, knot in the middle.
16	Gr11Q66k	D116K	linen	10	0.25	S2z	Fibres not well separated, double knot at one end.
17	Gr11Q66l	D116L	linen	9	0.3	Z3s	Fibres not well separated.
18	Gr11Q75	D053	linen	50	0.2	S3z(4s)	It ties a corner of the textile D053, the final part is unraveled and partially knotted.
19	Gr11Q79	814859	linen	14	0.15	S3z (2z)	The string knotted to the textile.
20	Gr11Q97	814852	linen	14.5	0.5	Not identified	Bad condition.
21	Gr11Q98	577250	linen			S2z	Bleaching.
22	Gr11Q99	864407	linen	2.4	0.3	(S2z)2	The string tied to the textile.

Abbreviations used in tables

Gr11Q N (= number) item from De Vaux's excavations 1956
P11Q N item from Patrich's excavations 1988, 1991
FB11Q N item from Fidanzio - Bahat's excavations 2017
WA = Warp; WE = Weft
Spinning tightness: L = Loose; M = Medium; T = Tight.
TPC = threads per centimeter
Weaving technique: T – Tabby; BAL = Balanced tabby; WE.F = Weft Faced Tabby; WA.F = Warp Faced Tabby
D = Density of weaving D = Dense M = Medium L = Loose
Color: BL = Blue C = Cream U = Undyed W = White

be grown in the Jordan Valley, Beth She'an Valley, Tiberias, etc.,[62] as the plant requires plenty of water and a hot climate. The Talmud also states that flax was grown specifically in the Galilee region, while Judaea was characterized by woolen textiles: "They take garments of wool from the women in Judea and of linen in Galilee."[63] It is thus likely that they were not produced locally by the inhabitants of Qumran. Spindle whorls and loom weights (indicators of spinning and weaving) were not found in Cave 11Q nor elsewhere at Qumran.[64] Hence, we can assume that the textiles were brought to Qumran from another place in Israel.[65]

As aforementioned, one textile (Gr11Q132; see Fig. 13) has a darning that is more characteristic of Egyptian production. It may be taken into account that imported garments supplied specialized and fashionable tastes in antiquity. Some foreign textiles were available for people who could afford them, e.g. the fine linens of Pelusium and India worn by high priests.[66] According to Talmudic sources, flax was also imported into Judaea from Syria, especially in sabbatical years.[67] At the same time it is hard to determine whether this textile (Gr11Q132) was imported from Egypt, according to only one parameter, while all the other parameters in the textiles from Cave 11Q suggest Israeli production.

3.3 *Quality of the Textiles*

The weaving technique is very simple in all the textiles, and the differences in linen textiles in general are not as prominent as in woolen textiles. Sewing, patches and mending, as discussed above, indicate that the quality of the textiles is not identical. Some of the textiles show higher ability of weaving than other simpler textiles. As mentioned before, some textiles present a high number of threads, homogeneity in thickness, bleaching etc., while others are much coarser. Thickness of the threads is not uniform as well as the regularity of the thread interlacing in the warp and weft which defines the final quality of the woven fabric are not identical. Different qualities are also attested in Talmudic sources: in contrast to Beth She'an's (Scythopolis) excellence, the linen garments produced at Arbel in the Lower Galilee were coarse and cheap.[68]

A number of textiles found at Qumran presents irregularities in warp and weft (see Fig. 5) determining weaving faults. Sometimes a weft thread passes over

62. T. Schick, "The Early Basketry and Textiles from Cave in the Northern Judean Desert," *'Atiqot* 41 (2002) 223-39, on p. 238; Shamir, "Textiles from the Chalcolithic Period," 21; M. Kislev et al., "Flax Seed Production: Evidence from the Early Iron Age Site of Tel Beth-Shean, Israel and from Written Sources," *VHA* 20/6 (2011) 579-84.
63. b. B. Qam. 119a.
64. De Vaux published only two spindles from Qumran: J.-B. Humbert and A. Chambon (ed.), *Fouilles de Khirbet Qumrân et de 'Aïn Feshkha: Vol. I: Album de photographies. Répertoire du fonds photographique. Synthèse des notes de chantier du Père Roland de Vaux OP* (NTOA.SA 1; Fribourg/Göttingen: Éditions Universitaires/Vandenhoeck & Ruprecht, 1994), 294.
65. See also Shamir and Sukenik, "Qumran Textiles," 220-2.
66. Mishnah, Yoma 3, 7; See also Shamir, "Textile Trade to Palestine in the Roman Period," 233.
67. The seven-year agricultural cycle was mandated by the Bible for the Land of Israel, and is still observed in contemporary Judaism. During a sabbatical year, the land is left to lie fallow, and all agricultural activity, including ploughing, planting and harvesting, is forbidden by Jewish law.
68. Jerusalem Talmud 7:7, 31c/30; See also: Bereshit Rabba 19:1.

two warp threads (e.g. textile no. Gr11Q75, Fig. 18). Weaving faults are very rare in the Roman Period in the Land of Israel, though they do occur, e.g. in 'En Rahel,[69] and in Mo'a;[70] Crowfoot suggested that faults may have been due to inexperience of the weavers during the transition from the warp-weighted to the upright loom.[71] Faults could also indicate separation between warps and wefts or incorrect tying of the cross-beams.[72]

Fig. 18. Detail of textile Gr11Q75 with weaving faults (Photo by Naama Sukenik by Dino-Lite)

More than 65 percent of the textiles in our assemblage have a white color (see Table 1; e.g. see Figs 2, 10, 12),[73] which was probably obtained due to a long process called bleaching. During this process, the natural greyish-brown color of the linen changed to white. The textiles were soaked in cleaning and whitening chemicals including sodium carbonate, wood ash or some plants, such as *Anabasis setifera* or *Mesembryanthemum nodiflorum*, with a high sodium content (potash).[74] Additionally, the procedure includes exposing the textile in sunlight for weeks to complete the bleaching process.[75] This practice took a number of days and required a lot of effort.[76] The process of bleaching was quite common in Egypt, where there was a specialization in the linen textile industry, and most production was made for clothing.[77] Tomb paintings and models from Egypt depict the repetitive process of putting the wet linen cloth into ash, rubbing it with detergent and so on; finally laying it out to bleach dry in the hot sun.[78] The bleaching process is also depicted on wall paintings at Pompeii,[79] taking place during the fulling process.[80] Although it is difficult to know the extent of bleaching in textile industry in the land of Israel, we can assume that textiles employed for simple purposes such as sacks or shrouds were not bleached and were left in their natural color.[81] Bleached textiles have been found only at a number of sites in the Roman period in

69. Shamir, "Textiles, Basketry, and Cordage from 'En Rahel," 101.

70. Shamir, "Textiles, Basketry, Cordage and Whorls from Mo'a (Moje Awad)," 100.

71. Crowfoot, "Linen Textiles," 61.

72. J.P. Wild, *Textile Manufacture in the Northern Roman Provinces* (Cambridge: Cambridge University Press, 1970), 64.

73. We don't think the textiles got their whitish color from the chalk at the cave, because the bleaching is uniform.

74. N. Sukenik et al., "Early Evidence (Late 2nd millennium BCE) of Plant-Based Dyeing of Textiles from Timna, Israel," *PLOS ONE* 12/6 (2017), doi.org/10.1371/journal.pone.0179014; E. Soriga, "A Diachronic View on Fulling Technology in the Mediterranean and the Ancient Near East: Tools, Raw Materials and Natural Resources for the Finishing of Textiles," in S. Gaspa, C. Michel, and M.-L. Nosch (ed.), *Textile Terminologies from the Orient to the Mediterranean and Europe, 1000 BC to 1000 AD* (Lincoln, NE: Zea Books, 2017) 24-46, on pp. 32-36.

75. Forbes, *Studies in Ancient Technology*, 95; B.J. Kemp and G. Vogelsang-Eastwood, *The Ancient Textile Industry at Amarna* (London: Egypt Exploration Society, 2001), 158; A.A.H. Poot, "Chemical Bleaching of Ancient Textiles," *Studies in Conservation* 9 (1964), 53-64.

76. L. Cleland, G. Davies, and L. Llewellyn-Jones, *Greek and Roman Dress from A to Z* (London: Routledge, 2007), 211; Poot, "Chemical Bleaching," 54.

77. Forbes, *Studies in Ancient Technology*, 27-30; R. Hall, *Egyptian Textiles* (Shire Egyptology 4; London: Shire Publications, 1986), 9.

78. https://www.decktowel.com/pages/linen-history, accessed 14/08/2018.

79. M. Flohr, *The World of the Fullo: Work, Economy and Society in Roman Italy* (Oxford Studies on the Roman Economy; Oxford: Oxford University Press, 2013), 113-5, Figs 26-7.

80. Soriga, "Diachronic View on Fulling Technology."

81. For example, the linen textiles in 'En Tamar used as simple shrouds were left in their natural color: see O. Shamir, "Textiles, Basketry, Cordage and Fruits from `En Tamar: Preliminary Report," in P. Bienkowski and K. Galor (ed.), *Crossing the Rift: Resources, Settlements, Patterns and Interaction in the Wadi Arabah* (LSS 3; Oxford: Oxbow, 2006), 191-4, as well as the sacks from the Cave of the Letters have natural color: Yadin, *Finds from the Bar Kokhba Period*.

Israel, including 'En Rahel on the Spice Route[82] and the El Masaia cave in Nahal Deragot.[83]

The evidence of bleaching and the fact that a lot of textiles with hem were made by rolling and whipping with sewing threads – in most cases with irregular, coarse, and uneven stitches with irregular intervals between them – indicate a secondary use, being probably cut from bleached garment. More than that, we can assume that the textile findings from Qumran probably provide an insight into the clothing that was worn by the members of the community.[84] In ancient times garments were too costly to be thrown away, thus the secondary use clothing industry flourished.[85] When the garment could no longer be mended, it was cut into pieces and used as patches or for other purposes.[86]

The low number of patches could indicate textile quality and economic status of the site, but we can also assume that for textiles in secondary use, someone selected a portion of textile without any repairs and sewing, cutting it into smaller parts and realizing a new textile. Some of the patches are found in textiles with decorations (e.g. textiles Gr11Q36a, Gr11Q31, Fig. 15): this could have been an effort to preserve the decoration.

3.4 *The Uses of the Textiles*

Another important questions is the function of the textiles found in Cave 11Q. Although no item was found complete, we propose that most of the textile fragments from Cave 11Q were used as a wrapper or as padding to protect the scrolls deposited in the cave. Eight small textiles were found adherent to a scroll fragment (the biggest one is 6 x 6 cm): this could account for the function of these textiles as scroll wrappers (Fig. 19). Additionally, as already stated, the textile reported by the Bedouins to have been found together with the Temple Scroll was identified as a scroll wrapper, too.[87] This function was also proposed by Crowfoot, for most of the textiles found in Cave 1Q: "Some of them were certainly scroll wrappers… one scroll was found still wrapped in small square of linen."[88] Scroll wrappers are mentioned in the Talmud and the Mishnah, where they are named "*Mitpehoth Sepharim*" (Book kerchief),[89] strengthening the idea that the wrappers were made of textiles. Another material used as a scroll wrapper is leather, which wrapped papyrus scrolls. Scrolls made of papyrus which is weaker than parchment and needs greater protection than the one provided by textile.[90] In Mishnaic times, scroll wrappers were regarded as holy artefacts: they were not discarded after they had been worn out; instead, as was customary with sacred objects such as holy books, they were stored in a repository for sacred objects known as *genizah*.[91]

Fig. 19. Textile fragment adherent to a scroll fragment (Courtesy of The Leon Levy Dead Sea Scrolls Digital Library IAA, Photo by Shai Halevi)

82. Shamir, "Textiles, Basketry, and Cordage from 'En Rahel," 96.

83. O. Shamir, *Textile in the Land of Israel From the Roman Period till the Early Islamic Period in the Light of the Archaeological Find* (PhD. diss., Hebrew University, 2006), 160.

84. Shamir and Sukenik, "Qumran Textiles and the Garments," 218-20.

85. A.T. Croom, *Roman Clothing and Fashion* (Stroud: Tempus, 2010), 24-5.

86. Shamir and Sukenik, "Qumran Textiles and the Garments," 219.

87. Sukenik, "Temple Scroll Wrapper."

88. Crowfoot, "Linen Textiles," 18.

89. Mishnah, Kil 9.3; Meg. 3.1.

90. Crowfoot, "Linen Textiles," 24; Sukenik, "Temple Scroll Wrapper."

91. For example: "Wrappings of scrolls which are worn out may be used for making shrouds for a Meth Mitzvah; and this act constitutes their 'stowing away'" (b. Meg. 26b).

The interpretation of textile Gr11Q75 (Fig. 17) as a scroll wrapper[92] raises questions about the function of Qumran textiles as described by Crowfoot as a jar cover.[93] Cautiously, it is possible to assume that some other fabrics in the cave were used also as a scroll wrapper. Textiles similar to Gr11Q75 were found in Cave 11Q, including Gr11Q46b (Fig. 20), Gr11Q26 which has a tied corner (Fig. 10) but without strings that did not survive, and fragments Gr11Q79 and Gr11Q99 that have a little string tied to the textile corner. A large number of fragments with similar hem was manufactured in analogous technique by cutting, rolling and whipping the edge, such as the hem found in the Temple Scroll wrapper,[94] and the hem in textiles identified by Crowfoot as scroll wrappers from Cave 1Q;[95] which could suggest a similar function for the textiles in our assemblage. This is also true for the large number of strings found in Cave 11Q that may have been used to tie the scroll wrapper, as the cord in textile Gr11Q75 or in the Temple Scroll wrapper.[96] Anyway, currently this is only a hypothesis, and only after thorough examination of the assemblage from Qumran we will be able to establish the function of all those textiles.

Fig. 20. Detail of textile Gr11Q46b with tied corner (Photo by Naama Sukenik by Dino-Lite)

92. See M. Fidanzio and N. Sukenik, "Linen textile Gr11Q75 : a scroll wrapper from cave 11Q," in this volume.

93. Crowfoot, "Linen Textiles," 19, Pl. V.12.

94. Sukenik, "Temple Scroll Wrapper."

95. Crowfoot, "Linen Textiles," nos 41, 42.

96. Sukenik, "Temple Scroll Wrapper;" we must emphasize that Crowfoot's catalogue does not include strings or cords. We can assume that they were not considered important items.

3.5 *The Textiles from Cave 11Q Compared to Cave 1Q*

The textiles from Cave 11Q can be compared to those found in Cave 1Q, relying on Crowfoot's report. Although only a preliminary publication of 77 textiles, a Crowfoot's comprehensive report had great importance for the next stages of research. Even though the textiles from Cave 1Q are in better state of preservation than those from Cave 11Q, the assemblage from the latter is very similar to that of the former. It should be emphasized that the textiles from Cave 11Q were not found with rat and mouse excrements like the textiles from 1Q which were only exposed to soil, probably indicating they had perhaps for most of the time been protected in a closed place like a jar or under fallen rocks. In both caves, linen textiles were made in tabby weaving in a similar way, and most of the edges were made by the same practice of cutting, rolling and whipping with linen strings. Therefore, we can suggest that some of the textiles from Cave 11Q were used to protect scrolls as the textiles from Cave 1Q.[97]

Despite the lack of explicit reference to bleaching in Crowfoot's catalogue, she mentions the white color of some textiles.[98] The two similar assemblages from caves 1Q and 11Q, as far as the textiles are concerned, strengthen our assumption about ideological motivations behind the use of white linen fibers and refraining from using wool textiles (predominant material in other Roman sites and widely used in this period). Qumran textiles were free from Hellenistic features, which are so common in other Jewish sites.[99]

Further, we can highlight three differences between Cave 11Q and Cave 1Q:

1. The textiles in cave 11Q bear fringe borders which were not found in the textiles from cave 1Q;[100]

97. Crowfoot, "Linen Textiles," 18-9.

98. Crowfoot, "Linen Textiles," e.g. nos 7, 30, 15, 36.

99. Shamir and Sukenik, "Qumran Textiles and the Garments;" Sukenik, "Temple Scroll Wrapper;" O. Shamir and N. Sukenik, "The Christmas Cave Textiles Compared to Qumran Textiles," *ATN* 51 (2010) 26-30.

100. Crowfoot, "Linen Textiles," 20; this is true for other fringes, too, except for the Temple Scroll wrapper. Sukenik suggested the presence of fringes: Sukenik, "Temple Scroll Wrapper."

2. In Cave 11Q only a few blue threads decorating the textiles were found, differing from Cave 1Q, which yielded many more blue bands and stripes;[101]
3. The number of patches in Cave 11Q is a little higher than in Cave 1Q, which yielded only one patch.[102]

It is hard to know if these differences are accidental or caused by the poor state of preservation of the textiles (e.g. the fragility of the fringes) or indicate a slightly different assemblage of textiles. We can assume that decorated wrappers with a unique pattern in blue color probably mark a particular scroll. Moreover, if we accept that the textiles with blue decoration were conceived as scroll wrappers since the beginning, while most of the other textiles were employed as a wrapper in secondary use, we can assume that the assemblage of the scrolls in cave 1Q is slightly different from cave 11Q, and probably more important. Anyway, it is only a hypothetical assumption, so far.

101. Crowfoot, "Linen Textiles," 20.

102. Crowfoot, "Linen Textiles," 36, no. 36.

Conclusions

So far, the textile assemblage found in Cave 11Q is the largest from all Qumran caves. It is entirely published here for the first time and includes a lot of fragments of textiles and cords used in most cases to protect the scrolls. This leads us to propose a main function of the cave as a storage place.

We can assume that the scrolls had double protection: at a first stage, the scroll was wrapped with linen textiles; at a second stage, scrolls were placed in a jar. This practice is still in use today, when wrapping biblical scrolls in synagogues.[103] Moreover, the function of the textiles may have been more for protection than for aesthetic purposes. We can also point out that only linen fibers, in most cases bleached, were used, showing the peculiarity of Qumran compared to any other assemblages from the Roman period. Further research on other Qumran textiles might help us to better understand this phenomenon, and to determine the function of the fabrics.

103. B. Yaniv, "From Spain to the Balkans: Textile Torah Scroll Accessories in the Sephardi Communities of the Balkans," *Sefarad* 66/2 (2006) 407-42.

Chapter Four
Appendix A

Linen Textile Gr11Q75: A Scroll Wrapper from Cave 11Q

Marcello FIDANZIO and Naama SUKENIK

The textile Gr11Q75 is the best preserved and the most complete among those found by archaeologists in Cave 11Q.[1] Herewith, we investigate the function of textile Gr11Q75, which we interpret as a scroll wrapper bearing some peculiar features.

1. Description

Textile Gr11Q75 preserves portions of three hems, while the fourth edge is missing. The preserved part of the textile has a rectangular shape and measures 33 cm x > 26 cm. The threads are S-spun medium, a spinning technique characteristic of other linen textiles generally found in the Judaean Desert, and at Qumran in particular.[2] The thickness of the threads is non-uniform, standing on ca. 0.1 mm - 0.5 mm (Fig. 2),[3] and the threads were woven by a simple technique called "balanced tabby."[4] The weave is medium, with a density of 14 threads per cm on the warp and the weft. The textile is bleached white without any decoration and some stains were observed.

Although the fabric is bleached, and although no weaving mistakes were found, the number of threads per cm, in addition to the thickness of the threads and the quality of the stitches, define Gr11Q75 as a simple (not high-quality) textile. Among the other textiles found in caves 11Q and 1Q, there are items showing clear differences in quality. The finest one, Gr11Q59b, is a tightly-spun, evenly woven fabric with high number of thin threads per cm – count of 26 warps and 20 wefts per cm; on the opposite, textile Gr11Q189 has 8 x 8 threads per cm: the more coarse and uneven the yarn, the lower the count. Therefore, Gr11Q75 could probably fit the second group of textiles defined by Grace M. Crowfoot: i.e., scroll wrappers with plain weaving, used to protect the scroll.[5]

1. For the Temple Scroll wrapper purchased from the Kando family see N. Sukenik, "The Temple Scroll Wrapper from Cave 11: MS 5095/2, MS 5095/4, MS 5095/1," in T. Elgvin, K. Davis, and M. Langlois (ed.), *Gleanings from the Caves: Dead Sea Scrolls and Artefacts from the Schøyen Collection* (LSTS 71; London: Bloomsbury T&T Clark, 2016) 339-50.

2. A. Sheffer and H. Granger-Taylor, "Textiles from Masada: A Preliminary Selection," in J. Aviram, G. Foerster, and E. Netzer (ed.), *Masada IV: The Yigael Yadin Excavations 1963-1965: Final Reports* (Jerusalem: Israel Exploration Society/Hebrew University, 1994) 149-256, on p. 162; O. Shamir and N. Sukenik, "Qumran Textiles and the Garments of Qumran's Inhabitants," *DSD* 18 (2011) 206-25.

3. G.M. Crowfoot, "The Linen Textiles," in D. Barthélemy and J.T. Milik, *Qumran Cave 1* (DJD 1; Oxford: Clarendon, 1955) 18-38, on p. 19.

4. The count of the warp threads [per cm] is the same or [closely] similar to that of the weft.

5. Crowfoot, "Linen Textile," 19.

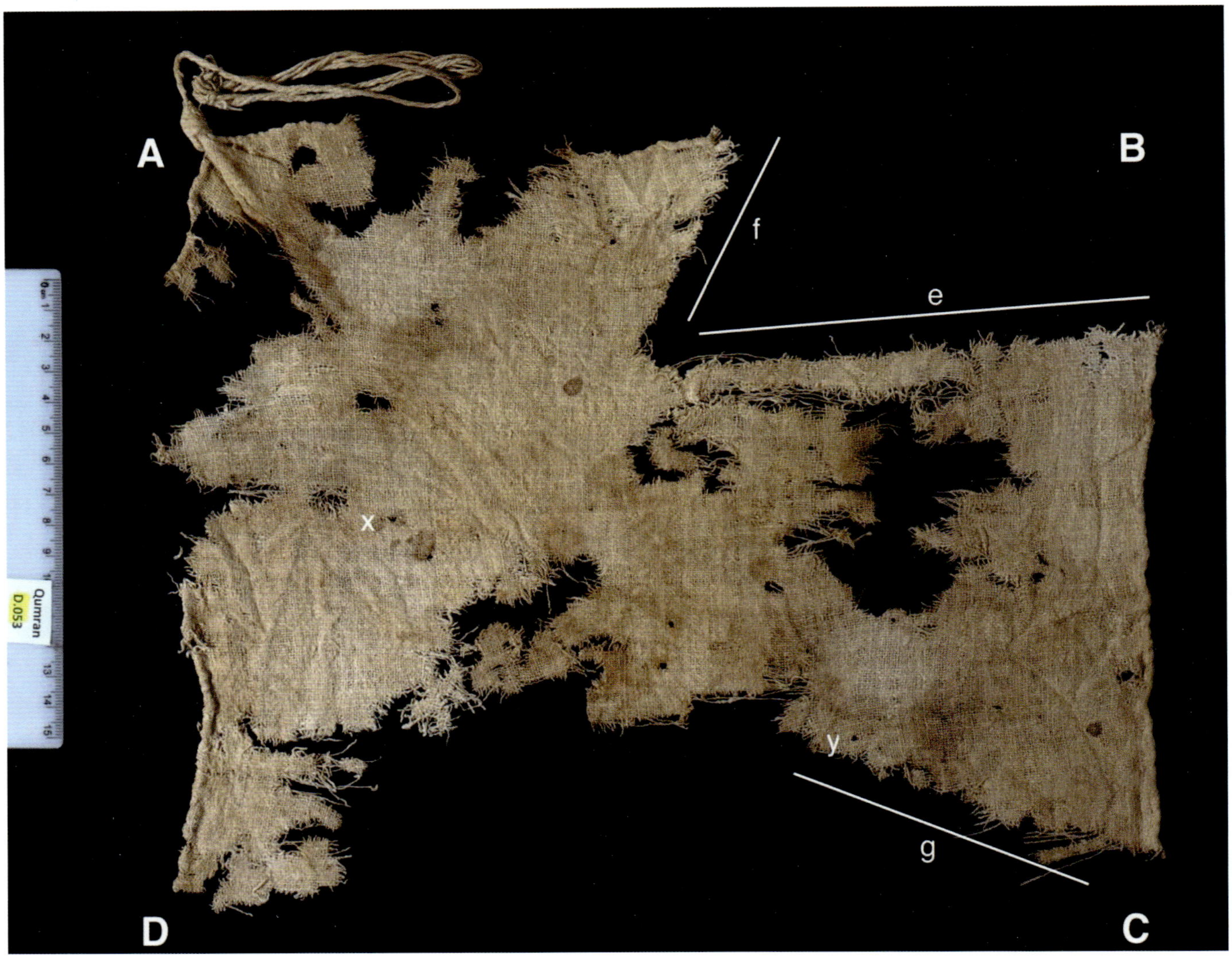

Fig. 1. Textile Gr11Q75 (Photo by Clara Amit, courtesy IAA)

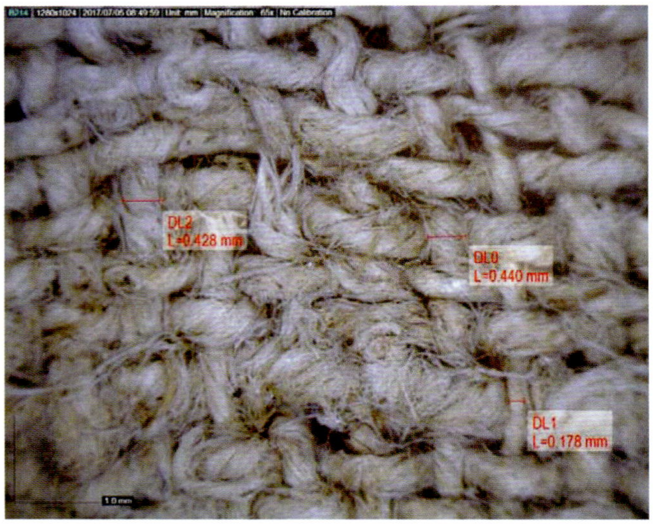

Fig. 2. Gr11Q75 Dino-Lite x 60 (Photo by Naama Sukenik)

The three preserved hems were rolled up, sewn and whipped by single linen thread. This technique was identified in many other textiles found in Cave 1Q including nos 3, 5, 7, 15, 17, 26, 30, 37 etc. The stitches are irregular, the space between the stitches is non-uniform and the seam is not straight, attesting an unskilled or careless hand.

The only preserved corner (A, Fig. 1) is rolled and knotted on itself with a long string hanging from it (Fig. 3). The string measures about 50 cm, 1.2 mm in diameter. It is made of three Z4s plied together to S-plied, (S4z)3S (Fig. 4). The final part of the string is closed on itself delimiting a circular area with a diameter of 5.4 cm (Fig. 5). We think that it tied a cylindrical object (Fig. 6).

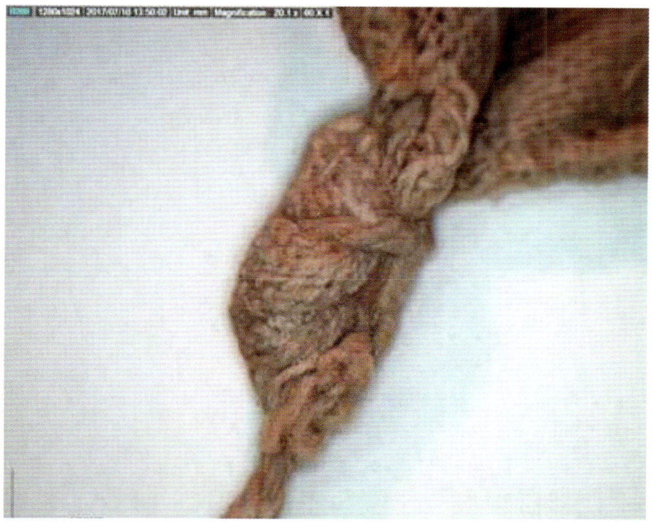

Fig. 3. Knot (A) Dino-Lite x 60 (Photo by Naama Sukenik)

Fig. 5. Final part of the string (Photo by Giorgio Skory)

Fig. 4. String Dino-Lite x 60 (Photo by Naama Sukenik)

Fig. 6. String function and diameter measure (Photo by Dennis Mizzi)

The string could have been pulled to wrap and fasten the textile along the diagonal A – C (Fig. 1).[6] The textile shows signs of cuts (e, f, and g Fig. 1) in connection with the unpreserved corner (B), and on the opposite incomplete side (C – D). The cuts were made by knife or scissors, probably in order to take out the textile content, i.e. the scroll.

Textile Gr11Q75 does not show any circular marks or traces suggesting long time contact with a neck of a jar and any possible lid, as one might expect from a textile used as jar cover.

6. Additionally, some holes were noticed on the textile, probably caused by worms. The gap between them (x and y in Fig. 1) is 16.7 cm. This measurement fits the final part of the string. Worm holes are attested on Dead Sea Scrolls (see e.g. 11QPs[a]): we can suppose that a worm passed through a scroll wrapped by a textile. Admittedly, at least two weak points remain: 1) on textile Gr11Q75 there are more holes at different distances; 2) it is not certain that the worm passed through the scroll and its wrapper along the diameter.

2. Function

According to the aforementioned features of the textile, we suggest that Gr11Q75 was used as a scroll wrapper, tied by the attached string. The position of the knot and the string at the edge of the fabric possibly indicates the way the scroll wrapper was tied and wrapped (Fig. 7). If we are right, the outermost part of the string, still closed, attests the diameter of the scroll wrapped inside.

In Cave 1Q a scroll was found still wrapped in its linen textile. The photos published in DJD 1 pl. I show the corner of the textile placed at the center of the scroll as in the reconstruction we suggest for Gr11Q75, even though there is no string attached to the corner.

This supposed system of wrapping the scroll diverges from the reconstruction of the Temple Scroll wrapper[7], and also from that of a scroll wrapper found at Masada[8]. In both cases, the reconstruction places the scroll parallel to the edge of the textile (and not diagonal such as the textile photographed in DJD 1 or our reconstruction of Gr11Q75): apparently, several ways to wrap a scroll were in use at Qumran.

Our reconstruction calls into question the interpretation of the function of some textiles from Cave 1Q, which Crowfoot assigned to her third group and identified as jar covers,[9] e.g. Crowfoot textile no. 15 (IAA no. 351288). This topic shall be further developed in the next volume, presenting a new study of textiles found in Cave 1Q.

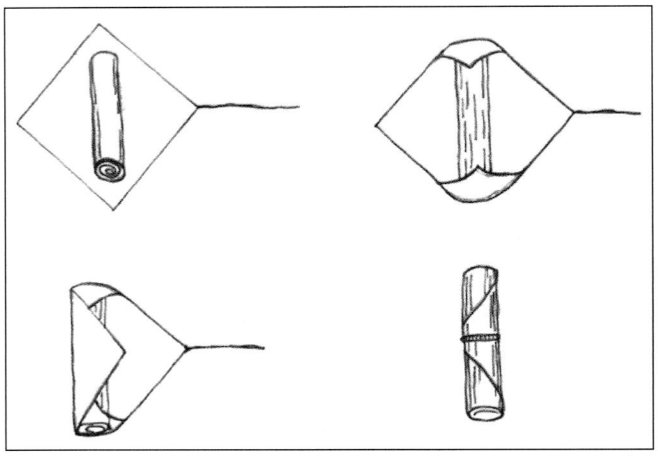

Fig. 7. The system of scroll wrapping (Drawings by Amnon Bahat)

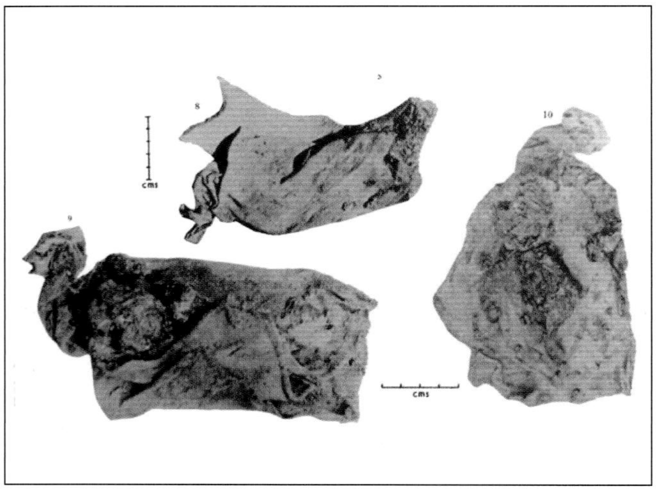

Fig. 8. Remains of a scroll in its linen wrapper, DJD 1, Pl. I

7. Sukenik, "Temple Scroll Wrapper."

8. Sheffer and Granger-Taylor, "Textiles from Masada," 223-6.

9. Crowfoot, "Linen Textiles," 19.

Chapter Four

Appendix B

Analysis of the Blue Color from Textile Gr11Q31a

Naama SUKENIK, Alexander VARVAK, Zohar AMAR, and Iluz DAVID

The blue color from textile Gr11Q31 was analyzed at Bar Ilan University, in the HPLC Unit, Faculty of Life Sciences, using HPLC-DAD (Hitachi LaChromElite Chromatography) system,[1] a method that has been widely used since 1985 for the identification of dyes found in archaeological artefacts.[2] The HPLC is considered the most appropriate method for archaeological textiles since it requires only a small sample, ensuring minimal destruction. At the same time this method is reliable, with a high degree of accuracy and separation capability, qualities which are crucial for the identification of minor compounds in archeological textiles.[3] The identification of dyes was based on a database containing the "fingerprint" of the known dyes and based on the retention time, and their UV–visible absorbance spectra.[4] Minute sample weighing 2 mg was taken from the blue fiber and was dissolved in 150 µL DMSO, and heated for 10 min at 95°C. The liquid was then separated from the sample via centrifugation and transferred to a sterile Eppendorf 1.5 mL microtube to be processed by HPLC. An amount of 20µl of the sample was injecte.[5]

The blue color from textile Gr11Q31 was identified as Indigo (IND) (RT= 8.8 min, Pics: 242 nm, 286 nm, 334nm and 613nm), and Indurubin (RT= 10.1 min, Pics: 289nm, 362nm, 540nm). These components were found in many indigo plants in the world, but in particular from two different species that were known in the ancient world in the Mediterranean area: Woad (*Isatis tinctoria* L.) and Indigo (*Indigofera tinctoria* L.),[6] additionally, they were

1. HPLC system (running EZ Chrom Elite v. 3.2.1 software) consisted of an L-2130 binary pump, an L-2200 autosampler, an L-2300 column oven (column temperature of 30°C was used for all analyses), and an L-2455 Diode Array Detector. The chromatographic column was a GraceSmart RP18, 5 µm, 250 mm × 4.6 mm ID.

2. J. Wouters, "High Performance Liquid Chromatography of Anthraquinones: Analysis of Plant and Insect Extracts and Dyed Textiles," *Studies in Conservation* 30 (1985) 119-28.

3. Z.C. Koren, "An Efficient HPLC Analysis Scheme for Plant and Animal Red, Blue and Purple Dyes," *DHA* 13 (1994) 27-37; J.H. Hofenk de Graaff, W.G. Roelofs, and M.R. van Bommel, *The Colourful Past: The Origins, Chemistry and Identification of Natural Dyestuffs* (London/Riggisberg: Archetype Publications/Abegg-Stiftung, 2004), 25-34.

4. N. Sukenik et al., "Early Evidence (Late 2nd millennium BCE) of Plant-Based Dyeing of Textiles from Timna, Israel," *PLOS ONE* 12/6 (2017)," Appendix A.

5. For the analysis protocol see: N. Sukenik et al., "New Evidence of the Purple-Dye Industry at Tel Shiqmona, Israel," *Archaeometry* 59/4 (2017) 775-85, on p. 780.

6. Z.C. Koren, "HPLC-PDA Analysis of Brominated Indirubinoid, Indigoid, and Isatinoid Dyes," in L. Meijer et al., *Indirubin, the Red Shade of Indigo* (Roscoff: Life in Progress Editions, 2006) 45-53.

also known from species of murex snails that were used to produce the purple dye.[7] However, according to the results, no compounds unique to the murex species, such as monobromoindigotin or dibromoindigotin were found in the sample. Therefore, it is possible to conclude that the blue decoration was dyed with indigotin from a plant source.[8] Similar result was obtained from the blue decoration of the scroll wrapper from Cave 1Q (textile no. 464131).[9] To date, using the analytical tools available to us, it has not been possible to determine which of the plants had been used (Woad or Indigo).[10] Despite the limitation of analytical instruments, the choice seems to point to Woad (*Isatis tinctoria* L.), which was well-known in the Roman period and mentioned in many different sources, including Jewish ones,[11] and was widely cultivated in Israel as an agricultural crop.[12] By comparison, the Indigo plant was little known during the Roman period, when they had just begun to import it from India.[13] The blue indigo pigment which was extracted from the leaves was considered as a "vat dye," indicating a complex and comprehensive process of dyeing which includes reduction and oxidation. The dyeing process took several days in antiquity, and indigo was among the earliest pigments from dyed plants which were known in the dyeing craft.[14]

7. Koren, "HPLC-PDA Analysis of Brominated Indirubinoid, Indigoid, and Isatinoid Dyes;" N. Sukenik et al., "Chemical Analysis of Murex-Dyed Textiles from Wadi Murabba'at, Israel," *JASR* 3 (2015) 565-70.

8. N. Sukenik et al., "A Re-Evaluation of the Textile Dyes in the Cave of Letters," in J. Ortiz et al., *Textiles, Basketry and Dyes in the Ancient Mediterranean World: Proceedings of the Vth International Symposium on Textiles and Dyes in the Ancient Mediterranean World (Montserrat, 19-22 March, 2014)* (Purpureae Vestes V: Textiles and Dyes in Antiquity; Valencia: Universitat de València, 2016) 263-73, on pp. 267-8.

9. N. Sukenik, *Dyes in Textiles from the Early Roman Period Found in the Judean Desert Caves: Chemical, Historical and Archaeological Aspects* (PhD diss.; Ramat Gan: Bar-Ilan University, 2013) (Hebrew), 256-7; this confirms the result obtained in the past by Crowfoot; see Crowfoot, "Linen Textiles," 19.

10. Hofenk de Graaff, *The Colourful Past*, 257.

11. See for example: Mishnah, Sh'vi'it, 7, 1; Mishnah, Shabbat, 9, 5; Mishnah, Megilla, 4, 7; J Talmud, Sh'vi'it, 7, 1 (37a).

12. D. Zohary, M. Hopf, and E. Weiss, *Domestication of Plants in the Old World* (Oxford: Oxford University Press, ^{4}2013), 166-7.

13. Plinius NH, XXXIII, 163; Sukenik et al., "A Re-Evaluation of the Textile Dyes," 268; one cannot rule out the possibility that they used a different variety, such as *Indigofera articulata*, which may have been known in the Land of Israel already in ancient times; Y. Melamed and M. Kislev, "Remain of Seeds, Fruits Insects from the Excavation in the Village of 'En Gedi," *JSRS* 49 (2005) 89*-102* (Hebrew).

14. Sukenik et al., "Early Evidence (Late 2nd millennium BCE) of Plant-Based Dyeing."

Chapter Five A

Organic Materials from Cave 11Q: A. Leather, Basketry, Ropes, Wood and Seeds

Joan E. TAYLOR and Naama SUKENIK

As well as textiles, string and manuscripts other organic items were also brought to light in Cave 11Q.[1] This material survived well over many centuries, due to the high temperature and dry climate of the Judaean desert and Dead Sea area. Despite the small number of the objects found (see Table 1), they contribute to the study and understanding the function of Cave 11Q.

1. Leather

1.1 *Tabs and Thongs*

There is a small collection of pieces of leather, some being tabs or ties from scrolls (Gr11Q20a,b,c, Gr11Q200; Table 1: 1 and 2). Similar thongs (ties) and tabs, with the same measurements, were found in the other Qumran caves (Cave 1Q,[2] Cave 4Q and 8Q[3]). Two scrolls from Cave 4Q (4QDa and 4QApocryphal Psalm and Prayer) still had their tabs attached. Other remains are similar to the items of the Schøyen collection.[4] The tabs from 11Q, like the other items from Qumran, are made of folded rectangular leather in which a thong is inserted through two slots. The thong is without any signs of sewing (as in sandals). These were used to bind up and secure individual scrolls. Thongs/ties could be tightened against the tab and then wound around the scroll.[5] We can assume then that the scrolls in Cave 11Q were first closed tightly with leather ties, and then wrapped in textiles that were wound around with linen cord (see Chapter 4).

1. Excavations took place under the auspices of the Jordan Department of Antiquities and the École biblique et archéologique française, with a preliminary report published by Roland de Vaux, in R. de Vaux, "Fouilles de Khirbet Qumrân: rapport préliminaire sur les 3e, 4e, et 5e campagnes," *RB* 63 (1956) 533-77. Further material was published by J. Patrich, "Khirbet Qumran in the Light of New Archaeological Explorations in the Qumran Caves," in M.O. Wise et al. (ed.), *Methods of Investigation of the Dead Sea Scrolls and the Khirbet Qumran Site: Present Realities and Future Prospects* (ANYAS 722; New York: New York Academy of Sciences, 1994) 73-95.

2. D. Barthélemy and J.T. Milik, *Qumran Cave 1* (DJD 1; Oxford: Clarendon, 1955), 7.

3. J. Carswell, "Fastenings on the Qumrân Manuscripts," in R. de Vaux and J.T. Milik, *Qumrân Grotte 4.II: I. Archéologie. II. Tefillin, Mezuzot et Targums (4Q128-4Q157)* (DJD 6; Oxford: Clarendon, 1977) 23-8, Pl. 5.

4. T. Elgvin, "Leather Cord from Qumran, Shoe Remains: MS 5095/6, MS 1655/5," in Id., K. Davis, M. Langlois (ed.), *Gleanings from the Caves: Dead Sea Scrolls and Artefacts from the Schøyen Collection* (LSTS 71; London: Bloomsbury T&T Clark, 2016) 323-38, on pp. 323-4.

5. O. Shamir, "Organic Materials," in D.T. Ariel (ed.), *The Dead Sea Scrolls* (Exhibition Catalogue; Jerusalem: Israel Antiquities Authority, 2008) 116-33, on pp. 130-1; Elgvin, "Leather Cord," 323.

This double tying practice is evidenced in the case of the Temple Scroll, where the wrapper and the linen cord were found.[6]

1.2 *Sandals*

There are also fragments of leather from sandals or shoes (Table 1: 3, 4, 5, 6). Some pieces made of leather most likely derive from the soles of sandals (Gr11Q21a, Gr11Q21b). Fragments of *soleae* sandals were found in many sites in Israel, for example in the Cave of the Letters,[7] the Cave of Horror[8] and in the Cave of the Spear.[9] In the Roman period the layers of the sole were sewn together by leather bindings,[10] as probably represented by Gr11Q21b.

Another fragment (Gr11Q21d) comes from the tabs near the heel, called 'ears' in the Mishnah (m. Kelim 26:4). These tabs, one on either side, entered the upper sole through slits in the inner sole and were secured by the stitching joining the soles.[11] The upper part of each tab was cut with one or two slits, and the main strap was threaded through the slits and then again to another tab on the upper part of the sandal, by the toes, where the strap ends were tied together, securing the foot. Gr11Q21d consists of two pieces of leather sewn together with small stitches with a slit in the centre appearing like a button hole. A thong or tie could be passed through it. Two complete sandals are in storage in the Israel Antiquities Authority (IAA 351270-351271),[12] and these preserve two and three layers of soles fastened together by leather thongs (see Fig. 1).[13] There are also examples from Qumran Cave 4Q (IAA 464295) and from Cave 2Q (IAA 477613). Possible shoe remains deriving from Qumran are also among the items of the Schøyen collection.[14] Sandal-straps are also found commonly in leather collections from the Roman period like in the Cave of the letters in the Judaean Desert.[15]

Fig. 1. Sandal 96-9105 from the Cave of the Letters (Photo by Clara Amit, courtesy IAA)

Fig. 2. Two sandals of the Early Roman period from the Dead Sea area: Sandal A (below) and Sandal B (above). (Photo by Clara Amit)

6. N. Sukenik, "The Temple Scroll Wrapper from Cave 11: MS 5095/2, MS 5095/4, MS 5095/1," in Elgvin, Davis, and Langlois, *Gleanings*, 339-50.

7. Y. Yadin, *The Finds from the Bar Kokhba Period in the Cave of Letters* (Jerusalem: Israel Exploration Society, 1963), 165-8.

8. Y. Aharoni, "Expedition B: The Cave of Horror," *IEJ* 12 (1962) 186-99, Pl. 28:D.

9. R. Porat, H. Eshel, and A. Frumkin, "The 'Caves of the Spear': Refuge Caves from the Bar-Kokhba Revolt North of 'En-Gedi," *IEJ* 59 (2009) 21-46.

10. Yadin, *Finds from the Bar Kokhba Period*, 166; Elgvin, "Leather Cord," 324.

11. Yadin, *Finds from the Bar Kokhba Period*, 167; R. Rosenthal-Heginbotham, "'A Man Must Not Go Out with a Nail-Studded Sandal': Footwear in Jewish Sources and from Archaeological Remains," in A. De Moor, C. Fluck, and P. Linscheid (ed.), *Drawing the Threads Together: Textiles and Footwear of the 1st Millennium AD from Egypt* (Tielt, Lannoo Publishers, 2013) 268-75, on p. 269.

12. They are designated "Sandal A" and "Sandal B." The dimensions are: Sandal A: length 22 cm (8 5/8 in.), width 6.8 cm (2 5/8 in.). Sandal B: length 21 cm (8 1/4 in.), width 5.5 cm (2 1/8 in.). Unfortunately, it is unclear the exact place where the sandals were found.

13. Shamir, "Organic Materials," 128-9.

14. See Elgvin, "Leather Cord," 324.

15. Yadin, *Finds from the Bar Kokhba Period*, 165-8; Rosenthal-Heginbotham, "'Footwear in Jewish Sources."

2. Ties and Knots

Items Gr11Q25, Gr11Q9/1 and Gr11Q9/2 involve ties or knots. Item Gr11Q25 (Table 1: 8) has skin that appears to be leather, since it is similar to remains from sandals, scroll tabs and ties. It may be that linen string used for a scroll wrapper was wound up with a leather tie attached to a scroll, and this binding has held together after the linen wrapper was removed.

However, Gr11Q9/1 and 2 (see Table 1: 9, 10) unusually combine animal tissue with linen string. These are discussed together separately in Chapter 5, where it is suggested that they are Bedouin amulets; the radiocarbon dating of these has indicated that they are from the early modern period.

3. Basketry and Ropes

Two fragments of basketry (Gr11Q202, Gr11Q203; Table 1: 11, 12) may come from the same object, used as a basket or mat. This basketry was found at the entrance of Cave 11Q, and has been discussed already by Orit Shamir in the catalogue for the IAA touring Dead Sea Scrolls exhibition.[16]

The basketry was made of date palm leaflets and date fibres in twill braid plaiting technique that was very common in the Roman period. Baskets woven in this way were used for storage or carrying loads, and a comparable example with a very similar size of palm leaf braids and technique has been found in Cave of Letters in the Judaean Desert (see Fig. 3) and is very well preserved,[17] Hundreds of fragments of similar basketry were found in Masada,[18] also in other sites that date to the Roman period including Murabba'at,[19] M'oa,[20] and Ein Rachel.[21] However, this example is made with narrower braids and therefore appears finer in quality. In this technique, long flat braids were attached as weaving progressively enclosed a cord. The cords, that become invisible, are encased in the braid edge to give a horizontal ribbed texture.[22] These cords are usually made of two plied strings (in S or Z) made of date fibres. Arched plaited handles were attached, made of palm-fibre cords attached to rims by threading cords through the weaving of the basket.[23] Thin date fibre cords were found in Cave 11Q (Gr11Q204: Table 1: 13), which probably came from basketry done with the same technique.

Fig. 3. Basket from the Cave of the Letters. (Photo by Clara Amit, courtesy IAA)

In addition, there are thicker cords made of date fibres (Gr11Q205, Gr11Q206; Table 1: 14, 15) and the uses of these for binding cannot be determined with precision.

16. Shamir, "Organic Materials." This discussion is also found in the online catalogue http://www.loc.gov/exhibits/scrolls/art2.html. Note that in the photograph in this catalogue the two pieces are laid over each other to give an impression of one large piece, and an intermediate piece (currently unidentified) has been placed in between.

17. Yadin, *Finds from the Bar Kokhba Period*, 136-49.

18. K. Bernick, "Masada Basketry, Cordage and Related Artifacts," in J. Aviram, G. Foerster, and E. Netzer (ed.), *Masada IV: The Yigael Yadin Excavations 1963-1965: Final Reports* (Jerusalem: Israel Exploration Society/Hebrew University, 1994) 284-317, on pp. 297-304.

19. G.M. Crowfoot and E. Crowfoot, "The Textiles and Basketry," in P. Benoit, J.T. Milik, and R. de Vaux, *Les Grottes de Murabba'ât* (DJD 2; Oxford: Clarendon, 1961) 51-63, on p. 63.

20. O. Shamir, "Textiles, Basketry, Cordage and Whorls from Mo'a (Moje Awad)," *'Atiqot* 50 (2005) 99-152, on pp. 107-8.

21. O. Shamir, "Textiles, Basketry and Cordage from 'En Rahel," *'Atiqot* 38 (1999) 91-123, on pp. 101-4; and see O. Shamir, "Textiles, Basketry, Cordage and Fruits from 'En Tamar: Preliminary Report," in P. Bienkowski and K. Galor, *Crossing the Rift: Resources, Settlements, Patterns and Interaction in the Wadi Arabah* (LSS 3; Oxford: Oxbow, 2006) 191-4.

22. Bernick, "Masada Basketry," 299.

23. Shamir, "Organic Materials," 122-3.

4. Wood

Various pieces of wood were found in the cave. Two of the wood items are natural (Gr11Q22b and Gr11Q22c; Table 1: 16, 17). Item Gr11Q22c, has some black staining and a central hole. One wooden object is clearly manufactured: item Gr11Q22a (Table 1: 19) This appears to be a sharp object that has suffered some damage to the point, and it has some black staining near the tip which may indicate burning.[24] This was radiocarbon dated in 2004 and it can be seen clearly on artefact Gr11Q22a, the wooden point, that two samples were taken from it. These two samples from the same object appear to have been tested separately, yielding almost identical results. These place the wooden point most likely in the 10th century CE (Gr11Q22b, 68.2% probability dated to 890-985 CE and 95.4% probability between 820-1020 CE; Gr11Q22c, 68.5% probability dated between 885-980 CE and 95% probability between 770-1020 CE).

A piece of the natural wood was also radiocarbon dated: a sample of Gr11Q22c was taken (and also labelled as D024). The final dating of this was 1770-1640 BCE (68.2% probability) or 1880-1610 BCE (95.4% probability).[25] This result will be discussed further in the chapter on radiocarbon dating results.

New excavations in the cave in 2017[26] brought to light another piece of wood. This example (FB11Q5; Table 1: 19) is a tube-shaped object which shows some evidence of cutting at the thin end.

5. Seeds and Stones

Along with the other organic material a few seeds and stones were found in both de Vaux's and Fidanzio's excavation. The collection includes some Egyptian Balsam seeds (Gr11Q207; FB11Q3; Table 1: 20). The tree (*Balanites aegyptiaca*) grows in hot places in desert oases along the Jordan Rift and similar seeds were found in other sites close to the Dead Sea in the Roman period: Ein Tamar,[27] Qarantal,[28] and Qasr el-Yahoud.[29] The fruit of this tree, called *balanos*, was and is used for food. The fruit, which is slightly bitter, can be crushed in a mortar and the pulp used also for medicine and spices. The oil is considered medicinal.[30]

The cave also yielded date stones (*Phoenix dactylifera*) (Gr11Q208, Table 1: 21), which were found both at Qumran and in other sites in the Dead Sea area like Masada.[31] The date palm of various types was cultivated in oases and also grows wild in places around the Dead Sea where sufficient water supports it, most frequently on the eastern side. It had a variety of uses as well as being consumed for food, for example making basketry and rope, or for making date honey and medicine.[32] The wood of the date palm was used for ceiling beams.[33]

24. A fairly recent identifying note for these items, made by Mireille Bélis, reads 'D024 G.11 Q22 bois' (Cave 11 Q22 wood). D024 and Q22 have been written on the boxes. The designation D024 relates to the fact that certain wood samples were tested in a batch of other items in 2004 and this identifier is recorded. K.L. Rasmussen et al., "Cleaning and Radiocarbon Dating of Material from Khirbet Qumran," in J. Gunneweg, C. Greenblatt, and A. Adriaens (ed.), *Bio- and Material Cultures at Qumran: Papers from a COST Action G8 Working Group Meeting Held in Jerusalem, Israel on 22-23 May 2005* (Stuttgart: Fraunhofer IRB, 2006) 139-64.

25. Rasmussen et al., "Cleaning and Radiocarbon Dating."

26. Undertaken by the Istituto di Cultura e Archeologia delle Terre Bibliche of the Facoltà di Teologia di Lugano (ISCAB FTL) and the Università della Svizzera Italiana (USI), and headed by M. Fidanzio (Director of the ISCAB FTL) and D. Bahat (ISCAB FTL).

27. Shamir, "Textiles, Basketry, Cordage and Fruits from 'En Tamar," 162.

28. Y. Melamed, "Chalcolithic and Hellenistic Plant Remains from Cave V/49," *'Atiqot* 41 (2002) 101-8.

29. Z. Amar and O. Shamir, "Egyptian Balsam and its Use in the Jordan Rift Region," *JSRS* 22 (2013) 369-76 (Hebrew); O. Shamir, "Egyptian and Nubian Textiles from Qasr el-Yahud, 9th century AD," in A. De Moor, C. Fluck, and P. Linscheid (ed.), *Textiles, Tools and Techniques of the 1st millennium AD from Egypt and Neighbouring Countries: Proceedings of the 8th Conference of the Research Group "Textiles from the Nile Valley", Antwerp, 4-6 October 2013* (Tielt: Lannoo, 2015) 48-60.

30. Amar and Shamir, "Egyptian Balsam;" N.F. Hepper and J.E. Taylor, "Date Palms and Opobalsam in the Madaba Mosaic Map," *PEQ* 136 (2004) 35-44, on p. 43; J.E. Taylor, *The Essenes, the Scrolls and the Dead Sea* (Oxford: Oxford University Press; rev. paperback edn, 2014), 315.

31. M. Kislev and O. Simchoni, "Hygiene and Insect Damage of Crops and Food at Masada," in J. Aviram et al. (ed.), *Masada VIII: The Yigael Yadin Excavations 1963-1965, Final Reports* (Jerusalem: Israel Exploration Society/Hebrew University, 2007) 133-70.

32. See Taylor, *Essenes*, 313-14.

33. B. Wagemakers and J.E. Taylor, "New Photographs of the

Two other seeds of fruit came from the plant *Ziziphus spina-christi* (Gr11Q209; FB11Q4; Table 1: 22), or jujube, which also had medicinal uses.[34]

Since the cave was (and is) frequented by bats, we consulted with the most noted specialist on these bats, Prof. Yoram Yom-Tov, Professor of Zoology at Tel Aviv University, to ask if it was possible that fruit was brought here by these animals. However, he informed us (email of 5/3/2016) that in this cave there are two species of bats: several hundreds of *Taphozous perforatus* and few *Rhinopoma hardweckei*. These bats - the Egyptian Tomb Bat and the Lesser Mouse-Tailed Bat respectively - are insectivores. The tree *Balanities aegyptiaca* is, however, eaten by ruminants (sheep and goats) even today, and it is possible some seeds could have been carried by these animals at certain times when the cave was accessible. The holes in the seeds could be caused by humans puncturing the seed cask to extract the oil, or else could be the result of (animal) teeth biting into these. The times of the different seeds' arrival in the cave has not yet been ascertained on the basis of radiocarbon dating. It would be too costly to test for each of these: unless dates and seeds are found in a clear cluster, any individual item may not be related to another. There is no stratigraphy that relates to their appearance in the cave.

Conclusion

We can conclude that the basketry and fragments of sandals likely come from the Roman period on the basis of their parallels. However, the radiocarbon dating of the wood indicates quite different ages. The plant remains (seeds and stones) cannot be definitively ascribed to the Hellenistic to Roman period, and may perhaps relate to the wood and cotton from the 9th century, given the appearance of such seeds in Qasr el-Yahoud at this time,[35] but the typology of the basketry and the sandal remains would suggest that they could belong with the linen textiles identified as scroll wrappers, packing and string, and also the manuscripts, or else they came from around about the same period. The scroll tabs and ties should be definitively associated with the scrolls. The state of the organic objects uncovered in Cave 11Q, including the manuscripts and textiles, indicates that it was an environment allowing good preservation of organic materials. Thus, these remains reflect reliably the use of the cave. The number of organic materials not directly related to scrolls or textiles are quite minimal, and hence in our opinion this reinforces the research assumption that the cave was not used for dwelling in the Roman period but was primarily used for scroll placement. However, the basketry, date rope, sandal pieces and/or seeds might also relate to a use of the cave as a temporary hide-out. Some of these items may also possibly come from later or earlier periods, given the range of radiocarbon dating results.

Qumran Excavations from 1954 and Interpretations of L.77 and L.86," *PEQ* 143 (2011) 134-56.

34. E. Lev and Z. Amar, *Practical Materia Medica of the Medieval Eastern Mediterranean According to the Cairo Genizah* (Sir Henry Wellcome Asian Series 7; Leiden: Brill, 2007), 381-2; Taylor, *Essenes*, 327.

35. See Shamir, "Egyptian and Nubian Textiles."

Table 1: List of organic objects from Cave 11Q

(Photos by Clara Amit, courtesy of the Israel Antiquities Authority)

	Inventory No.	Other No.	Object	Material	Dimensions (in cm)	Photo
1.	Gr11Q20a, b, c	864398	Tab and two thongs from scrolls	Leather	Tab: L. 2; W. 2.3 Thong: L. 8; W. 0.35 Thong: L. 3.75; W. 0.5	
2.	Gr11Q200	870781	Two fragments of thongs from scroll ties	Leather	1. L. 4 W. 0.55 2. L. 3.2 W. 0.4	
3.	Gr11Q21a	864363	Two fragments of sandal sole with holes for thread	Leather	L. 7; W. 4	
4.	Gr11Q21b	864362	Fragment of leather with holes for tabs, binding for sole?	Leather	L. 4; W 4 H. 0.2	
5.	Gr11Q21c	870772	Fragment of leather sole (sandal?)	Leather	L. 4.3; W. 5 H. 0.25	

6.	Gr11Q21d	870782	Fragment of sandal	Leather, linen thread	L. 3.8;W. 1.2 H. 0.32	
7.	Gr11Q201	477617	Fragments of leather	Leather		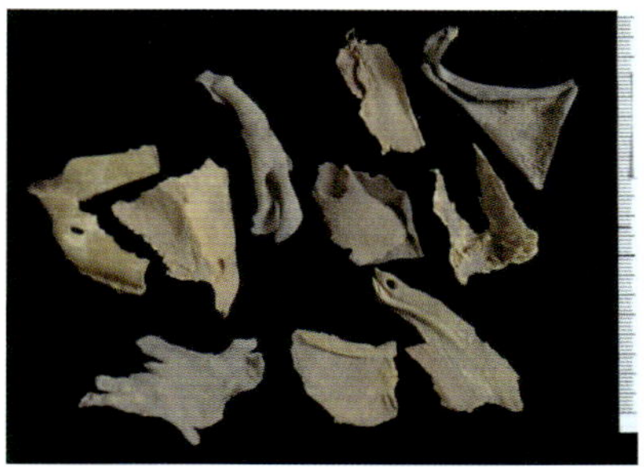
8.	Gr11Q25	864394	Strip of leather tied with linen string	Leather and linen	L. 2.55 cm W. 1 cm	
9.	Gr11Q9/1	464628*	Knots	Animal tissue, linen	L. 3.35; W. 3.2; H: 3.35	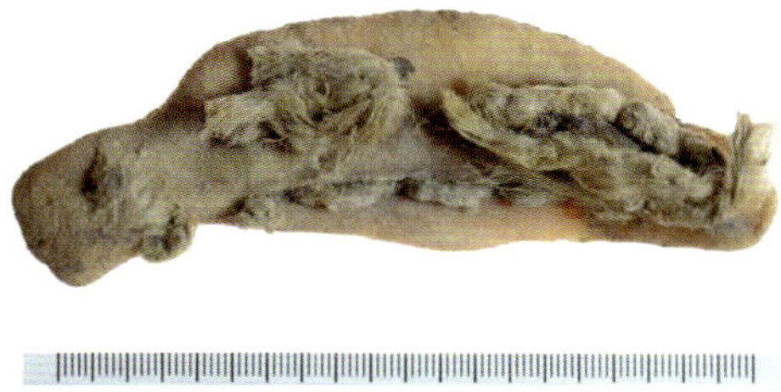
10.	Gr11Q9/2	464629*	Knots	Animal tissue, linen	L. 4.35; W. 3; H. 2.25	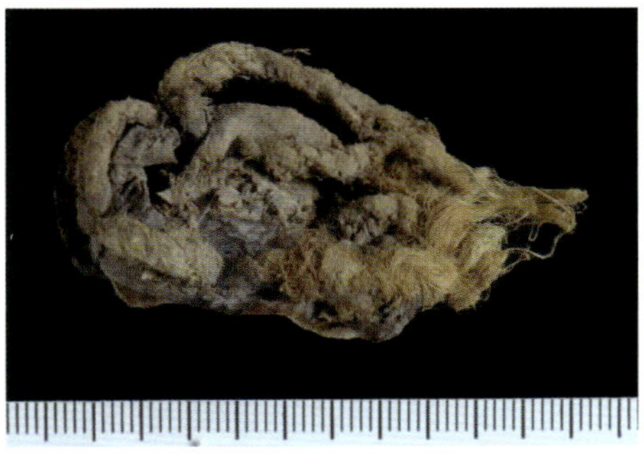
11.	Gr11Q202	351300	Basketry	Fibre of date palm	L. 28.5 W. 16	

12.	Gr11Q203	351301	Basketry	Fibre of date palm	L. 21 W. 22	
13.	Gr11Q204	864358	Thin cord	Fibre of date palm	The longest rope L. 22 W. 0.25	
14.	Gr11Q205	864357	Thick cord	Fibre of date palm	L. 18 W. 0.6	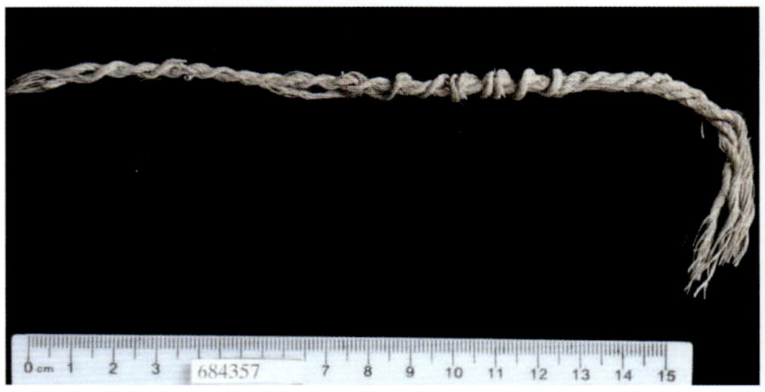
15.	Gr11Q206	864359	Two ropes	Fibre of date palm	1. L. 15; W. 0.8 2. L. 9.3; W. 2.3	
16.	Gr11Q22b (=D024)	864397	Roots/ tendrils (?) of tree	Wood		
17.	Gr11Q22c (= D024)	864396	Piece of object with black staining	Wood	L. 3.3; W. 2; H. 1.45	

18.	Gr11Q22a (=D024)	864395	Wooden point with some black staining	Wood	L. 12.3 W. 2.5 H. 0.8	
19	FB11Q5	B. 201.F2	Wooden object with indications of cutting	Wood	L. 9.6 W. 1.5 H. 1.5	
20.	Gr11Q207 FB11Q3	477618	8 seeds 10 seeds	*Balanites aegyptiaca*		
21.	Gr11Q208 FB11Q4	848775	2 seeds 5 seeds	*Ziziphus spina-christi*		
22.	Gr11Q209	848771	1 seed	*Phoenix dactylifera*		

Chapter Five B

Organic Materials from Cave 11Q: B. Gr11Q9/1 and 2

Joan E. TAYLOR

When excavators came to Cave 11Q in 1956 and salvaged what was left after the initial work done by Bedouin, two items identified as being made of leather or hide were among the artefacts retrieved: Gr11Q9/1 and 2. As they form part of the key 'Q' list of items designated in the cave they deserve special attention. These objects have remained unstudied ever since they were found.

Naama Sukenik of the Israel Antiquities Authority and the present author made an initial inspection of the two artefacts in July 2014. This was followed by scientific tests and a further joint examination of the artefacts in July 2015. I am very grateful to Dr Sukenik for her careful study and help, and for being a great conversation partner in this work. As a result of these examinations and tests, some tentative conclusions are possible.

1. The Artefacts within the Cave Environment

According to the published inventory of Cave 11Q the items are: 'deux fragments de peau', indicating two fragments of hide (skin). However, this does not describe them fully or accurately. In the excavation card (Figure 1) and original inventory the discovery site is identified as being in the interior of the cave to the right of the (interior) entrance, and the card is dated 11 March 1956. This identification of the find spot is very important.

The description reads: 'Deux fragments de cuir (?) très durci dans lesquels une corde est passée plusieurs fois'. 'Cuir?' appears at the top of the card also. The question mark is significant because the nature of the organic material is something that needs careful examination. The mention of a single cord in the description on the card might indicate that these objects were considered to have been joined together, and the fact that they are given the same object number would likewise suggest this. However, now they are separated.

In de Vaux's diary notes of his excavation of Cave 11Q it is stated in the entry for 26 February, 1956, that certain 'fragments de cuir' were found at the entrance of the cave along with basketry and potsherds of the Qumran type, cloth fragments, a nail, a knife blade and inscribed fragments. This mention of such leather fragments at the cave entrance refers to other leather pieces (e.g. from shoes), and may confuse scholars and their assessment of the find spot, since de Vaux did not in his field notes record the discovery of the items Gr11Q9/1 and 2 where they were in fact located, inside the cave, on 11 March. On this day, he wrote simply,

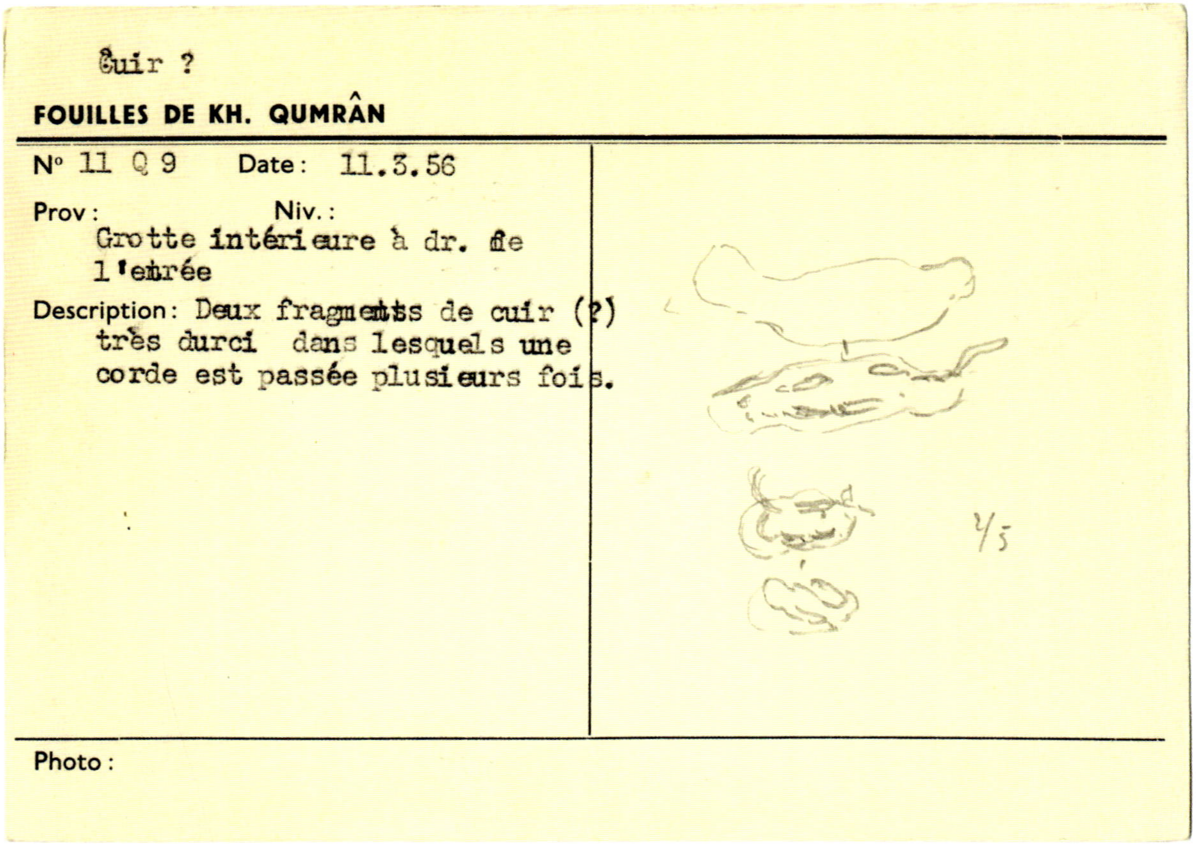

Cuir ?

FOUILLES DE KH. QUMRÂN

N° 11 Q 9 Date: 11.3.56

Prov: Niv.:
Grotte intérieure à dr. de l'entrée

Description: Deux fragments de cuir (?) très durci dans lesquels une corde est passée plusieurs fois.

1/5

Photo:

Fig. 1. De Vaux's inventory: card noting discovery of Gr11Q9

'Nettoyage de la grotte.' On 12 March, the day after the discovery of Gr11Q9/1 and 2, he wrote: 'On nettoie la grotte intérieure et à droite de l'entrée, gisent quelques tessons typiques de Qumran et une clé de fer.' It should be noted that the attested pottery pieces were not given excavation numbers, and the list of items actually includes one iron key (Gr11Q11) and one malachite bead (Gr11Q12), the latter presumably deriving from a woman's bracelet or necklace. Preceding these is another item, a 'tige de fer' – an iron rod or awl (Gr11Q10) - which may be associated with them or with the 'hide' pieces. The location of the pottery pieces and key is the same as given on the card for Gr11Q9/1 and 2, and studies show that they should be placed in the Roman period. However, they may have been reached at a deeper level than the discovery of the 'hide' objects Gr11Q9/1 and 2 found on 11 March, or indeed the awl (Gr11Q10). Prior to the clearing of the area just to the right of the entrance, de Vaux notes discoveries dating to Iron Age II (Gr11Q5, Gr11Q7 and Gr11Q8), and it appears that after their discovery on 3 March and recording, a new area was opened up, with Gr11Q9/1 and 2 being found first. This lack of clarity in terms of the findings leaves the dating of Gr11Q9/1 and 2 in doubt.

De Vaux does not associate Gr11Q9/1 and 2 with any of the pottery he mentions in his summary in Revue Biblique where he distinguishes three periods of occupation: the Chalcolithic, Iron Age II (7th century BCE) and Roman periods. Presumably he considered the items to belong to one of these three eras.

2. Description of Artefacts

2.1 *Gr11Q9/1*

Item Gr11Q9/1 (IAA 464628, see Fig. 2) is 10.4 cm long and 3.35 cm wide, with a maximum thickness of 1.5 cm. Its total weight is 20.37 g. It is more curved in shape and thinner on one side and is bent

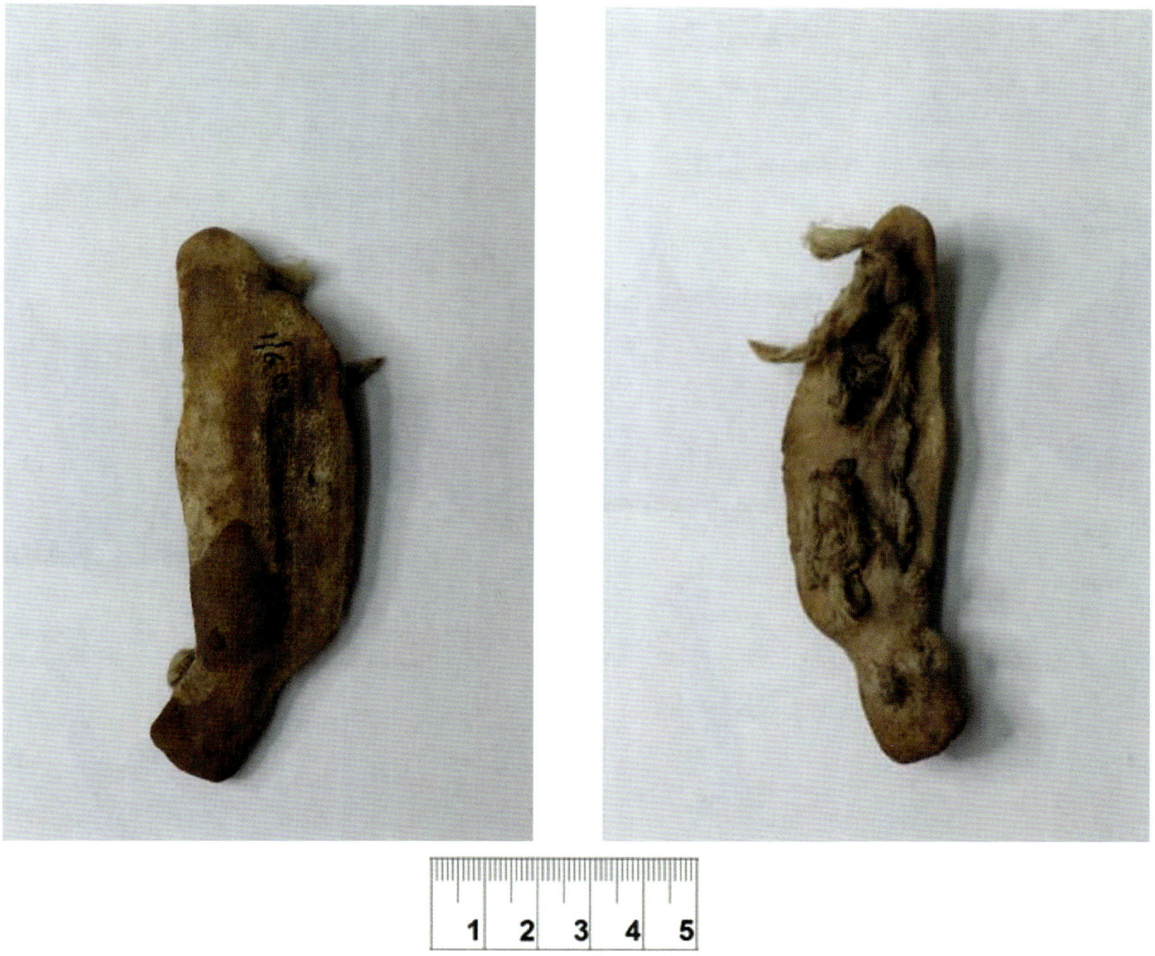

Fig. 2. Gr11Q9/1, back and front showing string puncturing artefact and knots. (Photo by J.E. Taylor)

in form, in that it does not lie flat. While now the material is very dry and hard, it was originally soft enough to allow for holes to be punched, through which linen string has been passed and knotted. There are areas of dark brown discoloration on the back of the object.

In some ways the object appears as if it might be a tiny pouch. It has a slight ridge on the back which seems to show a cylindrical shaping. In order to determine if anything was inside the object, it was examined by x-ray (Figure 3). The x-ray showed clearly the lines of the string and 6 knots spaced evenly, with the lightness indicating intrusive particles in the string that create a higher density along the string and knots than in the surrounding material. The x-ray can be overlaid on the object to show where the higher density areas are found in relation to the string. The shaping of the string and knots seemed to have given rise to the ridges on the back of the object, but there was apparently nothing inside it: it appears as solid.

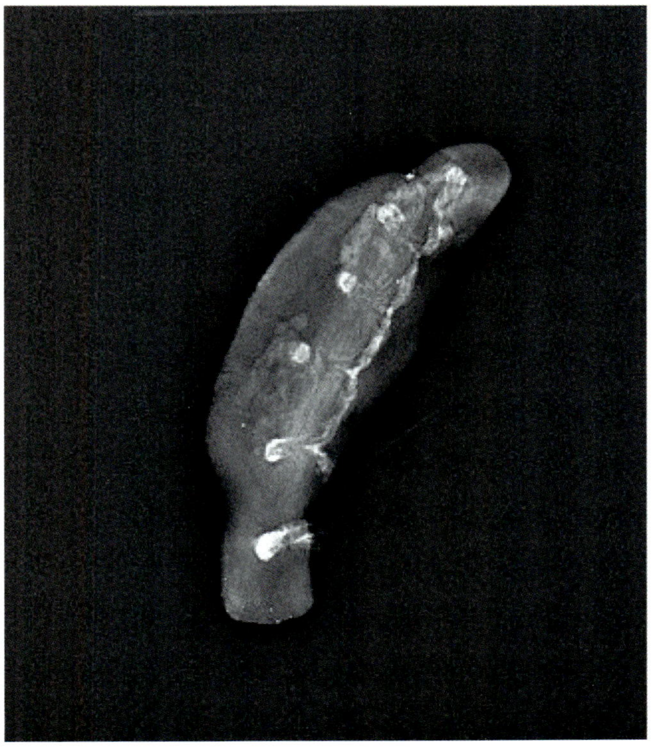

Fig. 3. X-Ray of object Gr11Q9/1

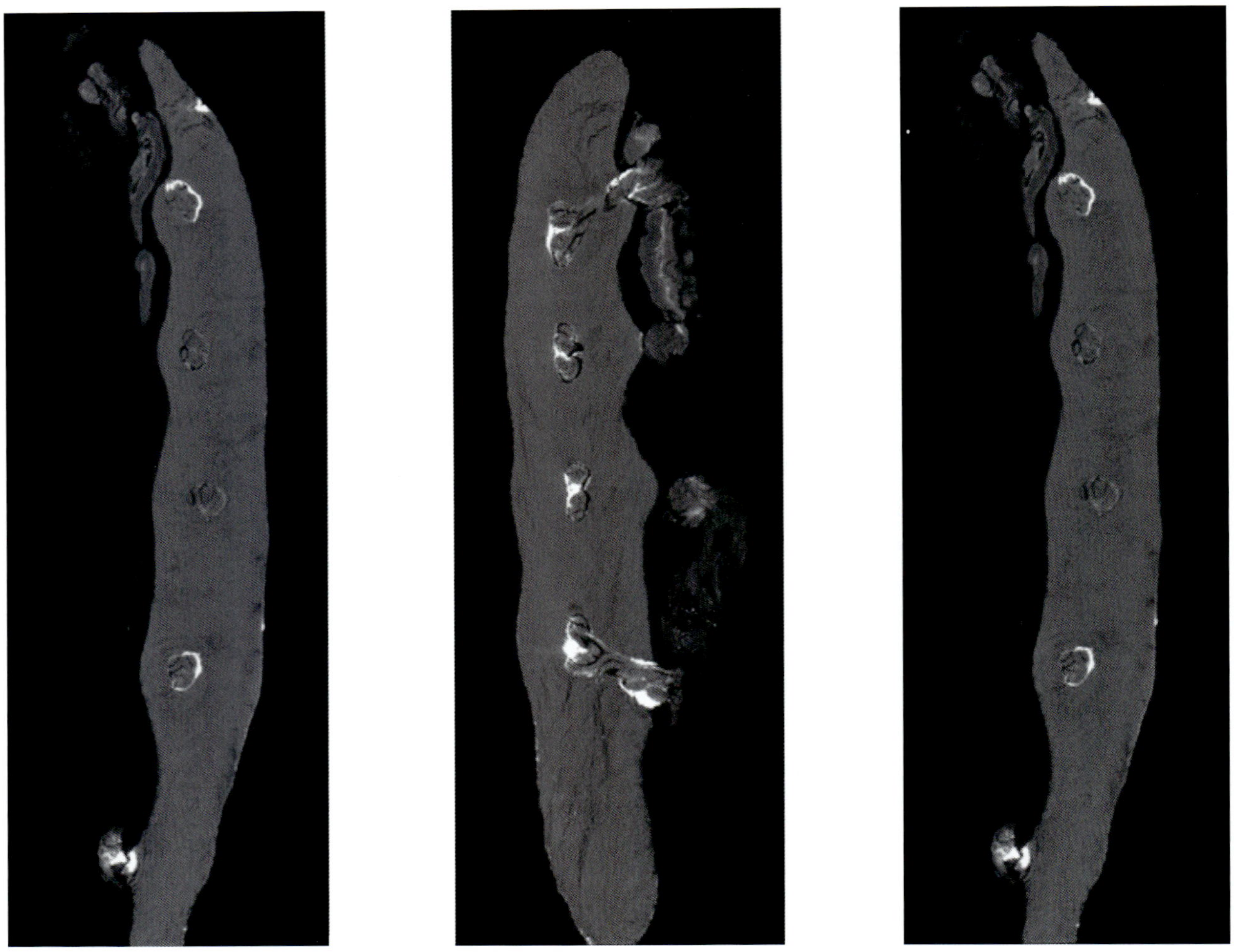

Fig. 4. CT scans of the object Gr11Q9/1

In order to further clarify the nature of the object it was micro-scanned by X-ray computed tomography (CT), and images here reproduced show three different cuts (Figure 4: a, b and c). These indicate also the conglomeration of high-density residue in the 6 knots more clearly. These conclusively show that the object is entirely solid. It is not made up of a folded piece of skin but it is one thick piece of organic tissue.

Following this, further observation by eye and under the microscope in the laboratory confirmed that there are no joins anywhere on the object, and no features on the surface that would indicate skin (such as pores or hair follicles). The object was photographed for the purposes of research records and for further study.

The organic material has rounded edges that are intact throughout. Its thickness is entirely composed of solid tissue through which the string has been passed and knotted. The string may indicate that it was sewn on to another object (either Gr11Q9/2 or something else), though this cannot be proven. Around the edges of two of the holes, however, it is possible to see what appears to be a congealed substance or remains of an organic connecting tube (Figure 5). It was thought that the nature of the organic tissue was not possible to determine without incisions that would damage the object. However, it would best correspond with an internal organ of the body of an animal (see below).

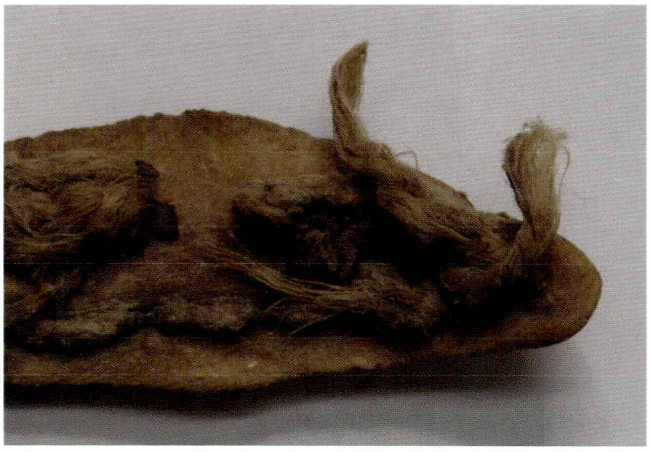

Fig. 5. Gr11Q9/1 magnification showing congealed substance or connecting tube between string knots (Photo by J.E. Taylor)

GrA	Sample Name	Age BP	Error ±	∂13C
64961	Gr11Q9/1	190	50	-24.40
64963	Gr11Q9/2	210	60	-24.96

Tab. 1. Radiocarbon results by Prof. Johannes van der Plicht at the Centre for Isotope Research

2.2 *Gr11Q9/2*

A second associated object (IAA464629) also has string passed through it, and the two objects may originally have been connected (see above). Gr11Q9/2 is smaller than Gr11Q9/1. It is only 4.35 cm long and 2.25 cm wide (without the string counted; 3.1 cm with the string), and weighs 4.06 g. It has a thickness of 1.5 cm.

This item is not made up of one substance, but has layers of different materials. This was clear under microscopic analysis and may be seen in Figure 6.

The lower level is a 'base' of linen string wound up to form a kind of loose knot. On this there appears to be organic tissue which is slightly decomposed to a black substance resembling bitumen at one end. This appearance is similar to leather scrolls which decompose to a similar substance.[1] On top of this the material may be bone or solidified fatty tissue of animal origin.

Fig. 6. Gr11Q9/2 magnification showing layers of organic material. (Photo by J.E. Taylor)

3. Radiocarbon Dating of Gr11Q9/1 and 2

Pieces of string from both these artefacts were taken for radiocarbon dating, with results determined in July 2015. The string from the objects was examined by Prof. Johannes van der Plicht at the Centre for Isotope Research, Groningen University, and radiocarbon results were obtained as indicated in Tab. 1 (see Appendix to this chapter). The results indicated that the objects were relatively modern in date. In order to verify these surprising results, another sample from Gr11Q9/1 was tested again in 2016 as part of the run of tests on 11Q linen with veritably identical results.[2] This shows conclusively that the objects were deposited in modern times, and are not ancient.

Given the nature of the results, it needs to be noted that the dating allows for the small possibility of these items being deposited even up to 1956 (and also from c.1642 onwards), but the highest probabilities (47.7%) are concentrated in the period 1724-1815. In addition, the description of the item as 'très durci', at the time of its discovery, corroborated by the actual appearance of the objects now, indicate that they were already extremely dried out (aged) at the time of their discovery. The objects were not considered by the excavators to be recent deposits, but part of a repertoire of ancient remains. The objects contain fine dust from the cave earth, indicating that they were dug up, like the other artefacts. Intrusive particles have also impregnated the string. The radiocarbon dating then needs to be balanced with such actual observations, in order to determine the most likely range of possible dates for the deposit, and the range of the highest probability some 200 years ago seems therefore most secure.

1. D. Barthélemy and J.T. Milik, *Qumran Cave 1* (DJD 1; Oxford: Clarendon, 1955), 7, 39.

2. See Taylor et al., "The Radiocarbon Dates of Samples from Qumran Cave 11Q," in this volume.

This is highly significant in terms of understanding the artefact repertoire of Cave 11Q, and it means we need to consider more recent times for objects found within it. If the cave was accessible in modern times (and perhaps for centuries before) then objects may have been taken out as well as taken in.

4. The Nature of the Objects Gr11Q9/1 and 2

One possible clue to the nature of the objects may be found in the knots, in that objects defined as 'knots' were used in healing and magic from antiquity and into modern Bedouin practice. In antiquity the most famous example is the Hercules knot that was believed to aid the healing of wounds (*Nat. Hist.* 28: 17 [63-64]).[3] Such knots could combine string and organic material: Pliny notes that sores caused by riding could be cured by three horse hairs tied in three knots, placed on the wound (*Nat. Hist.* 28: 61 [218]). To aid someone's recovery from quartan fever, a caterpillar is wrapped in linen and bound by a thread with three knots (*Nat. Hist.* 30: 30 [102]). A patient should make four or three knots on a heliotropium plant for quartan or tertian fever respectively, while offering a prayer that s/he may recover to untie them (Pliny, *Nat. Hist.* 22: 29 [61]). Seven or nine knots from a thread on a loom, each one named after a widow, should be attached to tumours on the groin (Pliny, *Nat Hist.* 28: 12 [48]). In the Egyptian magical text Papyrus Leiden I: 348, spells 4, 8 and 10 define knots for cures, and these knots are to be tied on to the body: to a big toe, foot or throat respectively.[4] The use of such knots as evidenced in Hebrew literature has been explored by Gandz.[5] Trachtenberg notes:

> binding knots was a common homeopathic device, and even served as a description of magic, which, in the Talmud, was said to consist of 'binding and loosing.' In the book of Daniel (5:12, 16) the ability 'to loose knots' is listed as one of the magician's accomplishments.[6]

The reference here is to Dan. 5:12 and 16 concerns the Aramaic expression מְשָׁרֵא קִטְרִין, 'untying knots', which in the LXX is found likewise as 'loosing knots', λύων συνδέσμους. Trachtenberg continues:

> Talmudic literature contains several examples of this knot-magic, and the commentaries on the well-known reference in the Koran (Sura 113) to the magical use of knots relate that a Jewish magician bewitched Mohammed by tying knots, so that he became weak, refused food and neglected his wives. Nor was the physical act of tying a knot required; the magician could produce the same effect by word of mouth.[7]

Trachtenberg's reference to 'Talmudic literature' refers to the use of the word שרא in relation to undoing spells (e.g. j.Moed 3: 81d; j.Sanh. 7: 25d).

While this makes a knot amulet appropriate for an assemblage from the Roman period, the 'knot spell' is one of the foundations of Arab magical practice.[8] Two Quranic Suras, known as *al-Mu'awwadhateyn*, are supplications for refuge and protection, in which there are prayers against those who 'blow upon knots': 'The Daybreak' (*al-Falaq*) and 'Mankind' (*al-Nas*) (Quran 2: 255, 113: 1-5 and 114: 1-6).[9] Relevant here is what Shah notes regarding how knots can also be used for cures:

> Just as evil can be 'bound' into knotted thread, so can good be done by the same means. Among the Central Asian [Arab] tribes, illness is cured by 'blowing upon knots'; and there is a regular ritual attached to the whole thing. A three-coloured cord is spun, in green, blue and red; one knot is tied every day. After seven days the spell is buried in an inaccessible spot, and the disease will then disappear.[10]

---

3. H. Clark Kee, *Medicine, Miracle and Magic in New Testament Times* (Cambridge: Cambridge University Press, 1988), 105-6. It was even used in the entrances to synagogues, G. Bohak, *Ancient Jewish Magic: A History* (Cambridge: Cambridge University Press, 2008), 322.

4. J.F. Borghouts, *The Magical Texts of Papyrus Leiden 1.348* (Leiden: Brill, 1971), 17-9.

5. S. Gandz, "The Knot in Hebrew Literature, or from the Knot to the Alphabet," *Isis* 14/1 (1930) 189-214.

6. J. Trachtenberg, *Jewish Magic and Superstition: A Study in Folk Religion* (New York: Behrman's Jewish Book House, 1939), 127, and see Bohak, *Ancient Jewish Magic*, 263, 272.

7. Trachtenberg, *Jewish Magic*, 127.

8. I. Shah, *Oriental Magic* (London: Octagon, 1956), 81-2; R. Campbell Thompson, *Semitic Magic: Its Origins and Development* (Luzac's Oriental Religions Series 3; London: Luzac & Co., 1908), 164-73, connects ancient knot magic with modern instances he encountered during the course of his research.

9. Shah, *Oriental Magic*, 82; A. Abu-Rabia, "The Evil Eye and Cultural Beliefs among the Bedouin Tribes of the Negev, Middle East," *Folklore* 116/3 (2005) 241-54, on p. 245.

10. Shah, *Oriental Magic*, 82.

While the knots can then be understood as forming amulets, they are in Gr11Q9/1 and 2 combined with the internal body parts of animals. That animal body parts could form parts of amulets/ligatures is identified in the 8th-9th century work of Costa ben Luca (Qusta Ibn Luca, a Syrian Melkite), *De physicis ligaturis*. They are found also in the 11th-century studies of Avicenna and the work of the 14th century scholar Ibn al-Durayhim, titled *Kitāb al-Manāfi' al-Ḥayawān*, 'Book on the Usefulness of Animals'. Given such attestations, it is most likely that these objects Gr11Q9/1 and 2 are to be identified as 'knot amulets' involving animal body parts. These may have been purposely buried in the cave.

5. Related Artefact

Marcello Fidanzio has kindly made available a photograph showing one of the excavators of Cave 11Q observing an object that seems to have a similar shape to item Gr11Q9/1 (Figure 7). However, it is not possible to match the outline of the shape in the photograph exactly with the known objects of this type in the current holdings of the IAA. For example, the item in the photograph appears slightly larger than Gr11Q9/1, there is a hole on the left side, the upper part is more rounded and the lower part is longer. The photograph is indistinct, and it is also not possible to distinguish any string attached to what may also be an animal organ of some kind, but a small part of the object being held seems indicated between the fingers of the man who holds it. This would suggest an additional small extension attached in some way, as Gr11Q9/2 may have been attached to Gr11Q9/1. At the present time this object is lost.

Fig. 7. Detail of photograph showing an item found during 11Q excavations, similar in shape to Gr11Q9/1.

Chapter Five B
Appendix

The Radiocarbon Dating of String from Gr11Q9/1 and 2

Johannes VAN DER PLICHT

In July 2015 two small pieces of linen string were taken from items Gr11Q9/1 and 2 respectively and were sent to the Centre for Isotope Research, Groningen University, for radiocarbon dating. A second test was completed in 2016 on string from Gr11Q9/1 in order to verify the results, as part of the run of tests done on the textiles from the cave[1].

1. Radiocarbon methodology

Before the actual ^{14}C measurement, the sample materials have to be chemically pretreated in order to isolate the datable fraction, and to remove contaminants. The routine treatment of samples consists the so-called "AAA" treatment: Acid-Alkali-Acid.[2]

Both linen samples Gr11Q9 however were too delicate to undergo this full treatment; this would dissolve all material. In such cases the cleaning is limited to "A", only one gentle acid bath (4% HCl at room temperature).

After the chemical pretreatment, the samples are combusted into CO_2 by an Elemental Analyzer (EA), coupled on-line with a stable isotope Mass Spectrometer (MS). The EA is also used for purifying the CO_2; the MS provides precise measurements of the $\delta^{13}C$-values.

Subsequently, the CO_2 is reduced to graphite by reacting under excess H_2 gas.[3] This graphite is then pressed into target holders which are placed in the ion source of the AMS (Accelerator Mass Spectrometer). The Groningen AMS facility is based on a 2.5 MV accelerator, and measures the ^{14}C concentration in the graphite.[4]

The results are reported in conventional Radiocarbon years (BP), which includes correction for isotopic fractionation and usage of the conventional half-life[5].

1. See Van der Plicht *et al.* in this volume.
2. M.G. Mook and H.J. Streurmann, "Physical and Chemical Aspects of Radiocarbon Dating," in W.G. Mook and H.T. Waterbolk (ed.), *Proceedings of the First International Symposium ^{14}C and Archaeology, Groningen 1981* (PACT 8; Strasbourg: Council of Europe, 1983) 31-55.
3. A.T. Aerts-Bijma, J. van der Plicht, and H.A.J. Meijer, "Automatic AMS Sample Combustion and CO_2 Collection," *Radiocarbon* 43/2A (2001) 293-8.
4. J. van der Plicht et al., "Status Report: The Groningen AMS Facility," *NIM B* 172 (2000) 58-65.
5. W.G. Mook and J. van der Plicht, "Reporting ^{14}C Activities and Concentrations," *Radiocarbon* 41/3 (1999) 227-39.

The ^{14}C dates (reported in BP) are calibrated into calendar ages using the presently recommended calibration curve IntCal13. [6] Both results (Gr11Q9/1 and Gr11Q9/2) are practically the same 190 ± 50 and 210 ± 60 respectively. Assuming they represent the same event, they can be averaged with result 200 ± 40 BP.

The calibration yields many possibilities between 1650 AD and modern times, because the natural ^{14}C content is strongly varying for this timeframe. Formally, the result is 1655-1680, 1740-1805, and 1935-1955. All numbers quoted here are rounded to the nearest 5, at 1-sigma (68.2%) confidence.

The calibration is shown in Figure 1. The ^{14}C timescale is plotted vertically, the calendar timescale horizontally. The (averaged) ^{14}C date is plotted in red; the calibration curve is the blue line. In grey is the probability distribution of the calibrated ^{14}C dates.

Given the surprising results for the researchers, it was decided to run a second radiocarbon test on string from Gr11Q9/1 in 2016. The same process was followed in regard to this test, and the results were very similar (see Figure 2). All three dates (Gr11Q9/1, 9/2 and again 9/1) yield the same date within error. The averaged result for the three is 220 BP with a measurement error of 30 (number rounded to 5). This means that the 14C measurement must be correct, there are no mistakes (like mixing up samples, wrong chemistry, wrong normalisation, etc). The linen string is sub-recent.

6. P.J. Reimer et al., "IntCal13 and Marine13 Radiocarbon Age Calibration Curves 0-50,000 Years cal BP," *Radiocarbon* 55/4 (2013) 1869-87.

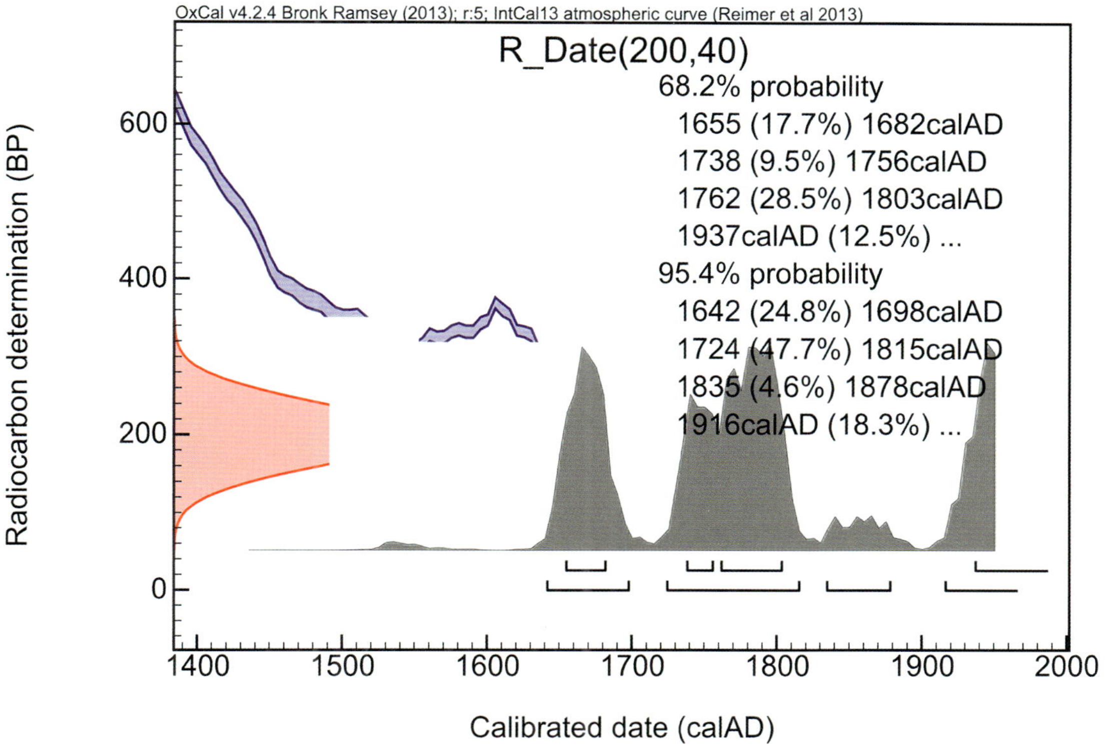

Fig. 1. Calibration curve showing averaged results on Gr11Q9/1 and Gr11Q9/2 linen thread

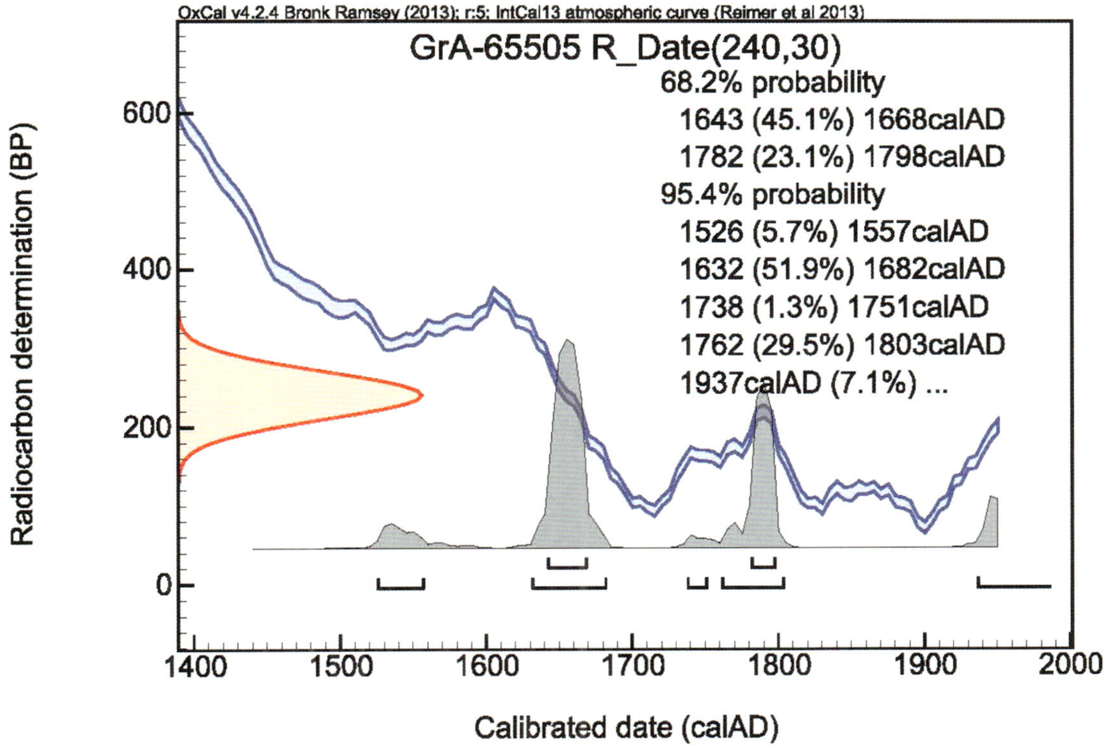

Fig. 2. Calibration curve for results of re-testing Gr11Q9/1

Chapter Six

The Radiocarbon Dates of Samples from Qumran Cave 11Q

Joan E. TAYLOR, Johannes VAN DER PLICHT, Kaare LUND RASMUSSEN, Naama SUKENIK, Orit SHAMIR, and Mireille BÉLIS

With permission from Jean-Baptiste Humbert (EBAF), Mireille Bélis (EBAF), and Orit Shamir (IAA), a batch of new radiocarbon tests were run in 2015 and 2016 to determine the dates of items from Cave 11Q. Samples were chosen and cut by Naama Sukenik at the IAA Organic Materials Unit, in collaboration with Joan Taylor of King's College London.[1] The tests were run at the Center for Isotope Research, Groningen University, under the supervision of Johannes van der Plicht, with a prior examination for chemical characteristics done under the supervision of Kaare Lund Rasmussen, Department of Physics, Chemistry and Pharmacy at the University of Southern Denmark. Additionally, with permission from Martin Schøyen, a sample from the Temple Scroll (11Q19) wrapper was acquired from the Schøyen Collection, Norway, and this was by agreement published initially in a volume dedicated to objects within this archive.[2] Funding was obtained from King's College London, Department of Theology and Religious Studies, supplemented by the Leverhulme International Network for Dispersed Qumran Caves Artefacts and Archives (a partnership between Joan E. Taylor, Marcello Fidanzio and Dennis Mizzi).

1. 11Q Samples

In Cave 11Q a large number of pieces of linen were discovered, in quite good condition. These linen fragments are now conserved in the holdings of the IAA's Organic Materials Unit, Jerusalem. Some of these have blue lines associated with scroll wrappers, while some may be from jar covers or from packing pieces. It was not absolutely clear that all these should be dated to the Roman period. For example, it was noted that one of these pieces (Gr11Q132, IAA 577293) is unusual in that it has a kind of mending which is very rare in Judaea during the Roman period and has been found in only one imported textile wrapper from Masada.[3] This mending, using two sewing threads, often ignores the warp and weft direction.[4]

1. We are grateful also to Gregory Doudna for his comments on a draft of this paper.

2. J.E. Taylor and J. van der Plicht, "Radiocarbon Dating of the Temple Scroll Wrapper and Cave 11Q," in T. Elgvin, K. Davis, and M. Langlois (ed.), *Gleanings from the Caves: Dead Sea Scrolls and Artefacts from The Schøyen Collection* (LSTS 71; London: Bloomsbury T&T Clark, 2016) 351-6.

3. A. Sheffer and H. Granger-Taylor, "Textiles from Masada: A Preliminary Selection," in J. Aviram, G. Foerster, and E. Netzer (ed.), *Masada IV: The Yigael Yadin Excavations 1963-1965: Final Reports* (Jerusalem: Israel Exploration Society/Hebrew University, 1994) 149-256, on pp. 223-5.

4. F. Letellier-Willemin, "The Long and Narrow Sleeved Tunic of the Mummy W14 of El Deir," in A. de Moor, C. Fluck, and P. Linscheid (ed.), *Textiles, Tools and Techniques of the 1st*

Six 11Q linen samples were taken for analysis (see Table 1), including the piece (Gr11Q132) that was thought might indicate a later period of occupation. They are as follows:

1. Bundle of strings (Gr11Q98) that are tied together. The fibres have been identified as flax (*Linum usitatissimum L.*). The string is made with two S–spun (clockwise direction) threads in Z ply (s2Z). The colour of the strings is very white and this probably indicates bleaching.

2. Fragment of textile (Gr11Q119).
Measurements: 12.5 cm x 10 cm. The fibres have been identified as flax (*Linum usitatissimum* L.) and the threads (warp and weft) were made in S-spun (clockwise direction) in tabby weaving. The colour of the textile is beige-white and this probably indicates bleaching. A few unidentified grey and purple stains were observed.[5]

3. Fragment of beige textile (Gr11Q132).
Measurements: 21.5 cm x 9 cm. The fibres have been identified as flax (*Linum usitatissimum* L.) and the threads (warp and weft) were made in S-spun (clockwise direction) in weft faced weaving, with warp predominating. In two places it has mending.

4. Fragment of textile (Gr11Q107).
Measurements: 6 cm x 4 cm. It is cut fabric in a square shape. The fibres have been identified as flax (*Linum usitatissimum* L.) and the threads (warp and weft) were made in S-spun (clockwise direction) in tabby weave. The textile is decorated with a faded blue band, composed of three rows of weft threads (as for example textile no. 43 from Cave 1Q[6]). The color of the textile is beige-white and this probably indicates bleaching.

5. Fragment of textile (Gr11Q76).
Measurements: 4 cm x 1.5cm. The fibres have been identified as flax (*Linum usitatissimum L.*) and the threads (warp and weft) were made in S-spun (clockwise direction) in tabby weave. The colour of the textile is very white and this probably indicates bleaching.

6. Fragment of linen textile (Gr11Q101).
Measurements: 7 cm x 3.8 cm. The fibres have been identified as flax (*Linum usitatissimum* L.) and the threads (warp and weft) were made in S-spun (clockwise direction) in tabby weave. The textile has a crowded selvedge that is made of warp threads without any special reinforcement. The colour of the textile is very white and this probably indicates bleaching.

In addition, there was one further sample included in the batch:

7. A piece of linen (IAA 585785) from the Christmas Cave, in the Wadi en-Nar (Kidron). From the splicing technique of the textile[7] it appears that this textile comes from the Chalcolithic/Early Bronze period. It was thought to be important because it could provide a more accurate dating within this period, and could function as an interesting comparison to the 11Q linen.

Samples (10, 11) were previously taken of objects Gr11Q9/1 and Gr11Q9/2[8] and a further sample of linen string from Gr11Q9/1 (8) was tested to ensure there was no error. As noted, a sample was also previously taken of the Temple Scroll wrapper in the Schøyen collection (MS 5095/1) and published elsewhere,[9] and this is included in Table 1 for completeness.

In terms of the any possible contamination of the linen samples, IAA conservator Raia Viniski explained that the linen from Cave 11Q did not require extensive cleaning, which is significant in a cave that was accessible to bats and covered in bat guano, since it cannot then have been covered with dung and substance. Some textiles were dirty with soil and dust

Millennium AD from Egypt and Neighbouring Countries: Proceedings of the 8th Conference of the Research Group 'Textiles from the Nile Valley': Antwerp, 4th-6th October 2013 (Tielt: Lannoo Publishers, 2015) 26-37, on p. 32.

5. For similar stains see M. Bélis, "The Unpublished Textiles from the Qumran Caves," in M. Fidanzio (ed.), *The Caves of Qumran: Proceedings of the International Conference, Lugano 2014* (STDJ 118; Leiden: Brill 2016) 123-36, on p. 133.

6. G.M. Crowfoot, "The Linen Textiles," in D. Barthélemy and J.T. Milik, *Qumran Cave 1* (DJD 1; Oxford: Clarendon, 1955) 18-38, on p. 35.

7. See O. Shamir, "Textiles from the Chalcolithic Period, Early and Middle Bronze Age in the Southern Levant - The Continuation of Splicing," *ATR* 57 (2015) 12-25, on p. 17, Fig. 6.

8. See J. Taylor, "Organic Items from Cave 11Q: B. Gr11Q9/1 and 2," in this volume.

9. Taylor and van der Plicht, "Radiocarbon Dating."

(perhaps from the Bedouin excavations), but not dung. This is different to the condition of linen found in Cave 1Q which reportedly was quite smelly and dirty, having been sometimes found under a thick layer of dung.[10] It is therefore unlikely that the 11Q textiles were exposed to the open cave environment for very long. Either they were protected below rockfall or they were pieces removed from jars and strewn in the cave as a result of the Bedouin's activities prior to the arrival of the archaeologists. The textiles required merely light cleaning (only with alcohol, as verified by Dr. Viniksi) and this good condition makes them particularly useful for radiocarbon dating.

2. Pre-testing of the Samples

The samples were all tested prior to radiocarbon treatment by Py-GC-MS in the search for conservational fluids or other modern contaminants. No contaminants were found. A second check of the possible presence of contaminants is tracing by the stable isotope of Carbon, ^{13}C (see next paragraph). These δ^{13}C values are all within the expected range.

3. The Radiocarbon Dating of the Samples

Dating by Radiocarbon (^{14}C) of organic samples provides a measure of time, to be more precise: the moment of death of the organism. Successful dating depends on the samples being cleaned thoroughly because they may contain foreign carbon with a different ^{14}C content, such as carbonate, humic substances and/or plant remains, and preservatives as applied in e.g. museums. These components must be removed in order to obtain the correct radiocarbon age of the organic material itself. Standard procedures for the chemical pretreatment of samples have been developed and are applied by all ^{14}C laboratories.[11]

The standard treatment of samples consists of the following steps: (i) Acid (HCl) in order to remove soil carbonate and possibly infiltrated humic acids; (ii) Alkali (NaOH) to remove e.g. soil humates; (iii) Acid (HCl) to remove any atmospheric CO_2 absorbed during step (ii). This pretreatment is referred to as the "AAA" (Acid-Alkali-Acid) treatment.

The pretreated and purified sample fraction is combusted into CO_2 gas using an Elemental Analyser, coupled to an Isotope Ratio Mass Spectrometer (IsoCube/IsoPrime). This EA/IRMS also provides the stable Carbon isotope value δ^{13}C. This is given as so-called delta-values, or δ^{13}C, defined as the deviation of the $^{13}C/^{12}C$ ratio from that of a standard material, expressed in permil.[12]

For ^{14}C analysis, part of the CO_2 is routed to a cryogenic trap to collect the samples for further processing. The CO_2 is transformed into graphite powder by the reaction $CO_2 + 2H_2 \rightarrow 2H_2O + C$ at a temperature of 600°C and using Fe powder as catalyst.[13]

Next, the graphite is pressed into target holders for the ion source of the AMS (Accelerator Mass Spectrometer). The Groningen AMS is based on a 2.5 MV particle accelerator built by High Voltage Engineering Europa.[14] The AMS measures the $^{14}C/^{12}C$ and $^{13}C/^{12}C$ isotope ratios of the graphite. From these numbers, the conventional ^{14}C age is determined.

By definition, the conventional ^{14}C age is based on the Libby halflife value, an international oxalic acid standard as a reference material and correction for isotopic fractionation using $^{13}C/^{12}C$. For a detailed explanation we refer to the literature.[15] These conventional ages are reported in the ^{14}C unit of time BP. The latter is not synchronous with calendar time because of past fluctuations in the natural ^{14}C concentration.[16]

10. J.E. Taylor et al., "Qumran Textiles in the Palestine Exploration Fund, London: Radiocarbon Dating Results," *PEQ* 137 (2005) 159-67.

11. W.G. Mook and H.J. Streurman, "Physical and Chemical Aspects of Radiocarbon Dating," in W.G. Mook and H.T. Waterbolk (ed.), *Proceedings of the First International Symposium ^{14}C and Archaeology, Groningen, 1981* (PACT 8; Strasbourg: Council of Europe, 1983) 31-55; M. van Styrdonck et al., "What's in a ^{14}C Date?," in J. Evin (ed.), *Actes du 3ème Congrès International ^{14}C et Archéologie, Lyon, 6-10 avril 1998* (Paris: Société Préhistorique Française, 1999) 433-48.

12. W.G. Mook, *Introduction to Isotope Hydrology: Stable and Radioactive Isotopes of Hydrogen, Carbon, and Oxygen* (London: Taylor and Francis, 2006).

13. A.T. Aerts-Bijma, J. van der Plicht, and H.A.J. Meijer, "Automatic AMS Sample Combustion and CO_2 Collection," *Radiocarbon* 43/2A (2001) 293-8.

14. J. van der Plicht et al., "Status Report: The Groningen AMS facility," *NIM B* 172 (2000) 58-65.

15. W.G. Mook and and J. van der Plicht, "Reporting ^{14}C Activities and Concentrations," *Radiocarbon* 41/3 (1999) 227-39.

16. For a treatise on "absolute dating" related to Qumran, we refer to J. van der Plicht and K.L. Rasmussen, "Radiocar-

For absolute dates, the conventional ^{14}C ages need to be calibrated into calendar ages. Calibration curves are obtained by paired dating of samples by ^{14}C and by dendrochronology, the latter being absolute. The presently recommended calibration curve is IntCal13.[17]

The calibration curve is non-linear, as can be seen in the example plot shown below (Figure 1). This results in non-gaussian probability distributions for the calendar age, sometimes yielding multiple solutions. The calibrated ages are reported in calBC or calAD, or simply BC or AD. All numbers (BP and BC/AD [for BCE/CE])[18] are rounded to the nearest 5. The measurement uncertainties are given as 1-sigma (68.2% confidence level).

The results of the dating are shown in Table 1. It shows the sample description, the IAA (Jerusalem) number, the KLR (Odense) number, the GrA (Groningen) number, the material analysed, the chemical treatment, the ^{14}C age (in BP) and its measurement uncertainty (1-sigma), the stable isotope ratio $\delta^{13}C$ (in ‰), the organic carbon content (C%) and the calibrated age in BC/AD (1-sigma range).

No samples could receive the full chemical pretreatment (AAA): 4% HCl, 1% NaOH and again 4% HCl, all at room temperature. They received only the first acid bath (A only) because they were very small or delicate or both. They would not survive the full treatment.

In general, good indicators for sample material integrity is the organic carbon content (the C% value) and the stable isotope content (the $\delta^{13}C$ value). Samples 10 and 11 (Gr11Q9/1 and Gr11Q9/2 = GrA-64961 and 64963) show a low C% value, which means the material (string) is partly degraded. In addition, these samples were very small, yielding larger measurement uncertainties. The measured $\delta^{13}C$ values are all within the expected range, and this lends credence that the pre-treatment procedure has been effective.

The calibrated age is given as 1-sigma range. To explain the calibration curve, Figure 1 is chosen as an illustration, representing Sample 1 (linen string sample, Gr11Q98 = GrA-65493 = QM GIIQ). The radiocarbon date (2160 ± 30 BP) is plotted in red along the vertical axis, the calibrated date in black along the horizontal axis. The relevant part of the calibration curve – the relationship between ^{14}C time and calendar time, IntCal13 – is shown in blue. The calibrated age range for this date is 350-300 and 230-165 BC. Both the ^{14}C age in BP, and the calibrated age range in calAD are reported at 1-sigma confidence level, with numbers rounded to the nearest significant 5, as in Table 1. At 2-sigma, the calibrated age range would be 358-279 and 259-108 BC.

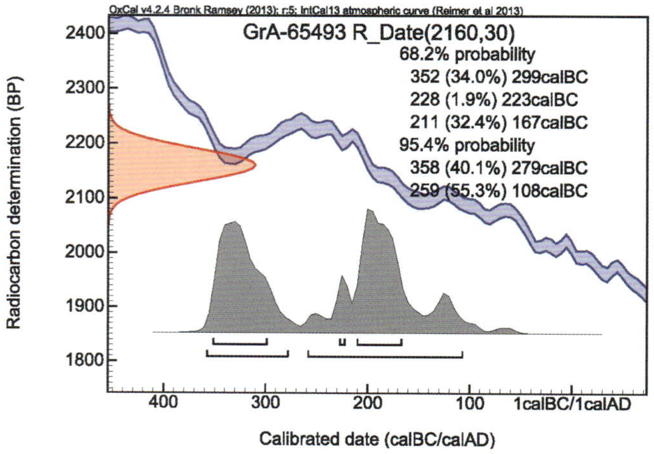

Fig. 1. Calibration curve for Sample 1: 11Q linen string, Gr11Q98, GrA 65493.

Figures 2-7 illustrate the calibration curves for the remainder of the linen samples tested, excepting Samples 8, 9 and 10 (Gr11Q9/1 and Gr11Q9/2; GrA-64961, 64963 and 65505; IAA nr. 464628 and 464629) which appear elsewhere in this volume in a separate discussion of these objects. These samples yielding subrecent datesoriginate from a time characterised by large and prolonged fluctuations in the natural ^{14}C content, going over in modern times with ^{14}C influenced by anthropogenic effects (fossil fuels and nuclear bomb tests). The calibration yields 3 eras, ca. 1660, ca. 1770 and younger than 1920.

bon Dating and Qumran," in J. Gunneweg, A. Adriaens, and J. Dik (ed.), *Holistic Qumran: Trans-Disciplinary Research of Qumran and the Dead Sea Scrolls: Proceedings of the NIAS-Lorentz Center Qumran Workshop 21-25 April 2008* (STDJ 87; Leiden: Brill, 2010) 99-121; and J. van der Plicht, "Radiocarbon dating and the Dead Sea Scrolls: A Comment on 'Redating'," *DSD* 14 (2007) 77-89.

17. P.J. Reimer et al., "IntCal13 and Marine13 Radiocarbon Age Calibration Curves 0-50,000 Years cal BP," *Radiocarbon* 55/4 (2013) 1869-87.

18. Note that in this chapter the conventional laboratory use of BC/AD is adopted except where historical discussion takes place.

Table 1

	Material	Inventory No.	IAA No.	Visual identifier at time of sampling (J.E. Taylor)	Sample identifier	KLR nr.	GrA nr.	Treatment	14C age (BP)	Sigma	δ13C (‰)	C%	Calibrated age at 1 sigma
1	11Q linen string	Gr11Q98	577250	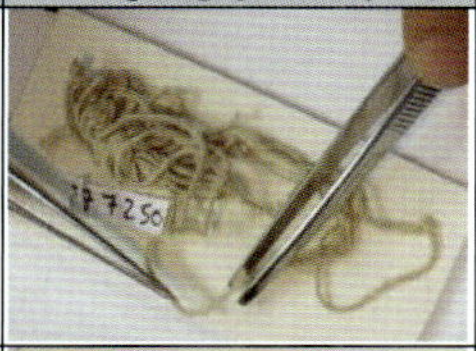	QM GIIQ	10423	65493	A	2160	30	-25.81	42.2	350-300, 230-165 BC
2	11Q linen	Gr11Q119	577264		QII	10424	65494	A	2085	30	-25.14	41.6	160-55 BC
3	11Q linen	Gr11Q132	577293		QII	10425	65495	A	1925	30	-25.11	41.9	55-125 AD
4	11Q linen	Gr11Q107	577252		QMGII	10426	65496	A	1990	30	-25.72	40.8	35 BC - 50 AD
5	11Q linen	Gr11Q76	577220	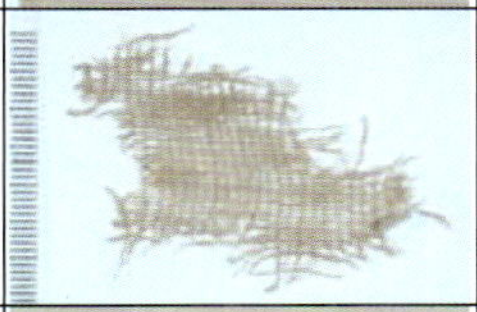	QMGII	10427	65497	A	2110	30	-24.84	42.9	180-90 BC
6	11Q linen	Gr11Q101	577245		QMGII	10428	65498	A	2025	30	-25.37	42.2	55 BC - 20 AD
7	Christmas Cave Linen		585785		QCC 585 785	10430	65501	A	4745	35	-24.32	43.1	3635-3515, 3395-3385 BC
8	11Q-9/1 linen string	Gr11Q9/1	464628	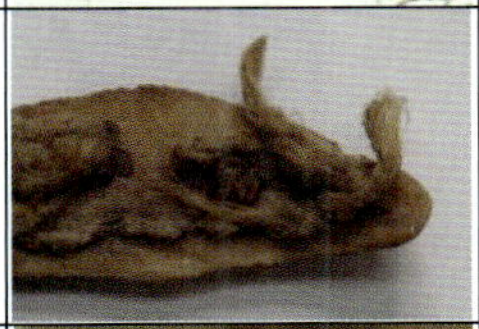	11Q-9/1	10432	65505	A	240	30	-24.30	44.0	1645-1670, 1780-1800 AD
9	Schøyen Linen wrapper		--	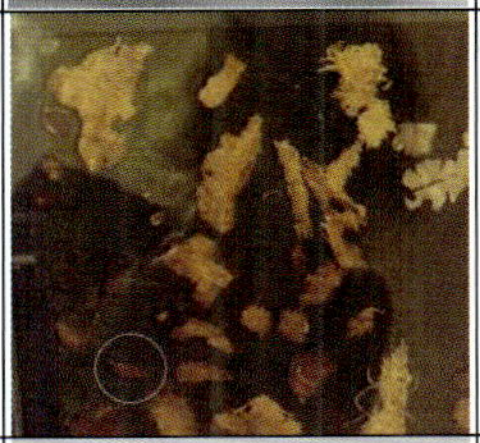	Schøyen 5095/1	--	62331	AAA	1900	30	-25.12	42.4	70-130 AD
10	11Q linen string		464628		11Q-9/1	--	64961	A	190	50	-24.40	29.6	>1655 AD
11	11Q linen String		464629		11Q-9/2	--	64963	A	210	60	-24.96	37.3	>1640 AD

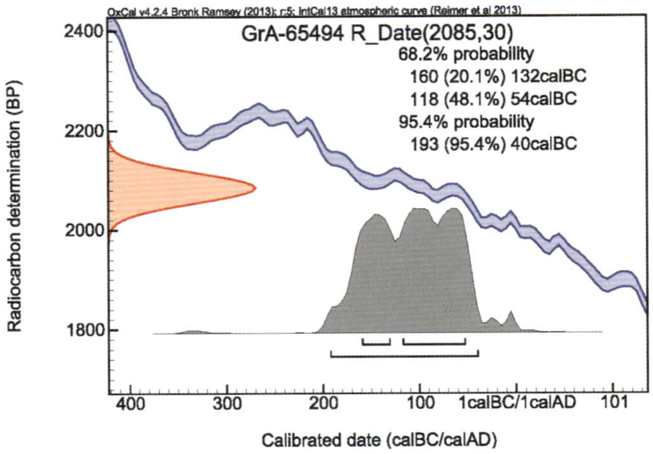

Fig. 2. Calibration curve for Sample 2: 11Q linen, Gr11Q119, GrA 65494

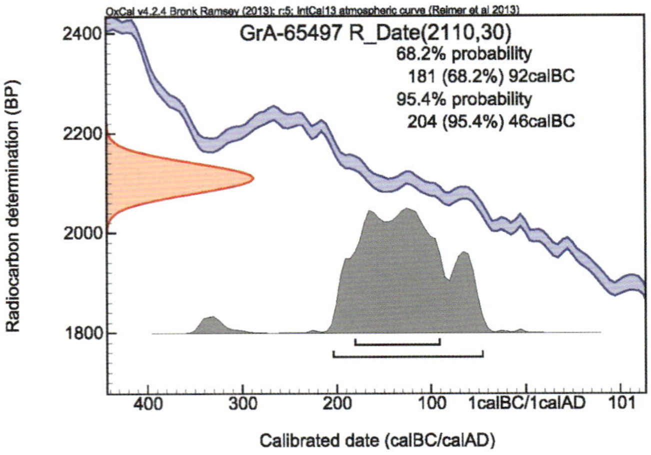

Fig. 5. Calibration curve for Sample 5: 11Q linen, Gr11Q76, GrA 65497

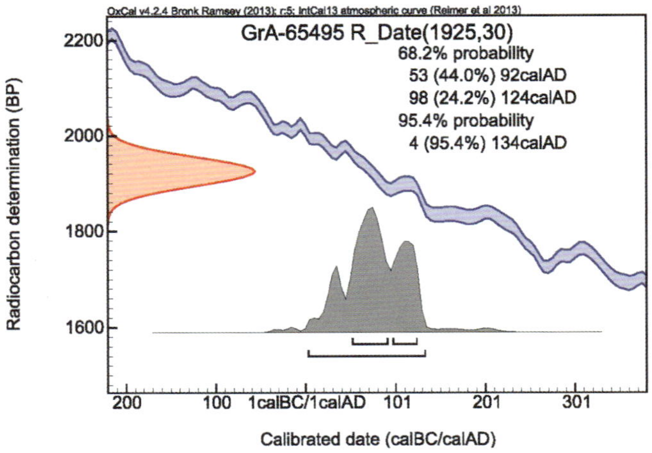

Fig. 3. Calibration curve for Sample 3: 11Q linen, Gr11Q132, GrA 65495

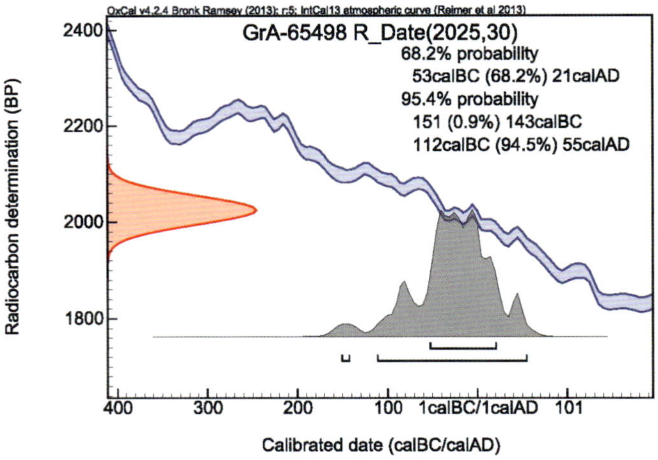

Fig. 6. Calibration curve for Sample 6: 11Q linen, Gr11Q101, GrA 65498

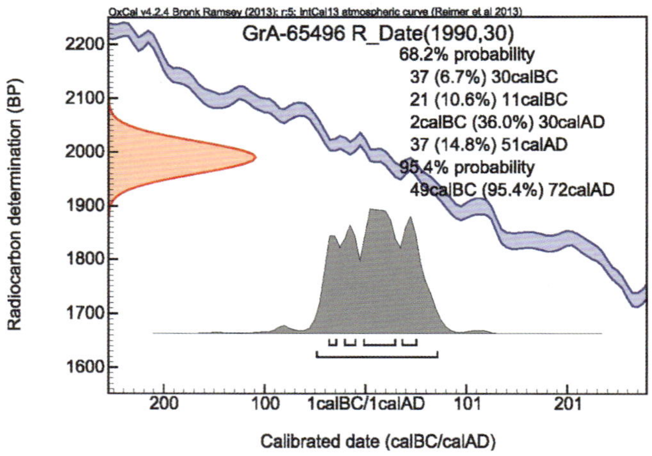

Fig. 4. Calibration curve for Sample 4: 11Q linen, Gr11Q107, GrA 65496

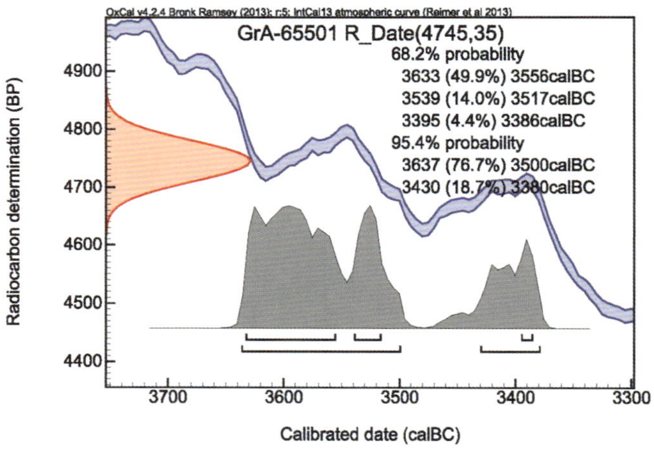

Fig. 7. Calibration curve for Sample 7: Christmas Cave linen, IAA 585785, GrA 65501

4. The Temple Scroll Wrapper

The Temple Scroll (11Q19) wrapper now in the Schøyen collection can be considered along with the dates obtained from material in the IAA holdings. This linen is unusual in being uncleaned, not even with light alcohol. While the main part of the wrapper (MS 5095/2) is preserved in one display unit, Martin Schøyen also retains numerous other small pieces from the wrapper (MS 5095/1) in another case, and permitted one of these to be taken for analysis, on the proviso that it was first published in the volume that focused on his collection.[19] The result from the radiocarbon testing of this wrapper provided a result of 1900 ± 30 BP, calibrated to 70-130 AD at 1 sigma, and 28-214 calAD at 2 sigma (95.4% probability), and within this range 88.5% confidence attached to a date between 50 and 180 calAD.

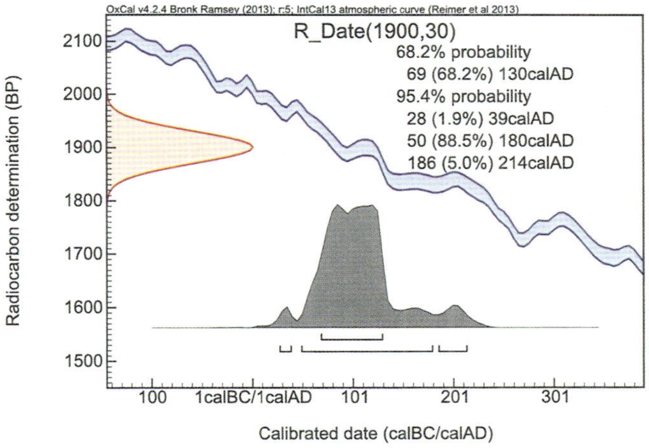

Fig. 8. Calibration curve for the Temple Scroll Wrapper (MS 5095/1).

This result needs to be compared to the radiocarbon date of the Temple Scroll (11Q19) itself. Gelatinised and ungelatinised samples from the manuscript were radiocarbon dated in the ETH Zurich laboratory in 1990 and provided a result of 2024 ± 49 (gelatinised) and 2066 ± 78 (ungelatinised) years BP, giving it an averaged result of 2030 ± 40 years BP, or date range of 97 BC-1 AD at 1 sigma, as calibrated using the dataset of this time.[20] The 2-sigma (95.4% probability) calibration of Gregory Doudna[21] done in 1998 indicated an averaged range of 166 BC-67 AD. Using the IntCal13 atmospheric curve,[22] the date of 2030 ± 40 years BP can now be plotted as providing a range from 164 BC to 57 AD at 2 sigma. The results present the possibility that the scroll was created some time earlier than the wrapper.

19. Taylor and van der Plicht, "Radiocarbon Dating."

20. G. Bonani et al., "Radiocarbon Dating of Fourteen Dead Sea Scrolls," *Radiocarbon* 34/3 (1992) 843-9, on p. 845.

21. G.L. Doudna, "Dating the Scrolls on the Basis of Radiocarbon Analysis," in P.W. Flint and J.C. VanderKam (ed.), *The Dead Sea Scrolls after Fifty Years: A Comprehensive Assessment: Vol. 1* (Leiden: Brill, 1998) 430-71.

22. Reimer et al., "IntCal13." The programme can be accessed at https://c14.arch.oc.ac.uk/oxcal.html.

5. Significance of Radiocarbon Dating Results for Cave 11Q

Radiocarbon dating of the organic materials of the Qumran caves should provide evidence for a clarification of the dating for the manufacture of the items. As noted, a radiocarbon date derives from the time of the death of the plant or animal used in the artefact. In regard to results, the actual date for the death of the organic material should lie before the *latest* date of a radiocarbon dating range. Thus, the date of a piece of linen textile created from flax harvested, prepared and spun in the year 10 CE should be indicated in a radiocarbon dating range in which the latest probable dates include a calibrated date designated as 10 AD at least. The 2 sigma (95.4%) radiocarbon dating results may well begin as late as 1 AD and range much later than this date, and within this range there may be clusters of higher and lower ranges of probabilities for dates, but the range should not start after or end before 10 AD. However, commonly only the 1 sigma range is given for the range, usually rounded to the nearest 5 as here. For more precise purposes the 2 sigma range should be consulted.

In terms of the comparative test sample, the Christmas Cave textile is a very old piece indeed, and in fact derives from the late Chalcolithic period (3637-3500 and 3430-3380 BC at 2 sigma, with a 76.7% probability within the older range). This result is consistent with objects found in the Christmas Cave that date to this era, including textiles.[23]

Hitherto, radiocarbon dating has largely focused on gaining further data to enable precise dating of the time of the writing of the scrolls, which can be used in parallel assessments from palaeography, but the high economic and religious value of scrolls and the difficulties of their manufacture would suggest their 'shelf-life' was comparably longer than textiles. Scroll wrappers may even have been designed for particular scrolls, meaning that their date of manufacture (preparation of linen) could be quite close to the time of the final use or deposit of a scroll. In the study of Shamir and Sukenik[24] it was noted that at least

23. See R. Porat, H. Eshel, and A. Frumkin, "The 'Caves of the Spear': Refuge Caves from the Bar-Kokhba Revolt North of 'En-Gedi," *IEJ* 59 (2009) 21-46; O. Shamir and N. Sukenik, "The Christmas Cave Textiles Compared to Qumran Textiles," *ATN* 51 (2010) 26-30.

24. O. Shamir and N. Sukenik, "Qumran Textiles and the Gar-

some of the linen textiles in the Qumran caves were previously used as garments. The linen textiles from scroll wrappers, packing and jar covers and string ties are particularly useful for radiocarbon dating as textiles usually have a relatively short 'shelf-life',[25] since they are easily worn out by use, thus previously used clothing and textiles then used for packing might have been just 10-20 years old at the time of their use in jars. Packing would normally be done with rags. One would nevertheless expect textile manufacture to be not that long before the time of their arrival in the caves, unless there was a particularly special or little used item of textile kept in storage. The question then is how old that special linen might be.

In terms of textiles and organic remains from Qumran Cave 11Q, a number of radiocarbon tests have already been run.[26] In the tests published in 2006, there were three results obtained from wood samples (from items with IAA numbers 864395 = Gr11Q22a and 864396 = Gr11Q22c).[27] The designation D024 in the published results relates to these.[28] A note associated with these wooden objects written at the time of the sampling defines them as 'D024 G.11 Q22 bois'. It can be readily seen on the pointed wooden artefact Gr11Q22a =864395[29] that two samples were taken from it. These two samples from the same object were then tested separately, and labelled QUM-515 and QUM-516 respectively. Not surprisingly these yielded almost identical results that places the object around the 10th century AD. QUM-515 (D024b) yielded a 68.2% (1 sigma) probability of 890-985 AD and 95.4% (2 sigma) probability of 820-1020 AD; QUM-516 (D024c) yielded a 68.2% (1 sigma) probability dated between 885-980 AD and 95.4% (2 sigma) probability between 770-1020 AD.

The other piece of sampled wood from 11Q (Gr11Q22c = 864396)[30] can also be identified by the cut still visible on the piece. It was identified as a piece of branch, also labelled as D024 (additionally labelled 'a' in the published sequence). The results of the dating of this were 1770-1640 BC (68.2% probability) or 1880-1610 BC (95.4% probability).[31] The piece of the tree, however, may not be assigned to human activity, as it may well be the residue of a living tree that grew proximate to (on top of?) the cave itself, at some point in the past. Cave collapse could have taken roots with it. The changing climatic conditions of the Dead Sea area mean different vegetation would have grown at different times, and the Middle Bronze II-III (c.1750-1550 BC) and the early phase of the Late Bronze periods were a time of comparative humidity with a wetter climate, when the Dead Sea level was also high.[32] Clearly, this item warrants further study by a botanical specialist. The likelihood of artefacts being dated variously may be understood already from what archaeologists have observed. The initial archaeological team already defined at least two earlier periods of cave use on the basis of pottery: part of a Chalcolithic small jar and fragments of jars and two lamps from the Iron Age.[33]

In addition to the three wood samples, three textile samples from 11Q were tested in the same batch of 2004. While the exact IAA numbers were not recorded, these comprised a piece of cotton, given the

ments of Qumran's Inhabitants," *DSD* 18 (2011) 206-25.

25. Y. Yadin, *The Finds from the Bar Kokhba Period in the Cave of Letters* (Jerusalem: Israel Exploration Society, 1963), 171.

26. K.L. Rasmussen et al., "Cleaning and Radiocarbon Dating of Material from Khirbet Qumran," in J. Gunneweg, C. Greenblatt, and A. Adriaens (ed.), *Bio- and Material Cultures at Qumran: Papers from a COST Action G8 Working Group Meeting Held in Jerusalem, Israel on 22-23 May 2005* (Stuttgart: Fraunhofer IRB, 2006) 139-64.

27. Two series of tests were run on the wood samples. In the cleaning of the wood samples, it was noted in regard to the first series of texts that the $\delta^{13}C$-values constituted a warning of the possible presence of contamination. Only the results of the second series, after renewed cleaning are reliable (Rasmussen *et al.*, "Cleaning and Radiocarbon Dating," 147-8).

28. Rasmussen et al., "Cleaning and Radiocarbon Dating," 148-52.

29. See also J. E. Taylor and N. Sukenik, "Organic Materials from Cave 11Q: A. Leather, Basketry, Ropes, Wood and Seeds," in this volume, Table 1.

30. Taylor and Sukenik, "Organic Materials from Cave 11Q."

31. Rasmussen et al., "Cleaning and Radiocarbon Dating," 148-52.

32. D. Langgut et al., "Vegetation and Climate Changes During the Bronze and Iron Ages (~3600-600 BCE) in the Southern Levant Based on Palynological Records," *Radiocarbon* 57/2 (2015) 217-35, on pp. 217, 227-8, 231.

33. R. de Vaux, "Fouilles de Khirbet Qumrân: rapport préliminaire sur les 3e, 4e, et 5e campagnes," *RB* 63 (1956) 533-77, on p. 574; J.-B. Humbert and A. Chambon (ed.), *Fouilles de Khirbet Qumrân et de 'Aïn Feshkha: Vol. I: Album de photographies. Répertoire du fonds photographique. Synthèse des notes de chantier du Père Roland de Vaux OP* (NTOA.SA 1; Fribourg/Göttingen: Éditions Universitaires/Vandenhoeck & Ruprecht, 1994), 265-6, on p. 344; see J.-B. Humbert, "Description de la poterie recueillie dans la grotte 11Q," in this volume.

designation QUM-533 (= Gr11Q35), and two pieces of linen labelled QUM-540 (= Gr11Q31b) and 541 (Gr11Q41).

The cotton piece was dated as follows (calibrated ages): Gr11Q35 (QUM-533 D037) 890 - 975 AD 1 sigma; 860 - 1020 AD 2 sigma.

This correlates well with the date of the wooden pointed artefact, placing both items around the 10th century, which suggests human activity in the cave in the Abbassid/Fatimid periods. The cave was therefore open before the deposit of the cotton piece and wooden artefact. This later dating can now be viewed alongside the result for Gr11Q9/1 and Gr11Q9/2. As noted above, analysis of Gr11Q9/1 and Gr11Q9/2 presented some surprises and provided further important indications that the cave was sufficiently open not only to bats but also to human visitors in the Ottoman period, most likely in the 17th or 18th centuries.[34] That the cave entrance could have been opened and closed over time is not surprising in an area of significant earthquake activity: an entrance once closed with stones could easily have been opened, and then closed again with rock fall. All evidence of original closures and openings can be erased by such activity. A massive earthquake of 746 destroyed Kh. el Mafjar near Jericho. Among others, there was a devastating earthquake affected the region in 1759.[35] One does not need to attribute the positioning or removal or rocks at an entrance to human activity. Passing wayfarers or herders may opportunistically have used (part of?) the cave when exposed. This would explain the diverse datings of the objects now examined. Cave 11Q was not a cave hermetically sealed from antiquity until the present day, with just a small opening accessible only to bats.

Of the materials likely to be associated with the scroll deposits, two linen textiles radiocarbon dated in 2004 yielded dates as follows:

A. Gr11Q31b (QUM-540 Cave 11Q D033b) 160 BC - 1 AD 1 sigma; 190 BC - 30 AD 2 sigma
B. Gr11Q41 (QUM-541 Cave 11Q D043) 50 BC - 25 AD 1 sigma; 100 BC - 70 AD 2 sigma

We add to this the Temple Scroll wrapper in the Schøyen Collection:

C. (MS 5095/1) 70-130 AD 1 sigma; 28-214 AD 2 sigma

These results can now be viewed along with the new set of radiocarbon dates which provide 2 sigma (95.4%) calibrated ranges as follows (see Figures 1-6):

1. Bundle of linen strings (Gr11Q98) 358-279 BC (40.1%) to 259-108 BC (55.3%).
2. Fragment of linen (Gr11Q119) 193-40 BC.
3. Fragment of linen textile with mended areas (Gr11Q132) 4-134 AD.
4. Fragment of linen textile with blue line (Gr11Q107) 49 BC-72 AD.
5. Fragment of linen textile (Gr11Q76) 204-46 BC.
6. Fragment of linen textile (Gr11Q101) 151-143 BC (0.9%); 112 BC-55 AD (94.5%).

The most striking element in the results from 11Q linen radiocarbon dating is the range of dates. Sample 1 from the bunch of linen strings (Gr11Q98) has a calibrated dating range at 2 sigma from 358 BC to 108 BC, with a probability dip in the middle of the curve (Figure 1). This string is not part of the packing but should form ties around a scroll wrapper or (possibly) string to tie on a jar lid in some way. Given this range there is no real possibility that the string was manufactured in the 1st century AD; even the very low probability trail peters out totally by the mid 1st century BC. Similarly early are Sample 2 linen (Gr11Q119), which has a 2 sigma range of 193-40 BC, and Sample 5, the piece of bleached linen (Gr11Q76), which yielded a range of 204-46 BC. Other dates in the 2 sigma ranges fall within the 1st century BC to 1st century AD, e.g. Sample 4 (the piece with the blue line Gr11Q107): 49 BC-72 AD and Sample 6 (Gr11Q101): 112 BC-55 AD at 94.5% probability. Sample 3, a piece that was thought to have later features in the sewing (with a mended area, not sampled) yielded a range spanning the 1st to mid-2nd century AD (Gr11Q132: 4-134 AD), as with the Temple Scroll wrapper. Importantly, even the outlying tiny probability trails of Sample 1 and Sample 3 do not intersect.

34. See Taylor, "Organic Items from Cave 11Q," in this volume.

35. D.H. Kallner-Amiran, "A Revised Earthquake-Catalogue of Palestine," *IEJ* 1 (1950-51) 223-46, on pp. 226-8; K.W. Russell, "The Earthquake Chronology of Palestine and Northwest Arabia from the 2nd through the Mid-8th Century A.D.," *BASOR* 260 (1985) 37-59, on pp. 47-9; I. Karcz, "Implications of Some Early Jewish Sources for Estimates of Earthquake Hazard in the Holy Land," *Annals of Geophysics* 47 (2004) 759-92, on pp. 778-81. There are numerous stories of cave entrances being opened by earthquakes, as in the case of the Drogarati caves in Kephalonia.

The dates indicate that the linen of Cave 11Q was manufactured at different times minimally stretching from 108 BC to 4 AD (using the outer parameters of 2 sigma ranges) but maximally stretching from 358 BC to 134 AD (likewise using these parameters). They do not cluster particularly strongly around certain dates, though they would generally correlate with the time of the Qumran settlement (early 1st century BC to end of 1st century AD). The conclusion must be that linen found in Cave 11Q was manufactured at different times over an extended period.

Given the significant variations of the dating of the linen, various questions may be asked: Were some scrolls (in their linen wrappers) deposited earlier than other scrolls in the same cave? Might there have been later uses of the cave, after some scrolls were deposited? Since caves have little stratigraphy the question of dating cave objects can be particularly difficult, and this is where radiocarbon dating can provide broad date parameters that can indicate whether an organic object comes from the Roman period, or the Iron Age, or even from the Mamluk period, when morphologies of artefacts (including textiles) can be ambiguous.

One may also ask how long a wrapper was in use prior to it being employed for depositing a scroll. Was the Temple Scroll given a fresh wrapper sometime prior to its deposit in a jar in Cave 11Q? Given that the palaeography of the Temple Scroll suggests that both this scroll and other manuscripts from Cave 11Q are relatively late, should we conclude, with Stökl Ben Ezra, that Cave 11Q is a 'young' cave?[36] We could note that it is the later part of manuscript radiocarbon range at 2 sigma that coheres with both the palaeography and indeed the earliest dating of the wrapper. The deposit of this material took place some time after this scroll and the wrapper was manufactured, and we do not know how long these were in use prior to their arrival in the cave. The Temple Scroll wrapper radiocarbon dating result would even raise the question of whether the linen was manufactured later than 68 AD, at a time corresponding to the occupation of Qumran in Period III, in de Vaux's system, or even the Bar Kokhba period; further tests could determine accuracy with greater precision.

However, arguing strongly against the view that 11Q is a 'young cave', exclusively, is indeed the evidence that suggests some of this linen is older than the 1st century AD. There may be various scenarios proposed to account for the early date range: for example, either (a) old scrolls now missing entirely were wrapped up in linen and stored for a long time before their placements in the cave, or (b) this older linen comes from extremely old rags used for packing, or (c) at least some of the scrolls were wrapped, packed and placed in jars in the cave already in the 1st century BC.[37] For this cave to have been used only in the 1st century AD one would have to argue that extremely old linen was used for storage and/or for rags, when rags would normally be torn from worn clothing or other textiles easily to hand. The question of how old a packing rag might be is impossible to answer, though normally linen cloth when worn is subject to quite rapid deterioration (from sweat, wearing and washing). Thus a more common approach would be to consider a radiocarbon date to be an indication of the time not only of manufacture but of use.

The dating range for samples from Cave 11Q, excluding those items that are from the 10th century or sub-modern, indicate that the manufacture and use of the linen of 11Q associated with scroll deposits did not likely take place all at the same time (e.g. either 1st century BC or 1st century AD).

36. D. Stökl Ben Ezra, "Further Reflections on Caves 1 and 11: A Response to Florentino García Martínez," in C. Hempel (ed.), *The Dead Sea Scrolls: Texts and Context* (STDJ 90; Leiden: Brill, 2010) 211-23; Id., "Old Caves and Young Caves: A Statistical Reevaluation of a Qumran Consensus," *DSD* 14 (2007) 313-33; cf. F. García Martínez, "Cave 11 in Context," in Hempel, *Dead Sea Scrolls*, 99-209, on p. 205.

37. See the arguments presented by G.L. Doudna, "The Legacy of an Error in Archaeological Interpretation: The Dating of the Qumran Cave Scroll Deposits," in K. Galor, J.-B. Humbert, and J. Zangenberg (ed.), *Qumran, the Site of the Dead Sea Scrolls: Archaeological Interpretations and Debates: Proceedings of the Conference Held at Brown University, November 17-19, 2002* (STDJ 57; Leiden: Brill, 2006) 147-57; Id., "Dating the Scroll Deposits of the Qumran Caves: A Question of Evidence," in Fidanzio, *The Caves of Qumran*, 238-46.

Chapter Seven

Metal and Stone Artefacts

Dennis Mizzi and Annalisa Faggi

This is a final report on a small assemblage of metal and stone artefacts excavated by Roland de Vaux from Qumran Cave 11Q. The small assemblage consists of six metal artefacts and one stone bead. All objects, except for Gr11Q6, are stored in the Rockefeller Museum.[1] Item Gr11Q6, on the other hand, is on display at the Shrine of the Book.[2] In this report, we make frequent references to de Vaux's official inventory,[3] the Typewritten Card Index (TCI),[4] de Vaux's handwritten field notes,[5] de Vaux's published field notes,[6] the finds list published together with the latter,[7] de Vaux's preliminary report published in *Revue*

1. We would like to thank Ms Alegre Savariego for her kind assistance with accessing the material stored in the Rockefeller Museum.

2. We would like to thank the staff at the Shrine of the Book, in particular Ms Galit Bennet and Ms Hasia Rimon, for giving us permission to study the object and for their kind assistance with handling it.

3. This is a typewritten booklet in which all catalogued items are listed according to their registration number, and accompanied by a brief description, some contextual information, and, occasionally, a drawing.

4. This index comprises a series of cards each of which contains the details (and sometimes a picture or a drawing) of a single registered object. The information in the TCI served as the basis for the official inventory (see previous note). Sometimes, minor errors were made in the transfer of information from the TCI to the inventory. For more information on the TCI, see M. Fidanzio and J.-B. Humbert, "Finds from the Qumran Caves: Roland de Vaux's Inventory of the Excavations (1949-1956)," in M. Fidanzio (ed.), *The Caves of Qumran: Proceedings of the International Conference, Lugano 2014* (STDJ 118; Leiden: Brill, 2016) 263-332, which also includes the full publication of the TCI. The cards for the 11Q objects can be found on pp. 330-2, and the pertinent ones are reproduced here.

5. These are de Vaux's original field notes, handwritten during the excavation of Cave 11Q. The notes were reproduced, with slight modifications, in J.-B. Humbert and A. Chambon (ed.), *Fouilles de Khirbet Qumrân et de 'Aïn Feshkha: Vol. I: Album de photographies. Répertoire du fonds photographique. Synthèse des notes de chantier du Père Roland de Vaux OP* (NTOA.SA 1; Fribourg/Göttingen: Éditions Universitaires/Vandenhoeck & Ruprecht, 1994), 344. An annotated transcription of the original notes has been prepared by M. Fidanzio for this volume. References to de Vaux's handwritten notes refer to this edition.

6. This refers to the French or English editions, published respectively in Humbert and Chambon, *Fouilles de Khirbet Qumrân et de 'Aïn Feshkha*, 344; J.-B. Humbert and A. Chambon (ed.), *The Excavations of Khirbet Qumran and 'Aïn Feshkha: Synthesis of Roland de Vaux's Field Notes* (NTOA.SA 1B; trans. and rev. S.J. Pfann; Fribourg/Göttingen: Éditions Universitaires/Vandenhoeck & Ruprecht, 2003), 67-8.

7. This refers to the list of registered objects appended to each locus or cave entry in the publication of de Vaux's notes. See previous note for bibliography.

Biblique,[8] and Alain Chambon's unpublished notes on the metal artefacts.[9]

The majority of the objects under examination cannot be dated through typology, either because no advanced typology exists or because their form has remained more or less consistent throughout the centuries, thereby defying precise typological classification. Consequently, the archaeological context – insofar as it can be reconstructed from de Vaux's notes and other archival sources – is the most valuable medium through which these artefacts could potentially be dated. Unfortunately, however, little progress can be made in this regard since these miscellaneous artefacts were found either out of their primary context or in mixed contexts. Accordingly, and in view of the fact that Cave 11Q was occupied or visited throughout various periods, the dating of the objects below should be considered nothing more than an educated guess, sometimes enhanced by typological and historical considerations.

1. Catalogue

This catalogue does not include the nail found on the first day of excavations,[10] for it was never registered in the inventory or the TCI and we were not able to find it among the Qumran objects stored at the Rockefeller. Nor does the catalogue include the arrowhead mentioned in the publication of de Vaux's field notes because it does not exist! The reference to an arrowhead is a mistake that apparently was made during the transcription of de Vaux's handwritten field notes, and what is described as "une pointe de fer romaine" or "a Roman arrowhead" is nothing more than item Gr11Q6 in our catalogue.[11]

Gr11Q2 (PAM Nº 43.734) [Pl. 1]

Knife blade.

Iron. Incomplete. Dimensions: length = 7.80 cm; maximum width = 1.70 cm; maximum thickness = 0.30 cm.

Registered on 28/02/1956

8. R. de Vaux, "Fouilles de Khirbet Qumrân: rapport préliminaire sur les 3e, 4e, et 5e campagnes," *RB* 63 (1956) 533-77, on pp. 573-4.

9. These are digital notes that Chambon had compiled when he started to study the metal artefacts from Qumran. The notes are kept at the École biblique et archéologique française de Jérusalem.

10. See de Vaux's field notes for 26/02/1956.

11. The publication of de Vaux's field notes makes reference to the discovery of "une pointe de fer romaine" (Humbert and Chambon, *Fouilles de Khirbet Qumrân et de Aïn Feshkha*, 344) or "a Roman arrowhead of iron" (Humbert and Chambon, *The Excavations of Khirbet Qumran and Ain Feshkha*, 67-8). The entry is dated to 03/03/1956. The significance of a Roman arrowhead inside Cave 11Q has been noted by a number of scholars (e.g., M. Popović, "Qumran as Scroll Storehouse in Times of Crisis? A Comparative Perspective on Judaean Desert Manuscript Collections," *JSJ* 43 (2012) 551-94, on p. 562; J.E. Taylor, "The Qumran Caves in their Regional Context: A Chronological Review with a Focus on Bar Kokhba Assemblages," in Fidanzio, *Caves of Qumran*, 9-33, on pp. 14, 25). Strangely, however, de Vaux ("Fouilles de Khirbet Qumrân: rapport préliminaire sur les 3e, 4e, et 5e campagnes," 574) makes no reference to this arrowhead in his preliminary report, and neither is the arrowhead registered in the inventory or the TCI. The only reference to it is de Vaux's published field notes, but significantly, it does not appear in the finds list published together with the notes. At first, we thought that de Vaux might have collected the arrowhead without registering it, akin to the situation with some of the material from the *khirbeh*. However, a thorough search through all the Qumran material stored at the Rockefeller proved in vain. De Vaux's handwritten notes provided us with the solution to this problem. De Vaux's entry for 03/03/1956 reads: "On avance dans la grotte intérieure. | Q.q [i.e. quelques] fragments écrits dt [i.e. dont] un petit rouleau très abîmé. **Une | piochon de fer (Romaine)** [*below the line*] **(hache de sapeur)**; une cruchette (Fer II)." It is evident that a 'scribal' error has been made when these notes were edited for publication. Apparently, "une piochon de fer (Romaine)" became "une pointe de fer romaine," whereas the "hache de sapeur" became a separate object. But it is clear that "hache de sapeur" is simply another description for, and thus identical with, the "piochon de fer (Romaine)" – indeed, in the TCI, both descriptors are used with reference to Gr11Q6 (see the TCI entry below). This explains why the list of those objects found on 03/03/1956 reads as follows in the published notes: "quelques fragment écrits et un petit rouleau très abîmé, *une pointe de fer romaine*, une cruchette du Fer II, *une hache de sapeur*" (our italics). This mistake was then replicated in the English translation, which refers to the discovery of "inscribed fragments and a small, very damaged scroll, *a Roman arrowhead of iron*, an Iron II juglet, and *a miner's axe*" (our italics). We thank Marcello Fidanzio for bringing this issue to our attention.

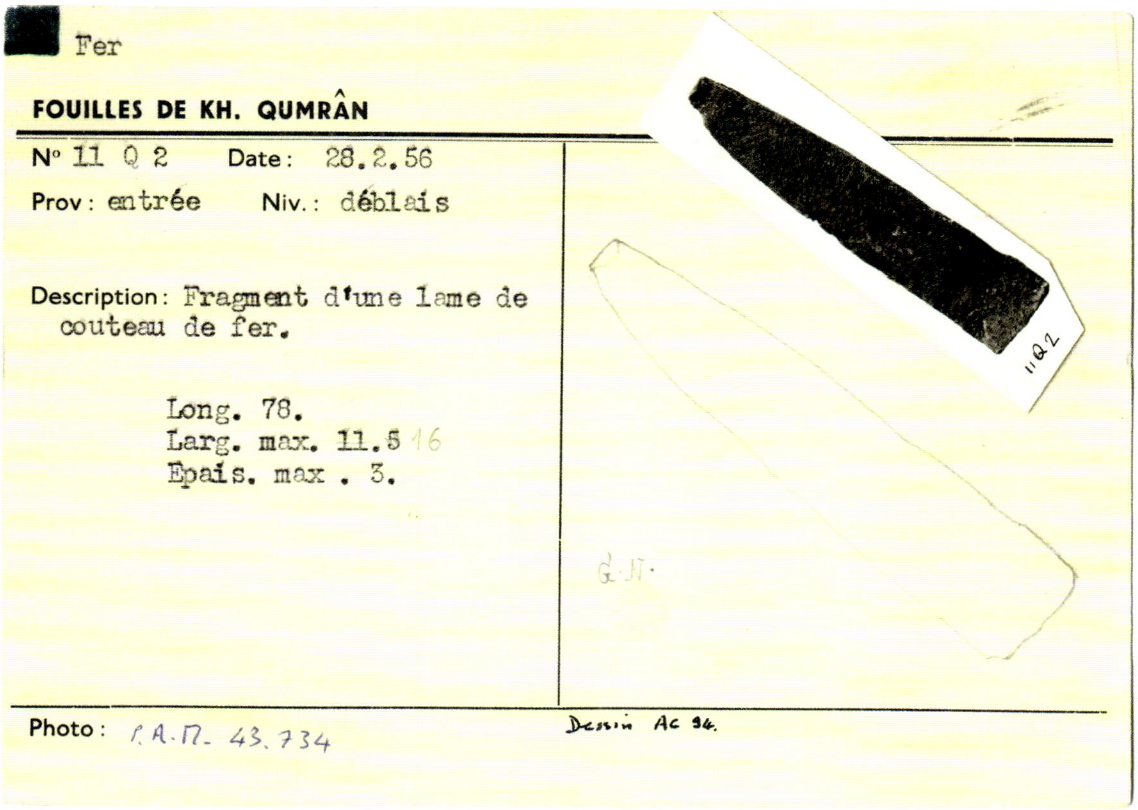

Fer

FOUILLES DE KH. QUMRÂN

N° 11 Q 2 Date: 28.2.56

Prov: entrée Niv.: déblais

Description: Fragment d'une lame de couteau de fer.

Long. 78.
Larg. max. 11.5 16
Epais. max . 3.

Photo: P.A.M. 43.734

Dessin AC 94.

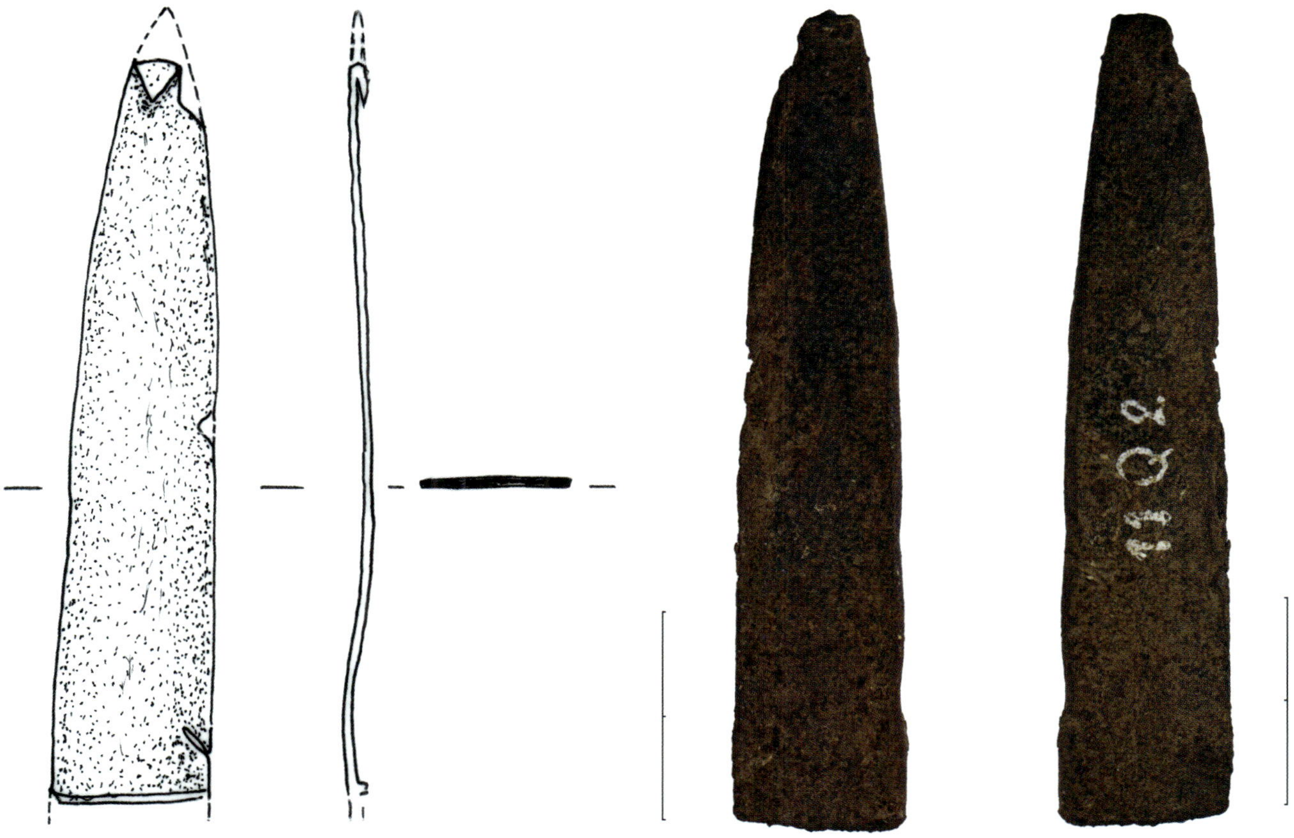

Pl. 1. Gr11Q2 - Knife blade

The TCI lists the context of Gr11Q2 as "Prov: entrée" and "Niv.: déblais." However, there is an incoherency between the date of registration in the TCI and de Vaux's field notes. According to the notes, the knife was found on 26/02/1956, when de Vaux's team dug the fill from the Bedouin's excavations – described as "déblais des fouilleurs clandestins devant l'entrée" – and collapsed rocks underneath it in front of the cave's entrance. Amidst these rocks, de Vaux retrieved two potsherds ("de l'époque de Qumrân," i.e., pottery typical of de Vaux's Periods Ib and II), several pieces of textiles, fragments of leather and basketry, scroll fragments, a nail, and a knife (Gr11Q2). On 28/02/1956, work was conducted inside the cave, specifically in the outer chamber – referred to as "la salle d'entrée" – and, there, the disturbed upper layer – also the result of the Bedouin's excavations and also referred to as "déblais des clandestins" – was cleared out, revealing a layer of yellow earth containing Chalcolithic pottery and a layer of stones and ash at its bottom. The contextual labels "entrée" and "déblais" fit both days of excavation, but the explicit reference to the discovery of Gr11Q2 on 26/02/1956 should be given preference over the date of its registration. It is most likely that de Vaux catalogued some (or all) of the objects found on 26/02/1956 two days later, on 28/06/1956. The fact that de Vaux notes that the "déblais" inside the cave was very poor in archaeological material is another strong indication that Gr11Q2 was found outside, not inside the cave, that is, on 26/02/1956. According to de Vaux, Gr11Q2 was found in between the rocks in front of the cave – therefore, under, not in, the fill of the Bedouin's excavations. This notwithstanding, the knife was probably thrown among the rocks (together with other objects) by the Bedouin from inside the cave, before getting covered by further material they excavated.

Date: Roman period?

It is not possible to date Gr11Q2 on the basis of typology (see below), and the context in which it was found seems to be a secondary one. It appears that Gr11Q2 was found in association with Qumran-type pottery, clumps of scroll fragments, pieces of textile, and fragments of leather and basketry, all of which were likely thrown out from inside the cave by the Bedouin. Although Cave 11Q contained Chalcolithic, Iron Age, Roman, and later material, the artefacts recovered in front of the cave's entrance seem to be predominantly Roman in date. The pottery dates to the first century BCE - CE, and the rest of the artefacts are typical of cave deposits from the Roman period in the region of Qumran (see further the other studies in this volume). In addition, it is most probable that the metal artefacts from Cave 11Q belong to one and the same assemblage (see Discussion), and some of these objects can be dated with varying degrees of confidence to the Roman period on the basis of typology and other considerations (see the entries for Gr11Q6 and Gr11Q11). Therefore, Gr11Q2 can be dated, albeit tentatively, to the Roman period.

Parallels: Tel Anafa (Hellenistic to Islamic periods);[12] Naḥal Ḥever, Cave of Letters (early second century CE);[13] Caesarea Maritima (sixth century CE).[14]

This is a single-edged, iron knife blade. It does not survive intact and is broken on the side of the tang, which is missing altogether. The blade is 1.70 cm wide, but close to the tip, the sharp edge curves inwards to a width of 0.50 cm. The blade is warped, and part of the sharp edge is damaged. The tip is blunt, but this is because it is bent and partially broken; originally, the blade had a pointed end.

The blade would have been attached to a wooden or bone handle by rivets placed in a row along a rectangular tang, or else it would have been fitted into the handle through a pointed tang. A metal collar may have secured the handle in place. It is unfortunate that the tang is missing as this might have helped secure the object's date if it had been of the rivet variety. Knife blades with three rivets are typically found in

12. G.S. Merker, "The Objects of Metal," in A.M. Berlin and S.C. Herbert (ed.), *Tel Anafa II, ii: Glass Vessels, Lamps, Objects of Metal, and Groundstone and Other Stone Tools and Vessels* (JRASS 10.2.1; Ann Arbor, MI: Kelsey Museum of the University of Michigan, 2012) 213-79, on pp. 225-6, Pls 5-6. The knife blades that resemble Gr11Q2 are M21 (except for the ridges along the blunt side of the blade), M21b, M21c, and M21d.

13. Y. Yadin, *The Finds from the Bar Kokhba Period in the Cave of Letters* (Jerusalem: Israel Exploration Society, 1963), 85, 88, Fig. 31:25-28, Pl. 24:25-28. All knives were found with their handles intact, some wooden, some made of bone. Three knives (nos 25-27) are attached to the handle via two rivets and they are much larger than our exemplar; the fourth (no. 28) is a small knife mounted onto its bone handle via a pointed tang.

14. K. Rafael, "The Metal Objects," in J. Patrich (ed.), *Archaeological Excavations at Caesarea Maritima: Areas CC, KK and NN. Final Reports: Vol. 1: The Objects* (Jerusalem: Israel Exploration Society, 2008) 433-69, on p. 449 (especially no. 246). This knife blade has a pointed tang with no rivet holes.

Iron Age contexts,[15] whereas blades in Roman and later contexts tend to have two rivets.[16]

Knives were versatile implements that would have been used for a variety of purposes, including food preparation and various crafts, such as carpentry, leatherworking, and weaving.[17] Interestingly, a number of the iron objects from Cave 11Q can be associated with one or various crafts. It is possible, therefore, that Gr11Q2 was part of a worker's toolkit.

Gr11Q3 (PAM Nº 43.734)[18] [Pl. 2]

Loop attachment?

Bronze. Incomplete. Dimensions: length = 2.60 cm; breadth = 3 cm; maximum width = 2.30 cm; maximum diameter of elliptical projection = 1.30 cm; diameter of circular projection = 0.80 cm; maximum internal diameter of loop = 1.10 cm.

Registered on 28/02/1956

Gr11Q3 is mentioned neither in de Vaux's field notes nor in his preliminary report, but it was registered in the TCI, which records its context as "Prov: entrée" and "Niv.: déblais," just like Gr11Q2. The date of registration is likewise identical. Therefore, Gr11Q3 might have been found in the same context as Gr11Q2. On the other hand, the fact that de Vaux never refers to Gr11Q3 in his daily narrative – while he mentions Gr11Q2 and numerous other objects in his entry for 26/02/1956 – suggests that Gr11Q3 could have actually been found on 28/02/1956 (unlike Gr11Q2, which was found on 26/02/1956 but registered on 28/02/1956), when work was underway in the cave's outer chamber ("la salle d'entrée"). The upper levels in the outer chamber contained soil and stone fills resulting from the Bedouin's excavations ("déblais des clandestins"). The contextual labels in the TCI fit both days of excavation (see the entry for Gr11Q2). In any case, the contextual label "déblais" in the TCI indicates that Gr11Q3 was found in a disturbed context.

Date: Roman period?

It is not possible to date Gr11Q3 on the basis of typology, and the context in which it was found seems to be a secondary one. Most probably, Gr11Q3 comes from the disturbed upper level in the cave's outer chamber, in which undated potsherds, fragments of an Iron Age II lamp, scroll fragments, and pieces of linen were found (see de Vaux's field notes for 28/02/1956, 29/02/1956, 01/03/1956).[19] Therefore, it is difficult to determine whether Gr11Q3 belongs to the Iron Age, the Roman period, or a later date. Nonetheless, it is most probable that the metal artefacts from Cave 11Q belong to one and the same assemblage (see Discussion), and some of these objects can be dated with varying degrees of confidence to the Roman period on the basis of typology and other considerations (see the entries for Gr11Q6 and Gr11Q11). Therefore, Gr11Q3 can be dated, albeit tentatively, to the Roman period.

Parallels: Manching, Germany (seventh to first century BCE).[20]

Gr11Q3 is a thick bronze loop with two broken projections (one circular, the other elliptical) whose ends would have been fused to another metal object,

15. See, for example, A. Mazar, *Excavations at Tell Qasile: Part Two: The Philistine Sanctuary: Various Finds, the Pottery, Conclusions, Appendixes* (Qedem 20; Jerusalem: Hebrew University, 1985), 6-8, Fig. 2:1, Photo 3; N. Yahalom-Mack and A. Mazar, "Various Finds from the Iron Age II Strata in Areas P and S," in A. Mazar (ed.), *Excavations at Tel Beth-Shean 1989-1996: Vol. 1: From the Late Bronze Age IIB to the Medieval Period* (Jerusalem: Israel Exploration Society/Hebrew University, 2006) 468-504, on pp. 494-6, Fig. 13.10:1, Photo 13.37.

16. Merker, "The Objects of Metal," 224.

17. For the use of knives in woodworking and leatherworking, see R.B. Ulrich, *Roman Woodworking* (New Haven: Yale University Press, 2007), 34, 36; W.H. Manning, "Industry," in L. Allason-Jones (ed.), *Artefacts in Roman Britain: Their Purpose and Use* (Cambridge: Cambridge University Press, 2011) 68-88, on p. 86. For the use of small knives (such as our exemplar) in weaving, see Yadin, *Finds from the Bar Kokhba Period*, 88. On the difficulty of assigning a specific function to knives, see also W.H. Manning, *Catalogue of the Romano-British Iron Tools, Fittings and Weapons in the British Museum* (London: British Museum Publications, 1985), 108.

18. In the TCI, the photograph of Gr11Q3 is mistakenly attached to the card of Gr11Q11 (see the TCI entry for the latter object below).

19. The excavation of the outer chamber was finished on 01/03/1956 not 29/02/1956. See note 23.

20. G. Jacobi, *Die Ausgrabungen in Manching: Band 5: Werkzeug und Gerät aus dem Oppidum von Manching* (Wiesbaden: Franz Steiner, 1974), 142-50, 297-9, Pls 39-42. These are not exact parallels, but they are close enough to possibly suggest a similar interpretation for Gr11Q3.

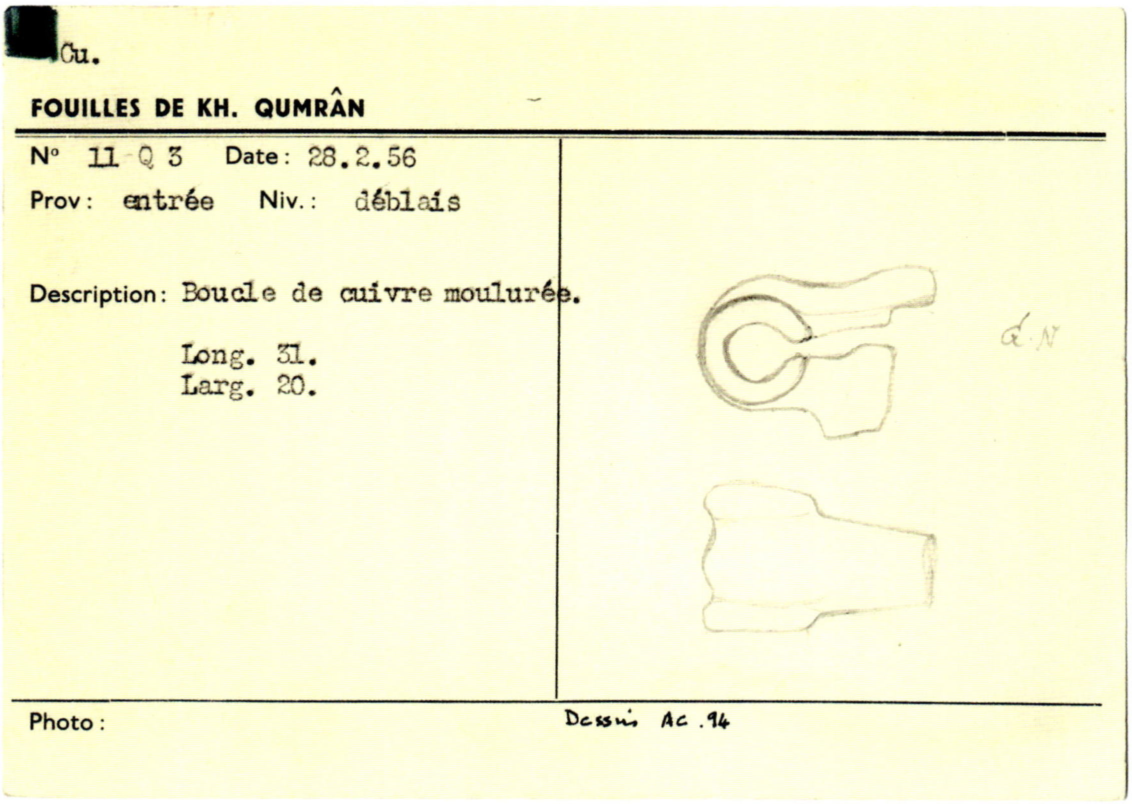

Cu.

FOUILLES DE KH. QUMRÂN

N° 11 Q 3 Date: 28.2.56

Prov: entrée Niv.: déblais

Description: Boucle de cuivre moulurée.

Long. 31.
Larg. 20.

Photo:

Dessin Ac. 94

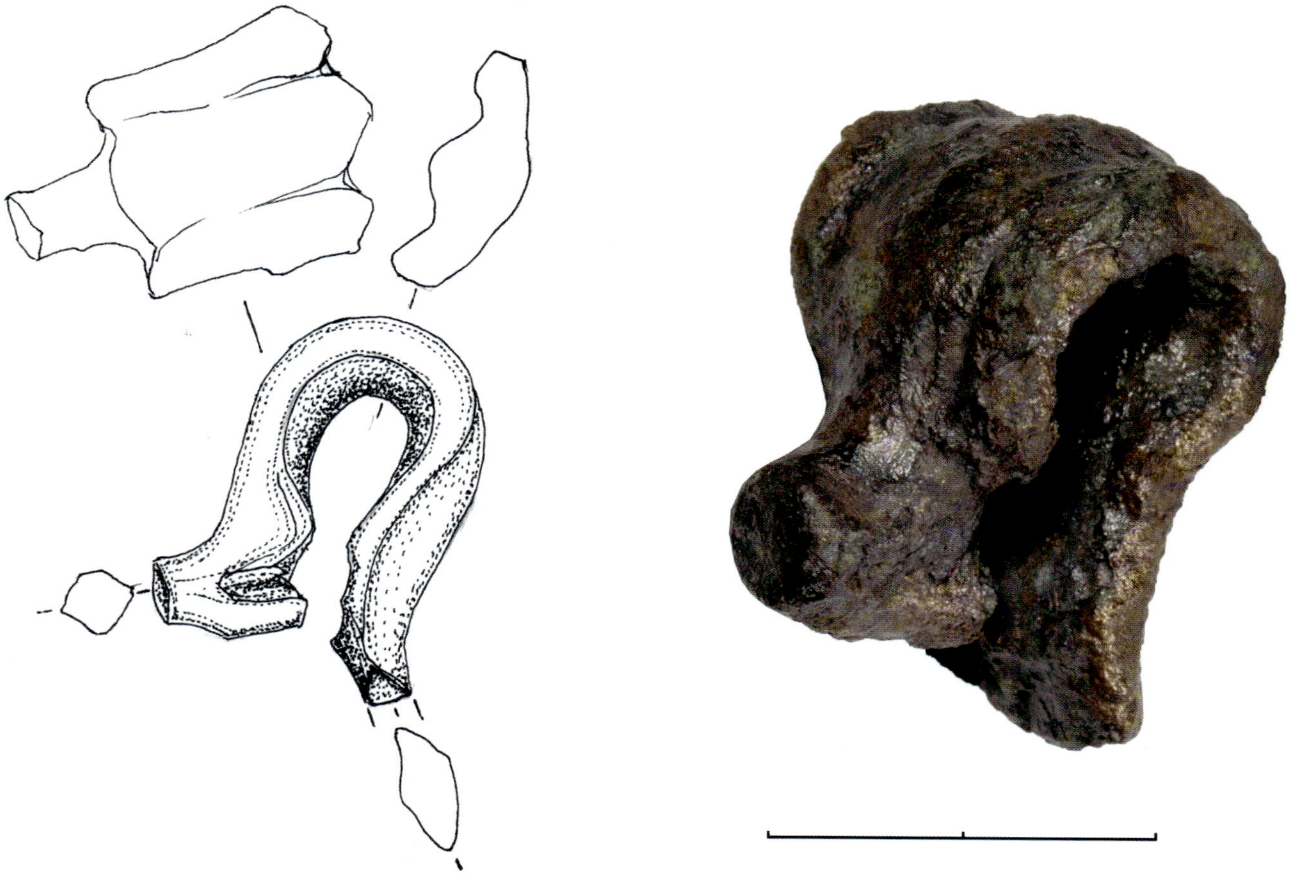

Pl. 2. Gr11Q3 - Loop attachment (?)

possibly a vessel. The outer side of the loop is decorated with two parallel grooves. The projections are perpendicular to one another, but the physical link between the two is now broken. On the inner side of the elliptical protrusion, there is a circular impression that mirrors the section profile of the other projection, indicating that the two originally joined at a right angle, closing the loop in the process.

In the official inventory and the TCI, this object is listed as "boucle de cuivre moulurée." This is how it is also listed in the finds list appended to de Vaux's published notes, which is based on the latter two sources. However, it is clear that this object is not a buckle.[21] In his unpublished notes on the metals, Alain Chambon refers to this object simply as a "pièce moulée." Parallels from other sites in ancient Palestine or the Mediterranean in general are hard to come by. Nonetheless, on the basis of similar objects from Manching, Germany, it is possible to interpret Gr11Q3 as an attachment loop that could have received one end of a handle. This bronze loop would have been fused to one side of a bronze vessel – which had to have had a curved profile (e.g., a cooking pot or a cauldron) – via its two projections, with an identical attachment on the other side of the vessel. The attachment loops from Manching are likewise grooved, but they have only a single jutting projection.

The interpretation of Gr11Q3 as an attachment loop remains highly tentative. If correct, however, it would mean that in Cave 11Q there was once a bronze vessel that has either degraded or, more likely, been looted.

Gr11Q4 (PAM Nº 43.734) [Pl. 3]

File/Chisel

Iron. Incomplete. Dimensions: length of file/chisel = 5 cm; width of file/chisel = 2.60 cm; maximum thickness of file/chisel = 0.60 cm; thickness of tip = 0.40 cm; maximum width of tang = 1.40 cm; thickness of tang = 0.50 cm.

Registered on 29/02/1956

Gr11Q4 is mentioned in de Vaux's preliminary report – where it is described as "un ciseau (ou une lime)" – but not in his field notes. In the TCI, the context is listed as "Prov: entrée" and "Niv.: déblais," as in the case of Gr11Q2 and Gr11Q3, but the date of registration is different. Although de Vaux never explicitly mentions Gr11Q4 in his daily narrative, his notes give us a clue as to its context. Assuming that the object was found on the day it was registered,[22] and taking into consideration the contextual labels in the TCI (for which see the entries for Gr11Q2 and Gr11Q3), Gr11Q4 is most likely to have been found in the disturbed upper level in the cave's outer chamber. Excavations in this part of the cave were finished on 01/03/1956.[23]

Date: Roman period?

It is not possible to date Gr11Q4 on the basis of typology, and the context in which it was found seems to be a secondary one. Most probably, Gr11Q4 comes from the disturbed upper level in the cave's outer chamber, in which undated potsherds, fragments of an Iron Age II lamp, scroll fragments, and pieces of linen were found (see de Vaux's field notes for 28/02/1956, 29/02/1956, 01/03/1956).[24] Therefore, it is difficult to determine whether Gr11Q4 belongs to the Iron Age, the Roman period, or a later date. Nonetheless, it is most probable that the metal artefacts from Cave 11Q belong to one and the same assemblage (see Discussion), and some of these objects can be dated with varying degrees of confidence to the Roman

21. Buckles are relatively common in Roman-period contexts, including Qumran, and they bear no resemblance to Gr11Q3. See, for example, R. Nenner-Soriano, "Metal Artifacts," in H. Geva (ed.), *Jewish Quarter Excavations in the Old City of Jerusalem conducted by Nahman Avigad, 1969-1982: Vol. 4: The Burnt House of Area B and Other Studies: Final Report* (Jerusalem: Israel Exploration Society/ Hebrew University, 2010) 248-60, on p. 250, Pl. 8.1:M8-9; Rafael, "The Metal Objects," 447-8.

22. The only artefacts not to be registered on the day of their discovery are those found on the first day of excavation.

23. In the entry for 29/02/1956, the published version of de Vaux's field notes reads: "On commence à dégager la grotte intérieure." However, in the original, handwritten notes, de Vaux actually states: "On commence à dégager l'entrée de la grotte intérieure," that is, the passageway between the outer and inner chambers. In the entry for 01/03/1956, the handwritten notes state further: "On finit de dégager la chambre d'entrée. On commence l'intérieur" (these remarks are missing from the published notes). It is therefore clear that the excavation of the outer part of the cave was finished on 01/03/1956 not on 29/02/1956.

24. The excavation of the outer chamber was finished on 01/03/1956. See note 23.

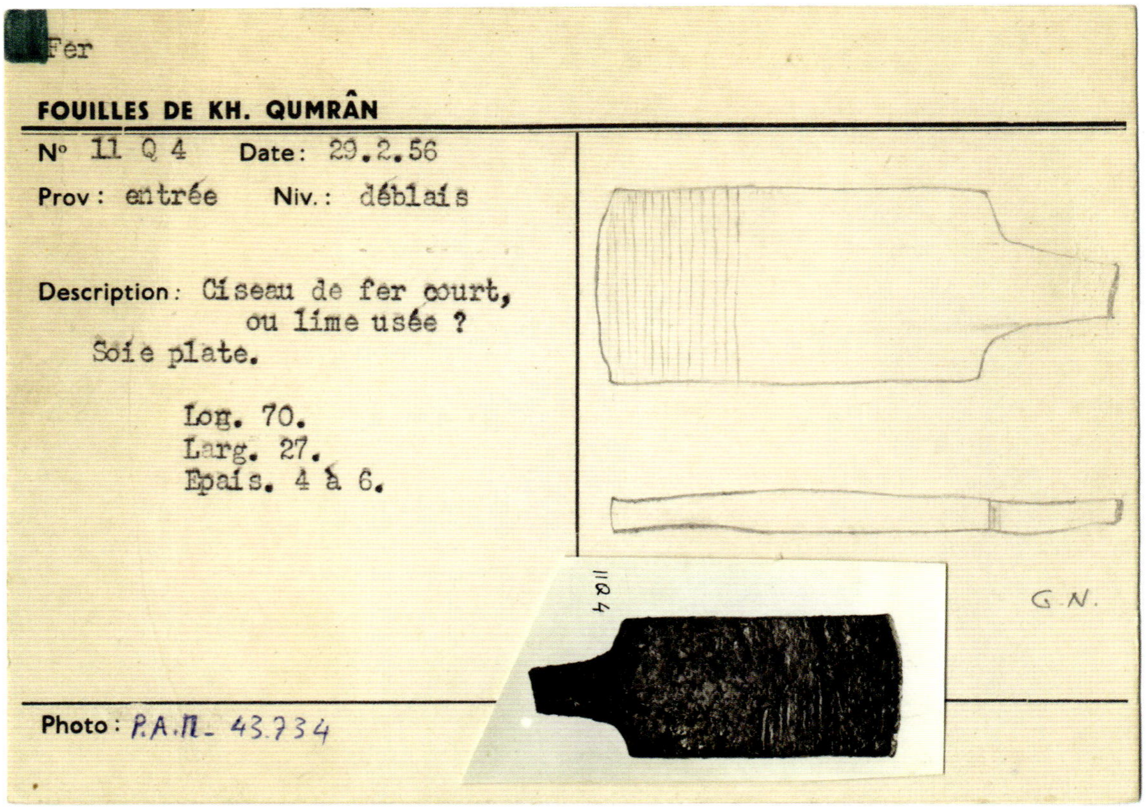

Fer

FOUILLES DE KH. QUMRÂN

N° 11 Q 4 Date : 29.2.56

Prov : entrée Niv. : déblais

Description : Ciseau de fer court, ou lime usée ?
Soie plate.

Long. 70.
Larg. 27.
Epais. 4 à 6.

Photo : P.A.M. 43.734

G.N.

11Q4

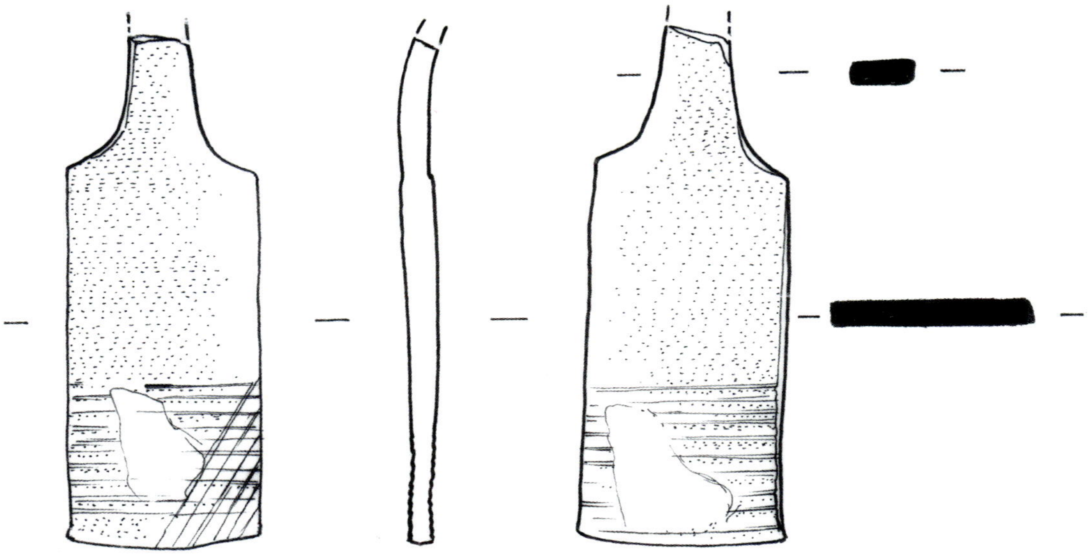

Pl. 3. Gr11Q4 - File/Chisel

period on the basis of typology and other considerations (see the entries for Gr11Q6 and Gr11Q11). Therefore, Gr11Q4 can be dated, albeit tentatively, to the Roman period.

Parallels: No parallels are known from sites in ancient Palestine, but files and chisels are commonly attested in Iron Age and Roman contexts at various sites in Europe and Britain,[25] although no exact or close parallels to Gr11Q4 could be found.

This is a small, rectangular, iron file/chisel with a pointed tang that is now broken. On both surfaces, the implement has a series of teeth (ca. 0.10 cm apart) near to and paralleling the tip. On one side, there are also parallel teeth stretching diagonally from one of the long edges down to the tip, intersecting with the horizontal teeth. The other side is too damaged to determine whether or not it had a similar set of diagonal teeth. In section, the instrument has a slight concave profile; it is thickest at the centre and tapers towards the edges. When still functional, it would have been mounted on a wooden or bone handle through its pointed tang. The file/chisel shows traces of use: the teeth on both surfaces are either abraded or completely smoothened; the tang is bent, possibly due to pounding; and the tip is slightly squashed, with its edges upturned.

In his preliminary report, de Vaux described Gr11Q4 as "un ciseau (ou une lime)," and similarly the TCI records the object as "ciseau de fer court, ou lime usée?". On the other hand, in the finds list appended to de Vaux's published notes, Gr11Q4 is listed as a "lame de fer," but this must be a typographical error ("lame" instead of "lime"). In any case, Gr11Q4 is certainly not a blade. The parallel and intersecting teeth on both surfaces clearly indicate that the implement is a file. It is also evident that Gr11Q4 doubled as a chisel, as indicated by the squashed upturned tip, which shows that it was hammered against (or into) other surfaces.

Files and chisels were used in various crafts, in particular carpentry, masonry, and metalworking.[26] The small nature of Gr11Q4 as well as the fact that it was mounted on a wooden or bone handle would seemingly indicate that it was used for woodworking. Chisels used by masons or metalsmiths typically had metal handles or socketed wooden handles in order to withstand heavy pounding. In contrast, carpenters used paring chisels simply by applying hand or shoulder pressure. On the other hand, Gr11Q4 has a rather blunt edge, which would not have been suitable for woodworking but adequate for cold metalworking (e.g., the repurposing of metal implements). In its function as a file, Gr11Q4 would have been well-suited for both woodworking and metalworking. Of course, it is not implausible that Gr11Q4 was a multipurpose instrument used for different purposes in different industries. In view of its small nature, it was probably employed as a chisel only for light operations, where moderate tapping (with a hammer or mallet) of the wooden or bone handle would have sufficed.

Gr11Q6 (PAM № 42.449, 450, 451) [Pls. 4 and 5]

Mattock

Iron. Complete. Dimensions: total length = 26 cm; length of adze/chisel = 15 cm; maximum width of adze/chisel = 2.10 cm; maximum thickness of adze/chisel = 1.70cm; length of axe = 8.20 cm; maximum width of axe = 5.80 cm; maximum thickness of axe = 2 cm; maximum diameter of hole = 3 cm.

Registered on 03/03/1956

On 03/03/1956, work was conducted in the interior part of the cave. The contextual information on the TCI reads: "grotte int. à dr. [i.e., droite] assez bas," which coheres with de Vaux's notes for the day and adds the extra information that Gr11Q6 was found in the right part of the inner chamber, at a fairly low level. Nonetheless, one should not make much of the contextual descriptor "assez bas" – this cannot be taken as an indication that Gr11Q6 was necessarily discovered in a secure context; indeed, this could refer to the fact that the surface level in the right part of the inner chamber is at a lower elevation than the rest of the interior.[27]

25. See, for example, Jacobi, *Die Ausgrabungen in Manching*, 15-24, 271-4, Pls 5-7; Manning, *Catalogue of the Romano-British Iron Tools*, 8-9, 11, 21-5, Pls 5-6, 10-11.

26. See Manning, *Catalogue of the Romano-British Iron Tools*, 8-9, 11, 21-5, Pls 5-6, 10-11; Id., "Industry," 78-9, 81, 84, 88; Ulrich, *Roman Woodworking*, 26-30.

27. See the cave's plan in this volume; and *cf.* de Vaux's field notes. The entry for 04-05/03/1956 in the handwritten notes reads: "Dans la grotte intérieure. Le rocher monte

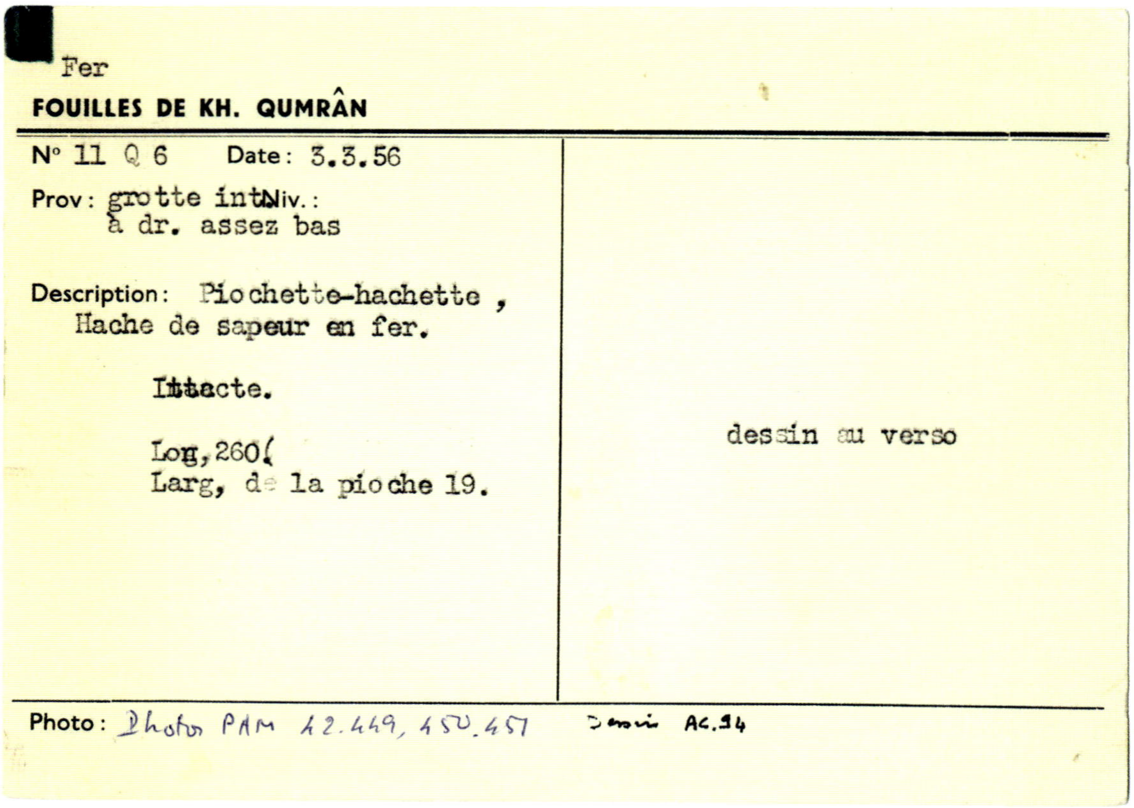

Fer

FOUILLES DE KH. QUMRÂN

N° 11 Q 6 Date : 3.3.56

Prov : grotte intNiv. :
à dr. assez bas

Description : Piochette-hachette ,
Hache de sapeur en fer.

Ittacte.

Log, 260(
Larg, de la pioche 19.

dessin au verso

Photo : Photo PAM 42.449, 450.451 Dessin AC.34

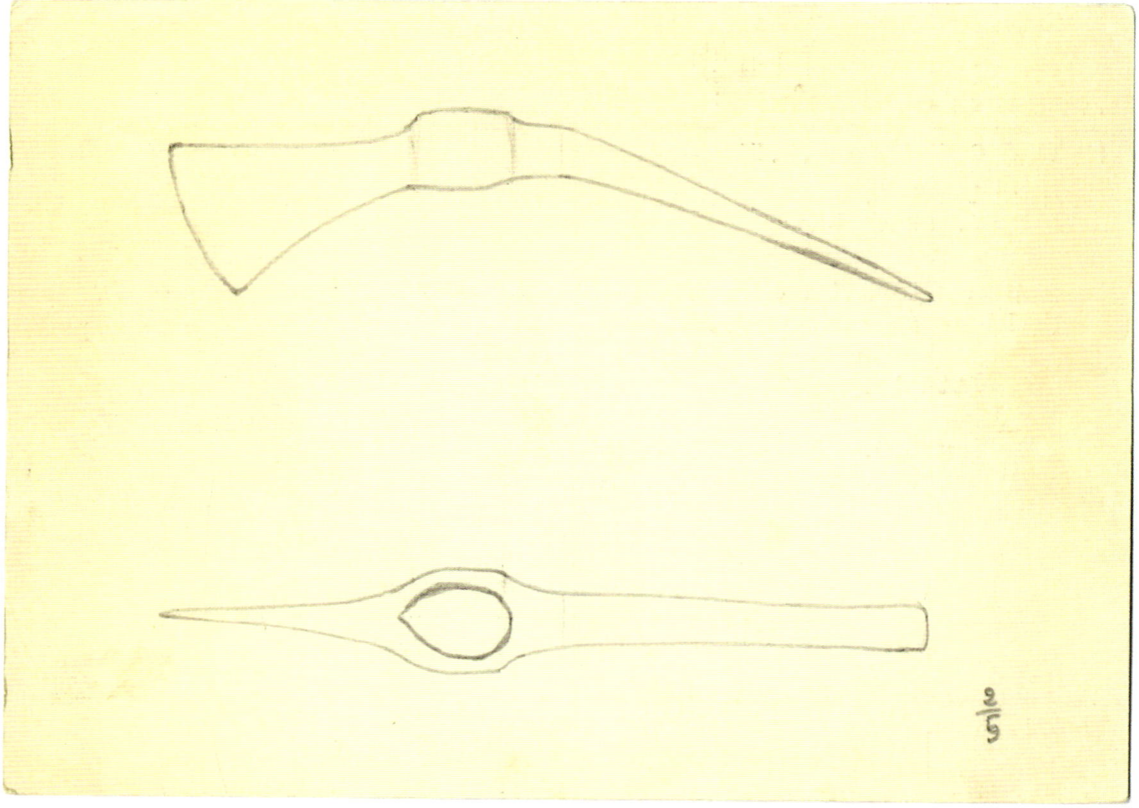

Pl. 4. Gr11Q6 - Mattock

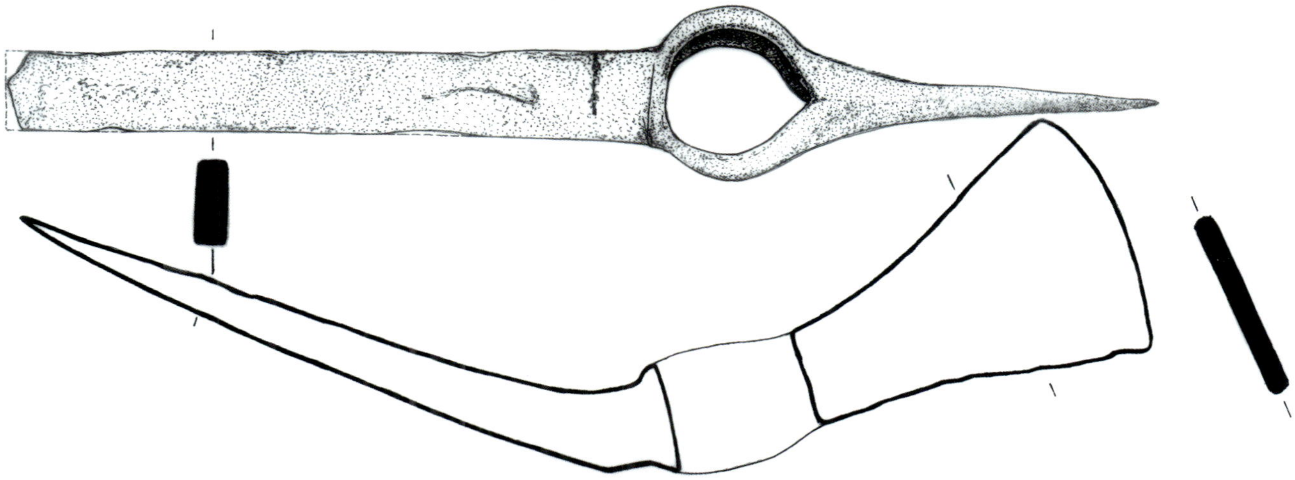

Pl. 5. Gr11Q6 - Mattock

Date: Roman period

On the basis of typology, Gr11Q6 can be dated, with a certain degree of confidence, to the Roman period. While mattocks or axe-adzes are already attested in Iron Age contexts, the few known exemplars are made of bronze and they are generally small and squat.[28] On the other hand, the profile of Gr11Q6 is well-attested in Roman and later contexts in ancient Palestine and the Mediterranean (see below). A Roman date for Gr11Q6 is strengthened further by the high probability that the metal artefacts from Cave 11Q belong to one and the same assemblage (see Discussion), which includes at least one object that can be dated securely to the Roman period on the basis of typology and other considerations (see the entry for Gr11Q11). Therefore, Gr11Q6 can be dated, somewhat more confidently than the other metal objects, to the Roman period.

Parallels: Jerusalem, Area E (Stratum 4: mid-first century BCE - second half of first century BCE);[29] Jerusalem, Nea Church (beneath foundations: Herodian period);[30] Jerusalem, Cardo (fills: sixth - twelfth century CE).[31] Large and small mattocks are also known from various Roman sites in Britain, northern Europe, and the Mediterranean.[32]

This is a double-bladed tool with a chisel or adze-like edge on one side and an axe on the other; the former would have been perpendicular to the haft, and the edge of the latter parallel to it. An oval hole for the fitting of a wooden haft separates the two blades. Close to the hole, both blades are thick, but they taper to a thin, sharp edge. The adze/chisel edge is more corroded than the axe, and it is also more worn out and partially notched off. This tool is best described as a type of mattock or an axe-adze.[33]

On the basis of its size, one can deduce that the mattock was mounted on a short haft. Probably, the tool would have been small enough to be held in one hand.[34] Determining the actual function(s) of this instrument is difficult owing to its myriad possible uses. For example, axes and adzes were prime carpenter tools,[35] but they were also used in agriculture,[36] by miners,[37] and by the Roman army.[38] In view of the small size of the implement and the presence of other tools in Cave 11Q, it is tempting to see Gr11Q6 as yet another piece of equipment from a craftsmen's toolkit. In contrast, it is unlikely that Gr11Q6 was deposited by a Roman soldier in the region. Relatively large objects like Gr11Q6 do not just get accidentally lost, and it is doubtful that a Roman soldier would have deposited, for no apparent reason, a mattock in Cave 11Q.[39] Furthermore, military mattocks tend to be larger than our exemplar.[40]

---

assez brusquement | vs [i.e., vers] l'intérieur." In the published version of the notes, the statement appears in the entry for 03/03/1956: "À l'intérieur de la grotte, le rocher monte assez brusquement vers le fond."

28. See, for example, Mazar, *Excavations at Tell Qasile*, 3-4, Fig. 1:1, Photo 1. But see Merker, "The Objects of Metal," Pl. 3:M10, who publishes an example from Tel Anafa which is not squat and resembles closely the profile of mattocks from the Roman period. As in ancient Palestine, mattocks are rare in the pre-Roman Iron Age in Britain. See S. Rees, "Agriculture," in Allason-Jones, *Artefacts in Roman Britain*, 89-113, on p. 98.

29. O. Gutfeld and R. Nenner-Soriano, "Metal Artifacts," in H. Geva (ed.), *Jewish Quarter Excavations in the Old City of Jerusalem Conducted by Nahman Avigad, 1969-1982: Vol. 3: Area E and Other Studies: Final Report* (Jerusalem: Israel Exploration Society/Hebrew University, 2006) 272-82, on p. 276, Pl. 12.2:M30.

30. Nenner-Soriano, "Metal Artifacts," 431, Pl. 16.3:M36. This is an incomplete specimen and it is made of bronze.

31. Nenner-Soriano, "Metal Artifacts," 431, Pl. 16.3:M34-35.

32. See the examples cited in R. de Vaux, "Une hachette essénienne?," *VT* 9 (1959) 399-407, on p. 399; and see also Manning, *Catalogue of the Romano-British Iron Tools*, 17-8, 30, 44, Fig. 6, Pls 8:B14, 9:B16, 17:F8; M.C. Bishop and J.C.N. Coulston, *Roman Military Equipment: From the Punic Wars to the Fall of Rome* (Oxford: Oxbow Books; ²2006), 117-8, 185, 187, Figs 68:2-5, 121:1-2; Rees, "Agriculture," Fig. 9g.

33. For a wide typological range of mattocks, see K.D. White, *Agricultural Implements of the Roman World* (Cambridge: Cambridge University Press, 1967), 36-68, esp. 61-4, Figs 35-39. See also Manning, *Catalogue of the Romano-British Iron Tools*, 17-8, 30, 44, Fig. 6, Pls 8:B14, 9:B16, 17:F8.

34. See also de Vaux, "Une hachette essénienne?," 399.

35. Ulrich, *Roman Woodworking*, 16-8; Manning, "Industry," 77-8.

36. White, *Agricultural Implements*, 63, 65; Rees, "Agriculture," 97-8, Fig. 9g.

37. White, *Agricultural Implements*, 63.

38. Bishop and Coulston, *Roman Military Equipment*, 117-8, 185, 187, Figs 68:2-5, 121:1-2.

39. Roman military equipment was typically reused and only rarely was it deposited while still intact. See the methodological discussion in M.C. Bishop, "Weaponry and Military Equipment," in Allason-Jones, *Artefacts in Roman Britain*, 114-32.

40. See Manning, *Catalogue of the Romano-British Iron Tools*, 44;

Gr11Q10 (PAM Nº 43.734) [Pl. 6]

Awl/Punch?

Iron. Incomplete. Dimensions: length = 6.30 cm; maximum thickness = 0.50 cm.

Registered on 12/03/1956

The TCI records the provenance of Gr11Q10 as "grotte int. à dr. [i.e., droite] de l'entrée," which matches the description of work in de Vaux's field notes for 12/03/1956. On this day, clearance work was carried out in the inner chamber, to the right of the entryway from the outer part of the cave. Here, Qumran-type pottery and an iron key (Gr11Q11) were found. Gr11Q10 is not mentioned in the field notes, but its contextual label in the TCI and the identical date of registration suggest that it may have been found together with these objects.

Date: Roman period?

It is not possible to date Gr11Q10 on the basis of typology. Nonetheless, Gr11Q10 seems to have been found in association with Qumran-type pottery – a descriptor which de Vaux uses for pottery typical of the first century BCE - CE (i.e., his Periods Ib and II) – and an iron key from the Roman period (see the entry for Gr11Q11). Furthermore, it is most probable that the metal artefacts from Cave 11Q belong to one and the same assemblage (see Discussion), and some of these objects can be dated with varying degrees of confidence to the Roman period on the basis of typology and other considerations (see the entries for Gr11Q6 and Gr11Q11). Therefore, Gr11Q10 can be dated, albeit tentatively, to the Roman period.

Parallels: No parallels are known from sites in ancient Palestine, but awls and punches are attested in Iron Age and Roman contexts at various sites in Europe and Britain.[41]

This is an iron rod, which is highly damaged and broken. The rod has a square or hexagonal section, but the acute nature of the deterioration precludes a more precise judgement. One of the ends is certainly broken, but the other may be the original, pointed end of the object. Most of the rod, except for the broken parts, is covered with a light brown patina, indicating that the damage to Gr11Q10 was incurred in modern times.

The function of this iron rod remains uncertain owing to its incomplete nature. The object is described as a "tige de fer" in the TCI, but de Vaux uses the term "tige" – translated as "rod" in the English edition of his notes – for various artefacts excavated from Qumran and the Judaean Desert, including cosmetic and medicinal utensils as well as metal rods of unknown purpose. It is quite probable that he described Gr11Q10 as a "tige" simply because he could not discern its function.

In the specific case of Gr11Q10, we can exclude its function as a cosmetic or medicinal stick since these implements are usually made of bronze and they are typically circular, not squarish or hexagonal.[42] Alain Chambon, in his notes on Gr11Q10, describes the object as a "poinçon," an awl or a punch, which is plausible. Awls and punches were used in a variety of industries, including leatherworking (e.g., to cut holes or to make depressions in the leather for decorative purposes) and woodworking (e.g., to make indentations in the wood).[43] Thus, this tentative identification would add yet another tool to the corpus of metals from Cave 11Q.

Bishop and Coulston, *Roman Military Equipment*, 117-8, 185, 187, Figs 68:2-5, 121:1-2.

41. See, for example, Jacobi, *Die Ausgrabungen in Manching*, 54-6, Pl. 11:182-225; Manning, *Catalogue of the Romano-British Iron Tools*, 39-42, Pls 15:E4-16:E34.

42. For spatulas and kohl sticks, see, for example, E. Chernov, "Metal Objects and Small Finds from En-Gedi," in Y. Hirschfeld (ed.), *En-Gedi Excavations II: Final Report (1996-2002)* (Jerusalem: Israel Exploration Society, 2007) 507-43, on pp. 509-11, Figs 8-13, Pl. 2; G. Hadas, "Nine Tombs of the Second Temple Period at 'En Gedi," *'Atiqot* 24 (1994) 3-65 (Hebrew), 1*-8* (English Summary), on Figs 15:26, 23:24-25, 50:28, 62:31; R. Nenner-Soriano, "The Metal Artifacts from the Hasmonean and Herodian Palaces at Jericho and Cypros," in R. Bar-Nathan and J. Gärtner (ed.), *Hasmonean and Herodian Palaces at Jericho: Final Reports of the 1973-1987 Excavations: Vol. 5: The Finds from Jericho and Cypros* (Jerusalem: Israel Exploration Society/Hebrew University, 2013) 270-84, on p. 273, Pl. 11.1:18-20; B.L. Johnson, "Clay, Stone, and Metal Objects from the Hellenistic to the Early Islamic Period," in Mazar, *Excavations at Tel Beth-Shean,* 654-74, on p. 662, Fig. 22.4:9-10, Photos 22.8c, 22.11; Rafael, "The Metal Objects," 446.

43. Manning, *Catalogue of the Romano-British Iron Tools*, 39-42; Id., "Industry," 87.

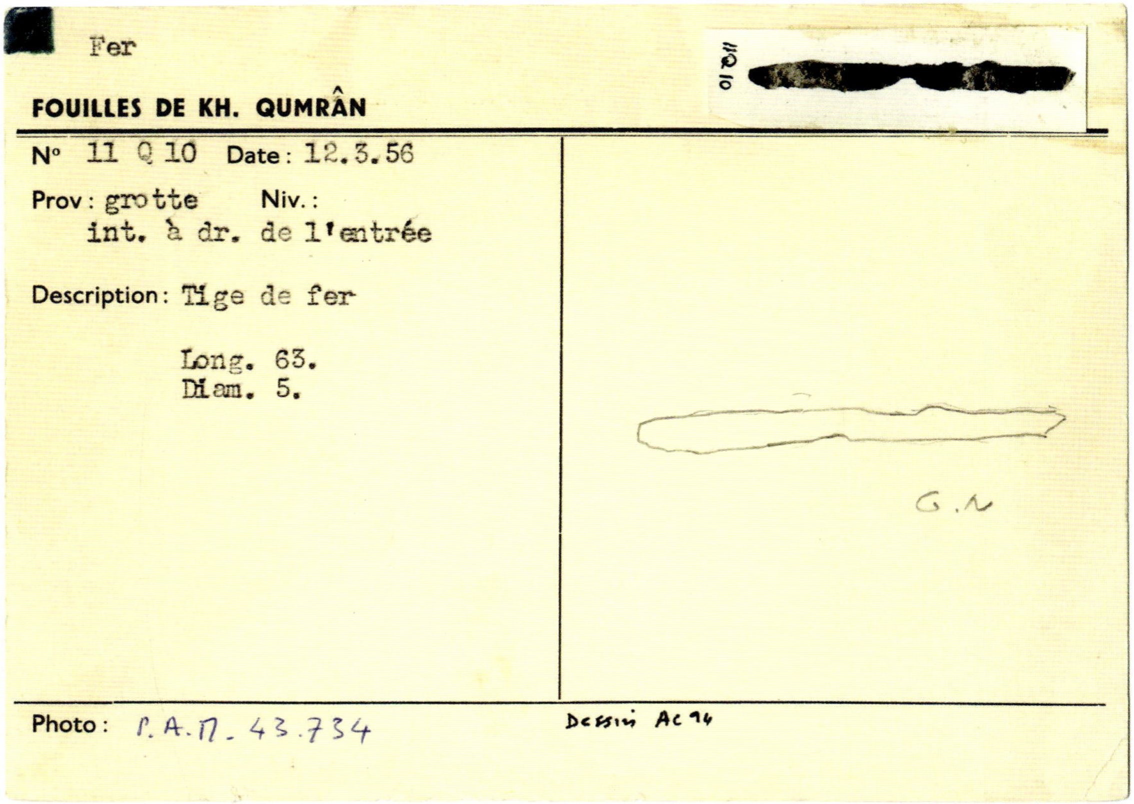

Fer

11Q10

FOUILLES DE KH. QUMRÂN

N° 11 Q 10 Date : 12.3.56

Prov : grotte Niv. :
int. à dr. de l'entrée

Description : Tige de fer

Long. 63.
Diam. 5.

G.N

Photo : P.A.M. 43.734

Dessin AC 94

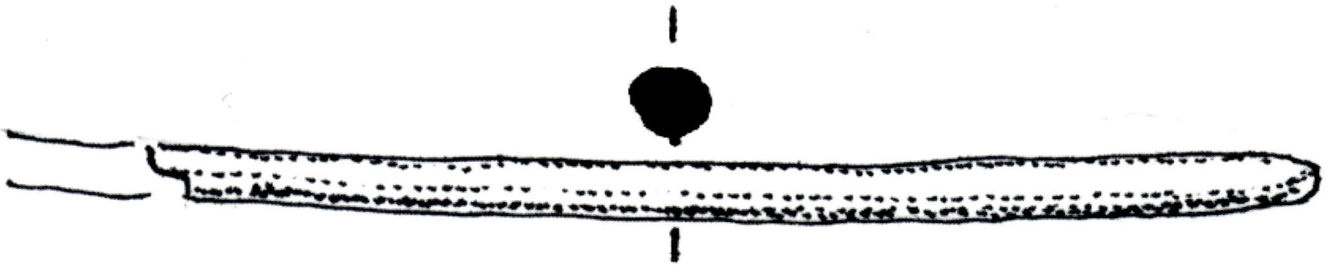

Pl. 6. Gr11Q10 - Awl/Punch (?)

Gr11Q11[44] (PAM Nº n/a[45]) [Pl. 7]

Key

Iron. Incomplete. Dimensions: length of shank = 4.50 cm; maximum thickness of shank = 1.50 cm; length of stem = 3 cm; maximum thickness of stem = 0.80 cm; extant length of bit = 2.70 cm; maximum thickness of tines = 1 cm; height of tines = 1.30 cm; diameter of loop handle = 1.40 cm.

Registered on 12/03/1956

The TCI records the provenance of Gr11Q11 as "grotte int. à dr. [i.e., droite] de l'entrée," which matches the description of work in de Vaux's notes for 12/03/1956. On this day, clearance work was carried out in the inner chamber, to the right of the entryway from the outer part of the cave. Here, Qumran-type pottery, possibly Gr11Q10, and Gr11Q11 were found.

Date: Roman period

On the basis of typology and its contextual association with Qumran-type pottery, Gr11Q11 can be dated, with a high degree of confidence, to the Roman period. Elbow keys of the same type as Gr11Q11 appear to have been a Roman innovation and they were commonly used throughout the Roman Mediterranean. They are attested as early as the first century BCE and continue to occur in late Roman and Byzantine contexts.[46] Such keys are also mentioned in the Mishnah (*m.Kelim* 14.8), attesting to their use in Jewish settings during the second and third centuries CE.

Parallels: Qumran (first century BCE - CE);[47] Nein (first century CE);[48] Nir Gallim (late first - early second century CE);[49] Naḥal Ḥever, Cave of Letters (second century CE);[50] Wadi Murabba'at, Cave 1 (second century CE).[51]

This is an iron elbow (or L-shaped) key made up of four main components: a shank, the longest component of key Gr11Q11; a loop handle (now partially broken) at the far end of the shank, which indicates that the key was either hung around the neck, or connected to a belt worn around the waist, or hung on a hook on the wall, or worn on the finger;[52] a short stem perpendicular to the shank; and a bit (carrying the key's tines) perpendicular to the stem. Three tines are preserved on the bit, but this is broken and, so, the key probably had more tines, possibly five, if regional parallels as well as keys from the built settlement at Qumran are any indication. The key's shank and stem have a rectangular section. Gr11Q11 is highly corroded and, interestingly, the level of corrosion is similar to that of Gr11Q10, which possibly corroborates the view that these two objects were found in the same context (i.e., in the same soil matrix).

Elbow keys would have been inserted through a lock plate in order to operate a tumbler lock mechanism installed on the interior side of a door or furniture unit. The key would have been used both to displace the tumbler pins out of the deadbolt and also to pull the deadbolt from its frame,

44. The finds list appended to the French edition of de Vaux's published field notes has two keys, designated as Gr11Q11 and Gr11Q12. This information has been replicated in the scholarly literature (e.g., Taylor, "The Qumran Caves in their Regional Context," 14). However, this is an error, and de Vaux's field notes, his official inventory, as well as the TCI refer to only one key, which is Gr11Q11. Moreover, there are no traces of a second (unregistered) key in the stores of the Rockefeller. The English edition of de Vaux's notes displays the correct information – the discovery of only one key, Gr11Q11. See also note 55.

45. There is no PAM photograph of Gr11Q11. The photograph attached to the TCI entry for Gr11Q11 is actually a picture of Gr11Q3.

46. Yadin, *The Finds from the Bar Kokhba Period*, 94; T.D. Pace, *A Typology of Roman Locks and Keys* (MA thesis; Southwestern Baptist Theological Seminary, 2014), 63-4.

47. Unpublished.

48. F. Abu Zidan, "Nein," *HA-ESI* 126 (2014), Fig. 4:1.

49. A. Dagot, "Nir Gallim," *HA-ESI* 126 (2014), Fig. 7.

50. Yadin, *Finds from the Bar Kokhba Period*, 92-100, Figs 33-37.

51. R. de Vaux, "Archéologie," in P. Benoit, J.T. Milik and R. de Vaux, *Les Grottes de Murabba'at* (DJD 2; Oxford: Clarendon, 1961) 3-50, on Fig. 10:7, Pl. XII:8.

52. See also Pace, *A Typology of Roman Locks and Keys*, 47-8. According to *t.Shabbat* 4.11, women were not to go out wearing keys on their finger on Shabbat. Such keys, must have had rings at the end of the shank, like our example. Nonetheless, with a diameter of 1.40 cm, Gr11Q11 might be too small for it to have been worn on the finger, unless (of course) it was worn on the little finger or on a small hand.

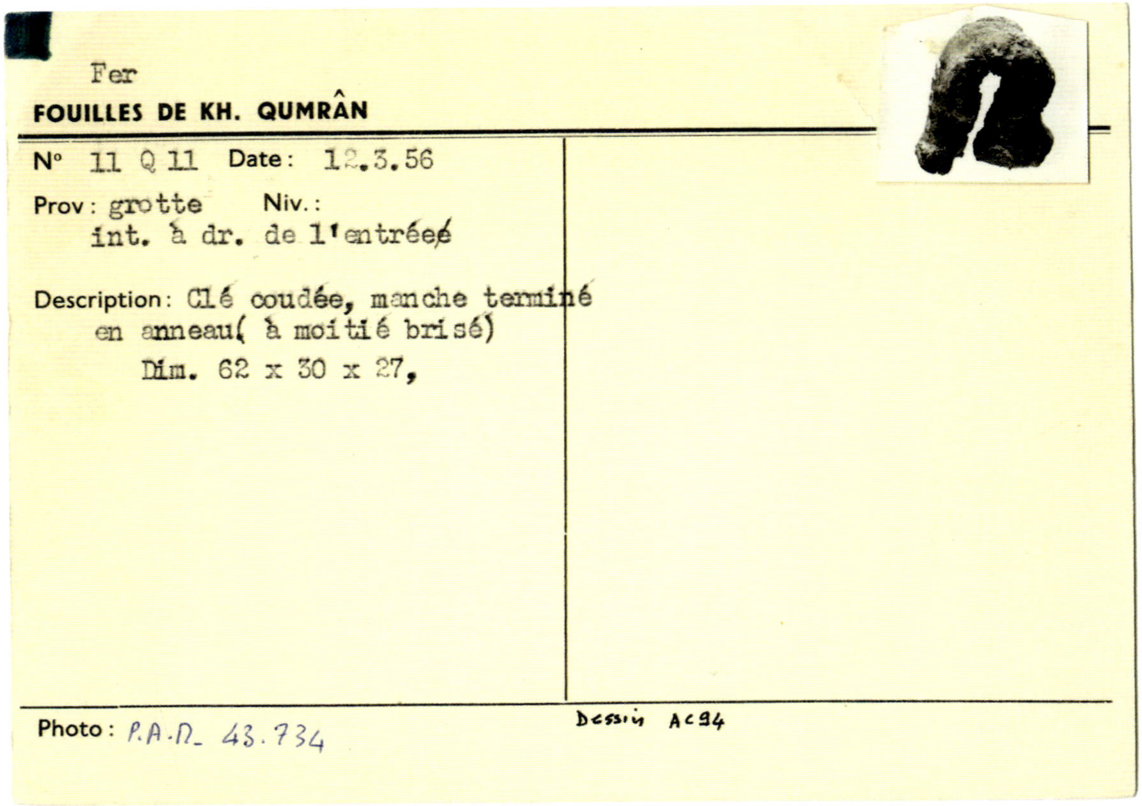

Fer

FOUILLES DE KH. QUMRÂN

N° 11 Q 11 Date: 12.3.56

Prov: grotte Niv.:
int. à dr. de l'entrée

Description: Clé coudée, manche terminé en anneau(à moitié brisé)
Dim. 62 x 30 x 27,

Photo: P.A.M. 43.734

Dessin AC94

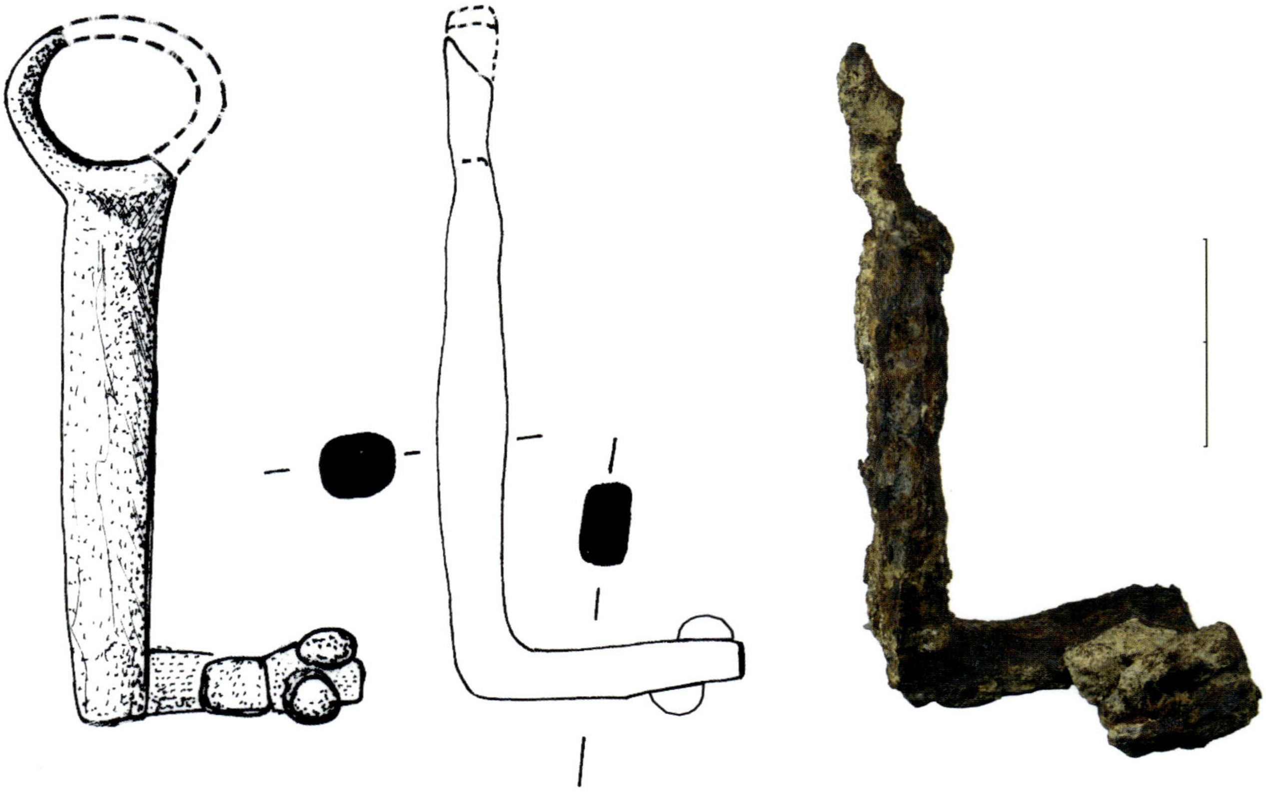

Pl. 7. Gr11Q11 - Key

thereby unlocking the unit.[53] For this reason, elbow or L-shaped keys are frequently referred to as slide keys. Since there were no locking mechanisms on the outer side – meaning that a key had to be inserted *through* the wooden panel (via a lock plate) in order to access the lock on in the inner side – the size of a key is usually indicative of the type of door or furniture unit on which it was used. That is, thick and heavy doors would have required large keys, which needed to be longer than the door's thickness and sturdy enough to displace the tumbler pins and slide the deadbolt without breaking. Naturally, small keys would have been used to unlock small doors, chests, cupboards, or cabinets.[54] Gr11Q11 is a small key and, therefore, it probably unlocked either a small door within a domestic settlement or a chest, cupboard, or cabinet.

Gr11Q12[55] (PAM Nº 43.734) [Pl. 8]

Bead

Malachite. Almost complete. Dimensions: length = 1.10 cm; width = 0.80 cm; diameter of hole = 0.30 cm.

Registered on 12/03/1956

The TCI lists the provenance of Gr11Q12 as "grotte intérieure," and the date of registration is identical to that of Gr11Q10 and Gr11Q11, which were found, together with Qumran-type pottery, to the right of the entryway of the cave's inner chamber. However, unlike Gr11Q10 and Gr11Q11, the contextual label of Gr11Q12 does not specify that it was found to the right of the entrance. Therefore, it remains unclear whether or not Gr11Q12 was found together with Gr11Q10, Gr11Q11, and the Qumran-type pottery.

Date: Iron Age II, Roman period, or later?

It is not possible to date Gr11Q12 on the basis of typology (its cylindrical shape is common, and it lacks any distinguishing characteristics, such as decorative patterns or incisions), and the context in which it was found is unclear. Nonetheless, it is worth recalling that on 12/03/1956, de Vaux's team finished the clearance of the disturbed upper level in the cave's inner chamber and that the prehistoric levels started to be excavated a day later, on 13/03/1956. Therefore, it is likely that Gr11Q12 comes from the mixed upper level containing Iron Age II, Roman, and later material (see de Vaux's entries from 01/03/1956 onwards).

Parallels: Malachite beads are typically found in Iron Age contexts in ancient Palestine,[56] although they are rare relative to beads made from other types of stone. Although there are no specimens (to our knowledge) from the Roman period in Palestine, malachite beads are attested in Graeco-Roman contexts in Egypt.[57]

This is a malachite bead.[58] It has a cylindrical profile and an elliptical section, but one side of its face is almost flat. The surface – which is partially chipped off – is dark green with patches of lighter green, and it is very smooth, indicating that it had been polished. A small hole for the string cuts right through the bead.

53. Yadin, *Finds from the Bar Kokhba Period*, 95; Manning, *Catalogue of the Romano-British Iron Tools*, 92-3; Pace, *A Typology of Roman Locks and Keys*, 58-9, 63-4.

54. See further Yadin, *Finds from the Bar Kokhba Period*, 100.

55. The finds list appended to the French edition of de Vaux's published field notes lists this as 11Q-13, but this is incorrect. This is because the finds list, erroneously, records two keys from Cave 11Q, designated as Gr11Q11 and Gr11Q12. However, de Vaux's field notes, his official inventory, as well as the TCI refer to only one key, which is Gr11Q11. The English edition of de Vaux's notes displays the correct information – the discovery of only one key (Gr11Q11) and the designation of the stone bead as Gr11Q12. See also note 44. A note has recently been added in pencil on the card of Gr11Q12 in the TCI, and this refers to the information in the French edition and re-designates the bead as Gr11Q13. However, in view of the above, this note should be ignored as it is clearly dependent on the erroneous information in the French edition.

56. See H. Ben-Basat, *Early Iron Age Beads at Tel Dor: A Comparative Study* (MA thesis; University of Haifa, 2011), available at http://dor.huji.ac.il/Download/Article/Ben-Basat-2011_eIR_bead.pdf.

57. N. Xia, *Ancient Egyptian Beads* (Heidelberg: Springer, 2014), 139.

58. The identification of the stone is further confirmed by X-Ray Flourescence (XRF) analysis, which indicates that the stone contains a high concentration of copper. The XRF analysis was conducted by Vincenzo Palleschi (National Research Council and University of Pisa, Italy). We are grateful for his assistance.

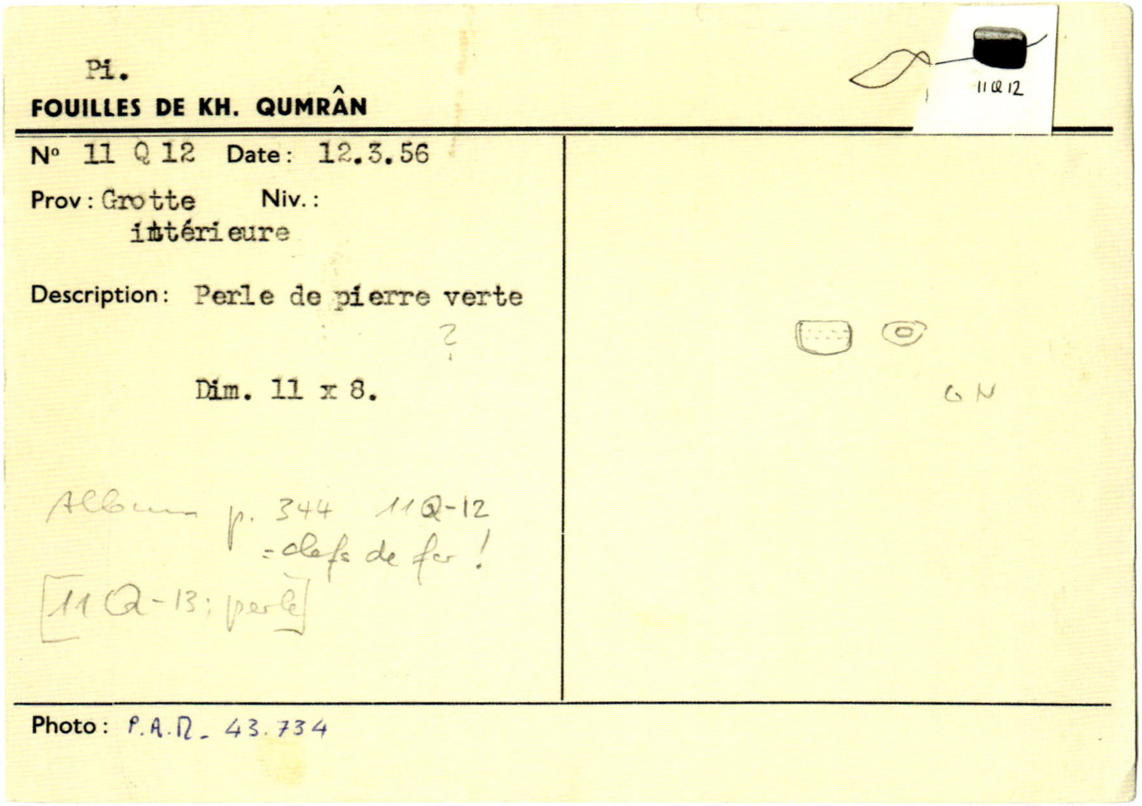

Pi.

FOUILLES DE KH. QUMRÂN

11 Q 12

N° 11 Q 12 Date : 12.3.56

Prov : Grotte intérieure Niv. :

Description : Perle de pierre verte ?

Dim. 11 x 8.

Album p. 344 11Q-12 = clefs de fer !

[11 Q-13 ; perle]

GN

Photo : P.A.M. 43.734

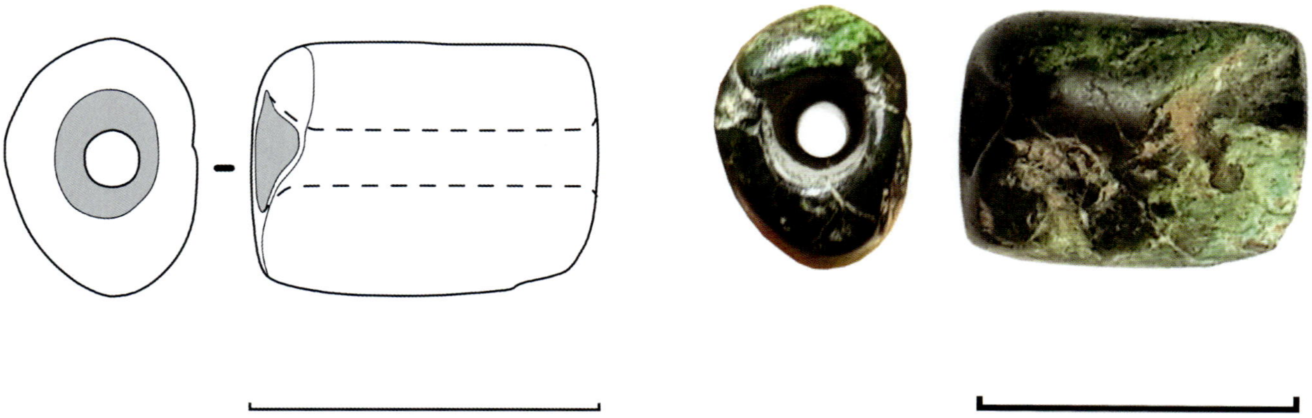

Pl. 8. Gr11Q12 - Bead

2. Discussion

Among the caves at Qumran, Cave 11Q is significant for the concentration of metal artefacts discovered in it. Indeed, this is one of only five caves in the region of Qumran to have yielded a relatively substantial number of miscellaneous artefacts.[59]

The fundamental difficulty with the assemblage of metals from Cave 11Q, however, is the uncertainty of its dating. In his preliminary report, de Vaux gives the impression that Cave 11Q had three clear strata containing Chalcolithic, Iron Age II, and Roman-period material, while noting that all metal artefacts came from the latter level.[60] Nevertheless, it is evident that, in the preliminary report, de Vaux presents a reconstructed stratigraphy of the cave. In reality, most of the metal objects were found in secondary or disturbed contexts. Therefore, their attribution to the Roman period is less certain than de Vaux implies. As we note above, our dating is only tentative and amounts to nothing more than an educated guess based on a number of considerations, namely: 1) the contextual association with Qumran-type pottery or other material from the Roman period; 2) the assumption that the metal artefacts belonged to one and the same assemblage; 3) the fact that two objects from this assemblage can be dated with varying degrees of confidence to the Roman period; and 4) the fact that the evidence from later visits to the cave is meagre.

The presence of a distinctive corpus of metal artefacts (which is anomalous among the Qumran caves) and the fact that many of the objects are tools encourages us to see the metals as part of one assemblage.[61] If this is correct, then an Iron Age II date for the metals can be excluded in view of Gr11Q11 and, to a less certain extent, Gr11Q6, whose typology puts them in the Roman period or later. Furthermore, while a later date cannot be excluded outright – especially in view of human activity at Qumran in the late first and early second centuries CE as well as in the late Roman/Byzantine, early Islamic, Medieval, and Ottoman periods – it is unlikely that the metal assemblage postdates the first century. The latter is by far the most represented period in Cave 11Q, with an assemblage comprising pottery, scrolls, and a relatively large corpus of linen textiles and cords.[62] In contrast, evidence from later periods is either non-existent or else too meagre. For instance, the possibility that the metals were deposited during the Second Revolt is doubtful considering that Cave 11Q lacks incontrovertible evidence of its use during the early second century CE, not to mention that it looks nothing like other Second Revolt caves in the Judaean Desert, which are typically characterized by a much larger repertoire of artefacts.[63] Evidence from the late Roman, Byzantine, and early Islamic periods is similarly lacking. As for the visits made to the cave in the Medieval and Ottoman periods,[64] not only do they seem to have been limited in scope, but the key (and, by extension, the whole assemblage, assuming the metals were part of a single cache) cannot be dated so late. The first century, therefore, seems to be the most plausible date of deposition. If we accept that this corpus represents a single cache of tools and implements, then we must also admit that it could not have been lost accidentally; rather, it must have been an intentional deposit. It is therefore tempting to associate it with the other intentional deposit in Cave 11Q – the scrolls.[65]

With these brief reflections in mind, what can we learn about Cave 11Q on the basis of the metal artefacts? Why were they deposited there? Metal tools and implements were valuable objects, and often they were re-sharpened or re-used, or otherwise melted and re-forged. They were also portable objects, and therefore they could have been carried away from a

59. See D. Mizzi, "Miscellaneous Artefacts from the Qumran Caves: An Exploration of their Significance," in Fidanzio, *Caves of Qumran*, 137-60.

60. De Vaux, "Fouilles de Khirbet Qumrân: rapport préliminaire sur les 3e, 4e, et 5e campagnes," 574.

61. The key (Gr11Q11) is not necessarily an outlier. A second-century shipwreck discovered along the Rhine, at Utrecht, yielded a tool chest with lock and key. Analogously, the key in Cave 11Q could have belonged to a wooden chest that contained the various metal implements found there, and thus it can be considered as an integral component of the metal assemblage. We thank Jürgen Zangenberg for bringing the Rhine shipwreck to our attention.

62. See the various contributions in this volume.

63. See Mizzi, "Miscellaneous Artefacts;" Taylor, "The Qumran Caves in their Regional Context."

64. See the contributions in this volume by Shamir, Sukenik, and Rottoli; Taylor and Sukenik; and Taylor et al.

65. Certainly, it is possible that the metal objects had no association with the scroll deposit. After all, evidence of multiple visits during the first centuries BCE and CE is attested in other caves in the region (e.g., Cave 1Q). Nonetheless, in the case of Cave 11Q, this argument is weakened by the absence of any explicit, supporting evidence in this regard.

site when it was abandoned. Nowhere is this clearer than at Pompeii and Herculaneum: despite the fact that both cities were destroyed abruptly by the eruption of Vesuvius in 79 CE and that many objects (as well as people) were found in situ as they lay in the final hours of both cities, very few metal tools have been found. It is evident that the craftsmen who managed to escape the destruction took their valuable tools with them.[66]

It is not implausible to imagine a similar scenario in the case of Cave 11Q – that is, people deposited more than just scrolls here. It is doubtful that the cave was used for habitation,[67] and neither are there any indications that the cave was utilized as a workshop. Accordingly, the deposition of such a cache of metal tools and implements must have been a deliberate act of hiding, with the express purpose of later retrieval. Although the assemblage seems to be random, it is quite possible that the original deposit was larger and included more objects. Some of this material could have been looted during later visits made to the cave, a possibility underlined by Gr11Q3, if its identification as a loop attachment is correct. If we link together the deposit of scrolls and metals, then it would mean that the scrolls, like the metals, were placed inside Cave 11Q with the aim of later recovery. In other words, the deposit was not meant to be permanent.[68]

Beyond possibly contributing to the debate concerning the history of deposition of the scrolls, the metal artefacts also shed light on daily life and industries. Importantly, the corpus adds to our knowledge of the types of metal tools and implements in circulation in the Roman period. Since metals do not fare very well in the archaeological record, relative to other artefacts, their discovery is always welcome.

What we have published here is a very small assemblage, but one which can still be potentially informative. It is regrettable, however, that we know so little about the archaeological context of these artefacts and that we are, therefore, severely restricted with regard to what we can say about them. The above discussion is meant to serve as a preliminary reflection on the corpus and by no means does it exhaust all possible avenues of interpretation. More importantly, we cannot claim that our arguments are conclusive owing to the problematic nature of the data, which is why we cannot exclude alternative interpretations. We only hope that the raw data we publish here inspires others to work with the material and, possibly, to draw out further conclusions. At the same time, we reiterate the fact that Cave 11Q did not yield a Roman arrowhead, and it contained only one, not two keys.

66. Ulrich, *Roman Woodworking*, 13-4.

67. See the discussion in Mizzi, "Miscellaneous Artefacts." And see also the conversation between F. García Martínez, "Cave 11 in Context," in C. Hempel (ed.), *The Dead Sea Scrolls: Texts and Context* (STDJ 90; Leiden: Brill, 2010) 199-209, on pp. 206-7; D. Stökl Ben Ezra, "Further Reflections on Caves 1 and 11: A Response to Florentino García Martínez," in Hempel, *The Dead Sea Scrolls*, 211-23, on p. 220; J.E. Taylor, *The Essenes, the Scrolls, and the Dead Sea* (Oxford: Oxford University Press, 2012), 279, n. 30.

68. The presence of Gr11Q11 strengthens this conclusion. Keys, whether they unlocked doors or smaller furniture units, are characteristic of assemblages deposited during wartime or periods of socio-political unrest (*cf.* the keys from the Bar Kokhba caves in Naḥal Ḥever, for which see Yadin, *Finds from the Bar Kokhba Period*, 92-100; some of the keys are smaller than Gr11Q11). Unless it was dropped by accident, the key in Cave 11Q reflects the hope that it would be retrieved and re-used at some future time. As suggested above in note 61, it is not implausible that the key could have belonged to a tool chest which contained the tools and implements found in the cave (and others which did not survive in the archaeological record).

Chapter Eight

The Preservation and Digitization of the Manuscripts Attributed to Cave 11Q

Pnina SHOR, Oren ABLEMAN, Orit ROSENGARTEN, Beatriz RIESTRA, Helena LIBMAN, Tanya BITLER, Tanya TREIGER, and Ashlyn OPRESCU

While other articles in this volume discuss the content and historical significance of the Dead Sea Scrolls attributed to Qumran Cave 11Q, this paper hopes to elucidate their conservation and preservation aspects, through the work carried out by the Israel Antiquities Authority. Even though this paper focuses primarily on the thirty Cave 11Q manuscripts, currently arranged in over one hundred plates and boxes, much of the work applied to them can equally be applied to the rest of the Dead Sea Scroll corpus. This work includes understanding how the history of the scrolls, both ancient and modern, has affected their current appearance and condition, carrying out interventive treatments in order to stabilize the scrolls and preserve them for future generations, and making use of modern technology to further those preservation goals.

1. Conservation and Condition

Despite their varied appearance and differing states of preservation, the condition concerns of the Dead Sea Scrolls in general, and the Cave 11Q scrolls in particular, can be divided into four main categories: thickness, surface appearance, cockling and delamination, and gelatinization. The thickness and surface appearance of the fragments are affected by a wide range of variables including the source animals, manufacturing process, ancient and modern storage conditions and the various treatments the scrolls have undergone since discovery. The source animal is a key variable as skin thickness varies across species, across age and size within the same species (younger and smaller animals have thinner skin) and across different areas of a single skin (thicker at the spine gradually thinning towards the belly area).[1] Ancient and modern storage conditions as well as the various past treatments will all have had effects on the surface appearance of the fragments be it colour, texture, or the condition of the ink. Because there are so many possible sources of surface alternation, it is impossible to definitively pinpoint all the causes and effects in play and explain why two fragments from the same scroll may have completely different appearances, or why two fragments from different scrolls may look the same.

Cockling and delamination occurs when parchment has absorbed and released moisture depending on the surrounding environment. This process causes the material to expand and contract across all dimensions. However, these motions are not perfect mirrors of each other, meaning that the parchment

1. B.M. Haines, "The Fibre Structure of Leather," in M. Kite and R. Thomson (ed.), *Conservation of Leather and Related Materials* (Oxford: Elsevier, 2006) 11-21, on pp. 9-12.

does not return to its original flat state, but rather becomes curled and wavy or cockled.[2] In extreme cases if one layer of the parchment expands and contracts at a different rate than the layer below it, it can become detached or delaminated. The tannin dressing used on the surface of the parchments from the Qumran caves resulted in clearly defined layers within each scroll fragment,[3] each with slightly different rates of expansion and contraction. This probably accounts for the delamination, especially of the writing surface, seen in some of the Dead Sea Scrolls.

Gelatinization is the end degradation product of parchment. When there is enough moisture present gelatinized parchment will be sticky and jelly-like, however in dry conditions this material shrinks, fuses together, blackens, hardens, and quite often crumbles away.[4] It is this process that is responsible for the blackened, uneven edges found on most of the Dead Sea Scroll fragments, as well as the fused state of some scrolls such as 11Q4 Ezek which "survived as a dense, unopenable mass."[5] H.J. Plenderleith, the first director of ICROM who was asked for assistance with this scroll, described it as having "become solidified into a pitch-like lump which breaks with a jet black lustrous or resinous fracture … gelatinized and later congealed to such an extent that the cross-section indicates no stratification whatever."[6]

Over the last 70 years numerous treatments were carried out on the scrolls, always with the best intentions, to unroll them, improve legibility, and hold them together. The most noteworthy treatments are the extensive use of pressure sensitive tape, and occasional use of castor oil and other surface treatments by the first scholars in the 1950s. In preparation for an exhibition at the British Museum, a conservator from this institution treated a few of the scrolls in the 1960s. Unfortunately, her use of British Museum Leather Dressing to reduce the brittleness of the fragments has also had detrimental consequences to their surface condition. In the 1970s conservators of the Israel Museum attempted to remove some of the tape and support fragile fragments with tissue paper adhered with acrylic Perspex glue to the versos of many fragments.

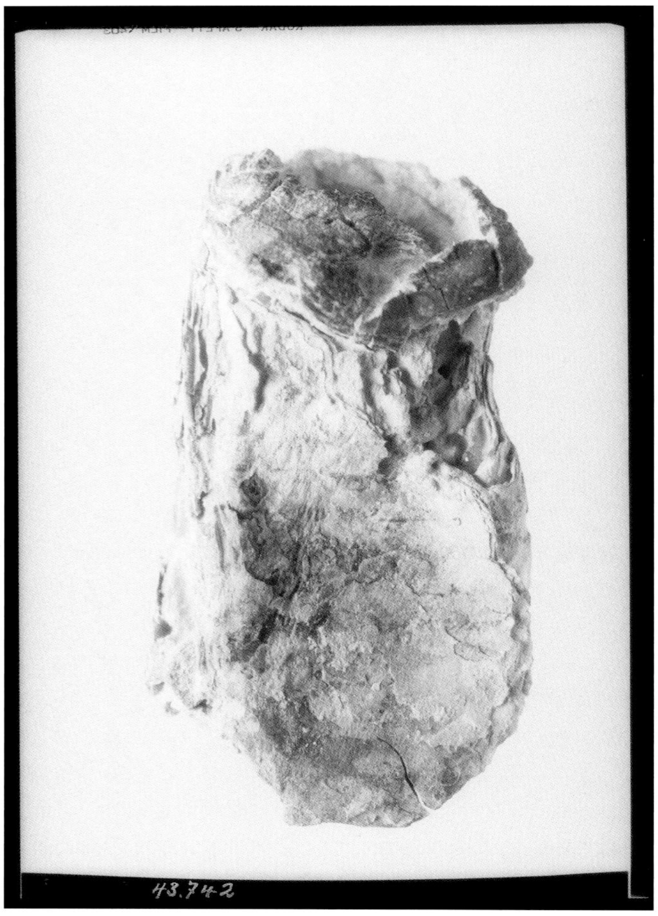

Fig. 1. 11Q4 Ezek. PAM 43.742. Photograph: Najib Albina[7]

Since the establishment of the Israel Antiquities Authority's (IAA) Dead Sea Scrolls (DSS) Conservation Lab in the 1990s, a designated team of conservators has been removing and reversing these previous treatments, when possible, with careful use of mechanical techniques and solvents.

2. C.S. Woods, "The Conservation of Parchment," in Kite and Thomson, *Conservation of Leather*, 200-24, on p. 205.

3. J.B. Poole and R. Reed, "The Preparation of Leather and Parchment by the Dead Sea Scrolls Community," *Technology and Culture* 3/1 (1962) 1-26, on pp. 1-20.

4. Woods, "Conservation of Parchment," 205.

5. E.D. Herbert, "11QEzekiel (Pls II, LIV)," in F. García Martínez, E.J.C Tigchelaar, and A.S. van der Woude, *Qumran Cave 11.II: 11Q2-18, 11Q20-31* (DJD 23; Oxford: Clarendon, 1998) 15-28, on p. 16.

6. H.J. Plenderleith, unpublished examination March 3, 1962.

7. All images, unless otherwise noted, are courtesy of The Leon Levy Dead Sea Scrolls Digital Library, IAA, photographer: Shai Halevi.

Fig. 2. Removal of pressure sensitive tape from a fragment

They then use Japanese tissue paper and methyl cellulose adhesive to support the edges and fragile areas of the scroll fragments to ensure their continued preservation. The thousands of fragments of the Dead Sea Scrolls are stored in a climate controlled storeroom. The majority are arranged on "plates" of archival materials and stored in Solander boxes; about a hundred are mounted for exhibition purposes.

2. State of Preservation of the Cave 11Q Scrolls

The scrolls of Cave 11Q present a diverse range of preservation states. On the one hand, there are scrolls in a similar condition to the well-preserved scrolls from Cave 1Q. On the other hand, there are extremely fragmentary and badly damaged scrolls at times in a worse condition than the material found in Cave 4Q, such as the unidentified fragments still in boxes. The following descriptions highlight interesting features of the major scrolls from Cave 11Q but should not be considered unique to the cave or the scroll.

A. Eight of the scrolls reached the scholars' hands while still partially or completely rolled. Two of them – 11Q5 Ps^a and 11Q10 tgJob – have an uninscribed area remaining at the end of the scroll, while four of them – 11Q1 paleoLev^a, 11Q11 apocrPs, 11Q17 ShirShabb, and 11Q19 T^a – have blank handle sheets at their end, although only two are intact. Of these eight scrolls, 11Q5 Ps^a, 11Q19 T^a, and 11Q1 paleoLev^a, proved to be the best preserved when unrolled. First and foremost, 11Q5 Ps^a was so well preserved that Sanders unrolled it within ten days and prepared it for publication within a year.[8] At 4.2 meters long it is probably the best-preserved scroll from Cave 11Q. According to Sanders, when the scroll was first unrolled the threads connecting the individual sheets were still intact but quickly disintegrated to dust upon exposure. Currently the manuscript consists mainly of the substantial fragments recovered from the rolled scroll, now divided into six plates which preserve 28 columns of text. In addition to these, the remnants of three additional columns were found on fragments A-D which were not physically connected to the rolled scroll. The majority of the fragments are a medium brown color and only the edges, particularly along the bottom, are blackened and gelatinized. In a few cases there are white dots on the gelatinized areas. There is also scattered insect damage, including some small holes, and some abrasion which may be from the original scribes scraping away mistakes. On a few fragments there are trace remnants of sewing. In the 1970s the fragments were backed with tissue paper and acrylic glue, which has been removed, where possible, and replaced with Japanese tissue paper by the IAA DSS Conservation Lab.

Y. Yadin also attributed to this scroll Fragment E, sent to him by mail as an enticement for purchasing the Temple Scroll. This fragment, with remains of three columns of text, is 37 cm long and is in poorer condition than the others. It is a darker shade of brown with a larger proportion of blackened and gelatinized areas, and edges that are especially fragile and uneven. There are also a number of holes, spots and delaminated areas on the surface as well as a light deposit of sand or dirt. The verso shows traces of previous conservation work done in the 1970s. In DJD 23 a sixth tiny fragment F was published in conjunction with Fragment E.[9] Another small fragment that is most likely connected with fragment E has been identified by O. Ableman and published in his paper in this volume.

8. J.A. Sanders, "The Scroll of Psalms (11QPss) From Cave 11: A Preliminary Report," *BASOR* 165 (1962) 5-11. Sanders later published a detailed report on his work of unrolling and publishing the scroll. See J.A. Sanders, "The Modern History of the Qumran Psalms Scroll and Canonical Criticism," in S.M. Paul et al. (ed.), *Emanuel: Studies in Hebrew Bible, Septuagint, and Dead Sea Scrolls in Honor of Emanuel Tov* (VTSup 94; Leiden: Brill, 2003) 393-411.

9. DJD 23, 29-36.

Fig. 3. 11Q5 Ps[a], Plate 975

Fig. 4. 11Q1 paleoLev[a], Plate 1039/1

11Q19 T[a], deposited at the Shrine of the Book, is at 8.14 meters the longest scroll found so far. Because it was hidden in a shoebox under Kando's shop floor for so many years it was severely damaged. It is preserved in eight plates in various states of preservation and divided into 67 columns. Soon after the Six Days War it was unrolled in the conservation lab of the Israel Museum where it was coated with Perspex glue and backed with tissue paper to strengthen it. Because most of it is extremely brittle, fragile, gelatinized, and in some instances transparent, the conservators of the IAA DSS Conservation Lab decided to try to stabilize it. Where possible, this was done by reinforcing the scroll through the old backing using Japanese tissue paper and methyl cellulose adhesive. This procedure simultaneously relaxed and flattened the parchment.

One of the fragments has three white spots which appear to be the remnants of insect nests. Of the Cave 11Q material, this was the only scroll singled out for scientific testing, and in the 1990s it was sampled for carbon-14 dating and DNA extraction. The carbon-14 analysis dated the scroll to 97 BCE-1 CE,[10] and the DNA extraction concluded that the scroll was manufactured from goat skins.[11]

11Q1 paleoLev[a] consists of four plates, the most impressive of which is catalogued as plate 1039/1. This single fragment is one meter long and preserves seven columns of the end of the scroll. It is a light brown color with some blackening and gelatinization especially along the scallop-shaped bottom edge. Some of the original stitching is visible to the right of the centre of the fragment. It was also attached to tissue paper with Perspex glue in the 1970s, however most of this has since been removed. In some cases where it was impossible to remove this tissue without damaging the scroll, it was left in place. The other parts of the scroll, numbering fourteen fragments for a total length of about 88 cm, are in similar condition, although five of them show considerably more gelatinization over the whole surface of the fragment.

10. G. Bonani et al., "Radiocarbon Dating of the Dead Sea Scrolls," *'Atiqot* 20 (1991) 27-32.

11. G. Kahila Bar-Gal, *Genetic Change in the* Capra *Species of Southern Levant over the Past 10,000 Years as Studied by DNA Analysis of Ancient and Modern Populations* (PhD diss.; Hebrew University, 2000), 3-72.

Fig. 5. 11Q11 apocrPs, Plate 61

Fig. 6. 11Q10 tgJob, Plates 631-624-634

B. 11Q11 apocrPs[a] 11Q10 tgJob, 11Q17 ShirShabb, and 11Q18 NJ also all originally found rolled, display interesting patterns of degradation caused by gelatinization. Both edges of each scroll were heavily gelatinized before discovery and subsequently crumbled away when they were moved and later unrolled, resulting in characteristic shapes for the fragments of each individual scroll.

11Q11 apocrPs[a] consists of six fragments in four plates and is approximately 80.5 cm long. The longest single fragment, 55 cm, is a medium brown color with some gelatinization at the edges. An uninscribed handle sheet was originally attached to the end of the scroll and according to DJD 23 it is attached to a wooden bar.[12] However, recent observations with both a microscope and multispectral imaging indicate that the edge of the uninscribed handle sheet consists only of tightly rolled parchment tied with a string; there are no signs of a wooden bar inside it. A further striking feature is that all the fragments of this scroll exhibit a snake-like shape due to heavy gelatinization that damaged both the upper and bottom edges of the scroll.

11Q10 tgJob provides the clearest example of how substantial gelatinization effects the contour of the scrolls. The longer better-preserved fragments of this manuscript exhibit heavily scalloped edges which develop first into large oval-shaped medallions and then into smaller oval-shaped medallions in the poorer preserved fragments. The entire scroll consists of 38 columns divided into seventeen plates. The longest single fragment is just over one meter, but is in very poor condition. All the fragments are dark brown with black gelatinized edges, and there are holes, creases and delaminated areas spread across the surface; the ink on most of the fragments is unstable. This scroll was also first treated in the 1970s and then re-treated by the IAA DSS Conservation Lab. To reduce the parchment's exposure to moisture a special mix of alcohol and water was used to make the methyl cellulose adhesive.

11Q17 ShirShabb shows yet a third pattern of deterioration: the larger fragments resemble arrowheads, while some of the smaller ones resemble an uppercase *lambda*. Unlike the two previously mentioned scrolls, which suffered gelatinization from both the top and bottom edges resulting in their rounded shapes, the gelatinization of 11Q17 ShirShabb occurred more as a triangular shape from one edge, resulting in its different pattern of deterioration. The fragments which remain are generally a medium brown color with some blackening

12. Cf. DJD 23, 181 and Pl. XXII.

and gelatinization of the edges. The ruled lines are very visible, and the text is clearly written below these lines. However, some of the fragments are in very poor condition having partially crumbled into powder-like particles.

Fig. 7. 11Q17 ShirShabb, Plate 609

11Q18 NJ also suffered the loss of its margins due to gelatinization. However the resulting fragments, which were cut loose from the petrified scroll following H.J. Plenderleith's consultancy,[13] have much more varied and irregular outlines. The gelatinization of some of the fragments has caused them to shrink and deform slightly, creating cracks running from the outer edges into the centre. The fragments are generally dark brown but with lighter centres. Some of the parchment is very thick and a few fragments have a white deposit on the surface.

Fig. 8. 11Q18 NJ, Plate 570

13. J.P.M. van der Ploeg, "Les manuscrits de la Grotte XI de Qumrân," *RdQ* 12/45 (1985) 3-15, on p. 14.

C. Other notable scrolls from Cave 11Q include 11Q14 Sefer ha-Milhamah, 11Q20 T^{b}, 11Q7 Ps^{c} and 11Q13 Melch.

Fig. 9. 11Q14 Sefer ha-Milhamah, Plate 607/1

11Q14 Sefer ha-Milhamah primarily consists of one well-preserved fragment and a few smaller ones. It is light brown with only minimal blackening around the edges, a few small holes, some slight delamination on the right edge, and some brown stains on the left of the front surface. Like many of the Cave 11Q scrolls it was treated in the 1970s and subsequently re-treated by the IAA DSS Conservation Lab.

Most of the fragments of 11Q20 T^{b} are light brown in color, although many of them have darker brown stains over large areas of their surface. There is some gelatinization of the edges which for a few fragments has resulted in slight shrinkage and some cracks. Several fragments have circular white deposits on their surface.

The fragments of 11Q7 Ps^{c} range in color from light brown to dark brown to black along the gelatinized edges, and they are brittle with a few spots, deposits, holes and cracks across the surface. The main feature of these fragments is the areas of delamination and abrasion on the surface, most likely from insects, which have caused the loss of some text.

11Q13 Melch is in the worst condition of the five, and has been treated by the IAA DSS Conservation Lab so that the edges and fragile areas are supported. All fragments show gelatinization on the edges,

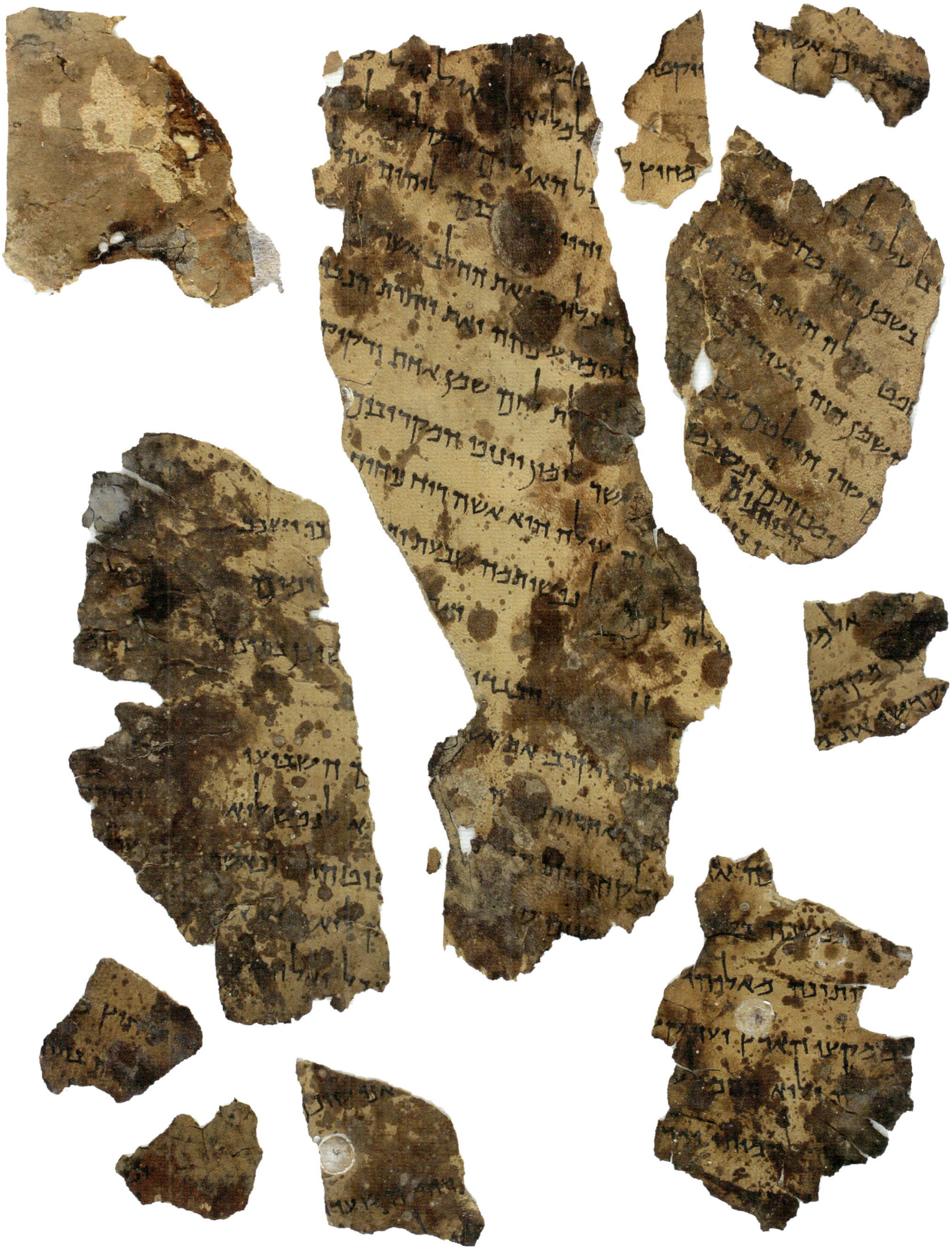

Fig. 10. 11Q20 T^{b}, Plate 580

Fig. 11. 11Q7 Ps^{c}, Plate 606/1

Fig. 12. 11Q13 Melch, Plate 579

particularly along the top, but some fragments are completely gelatinized. There are also a number of holes, cracks and white surface deposits. The key feature of this scroll is its extensive delamination some of which may have been caused or further exacerbated by insects. In several instances the thin upper writing layer has separated completely from the thicker lower layers of the parchment. As a result, a number of the fragments published in DJD 23 as single fragments have now been imaged and catalogued as two different entities, with the thicker lower layer preserving the original shape of the fragment.[14]

D. One of the phenomena of Cave 11Q are the thousands of scroll fragments still housed in boxes with the original dirt and debris from the cave; overall there are about 35 boxes attributed to Cave 11Q. While preparing the material for publication the editors of DJD 23 were aware of these boxes, so they combed through them and took out fragments with writing visible to the naked eye. These fragments were then arranged into plates, photographed in infra-red, and published in DJD 23.[15] Some of the fragments belong to the rolled scrolls e.g. 11Q17 ShirShabb or 11Q18 NJ, from which they were probably detached during the unrolling process.[16] Nevertheless, many of the boxes contain material that does not necessarily belong to these manuscripts. About three years ago the IAA began to catalogue items which had not yet been recorded with a focus on material still in boxes.[17] The individual cataloguing and treatment of these fragments is an ongoing project in itself.[18] One of its first outcomes is a renewed examination of the boxes attributed to Cave 11Q. A few dozen fragments with traces of writing on them were removed from one of these and several have been identified. Some of them are presented in O. Ableman's paper in this volume.

Fig. 13. Unidentified fragments from Cave 11Q in Box 1032A

E. Minute remnants of textiles probably belonging to scroll wrappers and still attached to tiny text fragments are also surfacing as a result of this survey. These fragments and textiles are reminiscent of the single fragment of 11Q24 Unidentified Text ar, published in DJD 23, which also has a textile attached to its verso.[19] They are very difficult to identify because most of them are adhered to the fragments due to a layer of hardened dirt. So far about seven samples have been identified. Besides these samples the only other example of a textile still wrapping a scroll is the unique, and larger, piece from Cave 1Q to which a tiny sherd of a pottery rim is also still attached.[20]

Fig. 14. Textile still attached to 11Q24, P567-Fg010-R -D20052014-color

14. DJD 23, 221.

15. The removal of fragments from the boxes is mentioned in DJD 23, 438. A summary of E. Tigchelaar's inspection of these boxes has been published in E. Tigchelaar, "Some More Small 11Q1 Fragments," *RdQ* 18/70 (1997) 325-30, on pp. 326-7, n. 5.

16. DJD 23, 305-6.

17. An inventory of these items was prepared by Oren Ableman and Lena Libman with the generous assistance of Prof. Hannah Cotton of the Hebrew University of Jerusalem.

18. For a brief explanation of the cataloguing process cf. O. Ableman, "Newly Identified Pentateuchal Fragments: 4QExod^{g} (4Q18, Exod 12:51-13:3), 4QDeut^{k3} (4Q38b, Deut 30:13-18)," *RdQ* 30/111 (2018) 91-100.

19. Cf. DJD 23, 421.

20. Cf. D. Barthélemy and J.T. Milik, *Qumran Cave 1* (DJD 1; Oxford: Clarendon, 1955), 7, 12, and Pl. I (8-10).

3. The Digitization Project

In the 1950s, soon after the discovery of the scrolls, the first scholars placed the individual fragments in glass plates primarily according to paleographic and physical similarities, thus creating about 1260 plates. The compilation of these plates was documented by the infrared photographs whose negatives became known as PAM negatives. These PAM negatives have served as the basis and reference for most of the research and publication of the scrolls until the beginning of the IAA's digitization project. Therefore, the first stage of the digitization project was to scan about 4000 PAM negatives in the best possible resolution. Many of the plates do indeed contain fragments from the same manuscript, and are mostly arranged in line with their final reconstruction as seen in the later PAM series numbered 43-44.000. However, there are a significant number of plates where unidentified fragments were grouped together even when it was clear that they belonged to different manuscripts. The editors would occasionally move fragments from plate to plate as they refined their reconstruction.

In 1981 E. Qimron began to assemble an inventory list which was updated by J. Strugnell in 1984-5. The final arrangement of scrolls on plates was set in 1991 once the inventory list was drawn,[21] and permanently frozen with the establishment of the IAA DSS Conservation Lab that same year. This final arrangement still included single manuscripts whose fragments were spread across 10-20 plates and single plates containing fragments from several different manuscripts. Therefore, after 1991, in order to present plates that reflect the correct reconstruction of the fragments, scholars created virtual plates combining fragments from various physical plates.[22]

In later volumes of the DJD series, DJD 23 included, the editors usually indicate the numbers of the PAM negatives in which the fragments appear, and the inventory number of the plates on which the fragments are physically arranged. However, there are some minor errors in recording the locations of some small fragments, and occasionally when the editors could not locate the physical fragment, they relied only on their PAM photograph.

Fig. 15. PAM negatives with fragments from various manuscripts, PAM 44.114 (Upper), PAM 42.177 (Lower)

In the beginning of the twenty-first century when the IAA began to computerize the data about the scrolls, a comparison between the published photographs and the physical plates was undertaken. This information was recorded manually on a copy of all the DJD plates and in the IAA's computerized database. Eventually it was integrated into the work procedure and metadata of our current digitization project.

21. Reed, S.A., *The Dead Sea Scrolls Catalogue: Documents, Photographs and Museum Inventory Numbers* (SBL RBS 32; ed. and rev. M.J. Lundberg with the collaboration of M.B. Phelps; Atlanta: Scholars, 1994).

22. E.g. the fragments of 11Q18 NJ are spread across fifteen plates; whereas, Pl. 567 contains fragments from 11 manuscripts.

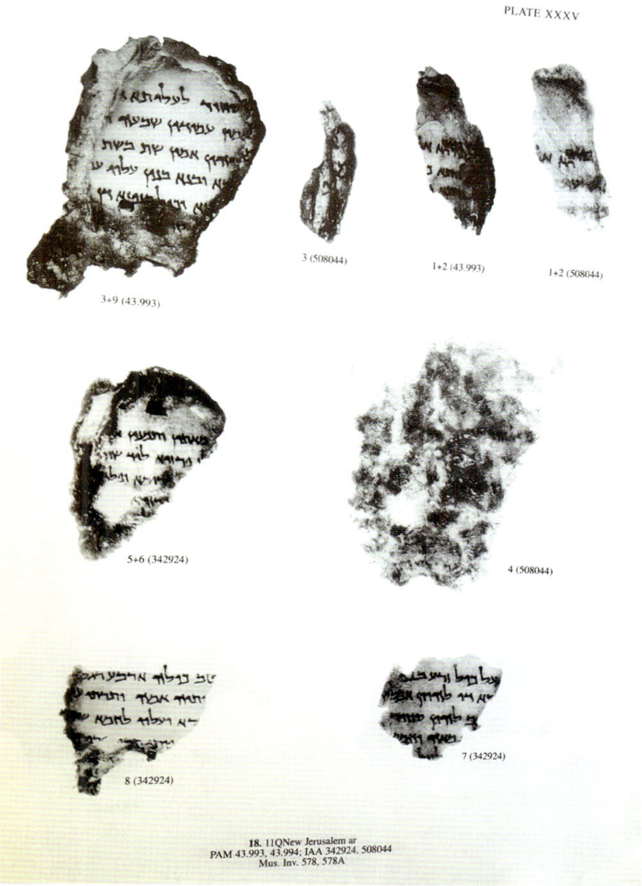

Fig. 16. DJD 23, Plate XXXV, a virtual plate that contains fragments of the same manuscripts from different Plates and PAMs

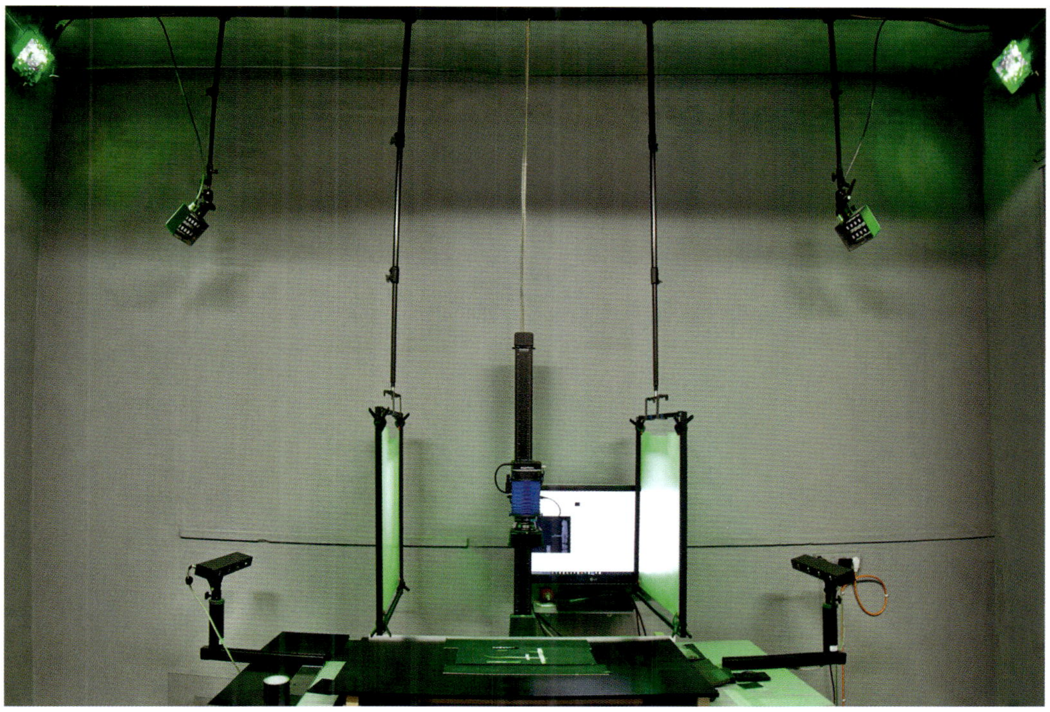

Fig. 17. The MegaVision Imaging System

On the occasion of the 60th anniversary of the discovery of the Scrolls, in November 2007, the IAA brought together an international team of experts for imaging and data management to assist and recommend how to go about the documentation of the scrolls both for conservation and research purposes.[23] In 2008 the IAA set out to choose the most advanced and adequate system and raise the funds to implement a project of such a scope.[24]

The systematic imaging of the thousands of scroll fragments was launched in September 2011. In December 2012 the images were first uploaded to a dedicated website: The Leon Levy Dead Sea Scrolls Digital Library, (www.deadseascrolls.org.il).[25] To date over 34,000 multispectral images have been uploaded. This website has become an indispensable resource for scholars, but a key function of this project is also to allow open access to the images of all the DSS for the public worldwide. One of the crucial decisions made when planning this digitization project was to image fragments rather than plates. This challenge necessitated the development of yet another cataloging system in which for the first time each fragment was viewed as a separate entity.

The digitization process begins with the preparation of each plate of fragments for imaging by the team of IAA DSS conservators. The plate is then imaged in color and a software, specifically adapted to our needs, identifies the fragments on the plate, numbers them, and creates a 'map' of the plate with the coordinates of each fragment. This information is then integrated into the MegaVision (MV) imaging system's database. Each fragment is imaged individually under twelve wavelengths: seven in the visible spectrum and five in the near infrared range, with 28 exposures from various angles and different lighting. The highest infrared wavelength of 924 nanometers, chosen to enable new readings beyond those of the PAM photographs, has already yielded new readings. The color image created from the seven bands in the visible spectrum also serves as a surrogate of the scroll. As such, along with the monitoring system that was developed based on these wavelengths, it is a key part of the IAA's preservation efforts.

Once the digitization process is completed the new data for each plate is integrated into the IAA database. Volunteers help update and correlate the various numbering systems given by the scholars in the DJD volumes, by the conservators, and by IAA's MV system. This step is crucial for creating and maintaining a single unified database that functions accurately with all the existing numbering systems.[26]

This new cataloguing system has led to occasional difficulties identifying fragments whose physical shape has changed from their appearance in the PAM negatives, such as those belonging to 11Q13 Melch. However, the decision to catalogue fragments individually has made it possible to sometimes identify supposedly "lost" fragments. An example of this from Cave 11Q can be seen in Plate XLVIII in DJD 23 which presents a collection of unidentified fragments in paleo-Hebrew located on various plates attributed to Cave 11Q. These fragments probably belong to the same manuscript so they were numbered 11Q22 paleoUnidentified Text. The fragments of this manuscript were recorded as being physically located on plates 614, 1020, and 1032, with fragments 1, 2 and 5 listed as missing.[27] Several years ago fragment 1 was identified on plate 1022 and is already noted in E. Tov's Revised List.[28] The location of fragment 2 is still unknown, whereas fragment 5 was recently discovered on plate 697 and is registered as number 15 on the new MegaVision "map" plate.

Most of the fragments on plate 697 belong to 4Q270 D^{e}, and are published in DJD 18. However, the plate also includes four additional unidentified fragments. Since one of these fragments is in paleo-Hebrew script, it was compared with other paleo-Hebrew manuscripts and eventually identified as the missing fragment 5 of 11Q22 paleoUnidentified Text. One

23. The committee was sponsored by the generous help of Yad Hanadiv.

24. The Leon Levy Foundation and the Arcadia Fund sponsored this multi-million $ project for the first five years.

25. The first version of the site was developed in collaboration with Google R&D Israel.

26. We would like to thank Barry Bowalsky Laura Worden and Matea Dautović, volunteers who have helped us with this issue. Their tedious efforts are instrumental for the successes of the project.

27. Cf. DJD 23, 415.

28. E. Tov, *Revised Lists of the Texts from the Judaean Desert* (Leiden: Brill, 2010), 77. Tov evidently could not locate the small fragment 7. A closer examination of Pl. 1032 with the aid of the new images confirmed that it is still there as registered in DJD 23.

Fig. 18. Plate 697, fragment 15 is circled

of the other unidentified fragments on plate 697 was then identified as fragment 1 of 11Q30, which also houses unclassified fragments. Both re-identified fragments appear in PAM 44.117 along with other fragments from Cave 11Q, but it is still unclear why and when they were moved to a plate that belongs to a different cave.

4. Conclusion

The goal of this paper was to present an overview of the scrolls attributed to Cave 11Q, discussing their similarities with the material from other caves and highlighting some of the exceptional features and phenomena particular to scrolls from this cave. While the discovery, treatment history, and general condition of the material from Cave 11Q is similar to that of the material from the other ten caves, the number of scrolls found rolled, the patterns of degradation found in half of them, and the existence of textile remnants count among the most remarkable of these exceptional features. It is hoped that this presentation will aid in the further analysis and understanding of these scrolls, as well as those from the other caves.

Additionally, this paper has provided an overview of the IAA's digitization project and how it has allowed for new discoveries in material which has hitherto been unidentified. The material from the Qumran caves includes thousands of small fragments with little or no writing, most of which were never published in the DJD series because they were not associated with specific manuscripts. In this respect DJD 23 is somewhat an exception since it did include some tiny fragments with minimal traces of writing.[29] However, with the availability of new technologies, such as those employed by the IAA's digitization project, more and more of these fragments with traces of ink can be identified, imaged, catalogued, and made accessible to scholars. Furthermore, it is hoped that additional technologies together with computer science algorithms will make it possible to study these newly identified fragments and connect them with previously identified and published manuscripts.

While the individual documentation of all the DSS fragments will doubtlessly be useful to scholars and will push forward the understanding of the content of the Dead Sea Scrolls, it may also provide essential data for future conservation efforts, ensuring that not only the scholarship, but the physical scrolls themselves, will endure for generations to come.

29. E.g. DJD 23, Pls XLIX-LI.

Chapter Eight
Appendix

Manuscripts from Cave 11Q: Photo Collections by Hunzinger and Allegro

Marcello FIDANZIO (ed.)

On 5 September 1957, the members of Cave 4Q team who were in Jerusalem (Allegro, Fitzmeyer, Hunzinger, Milik, and Strugnell) were allowed one hour to access the manuscripts from Cave 11Q stored at Rockefeller Museum. Two photo collections by Claus-Hunno Hunzinger and John Marco Allegro depict this event and show some manuscripts a year and a half after their discovery. Thanks to the work done by the network for Dispersed Qumran Caves Artefacts and Archival Sources (Joan Taylor, Dennis Mizzi, and Marcello Fidanzio) and by Alexander Schick these two collections are being made available here.

Manuscripts from Cave 11Q: 5 September 1957
Photos by John Marco Allegro (courtesy Estate John Allegro)

Fig. 1

Fig. 2

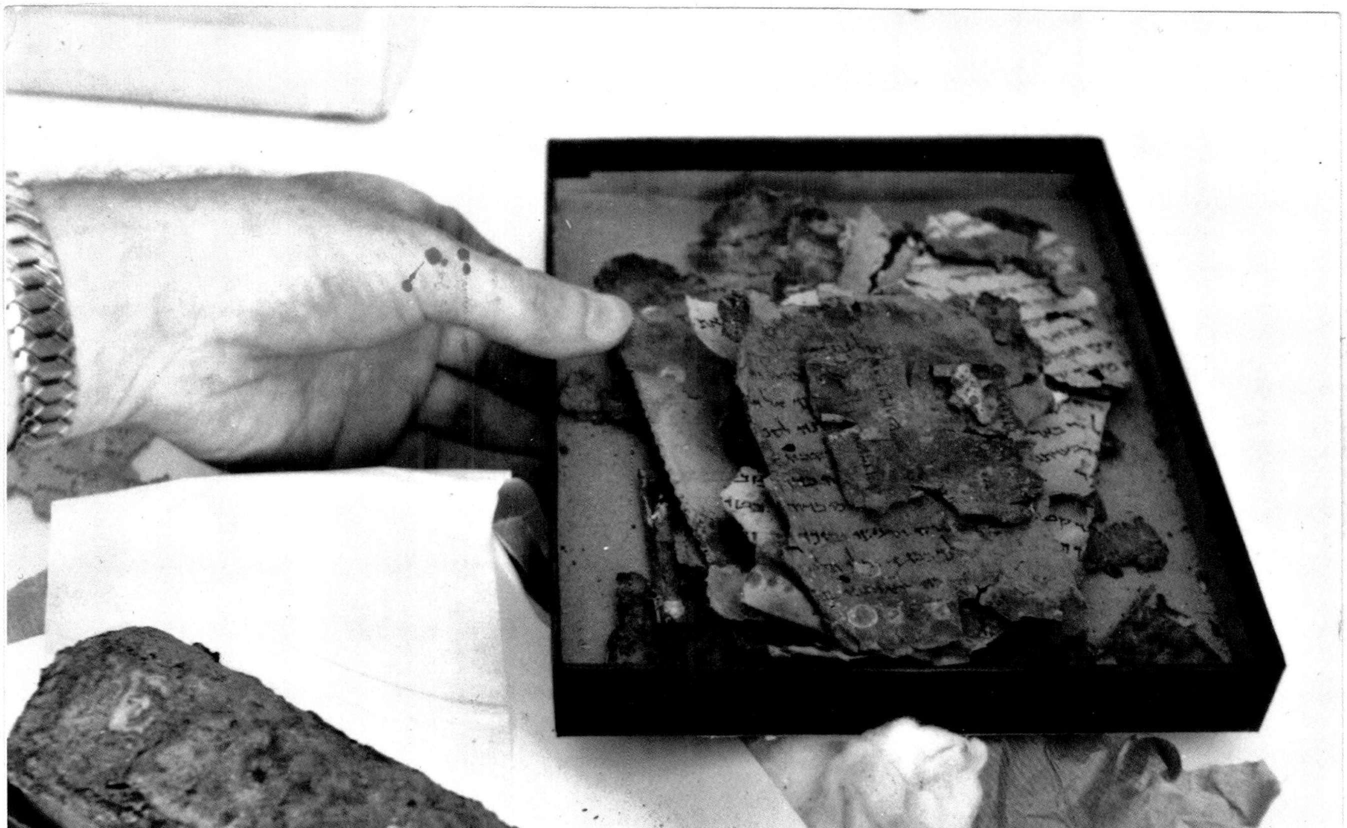

Fig. 3

Fig. 4

Fig. 5

Fig. 6

Fig. 7

Manuscripts from Cave 11Q: 5 September 1957
Photos by Claus-Hunno Hunzinger (courtesy Qumranarchive Alexander Schick)

Fig. 8

Fig. 9

Fig. 10

Fig. 11

Fig. 12

Chapter Nine

The Retrieval of Unknown Manuscript Fragments from Cave 11Q

Marcello Fidanzio

Three different batches of tiny fragments bearing inscribed text, attributed to Cave 11Q, have been retrieved over the past few years. The circumstances of the finding of the fragments and their provenance are clarified below.

1. Leather Fragments Collected During the Excavations: Cigar Box 4/3/1956

A batch of 74 tiny leather fragments, 32 of which bore letters,[1] was found by Mireille Bélis in July 2015 while she was studying the textiles from Cave 11Q. The fragments were initially kept in a cigar box stored in the same drawer together with the textiles collected during the excavations of Cave 11Q in 1956. After the excavations, the material remained at the Rockefeller Museum until Bélis began her work on the textiles in 1995. Subsequently, the Israel Antiquities Authority intervened to improve the storage conditions of the organic materials. The leather fragments were moved from the cigar box to a paper envelope. On the cigar box, there were several pieces of handwriting, most probably all dating from the time of excavation. The conservator(s) decided to take a photocopy of the box, thus saving the information.

On the box we can see three different handwritten texts: the longest sentence (in Arabic) was in all likelihood written by one of the workers: "the name of the owner of this box, Ali Hassan Al Khatib, shall remain long after the box." On the box lid, it states: on the left (in Arabic) "Ali Hasan Ali Subuh"; and on the right (in French) "Fragments mss". On the spine, it states (in French): "Grotte 11Q du 4/3" followed by a few marks difficult to read: "mss"? This text is readable when the box is closed; boxes were usually stored side-by-side on the shelves.

The handwriting in French on the lid and on the spine of the box is that of Roland de Vaux, and 4 March (1956) is one of the dates of the excavation at Cave 11Q.

It is therefore possible to argue that the fragments inside the box come from the excavations carried out in Cave 11Q by de Vaux and Gerald L. Harding. Some of these fragments,[2] which match other scroll fragments claimed to have been found in Cave 11Q by the Bedouins, may provide evidence for confirming the provenance of the latter from Cave 11Q.

1. E. Puech, "Nouveaux menus fragments de la Grotte XI (P1344, P1345 et P1038B)," in this volume.

2. Puech, "Nouveaux menus fragments."

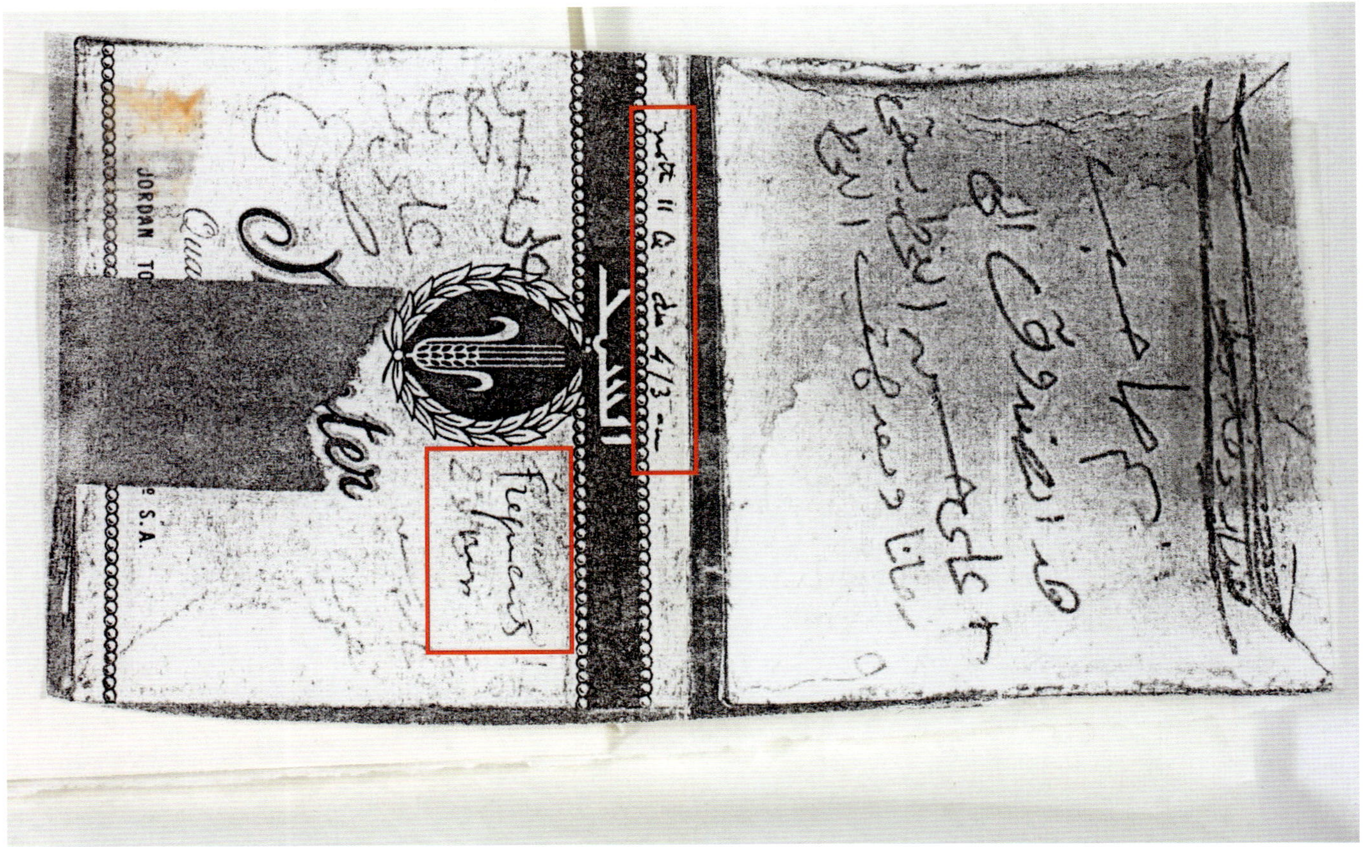

Fig. 1. Photocopy of the cigar box where the fragments were stored. Courtesy of the Israel Antiquities Authority. Photo: Shai Halevi

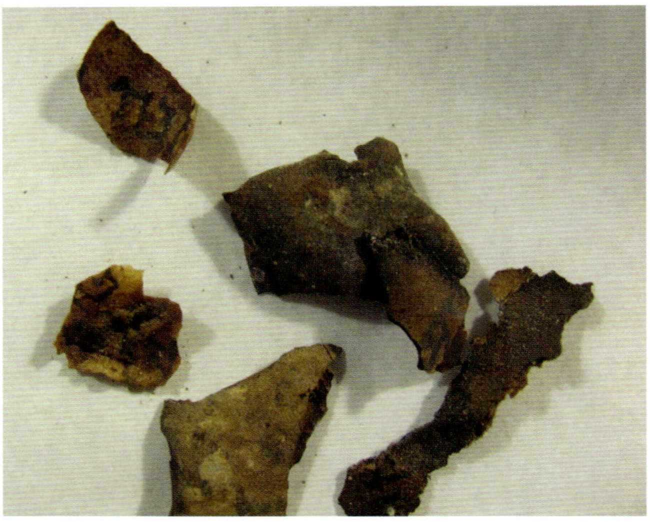

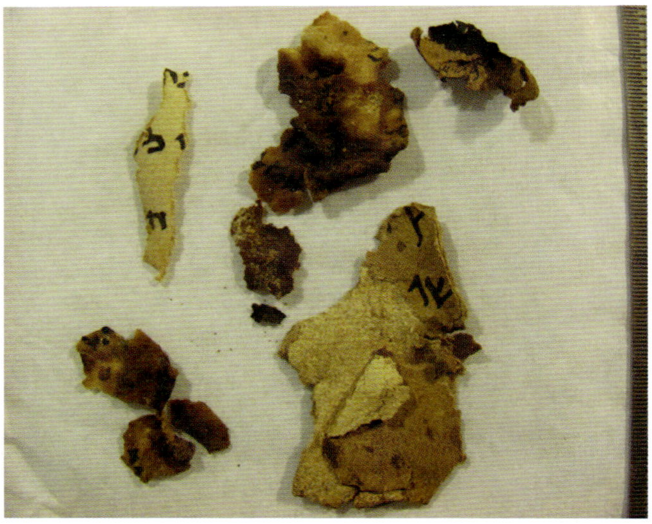

Figs. 2-3. A few of the tiny leather fragments, on the day of the retrieval, 5 July 2015. Photo: Mauro Rottoli

The date raises a few questions. On 4 March, de Vaux and his assistant Jourdain-Marie Rousée were not at Qumran. The *Chronique du Couvent de Saint Étienne* for Saturday 3 March, states: "Les Pères de Qumrân reviennent pour deux jours," and on Monday 5 March: "Les PP de Vaux et Rousée repartent pour Qumrân".[3] In the excavation diary, the two dates, 4 and 5, are combined into one single entry. It seems

3. EBAF's archives, for further details cfr. M. Fidanzio (ed.), "Archival Sources and First Publications on the Excavations of Cave 11Q," in this volume, 19, n. 12.

that the excavation continued in the absence of its director, probably led by his Arab foreman.

For the dates of 4 and 5 March, the diary reports the discovery of "quelques petits fragments inscrits". The cigar box we are dealing with, contained numerous fragments, but less than 32 feature written marks visible to the naked eye as revealed with multispectral imaging.

Émile Puech proposes compatibility between one fragment (P1344 – 12) and that described in the diary entry on 29 February: "un petit fragment avec 2 lettres phéniciennes".[4] Could it be that the cigar box contained all the fragments found in the excavation? "Un petit rouleau très abîmé" found on 3 March should have been stored separately. The "fragment de plusieurs épaisseurs collées: inscrits?" mentioned in the excavation diary on 26 February is also not to be found in the box. Moreover, it is unlikely that 4 March was the date chosen for recording all the manuscript fragments found up until then, because de Vaux was absent. In the event, further fragments were discovered on subsequent days. Probably, then, the fragments kept in the cigar box were actually found on the day in question.

2. Papyrus Fragments Box P1038B

Tiny papyrus fragments bearing letters were detected in box P1038B by Mauro Rottoli and Oren Ableman. The box and its contents were first recorded in the catalogue by Stephen Reed, and later mentioned by Eibert Tigchelaar in a list of all the boxes with tiny fragments attributed to Cave 11Q.[5] Oren Ableman retrieved this box in 2014 during a general inventory of the storeroom of the Dead Sea Scrolls Conservation Laboratory (DSSCL - IAA) he conducted together with Hannah Cotton in 2014. When the archaeobotanist Rottoli was invited to analyze some organic material in the DSSCL - IAA, Ableman decide to submit box P1038B where

Fig. 4. The tiny papyrus fragments stored in box 1038B.
Courtesy of the Israel Antiquities Authority. Photo: Shai Halevi

4. Puech, "Nouveaux menus fragments," 207.

5. "11QX11 Chunks with letters", S.A. Reed, *The Dead Sea Scrolls Catalogue: Documents, Photographs and Museum Inventory Numbers* (SBL RBS 32; ed. and rev. M.J. Lundberg with the collaboration of M.B. Phelps; Atlanta: Scholars, 1994), 515. "Very dark brown chunks with in total five or six, relatively large square letters. Not published in DJD XXIII", E.J.C. Tigchelaar, "Some More Small 11Q1 Fragments," *RdQ* 18/70 (1998) 325-30, on p. 327, n. 5. I am grateful to Oren Ableman for calling my attention on these references.

he suspected the possible presence of papyrus. On July 2015 Rottoli observed eight tiny inscribed papyrus fragments. The provenance of the contents of this box is listed as Cave 11Q but there are no indications as to whether these fragments came from the archaeological excavations or from the Bedouins. These fragments take their place alongside the two fragments of papyrus from Cave 11Q already published in DJD 23.

The leather fragments "cigar box 4/3/1956" (P1344 and P1345) and the papyrus fragments box P 1038B are studied in Puech's chapter.[6]

3. Leather Fragments Box 1032A

Many tiny leather fragments bearing letters were observed by Oren Ableman during the preparation of an inventory list of unidentified material in the IAA's scroll storeroom. 82 fragments stored in box 1032A were subject to an initial analysis, and several of them revealed traces of inscriptions.

The contents of box 1032A are listed as coming from Cave 11Q. Ableman's chapter[7] presents a preliminary edition of 12 fragments of interest.

Fig. 5. The tiny fragments stored in box 1032A. Courtesy of the IAA. Photo: Shai Halevi

6. Puech, "Nouveaux menus fragments."

7. O. Ableman, "Preliminary Publication of Cave 11 Fragments from Box 1032A," in this volume.

Chapter Ten

Nouveaux menus fragments de la Grotte 11Q (P1344, P1345 et P1038B)

Émile Puech

Quelque soixante quatorze menus fragments de cuir détachés des rouleaux de la Grotte 11Q ont été dernièrement retrouvés au cours de l'étude des trouvailles de la Grotte. Ils doivent être ce que le fouilleur R. de Vaux signale dans son journal de fouille du 29 février au 7 mars 1956 : « On commence à dégager l'entrée à la grotte ... quelques fragments inscrits sont récupérés dans les déblais dont un petit fragment avec deux lettres phéniciennes ; quelques fragments écrits ; encore quelques fragments inscrits, ... ».[1] Des reproductions en couleur et à l'infrarouge au laboratoire Leon Levy Dead Sea Scrolls Foundation Project of the Israel Antiquities Authority sur deux planches numérotées P1344 et P1345 ont révélé que seuls trente deux d'entre eux portaient des traces d'écriture, allant de parties de lettres jusqu'à un mot ou plus. Mais quarante deux autres fragments se sont révélés être anépigraphes. Sont présentés ici les restes de ces menus fragments avec écriture, en essayant d'identifier au mieux leur appartenance à des rouleaux connus.[2] Certains proviennent de rouleaux à écriture paléo-hébraïque, d'autres les plus nombreux à des rouleaux à écriture judéo-araméenne, mais certains témoignent d'un mélange de ces écritures, ou d'une écriture cryptique.

Une autre série de sept menus fragments de papyrus, P1038B, a été repérée par M. Rottoli et O. Ableman au Dead Sea Scrolls Conservation Laboratory, Israel Antiquities Authority. Ils sont présentés à la suite.

1. Voir R. de Vaux, « Journal de fouille », dans M. Fidanzio (ed.), «Archival Sources and First Publications on the Excavations of Cave 11Q» dans ce volume : (26-2-1956 entrée de la grotte) « 1 fragment de plusieurs épaisseurs collées : inscrits ? », (29-2-1956 grotte intérieure) « Quelques fragments inscrits récupérés dans les déblais dont un petit fragment avec deux lettres phéniciennes », (3-3-1956) « On avance dans la grotte intérieure. Quelques fragments écrits dont un petit rouleau très abîmé », (4 et 5-3-1956) « Dans la grotte intérieure. Le rocher monte ... quelques petits fragments inscrits », (6/7-3-1956) « De moins en moins de tessons ... et à peine de fragments inscrits ».

2. Voir J.A. Sanders, *The Psalms Scroll of Qumrân Cave 11 (11QPs^a)* (DJDJ IV ; Oxford : Clarendon, 1965) ; D.N. Freedman and K.A. Mathews with contributions by R.S. Hanson, *The Paleo-Hebrew Leviticus Scroll (11QpaleoLev)* (Winona Lake, IN : American Schools of Oriental Research, 1985) ; Y. Yadin, מגלת המקדש - *The Temple Scroll*, 3 Volumes with Supplementary Plates (Jerusalem : Israel Exploration Society, 1977-1983) ; E. Puech, « Notes en marge de 11Qpaléolévitique. Le fragment L, des fragments inédits et une jarre à manuscrits de la Grotte 11 », *RB* 96 (1989) 161-83 ; F. García Martínez, E.J.C. Tigchelaar, and A.S. van der Woude, *Qumran Cave 11.II: 11Q2-18 and 11Q20-31* (DJD XXIII ; Oxford : Clarendon, 1998).

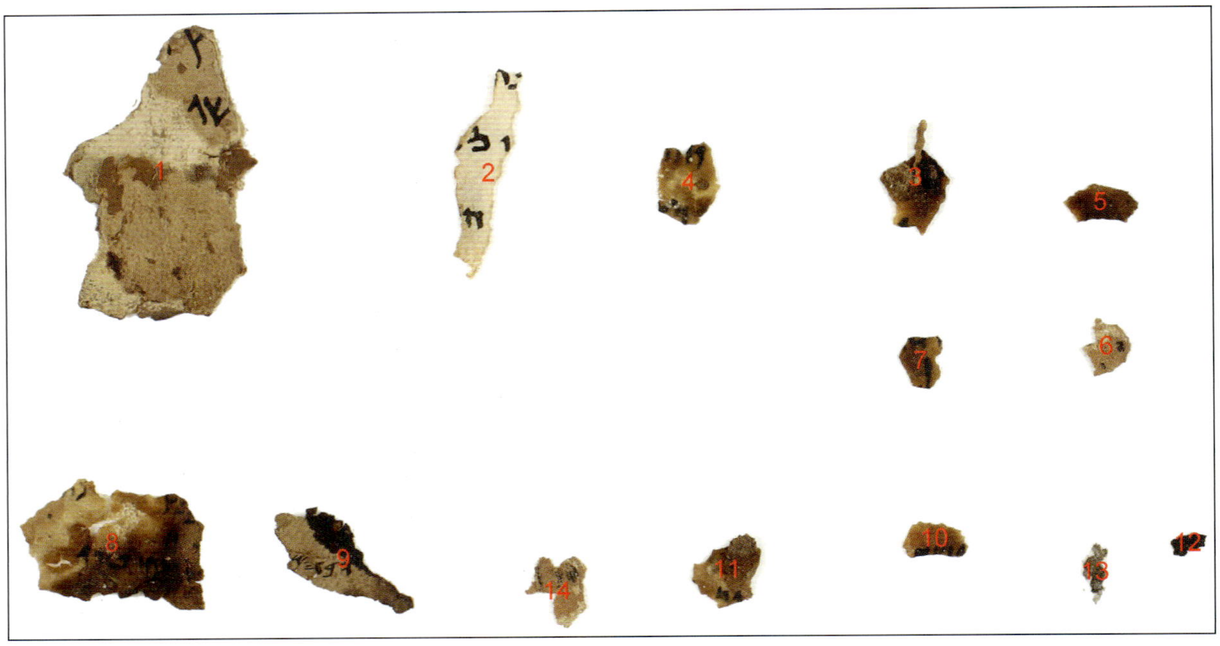

Planche P1344[3]

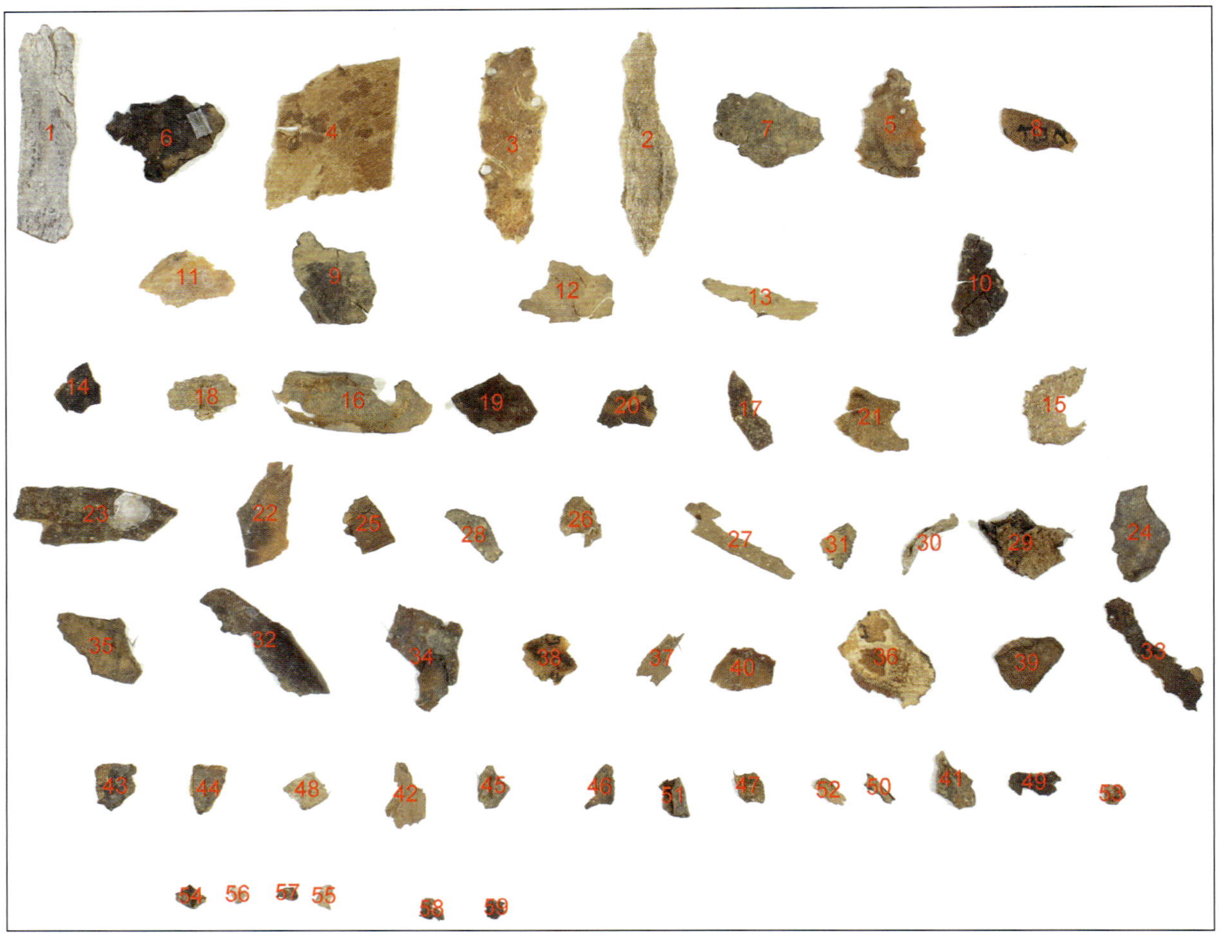

Planche P1345

3. Toutes les images sont reproduites avec l'aimable autorisation de The Leon Levy Dead Sea Scrolls Digital Library, Israel Antiquities Authority, photographe: Shai Halevi.

1. Fragments de cuir en écriture paléo-hébraïque

P1344 - 9 = *11Q22* 8

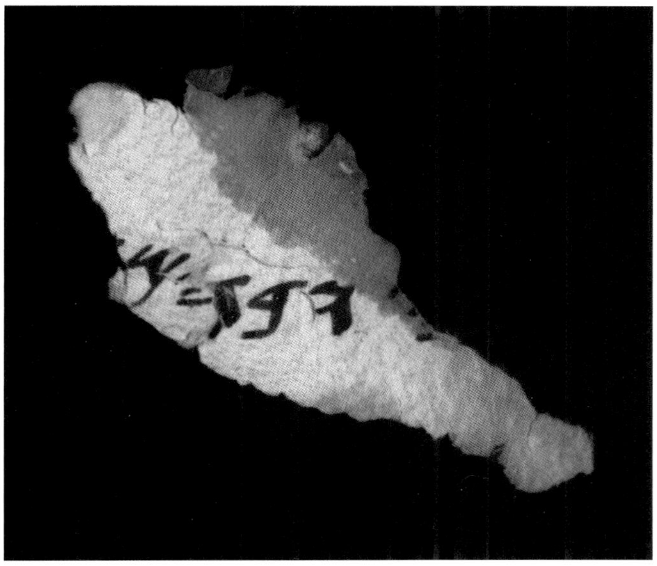

Fragment de peau brun clair avec une tache brune sombre dans la partie supérieure à droite, dos brun, longueur maximale (diamètre) 1,9 cm, épaisseur 0,1 mm. Surface réglée à la pointe sèche, écriture paléohébraïque sous la ligne. Restes de trois lignes d'écriture, interligne de *ca* 0,8 cm, hauteur des lettres, entre 1 et 2 mm. Belle écriture régulière qui peut dater *ca* 100 ou le début du premier siècle av. J.-C.

1]כ[·]ה[
2]ה·ובהמה[
3] ○[

À la ligne 1, bas de hampe fortement crossée à gauche, *kaf* le plus vraisemblable, préférable à *mem* ou *nun,* puis à quelque distance (le point séparatif), restes de haste et de trait oblique à gauche, *he* le plus vraisemblable (voir l. 2).

À la ligne 2, restes des trois obliques parallèles : *he*, puis point séparatif, et à la cassure de gauche, jambage au trait plein à droite avec le trait délié oblique supérieur dépassant à droite le départ du jambage : *he* très probable, plus difficilement *dalet.*

À la ligne 3, départ de trait à *ca* 30° à droite, *qof* ou *taw* possibles, *šin* plus difficile, mais sans séparatif auparavant, on devrait envisager un *vacat.*

²...]*h et le bétail*[...

La lecture de la ligne 2 est assurée, mais non son interprétation. Le substantif est possible mais dans les parallèles bibliques, il est très souvent précédé de **אדם**, pour la paire « l'homme et la bête », cependant le mot se retrouve en Jr 12,4 au singulier dans quelques manuscrits hébreux, le syriaque, le targum et la Vulgate, voir aussi la séquence en 2 Ch 32,28. On pourrait aussi envisager le pronom suffixe long avec la préposition au sens de « en » ou « contre » qui semblerait mieux convenir, voir Ml 2,17, cependant le suffixe court en כ- au frg. 1 2 ne favorise pas cette solution, bien au contraire.

Cette écriture et le cuir sont en tout comparables aux fragments de *11Q22*, non identifié. Comme plusieurs lectures sont à revoir, l'occasion se présente pour en proposer une réédition. Aucun joint ne semble possible.

11Q22 1

Les nouvelles reproductions P1022 (couleur et infra-rouge) permettent d'apporter quelques précisions de lecture. En gras et en italique les mots écrits à l'encre rouge.

1]ת/ה·הודעת·ישועה[·]א[ת·]מ[ל]כותו·[ל]ימ[י·]על[מ[
2a]   כי   {כ}   [
2 ***אלהי[מ*** vac ***תהיה·עדי ·נגה·באהבתכ·לאלהיכ*** vac וילב[שכ·
3]ר[מ]כתב·ערי·[ש]למו·ל[ע]ל[מ

Les restes de la première lettre peuvent être ceux de *taw* ou de *he*. La lecture **הודעת.** paraît préférable à **הודעו.**, le *ʿaïn* en triangle couché à droite est encore assez bien visible, puis *taw* préférable à *waw.* Ensuite viennent le point séparatif, le *yod* clair et le premier 'v' du *šin* dont le trait délié s'est un peu détaché, de légers restes de l'oblique du *waw*, le *ʿaïn* triangulaire que touche le jambage du *he*. Puis de bonnes traces de *alef.* Après une lacune que la cassure a quelque peu rapetissé (chevauchement des bords), restes d'une lettre à hampe à gauche bouclée (*kaf*/ *nun* ou mieux *mem* pour la lecture du mot), espace et restes d'une autre hampe à gauche bouclée avec un bas de jambage à l'extrémité de la boucle : *waw*(?), puis au mieux extrémité d'un croisillon de *taw* sur lequel s'appuie et que croise même le jambage droit de *waw* suivi d'un point séparatif à l'extrémité du trait oblique. Après un espace, une extrémité du croisillon de *taw* ou de *yod*, une hampe à gauche bouclée et un peu plus loin une longue hampe à gauche : *mem* le plus vraisemblable dont la tête n'est pas préservée.

La première lettre conservée au début de la ligne 2 est *mem* à l'encre rouge,[4] sans doute pour אלהי]ם voir plus loin לאלהיכ dans la même ligne. Suit un court *vacat* mais avec des lettres de dimension plus réduite dans l'interligne, כי, qui pourraient même avoir été quelque peu grattées, il est difficile de le prouver, voir la photographie P1022, tout comme plus loin au-dessus de l'autre *vacat*. Puis la lecture est assurée.

La première trace d'encre de la ligne 3 au-dessous de *he* de la ligne 2 peut être celle de la tête arrondie de *reš*, puis à la cassure suivante de bons restes du ductus de la tête de *kaf*, et à l'autre cassure tracé de *yod* (non de *kaf* des éditeurs). Après le *lamed*, tête de *mem* plus vraisemblable que *nun* étant donné la distance à la hampe du *lamed*, suivi de *waw* certain. La hampe du *lamed* suivant est écaillée ou grattée comme les lettres de l'interligne, et dans la lacune pour l'espace entre les deux *lamed*, *'aïn* très vraisemblable.

Traduction

1...]. *tu as* fait connaître le salut av[ec] sa r[o]yauté [*pour*] les jour[*s d'éterni*]*té*[... 2... **Die**]**u**, *vac.* ‹car›(?) tu seras un joyau rayonnant par ton amour **pour ton Dieu** *vac.* Et Il [te] revê[tiras de ... 3...].[ ]ton [*co*]*up* les villes de sa [pros]périté pour [*tou*]*jou*[*rs*.

À la ligne 1, les lectures paraissent certaines à l'exception du verbe à la deuxième personne du singulier, la ligne suivante favorise la lecture du singulier. Pour ל[ימ]י.על[מ], voir Is 63,9.11, versets 8-9 où apparaît la racine ישוע, Am 9,11, Mi 5,1 ; 7,14, et *1QH*[a] IX 17.

À la ligne 2, on peut lire *אלהי[מ*, ou même *אלהיכ[מ*, voir le fragment 6 3. Les deux courts *vacat* paraissent signifier une citation ou une explication.

À la ligne 3, La lecture ש]למו] semble s'imposer, « sa paix/prospérité », difficilement « Salomon » avec cette orthographe en *3Q15*. Le substantif ערי est au cas construit pluriel. Le mot précédent devrait être compris comme מכתב, « ton [co]up », vraisemblablement au singulier, allusion à une punition ou mieux à une victoire. Pour le sens, on pourrait restaurer le verbe [ותשמ.במ, ou [ותרפא.ממ, et à la fin comprendre sans doute ל[ע]ל[ם, « pour [tou]jou[rs] ».

Les éditeurs ont rapproché le *Testament d'Abraham* 17,7 pour l'expression de la ligne 2, et ils ont noté les emplois de עדי et de לב[ש dans un même verset en 2 S 1,24 et Is 49,18. Une allusion aux premiers temps de la royauté paraît raisonnable.

11Q22 2

1 ·את]·אוהבי·ופקד[תי·
2 ·]והייתי[·]ל[ו/המ·לאב·

À la ligne 1, bonne trace du trait supérieur de *dalet* sur PAM 44.006. À la ligne 2, trait supérieur de la tête de *waw* (non le point séparateur), et départ de la hampe du *lamed* assuré.

Traduction

1... *celui/ceux*]qui M'aime(*nt*), et [Je] visiterai[...2...]et J'*ai été*/Je *serai* pour[*lui/eux* un père, ...

À la ligne 1, comparer les constructions d'Ex 20,5-6 et Dt 5,9-10. Pour la ligne 2, voir Jr 31,9 et Pr 4,3, *4Q382* 104 3, *4Q418a* 19 3.

11Q22 3

1]א/תבו[
2]מ·ת[

La première lettre de la ligne 1 peut être lue *alef*, ou *taw*, difficilement *waw*, et à la ligne 2 *mem* est préférable à *nun* par l'angle et la hauteur de la tête.

11Q22 4

1]עוד·א[

On ne peut guère hésiter entre *lamed* et *'aïn* au tracé proche du *'aïn* au fragment 1 3 pour עוד[, le *lamed* a en général dans cette main un tracé plus bouclé, mais *bet* est totalement exclu.[5] Le mot עוד peut être adverbe ou verbe.

4. Les éditeurs, García Martínez, Tigchelaar, and van der Woude (voir DJD XXIII, 415), n'ont pas lu cette lettre, ni les traces dans l'interligne, et bien d'autres lettres de ce fragment.

5. Voir García Martínez, Tigchelaar, and van der Woude (DJD XXIII, 416), qui proposent même de lire כבוד.

11Q22 5

1]כ[
2]תיכ·ול[ ]ooo[

[2]...]tes[...]. et .[...]...[...

11Q22 6

1]ב/פ[
2]כ/נו·חרבותי[ו/ה/כ(מ)
3 ·*אלה*]י*כמ*[

Au-dessus du *reš*, reste de base de jambage de *bet* ou de *pe* étant donné sa position sous la ligne. À la ligne 2, probablement *nun* ou *kaf*, puis *bet* certain, non *pe* de l'édition. À la ligne 3, la fin du mot en rouge est de lecture assurée, le *mem* est moins bien préservé, à l'encre rouge[6] comme au fragment 1 2.

Traduction

[2]...].. [*t*/*s*e]s(/*leur*]s) ruines[... [3]...]**votre**[**Di**]**eu**, .[...

En lisant *nun* à la ligne 2, on pourrait renvoyer au fragment 1 3, et avec *kaf*, un verbe au pluriel.

11Q22 7

1 ·]ו/ב/מיהוה·

1 ...]*et*/*par*/*de* Yahvé

La trace d'encre à la cassure ressemble davantage à la tête de *waw*, de *bet* ou de *mem* qu'à un point. Le mot est près de la marge gauche de la colonne. Il n'y a pas de trace de hampe de *lamed* pour une ligne 2, mais un simple point ou tache d'encre.

Si le fragment appartient bien à ce manuscrit, comme il semble, il est surprenant de voir le tétragramme écrit à l'encre noire[7] et non à l'encre rouge comme *nomen sacrum*.

11Q22 9 - 11Qfr.paléo-hébreu

Par le ductus spécifique de plusieurs lettres et un interligne comparable, on doit joindre à ces huit (?) fragments en paléo-hébreu, celui de provenance inconnue aux mains de particuliers.[8]

1 להקלט[·]מאה·החל]ק
2 ויתרוממ·[
3 וימח[

[1]pour être ramassé de la par[t de ...]
[2]et il s'exaltera [...]
[3]et il *fera disparaître* [...]

La lettre après *mem* à la ligne 3 pourrait être lue *ḥet*. Le passage reste non identifié.

Parmi les manuscrits retrouvés à Qumrân, l'encre rouge est déjà attestée au moins dans cinq d'entre eux. Elle est présente dans deux manuscrits bibliques. En *4Q27 = 4QNb*^{b}, en début de paragraphe pour le verset entier ou une unité est à l'encre rouge, sur une ligne et même la première partie de la suivante, sans trop dépasser une demie ligne (Nb 20,22-23 ; 23,27), d'autres fois seule la première ligne est à l'encre rouge et le verset continue à l'encre noire à la ligne suivante (Nb 21,21a ; 22,21(?) ; 23,13(?) ; 31,25-26(?) ; 31,37-38(?) ; 31,48 ; 32,25 ; 33,1-2).[9] Parmi ces exemples de *4QNb*^{b}, seuls quatre correspondent à une coupure majeure de paragraphes, et quatre autres à des coupures mineures. Mais la fonction spéciale de cet usage en *4QNb*^{b} échappe en grande partie, usage liturgique ou ?

En *2Q14 - 2QPs*, les deux premières lignes du Psaume 103,1-4 sont écrites à l'encre rouge, soit quatre courts versets.

Parmi les manuscrits non bibliques, l'encre rouge est employée en *4Q270 - 4QD*^{e} 3 i 19, apparemment comme en-tête des prescriptions concernant la terre,[10]

6. García Martínez, Tigchelaar, and van der Woude (DJD XXIII, 418) écrivent : « The traces of the second line are very faint and are not visible on the fragment itself », et ils n'ont pas noté l'encre rouge pourtant bien visible sur la photographie couleur.

7. Voir DJD XXIII, 418.

8. Voir G. Lacerenza, « Un nouveau fragment en écriture paléo-hébraïque », *RdQ* 19/75 (2000) 441-7, et E. Puech, « Note additionnelle sur le fragment paléo-hébreu », *RdQ* 19/75 (2000) 449-51, où je rapprochais ce fragment de 11Q22 par la graphie de l'ensemble des lettres préservées. Ce rapprochement me paraît de plus en plus probable à défaut de certain.

9. N. Jastram, «27. 4QNum^b», in E. Ulrich *et al.*, *Qumran Cave 4. VII : Genesis to Numbers* (DJD XII ; Oxford : Clarendon, 1994) 205-67, p. 210-1, signale qu'on n'a pas d'exemple de moins d'une ligne en rouge, ni de plus d'une ligne et demie.

10. Voir J.M. Baumgarten, «270. 4QDamascus Document^e», in

mais à lire ainsi אלה חוקי אדמת ה]קודש à la suite de J.T. Milik.[11]

Et parmi les manuscrits non identifiés de la grotte 4, deux des sept fragments de *4Q481d* portent des restes d'écriture à l'encre rouge.[12] Mais à ces fragments, on doit joindre le fragment *4Q27* 109 qui n'appartient aucunement au manuscrit des *Nombres* par le contenu et la graphie.[13] Je note en passant que *4Q481a* 3 3-4 recoupe *4Q385a* 1a-b ii 6-7 (= *4QApocryphe de Jérémie C*). Les mots à l'encre rouge de *4Q481d* 1 et 2 semblent introduire une parole (divine ?) en début de paragraphe : lire ainsi frg. 1 i, ligne 1 אדון [, ligne 2 ם לחוק[, et 1 ii, ligne 1] תסע, et ceux du frg. 2, ligne 1]א ◦[, ligne 2]ן צור לכם[. [14]

À ces manuscrits non bibliques qumraniens avec des 'rubriques' de la grotte 4, —toutes ces copies sont datées de l'époque hérodienne ancienne—, il faut ajouter maintenant *11Q22* mais le seul en paléo-hébreu. Par ailleurs ce manuscrit use d'un procédé différent des emplois précédents en n'employant l'encre rouge que pour le substantif divin אלהי]ם, לאלהיכ et אלהיכמ, (mais apparemment pas pour le tétragramme si le fragment 7 est bien à intégrer à ce manuscrit). On peut comparer l'usage du paléo-hébreu à l'encre noire dans d'autres manuscrits pour souligner ces occurrences, voir par exemple le nom אלהכה en *4Q243 - 4QPseudo-Daniel* 1 2, ou אל(י) en *1QH^a^* VII 38 ; IX 28 ; X 36, XV 37 (*prima manu*), *1QH^b^* 1 5, *1Q27 - 1QMystères* 1 ii 11, *3Q14* 18 2, *4Q183* 1 ii 3, *6Q15 - 6QD* 3 4-5 (= *CD* V 21-VI 1-2), *6Q18 - Incantations* 6 5 ; 8 1 ; 10 3, mais en *4Q57 - 4QIs^c^* אל est en écriture araméenne en 27 2 alors que יהוה est toujours en paléo-hébreu, y compris les suffixes, comme אלוהים en 24 39, אלוהינו en 37 3, אלוהיכה en 35 10 mais pas en 47 16, ou encore (יהוה) צבאות en 24 38 ; 50 3 et 62 1 mais pas en 40 3 et 57 2, et (יהוה) אדוני en 9 i 25 ; 20 11 ; 63 2 mais pas en 9 ii 27.[15] Le scribe de *11Q5 - 11QPs^a^*, copie du 1er s. ap. J.-C., écrit le tétragramme en paléo-hébreu (qu'il a exponctué deux fois en XVI 8 et XXI 2 mais aussi effacé en XIV 9, parfaitement clair au deuxième grattage et apparemment une partie du tétragramme יהו dans le premier espace trop réduit laissé par le premier copiste)[16] mais non les prépositions devant le mot, alors que le nom divin אלוהים/ינו ou אל et même יה (XIV 8 et 14) sont en écriture araméenne. De son côté *1QpHa* écrit le tétragramme en paléo-hébreu dans la citation mais use d'un substitut dans l'interprétation, *e. g.* col XI 7 et 13.[17]

Ces exemples montrent que les copistes interviennent de différentes manières d'une part et, d'autre part, qu'une certaine évolution de la pratique s'est produite au moins au cours du 1er s. av. et de la première moitié du 1er s. ap. J.-C. L'usage de l'encre rouge à propos des *nomina sacra* en *11Q22* paraît être une autre manière de souligner ce phénomène en attirant encore davantage l'œil du lecteur, mais l'écriture du tétragramme à l'encre noire n'entrerait pas dans cette même catégorie, ce qui paraît surprenant si le fragment 7 appartenait à ce manuscrit. Quelles en sont les motivations ? Difficile de répondre, mais *1QS* VI 27 - VII 1 stipule que « celui qui profère un juron par le Nom vénérable au sujet de tout [...], ou qui blasphème soit qu'il est terrifié par l'épreuve ou pour tout autre raison, alors qu'il lit dans le livre ou qu'il prie, on l'expulsera ».

L'encre rouge qui a été analysée, est à base de cinabre, bien connue en Palestine au moins dès l'époque romaine, époque hérodienne ancienne, dont l'origine la plus vraisemblable est soit l'Asie Mineure, ou l'Espagne.[18]

Id., *Qumran Cave 4. XIII: The Damascus Document (4Q266-273) on the Basis of Transcriptions by J.T. Milik* (DJD XVIII ; Oxford : Clarendon, 1996) 137-68, p. 147.

11. Voir J.M. Baumgarten, «Corrigenda to the 4Q MSS of the *Damascus Document*», *RdQ* 19/74 (1999) 217-25, p. 217-8, où l'auteur revient au placement et à la lecture de Milik.

12. Voir E. Larson and L.H. Schiffman, «481d. 4QFragments with Red Ink», in G.J. Brooke *et al.*, *Qumran Cave 4. XVII: Parabiblical Texts: Part 3* (DJD XXII ; Oxford : Clarendon, 1996) 315-9.

13. Le frg. a été joint par les éditeurs à 4Q27 à cause de l'encre rouge d'abord repérée, bien que différent du reste.

14. La lecture de frg. 1 i 1, n'est pas assurée mais אחי paraît exclue, et en 1 ii 3 lire]בל ; au frg. 2 l. 3 בית[, et en 3 i]ה יד [. Les lectures de l'édition doivent être corrigées.

15. L'écriture hérodienne du 1er s. ap. J.-C. de cette copie explique-t-elle l'inconsistance du scribe comparé aux habitudes des copistes des siècles précédents?

16. Cela précède et déroge aux règles de Tannaïm dans l'usage du paléo-hébreu, *Yerushalmi Megillah* 1. 71d, voir J.P. Siegel, «The Employment of Palaeo-Hebrew Characters for the Divine Names at Qumran in the Light of Tannaitic Sources», *HUCA* 42 (1971) 159-72, où le paléo-hébreu ne peut être effacé de par sa sacralité (p. 169), or on connaît au moins un cas de grattage clair et un deuxième vraisemblable.

17. Pour d'autres exemples, voir E. Tov, *Scribal Practices and Approaches Reflected in the Texts Found in the Judean Desert* (STDJ 54 ; Leiden : Brill, 2004), 238-46 et Table 1, mais (p. 240) le *kaf* de אלהכה en 4Q243 est bien en paléo-hébreu, de tracé proche du tracé samaritain (avec Milik), et p. 245, pour le grattage du tétragramme en *4QPs^a^*, voir ci-dessus.

18. Voir Y. Nir-El and M. Broshi, «The Red Ink of the Dead Sea Scrolls», *Archaeometry* 38/1 (1996) 97-102. Leur analyse est

P1344 - 12 = *11Q1 - 11QpaléoLv* (frg.)

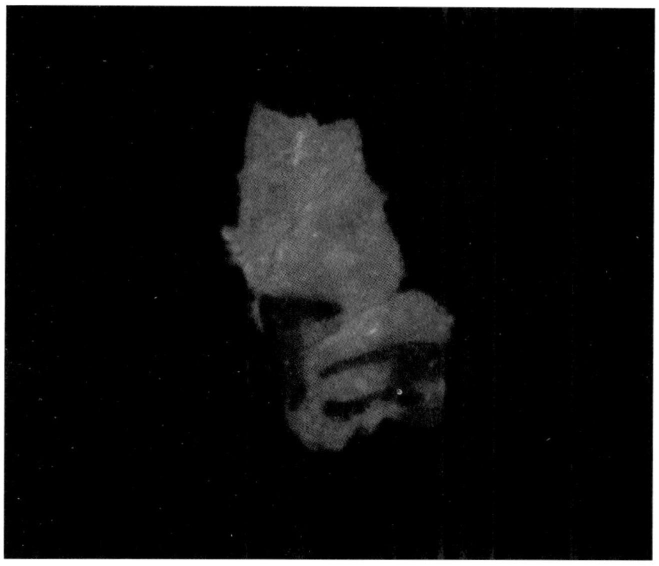

Fragment de peau brun très foncé. Largeur maximale de 0, 55 cm. Écriture paléohébraïque.

1]זה[

La première lettre est *zaïn*, suivi de *he* assuré. Comprendre soit]זה[« ceci », ou plusieurs restaurations possibles ?]זה[?.

La graphie ressemble fortement à plusieurs ductus de lettres de *11QpaléoLévitique - 11Q1*. La couleur brun foncé du fragment, épaisseur *ca* 0,2-0,3 mm, paraît s'accommoder avec la description qui en est donnée de *11Q1*.[19] Comme la partie extérieure du manuscrit a été retrouvée en fragments détachés, la partie intérieure n'ayant été déroulée qu'en 1970, on comprend que l'antiquaire ait pu vendre des fragments détachés.[20] Ce petit fragment P1344 - 12 ne joint pas à une cassure de ce qui est actuellement connu du rouleau, mais il pourrait être situé à gauche du fragment C (= Lv 11,27-32) à la ligne 3 = Lv 11,29. Dans ce cas la miette de cuir, à lire]זה[ו, se serait détachée lorsque les bédouins ont retiré le rouleau de son enveloppe de lin lors de la découverte en 1956. Mais elle peut aussi bien provenir d'une autre passage du début du rouleau, tels]זה[ח(ה) en 7,30.31.34 et 8,29 ou ב]זה[ה en 8,9, même sans restes désintégrés et récupérés par les premiers explorateurs.

Le fragment P1344 - 12, pourrait être celui que le fouilleur R. de Vaux signale dans son journal de fouille au 29 février 1956 « avec 2 lettres phéniciennes ».[21]

Par la même occasion, il est possible de replacer le fragment non identifié *11Q30* 18 en paléohébreu[22] à lire : 1]לא.[, et 2]במח[, en *11Q1* Frag. H = *11QpaléoLévitique* 17,2-3, avec un joint au-dessus du fragment *ad*[23] à droite du fragment H b aux lignes 4 et 5,[24] et restaurer :

4 ת·אליהמ·זה·הדבר·אשר·צ[וה·יהוה]·לאמר·איש·איש
·מבית·ישראל·ו[ה?])
5 אשר·ישחט·שור·או·כשב[·או·עז·]במח[נ]ה·או·אשר·
ישחט·מחוצ·למ
6 חנה·ואל·פתח·אהל·מוע[ד·]ל[א·הביא·]להקריב·
קרבנ·ליהוה·לפני·משכ

Étant donné le *waw* à la fin de la ligne 4, serait-il exclu que le scribe ait comblé un oubli ? Il semble que des restes de *he* ajouté sont encore visibles à gauche sous la tête du *waw*, et peut-être même effacé : le scribe aurait-il tenté de corriger dans la marge en accord avec le grec והגר הגר בתוככמ et de s'être ravisé ?

faite à partir de l'encre rouge des deux manuscrits bibliques et de 4Q270, alors bien repérés comme exemples de ce procédé.

19. Voir Freedman and Mathews, *Paleo-Hebrew Leviticus*, 3-4.

20. Par exemple le fragment L qui assure la jonction du fragment K à la partie encore enroulée. G. Roux avait acheté ce fragment en 1967 lors d'un de ses nombreux séjours dans le pays, et il me l'avait montré lors d'une première rencontre à Rodez en 1971, que j'ai publié ensuite dans la *RB* ; voir Freedman and Mathews, *Paleo-Hebrew Leviticus*, 2-3.

21. Voir ci-dessus, n. 1.

22. Voir DJD XXIII, 442, qui ont lu en écriture araméenne, l. 1]°°[, et l. 2]רמ[sans aucune hésitation.

23. Voir E.J.C. Tigchelaar, «Some More Small 11Q1 Fragments», *RdQ* 18/70 (1997) 325-30, fragment *ad*, p. 328. L'auteur a identifié parmi ces débris dans la boîte 988 les fragments *aa-ai* de *11QpaléoLévitique*.

24. Pour d'autres menus fragments identifiés et replacés à gauche et à droite des deux pièces du fragment H, voir Puech, « Notes en marge », 174, avec commentaire sur le *waw* en fin de ligne 4, variante du *textus receptus*, non signalé dans l'édition de Freedman and Mathews, *Paleo-Hebrew Leviticus*, 34. La photographie PAM 42.173 a conservé des restes non lus à la fin des lignes 3 ואמר, et 4-6 (voir *supra*, fines traces de la tête de *kaf*).

2. Fragment avec les deux types d'écriture ou assimilés

P1345 - 44

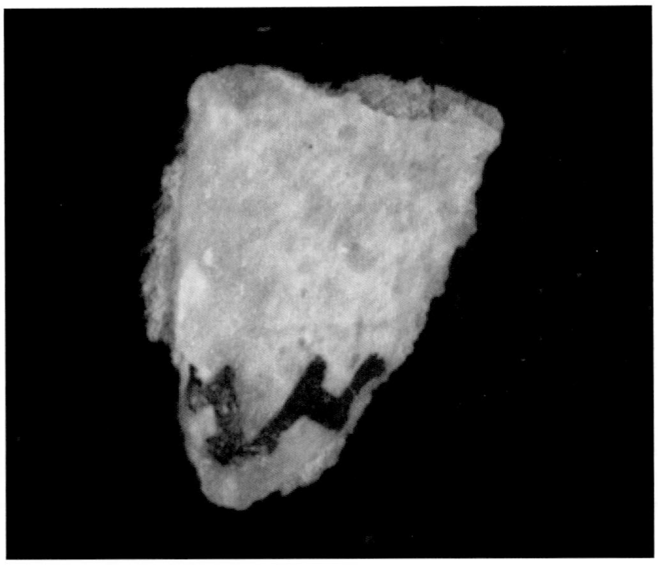

Fragment de cuir de couleur brun. Largeur maximale de 0,65 cm. Surface réglée, écriture sous la ligne. Restes d'une ligne d'écriture paléo-hébraïque, hauteur des lettres : *ca* 0,2 cm.

1]ככ[

Ductus d'une grande tête de *kaf* assez unique, les deux traits obliques à gauche réunis par un trait court à angle droit, le jambage de droite amorce un prolongement, mais non conservé par la cassure.

Puis vient un jambage vertical muni d'une tête étroite à gauche ouverte en forme de v, et d'un coude à angle droit, la cassure ne permet pas d'en connaître le prolongement à gauche, à lire sans doute *kaf* mais en écriture judéo-araméenne.[25]

Le *kaf* en écriture paléo-hébraïque pourrait être la fin du nom divin אלהי]כ, dans ce cas à ajouter aux exemples signalés ci-dessus.

25. Voir des ductus de *kaf* de *4Qpaléo-Exode* (*4Q22*) et de *11Q paléo-Lévitique* (*11Q1*).

P1345 - 7 = *11Q2* 10 - *11QLv*^b 10

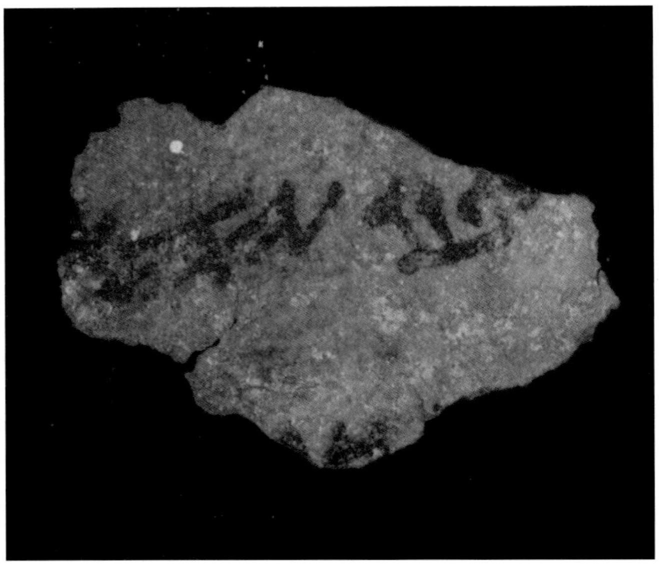

Fragment de peau grisâtre, dos noirci avec des traces de fibres. Longueur maximale 2,1 cm. Restes de deux lignes d'écriture, interligne de 0,9 cm, hauteur des lettres entre 0,55 et 0,6 cm. Lettres par transparence au verso.

Écriture araméenne avec le tétragramme écrit en paléohébreu comme il arrive souvent dans les manuscrits qumraniens. Écriture calligraphique hérodienne tardive, *ca* le deuxième quart du premier siècle A.D. Ce fragment appartient visiblement à *11Q2* - *11QLévitique*^b, = frg. 10,[26] à lire ainsi :

Frg. 10 - Lv 16,15 :

1 לעם]לפני *יהו*[*ה* והביא את דמו אל מבית לפרכת
2 ועשה א]ת דמ[ו כאשר עשה לדם הפר והזה אתו על

La lecture de la ligne 2 a gardé des traces du départ du *taw*, la tête caractéristique du *dalet* et l'épaule droite du *mem*.

[1]pour le peuple] devant Yahwe[h et il portera de son sang derrière le voile [2]et il fera ave]c [son] sang[comme il a fait avec celui du taureau et il l'aspergera sur [3]le propitiatoire...

L'identification de ce nouveau fragment de *11QLv*^b a son intérêt en ce qu'il atteste une variante avec le grec à la ligne 1 : ἔναντι Κυρίου = לפני יהו]ה. Il serait possible de placer le frg. 8 על[à la fin de la ligne 2,

26. Voir DJD XXIII, 1-9.

mais il manque d'appui pour une certitude, voir aussi frg. 2 2. Comparer *11Q2* 4 1-2 (Lv 14,16-17), et 2 2 et 6 avec מלפני.

Frg. 9 i-ii - *11Q2* - *11QLv*^{b} 17, 5-6.16 et 18,1(?)

C'est une occasion de reprendre la lecture du frg. 9 i-ii laissé comme non identifié dans l'*editio princeps*.[27]

À l'aide de PAM 44.114 et d'une nouvelle reproduction P567,[28] il est possible, semble-t-il, d'en proposer une identification.

Le frg. 9 i 1-3 a conservé des restes de la fin de trois lignes, à lire ainsi :

את זבחיהם אשר הם זבחים על פני השדה ו]הביאום 1
ליהוה אל פתח אהל מואד אל הכהן וזבחו זב]חי 2
שלמים *ליהוה* אותם וזרק הכהן את הדם] על 3

À la ligne 1, la lecture אום est assurée sur P567, ainsi que ב sur PAM 44.114 avec une bonne trace de la partie gauche de *he* préférable à *yod*, et des traces de *yod* entre *bet* et *alef*. À la ligne 2, *yod* paraît assuré, précédé du jambage gauche d'une lettre avec l'horizontale de la tête, *ḥet* répond à ce tracé. À la ligne 3, le *lamed* certain est précédé de traces de lettre qui correspondent assez bien à la tête de *'aïn*. Cette identification qui paraît à retenir, est témoin de la *scriptio plena* comme ailleurs de cette copie, y compris ici dans le *waw* de la troisième personne du pluriel.

Le fragment porte des restes de débuts de lignes d'une deuxième colonne, 9 ii, Lv 17,16-18,1, à lire :

יכבס] ובשרו לוא ירחץ ונשא עונו *vacat* 1
vac]*at* 2
ו]ידבר 3

La lecture de la ligne 1 semble s'imposer avec des restes de la partie droite convexe de *samek*. Le *vacat* à la ligne suivante, non signalé dans l'*editio princeps*, aide à identifier le verset 16 qui termine le chapitre avec une *petuḥah* dans le TM. La trace d'encre à la ligne 3 peut être celle de la tête de *waw* de ו]ידבר au début de 18,1.

Le fragment 9 vient se placer entre le nouveau fragment 10 et le fragment 7 de l'édition.

Par la même occasion, on peut aussi proposer de placer]על[du frg. 8 aux fragments 9 i 1 ou en 2 2.

P1345 - 34A = *11Q2* 11 - *11QLv*^{b} 11, Lv 18,11

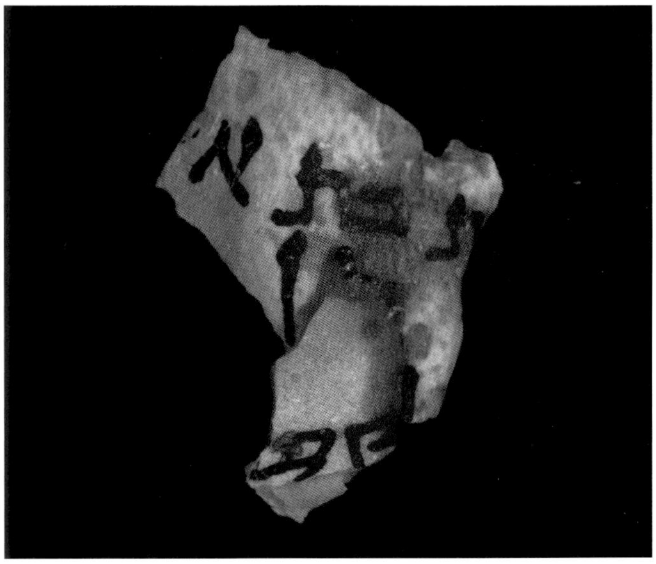

Fragment de peau de couleur brun rougeâtre avec des plages sombres, au départ partiellement recouvert par le fragment P1345-34B. La séparation des deux confirme la première proposition d'identification. Largeur maximale de 1,45 cm. Surface réglée à la pointe sèche. Restes de deux lignes d'écriture. Interligne de 0,85 cm, hauteur des lettres : *bet* 0,23 cm, *taw*/*alef* 0,35 cm. Écriture de l'époque hérodienne ancienne du dernier tiers du première siècle av. J.-C.

[11]ערו]ת בת אש]ת אביך מולדת אביך אחותך היא 1
לוא] תגל]ה עורתה *vacat* 2

À la cassure de la ligne 1, trait courbe de pied de *lamed* ou mieux du premier trait à droite de *šin*. À la ligne 2, *taw*, *gimel* avec une partie du pied, bas, encore visible, et *lamed*.

Le fragment porte des restes de Lv 18,11, et appartient au manuscrit *11Q2* - *11QLv*^{b}, avant le fragment 7. La longueur des lignes correspond à celles des autres fragments de cette copie. La mise en place du fragment appuie les *vacat-setumôt* avant et après ce verset 11, comme dans le TM. Mais la *scriptio plena* לוא comme partout ailleurs dans ce manuscrit semble devoir être retenue pour un meilleur alignement à la marge de droite. On restaure le féminin היא avec le

27. Voir DJD XXIII, 8-9.

28. Reproduction par The Lunder Family Dead Sea Scrolls Conservation Laboratory, Israel Antiquities Authority, mais sur cette dernière manque toute une bande droite du frg. 9 i 1-3 qui a disparu lors du dernier traitement du fragment.

qeré pour être en accord avec le substantif précédent. C'est le frg. *11Q2* 11.

P1345 - 34B attaché par dessus la ligne 2 de ce fragment, est lui aussi identifié à une copie du *Lévitique*, mais en écriture cryptique, voir *infra*.

P1345 - 36 = *11Q2* 12(?) - *11QLv*ᵇ 12(?)

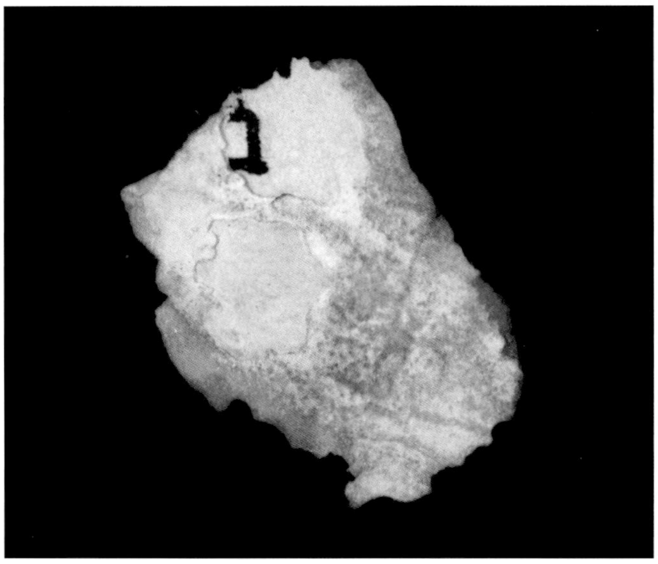

Fragment de peau de couleur brun, épiderme arraché sur la presque totalité de la surface. Largeur maximale 1,5 cm. Restes de deux lignes d'écriture, apparemment marge de droite et *vacat* ou marge inférieure. Hauteur du *bet* : 0,3 cm. Comme l'interligne paraît minime (*ca* 0,45 cm), on pourrait avoir affaire à une correction/addition supra-linéaire et mordant dans la marge de droite, à moins d'un *vacat* dans la ligne. Réglage non visible. Écriture d'époque hérodienne tardive (?).

1a אד/ק]
1 ב]

À la ligne 1, est visible la jonction du jambage vertical près du bas de la diagonale du *'alef.* Puis trace d'un jambage touchant la tête du *bet, kaf* final.

En lisant **אך**, ces restes peuvent être identifiés à Lv 27,26 après une *setumah* dans le TM :

1a אך]
1 ב]כור אשר יבכר ל*יהוה* בבהמה לוא יקדיש איש
אותו אם שור אם שה

Le tétragramme devait être écrit en paléohébreu en *11Q2*. Le samaritain et le grec ajoutent **כל**. Ce fragment recevrait alors le numéro 12 des fragments identifiés de ce rouleau : *11Q2* 12.

3. Fragments en écriture araméenne

P1344 - 1 = *11Q14* 5 - *11QSefer ha-Milḥamah* 5

Fragment de peau de couleur brun clair avec des taches brun-rougeâtre, à l'épiderme arraché par endroits, verso de même couleur. Largeur maximale de 1,6 cm, épaisseur de 0,5 mm. Surface réglée à la pointe sèche, écriture sous la ligne, interligne de 0,9 cm, et marge inférieure préservée de 2,6 cm. Hauteur des lettres de 0,35 cm.

1 [ץ ו/י]
2 [שו]
marge inférieure (?)

À la ligne 1, *ṣade* final, puis bas de jambage assez haut, *waw* ou *yod* préférable à *he*. La surface arrachée à la 'ligne 3' ne permet pas de savoir s'il y avait un *vacat*, ou la marge inférieure. Comme la graphie est en tout semblable à celle de *11Q14*, il a été possible de replacer le fragment en *11Q14* ii 14-15 pour lire (recoupement avec *4Q285* 8 10 souligné)[29] :

14 [האר]ץ ו[אין דב]ר בארצכם כיא אל עמכם ומלאכי
15 [קוד]שו [מתיצבי]ם בעדתכם ושם קודשו נקרא עליכם
marge inférieure

29. Voir DJD XXIII, 247.

[14]la ter]re, e[t il n'y aura plus de pes]te dans votre pays, car Dieu est avec vous et Ses[sain]ts [15]anges[se tienne]nt dans votre congrégation et Son saint Nom est invoqué sur vous.

P1344 - 2 = *11QRT*[a] - *11Q19*

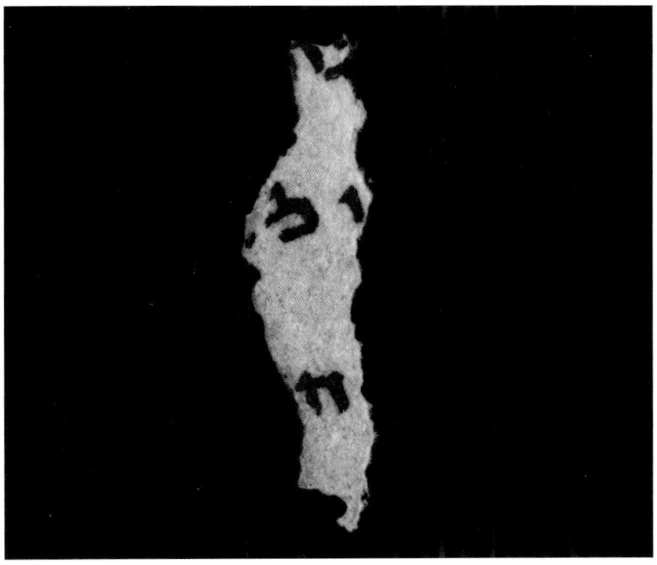

Languette de peau de couleur brun clair, transparence de l'encre au verso. Largeur maximale de 0,6 cm, épaisseur de 0,3 mm, réglage non visible, restes de trois lignes, interlignes de 0,85 à 0,95 cm. Écriture hérodienne tardive, *ca* première moitié/deuxième tiers du premier s. A.D.

1]מליט/ם[
2]כי מן[
3]ה○[

À la ligne 1, restes probables de *mem* (extrémités des deux traits, de l'oblique et de la base), puis extrémité du pied de *lamed* au-dessus de l'oblique du *mem*, *waw* ou *yod* et tracé légèrement convexe avec une base tracée en un deuxième mouvement, ainsi le *ṭet* et parfois le *mem* final dans cette main.

À la ligne 2, trace de la tête et de la jonction avec *yod* ou *waw* assez court, *bet* ou *kaf* possibles, puis trace de jambage légèrement à gauche, *nun* final possible, ou (?). Très légère trace d'encre de trait convexe en haut à la cassure à la ligne 3.

Le support, les interlignes et la graphie s'accordent pour l'appartenance du fragment à la première feuille de *11Q19* - *11QTemple*[a], feuille de V colonnes qui a remplacé la précédente probablement hors d'usage.

Cela se comprend d'autant mieux que le fragment provenant des premiers enroulements a dû tomber lors de l'extraction du rouleau de la jarre et de l'ouverture du tissu de lin.

P1344 - 3 (= *11Q7* - *11QPs*[c])

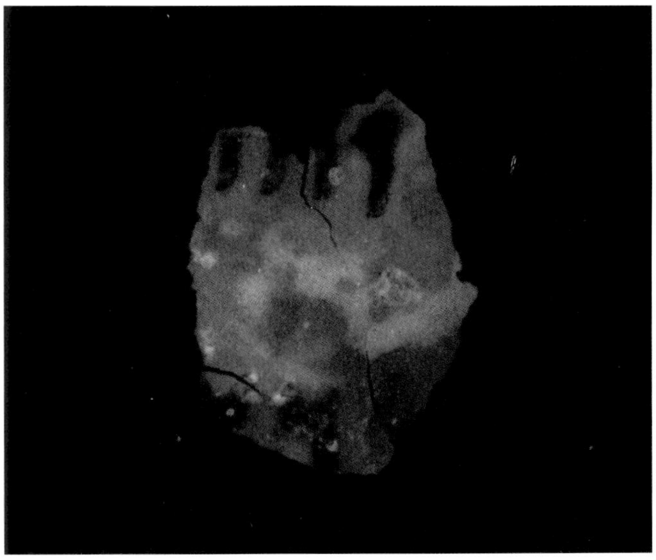

Fragment de peau de couleur brun clair avec des taches brunes rougeâtres. Largeur maximale de 0,7 cm. Restes de deux lignes d'écriture, interligne de 0,7cm, hauteur des lettres de 0,3 cm. Écriture hérodienne ancienne, dernier tiers du premier siècle av. J.-C. Le *alef* à la diagonale en sinusoïde et au jambage gauche coudé à droite, le *reš* et le *ṣade* au trait de droite à angle droit rappellent très étroitement *11Q7* - *11QPs*[c] au point de devoir attribuer le fragment à ce rouleau même sans joint matériel. La couleur et les interlignes seraient en plein accord, même si les réglures y sont à peine visibles.

1]וי/הו/י [
2]ארצ/ץ[

À la ligne 1, *waw* ou *yod*, *he* le plus probable (ou *ḥet*) et *yod* ou *waw*. À la ligne 2, restes plus effacés de *alef*, puis *dalet* ou *reš* et *ṣade* médian.

[1]...] *et il y eu*[*t* / *Yahv*[*é*(?) ... [2]...]la terre (de)[...

soit Ps 10,16-18 :

1]ועד אבדו גוים מארצו [17]תאות ענוים שמעת[יהו]ה
תכין לבם תקשיב אזנך [18]לשפוט[
2]יתום ודך בל יוסיף עוד לערוץ אנוש מן ה[ארץ
] *vacat* [

ou Ps 23,6-24,1-2 :

1 [ימי חיי ושבתי בבית] יהו[ה לאורך ימים *vacat* [
2 [¹לדויד מזמור ליהוה ה]ארץ[ומלואה תבל ויושבי בה
²כי הוא על ימים יסדה ועל

Dans le premier cas, le nouveau fragment se situerait entre les fragments 3 (Ps 9,3-7) et 4-7 (Ps 12,5-14,6, et dans le deuxième cas, entre les fragments 10 (Ps 19,4-8) et 11 (Ps 25,2-7). Les deux placements sont également possibles dans les dimensions des colonnes de ce manuscrit.[30]

P1344 - 4

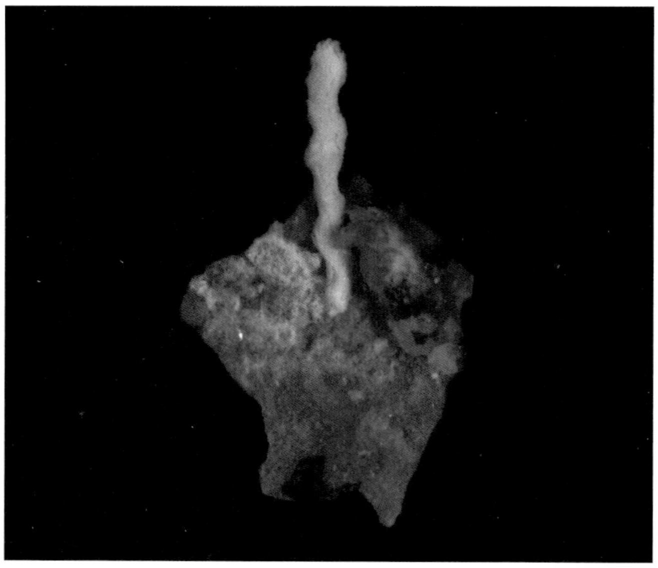

Petits fragments de peau, gélatineux, de couleur brun rougeâtre, avec des restes d'un fils de lin attaché. Lettres par transparence au verso. Sur la petite esquille en écriture hérodienne tardive : (*11Q11* ou *11Q12* ?)

1 [מ]

Sur le petit fragment :

1 [??]
2 [ד]

Lettre à petit pied à gauche, *taw* ou *ṣade* (?), puis traces de lettres recouvertes par l'esquille.

30. Voir DJD XXIII, 49-61.

P1344 - 5

Fragment de peau de couleur brun rougeâtre, transparent. Traces de lettres sur le bord inférieur.

1]○י○○○[

Traces de jambage, *taw* ou *nun* possible, tête de *yod* (?), puis départ de trois jambages : têtes de *alef* et de *reš* possibles, ou ?.

P1344 - 7 = *11Q20* 44 - *11QT*ᵇ 44

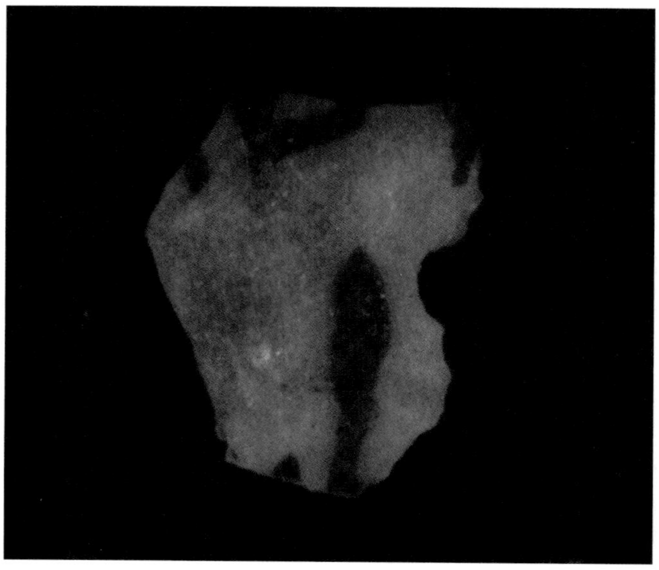

Fragment de peau de couleur brun foncé rougeâtre. Largeur maximale de 0,5 cm. Restes de deux lignes d'écriture, interligne de *ca* 0,8 cm.

1 [○○ש○]
2 [לוא(?)]

À la ligne 1, jambage de lettre, *yod* ou *waw* possibles que touche un trait oblique, *alef*(?), *šin* probable, et jambage de lettre, *waw*, *yod*, *reš*, ?. À la ligne 2, *lamed* à longue hampe à double boucle tracée en '8' très étiré,[31] et tête de lettre, *waw* ou *yod* possibles. et fines traces de lettre, *alef* possible. Comme la graphie la plus proche est celle de *11Q20*, il ne serait pas impossible, mais non certain à défaut de joint, de replacer ce fragment en *11Q20* XII 3-4 (fragment 21 i 1-2 mais avec un interligne comparable) en lisant (*11Q19* XLV 8-11 souligné)[32] :

3 בגדיו ורחץ ביום הר]אישו[ן וביום השלישי יכבס
בגדיו ורחץ ובאה השמש א]חר
4]יבוא אל המקדש ו]לוא[יבואו בנדת טמאתמה אל
מקדשי וטמאו ואיש]כי ישכב

Traduction

³ses habits et se lavera le p]remie[r jour. Le troisième jour, il nettoiera ses habits et se lavera au coucher du soleil, en]suite [⁴il pourra entrer dans le sanctuaire. Ils]n'[entreront]pas[dans mon sanctuaire souillés par du sang menstruel, ils se souilleraient. Un homme] s'il couche[⁵...

Le fragment devrait recevoir le numéro 44.[33]

P1344 - 8

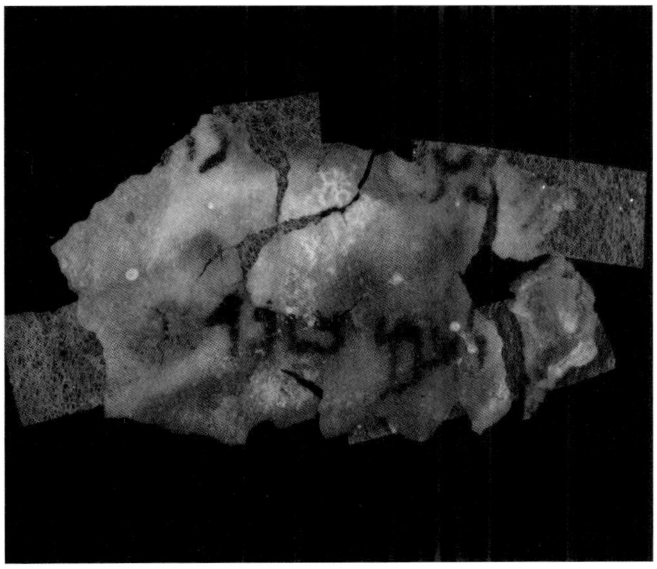

31. Comparer par exemple *11Q19* L 17 כלי.

32. Voir DJD XXIII, 390 : cette identification, si elle était retenue, demanderait une répartition un peu différente des lignes XII 1-3.

33. Voir DJD XXIII, 357-409, p. 409.

Fragment de peau de couleur brun clair à gauche et brun foncé rougeâtre à droite, éclaté. L'esquille en haut à droite n'est manifestement pas en place, il faut replacer l'autre esquille au-dessus de laquelle se trouve une troisième esquille pour retrouver les joints entre eux. Largeur maximale de 2,3 cm, épaisseur de 0,1 mm. Restes de deux lignes d'écriture, interligne de *ca* 0,8 cm, et marge gauche.

1]והתקבצו כול הנת[(?)
2]ועם בזוי

À la ligne 1, sur l'esquille supérieure de droite, non en place, restes probables de *yod*/*waw*, de *he*, et partie du coude de *taw* (?). Traces de la tête de *qof* sous l'esquille qui le recouvre, puis restes de la tête et de la base de *bet* vraisemblable, puis *ṣade*, jambage de *waw* probable, puis traces de lettres, et restes de *nun-taw* possibles : peut-être]כול הנת. À la ligne 2, la lecture est assurée.

¹...]et se sont rassemblés *tous les* ..[²...]et *un peuple* méprisé ³[...

Le premier mot peut se comprendre au mieux והתקבצו[. À la ligne 2, comprendre la préposition ou mieux le substantif suivi du participe passé « et un peuple méprisé » ; pour בזוי, voir Ps 22,7 ובזוי עם, et Jr 49,15 et Ab 2.

À la ligne 1, une restauration הנת]ושים serait possible. Cette graphie a des rapprochements avec les manuscrits du *Rouleau du Temple*, le fragment appartiendrait-il à *11Q20* ?

P1344 - 10

Fragment de peau de couleur brun foncé à rougeâtre, transparent. Largeur maximale de 0,75 cm. Surface réglée, restes d'une ligne d'écriture, sous la ligne. Graphie du type semi-formel rond de l'époque hérodienne ancienne.

1]ו/ישה[

La lecture paraît assurée, *waw* ou *yod*, difficilement une autre lettre, et on devrait restaurer ע]ושה « faisant », une orthographe pleine de מ]ושה, « Mo]-//ïse » fréquente dans les manuscrits qumraniens, ou (?).

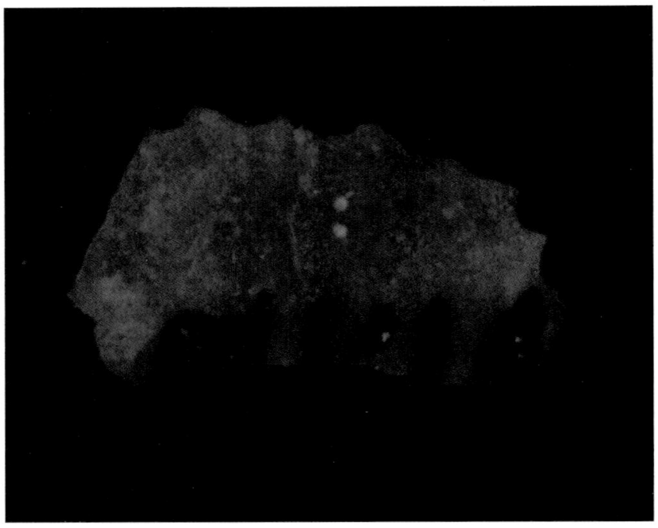

Une identification possible serait en *11Q2*, sous le fragment 1 ii à localiser en Lv 8,9, deuxième וישם, en lisant à la ligne suivante את מ]ושה, manuscrit à orthographe *plene*. Voir ci-dessus P1345 - 7 en Lv 16,15. Mais le *šin* y est d'un ductus légèrement différent.

La graphie est comparable à celle du copiste de *4Q27 - 4QNb^b^*, voir *e. g.* מושה, fragment 4 3,[34] toutefois différente de celle du scribe de *11Q6 - 11QPs^b^*, fragment 1 3, mais il n'y a pas d'autres restes des *Nombres* dans la grotte 11Q.

P1344 - 11

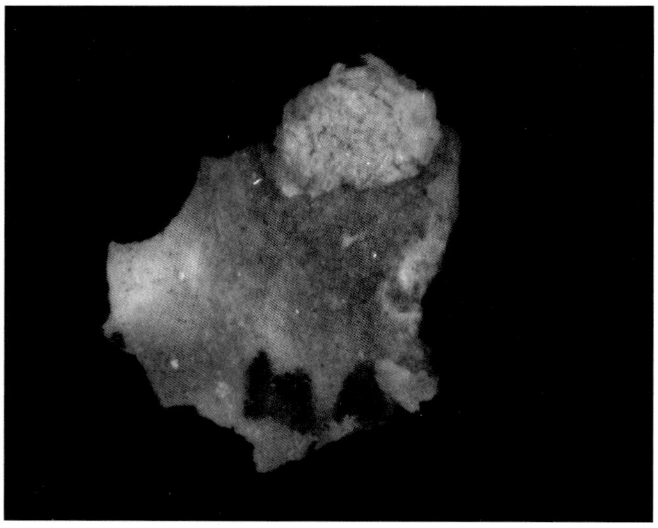

Fragment de peau de couleur brun clair avec des plages plus foncées, surface arrachée dans la partie supérieure. Largeur maximale de 0,7 cm. Restes d'une ligne d'écriture.

34. Voir Jastram, «27. 4QNum^b^».

1]○ יר/ו○[

Légère trace d'encre, puis tête de lettre, *yod* ou *waw*, puis de *dalet* ou *reš*, et à la cassure, départ d'un trait légèrement convexe. Une possible identification serait en *11Q4 - 11QÉzéchiel* pour la graphie.

P1345 - 6

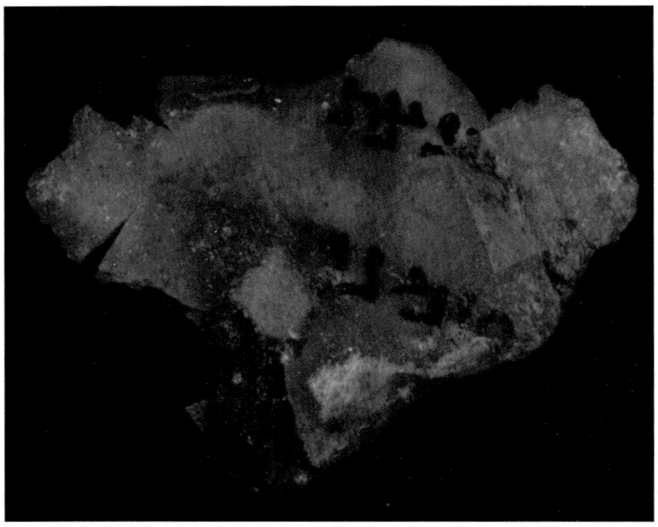

Fragment de peau brun très sombre à noirâtre, de même au verso. Largeur maximale de 2,3 cm. Restes de deux lignes d'écriture réglées à la pointe sèche, interligne de 0,6 cm, et marge gauche. Écriture calligraphique hérodienne tardive, du milieu du premier siècle.

1]○ו מעצת[]
2]טמנו []
3]○ ○[ ]

À la ligne 1, la première lettre peut être *nun*, *ṣade* ou *taw*(?), puis *waw* ou *yod*. À la ligne 2, *vacat* ou fin de ligne(?), et à la ligne 3 seraient possibles des traces de *šin* ou *ṣade*, puis de *lamed*(?).

1 ils]l'[excluront(?)] du conseil de 2[...] ils ont caché 3[...]..[...

Ce fragment devrait pouvoir être compris או]תו מעצת, voir *1QS* VIII 22 ישלחהו מעצת היחד et *11Q19/RT* LVIII 20 לוא יצא מעצת לבו. Il pourrait aussi appartenir au rouleau des *Hymnes 11Q16* sans parallèle connu, même interligne et graphie comparable autant qu'on puisse en juger avec si peu de texte, comparable aussi à *11Q8* (*Ps^d^*).

P1345 - 8 (= *11Q20 - 11QRT*[b] *8*)

Fragment de peau de couleur brun avec des taches rougeâtres. Largeur maximale de 1,25 cm. Restes d'une ligne d'écriture, hauteur des lettres : 0,3 cm. Calligraphie d'époque hérodienne.

מל]אכה נ[עשה/ו(?) 1

La lettre à la cassure est *nun* ou *zaïn*.

[1]... *un ou*]*vrage f*[*ait* (?)...

En retenant *nun*, on pourrait y lire 1 S 15,9 : וכול המל]אכה נ[מבזה. (TM et Grec, versions בזה), ou -פל]אכה נ[ראה, ou mieux encore מל]אכה נ[עשה/ו, expression connue de *11QRT*[a]*-11Q19* XXVII 6-7.10 ; la graphie étant comparable à celle de *11Q20* favorise cette identification.

En lisant *zaïn*, on pourrait y lire Esd 2,69 = Ne 7,70 : נתנו לאוצר המל]אכה ז[הב דרכמונים שתי רבות.[35] Mais *Samuel* ni *Esdras* ne sont encore attestés dans la grotte 11.

P1345 - 9

Fragment de peau de couleur brun gris foncé (une esquille est collé au verso). Épiderme arraché dans la partie supérieure. Largeur maximale 1,4 cm, surface réglée, écriture sous la ligne, hauteur des lettres : 0,3 cm. Écriture hérodienne tardive du type de *11Q8 - 11QPs*[d].

35. La lecture ה(מל]אכה ג[דולה se retrouve en Ne 6,3 et 1 Ch 29,1, mais *gimel* ne se recommande pas.

](?)*marge/vacat*[1
]○שם בכ[2
]ל[3

La lecture *bet-kaf* paraît assurée, suivie d'une trace d'encre à la hauteur de la tête du *kaf* qui peut être une trace du pied de *lamed* ou même de l'épaule de *bet* ou de *taw*. Puis départ de la hampe de *lamed* certain.

Si on a affaire à la marge supérieure de 0,8 cm préservée hors la surface de l'épiderme arrachée, on ne peut identifier les restes à So 3,19-20, faute de légères traces de la hampe du *lamed* pour]לשם בכל[, et aucun manuscrit de la grotte 11 n'atteste de restes des *Douze Prophètes*. On doit avoir affaire à un suffixe ם- ou ?.

P1345 - 14 = *11Q20* 45 - *11QRT*[b] 45

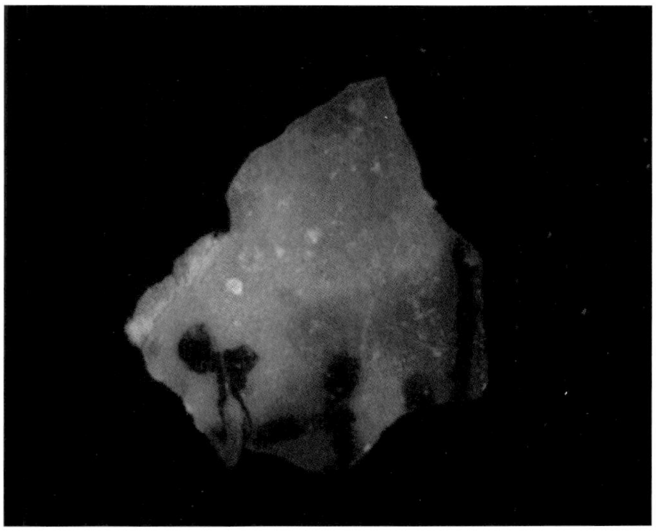

Fragment de peau très noirci, verso de couleur brun clair avec de grosses taches noires. Largeur maximale de 0,9 cm, restes d'une ligne d'écriture, hauteur des lettres de 0,3 cm.

Écriture d'époque hérodienne tardive.

1]*vac*[

2]לנגב[

²...]*au sud*[...

Le *bet* a le ductus des *bet* de *11Q20*, voir frgs 17 3, 18 2, etc. La séquence ne se retrouve qu'en 1 Ch 26,17, et en *4Q365* 32 10 où le TM de Nb 13,22 lit **בנגב**, et trois fois dans le *Rouleau du Temple*, en *11Q19* IV [2],[36] XXXVIII 14 et XXXIX 12, à moins d'une autre coupure des mots peu apparente. Cette main de scribe semble être celle du copiste de *11Q20 - 11QTemple*^{b}, et le fragment pourrait être identifié à un de ces derniers passages. En effet le fragment 17 de *11Q20* atteste des restes de *11Q19* XXXVII 9 -XXXVIII 10.

P1345 - 17 (= *11Q20 - 11QRT*^{b})

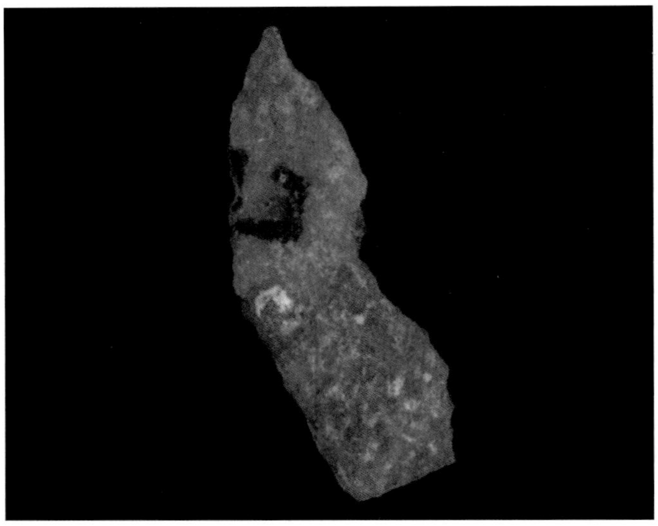

Fragment de peau de couleur brun foncé rougeâtre. Largeur maximale de 0,5 cm. Restes d'une ligne d'écriture, hauteur des lettres, 0,25 cm.

1]כב

La lettre à la cassure présente le ductus de *bet,* comme le plus probable, ou *mem*, et la marge droite (?).

La graphie est celle de *11Q20 - 11QTemple*^{b}, sans qu'il soit possible de proposer un joint direct avec d'autres fragments.

36. Voir la restauration de la colonne par L.H. Schiffman *et al.*, in J.H. Charlesworth *et al.* (ed.), The Dead Sea Scrolls: Hebrew, Aramaic, and Greek Texts with English Translation. Vol. 7: *Temple Scroll and Related Documents* (Tübingen/Louisville : Mohr Siebeck/Westminster John Knox, 2011), 270.

P1345 - 20

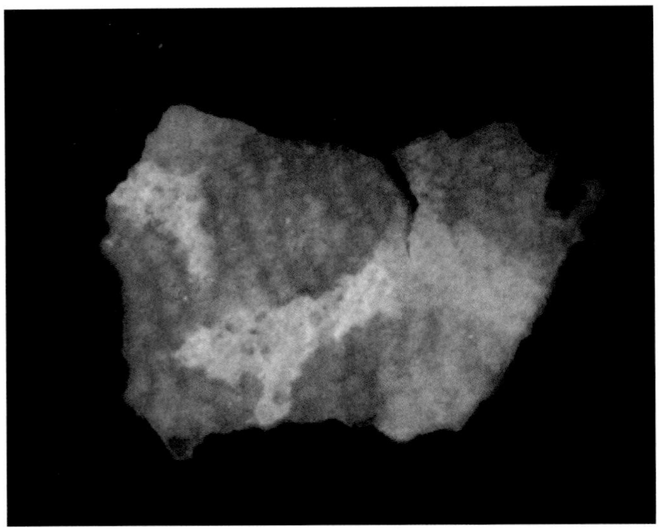

Fragment de peau de couleur brun clair avec des plages de brun foncé rougeâtre. Largeur maximale de 1,25 cm. Marge gauche préservée.

1 א[

Jambage gauche de *alef* avec léger trait de retour. Plusieurs *alef* de *11Q18-11Jérusalem Nouvelle* araméen ont ce même tracé, et difficilement *mem*.

P1345 - 24 = *11Q20* 46 - *11QRT*^{b} 46 - XIV 17-18

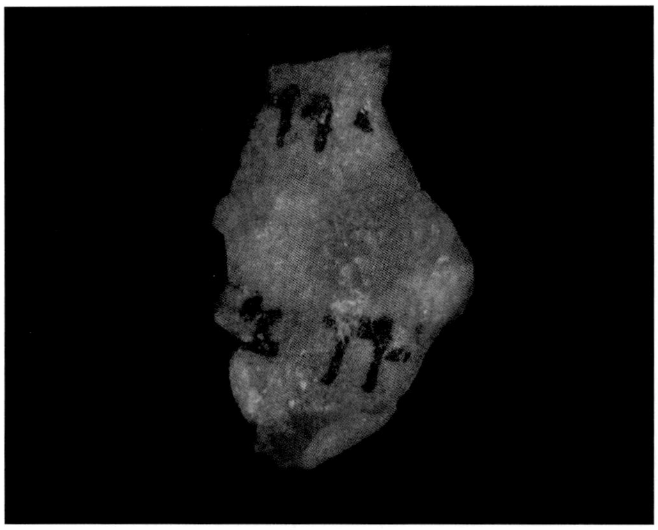

Fragment de peau de couleur brun très foncé. Largeur maximale de 1,15 cm. Restes de deux lignes d'écriture, interligne de 0,95 cm, hauteur des lettres *ca* 0,3 cm. La graphie de type formel hérodien du 1er siècle est celle du copiste de *11Q20 - 11QTemple*^{b}.

Le fragment prend place en *11Q20* XIV 17-18 (= *11Q19* L 18-21 souligné) :

1 יטהרו] עור עד לעולם *vac* כול שרץ הארץ תטמאו
החולד והעכ]בר וה[צב למינו והלטאה והכח]
2 והחמ]ט והתנשמת *vacat* כול איש אשר יגע
בה]מה במ[ותמה יטמה עד הערב וכבס]

1]◦ר וה[
2]מה ב◦[

À la ligne 1, trace d'encre à droite des restes du jambage de *dalet* ou *reš*, puis *waw* - *he* avec des restes du deuxième jambage. À la ligne 2, partie gauche de la tête de *mem*, et trace de lettre à gauche de *bet*, restes de départ de jambage cambré : *bet*, *nun*, *mem*, *kaf*.

Traduction

La vaisselle d'argile] [1]ne pourra plus être purifiée. *vacat* Vous tiendrez pour impures toutes les bestioles du sol : la taupe, la sou]ris et les [différentes espèces de grands lézards, le lézard vert, le lézard des sables, [2]le caméléon, le gecko. *vacat* Quiconque] les touche, une fois m[ortes, est impur jusqu'au soir et doit laver ...

P1345 - 28

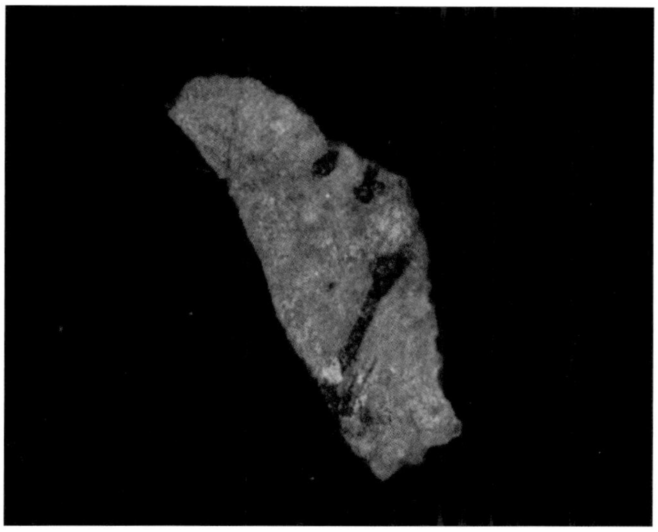

Fragment de peau de couleur brun foncé. Largeur maximale de 0,5 cm. Restes de deux lignes d'écriture. Longueur de la hampe du *lamed* : 0,5 cm. Interligne entre 0,8 et 0,9 cm. Brisure à gauche à *ca* 0,3 cm du dernier jambage de la ligne 1 : marge gauche à 0,5 cm ou simple espace entre des mots ? Écriture hérodienne.

1]עה [?]
2]ל◦[

À la ligne 1, bas de deux jambages parallèles, *he* le plus probable ou *waw-yod*, ou ?, précédés de restes de trait à gauche touchant la haste: *'aïn* préférable à *lamed*. À la ligne 2, trace de départ de trait à gauche du *lamed*. Ces caractéristiques rapprochent le frg. des manuscrits *11Q2-11QLv* ou de *11Q8-11QPs[d]*.

P1345 - 32

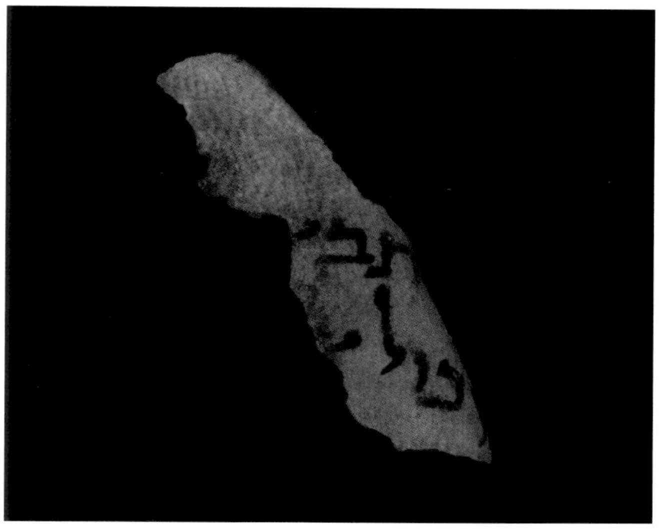

Fragment de peau de couleur brun très foncé. Largeur maximale de 1 cm. Restes de quatre lignes, surface réglée. Le bas du frg. à droite est replié et non visible sur la photographie. Interlignes de 0,7 cm. hauteur des lettres : *bet* 0,3 cm. Belle écriture hérodienne formelle de la première moitié du 1er siècle.

1]ל(?) [
2]*vac.*[
3]א יתבע/ש[
4]קן כול ש[

À la ligne 1, bas de jambage fin à gauche, *lamed* possible. *Vacat* à la ligne 2. À la ligne 3, *alef* est certain, puis le mot suivant commence par un *yod* à tête triangulaire bien marquée en trois tracés, et à la cassure suivante *'aïn* ou *šin*. À la ligne 4, tracé cambré de *nun* final précédé à la cassure apparemment du tracé de la partie gauche de *qof*, préférable à celui de *zaïn*, *ḥet* ou *samek*, puis *šin* certain à l'autre cassure.

Sans identification assurée, la langue peut être l'hébreu ou l'araméen. Si à la ligne 3 le *hitpe'el* de בעה « (il) *ne*]sera *pas*(?) recherché » paraît plausible, ne peut être exclu le *hitpa'al* de בשר, « il *ne*]sera *pas*(?) annoncé », la négation ל]א, possible, précédant le verbe. La ligne 4 est plus difficile à comprendre : une forme de תקן « redresser, corriger » paraît sous-jacente, puis peut-être une forme de ש]אר « chair », ש]גיאה « erreur », etc.

P1345 - 33

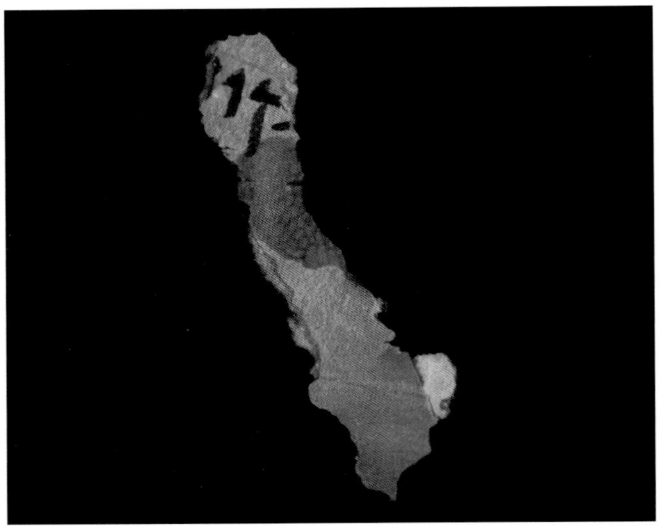

Languette de peau de couleur brun foncé à rougeâtre, tache sombre vers le centre, et brun clair en bas à droite. Largeur maximale de 0,7 cm. Surface réglée à la pointe sèche.

Restes de trois lignes, écriture sous la ligne. Interlignes de 0,75 cm. Hauteur du *waw* 0,25 cm.

Écriture calligraphique d'époque hérodienne tardive.

1]קוד/ה[
2] *vac* [
3]ה [

À la ligne 1, haste de *dalet* ou de *he* avec traces de trait horizontal de la tête. Ligne 2 *vacat*.

Restes de tête de *he* en bas à droite sur la partie de couleur brun clair.

Les restes favoriseraient un rattachement du fragment au rouleau *11Q5 - 11QPs*[a], sans qu'il ait été possible d'établir un joint, ou *à 11Q11 - 11QPsAp*[a].[37]

37. Les frgs 1 et 2 de ce rouleau sont réglés.

P1345 - 38

Fragment de peau de couleur brun rougeâtre avec des plages sombres. Fragment adhérant au verso. Largeur maximale de 0,9 cm. Restes de trois (?) lignes d'écriture (transparence au verso), interligne de 0,8 cm, hauteur du *bet* : 0,15 cm. Écriture d'époque hérodienne.

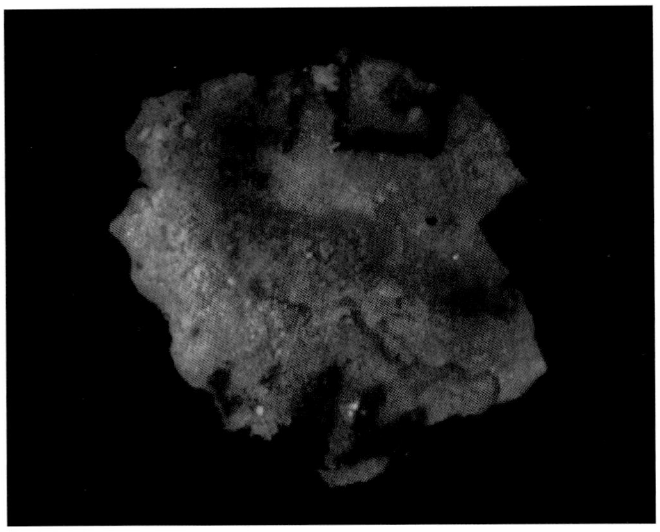

1]ד/ן[
2] ביניה[
3 ש]מו/יע[

[2]...] entre ..[... [3]...]*a prolamé*[...

À la ligne 1, extrémité d'une longue hampe de *kaf* final ou de *nun* final les plus vraisemblables à moins d'une correction supralinéaire. À la ligne 2, lire sans doute *yod* suivi de *nun*, d'un *yod* et de *he* (?). À la ligne 3, tête de *waw* ou de *yod*, puis *'aïn* préférable à *ṣade* final.

Plusieurs restaurations possibles pour une identification sans joint matériel.

P1345 - 43 = *11Q8* 18 - *11QPs*[d] 18

Fragment de peau de couleur brun foncé, épiderme arraché à gauche. Largeur maximale de 0,8 cm. Restes de deux lignes d'écriture, réglage à peine visible, interligne de 0,6 cm, hauteur des lettres : *bet*/*waw* 0,2 cm. Écriture d'époque hérodienne.

1]בול [
2]ה ו/י[

À la ligne 2, tête de lettre : *he/ḥet/samek*, puis jambage de lettre sur le bord de la surface arrachée, *waw* ou *yod* (?). Le fragment pourrait appartenir au manuscrit *11Q8* 18 - *11QPs*[d] 18 = Ps 29,10-11:

1 אמר כבוד [10]יהוה למ]בול [ישב וישב יהוה מלך לעולם
2 [11]יהוה עז לעמו יתן יהו]ה י[ברך את עמו לשבום *vacat*

P1345 - 49

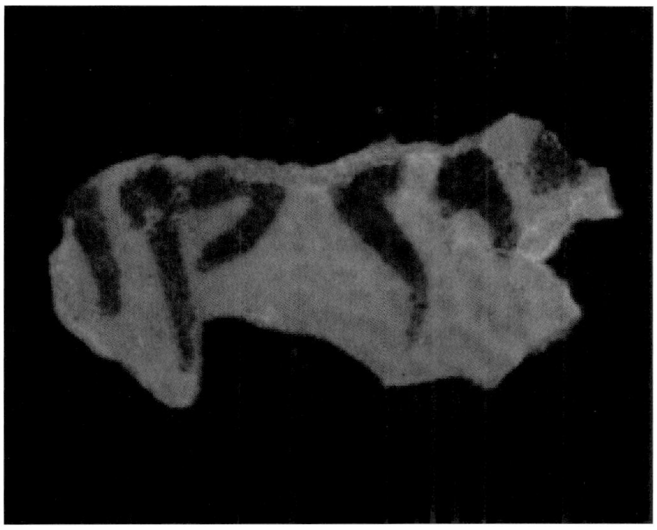

Fragment de peau brun très foncé. Largeur maximale de 1 cm. Restes d'une ligne d'écriture hérodienne tardive. Hauteur des lettres : *reš* 0,2 cm, *nun/qof* 0,35 cm. Même main que celle de *11Q10* - *11QTargum Job*, de*11Q11* - *11QPsAp*[a], et comparable à la main de la première feuille de *11Q19* - *11QTemple*[a].

1]דין קר[

À la première cassure, tête de *dalet* le plus probable ou *reš*, et à la deuxième cassure, jambage de *reš*.

Même si la séquence des lettres se retrouve en Dn 3,26 et 6,13, il est peu probable qu'il faille en faire l'unique petit reste d'un rouleau de *Daniel* dans la grotte 11.

P1345 - 51

Fragment de peau de couleur brun grisâtre. Largeur maximale de 0,45 cm, replié, semble porter une ligne : *lamed* précédé d'une trace de lettre, *mem* (?). Doit être déplié pour une meilleure lecture.

1]○ל[

P1345 - 54

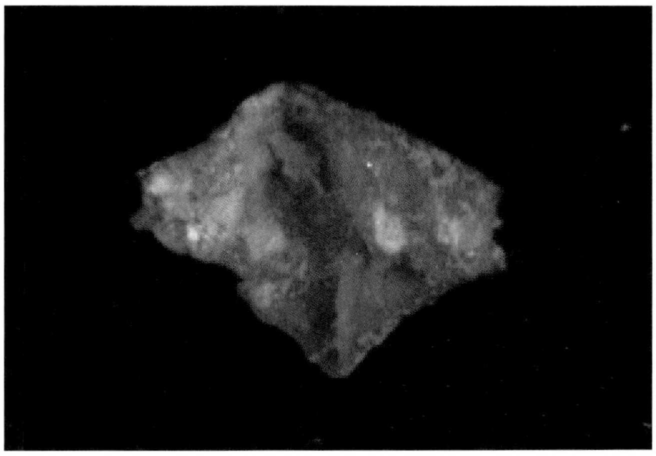

Fragment de peau de couleur brun avec des taches sombres. Largeur maximale de 0,55 cm, surface en partie arrachée. Restes d'une hampe de *lamed*, hampe de 0,45 cm, au ductus entre autres du copiste de *11Q20* - *11QTemple*[b].

1]ל[

P1345 - 58 = *11Q6/7 - 11QPs*$^{b/c}$(?)

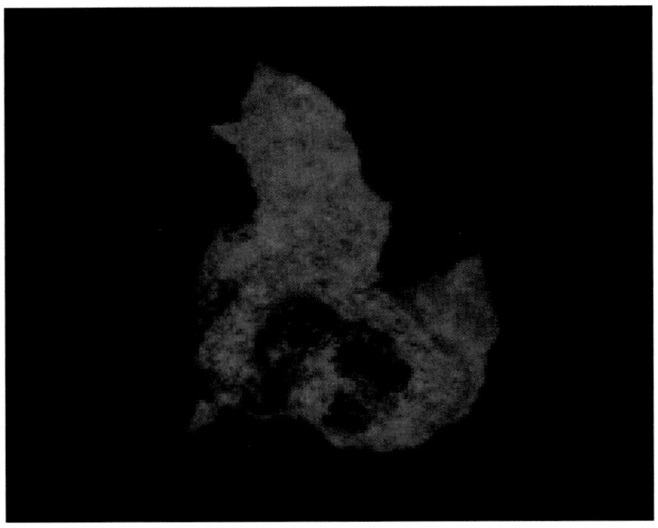

Deux petits fragments de peau collés de couleur brun foncé. Largeur maximale de 0,4 cm. Restes d'une ligne d'écriture, hauteur des lettres, un peu moins de 0,2 cm.

1]כנד[

La première lettre peut être lue *bet* ou mieux *kaf* (lettre étroite). À la cassure, *dalet* préférable à *ḥet*, le trait de gauche ne part pas du sommet du jambage pour le crochet de ces deux lettres. Le ductus des lettres est proche de celui de *11Q7 - 11QPs*^{c}. On suggérerait une lecture]כנד[en Ps 33,7 :[38]

1 7כונס]כנד[מי הים נותן באוצרות תהומות

Traduction

7Il rassemble]comme une digue[l'eau des mers, il met en réserve les abîmes.

Mais on ne peut exclure une plus grande proximité de tracé des trois lettres de *11Q6 - 11QPs*^{b} en lisant Ps 78,13 :

13 בקע ים ויעבירם ויצב מים] כנד[

Traduction

13Il fendit la mer et les fit passer, il dressa les eaux comme une digue.

38. Voir DJD XXIII, 49-61, restes des Pss 2, 9, 12-14, 17-18, 19 et 25.

avec une variante au lieu de כמו־נד du TM. En effet, le frg. 1 de *11Q6* a gardé des restes des Pss 77,18-78,1,[39] les frgs seraient dans ce cas plus rapprochés.

4. Fragments en écriture cryptique A

P1345 - 34B = *11Q23* 4- *11QcryptLv*^{c} 4

Petit fragment de peau de couleur brune avec une écriture cryptique qui était 'collé' sur un autre avec une écriture judéo-araméenne (*supra* P1345-34B). Fragment réglé. Largeur maximale de 0,7 cm et hauteur de 1 cm, interligne *circa* 0,8 cm.

1]מ ו[
2]סמ[

À la ligne 1, les restes à la cassure pourraient convenir aux extrémités du *mem*, plus difficilement à *dalet* en écriture cryptique A, alphabet magistralement déchiffré par J.T. Milik,[40] suivi par exemple du bas du jambage de *waw*. À la ligne 2, la première lettre a le tracé du *mem* en cryptique A, suivi de celui de *samek* au tracé complet à la cassure gauche. Au-dessus du *mem*, au bord de la cassure, une tache d'encre(?) semble être un point de préférence à une addition supra-linéaire.

Plusieurs possibilités de lectures se présentent, soit le substantif מס « tribut » (mais ce mot n'est pas présent dans le *Lévitique*, voir *infra*), soit avec une première ou une troisième consonne radicale non préservée, soit encore avec la préposition -מ. Comme trois autres petits fragments, portant des réglures à la pointe sèche, dans cette même écriture cryptique A ont été retrouvés dans la grotte 11, ce dernier devrait appartenir à ce même manuscrit *11Q23, 11QcryptiqueLv*.[41]

39. Voir DJD XXIII, 37-47, p. 40.

40. Voir « Józef Tadeusz Milik. Souvenirs de terrain », entretien réalisé par F. Mébarki, *MdB* 107 (1997) 11-5, p. 14b, et F.M. Cross, *The Ancient Library of Qumran* (Sheffield : Sheffield Academic Press, ^{3}1995), 45. J.T. Milik, à qui avaient été assignés ces fragments en écriture cryptique, avait repéré deux types différents, plus un autre plus naïf mélangeant les caractères grecs, phéniciens et autres, dans une écriture de gauche à droite, voir J.T. Milik, *Ten Years of Discovery in the Wilderness of Judaea* (SBT 26 ; London : SCM, 1959), 113.

41. Voir DJD XXIII, 419-20.

La datation paléographique de ces fragments doit être située dans la deuxième moitié du deuxième siècle ou *ca* 100 avant J.-C., ainsi que l'ensemble des attestations de copies dans cette écriture cryptique A, tels par exemple *4Q249 - 4QpapcryptA Midrash Sefer Moshe*,[42] *4Q249a-i - 4QRègle de la Congrégation[a-i]*,[43] *4Q317 - 4QcryptA Calendrier luni-solaire*[44], *4Q298 - 4QDires du Maskîl à tous les fils de l'aube*,[45] *4Q259 - 4QSe*,[46] et quelques autres copies dans cette écriture.[47]

11Q23 3 = Lv 4,7 :

1 מן הדם על [קר]נות מזבח קטרת
2 הסמים לפנ[י]יהוה אשר באהל מועד
3 ואת כל דם ה[פר י]שפך אל יסוד מזבח
4 העלה אשר פ[תח] אהל מועד

Notes de lecture

À la ligne 1, reste de jambage, *qof* possible, puis extrémité de jambage finissant légèrement à gauche comme c'est souvent le cas pour *reš* dans cette écriture.

À la ligne 2, *yod* est certain.

À la ligne 3, la fin de tracé oblique à gauche peut être celle de *pe* même si elle est un peu basse sous la ligne, puis tête de *reš* certain, ensuite après un espace, extrémité de tracé crochue (PAM 44.005) qui peut être celle de *yod*, bien attestée ailleurs.

À la ligne 4, le tracé horizontal à la hauteur de l'épaule du *ḥet* est typique du *taw*.

Cette lecture qui semble tout à fait recevable sur quatre lignes successives pour une largeur de colonne de *circa* 12 cm minimum, permet d'identifier le verset 7 du chapitre 4 du *Lévitique* dans cette écriture. Pourquoi user de cette écriture cryptée pour un texte connu par ailleurs aussi bien en paléohébreu qu'en écriture judéo-araméenne ? Une réponse pourrait être celle d'habituer le copiste et le lecteur à ce type d'écriture en vue du *midrash* sur ce livre, tel *4Q249 - 4QpapcryptA Midrash Sefer Moshe* à propos de *Lévitique* 14. Quoi qu'il

42. Voir S. Pfann, «249. 4Qpap cryptA Midrash Sefer Moshe», in J.M. Baumgarten *et al.*, *Qumran Cave 4. XXV: Halakhic Texts* (DJD XXXV ; Oxford : Clarendon, 1999) 1-24, mais contrairement à Pfann (p. 4-6), qui propose une datation au plus tard dans la première moitié du deuxième siècle, on retient la datation du carbone 14 dans la deuxième moitié, ce que confirment les autres copies. Le titre en écriture araméenne archaïsante se situe bien dans le troisième quart du deuxième siècle, et même s'il est un titre écrit après la copie en cryptique, cela ne signifie pas des décennies plus tard, c'est plutôt une affaire de jours ou de mois. On ne peut pas retenir la nouvelle proposition de correction du titre ספר מושה en מדרש {ספר}מושה par J. Ben-Dov and D. Stökl Ben Ezra, « 4Q249 Midrash Moshe: A New Reading and Some Implications», *DSD* 21 (2014) 131-49, à partir d'observations paléographiques plus que douteuses : leur analyse paléographique est faussée par plusieurs considérations, y compris la description des tracés qui ne respectent pas le ductus des lettres, le départ de la tête du premier *reš* a visiblement disparu ainsi que le bas du jambage du *dalet* par des écailles de la surface, le jambage gauche concave à gauche du *samek* tracé en dernier lieu a été déformé et compris comme une fausse base du *pe* tracé en deux fois alors que ce n'est pas le cas (elle pouvait aller jusqu'à la base du *reš*, mais un point en empêche la vérification), les deux *reš* ont un même tracé, le premier mot est donc bien écrit à l'horizontale alors que le dernier va en descendant légèrement. La distance entre les mots ne prouve rien (voir le titre de *1QS*), les points d'exponctuation seraient bizarrement placés : trois affecteraient le *reš*, le supérieur pas même au centre, un sous la tête et l'autre au bas du jambage, *pe* n'en serait pas affecté !) et ils ne seraient pas de la même encre que la supposée addition à droite, ce qui devrait être le cas. Que l'encre soit de teinte plus légère peut provenir du séjour de la conservation et des expositions depuis le dépôt. Enfin, que signifierait ספר מושה dans ce cas, puisque ce n'est pas un texte biblique à proprement parler ? Le seul titre acceptable est bel et bien מדרש ספר מושה sans correction ni traces de deux mains, on n'a pas affaire à une imprimerie ! Les auteurs sont à la peine pour montrer la signification du titre מדרש מושה, sans le mot ספר ou תורת (מושה), car ce n'est visiblement pas un 'Midrash de Moïse', et on ne peut pas invoquer l'ignorance du contenu du rouleau par le copiste qui a écrit le titre.

43. Voir S.J. Pfann, «Cryptic Texts», in *Id.*, *Qumran Cave 4. XXVI: Cryptic Texts* and P.S. Alexander *et al.*, *Miscellanea, Part 1* (DJD XXXVI ; Oxford : Clarendon, 2000) 515-700, p. 534-74.

44. Voir S.J. Pfann, «4QcryptA Lunisolar Calendar», in D.M. Gropp, *Wadi Daliyeh II: The Samaria Papyri from Wadi Daliyeh* and M. Bernstein *et al.*, *Qumran Cave 4. XXVIII: Miscellanea, Part 2* (DJD XXVIII ; Oxford : Clarendon, 2001) pls LII-LVIII.

45. Voir S.J. Pfann and M. Kister, «298. 4QcryptA Words of the Maskil to All Sons of Dawn», in T. Elgvin *et al.*, *Qumran Cave 4. XV: Sapiential Texts, Part 1* (DJD XX ; Oxford : Clarendon, 1997) 1-30.

46. Voir E. Puech, « L'alphabet cryptique A en 4QSe (4Q259) », *RdQ* 18/71 (1998) 429-35, un usage typiquement essénien dans leurs compositions.

47. Voir M. Fidanzio e E. Puech, «La grotta 11 di Qumran: Archeologia e frammenti manoscritti», in M. Crimella, G.C. Pagazzi e S. Romanello (ed.), *Extra ironiam nulla salus. Studi in onore di Roberto Vignolo in occasione del suo LXX compleanno* (Biblica 8 ; Milano : Glossa, 2016) 927-48, p. 940-5, et J. Ben-Dov, D. Stökl Ben Ezra, and A. Gayer, «Reconstruction of a Single Copy of the Qumran Cave 4 Cryptic-Script Serekh haEdah», *RdQ* 29/109 (2017) 21-77.

en soit, cet alphabet cryptique inconnu ailleurs est typiquement essénien et utilisé pour certaines de leurs propres compositions, ce qui laisse penser qu'il a été inventé par eux dès après leur séparation au désert en 152 av. J.-C.[48] pour leur propre usage, copier des textes réservés aux initiés, membres de la communauté.

Le fragment 1[49] a conservé la lecture]בח ◦[, qu'on proposerait d'identifier à]ל בח]צר[en Lv 6,19, l'extrémité du trait horizontal un peu au-dessous de l'épaule du *bet* peut très bien convenir au tracé du *lamed*. Ainsi le fragment 1 à lire תאכ]ל בח]צר ne serait pas trop éloigné du texte du fragment 3, (voir aussi frg. 2).

Le fragment 2 est à lire]צר[. Noter entre autres les 30 emplois du mot צרעת en *Lévitique* 13-14, et le chapitre 14 est l'objet d'un *midrash* en *4Q249* en cryptique A (ci-dessus). Mais le fragment pourrait aussi se ranger en Lv 6,9 בח[צר] ou, en complétant les lettres à *circa* 0,7 cm à gauche du fragment 1, en Lv 6,19 pour lire תאכ]ל בחצר].

Compte tenu de ces identifications possibles et même vraisemblables des fragments 1 à 3 de *11Q23* à des passages du *Lévitique*, il serait possible d'y joindre le nouveau fragment 4, à comprendre, ligne 1, הכהני]מ ו[, et ligne 2, מס]לת(ה)[, en Lv 2,2 (en lisant de préférence ממנה avec le samaritain et le grec à משם du TM pour l'espace à la marge, ligne 2) :

1 אל בני אהרן הכוהני]מ ו[קמץ
2 ממנה מלוא קומצו]מס[לתה

Ainsi on aurait des restes des chapitres 2, 4 et 6 du *Lévitique* en cryptique A. Il est important de noter la présence de cette écriture cryptique aussi dans la grotte 4 où plusieurs fragments paraissent appartenir à une copie du *Lévitique* (*4Q249j* - *4QpapcryptALv^{b}* ?), et d'autres citant des passages du *Lévitique* (*4Q249k-l* - *4QpapcryptA Texte citant Lv A-B*).[50]

Il faut aussi noter que les grottes 4 et 11 ont bien des traits communs qu'on ne peut trop vite classer en deux périodes distinctes.[51]

5. Série P1038B. Fragments de papyrus

P1038B. - Frag. 3 = *11QpapLv* 14,25-27 :

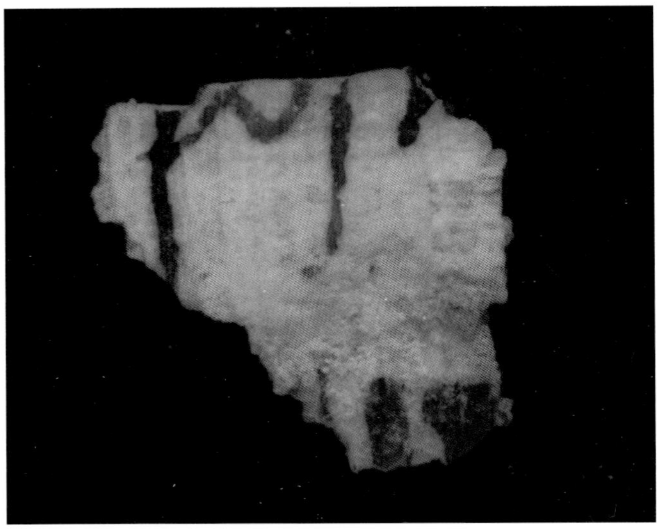

Fragment de papyrus de couleur brun avec des restes de deux lignes. Largeur maximale de 1,2 sur 1,2 cm. Interligne d'environ 1 cm. Écriture semi-cursive hasmonéenne tardive ou hérodienne ancienne, *circa* troisième quart du 1er siècle av. J.-C.

1]ת ומן [
2]הז/נה[

À la ligne 1, tracé typique de *taw* semi-cursif, puis après un espace vraisemblable un jambage longiligne de *waw* ou *zaïn* (mais trop long pour *yod*) suivi du tracé caractéristique de *mem* médian semi-cursif et d'un long jambage longiligne, *nun* final, puis un espace avant la cassure.

À la ligne 2, grande partie de la tête du *he* (*ḥet* est exclu par le tracé), départ de jambage longiligne, *zaïn* ou *nun* médian (*waw* paraît exclu sans esquisse de crochet), et départ de jambage vertical avec un tracé horizontal à gauche, difficilement *dalet*, *he* le plus probable.

Cette lecture convient au mieux à Lv 14,25-27 :

48. Voir E. Puech, « La Lettre essénienne MMT dans le manuscrit 4Q397 et les parallèles », *RdQ* 27/105 (2015) 99-135, où il est montré que la datation de la composition doit se situer entre la séparation et la rupture définitive, soit entre 152 et 150.

49. Voir DJD XXIII, 419, et pl. XLVIII (intervertir frgs 1 et 2).

50. Voir Pfann, «Cryptic Texts», 578-82.

51. Malgré D. Stökl Ben Ezra, «Old Caves and Young Caves: A Statistical Reevaluation of a Qumran Consensus», *DSD* 14 (2007) 313-33.

Planche P1038B

1 רגלו הימני]ת [26]ומן [השמן יצק הכהן על כף הכהן
2 השמאלית [27]ו]הזה[הכהן באצבעו הימנית מן השמן

Mais ne peuvent être retenus Ha 3,3 ou Ps 78,26-26 en lisant]תימן[, ligne 1, et soit ו]הוד[soit]חנה[מ, ligne 2. Ce fragment de papyrus est le quatrième exemplaire du *Lévitique* dans la grotte 11. (Voir *infra* P1038B Frag. 8 ?)

P1038B. - Frag. 5 = *11Q28* 3 - *11QpapJg* 12,6-7 (?) :

Fragment de papyrus de couleur brun, avec des restes de deux lignes d'écriture. Largeur maximale de 0,9 cm, interligne de 0,9 cm et hauteur du *šin circa* 0,3 cm.

1]ן[
2]שש[ ]

À la ligne 1, reste d'un long jambage : *nun* final, *kaf* final, ou (?). À la ligne 2, trace après une cassure, restes du jambage gauche de *sin* (?) puis *šin* certain. Ce fragment pourrait prendre place en Jg 12,6-7, en lisant ainsi :

1 אל מעברות הירד]ן[ויפל בעת ההיא מאפרים
ארבעים ושנים אלף [7]וישפט
2 יפחת את ישראל]שש[שנים וימת יפחת הגלעדי
ויקבר בערי גלעד *vacat*

P1038B. - Frag. 9 = *11Q28* 4 - *11QpapJg* 13,23-24 (?) :

Fragment de papyrus de couleur brun avec des restes de deux lignes. Largeur maximale de 0,9 cm, hauteur maximale de 1,3 cm. Interligne de 0,65 cm, hauteur du *kaf* : 0,4 cm.

Écriture semi-cursive d'époque hérodienne ancienne.

1]וכע[ ]
2]○מ○[

À la ligne 1, la lecture est assurée, et à la ligne 2, une trace de lettre, tête de *mem* assurée par le tracé, suivi d'un départ de trait convexe de gauche à droite, *'aïn* ou *šin*, plus difficilement de *alef*. Parmi les identifications possibles de passages bibliques, d'après le texte hébreu de la Bible, Jg 13,23-24 en lisant :

1 [וכע]ת לא השמיענו כזאת
2 ותלד האישה בן ותקרא את שמו]שמש[ון ויגדל הנער ויברכהו

Cette proposition est préférable à une identification à Jb 30,15-16, en lisant ligne 1: וכע]ס [, et ligne 2:]ימי[, et à Pr 27,3-4, en lisant ligne 1 : וכע]ס [, et ligne 2:]ומי[.

P1038B. - Frag. 4 = *11Q28* 5 - *11QpapJg* 16,4-5 :

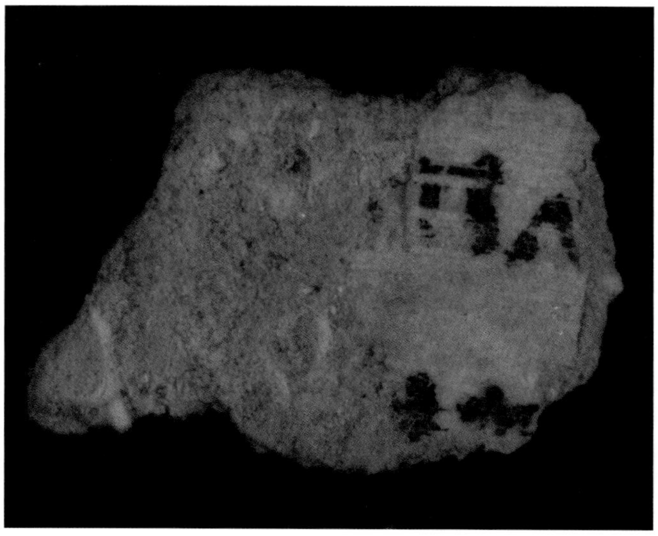

Fragment de papyrus de couleur brun, surface en partie arrachée à gauche, avec des restes de deux lignes d'écriture. Largeur maximale de 2,3 cm sur 1,6 cm, interligne de 0,85 cm, hauteur du *he* 0,4 cm. Écriture hérodienne ancienne.

1]אהב א[
2]ים[

À la ligne 1, *alef* n'est pas totalement préservé mais de lecture assurée, *he* certain, et traces du jambage et de base de *bet* probable, puis faible trace de lettre, *alef* possible. À la ligne 2, crochet de lettre et tête de *mem* final assurée. Le fragment pourrait trouver place en Jg 16,4-5 en lisant :

1 [4]ויהי אחרי כן וי]אהב א[שה בנחל שרק ושמה דלילה [5]ויעלו
2 אליה סרני פלשת]ים[ויאמרו לה פתי אותו וראי במה כחו

11Q28 1 - *11QpapJg* 17,1-2 (?) :

Les éditeurs ont donné à l'unique fragment de papyrus de la grotte 11 le sigle « 11Q28 - 11QpapUnidentified Text D ».[52] Ce fragment mesurant 1,2 cm de largeur sur 0,5 cm de hauteur, hauteur des *he-waw* 0,4 cm, en écriture hasmonéenne tardive ou hérodienne ancienne *circa* 50-25 av. J.-C., a été laissé sans proposition de lecture, il devrait cependant pouvoir être lu ainsi :

1]יהו [
2]אמ ○[

À la ligne 1, restes d'un tracé à gauche, crochet probable de *yod*, puis *he* et *waw* assurés. À la ligne 2, tête de lettre au tracé à droite *reš*, *mem* final ou *qof* préférables à *dalet*, puis *alef*, et *mem* médian au tracé semi-cursif le plus probable malgré l'écaille de la surface.

La lecture permettrait d'identifier le fragment avec Jg 17,1-2 en lisant :

1 ויהי איש מהר אפרים ושמו מיכ]יהו[[2]ויאמר לאמו אלף ומאה
2 הכסף אשר לקח לך ואתי אלית וג]ם אמ[רת באזני הנה הכסף

Pour la longueur des lignes comparables à celle des autres colonnes, cette proposition est préférable à Jg 17,2-3 qui suppose une variante orthographique dans le suffixe du verbe, contrairement au TM à la ligne 1 :

1 אתי אני לקחת]יהו [ותאמר אמו ברוך בני ליהוה
[3]וישב את אלף ומאה הכסף
2 לאמו ותאמ]ר אמ[ו הקדש הקדשתי את הכסף
ליהוה מידי לבני לעשות פסל

Cette proposition d'identification n'est pas certaine, car on ne peut exclure une correction supra-linéaire à la ligne 2 et de devoir restaurer la ligne différemment tout en gardant la même lecture. Toutefois, le fragment *11Q28* 1 en Jg 17,1-2(?) à rapprocher de quelques autres comme pouvant eux aussi appartenir à une copie de *Juges*, dont les fragments P1038B 9, 5, 6 et 7 : Jg 13,23-24(?) et Jg 14,13-14(?), restes de chapitres assez proches, comme uniques témoins d'un manuscrit sur papyrus, ne laisse pas d'intriguer. La proposition paraît au moins devoir être formulée, à défaut d'être plus affirmative.[53]

P1038B. - Frag. 6 = *11Q28* 6 - *11QpapJg* 18,5 (?) :

Fragment de papyrus de couleur brun foncé à droite, un peu plus clair à gauche. Restes d'une ligne d'écriture. Largeur maximale de 0,8 cm, hauteur du *he* 0,3 cm sur 0,4 de largeur. Écriture de période hasmonéenne tardive ou hérodienne ancienne, 2e moitié du 1er siècle av. J.-C.

]ליה: [

52. García Martínez, Tigchelaar, and van der Woude (DJD XXIII, 431) écrivent : «BOX 988 in the Rockefeller Museum contains eight small and two minute unpublished fragments of 11Q1, some small remains of wrappings, one unclassified fragment (11Q28 19), as well as two small papyrus fragments. In view of the absence of any other papyrus fragments among the finds in cave 11, the origin of these two fragments may seem suspect, but their placement in the same box as 11Q1 fragments warrants their publication as cave 11 fragments. Frg. 2 reveals only faint traces of ink, whereas frg. 1 has clear traces which are, however, difficult to identify». Il est impossible de savoir à quel fragment renvoie la mention «unclassified fragment (11Q28 19)» dont les éditeurs ne donnent nulle reproduction, puisque le sigle *11Q28* ne donne que la reproduction des fragments 1 et 2 du papyrus en question (Mus. inv. 988) d'une part et, d'autre part, il est difficile de retrouver des traces d'encre sur le frg. 2 d'après la photographie B-367189. Les fragments de *11QpaléoLévitique* ont été publiés par Tigchelaar, «Some More Small 11Q1 Fragments», 326. En conséquence on donne ici une numérotation en suivant aux nouveaux fragments de papyrus appartenant à une copie des *Juges*.

53. Tigchelaar, «Some More Small 11Q1 Fragments», 326 n. 20 : l'auteur signale dans la boîte 988, la présence d'un petit fragment en écriture araméenne «with square script, which was accidentally not included in DJD XXIII, is very dark, measures 4.5 × 3.5 mm, and reads]בא[». Aucune trace de ce fragment ne figure parmi ceux recueillis en 2015.

Seul un tracé oblique à gauche est visible à la cassure : *lamed* ou *yod*/*waw*, difficilement *mem* ou *pe*, puis *yod* le plus vraisemblable par la tête bien marquée suivi d'un *he* à large tête aux deux traits horizontaux fondus. Suivent deux ou même trois points superposés à gauche du *he* : fin de ligne ou séparation de mots (?), on a un tel usage en écriture samaritaine à la fin de versets, difficilement des points de couture.[54]

Si on retient *lamed* à la cassure, le fragment pourrait se placer en fin du verset Jg 18,5 :

1 שאל נא באלהים ונדעה התצליח דרכנו אשר אנחנו
הלכים ע]ליה : [

P1038B. - Frag. 7 = *11Q28* 7 - *11QpapJg* 18,27 :

Fragment de papyrus de couleur brun, avec des restes de deux lignes d'écriture. Largeur maximale de 1,9 sur 1,6 cm, hauteur des lettres 0,35 cm, interligne minimum 1 cm.

1 [○○]
2 [שר]

À la ligne 1, légère trace de trait oblique à gauche touchant le jambage vertical à la cassure : *lamed* possible et ?.

À la ligne 2, *šin* et *reš*. Le fragment devrait être replacé à la marge en Jg 18,27 :

1 לי]ש על עם שקט ובטח ויכו אותם לפי חרב ואת העיר
2 שר]פו באש[28]ואין מציל כי רחוקה היא מצידון ודבר אין

P1038B. - Frag. 8 = *11Q28* 8 - *11QpapJg* (?) ou *11QpapLv* (?) :

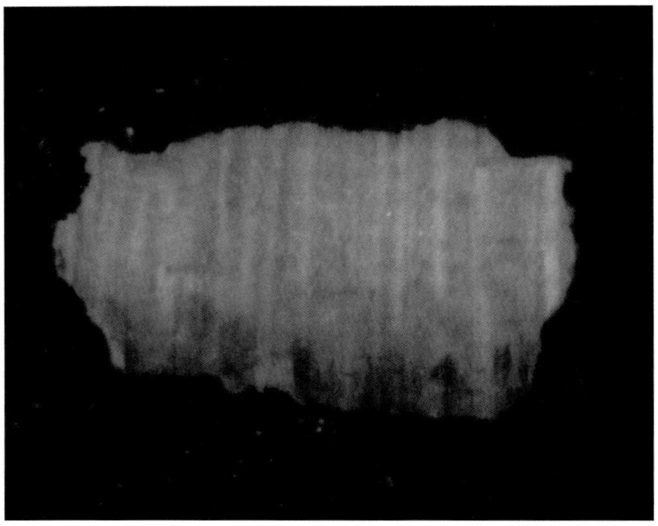

Fragment de papyrus de couleur brun, avec des restes d'une ligne d'écriture. Largeur maximale de 1,1 sur 0,35 cm. Ne sont visibles que sept à huit départs de jambages souvent indistincts, dont une lettre finale, *mem* à la cassure de droite suivi de *waw* probable.

1 [ם ו ○○○○ ○]

Sans joint direct, son identification est impossible, mais le fragment pourrait appartenir à *11QpapJg* ou même à l'écriture semi-cursive de *11QpapLv 28 6*.

Si ces identifications sont bien à retenir, ce seraient les seuls (six ou sept) fragments en papyrus du rouleau des *Juges* dans la grotte 11, et le rouleau viendrait

54. Comme cette ponctuation n'est pas comparable au point au-dessus ou en haut et en bas dans d'autres copies, voir Tov, *Scribal Practices*, 211, ne devrait-on pas y voir un premier usage de deux points séparant les « versets » comme il en sera plus tard avec les rouleaux samaritains à l'époque byzantine ?

s'ajouter aux manuscrits *1Q6, 4Q49, 4Q50 et 4Q50a* et *XJg*.[55]

Les frgs de papyrus 1 et 2 anépigraphe sont ceux de *DJD XXIII* Pl. L, 28, et les frgs 10 - 11 de P1038B ne sont pas étudiés ici.

Cette publication de nouveaux petits frgs m'est l'occasion de présenter l'identification de *11Q30* 17 (*DJD XXIII* Pl. LI) à Ez 4,4-6, entre les frgs de *11Q4* 2 et 3a :[56] Lire ainsi ces trois frgs réintégrés dans la même colonne = Ez 4,3-6 :

1 פניך אליה והית במצור [וצרת עליה] אות היא לבית
ישראל *vacat*
2 [4]ואהת שכב על צדך השמ[אלי ושמ]ת את עון בית
י[שר]אל עליו מספר הימים אשר תשכב
3 עליו תשא את עונם [5]ואני נת[תי לך א]ת שני עונם
[למספר י]מים שלש מאות ותשעים יום
4 ונשאת עון בית ישראל [6]וכלית את אל[ה ו]שכבת
על צ[דך ה]ימיני שנית ונשאת את עון בית
5 יהודה ארבעים יום יום לשנה [יום לשנה נתתיו לך]
[7]ואל מצור ירושלם תכין פניך וזרעך

Le frg. 11Q30 17 a gardé des traces de *šin* et de *reš*, ligne 1, à la ligne 2, bas de jambage du *yod*, et ligne 3, le départ du tracé de *dalet*. Avec les lectures révisées des restes des frgs 2 et 3a en miettes, il est possible de restaurer 5 lignes d'Ez 4,3-6, longueur des lignes *ca* 13 cm, en notant le *vacat-setumah* du TM.[57] La mise en colonne du passage appuie les leçons des TM, Syriaque et Vulgate contre le grec pour le nombre des années.[58]

55. Voir E. Puech, « Le livre des *Juges* dans les copies qumraniennes (*4Q559* 4–6, *1Q6, 4Q49–50–50^{a}*) », *RB* 124 (2017) 342-68.

56. García Martínez, Tigchelaar, and van der Woude (DJD XXIII, 442) écrivent : «The remnants may be a quote from Ez 4:5-6», sans plus.

57. Voir DJD XXIII, 18-21, pour des estimations différentes des longueurs des lignes.

58. Les chiffres différents des années du TM et du grec en Ez 4,5 pourraient ne pas être sans signification contrairement à des commentaires ; en effet, 190 années (grec) retranchées à 722, la chute de Samarie, rejoint le résultat des 40 années de la chute de Jérusalem et de Juda retranchées à 587, pour obtenir chaque fois le chiffre 532.

6. En conclusion

Parmi les fragments de rouleaux de cuir, dix-sept ont pu être identifiés à des manuscrits provenant de la grotte 11. Ce sont un frg. de *11Q1* (*11Qpaléo-Lévitique*), trois frgs de *11Q2* (*11QLv*), un frg. de *11Q14* (*11QSefer haMilḥamah*), un frg. de *11Q19* (*11QRT^{a}*), cinq frgs de *11Q20* (*11QRT^{b}*), un frg. de *11Q7* (*11QPs^{c}*), *11Q18* 8 (*11QPs^{d}*), *11Q6* 17 (*11QPs$^{b/c}$*) un frg. de *11Q22* (*11Qpaléo-hébreu* non identifié), *11Q22* 4 (*11QcryptLv^{f}* 4). Ces identifications ont même permis d'identifier et de relire des fragments laissés sans identification dans l'*editio princeps* : *11Q30* 18 (= *11Q1 - 11Qpaléo-Lévitique*), *11Q2* 9 i-ii (*11QLv*), *11Q23* 1-3 (*11QcryptLv*), *11Q30* 17 (*11Q4 - 11QEz*). Mais dix-neuf autres n'ont pu être identifiés avec quelque certitude, même si des propositions ont été suggérées pour plusieurs d'entre eux.

Parmi les fragments de papyrus, un fragment a été identifié comme appartenant à *11QpapLévitique*, et 5(/6) à *11Q28 - 11QpapJuges* permettant de récupérer *11Q28* 1(-2 anépigraphe) non identifiés. Reste un autre fragment qui peut provenir de l'un ou l'autre rouleau de papyrus. L'identification de ces fragments de papyrus a été une réelle surprise.

Même si des menus fragments de *11Q24-25-26-27* et *29-30-31* restent encore à identifier pour compléter le corpus des rouleaux de cette grotte, les fragments provenant des trouvailles de R. de Vaux, aussi menus soient-ils, assurent toutefois la provenance de la plupart des manuscrits découverts par les bédouins dans cette grotte en 1956, ce qui n'est pas sans importance historique, en confirmant les dires des bédouins. Par ailleurs la provenance et l'appartenance de tissu de lin ayant enveloppé le grand rouleau *11Q19-11QRT^{a}* au dire des bédouins et de l'antiquaire Iskandar Shahin ont été confirmées par les analyses spectrométriques et de fluorescence aux rayons X.[59] Ces menues trouvailles ajoutent même l'existence de rouleaux des *Juges* et du *Lévitique* (?) sur papyrus dont on n'avait jusque là nulle connaissance.

Il faut maintenant ajouter la série des fragments étudiés par O. Ableman.[60] Le travail de patience est à poursuivre.

59. Voir I. Rabin, «Archaeometry of the Dead Sea Scrolls», *DSD* 20 (2013) 124-42, p.134-6, confirmant même la différence de préparation de la première feuille du manuscrit, voir ici le frg. P1344-2 appartenant à cette première feuille.

60. Voir, dans ce volume, O. Ableman, «Preliminary Publication of Cave 11Q Fragments from Box 1032A».

Chapter Eleven

Preliminary Publication of Cave 11Q Fragments from Box 1032A

Oren ABLEMAN*

While working on compiling an inventory list of unidentified material in the Israel Antiquities Authority (IAA) scrolls' storeroom I came across various boxes with fragments that have apparently never been published or photographed.[1] Several of these boxes were listed in Reed's catalogue as containing material from Cave 11Q.[2] These boxes were inspected during the preparation of DJD 23 and some fragments with visible letters were removed and placed on plates.[3] Some of these fragments were identified with other Cave 11Q manuscripts and subsequently published in DJD 23. Many other fragments from Cave 11Q remained in boxes and have never been properly studied. It should be noted that the majority of unsorted material in boxes from the Qumran caves is attributed to Cave 11Q. In the following paper, I will present the work I have done so far on one of these boxes.

The box in question is numbered 1032A. The fragments now located on plate 1032 were originally taken out of this box. The inscribed fragments on plate 1032 were all published in DJD 23 and are identified with several different manuscripts (11Q2, 11Q6, 11Q8, 11Q11, 11Q13, 11Q17, 11Q20, 11Q22, 11Q25, and 11Q30). Box 1032A still contains a lot of unsorted material. With a few hundred fragments, this box contains the most substantial amount of material of all the boxes attributed to Cave 11Q and could perhaps be considered to be a cross-section of scroll-related material from Cave 11Q.

* I would like to thank the Dead Sea Scrolls team of the Israel Antiquities Authority for all the help with my work in general and this paper in particular. To Pnina Shor, Curator and Head of Dead Sea Scrolls Projects; to my fellow scrolls researchers Orit Rosengarten and Beatriz Riestra; to the conservators Lena Libman, Tanya Bitler, Tanya Treiger, Yana Frumkin, Asia Vexler, and Ashlyn Oprescu; and to the photographer Shai Halevi. All images are courtesy of the Leon Levy Dead Sea Scrolls Digital Library, IAA. They were photographed by Shai Halevi, unless noted otherwise.

1. The inventory list was prepared with the generous aid of Prof. Hannah Cotton, The Hebrew University of Jerusalem.

2. S.A. Reed, *The Dead Sea Scrolls Catalogue: Documents, Photographs and Museum Inventory Numbers* (SBL RBS 32; ed. and rev. M.J. Lundberg with the collaboration of M.B. Phelps; Atlanta: Scholars, 1994). Most of the information regarding the Cave 11Q boxes can be found on pp. 514-5.

3. The removal of fragments from the boxes is mentioned briefly in F. García Martínez, E.J.C. Tigchelaar, and A.S. van der Woude, *Qumran Cave 11.II: 11Q2-18, 11Q20-31* (DJD 23; Oxford: Clarendon, 1998), 438. I would like to thank Prof. Eibert Tigchelaar for confirming that he removed these fragments from the boxes and for helping identify their current placement on the plates. A summary of Tigchelaar's inspection of the boxes has been published in E.J.C. Tigchelaar, "Some More Small 11Q1 Fragments," *RdQ* 18/70 (1998) 325-30, on pp. 326-7, n. 5.

The fragments in box 1032A have never been subject to any form of treatment. Many of the fragments are still covered with a layer of dirt and other debris. All fragments in the box appear to be parchment, although final conclusions will be drawn only after all fragments have been fully studied. Many of the fragments are wads with a few layers of petrified parchment. They look like small stone pebbles or burnt pieces of wood. So far, no attempt has been made to separate these layers. Also, no attempt has been made to flatten any fragment. Thus, most fragments have a very uneven surface. Some fragments have a noticeably concave surface.

The box also contains several small fragments of textile, some of them still stuck to parchment fragments or wads. In general, the box contains a fair amount of dirt and other debris. Most of it is still stuck to the fragments, but some has become detached and is gathering at the bottom of the box. Some of the debris also seems to be of organic materials.

Fig. 1. Box 1032A

To study the content of the box more closely I removed 82 fragments and placed them on an acidic free cardboard plate, which is now numbered plate 1032A/1.[4] At first, I examined and imaged each fragment with a Dino-Lite digital microscope. Later, all the fragments on the new plate were imaged with the multispectral imaging system, built specifically for imaging the scrolls by MegaVision inc.[5] Traces of ink were found on many of the fragments under IR light already during the initial examination with the Dino-Lite. In most cases the script was not visible to the naked eye. With the help of the MegaVision images it was possible to decipher the text on some of these fragments.

The following is a preliminary edition of some fragments of interest now placed on plate 1032A/1. It is not a full report on all 82 fragments removed from the box, which is beyond the scope of the current paper. My paper focuses on cases where a substantial amount of text could be deciphered. Included here are their short physical descriptions, preliminary palaeographic analysis, transcriptions, and tentative identifications of texts and manuscripts when possible. Other fragments on plate 1032A/1 yielded only very little text, or no text at all.

The fragments are numbered according to the number given to them by the MegaVision imaging system.

Fragment 1

Physical Description: A parchment wad consisting of at least three layers with a slightly concave surface. Its colour is tan to dark brown with some black spots at the left edge. The wad may be petrified, but it does not seem to be as stiff as some of the other wads in the box. Its measurements are c. 3 × 2 cm. At least one stitching thread connecting two sheets can be seen clearly. One line of script can be identified on what appears to be the layer under the stitching. Remnants of three lines can be identified on yet

4. These 82 fragments were selected partially at random and partially due to a first impression that they could contain script. In many cases, this first impression proved to be wrong, although in a few cases this impression was correct. Most of the fragments can be clearly identified as parchment. Some are wads, while others contain only one layer. In one case, a fragment seems to be too thin and brittle to be parchment (no. 53). It may be a petrified remain of an animal skin that has 'split', or it may be some other material. In one case, a small chunk turned out to be a small animal bone (no. 10).

5. For a previous comprehensive report about the digitization aspects of the project see P. Shor et al., "The Leon Levy Dead Sea Scrolls Digital Library: The Digitization Project of the Dead Sea Scrolls," *JEMAHS* 2/2 (2014) 71-89.

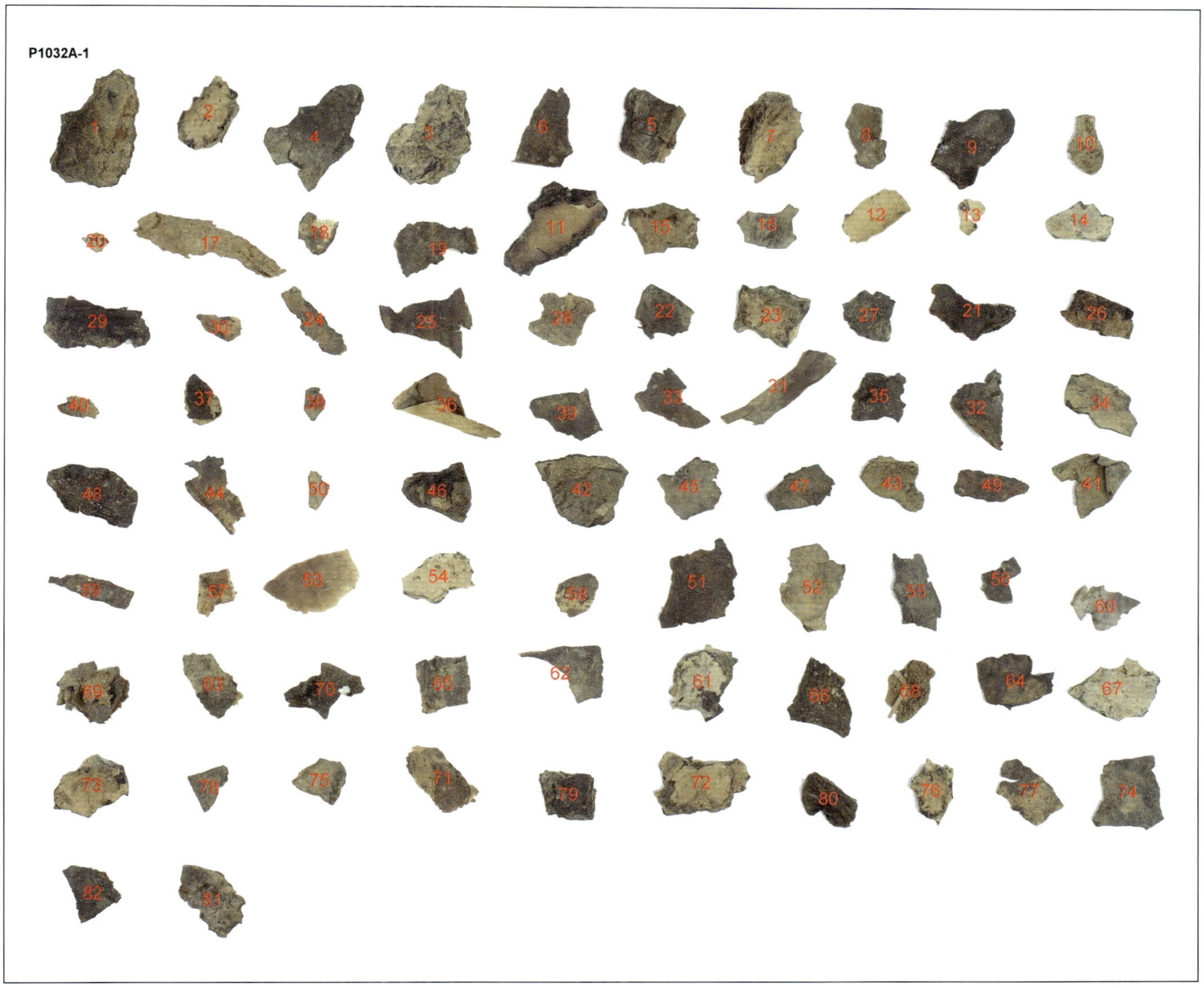

Fig. 2. Plate 1032A/1 – Fragments Removed from Box 1032A

another lower layer. At times, it is difficult to determine to which layer a letter belongs.

Palaeography: The top layer (with the thread) may have two letters that cannot be deciphered. However, these may just be dark spots. Three lines of text were identified on the bottom layer (layer 3). The clearest letters are on the middle layer (layer 2). All lines of script are on the bottom third of the fragment. This may indicate that a top margin is preserved here. However, the poor state of preservation and the difficulty to read the text caused by the different layers may have obstructed our view of additional lines of script. Moreover, there are a few spots above the lines that could perhaps be traces of ink.

The average letter height is c. 2 mm, although exact measurements are difficult to determine. The script can perhaps be characterized as semi-formal Herodian (or perhaps even late Herodian).

Fig. 3. Fragment 1

Transcription:

Layer 2:

1 [על תׄס֯]

Layer 3:

1 [◦ך֯]
2 [◦י֯ן ◦]
3 [◦◦ ל֯ ◦]

Identification: The poor state of the fragment makes it difficult to offer any suggestion for now.

Fragment 5

Physical Description: A petrified parchment wad with several layers. The measurements of the wad are c. 2 × 1.5 cm. The wad has a slightly concave shape and is rounded in certain areas. This is particularly pronounced at the right edge, which has a ridge-like shape. This ridge cast a shadow on certain parts of the surface when the fragment was imaged.

The colour of the upper layer on the *recto* is dark grey to black. No script is visible to the naked eye, but at least three lines were identified with IR light. The colour of the *verso* is mainly tan to dark brown with many dark grey spots. There is also some dirt stuck to it. A thread is stuck between the parchment layers on the right side of the wad. Another thread is probably stuck towards the top left corner of the *verso*. Some fibres stuck to the *verso* appear to be remnants of a linen wrap.

Fig. 4. Fragment 5

Palaeography: The script on the right side of the fragment is difficult to decipher due to the dark colour of the surface and the shadow in the images. Clear script was identified on the upper layer of the wad, but traces of letters that could not be deciphered were identified also on the next layer.

The average letter height is c. 2 mm. The script is formal Herodian or late Herodian.

Transcription:

1]ת֯ס֯[
2]○○ולאׄ[
3]מ֯ד֯ה֯[6]

Notes on Reading: The second letter on line 2 could not be deciphered mainly due to the problematic curve of the wad that made the images unclear at this point. The possible readings for this letter are: *gimel*, *nun*, *pe*, or *ayin*.

Identification: There are not enough letters for any conclusions about the text or the manuscript it belonged to. Still, the rather well written formal Herodian script is similar to that of some Cave 11Q manuscripts.

If the reading of the word מדה on line 3 is correct, then this could indicate that the fragment belongs to a copy of the *Temple Scroll*. A less likely possibility is that it belongs to a copy of Ezekiel. The word מדה appears many times both in the Hebrew Bible and in several of the non-biblical Qumran texts. Within the Hebrew Bible it is most common in Ezekiel 40-48. This raises the possibility that the fragment belongs to 11Q4. As noted above, this fragment is a petrified wad and it does indeed resemble the unopened scroll of 11Q4 now placed in box 1013a.[7] Still, when the paleography of the new fragment is compared with that of the few fragments that were recovered from 11Q4 some small differences are noticeable. This is most pronounced when comparing the one extant *lamed* in the new fragment – which appears to have a hook at its tip – with the wide shoulders of some of the *lameds* in 11Q4.[8] The comparison of both the physical and paleographic features of these fragments is however problematic due to the poor state of both 11Q4 and the new fragment. Identifying the fragment with 11Q4 therefore seems to me like a possibility that should be kept in mind, but that is not very likely.

A more likely identification for the new fragment is with 11Q21. The word מדה appears over a dozen times in the *Temple Scroll*,[9] far more than in any other non-biblical text found at Qumran. When the scribal hand of the new fragment is compared with those of the Cave 11Q manuscripts of the *Temple Scroll*, there are noticeable differences with 11Q19 and 11Q20. However, the scribal hand of 11Q21 seems almost identical. Not enough letters have survived on the new fragments to confirm this identification, but with the images currently available it seems to be the most likely one.

Fragment 8

Physical Description: A parchment fragment that has curled at the top and bottom edges. There seems to be part of another layer of the scroll on the *verso*, but this could also be a fold in the parchment. The fragment is dark brown. What seems to the naked eye like black spots turned out to be parts of two lines of script preserved on the *recto*. Due to the curling at the edges, the fragment needed to be tilted a bit to make all letters visible to the camera lens. This could only be done when using the Dino-Lite. Due to the curling the fragments height could not be determined exactly, but it is probably c. 1 cm. The width is c. 1.8 cm.

Palaeography: The average letter height is c. 2 mm, and the distance between the two lines is c. 4 mm. The script is formal Herodian. The developed *keraia* on *bet* and *resh* seem to indicate a later Herodian script. In contrast, the *ayin* and final *tsadi* do not seem to match the developments these letters underwent towards the later Herodian period.

6. The reading of line 3 was first suggested by Prof. Émile Puech in his response to this paper also published in this volume. I now accept this reading and would like to thank Prof. Puech for his comments and for making his response available to me before publication.

7. For physical descriptions of 11Q4 and the attempts to open it see DJD 23, 15-7; W.H Brownlee, "The Scroll of Ezekiel from the Eleventh Qumran Cave," *RdQ* 4/13 (1963) 11-28, on pp. 11-4.

8. Cf. DJD 23, 21; Brownlee, "Scroll of Ezekiel," 25.

9. Some of the appearances of מדה in 11Q19 are reconstructed. Its prevalence is due to the *Temple Scroll*'s dependency on Ezekiel 40-48.

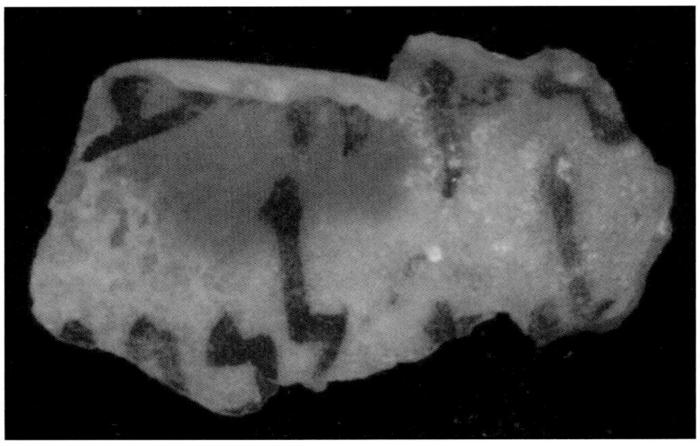

Fig. 5. Fragment 8 – 11Q8, Ps 37:3-4

Fig. 6. Fragment 8, tilted view (Photographer: Oren Ableman)

Transcription:

1]○רץ ורע[
2]לו○ לב○○[

Identification: The scribal hand is most certainly closer to 11Q8 than any other manuscript from Cave 11Q. However, there are no remnants of the clear ruling found on 11Q8. This could perhaps be the result of the fragment's very dark colour.

The preserved text seems to be Ps 37:3-4. This would lead to the following reconstruction of the text on the fragment:

1]ארץ ורע[ה
2 משא]לות לבכה[

If this identification is correct then this fragment almost certainly belongs to 11Q8 and should be placed to the right of frg. 5:5-6. The two fragments cannot be joined directly, but the lacuna between them is probably only a few millimetres. The result is that the reconstruction offered in DJD 23 should be slightly amended.[10] I would suggest the following combined reconstruction:[11]

1 קו[ם va]cat
2 va[cat לדויד א]ל תתחר
3 במרעים א[ל תקנא בעש]י עולה כי כחציר מהרה
4 ימלו וכירק ד[שא יבלון בט]ח ביהוה ועשה טוב
5 שכן [ארץ ורע] [ה אמונה וה]תענג על יהוה ויתן לכה
6 משא[לות לבכה] גו[ל] על יהוה

Fig. 7. 11Q8 frg. 5, Ps 36:13-37:4 (5?)

10. Cf. DJD 23, 68. The main difference between my own reconstruction and that of DJD is that I have placed frg. 5 towards the middle of the column instead of at its right margin.

11. As already noted in DJD 23, the lines cannot be fully reconstructed on the basis of MT. The addition of the new fragment strengthens the supposition that this text follows a slightly different version than MT. The following reconstruction assumes that there were some unknown pluses that did not survive in the lacunas.

Fragment 24

Physical Description: A small fragment with a slight curl at its bottom right edge. Its measurements are c. 2.1 × 0.65 cm. The fragment's colour is tan brown with some lighter spots. Remnants of three lines of script have survived on the fragment. Only three letters have survived on each line (and some of those only partially). There seem to be traces of ruling in the second line.

Palaeography: The letters have an average height of c. 3 mm. The distance between the lines is c. 3.5 mm. The script is Herodian, and should probably be classified as late Herodian. Still, there are not enough surviving letters to reach a more accurate dating.

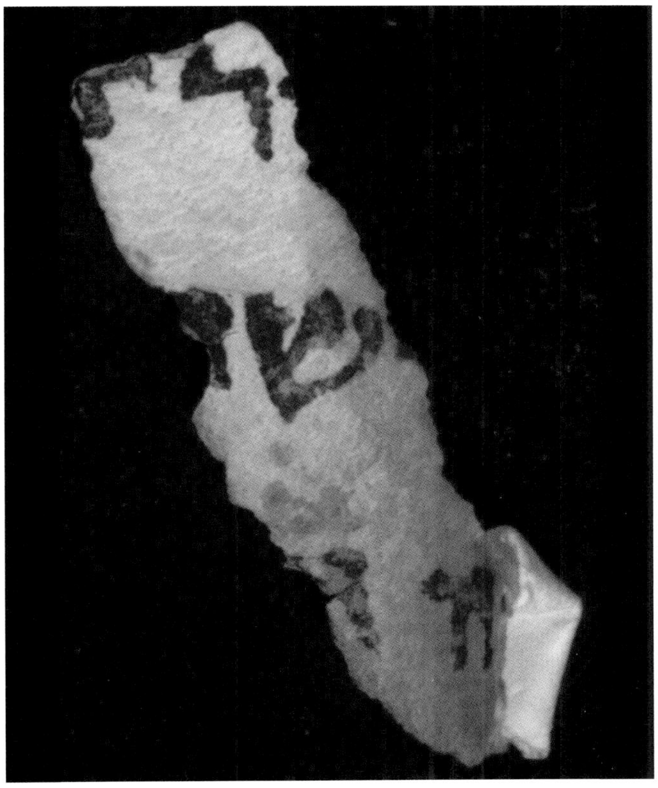

Fig. 8. Fragment 24 – 11Q11(?)

Transcription:

]◦רצׄ[1
]◦שה֯[2
]◦ה ה֯[3

Identification: The fragment seems to belong to 11Q11. This identification is based on the similarity of the scribal hand as well as physical similarities. The long and narrow shape of the fragment is typical of 11Q11 and 11Q17. However, the script is distinctively different from that of 11Q17.

Based on the shape of the fragment it probably originated somewhere in col. I-II of 11Q11.[12] The *shin* on this fragment is also most similar to the examples from these columns. The fragment most certainly does not come from the end of the scroll – which contains Ps 91 – since nothing in the text of the fragment matches that biblical text.

Fragment 37

Physical Description: A small parchment fragment with a concave shaped surface. Its measurements are c. 1.8 × 0.9 cm. The fragment contains only one layer, but this layer is in the process of splitting into two. The upper layer is very dark brown or black. In contrast, the bottom layer is very light sandy brown. The light colour is also evident on the *verso*, but there are some darker patches and spots. Remnants of two lines of script have survived on the very dark *recto*. They are visible only in IR images. There is a fold towards the bottom right edge of the fragment. This fold seems to cover additional letters of the second line.

Palaeography: To date, this is the only fragment taken out of the box that contains paleo-Hebrew script (however note that 11Q22 frg. 7 also came out of this box). Only three full letters have survived, but since they are from two different lines it is safe to assume that the entire scroll was written in this script. The letters have an average height of c. 1.5 mm. The distance between the lines is slightly under c. 1.5 mm. The script is similar to other Qumran paleo-Hebrew fragments, although some features seem closer to the contemporary square Hebrew script. The *qop* in particular seems almost identical to its form in square script. It has a small triangular "loop" on its right side, and a pronounced tick at its top left corner. These are typical features of late Hasmonean and Herodian script.[13]

12. In his comments to this paper Émile Puech suggests that this fragment can be physically joined to col. II of 11Q11 where he argues that traces of the head of the *sade* are visible. While this join is possible I think that it is not certain. The outline of the top of the new fragment does not easily fit with that of the larger fragment. Moreover, the ink traces in col. II that Puech identifies as the head of a *sade* are in my opinion too minuscule for a meaningful reading.

13. See F.M. Cross, "The Development of the Jewish Scripts," in Id., *Leaves from an Epigrapher's Notebook: Collected Papers in*

This leads me to the conclusion that this fragment should probably be dated to this period. This would give the fragment a slightly later date than most other paleo-Hebrew manuscripts from Qumran.

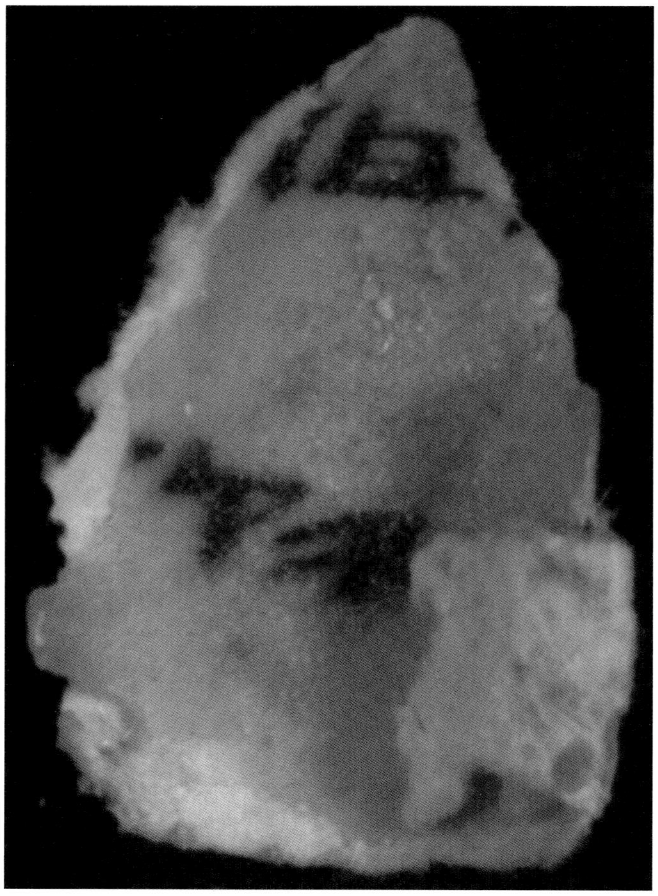

Fig. 9. Fragment 37

Transcription:

1
]○ח○[2
]○קי[

Identification: The script is noticeably different than that of 11Q1 and clearly does not belong to it. It is rather similar to the few fragments of 11Q22. However, despite the similarity of script, there are some slight differences. These can be seen when comparing the *het* and *qop* of the new fragment, to the examples of these letters in fragments 6 and 2 (respectively) of 11Q22. Unfortunately, these are the only other examples of these letters in 11Q22. This is not enough to reach a conclusion one way or another. Identification with 11Q22 can probably be ruled out due to the fragment's very dark colour. 11Q22 is for the most part much lighter. This difference can however be explained as resulting from different types of damage that affected different parts of the same manuscript.

Fragment 41

Physical Description: A small triangular shaped fragment that is folded at two of its three edges. The surface is also curved. Its measurements are c. 2.1 × 1.7 cm, but if unfolded the fragment would be slightly wider.

The *recto* has a dark brown colour with some black splotches. The *verso* is light brown and seems to be covered with a thin layer of sand. Two lines of script are visible on the *recto* in IR images. Due to the folds in the fragment, certain parts of the top line appear in the images of the *verso*. Some dark lines on the *verso* could perhaps also be remnants of ink.

Palaeography: The average letter height is c. 3 mm. The distance between the two lines is c. 4.5 mm. The script is formal Herodian, although some letters bare some similarity to the 'Round' semiformal script. Characterization of the script is a bit difficult due to the fragments curved surface.

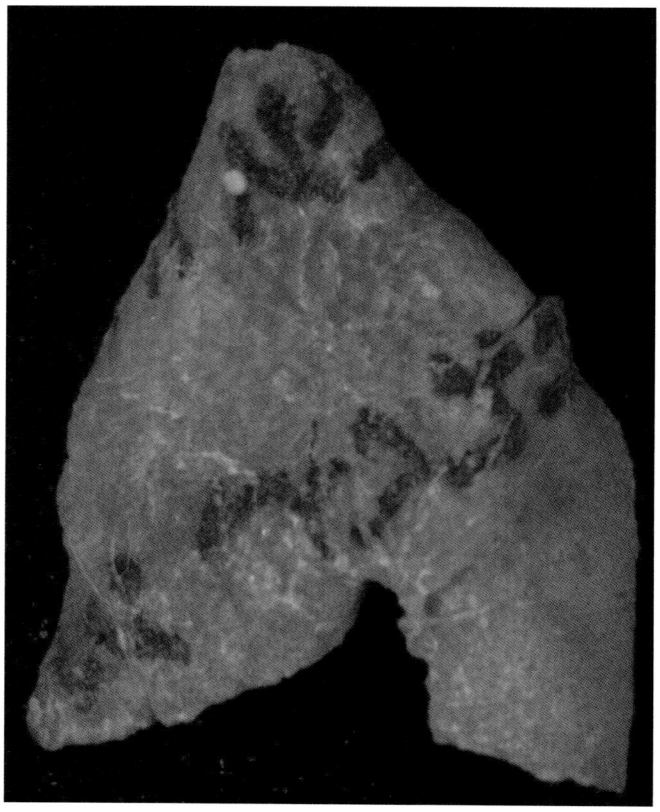

Fig. 10. Fragment 41 – Lev 13:51-52, 11Q2(?)

Hebrew and West Semitic Palaeography and Epigraphy (HSS 51; Winona Lake, IN: Eisenbrauns, 2003) 3-43, on pp. 31, 37.

Transcription: In this case, there are two possible transcriptions. Each transcription will yield an identification of the fragment with a different text and manuscript.

Option 1

1]מׄא ה֯וׄ◦[
2]כׄצפׄור א◦[

Option 2

1]מׄא ה֯וׄא֯[
2]בׄצמׄר או֯[

Identification: The main difference between the two options is if on line 2 one should read a *pe* and *waw* or a *mem*.

If option 1 is accepted, then the fragment is most similar to 11Q18. Still, an identification with 11Q18 is only tentative since there are not enough complete letters to reach final conclusions. The resulting text does not correspond to anything in the New Jerusalem text.

If option 2 is accepted, then the fragment probably belongs to 11Q2. This identification is not possible for option 1 since the *pe* in 11Q2 is significantly different from the example in this fragment. The identification of the fragment with 11Q2 could perhaps be questioned due to the shape of the right arm of the *tsadi*. The shape of the example on this fragment is noticeably different than 11Q2, but could be explained by the shape of the fragment and its curved surface.

It seems that option 2 should be preferred for both physical and textual reasons. The colour and texture of the fragment is noticeably similar to 11Q2 frg. 3.[14] Moreover, the text that results from option 2 corresponds exactly with Lev 13:51-52. The resulting line width is also identical to that of 11Q2. It seems therefore reasonable to assume that this fragment should be placed several lines before 11Q2 frg. 3 (=Lev 13:58-59), or in the preceding column.

If option 2 is correct, then the text of the fragment can perhaps be reconstructed as follows:[15]

1 נגע ט]מׄא ה֯וׄא֯[ושרף את הבגד או את השתי או את
2 הערב]בׄצמׄר או֯[בפושתים או את כול כלי עור

Fragment 47

Physical Description: A petrified wad of parchment with a slightly convex surface. Its measurements are c. 1 × 1.6 cm. The wad contains at least four layers. The parchment is very darkened and is mostly black with some patches of dark grey or brown. The *verso* is partially covered with dirt. On the *recto*, traces of script were identified on the top two layers of the wad.

Palaeography: The script is very difficult to decipher due to the fragment's dark colour. At least one certain line of script was identified on each of the top two layers of the wad. There may be traces of another line at the bottom of the upper layer, but the dark colour of the wad makes it difficult to determine whether these are indeed traces of ink or something else. Only the script on the top layer could be deciphered for now. The average letter height is c. 2 mm. The script is a formal Herodian hand.

Fig. 11. Fragment 47 – 11Q17

Transcription:

Layer 1:

1]◦ פלאי֯[

Identification: The script seems to be identical with the hand of 11Q17. The root פלא is also rather common in the *Sabbath Songs*. This identification

14. I would like to thank Lena Libman for making this observation.

15. This reconstruction assumes close correspondence with MT while also taking into account the orthography of the rest of 11Q2. The manuscript uses *plene* spelling, and in frg. 3 tend to omit the article. Cf. DJD 23, 2 and 5-6.

therefore seems almost certain. Nothing can be said about the placement of the fragment within the text based only on this single word.

Fragment 48

Physical Description: This is a parchment fragment covered with a thin layer of gummy material. This gives the fragment an almost completely black colour and a very uneven surface. Under the layer of gummy material the *recto* seems to be dark brown and the *verso* seems to be light brown. The measurements of the fragment are c. 2.3 × 1.3 cm. Two clear lines of script can be seen in IR images, as well as traces of two letters from two additional lines.

Palaeography: The letters have an average height of c. 3 mm. The distance between the lines is c. 5 mm. The script is formal Herodian, probably from the later part of the period.

Fig. 12. Fragment 48

Transcription:

1 [○]
2 [○שיה א֯]
3 [○רץ אז מׄ]
4 [ל֯]

Notes on Reading: The first letter in line 2 is *gimel*, *mem*, or *ayin*. *Ayin* seems most likely both as far as shape and possible reconstructions. *Alef* also seemed possible at first, but should be ruled out due to the noticeable differences with the two other examples of the letter in this fragment. The most probable reconstruction of this word is: מעשיה.[16] The first letter on line 3 should almost certainly be reconstructed as *alef*. The reading is therefore probably ארץ אז.

Identification: For now, I have not been able to match the text or script with anything else from Cave 11. The layer of gummy material makes it difficult to compare the script with those of other manuscripts. The script is similar to 11Q5 and the first scribe of 11Q19. This similarity is however superficial and this fragment could have potentially originated from other manuscripts.

A possibility that should be considered is that this fragment could be connected to the text of 4Q381 (*Non-Canonical Psalms B*) frg. 69. The word sequence ארץ אז appears only here and in 4Q381 frg. 69:6. Moreover, if the word in line 2 is indeed מעשיה then this could be similar to the word ממעשי that appears in 4Q381 frg.69:5^{sup}. Both fragments do not preserve the same exact text. It is however possible that both preserve different versions of the same text.

Fragment 55

Physical Description: A small parchment fragment. Its measurements are c. 1.2 × 1.7 cm. The *recto* is a dark brown with a slightly reddish tint in certain places. The *verso* is a more uniform mid-brown colour. The *recto* contains remnants of three lines of script. The script is clearly visible in IR light, but parts of it can be recognized also in colour images.

Palaeography: The size of the letters is not uniform and they range in height between c. 2-3 mm. The distance between the lines is c. 3.5 mm. There is a noticeable difference in the thickness of the lines between the two words on line 2. This could perhaps be the result of the scribe starting to use a different quill at this point. The script seems to be formal mid to late Herodian.

16. This was suggested with thanks by Émile Puech in his comments on this paper.

Fig. 13. Fragment 55 – Deut 19:5 (?), 11Q3(?)

Transcription:

1] הו[ ]○[
2]את̇ מ̇צא[
3]○[

Identification: The word sequence מצא את appears several times in the Hebrew Bible. When taking the two letters on line 1 into consideration, the closest correspondence is Deut 19:5. If this is correct, then the word on line 1 should be reconstructed as רעהו. This raises the possibility that the fragment belongs to 11Q3. The fragment is indeed physically similar to the fragments of that manuscript. The palaeography is also similar, but not identical. This identification therefore seems possible, but not certain.

Fragment 62

Physical Description: A parchment fragment with a slightly curved surface. Its measurements are c. 1.5 × 1.2 cm. The colour is mostly dark brown with some black blemishes. Two lines of script can be seen clearly in IR images. Some traces of ink are visible to the naked eye, but are difficult to distinguish from the dark surface of the fragment.

Palaeography: Most of the ink seems to be smudged. This makes the decipherment of some letters uncertain. The average letter height is c. 2.5 mm. The distance between the two lines is c. 4.2 mm. The script is formal Herodian. Further accuracy is difficult to determine due to the smudged ink and the low number of letters that have fully survived.

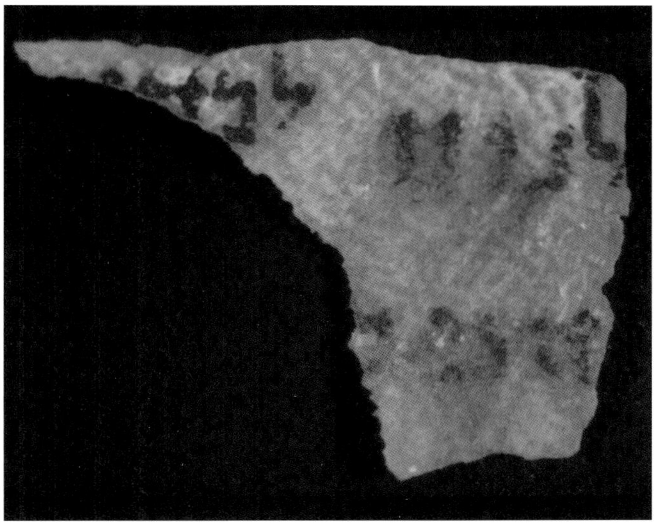

Fig. 14. Fragment 62 – Jubilees 5:19 (?), 11Q12(?)

Transcription:

1]לנוח̇ לב̇ד̇ו֯ן[
2]ה̇מ֯ב֯[17]

Identification: The text of line 1 seems to match *Jubilees* 5:19. Other identifications are possible, but this one seems to be the most plausible. If this is correct than this fragment perhaps belongs to 11Q12. The palaeography does seem to match, but the smudged ink makes it difficult to determine how plausible this identification is.

Fragment 68

Physical Description: A small parchment fragment with a lot of dirt stuck to its *verso*. Its measurements are c. 1.7 × 1.1 cm. The *recto* has a very dark brown to black colour. The *verso* is not visible due to the dirt stuck to it. Within the dirt are two (possibly connected) small pieces of organic material. They may be tiny wood splinters or papyrus fibres, but the later seems unlikely due to their colour and thickness. Remains of three lines of script can be seen on the *recto* in IR images.

Palaeography: The average letter height is c. 2 mm. The distance between the lines is c. 4.5 mm. The script is formal Herodian, and could perhaps

17. Originally I offered the following reading of line 3:]הּם֯ ל֯[. Following the comments to this paper by Émile Puech I find his reading to be more plausible. Puech also offers a possible reconstruction of the text based on *Jubilees* 5:19.

be more precisely characterized as late Herodian. However, there are not enough letters to be certain of this narrow dating.

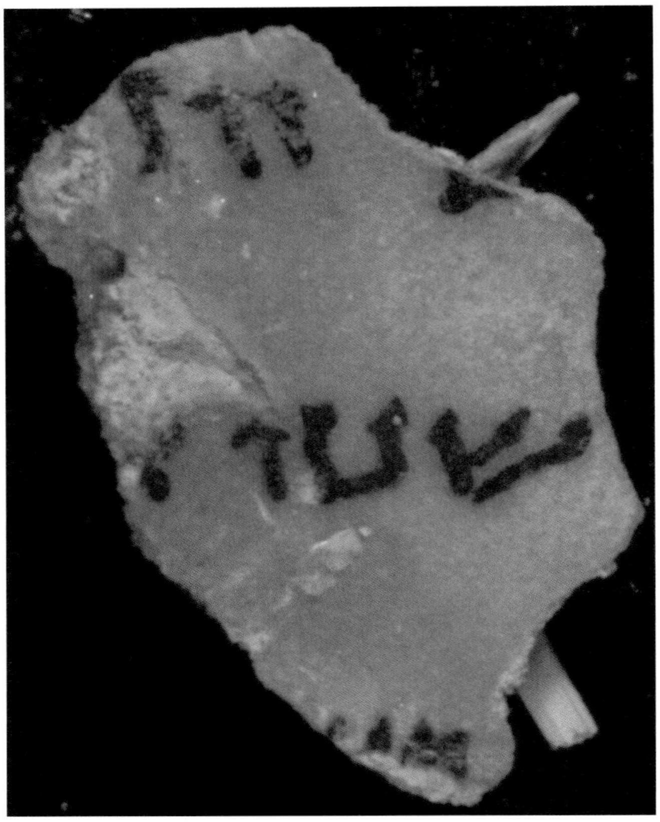

Fig. 15. Fragment 68 – 11Q21, Temple Scroll 22:13-14

Transcription:

1]ם̊ הז̇[
2]שנ̇ה א̇[
3]∘∘ [

Identification: The script is most similar to the scribal hand of 11Q21. The colour of the fragment and the physical characteristics of the parchment also seem to be similar. Still, the distance between the lines is slightly larger in this fragment and there are no traces of ruling like in 11Q21.

The identification with 11Q21 is also supported by the deciphered text. This string of letters closely corresponds with 11Q19 col. 22:13-14 (=11Q20 col. 6:6-7). Nothing else similar could be identified in the Hebrew Bible or in other Qumran texts. If this identification is correct, then it would support the identification of 11Q21 as a third Cave 11Q copy of the *Temple Scroll*. Still, if the text were identical to that of 11Q19 there should have been traces of a *bet* before the *shin* at the beginning of line 2. This absence can however be explained as a result of a slightly wider than normal gap between the letters. Another possibility is that the scribe skipped a word here and wrote שנה instead of שנה בשנה.

Based on the arguments above I would offer the following tentative reconstruction of the text:

1 ואכלום ביו]ם̊ הז̇[ה בחצר החיצונה לפני יהוה חוקת עולם
2 לדורותיהמה שנה ב]שנ̇ה א̇[חר יואכלו
3]∘∘[

Fragment 81

Physical Description: A small parchment fragment with an uneven surface. The fragment is a bit 'crumpled' and this has caused some folds at the edges. Its measurements are c. 1.2 × 1.7 cm. The fragment is very dark brown with a bit of a reddish tinge. Remains of one line of script, and small traces of another one, can be seen in IR images on the *recto*. A fold at the top left edge of the fragments probably covers one or two additional letters of the first line.

Palaeography: The average letter height is c. 2.7 mm. The distance between the two lines is c. 6 mm. The script is a formal Herodian hand. Some letters are not fully visible due to the folds in the parchment.

Fig. 16. Fragment 81 – 11Q5, Ps 147:1-2

Transcription:

1]∘ זמרה̇[
2]ש̊∘[ ]ל̊[

Identification: The word זמרה is relatively rare. In the Hebrew Bible it appears only in Isa 51:3, Ps 81:3, 98:5, and 147:1. It also appears in 4Q443 frg. 1:2. The first unidentified letter of line 1 seems to have a base stroke. This would seem to fit only Ps 147:1. Moreover, the partial letters in line 2 can perhaps be placed in 147:2.

The script of this fragment seems to be identical to 11Q5, although there are not enough letters to be certain. Part of Ps 147:1 has survived in 11Q5 frg. E col. 2:16. The word זמרה is not part of the surviving text there. If this fragment does indeed belong to 11Q5, then it should probably be placed a bit to the right of the bottom line of col. 2 of frg. E.[18] The text could then be reconstructed as follows:

16 הללויה כי טו]ב̊ זמרה̇[אלוהינו כי נעים ת]הלה בונה ירושלים
17 יהוה נדחי י]ש̊ר̊[א]ל̊[יכנס

It should be noted that this reconstruction differs from MT and the reconstruction proposed in DJD 23.[19] By my calculation, in order for the word ישראל to be located directly under זמרה in the previous line, זמרה must be located a bit further to the left than in the reconstruction in DJD 23. This is possible if we assume that הללויה was located at the beginning of line 16 instead of line 15 as proposed in DJD 23. This seems to me reasonable, since as noted in DJD 23, there is no other example in 11Q5 of הללויה being written on a separate line that was then left empty.

The problem with my reconstruction is that I must assume some sort of variant reading or omission in line 16. As noted in DJD 23, the full text of MT 147:1 does not fit in the lacuna at the beginning of the line. However, LXX for this verse omits either נעים or נאוה.[20] I have accordingly omitted נאוה, but omitting נעים instead is also possible. The resulting line is also slightly longer than the average for this column and therefore we should perhaps consider the possibility that כי was also omitted. Despite these difficulties I think that any reconstruction of this line must assume a variant that is one word shorter than MT and this seems to be the most plausible reconstruction.

Conclusions

My study of box 1032A has brought to light some unexpected new discoveries. It demonstrates that even what appears at first sight to be nothing more than odds and ends, can turn out to be fragments with text. In some cases, even such tiny fragments can be identified with known manuscripts and give us new insights about their text.

It must be emphasized that my study of these fragments is possible thanks to equipment and technologies that until recently were not available to scholars of the Dead Sea Scrolls. As we have just seen, even with these new options there are many difficulties when attempting to decipher the barely legible script on these severely damaged fragments. The Israel Antiquities Authority continues to move forward utilizing yet more advanced imaging technologies, such as X-ray Microtomography and Reflection Transformation Imaging (RTI). These will hopefully allow us to decipher even more of the script on these fragments.

This paper is a first step in the renewed study of the boxes from Cave 11Q. I have presented here just a sample of the fragments already removed from box 1032A. There is still a lot of work to be done, the box still contains hundreds of fragments that have yet to be examined, and perhaps some minuscule treasures are waiting to be discovered.

18. In his comments to this paper Émile Puech (below, Chapter 11 Appendix) suggests that this fragment should be physically joined to the bottom of 11Q5 frg. D. This join seems to me impossible. The outlines of both fragments do not connect in any obvious way. Moreover, Puech argues that the fold at the top left corner of the new fragment covers several letters. This fold is in fact much smaller and covers only one or two letters. It therefore seems far more reasonable to connect this new fragment to 11Q5 frg. E as suggested above.

19. Cf. DJD 23, 33-5.

20. Cf. J. Blau, "Nāwā Ṯhillā (Ps. CXLVII 1): Lobpreisen," *VT* 4/4 (1954) 410-1, on p. 410, n. 2.

Chapter Eleven
Appendix

Nouveaux menus fragments de la Grotte 11Q (boîte 1032A/1)

Émile PUECH

Ces lignes voudraient apporter quelques compléments à l'édition de nouveaux menus fragments de la boîte 1032A/1 de la grotte 11, dont les plus significatifs ont été publiés ci-dessus par O. Ableman.[1] On peut regretter que l'ensemble n'ait pas été présenté et que l'auteur en soit resté à une édition préliminaire.

1. Fragment de cuir en écriture paléo-hébraïque

- Frg. 37 : C'est le seul fragment en écriture paléo-hébraïque de cette série et l'éditeur, tout en le comparant aux fragments de *11Q22*, estime qu'il ne peut leur être joint à cause de la couleur sombre de la surface. Celle-ci est toute relative à ce propos et dépend du contexte de la découverte. Il est tout de même à noter que les dimensions des lettres et l'écartement des lignes sont comparables à celles de *11Q22* où de légères traces de réglure sont présentes. Il est regrettable que l'éditeur n'ait pas lu les restes de lettres sous les plis du cuir, lecture maintenant possible au laboratoire comme il le signale lui-même plusieurs fois. Il semble que la ligne 1 ait conservé une partie de *taw*, et soit *dalet* ou mieux *he* à l'autre cassure. Au moins une lettre devait être préservée sous le pli, ligne 2, et à l'autre cassure restes de *bet* ou de *taw*. *In fine* l'appartenance au groupe de fragments de *11Q22* paraît très probable.

2. Fragments en écriture araméenne

- Frg. 1 : Pour une étude appropriée et utile de ce frg., il est nécessaire de séparer les trois couches de cuir inscrites, ce qui est maintenant possible avec les nouveaux procédés d'étude.

- Frg. 5 : À la ligne 3, lire au mieux]מדה[. Pour une meilleure lecture et identification, il est indispensable de séparer les diverses couches d'enroulement et de disposer de tout le texte récupérable.

- Frg. 8 : L'identification du frg. à *11Q8 - 11QPs*^{d} est assurée, et il appartient à Ps 37,3-4. Avec le frg. 7, la nouvelle mise en colonne paraît à retenir, même si celle de la ligne 2 ne va pas sans difficulté. Proposer alors la restauration du Ps 36,13 : ולוא יכלו קו[ם à la ligne 1 de cet ensemble.

- Frg. 24 : Ce fragment étroit et allongé de gauche à droite non seulement semble appartenir à *11Q11*, mais il joint à la bande de *11Q11 - 11QPsAp* colonne II, où est encore visible la tête en 'v ' évasé du *ṣadé*, suivie d'un départ de jambage, donnant des restes de

1. O. Ableman, « Preliminary Publication of Cave 11 Fragments from Box 1032A » dans ce volume.

quatre lettres à ce joint. À la ligne 3, on aimerait pouvoir lire les lettres cachées par le repli du cuir, ce qui est possible au laboratoire avec les nouveaux procédés, et la lettre à gauche ne peut être *he*, mais *ḥet* préférable à *dalet*. Serait-il possible de restaurer ח]זק comme en fin de ligne en attendant de pouvoir proposer quelque séquence ?

- Frg. 41 : Ce fragment a conservé des restes de 2 lignes, mais une fois dépliée, la ligne 1 devrait permettre de lire au moins deux à trois lettres de plus. D'ores et déjà cependant la lecture de la ligne 2 confirme l'identification et l'appartenance à *11Q2 - 11QLv*^{b} 13,51-52. L'hésitation de l'éditeur n'est pas permise, *mem* est assuré, excluant *pe*. Ce fragment est à joindre aux autres récemment identifiés en P1345.[2]

- Frg. 47 : La ligne à peine visible sur la première surface peut aussi bien être lue ת]הפלאו[, mais on doit encore séparer les quatre couches et pouvoir lire les trois passages sous-jacents, pour assurer l'identification probable à *11Q17*.

- Frg. 48 : Des restes de 4 lignes, la lecture de la ligne 2 de l'éditeur est loin d'être assurée. À la cassure de gauche *gimel* est certain, non *'alef*, et à celle de droite, *mem* semble difficile, l'oblique est trop longue et basse, l'oblique du *'aïn* est un peu trop haute pour retrouver l'*habitus* du scribe de *11Q5*, toutefois cette lecture est à retenir par le tracé court du trait gauche rejoignant l'oblique, qui ne semble pas se poursuivre pour le tracé du *gimel*, מ]עשיה ג[, lecture préférable à נו]גשיה ג[.

- Frg. 55 : Ce fragment qui est à identifier à Dt 19,5-6, semble pouvoir être rattaché à *11Q3 - 11QDt*. Lire ainsi sur trois lignes :

1 את]ר[ע]הו [ביער לחטוב עצים ונדחה ידו בגרזן
לכרות העץ ונשל הברזל מן העץ

2 ו]מצא את[רעהו ומת הוא ינוס אל אחת הערים
האלה וחי ^{6}פן ירדוף גאל הדם אחרי

3 הרוצ]ח[כי יחם לבבו

La paléographie étant comparable, des différences sont même marquées pour des lettres sur le fragment lui-même. La grande différence est la largeur de la colonne comparée à celle des frgs 1 et 2 aux deux premiers chapitres de *Deutéronome*. Le frg. 1 porte encore les réglures, alors qu'elles ne sont plus visibles sur les frgs 2 et 3, et le module des lettres paraît un peu plus petit sur ce nouveau fragment. Il est plus incertain d'en faire le seul fragment d'un autre rouleau du *Deutéronome 11Q3a - 11QDt*^{a}.

- Frg. 62 : Si la première ligne a été bien lue, il faut corriger celle de la ligne 2 où la lecture המב]ול[est assurée, *mem* médian (non final) et *bet* (non *lamed*). L'identification du frg. à *Jubilés* 5,19 est certaine. On peut tenter une reconstruction assez littérale à partir du ge'ez[3] :

1 לפני המבול לוא נשא להם פנים רק]לנוח לבדו
כיא נשא אליו[

2 פניו בעבור בניו אשר הושיעם ממי]המב[ול
בעבורו כיא צדיק

Si cette rétroversion du ge'ez en hébreu est acceptable, la largeur de la colonne est alors comparable à celle des autres fragments identifiés en *11Q12*.[4]

- Frg. 68 : Des restes de trois lignes, l'éditeur ne propose aucune lecture de la ligne 3, à lire selon toute vraisemblance *bet-šin*, mais en l'absence de trace de lettre avant le *bet*, une lecture כבש n'est pas possible. En revanche est probable une lecture בש]נה [, mot bien attesté en *11Q19 - RT* XXII 14. Mais on ne peut pas en faire une copie de ce passage à moins de plusieurs variantes importantes non attestées en *11Q19* et *11Q20* dans les parties conservées. Une appartenance à la première feuille de *11Q19* serait-elle exclue ? La graphie montre quelques divergences avec *11Q21*, et le fragment n'est pas réglé, ce qui n'appuie pas une claire identification à cette troisième copie dont l'identification n'est elle aussi qu'une proposition des éditeurs. S'agirait-il d'une réécriture du passage en question ?

2. Voir E. Puech, « Nouveaux menus fragments de la Grotte XI (P1344, P1345 et P1038B) » dans ce volume.

3. Voir J.C. VanderKam, *The Book of Jubilees* (Scriptores Æthiopici 87-88/CSCO 510-511; Leuven: Peeters, 1989), Tom. 87, p. 32, et Tom. 88, p. 34-5.

4. Aux fragments identifiés par les éditeurs (DJD XXIII), on doit y joindre un autre fragment identifié plus tard, voir H. Eshel, «Three New Fragments from Qumran Cave 11», *DSD* 8 (2001) 1-8, frg. p. 3-5.

- Frg. 81 : L'auteur a proposé d'identifier ce fragment de 1,2 × 1,7 cm avec des restes de 2 lignes au Ps 147,1-2, mais sans en être certain. En effet, la reconstruction ne permet aucun alignement dans la disposition du fragment E de DJD XXIII où il ne peut également prendre place. Pour ce faire l'éditeur doit admettre plusieurs variantes ou omissions. Dans une étude de reconstructions de rouleaux, j'ai proposé de ne pas attribuer le fragment E à *11Q5*, mais d'en faire des restes d'un autre rouleau *11Q5a*, écrit par le même scribe avec une séquence différente des Psaumes.[5] Or ce fragment viendrait confirmer la mise en ordre et les identifications de ces diverses copies.[6] Le fragment 81 dont la partie gauche n'a pas été dépliée et qui recouvre jusqu'au *he* et même davantage dans la partie supérieure, devrait porter des restes de plusieurs lettres du mot suivant ; il est certainement à replacer sous le fragment D avec lequel il semblerait avoir un joint matériel correspondant au bas des fragments B et C, ligne 12, mais il ne peut en aucune façon se trouver isolé ailleurs à droite dans la colonne. Lire ainsi en *11Q5* IV13-14 :

הללו יה כי טו]ב זמרה אלו[הינו 13

כי ‹נעים?› נאוה תהלה בונה ירושלים יהוה נדחי י] 14
שר[א]ל[יכנס

Le Psaume 147 commençait dans la deuxième moitié de la ligne 13, comme il arrive plusieurs fois dans ce rouleau. Une seule variante peut être envisagée, ligne 14 avec le grec qui ne semble pas connaître **נעים** de l'hébreu (texte massorétique) et *11Q5a*, à moins d'une correction supra-linéaire,[7] pour d'autres corrections voir col. XII 15, XIII 6-7, XVI 11.11.16, XVII 6, XIX 8, XX 9, XXIII 6.12, XXV 9.12, sans compter nombre de lettres et de mots effacés/grattés. La copie *4Q86-4QPs^{d}* I 6-7 a un texte quelque peu confus, la dittographie apparente pourrait venir d'un original corrigé ou au moins au texte peu assuré où **נאוה** vient en tête et **נעים** comme correction insérée ensuite, ligne 6 :

הללו]יה כי טוב זמרה אלהינו נאוה[זמרה]

et ligne 7 :

אלהי]נו נאוה נעים תהלה [בונה ירושלם.[8]

5. Voir E. Puech, « Édition et reconstruction des manuscrits », in *Nuove luci sulla Bibbia e l'Ebraismo: i manoscritti di Qumran a settant'anni dalla scoperta (1947-2017) e il Sefer Torah della Biblioteca Universitaria di Bologna, Ravenna, 20 settembre, Bologna, 21-22 settembre 2016*, *Hen* 39 (2017) 105-25.

6. Note à paraître.

7. Sur ce v. 1 discuté, voir H.-J. Kraus, *Psalmen. 2. Teilband Psalmen 60-150* (BKAT XV/2; Neukirchen-Vluyn: Neukirchener Verlag, ^{5}1978), 1134-6.

8. Voir P.W. Skehan, E. Ulrich, and P.W. Flint, «86. 4QPs^{d}», in E. Ulrich *et al.*, *Qumran Cave 4. XI: Psalms to Chronicles* (DJD XVI; Oxford: Clarendon, 2000) 63-71, p. 66.

Chapter Twelve

Revisiting the Manuscripts and Fragments from Qumran Cave 11Q

Eibert TIGCHELAAR

1. Manuscript Remains: Scrolls and Fragments

Which scroll materials were found in Qumran Cave 11Q? The most recent and most comprehensive overview of the manuscript remains from Cave 11Q is presented in the form of a list in Emanuel Tov's *Revised Lists*.[1] The list gives thirty-one items, from 11Q1 through 11Q31. Twenty-eight of those have been fully published in DJD 23.[2] The exceptions are 11Q1 (the Paleo-Leviticus scroll),[3] 11Q5 (the Great Psalms Scroll),[4] 11Q19 (the Temple Scroll),[5] and a few purported Cave 11 fragments which turned up since the publication of DJD 23.[6] Of these thirty-one items, twenty-nine were identified as separate manuscripts, ranging from scrolls to single fragments. 11Q30 "Unclassified Fragments" contains various fragments, some of which might belong to those twenty-nine manuscripts, while others may be the last remains of one or more other manuscripts.[7] The material referred to as 11Q31 "Unidentified Wads" is

1. E. Tov, *Revised Lists of the Texts from the Judaean Desert* (Leiden: Brill, 2010), 64-78, replacing his earlier "Lists of the Texts from the Judaean Desert," in Id. (ed.), *The Texts from the Judaean Desert: Indices and an Introduction to the Discoveries in the Judaean Desert Series* (DJD 39; Oxford: Clarendon, 2002) 27-114, on pp. 77-89.
2. F. García Martínez, E.J.C. Tigchelaar, and A.S. van der Woude, *Qumran Cave 11.II: 11Q2-18, 11Q20-31* (DJD 23; Oxford: Clarendon, 1998).
3. D.N. Freedman and K.A. Mathews, *The Paleo-Hebrew Leviticus Scroll (11QpaleoLev)* (Winona Lake, IN: American Schools of Oriental Research, 1985). See, in addition: E. Puech, "Notes en marge de 11QPaléoLévitique: Le fragment L, des fragments inédits et une jarre de la Grotte 11," *RB* 96 (1989) 161-83, Pls 1-3; E.J.C. Tigchelaar, "Some More Small 11Q1 Fragments," *RdQ* 18/70 (1997) 325-30, Pl. 2.
4. J.A. Sanders, *The Psalms Scroll of Qumrân Cave 11 (11QPs^a)* (DJD 4; Oxford: Clarendon, 1965) published the scroll and fragments A through D. Y. Yadin, "Another Fragment (E) of the Psalms Scroll from Qumran Cave 11 (11QPs^a)," *Textus* 5 (1966) 1-10, Pls 1-5 published the large fragment E. Sanders incorporated fragment E in his *The Dead Sea Psalms Scroll* (Ithaca, NY: Cornell University Press, 1967). García Martínez, Tigchelaar, and van der Woude presented a revised edition of fragment E, and published the tiny fragment F, in DJD 23.
5. First publication by Y. Yadin, *The Temple Scroll*, 3 Vols. (Jerusalem: Israel Exploration Society, 1977) [Hebrew], and *The Temple Scroll*, 3 Vols. (Jerusalem: Israel Exploration Society, 1983) [English].
6. In Tov, *Revised Lists*, those are 11Q7 frags. 3a + 3b; 11Q12 frag. 7a; 11Q16 frag. 2.
7. For example, frag. 8-10. Cf. DJD 23, 438 and H. Jacobson, "11Q30, Fgs. 8-10," *RdQ* 18/72 (1998) 595.

probably all from the same manuscript, but has only a few letters that are visible to the naked eye.

Tov's list includes eight manuscripts that were found as partially or entirely rolled up scrolls. In order of their sigla they are: 11Q1 the Paleo-Leviticus scroll, 11Q4 the Ezekiel scroll, 11Q5 the Great Psalms Scroll, 11Q10 the Job Targum scroll, 11Q11 the Apocryphal Psalms scroll, 11Q17 the Shirot Olat ha-Shabbat scroll, 11Q18 the New Jerusalem scroll, and, finally, 11Q19 the Temple Scroll. There are photographs of all those scrolls in their unopened condition,[8] with the exception, to my knowledge, of 11Q1.[9] Six of the scrolls were sold through Khalil Iskander Shahin (Kando) to the Palestine Archaeological Museum; a seventh, 11Q11, was recovered during de Vaux's excavations of Cave 11Q in March 1956;[10] the eighth, the Temple Scroll, was seized from Shahin during the Six-Day War in June 1967. One should note, though, that from the first years after the discovery of Cave 11Q onwards, there have been reports about more scrolls. In his description of the Cave 11Q finds, Lankester Harding already referred to "rumours of other good scrolls from the same cave" and "reports of two nearly complete copies of the Book of Daniel among these."[11] Joseph Uhrig, or Mr. Z., the middleman between Shahin and Yadin, provided lists of Cave 11Q scrolls for sale that outnumber the ones we know now. Those lists may be seen as unreliable, but even the official second agreement signed 12 December, 1962, between the Palestine Archaeological Museum and the Dutch Royal Academy of Arts and Sciences mentions a higher number of scrolls than eventually were acquired. Either all those accounts were fabricated or exaggerated, or there actually were one or more small scrolls, that now are unknown to us.

The publication rights of the three "biblical" scrolls were all sold to American institutions, the American Schools of Oriental Research and the Claremont Graduate School. The publication rights of the Job Targum were acquired by the Dutch Royal Academy of Arts and Sciences and the Organisation of Scientific Research on 11 December 1961. One year later the publication rights of the remnant of the other Cave 11Q manuscripts, that is, the other scrolls (except 11Q1) and fragments, were also acquired by the Dutch institutions.[12] The Temple Scroll came into Israeli hands in 1967.

Most of the materials had been found by the Bedouin, and were sold in two stages to the Palestine Archaeological Museum, namely on May 19 and July 17, 1956. According to de Vaux's short notes, a few

8. 11Q4 on PAM 43.731 and 43.742, DJD 23, Pl. 54; 11Q5 on PAM 43.772-43.775, DJD 4, Pl. 1 shows 43.774; 11Q10 on PAM 43.796-43.799 (in the middle of the photographs); 11Q11, 11Q17, and 11Q18 on PAM 43.981, DJD 23, Pl. 53; 11Q19, Yadin, *Temple Scroll,* Vol. 3, Pl. 4.1.

9. The earliest photographs, PAM 42.171 and 42.172, taken in July 1956, show cols. 2-3, and cols. 5 (left part) and 6 of the unrolled scroll. On these photos there is a support behind the scroll, indicating it had been unrolled and supported earlier, before photographing. The scroll had been purchased on 19 May 1956.

10. R. de Vaux, "Fouilles de Khirbet Qumrân: Rapport préliminaire sur les 3e, 4e et 5e campagnes," *RB* 63 (1956) 533-77, on p. 574, refers to the recovery of a document in the shape of a hardened and blackened cigar (in his excavation diary he refers on 3/3 to "un petit rouleau très abîmé." This has occasionally been mistaken for a reference to the Cave 11 Ezekiel scroll (11Q4). See, e.g., W.W. Fields, *The Dead Sea Scrolls: A Full History: Vol. 1: 1947-1960* (Leiden: Brill, 2009), 299. However, the unopened 11Q4 scroll does not look at all like a cigar, while the unopened 11Q11 scroll immediately reminds one of a *bolknak* type of cigar (see the left scroll on PAM 43.981). See also J.P.M. van der Ploeg, "L'édition des manuscrits de la Grotte XI de Qumrân par l'Académie Royale des Sciences des Pays-Bas," in P.W. Pestman (ed.), *Acta Orientalia Neerlandica: Proceedings of the Congress of the Dutch Oriental Society Held in Leiden on the Occasion of its 50th Anniversary, 8th-9th May 1970* (Leiden: Brill, 1971) 43-5, on p. 44 who states: "Parmi les rouleaux découverts dans la grotte XI, nous avons trouvé un petit rouleau fort endommagé qui avait la forme d'un petit cigare trapu. Il contient des psaumes apocryphes."

11. "Notes and News," *PEQ* 89 (1957) 93-6, on p. 95. Cf. in largely the same words also G.L. Harding, "Recent Discoveries in Jordan," *PEQ* 90 (1958) 7-18, on p. 17, but without the reference to Daniel. Rumours on the existence of additional Cave 11Q scrolls, especially of either Daniel or Enoch scrolls, persist to the present day. See, for example, the interview with John Strugnell in the *Biblical Archaeology Review* (July/August 1994), in which he also states that he "wouldn't be surprised if there were five other manuscripts from Cave 11 sometime to be found in the near future."

12. The agreement of 12 December 1962 lists them as follows:
a. Unopened scroll and fragments containing Aramaic text about the New Jerusalem
b. Unopened scroll and fragments containing a text provisionally denoted "Olat ha-Shabbat"
c. Numerous fragments containing biblical texts in square Hebrew (Leviticus, Deuteronomium, Psalms) and non-biblical texts
d. Two unopened scrolls of unknown content
e. Some small scrolls and fragments also found in Cave 11.

parchment fragments, including some written in paleo-Hebrew, as well as a cigar-like scroll were found during the excavation. Whereas the cigar-like scroll (11Q11) apparently was added to the Cave 11Q collection purchased from the Bedouin, there was no clarity about the identity or whereabouts of the excavated fragments. It was assumed these were incorporated into the Museum collection,[13] but Mireille Bélis discovered Cave 11Q fragments among the Cave 11Q textiles at the École biblique et archéologique, which have been published now by Émile Puech.[14] However, also after the 1956 purchase of Cave 11Q materials from Shahin and the archaeological excavation by de Vaux, other fragments have turned up, which, without any doubt, could be assigned to the Cave 11Q manuscripts. This indicates that not all the materials found by the Bedouin had been sold through or by Shahin in 1956 to the Palestine Archaeological Museum. This seems to be confirmed by Frank Cross's report of Cave 11Q fragments that were shown to him in Beirut in 1967.[15]

Most famous of the fragments that turned up later are the large fragment E of the Psalms Scroll, which was sold, through Joseph Uhrig, to Yigael Yadin in 1960 and the large fragment L of the Paleo-Leviticus scroll which was sold (apparently in 1967) to Georges Roux. One of the 11Q10 fragments which was presumably seized from Shahin in 1967, was brought to the Shrine of the Book, and eventually identified in 1992 and published in 1993.[16] Another example is the Vatican Paleo-Hebrew fragment, bought by Salvatore Garofalo, perhaps already in the 1950s, which should be assigned to 11Q22.[17] In the case of the Temple Scroll, two fragments from subsequent layers of the scroll were broken off from the scroll. Uhrig reports that he himself broke off, late 1960 or early 1961, one fragment from the scroll, which he sent to Yadin as a sample of the scroll that was for sale (this fragment is from col. 15).[18] The other fragment (from col. 14) ended up in the collection of Arnold Spaer, and was published by André Lemaire.[19] This raises the question whether there are still more Cave 11Q fragments that were not sold to the Museum or seized in 1967.

Tov's list reports of a series of such fragments potentially from Cave 11Q. One such fragment, found in the desk of Yadin, was published in DJD 23 as 11Q8 frag. 3.[20] Two other fragments from Yadin's desk drawer are listed twice in Tov's list, namely both as XQ5a and XQ5b with the sigla they received in DJD 36, and as 11Q12 (11QJub) 7a resp. 11Q16 (11QHymns^{b}) 2, the identification proposed by Hanan Eshel. The 11Q8 identification is plausible but not certain. Eshel's two other identifications are clearly erroneous, both textually and palaeographically, and XQ5b has now been identified as a 4Q285 fragment.[21] Nonetheless, some of the unpublished small fragments from the same plate (IAA X78-X79) can plausibly be assigned to 11Q20. It remains a question how

13. See, for example, Sanders, *Dead Sea Psalms Scroll*, 6: "On November 20 [1961], Father de Vaux … asked Mr. Saad to bring the loose fragments from Cave 11, some of which had been purchased with the [11Q5] scroll and some of which had been recovered when the archaeologists subsequently excavated the cave."

14. See, in this volume, E. Puech, "Nouveaux menus fragments de la Grotte XI (P1344, P1345 et P1038B)," and M. Fidanzio, "The Retrieval of Unknown Manuscript Fragments from Cave 11Q."

15. F.M. Cross, "Reminiscences of the Early Days in the Discovery and Study of the Dead Sea Scrolls," in L.H. Schiffman, E. Tov, and J.C. VanderKam (ed.), *The Dead Sea Scrolls Fifty Years After Their Discovery: Proceedings of the Jerusalem Congress, July 20-25, 1997* (Jerusalem: Israel Exploration Society, 2000) 932-43, on pp. 941-2. It remains unclear whether Cross recognized the fragments as Cave 11Q fragments, or simple assumed they were from Cave 11Q, or whether their provenance was told to him.

16. B. Zuckerman and S.A. Reed, "A Fragment of an Unstudied Column of 11QtgJob: A Preliminary Report," *CAL Newsletter* 10 (1993) 1-7. One may note that the first photographs of the 11Q10 materials in PAM 43.796-799 show piles of the 11Q10 fragments, in complete disorder, indicating that a fragment might easily have been kept apart.

17. G. Lacerenza, "Un nouveau fragment en écriture paléo-hébraïque," *RdQ* 19/75 (2000) 441-7; E. Puech, "Note additionnelle sur le fragment en paléo-hébreu," *RdQ* 19/75 (2000) 449-51.

18. See the fragment depicted in Yadin, *Temple Scroll*, Vol. 3, Pl. 3.3-4.

19. A. Lemaire, "Nouveaux fragments du Rouleau du Temple de Qumrân," *RdQ* 17/65-68 (1996) 271-4.

20. S.A. Reed, *The Dead Sea Scrolls Catalogue: Documents, Photographs and Museum Inventory Numbers* (SBL RBS 32; ed. and rev. M.J. Lundberg with the collaboration of M.B. Phelps; Atlanta: Scholars, 1994), 185, 460 referred to this fragment as "Mas1g," and later the fragment was referred to as "XQPs." These old sigla are still mentioned in Tov, *Revised Lists*, 70.

21. E.J.C. Tigchelaar, "Notes on the Three Qumran-Type Yadin Fragments Leading to a Discussion of Identification, Attribution, Provenance, and Names," *DSD* 19 (2012) 198-214; Id., "The Yadin Qumran Fragment XQ5b (XQText B) Identified as a Fragment of 4Q285 (4QSefer ha-Milḥamah)," *RdQ* 29/110 (2017) 281-6.

Yadin got hold of these fragments and where they are from. It is easiest to assume that these fragments originate from the Shahin collection. One remote possibility is that at the same time when the Temple Scroll and the Job Targum were seized from Shahin, also those smaller fragments were confiscated. But then, why were they not brought to the Shrine of the Book? It is more likely that Yadin purchased them, just as he also acquired Bar Kokhba period documents from Shahin.[22] If the Yadin Hebrew and Aramaic fragments on IAA X78-X79 and X80 came from Shahin, there would be no need to assume they all came from the same cave. In sum, the Yadin fragment XQ5a, which was identified by Hanan Eshel as 11Q12, could either come from Cave 11Q, in which case it would represent an additional manuscript from this cave, or from another findplace, such as Qumran Cave 4Q.

Tov's list of Cave 11Q items also contains other questionable references. The list mentions two fragments, one from the Ashland Theological Library and the other presently belonging to The Museum of the Bible, which Hanan and Esther Eshel identified as 11Q7 frags. 3a-b.[23] The Museum of the Bible fragment has recently been published, and the style of the hand is clearly different from 11Q7, so that there is no reason to assign the fragment to Cave 11Q.[24] It is not even certain the fragment is authentic.[25] Tov's list also includes references to Schøyen 5095/1 as preserving fragments from 11QT cols. 2 and 3. Schøyen himself quotes a signed statement of William Kando, claiming that these fragments were found in the same jar in which the Temple Scroll was found, and were presented in 1961 to a customer in Zurich.[26] The editors, Torleif Elgvin and Kipp Davis, describe Schøyen 5095/1 as "Wads from 11QT^{a}, Unidentified Fragments from Cave 11" and argue that at least one of the wads (Wad Z) has several correspondences with 11QT^{a}, so that it might stem from the beginning of the Temple Scroll.[27] The claim is largely based on the analysis of the wrappings which were unified with a wad.[28]

On the basis of physical research which showed the presence of magnesium ammonium phosphate, or struvite, which is specifically associated with bat and seebird guano, Elgvin also tentatively assigns Schøyen 4612/3, which Puech had earlier published as 4Q587 4QTestament^{d},[29] to Cave 11Q, and calls it 11Q(?) Eschatological Fragment.[30] On palaeographic and visual grounds, Puech identified the Schøyen fragment and a fragment published by Lemaire (from the Spaer collection)[31] as coming from the same manuscript. It is tempting to associate these two small Aramaic fragments,[32] but Esther Eshel correctly observed that the fragments have different ways of writing the *mem*.[33] We should be cautious with respect to all

22. See, briefly, H. Eshel, "Gleaning of Scrolls from the Judean Desert," in C. Hempel (ed.), *The Dead Sea Scrolls: Texts and Context* (STDJ 90; Leiden: Brill, 2010) 49-87, on pp. 78-9.

23. E. Eshel and H. Eshel, "A Preliminary Report on Seven New Fragments from Qumran," *Meghillot* 5-6 (2007) 271-8, on pp. 276-7; Eshel, "Gleaning of Scrolls," 74.

24. L.M. Wolfe et al., "Psalm 11:1-4 (Inv. MOTB.SCR.000121)," in E. Tov, K. Davis, and R. Duke (ed.), *Dead Sea Scrolls Fragments in the Museum Collection* (PMB 1; Leiden: Brill, 2016) 190-9.

25. Most of the fragments acquired after 2002 by private collectors are most probably forgeries. See E. Tigchelaar, "A Provisional List of Unprovenanced, Twenty-First Century, Dead Sea Scrolls-like Fragments," *DSD* 24 (2017) 173-88; K. Davis et al., "Nine Dubious 'Dead Sea Scrolls' Fragments from the Twenty-First Century," *DSD* 24 (2017) 189-228; K. Davis, "Caves of Dispute: Patterns of Correspondence and Suspicion in the Post-2002 'Dead Sea Scrolls' Fragments," *DSD* 24 (2017) 229-70.

26. M. Schøyen, "Acquisition and Ownership History: A Personal Reflection," in T. Elgvin, K. Davis, and M. Langlois (ed.), *Gleanings from the Caves: Dead Sea Scrolls and Artefacts from The Schøyen Collection* (LSTS 71; London: Bloomsbury T&T Clark, 2016) 25-31, on p. 29.

27. T. Elgvin and K. Davis, "MS 5095/1, MS 5095/4. Wads from 11QT^{a}, Unidentified Fragments from Cave 11," in Elgvin, Davies, and Langlois, *Gleanings*, 301-8, on p. 302.

28. On these claims, see more specifically my review of *Gleanings* in *RdQ* 29/110 (2017) 314-22.

29. E. Puech, *Qumrân Grotte 4. XXVII: Textes araméens: Deuxième partie* (DJD 27; Oxford: Clarendon, 2009), 501-4.

30. T. Elgvin, "Texts and Artefacts from the Judaean Desert in The Schøyen Collection: An Overview," in Elgvin, Davies, and Langlois, *Gleanings*, 51-60, on pp. 53-4; E. Eshel, "MS 4612/3. 11Q(?)Eschatological Fragment ar," in *Gleanings*, 295-8.

31. A. Lemaire, "Un fragment araméen inédit de Qumrân," *RdQ* 18/70 (1997) 331-3; Id., "XQ6. XQOffering ar," in S.J. Pfann, *Qumran Cave 4. XXVI: Cryptic Texts* and P.S. Alexander et al., *Miscellanea: Part 1* (DJD 36; Oxford: Clarendon, 2000) 490-1.

32. Puech stated that both fragments have the same kind of whitish spots on the surface. It could easily be tested whether those white spots on both fragments are struvite. But even then, this would not be conclusive.

33. In most documents there is evidence of variation in the writing of letters, but here we are dealing with two different forms of the head and diagonal of *mem*.

those recent identifications. Some identifications are patently wrong, and it certainly would have been best not to include these fragments in the official lists as either Cave 11Q or Cave 4Q fragments.

However, even DJD 23 contains incorrect assignments. A clearly mistaken identification in DJD 23 is my own. I assumed that the object on PAM 44.012 came from Cave 11Q,[34] and preserved the offprint (in mirror) of part of a Cave 11Q manuscript. Since the preserved words correspond to Ps 6, I associated the offprint with 11Q8. Hanan Eshel pointed out that the photographed object, which may still be at the Rockefeller Museum but up to date has not been located, was probably a marl object, and hence incompatible with Cave 11Q, and that the hand of the writing was not similar to 11Q8.[35]

It seems to me that of all the fragments published after DJD 23, only one fragment can with certainty be assigned to Cave 11Q, namely the Paleo-Hebrew fragment in the Vatican library (formerly Garofalo) as belonging to 11Q22. All other post-DJD 23 associations of fragments with Cave 11Q are either based on incorrect identifications with Cave 11Q manuscripts or on insufficient evidence. There are, however, three or four collections of hitherto unpublished tiny Cave 11Q manuscripts. First, there are the many boxes with small fragments at the Israel Antiquities Authority. Stephen Reed catalogued them in the early 1990s; I went through twelve boxes in December 1996, and got permission to select from those boxes the most important ones which I wanted to have photographed.[36] Most recently, the IAA conducted a pilot study, and Oren Ableman has been able to identify a series of fragments.[37] Second, what seem to be Qumran Cave 11Q fragments from the 1956 de Vaux excavation have recently turned up at the École biblique et archéologique and are now published in this volume.[38] Third, many tiny fragments of the Temple Scroll at the Shrine of the Book have not been published. This holds true for a few of the fragments from the cigar-box which was photographed in 1967.[39] Some of those fragments, as well as other ones which have broken off from the scroll, in total about fifty unpublished small to minute fragments, have been placed on a museum plate with the tag "LII (15)" which was photographed in the late 2000s.[40] Fourth, the IAA plate X78-X79 contains two of the three so-called Yadin fragments, but also nine small to minute fragments, some of which plausibly come from Qumran Cave 11Q.[41]

2. Major Publications

2.1 The 1965 DJD 4 edition by James A. Sanders of the large Cave 11Q Psalms Scroll (11Q5) suffered from the absence of the large frag. E, which was published by Yadin in 1966, and republished in DJD 23.[42] Also, the edition could not take into account either the then not yet published parallel manuscript 11Q6, or the Cave 4Q Psalms scrolls. No published edition has images of both the DJD 4 materials and the Yadin frag. E. Only a few editions of 11QPs[a] transcribe the full text of the manuscript.[43] Newer photographs sometimes allow one to improve on the readings. For example, a new photo shows more clearly the first two lines of frag. D, which were ignored by Sanders, Dahmen and Ulrich. Thus, in the line above line 1 of the edition read]נ̊פשי ואתה̊[.[44]

34. PAM 43.975-44.011 as well as 44.013 are photographs of Cave 11 manuscripts, which suggests that PAM 44.012 would also be related to Cave 11Q. Reed, *Dead Sea Scrolls Catalogue,* 394, described the photographed object as "11Q? One frg., seemingly reverse image on stone or plaster."

35. H. Eshel, "A Note on 11QPs[d] Fragment 1," *RdQ* 23/92 (2008) 529-31.

36. I reported on those boxes in Tigchelaar, "Some More Small 11Q1 Fragments," 326-7, n. 5, and in DJD 23, 438. For another IAA box found by Mauro Rottoli with – purportedly – Cave 11Q fragments see, in this volume, Fidanzio, "Retrieval."

37. See, in this volume, O. Ableman, "Preliminary Publication of Cave 11Q Fragments from Box 1032A."

38. See Puech, "Nouveaux menus fragments."

39. Yadin, *Temple Scroll*, Vol. 3, Pl. 3.2. See also the photograph SHR 6314.

40. See section 4, below.

41. See section 5, below.

42. See above, note 4.

43. U. Dahmen, *Psalmen- und Psalter-Rezeption im Frühjudentum: Rekonstruktion, Textbestand, Struktur und Pragmatik der Psalmenrolle 11QPs[a] aus Qumran* (STDJ 49; Leiden: Brill, 2003); E. Ulrich, *The Biblical Qumran Scrolls: Transcriptions and Textual Variants* (VTSup 134; Leiden: Brill, 2010), 694-726.

44. See http://www.deadseascrolls.org.il/explore-the-archive/image/B-367150. The presence of traces in the top two lines was already suggested in DJD 23, 31; E. Puech, "Review of Ulrich Dahmen, *Psalmen- und Psalter-Rezeption*," *RdQ* 22/86 (2005) 279-81, on p. 280 tentatively but incorrectly suggested, on the basis of less legible photographs,]רע על נפש]י[.

The textual or material reconstruction of the scroll remains debated, both with respect to the question whether the scroll began with Ps 101, and with respect to the amount of missing columns (and their content) before and after frag. D.[45]

2.2 The 1977 three-volume Israel Exploration Society edition by Yigael Yadin of the large Temple Scroll, generally believed to stem from Cave 11Q (11QT^{a} or 11Q19) was a true tour de force, if only because of the detrimental state of the scroll.[46] The 1983 English edition already contained many improvements, and Elisha Qimron's subsequent transcriptions of 1996 and 2010, based on extensive study of different sets of photographs and of the original, and on the parallel texts from other manuscripts, provided a great advance.[47] A new full edition will be published by Lawrence Schiffman and Andrew Gross. There are still minor unpublished fragments at the Shrine of the Book which have broken from the scroll, and the old photographs frequently show small pieces with text that is not included in the editions. It is debatable, however, whether one should transcribe such minute fragments or small amount of letters without any context.

2.3 The 1985 ASOR edition of the Paleo-Hebrew Leviticus Scroll (11Q1)[48] by David Noel Freedman and K.A. Mathews suffered from many shortcomings. Only at a late stage in the publication of the volume the editors became aware of another major fragment at the Rockefeller Museum and of the private fragment of Georges Roux, which they could only study from a dark photograph. They also ignored the many small fragments at the Rockefeller that had broken off from the scroll. Puech's article presents many improvements on the transcriptions of the 1985 ASOR edition, and became an indispensable companion. The paleographical study by R.S. Hanson was done in 1977, and the volume does not engage the more advanced approach and the dates of McLean.[49] The edition gives a long and programmatic proposal of four different orthographical systems to be found in the scrolls, but it does not discuss the textual affiliation of the scroll, and could not yet relate the scroll to the other Leviticus materials from Qumran. Ulrich's *The Biblical Qumran Scrolls* now presents a transcription which incorporates Puech's readings and proposals,[50] but we still have no plates with all the fragments, nor an up-to-date full analysis of the text.

2.4 The 1998 DJD edition was based on many earlier editions by J. van der Ploeg, A.S. van der Woude, and Florentino García Martínez. It includes the Dutch materials as well as the few fragments that could be broken off from the Ezekiel scroll (edited by Ted Herbert) and the 11Q5 fragment E. The DJD edition was prepared by me in collaboration with García Martínez. In this edition, most attention was paid to matters of identification and reading of fragments, and possible reconstruction of manuscripts, and less to matters of content and the commentary. Looking back, twenty years later, I see a range of shortcomings and areas of improvement, of which I will only mention a few.

a. In some cases fragments may have been assigned to the wrong manuscript. This certainly goes for 11Q8 frag. 1, and perhaps for 11Q8 frag. 3.[51] Over the years I have never been entirely confident about our assignment of 11Q6 frag. 1.[52] Originally van der Ploeg assigned this fragment, with remnants of Ps 77:18-18:21, probably on material grounds to 11Q7,[53] but I reassigned it to 11Q6 because paleographically

45. See most recently, E. Jain, *Psalmen oder Psalter? Materielle Rekonstruktion und inhaltliche Untersuchung der Psalmenhandschriften aus der Wüste Juda* (STDJ 109; Leiden: Brill, 2014), 159-77 (with survey of previous scholarship).

46. See above, note 5.

47. E. Qimron, *The Temple Scroll: A Critical Edition with Extensive Reconstructions* (Beer Sheva/Jerusalem: Ben Gurion University of the Negev Press/Israel Exploration Society, 1996); thoroughly revised in Id., *The Dead Sea Scrolls: The Hebrew Writings: Vol. 1* (Jerusalem: Yad Ben Zvi, 2010).

48. See above, note 3.

49. M.D. McLean, *The Use and Development of Palaeo-Hebrew in the Hellenistic and Roman Periods* (PhD diss.; Harvard University, 1982). Note that Hanson dated the hand of the scroll to around 100 BCE as opposed to McLean ca. 1-50 CE!

50. Ulrich's transcription based on Puech's work is reproduced in R.A. Kugler and K.S. Baek, *Leviticus at Qumran: Text and Interpretation* (VTSup 173; Leiden: Brill, 2016).

51. Since both fragments were added at the very last stage in the drafts, we overlooked a number of errors in the transcription. In the reconstruction in frag. 1 line 1 the tetragrammaton was omitted. In frag. 3 line the word עם was omitted from the transcription, and in line 3 read תאיר rather than האיר.

52. See also Jain, *Psalmen oder Psalter?,* 181.

53. J.P.M. van der Ploeg, "Fragments de Psaumes de Qumrân," in Z.J. Kapera (ed.), *Intertestamental Essays in Honour of Józef Tadeusz Milik* (Qumranica Mogilanensia 6; Kraków: Enigma, 1992) 233-7.

the hand of the fragment did not fit well with 11Q7, and looked more like that of 11Q6. However, the execution of the letters in 11Q6 frag. 1 is not always identical to the usual execution in the other 11Q6 fragments, and the material differences indicate that other scenarios are possible, such as 11Q6 frag. 1 being the single preserved fragment of yet another Psalms scroll, or belonging to the 11Q7 manuscript written by two different hands. This issue is more important than it would seem. The other fragments of 11Q6 attest to the same Psalter collection we find in 11Q5 which according to most scholars started with Ps 101. 11Q6 frag. 1 would then indicate that this form of the Psalter could also comprise earlier parts of the Psalter. However, given the multiple alternative possible assignments of 11Q6 frag. 1, its assignment in DJD 23 cannot be used as ground truth in discussions about the psalters.

b. In some cases the placement of fragments is questionable. For example, the placement of 11Q10 frag. A6 in 11Q10 col. XVII, and of 11Q17 frag. 18 in 11Q17 col. VII do not agree with the damage patterns of those scrolls. Also (see below), the tentative reconstruction of 11Q20 can be improved upon.

c. There are several misreadings of the Hebrew letters, and the new IAA photographs often enable better readings. In 11Q11 V 8 read, with Qimron, הצ̊ב̊א rather than הצ̊ב̊ה of the DJD edition.[54] In 11Q15 we simply followed van der Ploeg in reading בחדריכה, which should be read, as indicated by Qimron, as בחיריכה.[55] For our misreading of 11Q18 17 ii (תרת̇ין rather than תרע̇ין) see Lukaszewski.[56] In 11Q22 frag. 6 read חרבותי rather than חרפותי. In many other cases the new IAA photographs make it much easier to read the writing on the fragments, which enables us to either confirm the DJD readings or to improve on them.[57] With the help of the new IAA photograph B-483154, the entire fragment 11Q24 should be retranscribed.

d. Andrew Gross has gone over all the 11Q20 fragments and the 11Q20 reconstruction, and has discussed some of his findings with me. The new IAA photographs clearly enable better readings in a series of cases,[58] which sometimes affect the reconstruction of the columns.[59]

e. When preparing the DJD 23 edition, three of the 11Q22 (11QpaleoUnidentified text) fragments could not be located. In the meantime, all but one have resurfaced, and the new IAA photographs show the use of red ink.[60] The Vatican Paleo-Hebrew fragment should also be assigned to this manuscript, as well as some of the tiny fragments rediscovered at the École biblique et archéologique. All of this necessitates a new edition of 11Q22. In this volume, Puech gives new transcriptions of most 11Q22 fragments, but not of the Vatican one.[61]

f. Like many editors in the DJD series, we were too dependent on Cross's paleography in two respects. First practically, by comparing letters of manuscripts

54. E. Qimron, *The Dead Sea Scrolls: The Hebrew Writings: Vol. 2* (Jerusalem: Yad Ben Zvi, 2013), 346. Not all of Qimron's corrections should be followed. E.g., in 11Q13 III 7 palaeographically יתממ]ו of DJD should be preferred above Qimron's correction יתמו which grammatically would be easier (Qimron, *Hebrew Writings: Vol. 2*, 280). Because of damage of the upper layer of the skin, many readings in this fragment are disputed.

55. J.P.M. van der Ploeg, "Les manuscrits de la Grotte XI de Qumrân," *RdQ* 12/45 (1985) 3-15, on p. 7; E. Qimron, *The Dead Sea Scrolls: The Hebrew Writings: Vol.3* (Jerusalem: Yad Ben Zvi, 2015), 247. Admittedly, the *yod* was somewhat damaged, but we should not have considered *dalet*.

56. A.L. Lukaszewski, "An Alternative Reading of 11Q18 Fragment 17 (11QNew Jerusalem)," *RdQ* 21/82 (2003) 321-3.

57. For example, DJD 23 read]מלא̊ב̊י̊[in 11Q17 IX 9; Qimron, *Hebrew Writings: Vol. 2*, 379 corrected this to]מלוב[ש, but the new IAA photograph B-365378 clearly reads]לאכי[, the piece with the *mem* having broken off between 1961 and 2013. Overall, I consider most of Qimron's improvements on the reading of 11Q17 IX as problematic, but, in contrast, all his corrections to the reading of col. X as justified.

58. For example, several letters of 11Q20 frag. 6a which were faded away on the old infrared PAM photographs are clearly visible on the new IAA photograph, B-365328.

59. For example, the rearrangement of frag. 25 vis-à-vis frag. 21 ii, on the basis of supralinear writing found on both fragments and detected by Andrew Gross. For the reading of the top line of frag. 21 ii (11Q20 XIII 3) which DJD read as וה|באים, one has to interpret the traces before ב not as a vertical line, but as two *zayins*, one on top of the other. The scribe originally wrote באים, and added before this word the letters והז, but apparently considered the cramped *zayin* as unclear, and therefore once again wrote the letter *zayin* above the earlier one. (A similar kind of supralinearly explicating a reading is found repeatedly in 1QIs[a]).

60. Observed both by E. Puech (forthcoming) and A. Perrot. See on the red ink in frag. 6: A. Perrot, D. Stökl Ben Ezra, and E.J.C. Tigchelaar, "More Red Ink on the Qumran Manuscript 11Q22," *COMSt Bulletin* 1/1 (2015) 29-33.

61. Puech, "Nouveaux menus fragments."

with the few lines in Cross's figures, and second methodologically by accepting his typological dating.[62]

3. The Cave Collection as a Whole and Its Interpretation

What can we say about the collection of Cave 11Q as a whole and its relation to the collections from the other caves? There may have been more manuscripts in Cave 11Q than have been preserved. One therefore should be careful with claims based on the absence of specific manuscripts. We can therefore only say something on the basis of what we have now. I am very reluctant to identify minute fragments with literary works on the basis of correspondences of a few letters, and I therefore ignore new proposals such as Puech's one of the identification of the fragments written in the so-called Cryptic A script.[63] I also ignore the Yadin and the Schøyen fragments.

3.1 *Interpretations of Cave 11: A Status Quaestionis*

In the proceedings of the 2014 Lugano conference on the caves of Qumran, Florentino García Martínez extensively surveyed the different observations about the different caves, including Cave 11, on which he had written previously.[64] I will only briefly summarize some earlier suggestions. Hartmut Stegemann argued that all texts came from the Qumran library. The distribution over the caves was dependent on the hasty decisions taken in the few days when the Romans approached the settlement.[65] Emanuel Tov claimed that fourteen of the Cave 11Q manuscripts were written according to what he calls the Qumran Scribal Practice, and that four more manuscripts reflect sectarian ideas or terminology. He therefore claimed "a strong sectarian connection of the fragments from Cave 11Q, stronger than that of the other caves" which would suggest that "the collection of texts in Cave 11Q must have come as a whole from the Qumran community itself, possibly brought from a specific location."[66] García Martínez responded that the sectarian texts par excellence are hardly attested in Cave 11Q, and demonstrated that from a different perspective, namely distribution of manuscripts with regard to type and content, Cave 11Q would be comparable to Cave 1Q. He proposed that the inhabitant of Cave 11Q "brought some of the holdings of the library of the Khirbet to Cave 11Q for safe keeping."[67] Daniel Stökl Ben Ezra distinguished between "old caves" and "young caves" and argued that Caves 2Q, 3Q, 5Q, 6Q and 11Q represented the library of the community of Qumran in the first century CE, whereas Caves 1Q and 4Q essentially contain the holdings of the library at the end of the first century BCE.[68] Stephen Pfann tried to assign the collections of the individual caves to a range of different groups. He associates the contents of Cave 11Q with those of Cave 3Q, both of which would have been brought by Zealots to those caves.[69] Unlike other scholars Joan Taylor does not connect the scrolls in the caves with hasty rescue operations during the Jewish war, but with preservation-burials of manuscripts from the libraries of Essenes from all over Judaea. In Taylor's hypothesis, the collections in Caves 1Q, 2Q, 3Q, 6Q, and 11Q (that is the natural caves with indication of presence of cylindrical jars) were such burial places.[70] Sidnie

62. F.M. Cross, "The Development of the Jewish Scripts," in G.E. Wright (ed.), *The Bible and the Ancient Near East: Essays in Honor of William Foxwell Albright* (Garden City, NY: Doubleday, 1961) 133-202; repr. with some revisions in F.M. Cross, *Leaves from an Epigrapher's Notebook: Collected Papers in Hebrew and West Semitic Palaeography and Epigraphy* (HSS 51; Winona Lake, IN: Eisenbrauns, 2003), 3-43.

63. Puech, "Nouveaux menus fragments."

64. F. García Martínez, "The Contents of the Manuscripts from the Caves of Qumran," in M. Fidanzio (ed.), *The Caves of Qumran: Proceedings of the International Conference, Lugano 2014* (Leiden: Brill, 2016) 67-79; F. García Martínez, "Cave 11 in Context," in C. Hempel (ed.), *The Dead Sea Scrolls: Texts and Context* (STDJ 90; Leiden: Brill, 2010) 199-209.

65. H. Stegemann, *The Library of Qumran: On the Essenes, Qumran, John the Baptist, and Jesus* (Grand Rapids, MI: Eerdmans, 1998), 61-2.

66. E. Tov, "The Special Character of the Texts Found in Qumran Cave 11," in E. Chazon, D. Satran, and R. Clements (ed.), *Things Revealed: Studies in Early Jewish and Christian Literature in Honor of Michael E. Stone* (JSJSup 89; Leiden: Brill, 2004) 187-96, on p. 196.

67. García Martínez, "Cave 11 in Context," 208.

68. D. Stökl Ben Ezra, "Old Caves and Young Caves: A Statistical Reevaluation of a Qumran Consensus," *DSD* 14 (2007) 313-33.

69. S.J. Pfann, "Reassessing the Judean Desert Caves: Libraries, Archives, *Genizas* and Hiding Places," *BAIAS* 25 (2007) 147-70, esp. 161.

70. J.E. Taylor, "Buried Manuscripts and Empty Tombs: The Qumran *Genizah* Theory Revisited," in A.M. Maeir, J. Magness, and L.H. Schiffman (ed.), *"Go Out and Study the Land" (Judges 18:2): Archaeological, Historical and Textual Studies in Honor*

White Crawford[71] and Mladen Popović[72] both do connect the disposal of manuscripts in the caves with the time of distress in the Jewish War. White Crawford still upholds Cross's model, while Popović emphatically allows for the possibility that the scrolls were brought from elsewhere. I will not offer a new thesis, but rather offer some comments and highlight some features.

3.2 *The Profile of Cave 11Q in Relation to the Other Qumran Caves*

First, as with the collections from most other Qumran caves, the collection consists exclusively of literary, that is, non-documentary texts.[73] In a general sense, the literary constellation of the Cave 11Q collection is comparable to that of most other Caves. As spelled out by, e.g., García Martínez, Cave 11Q has the same kinds of Hebrew and Aramaic texts as many other caves. Many of the identified works are also found in Cave 4Q and some also in other caves, such as its biblical works, an Aramaic translation of Job, Jubilees, the Songs of the Sabbath Sacrifice, the Aramaic New Jerusalem, and the Temple Scroll. Also, Cave 11Q has a few small fragments with the same kind of Cryptic A script as found in Cave 4Q. One may comment that those are general observations, but that we should look at the details. Many have observed the absence of copies of the Hodayot, and the Rule of the Community or the Damascus Document. However, the small fragment 11Q29 preserved a few words which indicate a penal code similar to that attested in the Rule of the Community, the Damascus Document, and in 4Q265. Compared to Cave 4Q, there are neither Greek texts, nor calendrical fragments or sapiential texts. This may be true, but the absence of certain works or types of texts is given the small amount of Cave 11Q texts hardly significant. The data of Cave 11Q are too limited to draw large conclusions. The most remarkable feature would be the presence of three copies of the Temple Scroll in Cave 11Q (11Q19, 11Q20, 11Q21), as against one from all the other caves (4Q524). In brief, attempts to define the specific literary or religious character of the collection, can do so only by overemphasizing one perspective and ignoring other ones.

The correlation of the collection of Cave 11Q manuscripts with those in the other Qumran Caves holds true not only for the literary character, or for the variation of scripts, but also for orthography and scribal practices. Tov correctly observes that the scribal practices attested in most of the Cave 11Q manuscripts are similar to those from the other caves, even though I disagree methodologically with his construct of a Qumran Scribal Practice.[74] Of special interest would be those cases where we may identify a scribe who penned a manuscript from Cave 11Q as well as one or more from other caves.

3.3 *Scribes*

Already van der Ploeg stated that one and the same scribe copied the Cave 1 Habakkuk pesher (1QpHab) and 11Q20,[75] and the arguments were described in more detail in DJD 23. One may add to the DJD 23 description still other idiosyncracies which indicate we are dealing with one scribe. For example, in both manuscripts the scribe repeatedly fails to neatly join the strokes of the letters. Thus, the right arm of *shin* does not always reach to the left downstroke. Even more often, the final *mem* is not entirely closed, because at the bottom left the strokes are not joined.

of Hanan Eshel (JSJSup 148; Leiden: Brill, 2012) 269-315.

71. S. White Crawford, "Qumran: Caves, Scrolls, and Buildings," in E.F. Mason (ed.), *A Teacher for All Generations: Essays in Honor of James C. VanderKam* (JSJSup 153; Leiden: Brill, 2011) 253-73; similarly, S. White Crawford, "The Qumran Collection as a Scribal Library," in S. White Crawford and C. Wassen (ed.), *The Dead Sea Scrolls at Qumran and the Concept of a Library* (STDJ 116; Leiden: Brill, 2016) 109-31.

72. M. Popović, "Qumran as Scroll Storehouse in Times of Crisis? A Comparative Perspective on Judaean Desert Manuscripts," *JSJ* 43 (2012) 551-94.

73. That is, "texts not specifically produced for a specific pragmatic purpose of daily life like legal deeds, economic receipts and lists, letters, and so forth." See H. Gzella, *A Cultural History of Aramaic: From the Beginnings to the Advent of Islam* (HdO 111; Leiden: Brill, 2015), 201.

74. See already E. Tigchelaar, "Assessing Emanuel Tov's 'Qumran Scribal Practice'," in S. Metso, H. Najman, and E. Schuller (ed.), *The Dead Sea Scrolls: Transmission of Traditions and Production of Texts* (STDJ 92; Leiden: Brill, 2010) 173-207.

75. J.P.M. van der Ploeg, "Une halakha inédite de Qumrân," in M. Delcor (ed.), *Qumran, sa piété, sa théologie et son milieu* (BETL 46; Paris-Gembloux/Leuven: Duculot/Leuven University Press, 1978) 107-13, on p. 107; Id., "Manuscrits de la Grotte XI," 9. Yadin, *Temple Scroll*, Vol. 1, 20 noted the resemblance, and stated that "The two scripts undoubtedly belong to one scribal school."

Eugene Ulrich argued that one scribe was responsible for copying 1Q11 (1QPs^{b}), 4Q57 (4QIsa^{c}), and 11Q14 (11QSM),[76] and is reported to have added to this list also 4Q113 (4QDan^{b}).[77] Morphologically, the formal hands of those manuscripts have much in common, but the finer pen in 11Q14 and smaller size of the letters in 1Q11, make it more difficult to ascertain whether these correspondences should be assigned to the formal character, or to an individual hand.

11Q18 is one of the many manuscripts which according to Ada Yardeni was written by one and the same proliferous Qumran scribe.[78] Yardeni's approach suffers from the absence of a methodological discussion about the relation between style, type, and individual hand, and by a focus on only a few letters. Of all the manuscripts mentioned by Yardeni, the hand of 11Q18 seems virtually identical to that of 4Q475 (4QRenewed Earth), and quite similar, but with some differences, to 4Q397 (4QMMT^{d}), Yardeni's base example of her Qumran scribe.[79]

The discovery of manuscripts written by one and the same scribe in different caves, including Cave 11Q, strongly suggests some kind of relationship between the collections in the different Caves. However, it neither of necessity indicates that those scribes were actually copying the manuscripts at Qumran, nor requires a shared origin of the scrolls before they were deposited in the different caves. Texts copied by the same scribe could have ended up in different subcommunities of a larger movement.

3.4 *Dates of the Manuscripts*

The majority of the Cave 11Q manuscripts are much younger than the average manuscript from Cave 1Q or 4Q. If one accepts Cross's palaeographic typology, all but three or four out of twenty-six manuscripts written in the "Judean script" are Herodian, the majority developed or late. It is possible that the DJD 23 editors too often have characterized the hands as "late Herodian," but most are certainly – according to Cross's dating – from the first century CE. The few manuscripts that conform to the so-called Hasmonaean type of script are 11Q13, for which I refer to Puech who sees it as late Hasmonaean,[80] and 11Q24 and 11Q27, both consisting of one fragment. In DJD 23 we qualified also 11Q29, which only has a few letters, as Hasmonaean, but the keraia on the *alef* would contradict this proposal.

Interestingly, the paleo-Hebrew Leviticus scroll seems also the palaeographically youngest of the paleo-Hebrew scrolls from Qumran, probably to be dated between the middle of the first century BCE and the Jewish War.[81] Given that the Cave 11Q manuscripts are with only very few exceptions from the first century CE, one must agree with Stökl Ben Ezra that the Cave 11Q materials cannot have been a random selection from a larger collection which also included the Cave 1Q and 4Q manuscripts. Any further conclusions should be part of a more comprehensive hypothesis.

76. E. Ulrich, "Identification of a Scribe Active at Qumran: 1QPs^{b}-4QIsa^{c}-11QM," *Meghillot* 5-6 (2008) *201-*10.

77. White Crawford, "Qumran Collection," 124 n. 57. For 4Q113 (4QDan^{b}), cf. the drawings of Cross, "Development of the Jewish Scripts," fig. 2, line 6, where the hand is described as "a developed Herodian formal script" of circa 20-50 CE, while in the text the hand of 4QDan^{b} is qualified as "late Herodian." One may note that Ulrich was the editor of both 4Q57 and 4Q113 in the DJD series, but when he edited those manuscripts he did not comment on the possibility that both were copied by the same scribe.

78. A. Yardeni, "A Note on a Qumran Scribe," in M. Lubetski (ed.), *New Seals and Inscriptions: Hebrew, Idumean and Cuneiform* (HBM 8; Sheffield: Phoenix, 2007) 287-98. Yardeni also mentions one other Cave 11 manuscript, 11Q15, as possibly written by this scribe, but this must be one of the several typos in her list.

79. See comparison between 11Q18 and 4Q397 in DJD 23, 309. Note, e.g., the different writing of *bet* or *taw*, which suggest a different execution of the writing of the letters. However, according to Gemma Hayes (University of Groningen; ERC Project "The Hands That Wrote the Bible"), who analyses the manuscripts of Yardeni's Qumran scribe, cautions that the Groningen artificial intelligence approaches indicate that 11Q18 and 4Q475 were not written by the same scribe (private communication, 2019).

80. Cf. DJD 23, 223, which unfortunately overlooked the discussion of the palaeographic dating in E. Puech, "Notes sur le manuscrit de 11QMelkîsédeq," *RdQ* 12/48 (1987) 483-513, on pp. 507-8. As a modest correction of Milik, who suggested an origin in the mid-first century BCE, perhaps even 75-50 BCE, Puech argues for a late Hasmonaean date, in the mid-first century BCE or slightly later.

81. According to the forthcoming work of M. Richelle and A. Perrot.

Appendices

4. The Cigar Box and the LII Photograph Temple Scroll (11Q19) Fragments

4.1 *The Cigar Box*

Yadin, Pl. 3.2 and the photograph SHR 6314 show a series of fragments in the Karel I Elegant cigar box which was seized from Shahin. I am not aware of any systematic listing of the fragments in this cigar box. Yadin, Pl. 3.2. shows the following fragments:

(a) top left, a fragment with mainly lower margin, and the letters כוהנים, or perhaps ל֯כוהנים. This fragment has not been published in any edition. The fragment lies on top of another fragment without any visible writing. The two fragments are separated on SHR 6314, and the fragment with ל֯כוהנים is found, in two pieces, in the LII photograph (see below, 4.2.).

(b) below this fragment, on the left side of the plate, a fragment that has been placed in col. 13 lines 16-17 and bottom margin (cf. Yadin, Vol. 3, Pl. 28).

(c) below that fragment, on the left side of the plate, a larger fragment that has part of col. 18 lines 8-11 (Yadin, Vol. 3, Pl. 33), and, on top of this larger fragment, a small fragment which Yadin placed at the beginning of col. 19 7 and read as ביבות (Yadin, Vol. 3, Pl. 34). Comparison with Pl. 10*:3-4 and the present Shrine of the Book image casts doubt on the placement and reading of this small fragment. It seems to more likely that this fragment belongs to col. 18 line 7. At the end one might read כול ע֯, which would fit the reading כול עם which was proposed by Qimron, who probably also identified this small fragment as belonging to col. 18 line 7. However, in spite of the fixed phrase כפר בו על כול עם הקהל, it is difficult to read the preceding traces as על.

(d) bottom of plate, the large "wad x." Note, however, that in Pl. 3.4 the sequence of the layers (with a large part of col. 13 on top of cols. 14 and 15) is exactly opposite to the sequence in Pl. 7.1 where, as one would expect, the writing of col. 15 covers that of col. 14 and of col. 13.

(e) very middle of the plate, small fragment with parts of two lines, which has been fitted in col. 21 lines 13-14 (Pl. 36).

(f) just below that fragment a small fragment with יח ניחוח which has been joined in col. 15 line 13.

(g) entire right side of the plate: bits and pieces of what came to be known as the "domino." Cf. Pl. 8.

4.2 *The LII Photograph*[82]

A plate at the Shrine of the Book labelled "LII (15)" was photographed by Ira Rabin in the late 2000s, some of the fragments of which were used for material research.[83] On the plate are almost fifty small to minute fragments, two of which were photographed in the above described cigar box while some others have broken off from the so-called "Wad X," which can be restored to their proper place in cols. 14 and 15.[84]

The fragment on the top of Pl. 3.2 of the cigar box, reading כוהנים, or perhaps ל֯כוהנים, has broken into several parts. The letters נים are in the left column of fragments in the LII photograph, second row. The letters ל֯כוה are in the fifth column from the left, second row. Apparently the piece with those letters was on the top of a wad, and one can also read the layer underneath it ל֯כ֯בש. Given the words and the bottom margin of the fragment, these two fragments can easily be fit in col. 15 line 18 and col. 14 line 18. Hence, one can now transcribe the beginning of these lines as follows:

14:18 [ההין]ל֯כבש ה֯אחד ל[שב]ע֯ת ה֯כ֯ב֯שים ולשע֯[ר ...
15:18 ל֯כוהנים בריאש֯[ונה] וסמכו זקני הכוהנ[ים ...

Given the "LII" tag, it makes sense to also consider possible joins of the fragments in col. 52. One certain candidate is the fragment in the middle column, second/third from the bottom, reading]מש֯[, which fits perfectly at the beginning of col. 52 line 3, משכית.

82. Permission to include the photograph in this publication was granted by the Israel Museum, holder of the plate with the fragments, and by Dr. Ira Rabin, who took the photograph and owns the copyright.

83. I. Rabin et al., "Analysis of an antique alum tawed parchment," in E. Janssen et al. (ed.), *Proceedings of the Joint Interim Meeting Multidisciplinary Conservation: A Holistic View For Historic Interiors, Rome 23-26 March 2010* (ICOM-CC, 2010), available from http://www.icom-cc.org/54/document/analysis-of-an%20antique-alum-tawed-parchment/?id=795#.WYyoJtOGMUE.

84. Therefore, Rabin's assumption that all fragments on this plate are from col. 52 is incorrect.

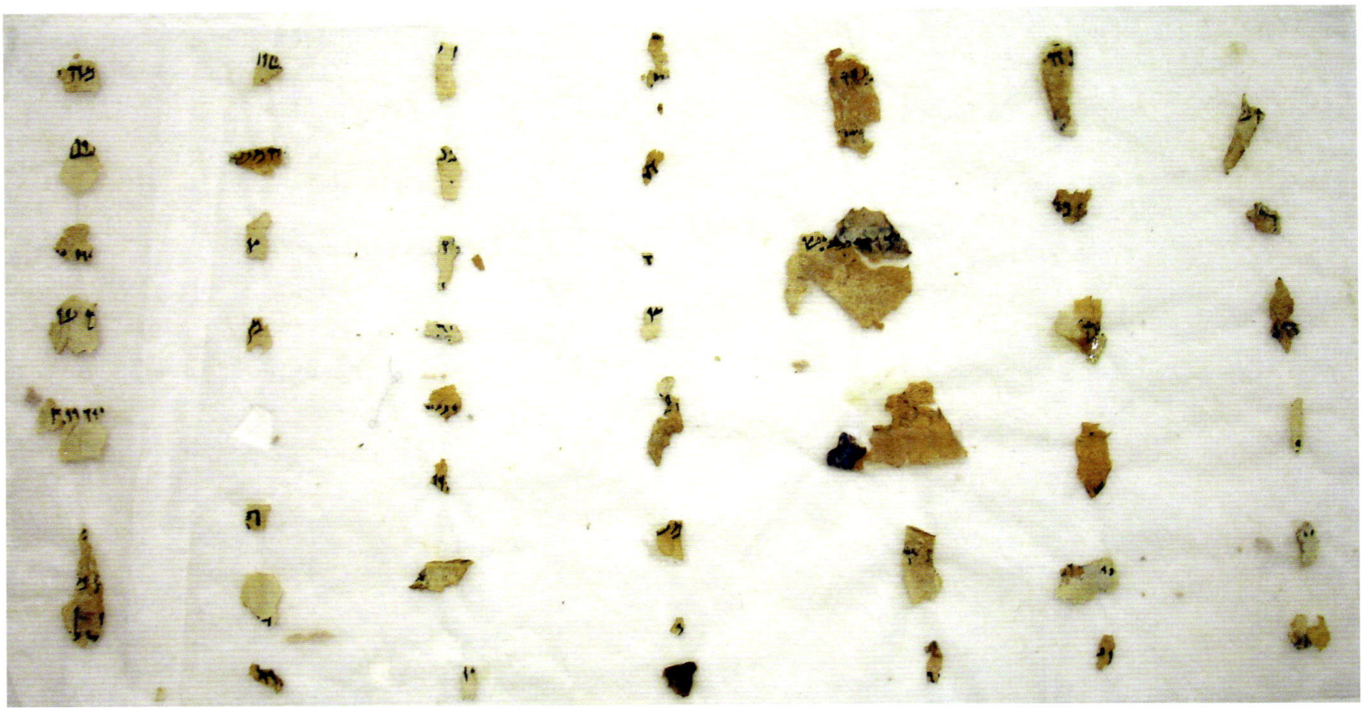

Fig. 1. The LII Photograph

5. The Yadin Fragments

The 1992 photograph JWS 97 shows the 4Q285 fragment published as XQ5b.[85] The photograph JWS 98 shows six fragments, namely, at the left the still partially rolled or folded fragment which would be published as XQ5a,[86] at the right the fragment which would be published as 11Q8 frag. 3, and in between four hitherto unpublished tiny fragments. Those fragments are presently on the IAA Plates X80 (only the now unfolded XQ5a fragment) and X78-X79, with the other abovementioned fragments, as well as five more minute frags. I will use the reference numbers given by the IAA.[87]

IAA PX78-X79 frags. 2 and 3 are respectively XQ5b/4Q285 and 11Q8.

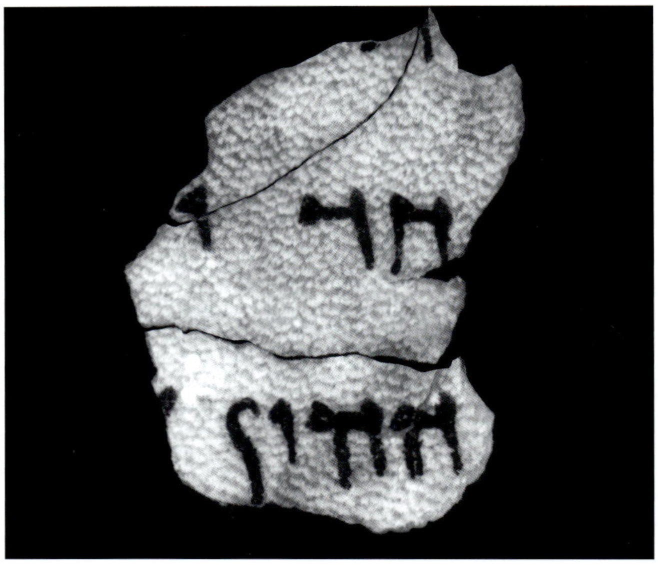

Fig. 2. Courtesy of The Leon Levy Dead Sea Scrolls Digital Library, Israel Antiquities Authority, photo: Shai Halevi. Joining of the separate photos to one image: Drew Longacre, University of Groningen

IAA PX78-X79 frag. 1 is a small fragment, of the same colour as frag. 3 (11Q8), with three letters:]מי/וע̊[.

However, it lacks the characteristic ruling of 11Q8. IAA PX78-X79 frag. 5 (also on JWS 98B) can easily be associated on material and palaeographical

85. DJD 36, 487-9, incorrectly identified as 11QHymns[b] frg. 2. See now Tigchelaar, "The Yadin Qumran Fragment XQ5b."

86. DJD 36, 485-6, incorrectly identified as 11QJub frag. 7a. See, in detail, Tigchelaar, "Three Qumran-Type Yadin Fragments."

87. The IAA images of plates X78-X79 are not yet accessible through the Leon Levy Dead Sea Scrolls Digital Library. I am grateful to the IAA for having given me access to the newly-made photographs of that plate.

grounds with frag. 3 (11Q8). Read in line 1]לׄ [, and in line 2]○י/מׄו[.

IAA PX78-X79 frags. 4, 8, and 9 (the first two also on JWS 98B) should be joined. They read as follows:

1]ו֯ל֯[
2]א]חד ו[
3]ההין ע֯[

The combination of the hand and the remaining vocabulary indicate these fragments should be assigned to 11Q20. In line 2, the spacing between א]חד and the following ו is larger than a normal word-dividing space in 11Q20. The trace at the left end of line 3 must be from *ayin* or *shin*, indicating ההין ע֯]ל or ההין ש֯]מן. It is most likely that these fragments correspond to some lines of 11QT[a] 14, even though the text does not exactly correspond with the reconstructions of either Yadin or Qimron.

IAA PX78-X79 frags. 6 and 7 have no legible traces. IAA PX78-X79 frag. 10 (also on JWS 98b) has a *he* at the end of the line and part of the margin. IAA PX78-X79 frag. 11 may be read]שׁקׄ[, but it cannot be associated with the other fragments on this plate.

Bibliography

Ableman, O., "Newly Identified Pentateuchal Fragments: 4QExod[g] (4Q18, Exod 12:51-13:3), 4QDeut[k3] (4Q38b, Deut 30:13-18)," *RdQ* 30/111 (2018) 91-100.

Abu Zidan, F., "Nein," *HA-ESI* 126 (2014).

Abu-Rabia, A., "The Evil Eye and Cultural Beliefs Among the Bedouin Tribes of the Negev, Middle East," *Folklore* 116/3 (2005) 241-54.

Aerts-Bijma, A.T., J. van der Plicht, and H.A.J. Meijer, "Automatic AMS Sample Combustion and CO_2 Collection," *Radiocarbon* 43/2A (2001) 293-8.

Aharoni, Y., "Expedition B: The Cave of Horror," *IEJ* 12 (1962) 186-99.

Aharoni, Y., *Excavations at Ramat Raḥel: Seasons 1961 and 1962* (Serie Archeologica 6; Roma: Centro di Studi Semitici, 1964).

Aharoni, Y. (ed.), *Beer-Sheba I: Excavations at Tel Beer-Sheba: 1969-1971 Seasons* (Publications of the Institute of Archaeology 2; Tel Aviv: Tel Aviv University, Institute of Archaeology, 1973).

Amar, Z. and O. Shamir, "Egyptian Balsam and its Use in the Jordan Rift Region," *JSRS* 22 (2013) 369-76 (Hebrew).

Avigad, N., "Expedition A - Nahal David," *IEJ* 12 (1962) 16-83.

Bar-Adon, P., *The Cave of the Treasure: The Finds from the Caves in Naḥal Mishmar* (Jerusalem: Israel Exploration Society, 1980).

Baillet, M., "Textes des grottes 2Q, 3Q, 6Q, 7Q à 10Q," in Id., J.T. Milik, and R. de Vaux, *Les 'petites grottes' de Qumrân: Exploration de la falaise. Les grottes 2Q, 3Q, 5Q, 6Q, 7Q à 10Q. Le rouleau de cuivre* (DJD 3; Oxford: Clarendon, 1962) 45-164.

Barthélemy, D. and J.T. Milik, *Qumran Cave 1* (DJD 1; Oxford: Clarendon, 1955).

Baumgarten, J.M., "270. 4QDamascus Document[e]," in Id., *Qumran Cave 4. XIII: The Damascus Document (4Q266-273)* (DJD 18; Oxford: Clarendon, 1996) 137-68.

Baumgarten, J.M., "Corrigenda to the 4Q MSS of the *Damascus Document*," *RdQ* 19/74 (1999) 217-25.

Bélis, M., "Des Textiles: Catalogues et Commentaires," in J.-B. Humbert and J. Gunneweg (ed.), *Khirbet Qumrân et 'Aïn Feshkha: Vol. II: Études d'anthropologie, de physique et de chimie* (NTOA.SA 3; Fribourg/Göttingen: Éditions Universitaires/Vandenhoeck & Ruprecht, 2003) 207-76.

Bélis, M., "The Unpublished Textiles from the Qumran Caves," in M. Fidanzio (ed.), *The Caves of Qumran: Proceedings of the International Conference, Lugano 2014* (STDJ 118; Leiden: Brill, 2016) 123-36.

Ben-Ami, D., "The Iron Age Pottery," in Id., *Jerusalem: Excavations in the Tyropoeon Valley (Giv'ati Parking Lot): Vol. 1* (IAA Reports 52; Jerusalem: Israel Antiquities Authority, 2013) 63-82.

Ben-Basat, H., *Early Iron Age Beads at Tel Dor: A Comparative Study* (MA thesis; University of Haifa, 2011).

Ben-Dov, J. and D. Stökl Ben Ezra, "4Q249 Midrash Moshe: A New Reading and Some Implications," *DSD* 21 (2014) 131-49.

Ben-Dov, J., D. Stökl Ben Ezra, and A. Gayer, "Reconstruction of a Single Copy of the Qumran Cave 4 Cryptic-Script Serekh haEdah," *RdQ* 29/109 (2017) 21-77.

Benoit, P., "Préface," in R. de Vaux and J.T. Milik, *Qumrân Grotte 4.II: I. Archéologie. II. Tefillin, Mezuzot et Targums (4Q128-4Q157)* (DJD 6; Oxford: Clarendon, 1977) v-vi.

Bernick, K., "Masada Basketry, Cordage and Related Artifacts," in Y. Aviram, G. Foerster, and E. Netzer (ed.), *Masada IV: The Yigael Yadin Excavations 1963-1965: Final Reports* (Jerusalem: Israel Exploration Society/Hebrew University, 1994) 284-317.

Bernick-Greenberg, H., "The Ceramic Assemblages and the Wheel-Made Pottery Typology," in R. Cohen and H. Bernick-Greenberg, *Excavations at Kadesh Barnea (Tell el-Qudeirat) 1976-1982* (IAA Reports 34; Jerusalem: Israel Antiquities Authority, 2007) 131-85.

Bishop, M.C., "Weaponry and Military Equipment," in L. Allason-Jones (ed.), *Artefacts in Roman Britain: Their Purpose and Use* (Cambridge: Cambridge University Press, 2011) 114-32.

Bishop, M.C. and J.C.N. Coulston, *Roman Military Equipment: From the Punic Wars to the Fall of Rome* (Oxford: Oxbow, [2]2006).

Blau, J., "Nāwā Ṯhillā (Ps. CXLVII 1): Lobpreisen," *VT* 4/4 (1954) 410-1.

Bohak, G., *Ancient Jewish Magic: A History* (Cambridge: Cambridge University Press, 2008).

Bonani, G. et al., "Radiocarbon Dating of the Dead Sea Scrolls," *'Atiqot* 20 (1991) 27-32.

Bonani, G. et al., "Radiocarbon Dating of Fourteen Dead Sea Scrolls," *Radiocarbon* 34/3 (1992) 843-9.

Borghouts, J.F., *The Magical Texts of Papyrus Leiden 1.348* (Leiden: Brill, 1971).

Brownlee, W.H., "The Scroll of Ezekiel from the Eleventh Qumran Cave," *RdQ* 4/13 (1963) 11-28.

Broshi, M. and H. Eshel, "Residential Caves at Qumran," *DSD* 6 (1999) 328-48.

Callegher, B., "The Coins of Khirbet Qumran from the Digs of Roland de Vaux: Returning to Henri Seyrig and Augustus Spijkerman," in M. Fidanzio (ed.), *The Caves of Qumran: Proceedings of the International Conference, Lugano 2014* (STDJ 118; Leiden: Brill, 2016) 221-37.

Campbell Thompson, R., *Semitic Magic: Its Origins and Development* (Luzac's Oriental Religions Series 3; London: Luzac & Co., 1908).

Carswell, J., "Fastenings on the Qumrân Manuscripts," in R. de Vaux and J.T. Milik, *Qumrân Grotte 4.II: I. Archéologie. II. Tefillin, Mezuzot et Targums (4Q128-4Q157)* (DJD 6; Oxford: Clarendon, 1977) 23-8.

Charlesworth, J.H et al. (ed.), *The Dead Sea Scrolls: Hebrew, Aramaic, and Greek Texts with English Translation: Vol. 7: Temple Scroll and Related Documents* (Tübingen/Louisville: Mohr Siebeck/ Westminster John Knox, 2011).

Chernov, E., "Metal Objects and Small Finds from En-Gedi," in Y. Hirschfeld (ed.), *En-Gedi Excavations II: Final Report (1996-2002)* (Jerusalem: Israel Exploration Society, 2007) 507-43.

Clark Kee, H., *Medicine, Miracle and Magic in New Testament Times* (Cambridge: Cambridge University Press, 1988).

Cleland, L., G. Davies, and L. Llewellyn-Jones, *Greek and Roman Dress from A to Z* (London: Routledge, 2007).

Commenge-Pellerin, C., *La poterie d'Abou Matar et de l'Ouadi Zoumeili (Beersheva) au IVe millénaire avant l'ère chrétienne* (Cahiers du CRFJ 3; Paris: Association Paléorient, 1987).

Commenge-Pellerin, C., *La poterie de Safadi (Beersheva) au IVe millénaire avant l'ère chrétienne* (Cahiers du CRFJ 5; Paris: Association Paléorient, 1990).

Croom, A.T., *Roman Clothing and Fashion* (Stroud: Tempus, 2010).

Cross, F.M., "The Development of the Jewish Scripts," in G.E. Wright (ed.), *The Bible and the Ancient Near East: Essays in Honor of William Foxwell Albright* (Garden City, NY: Doubleday, 1961) 133-202.

Cross, F.M., *The Ancient Library of Qumran* (Sheffield: Sheffield Academic Press, ^{3}1995).

Cross, F.M., "Reminiscences of the Early Days in the Discovery and Study of the Dead Sea Scrolls," in L.H. Schiffman, E. Tov, and J.C. VanderKam (ed.), *The Dead Sea Scrolls Fifty Years After Their Discovery: Proceedings of the Jerusalem Congress, July 20-25, 1997* (Jerusalem: Israel Exploration Society, 2000) 932-43.

Cross, F.M., "The Development of the Jewish Scripts," in Id., *Leaves from an Epigrapher's Notebook: Collected Papers in Hebrew and West Semitic Palaeography and Epigraphy* (HSS 51; Winona Lake, IN: Eisenbrauns, 2003) 3-43.

Crowfoot, G.M., "The Linen Textiles," in D. Barthélemy and J.T. Milik, *Qumran Cave 1* (DJD 1; Oxford: Clarendon, 1955) 18-38.

Crowfoot, G.M. and E. Crowfoot, "The Textile and Basketry," in P. Benoit, J.T. Milik, and R. de Vaux, *Les Grottes de Murabba'*ât (DJD 2; Oxford: Clarendon, 1961) 51-63.

Dagot, A., "Nir Gallim," *HA-ESI* 126 (2014).

Dahmen, U., *Psalmen- und Psalter-Rezeption im Frühjudentum: Rekonstruktion, Textbestand, Struktur und Pragmatik der Psalmenrolle 11QPs*[a] *aus Qumran* (STDJ 49; Leiden: Brill, 2003).

Davis, K., "Caves of Dispute: Patterns of Correspondence and Suspicion in the Post-2002 'Dead Sea Scrolls' Fragments," *DSD* 24 (2017) 229-70.

Davis, K. et al., "Nine Dubious 'Dead Sea Scrolls' Fragments from the Twenty-First Century," *DSD* 24 (2017) 189-228.

De Groot, A., G. Hillel, and I. Yezerski, "Iron Age II Pottery," in H. Geva (ed.), *Jewish Quarter Excavations in the Old City of Jerusalem Conducted by Nahman Avigad, 1969-1982: Vol. 2: The Finds from Areas A, W and X-2: Final Report* (Jerusalem: Israel Exploration Society/Hebrew University, 2003) 1-49.

Donceel, R., "Reprise des travaux de publication des fouilles au Khirbet Qumrân," *RB* 99 (1992) 557-73.

Doudna, G.L., "Dating the Scrolls on the Basis of Radiocarbon Analysis," in P.W. Flint and J.C. VanderKam (ed.), *The Dead Sea Scrolls after Fifty Years: A Comprehensive Assessment: Vol. 1* (Leiden: Brill, 1998) 430-71.

Doudna, G.L., "The Legacy of an Error in Archaeological Interpretation: The Dating of the Qumran Cave Scroll Deposits," in K. Galor, J.-B. Humbert, and J. Zangenberg (ed.), *Qumran, the Site of the Dead Sea Scrolls: Archaeological Interpretations and Debates: Proceedings of the Conference Held at Brown University, November 17-19, 2002* (STDJ 57; Leiden: Brill, 2006) 147-57.

Doudna, G.L., "Dating the Scroll Deposits of the Qumran Caves: A Question of Evidence," in M. Fidanzio (ed.), *The Caves of Qumran: Proceedings of the International Conference, Lugano 2014* (STDJ 118; Leiden: Brill, 2016) 238-46.

Elgvin, T., "Texts and Artefacts from the Judaean desert in The Schøyen Collection: An Overview," in Id., K. Davis, and M. Langlois (ed.), *Gleanings from the Caves: Dead Sea Scrolls and Artefacts from the Schøyen Collection* (LSTS 71; London: Bloomsbury T&T Clark, 2016) 51-60.

Elgvin, T., "Leather Cord from Qumran, Shoe Remains: MS 5095/6, MS 1655/5," in Id., K. Davis, and M. Langlois (ed.), *Gleanings from the Caves: Dead Sea Scrolls and Artefacts from the Schøyen Collection* (LSTS 71; London: Bloomsbury T&T Clark, 2016) 323-38.

Elgvin, T. and K. Davis, "MS 5095/1, MS 5095/4: Wads from 11QT[a], Unidentified Fragments from Cave 11," in Id, K. Davis, and M. Langlois (ed.), *Gleanings from the Caves: Dead Sea Scrolls and Artefacts from the Schøyen Collection* (LSTS 71; London: Bloomsbury T&T Clark, 2016) 301-8.

Eshel, E., "MS 4612/3: 11Q(?)Eschatological Fragment ar," in T. Elgvin, K. Davis, and M. Langlois (ed.), *Gleanings from the Caves: Dead Sea Scrolls and Artefacts from the Schøyen Collection* (LSTS 71; London: Bloomsbury T&T Clark, 2016) 295-8.

Eshel, E. and H. Eshel, "A Preliminary Report on Seven New Fragments from Qumran," *Meghillot* 5-6 (2007) 271-8.

Eshel, H., "Three New Fragments from Qumran Cave 11," *DSD* 8 (2001) 1-8.

Eshel, H., "A Note on 11QPs[d] Fragment 1," *RdQ* 23/92 (2008) 529-31.

Eshel, H., "Gleaning of Scrolls from the Judean Desert," in C. Hempel (ed.), *The Dead Sea Scrolls: Texts and Context* (STDJ 90; Leiden: Brill, 2010) 49-87.

Fidanzio, M., "Which Cave Does This Pottery Come From? The Information Written on the Pottery Found in the Qumran Caves (R. de Vaux Excavations 1949-1956)," *RB* 122 (2015) 128-31.

Fidanzio, M., "L'agenda di Qumran," in G. Paximadi and M. Fidanzio (ed.), *TerraSancta II: Ricerche storiche ed Archeologiche: Atti dei convegni 2012-2014* (ISCAB.SA 2; Lugano/Siena: Eupress FTL/Cantagalli 2017) 151-67.

Fidanzio, M. and J.-B. Humbert, "Finds from the Qumran Caves: Roland de Vaux's Inventory of the Excavations (1949-1956)," in M. Fidanzio (ed.), *The Caves of Qumran: Proceedings of the International Conference, Lugano 2014* (STDJ 118; Leiden: Brill, 2016) 263-332.

Fidanzio, M. and E. Puech, "La grotta 11 di Qumran: Archeologia e frammenti manoscritti," in M. Crimella, G.C. Pagazzi, and S. Romanello (ed.), *Extra ironiam nulla salus: Studi in onore di Roberto Vignolo in occasione del suo LXX compleanno* (Biblica 8; Milano: Glossa, 2016) 927-48.

Fidanzio, M. et al., "Campagna di scavi ISCAB-FTL e USI alla grotta 11Q di Qumran, marzo 2017," *RTLu* 22 (2017) 437-66.

Fidanzio, M. (ed.), *The Caves of Qumran: Proceedings of the International Conference, Lugano 2014* (STDJ 118; Leiden: Brill, 2016).

Fields, W.W., *The Dead Sea Scrolls: A Full History: Vol. 1: 1947-1960* (Leiden: Brill, 2009).

Fitzmyer, J.A., *Responses to 101 Questions on the Dead Sea Scrolls* (New York: Paulist, 1992).

Flohr, M., *The World of the Fullo: Work, Economy and Society in Roman Italy* (Oxford Studies on the Roman Economy; Oxford: Oxford University Press, 2013).

Forbes, R.J., *Studies in Ancient Technology: Vol. 5* (Leiden: Brill, 1956).

Franken, H.J., "The Twelve Pottery Classes," in Id. and M.L. Steiner, *Excavations in Jerusalem 1961-1967: Vol. 2: The Iron Age Extramural Quarter on the South-East Hill* (Oxford: Oxford University Press, 1990) 99-121.

Franken, H.J. and M.L. Steiner, *Excavations in Jerusalem 1961-1967: Vol. 2: The Iron Age Extramural Quarter on the South-East Hill* (Oxford: Oxford University Press, 1990).

Freedman, D.N. and K.A. Mathews, *The Paleo-Hebrew Leviticus Scroll (11QpaleoLev)* (Winona Lake, IN: American Schools of Oriental Research, 1985).

Freud, L., "Pottery. 2. Iron Age," in I. Beit-Arieh (ed.), *Tel* 'Ira*: A Stronghold in the Biblical Negev* (MSSMNIA 15; Tel Aviv: Emery and Claire Yass Publications in Archaeology, 1999) 189-289.

Galor, K. and J. Zangenberg, "Qumran Archaeology in Search of a Consensus," in K. Galor, J.-B. Humbert, and J. Zangenberg (ed.), *Qumran: The Site of the Dead Sea Scrolls: Archaeological Interpretations and Debates* (STDJ 57; Leiden: Brill, 2006) 1-15.

Gandz, S., "The Knot in Hebrew Literature, or from the Knot to the Alphabet," *Isis* 14/1 (1930) 189-214.

García Martínez, F., "Cave 11 in Context," in C. Hempel (ed.), *The Dead Sea Scrolls: Texts and Context* (STDJ 90; Leiden: Brill, 2010) 199-209.

García Martínez, F., "The Contents of the Manuscripts from the Caves of Qumran," in M. Fidanzio (ed.), *The Caves of Qumran: Proceedings of the International Conference, Lugano 2014* (Leiden: Brill, 2016) 67-79.

García Martínez, F., E.J.C. Tigchelaar, and A.S. van der Woude, *Qumran Cave 11.II: 11Q2-18, 11Q20-31* (DJD 23; Oxford: Clarendon, 1998).

Gitin, S., *Gezer III: A Ceramic Typology of the Late Iron II, Persian and Hellenistic Periods at Tell Gezer* (ANGSBA 3; Jerusalem: Hebrew Union College, 1990).

Granger-Taylor, H., "Weaving Clothes to Shape in the Ancient World: The Tunic and Toga of the Arringatore," *Textile History* 13 (1982) 13-25.

Gutfeld, O. and R. Nenner-Soriano, "Metal Artifacts," in H. Geva (ed.), *Jewish Quarter Excavations in the Old City of Jerusalem Conducted by Nahman Avigad, 1969-1982: Vol. 3: Area E and Other Studies: Final Report* (Jerusalem: Israel Exploration Society/Hebrew University, 2006) 272-82.

Gzella, H., *A Cultural History of Aramaic: From the Beginnings to the Advent of Islam* (HdO 111; Leiden: Brill, 2015).

Hadas, G., "Nine Tombs of the Second Temple Period at 'En Gedi," *'Atiqot* 24 (1994) 3-65 (Hebrew), 1*-8* (English Summary).

Haines, B.M., "The Fibre Structure of Leather," in M. Kite and R. Thomson (ed.), *Conservation of Leather and Related Materials* (Oxford: Elsevier, 2006) 11-21.

Hall, R., *Egyptian Textiles* (Shire Egyptology 4; London: Shire, 1986).

Harding, G.L., "Foreword," in D. Barthélemy and J.T. Milik, *Qumran Cave 1* (DJD 1; Oxford: Clarendon, 1955) v.

Harding, G.L., "Recent Discoveries in Jordan," *PEQ* 90 (1958) 7-18.

Hepper, N.F. and J.E. Taylor, "Date Palms and Opobalsam in the Madaba Mosaic Map," *PEQ* 136 (2004) 35-44.

Herbert, E.D., "11QEzekiel (Pls. II, LIV)," in F. García Martínez, E.J.C Tigchelaar, and A.S. van der Woude, *Qumran Cave 11.II: 11Q2-18, 11Q20-31* (DJD 23; Oxford: Clarendon, 1998) 15-28.

Herzog, Z. et al., "The Israelite Fortress at Arad," *BASOR* 254 (1984) 1-34.

Hofenk de Graaff, J.H., W.G. Roelofs, and M.R. van Bommel, *The Colourful Past: The Origins, Chemistry and Identification of Natural Dyestuffs* (London/Riggisberg: Archetype/Abegg-Stiftung, 2004).

Humbert, J.-B., "Introduction," in Id. and A. Chambon (ed.), *The Excavations of Khirbet Qumran and 'Aïn Feshkha: Synthesis of Roland de Vaux's Field Notes* (NTOA.SA 1B; trans. and rev. S.J. Pfann; Fribourg/Göttingen: Éditions Universitaires/Vandenhoeck & Ruprecht, 2003) xiii-xiv.

Humbert, J.-B., "Cacher et se cacher à Qumrân: grottes et refuges. Morphologie, fonctions, anthropologie," in M. Fidanzio (ed.), *The Caves of Qumran: Proceedings of the International Conference, Lugano 2014* (STDJ 118; Leiden: Brill, 2016) 34-63.

Humbert, J.-B., "Introduction," in Id., A. Chambon, and J. Młynarczyk, *Khirbet Qumrân et 'Aïn Feshkha: Vol. IIIA: L'archéologie de Qumrân: Reconsidération de l'interprétation. Les installations périphériques de Khirbet Qumrân. Qumran Terracotta Oil Lamps* (NTOA.SA 5A; Göttingen: Vandenhoeck & Ruprecht, 2016) 13-21.

Humbert, J.-B. and E. Villeneuve, *L'affaire Qumrân: Les découvertes de la mer Morte* (Découvertes Gallimard 498; Paris: Gallimard, 2006).

Humbert, J.-B. and A. Chambon (ed.), *Fouilles de Khirbet Qumrân et de 'Aïn Feshkha: Vol. I: Album de photographies. Répertoire du fonds photographique. Synthèse des notes de chantier du Père Roland de Vaux OP* (NTOA.SA 1; Fribourg/Göttingen: Éditions Universitaires/Vandenhoeck & Ruprecht, 1994).

Humbert, J.-B. and A. Chambon (ed.), *The Excavations of Khirbet Qumran and 'Aïn Feshkha: Synthesis of Roland de Vaux's Field Notes* (NTOA.SA 1B; trans. and rev. S.J. Pfann; Fribourg/Göttingen: Éditions Universitaires/Vandenhoeck & Ruprecht, 2003).

Jacobi, G., *Die Ausgrabungen in Manching: Band 5: Werkzeug und Gerät aus dem Oppidum von Manching* (Wiesbaden: Franz Steiner, 1974).

Jacobson, H., "11Q30, Fgs. 8-10," *RdQ* 18/72 (1998) 595.

Jain, E., *Psalmen oder Psalter? Materielle Rekonstruktion und inhaltliche Untersuchung der Psalmenhandschriften aus der Wüste Juda* (STDJ 109; Leiden: Brill, 2014).

Jastram, N., "27. 4QNum[b]," in E. Ulrich et al., *Qumran Cave 4. VII: Genesis to Numbers* (DJD 12; Oxford: Clarendon, 1994) 205-67.

Johnson, B.L., "Clay, Stone, and Metal Objects from the Hellenistic to the Early Islamic Period," in A. Mazar (ed.), *Excavations at Tel Beth-Shean 1989-1996: Vol. 1: From the Late Bronze Age IIB to the Medieval Period* (Jerusalem: Israel Exploration Society/Hebrew University, 2006) 654-74.

Kahila Bar-Gal, G., *Genetic Change in the* Capra *Species of Southern Levant over the Past 10,000 Years as Studied by DNA Analysis of Ancient and Modern Populations* (PhD diss.; Hebrew University, 2000).

Kallner-Amiran, D.H., "A Revised Earthquake-Catalogue of Palestine," *IEJ* 1 (1950-51) 223-46.

Karcz, I., "Implications of Some Early Jewish Sources for Estimates of Earthquake Hazard in the Holy Land," *Annals of Geophysics* 47 (2004) 759-92.

Kemp, B.J. and G. Vogelsang-Eastwood, *The Ancient Textile Industry at Amarna* (London: Egypt Exploration Society, 2001).

Kislev, M. and O. Simchoni, "Hygiene and Insect Damage of Crops and Food at Masada," in J. Aviram et al. (ed.), *Masada VIII: The Yigael Yadin Excavations 1963-1965: Final Reports* (Jerusalem: Israel Exploration Society/Hebrew University, 2007) 133-70.

Kislev, M. et al., "Flax Seed Production: Evidence from the Early Iron Age Site of Tel Beth-Shean, Israel and from Written Sources," *VHA* 20/6 (2011) 579-84.

Koren, Z.C., "An Efficient HPLC Analysis Scheme for Plant and Animal Red, Blue and Purple Dyes," *DHA* 13 (1994) 27-37.

Koren, Z.C., "HPLC-PDA Analysis of Brominated Indirubinoid, Indigoid, and Isatinoid Dyes," in L. Meijer et al. (ed.), *Indirubin, the Red Shade of Indigo* (Roscoff: Life in Progress Editions, 2006) 45-53.

Kraus, H.-J., *Psalmen: Vol. 2: Teilband Psalmen 60-150* (BKAT 15/2; Neukirchen-Vluyn: Neukirchener Verlag, ^{5}1978).

Kugler, R.A. and K.S. Baek, *Leviticus at Qumran: Text and Interpretation* (VTSup 173; Leiden: Brill, 2016).

Lacerenza, G., "Un nouveau fragment en écriture paléo-hébraïque," *RdQ* 19/75 (2000) 441-7.

Lamon, R.S. and G.A. Shipton, *Megiddo I: Seasons of 1925-34: Strata I-V* (OIP 42; Chicago: University of Chicago Press, 1939).

Langgut, D. et al., "Vegetation and Climate Changes During the Bronze and Iron Ages (~3600-600 BCE) in the Southern Levant Based on Palynological Records," *Radiocarbon* 57/2 (2015) 217-35.

Lapp, N.L., *The Third Campaign at Tell el-Ful: The Excavations of 1964* (AASOR 45; Cambridge, MA: American Schools of Oriental Research, 1981).

Lapp, P.W., *Palestinian Ceramic Chronology 200 B.C.-A.D. 70* (New Haven: American Schools of Oriental Research, 1961).

Larson, E. and L.H. Schiffman, "481d. 4QFragments with Red Ink," in G.J. Brooke et al., *Qumran Cave 4. XVII: Parabiblical Texts: Part 3* (DJD 22; Oxford: Clarendon, 1996) 315-9.

Lemaire, A., "Nouveaux fragments du Rouleau du Temple de Qumrân," *RdQ* 17/65-68 (1996) 271-4.

Lemaire, A., "Un fragment araméen inédit de Qumrân," *RdQ* 18/70 (1997) 331-3.

Lemaire, A., "XQ6. XQOffering ar," in S.J. Pfann and P. Alexander et al., *Qumran Cave 4. XXVI: Cryptic Texts. Miscellanea: Part 1* (DJD 36; Oxford: Clarendon, 2000) 490-1.

Lemaire, A., "Inscriptions du Khirbeh, des grottes et de 'Aïn Feshkha," in J.-B. Humbert and J. Gunneweg (ed.), *Khirbet Qumrân et 'Aïn Feshkha: Vol. II: Études d'anthropologie, de physique et de chimie* (NTOA.SA 3; Fribourg/Göttingen: Éditions Universitaires/Vandenhoeck & Ruprecht, 2003) 341-88.

Letellier-Willemin, F., "The Long and Narrow Sleeved Tunic of the Mummy W14 of El Deir," in A. de Moor, C. Fluck, and P. Linscheid (ed.), *Textiles, Tools and Techniques of the 1st Millennium AD from Egypt and Neighbouring Countries: Proceedings of the 8th Conference of the Research Group 'Textiles from the Nile Valley': Antwerp, 4th-6th October 2013* (Tielt: Lannoo Publishers, 2015) 26-37.

Lev, E. and Z. Amar, *Practical Materia Medica of the Medieval Eastern Mediterranean According to the Cairo Genizah* (Sir Henry Wellcome Asian Series 7; Leiden: Brill, 2007).

Linscheid, P. and C. Fluck, "Textiles from Krokodilopolis and Herakleopolis Magna in the Museum für Spätantike und Byzantinische Kunst, Berlin," *ATN* 21 (1995) 15-7.

Lukaszewski, A.L., "An Alternative Reading of 11Q18 Fragment 17 (11QNew Jerusalem)," *RdQ* 21/83 (2003) 321-3.

Mannering, U., "The Roman Tradition of Weaving and Sewing: A Guide to Function?," *ATN* 30 (2000) 10-6.

Manning, W.H., *Catalogue of the Romano-British Iron Tools, Fittings and Weapons in the British Museum* (London: British Museum Publications, 1985).

Manning, W.H., "Industry," in L. Allason-Jones (ed.), *Artefacts in Roman Britain: Their Purpose and Use* (Cambridge: Cambridge University Press, 2011) 68-88.

Mazar, A., *Excavations at Tell Qasile: Part Two: The Philistine Sanctuary: Various Finds, the Pottery, Conclusions, Appendixes* (Qedem 20; Jerusalem: Hebrew University, 1985).

Mazar, A. and N. Panitz-Cohen, *Timnah (Tel Batash) II: The Finds from the First Millennium BCE* (Qedem 42; Jerusalem: Hebrew University, 2001).

Mazar, E. and B. Mazar, *Excavations in the South of the Temple Mount: The Ophel of Biblical* Jerusalem (Qedem 29; Jerusalem: The Hebrew University, 1989).

McLean, M.D., *The Use and Development of Palaeo-Hebrew in the Hellenistic and Roman Periods* (PhD diss.; Harvard University, 1982).

Mébarki, F., "Józef Tadeusz Milik: Souvenirs de terrain," *MdB* 107 (1997) 11-5.

Melamed, Y., "Chalcolithic and Hellenistic Plant Remains from Cave V/49," *'Atiqot* 41 (2002) 101-8.

Melamed, Y. and M. Kislev, "Remain of Seeds, Fruits Insects from the Excavation in the Village of 'En Gedi," *JSRS* 49 (2005) 89*-102* (Hebrew).

Merker, G.S., "The Objects of Metal," in A.M. Berlin and S.C. Herbert (ed.), *Tel Anafa II, ii: Glass Vessels, Lamps, Objects of Metal, and Groundstone and Other Stone Tools and Vessels* (JRASS 10.2.1; Ann Arbor, MI: Kelsey Museum of the University of Michigan, 2012) 213-79.

Milik, J.T., *Ten Years of Discovery in the Wilderness of Judaea* (SBT 26; London: SCM, 1959).

Mizzi, D., "Miscellaneous Artefacts from the Qumran Caves: An Exploration of Their Significance," in M. Fidanzio (ed.), *The Caves of Qumran: Proceedings of the International Conference, Lugano 2014* (STDJ 118; Leiden: Brill, 2016) 137-60.

Mook, W.G., *Introduction to Isotope Hydrology: Stable and Radioactive Isotopes of Hydrogen, Carbon, and Oxygen* (London: Taylor and Francis, 2006).

Mook, W.G. and J. van der Plicht, "Reporting ^{14}C Activities and Concentrations," *Radiocarbon* 41/3 (1999) 227-39.

Mook, W.G. and H.J. Streurman, "Physical and Chemical Aspects of Radiocarbon Dating," in W.G. Mook and H.T. Waterbolk (ed.), *Proceedings of the First International Symposium ^{14}C and Archaeology, Groningen 1981* (PACT 8; Strasbourg: Conseil de l'Europe, 1983) 31-55.

Morrell, A., *The ATN Guide to Structural Sewing: Terms and Techniques* (Manchester: Manchester Polytechnic, 1990).

Müller, M. et al., "Identification of Ancient Textile Fibres from Khirbet Qumran Caves Using Synchrotron Radiation Microbeam Diffraction," *Spectrochimica Acta Part B: Atomic Spectroscopy* 59/10-11 (2004) 1669-74.

Nenner-Soriano, R., "Metal Artifacts," in H. Geva (ed.), *Jewish Quarter Excavations in the Old City of Jerusalem Conducted by Nahman Avigad, 1969-1982: Vol. 4: The Burnt House of Area B and Other Studies: Final Report* (Jerusalem: Israel Exploration Society/Hebrew University, 2010) 248-60.

Nenner-Soriano, R., "Metal Artifacts from the Cardo and the Nea Church," in O. Gutfeld (ed.), *Jewish Quarter Excavations in the Old City of Jerusalem conducted by Nahman Avigad, 1969-1982: Vol. 5: The Cardo (Area X) and the Nea Church (Areas D and T): Final Report* (Jerusalem: Israel Exploration Society/Hebrew University, 2012) 426-36.

Nenner-Soriano, R., "The Metal Artifacts from the Hasmonean and Herodian Palaces at Jericho and Cypros," in R. Bar-Nathan and J. Gärtner (ed.), *Hasmonean and Herodian Palaces at Jericho: Final Reports of the 1973-1987 Excavations: Vol. 5: The Finds from Jericho and Cypros* (Jerusalem: Israel Exploration Society/Hebrew University, 2013) 270-84.

Nir-El, Y. and M. Broshi, "The Red Ink of the Dead Sea Scrolls," *Archaeometry* 38/1 (1996) 97-102.

Pace, T.D., *A Typology of Roman Locks and Keys* (MA thesis; Southwestern Baptist Theological Seminary, 2014).

Patrich, J., "Khirbet Qumran in the Light of New Archaeological Explorations in the Qumran Caves," in M.O. Wise et al. (ed.), *Methods of Investigation of the Dead Sea Scrolls and the Khirbet Qumran Site: Present Realities and Future Prospects* (ANYAS 722; New York: New York Academy of Sciences, 1994) 73-95.

Patrich, J., "Did Extra-Mural Dwelling Quarters exist at Qumran?,"in L.H. Schiffman, E. Tov, and J.C. VanderKam (ed.), *The Dead Sea Scrolls Fifty Years After Their Discovery: Proceedings of the Jerusalem Congress, July 20-25, 1997* (Jerusalem: Israel Exploration Society, 2000) 720–7.

Perrot, A., D. Stökl Ben Ezra, and E.J.C. Tigchelaar, "More Red Ink on the Qumran Manuscript 11Q22," *COMSt Bull* 1/1 (2015) 29-33.

Perrot, J., "Umm Qatafa and Umm Qala'a: Two 'Ghassulian' Caves in the Desert of Judea," *EI* (1992) 100-11.

Pfann, S.J., "249. 4Qpap cryptA Midrash Sefer Moshe," in J.M. Baumgarten et al., *Qumran Cave 4. XXV: Halakhic Texts* (DJD 35; Oxford: Clarendon, 1999) 1-24.

Pfann, S.J., "Cryptic Texts," in Id. and P. Alexander et al., *Qumran Cave 4. XXVI: Cryptic Texts. Miscellanea: Part 1* (DJD 36; Oxford: Clarendon, 2000) 515-700.

Pfann, S.J., "4QcryptA Lunisolar Calendar," in D.M. Gropp, *Wadi Daliyeh II: The Samaria Papyri from Wadi Daliyeh* and M. Bernstein et al., *Qumran Cave 4. XXVIII: Miscellanea: Part 2* (DJD 28; Oxford: Clarendon, 2001) Pls LII-LVIII.

Pfann, S.J., "Preface to the English Edition," in J-B. Humbert and A. Chambon (ed.), *The Excavations of Khirbet Qumran and 'Aïn Feshkha: Synthesis of Roland de Vaux's Field Notes* (NTOA. SA 1B; trans. and rev. S.J. Pfann; Fribourg/Göttingen: Éditions Universitaires/Vandenhoeck & Ruprecht, 2003) xv-xviii.

Pfann, S.J., "Reassessing the Judean Desert Caves: Libraries, Archives, Genizas and Hiding Places," *BAIAS* 25 (2007) 147-70.

Pfann, S.J. and M. Kister, "298. 4QcryptA Words of the Maskil to All Sons of Dawn," in T. Elgvin et al., *Qumran Cave 4. XV: Sapiential Texts: Part 1* (DJD 20; Oxford: Clarendon, 1997) 1-30.

Poole, J.B. and R. Reed. "The Preparation of Leather and Parchment by the Dead Sea Scrolls Community," *Technology and Culture* 3/1 (1962) 1-26.

Poot, A.A.H. "Chemical Bleaching of Ancient Textiles," *Studies in Conservation* 9 (1964) 53-64.

Popović, M., "Qumran as Scroll Storehouse in Times of Crisis? A Comparative Perspective on Judaean Desert Manuscript Collections," *JSJ* 43 (2012) 551-94.

Porat, R., H. Eshel, and A. Frumkin, "The 'Caves of the Spear': Refuge Caves from the Bar-Kokhba Revolt North of 'En-Gedi," *IEJ* 59 (2009) 21-46.

Puech, E., "Notes sur le manuscrit de 11QMelkîsédeq," *RdQ* 12/48 (1987) 483-513.

Puech, E., "Notes en marge de 11QpaléoLévitique: Le fragment L, des fragments inédits et une jarre de la Grotte 11," *RB* 96 (1989) 161-83.

Puech, E., "L'alphabet cryptique A en 4QSe (4Q259)," *RdQ* 18/71 (1998) 429-35.

Puech, E., "Note additionnelle sur le fragment paléo-hébreu," *RdQ* 19/75 (2000) 449-51.

Puech, E., "Review of Ulrich Dahmen: *Psalmen- und Psalter-Rezeption*," *RdQ* 22/86 (2005) 279-81.

Puech, E., *Qumrân Grotte 4. XXVII: Textes araméens: Deuxième partie* (DJD 37; Oxford: Clarendon, 2009).

Puech, E., “La Lettre essénienne MMT dans le manuscrit 4Q397 et les parallèles,” *RdQ* 27/105 (2015) 99-135.

Puech, E., “Édition et reconstruction des manuscrits,” in *Nuove luci sulla Bibbia e l’Ebraismo: i manoscritti di Qumran a settant’anni dalla scoperta (1947-2017) e il Sefer Torah della Biblioteca Universitaria di Bologna, Ravenna, 20 settembre, Bologna, 21-22 settembre 2016*, *Hen* 39 (2017) 105-25.

Puech, E., “Le livre des *Juges* dans les copies qumraniennes (*4Q559* 4-6, *1Q6, 4Q49-50-50^a^*),” *RB* 124 (2017) 342-68.

Qimron, E., *The Temple Scroll: A Critical Edition with Extensive Reconstructions* (Beer Sheva/Jerusalem: Ben Gurion University of the Negev Press/Israel Exploration Society, 1996).

Qimron, E., *The Dead Sea Scrolls: The Hebrew Writings: Vols 1-3* (Jerusalem: Yad Ben Zvi, 2010, 2013, 2015).

Rabin, I., “Archaeometry of the Dead Sea Scrolls,” *DSD* 20 (2013) 124-42.

Rabin, I. et al., “Analysis of an Antique Alum Tawed Parchment,” in E. Janssen et al. (ed.), *Proceedings of the Joint Interim Meeting Multidisciplinary Conservation: A Holistic View for Historic Interiors, Rome 23-26 March 2010* (ICOM-CC, 2010), http://www.icom-cc.org/54/document/analysis-of-an-antique-alum-tawed-parchment/?id=795#.XCOKRC2h10s.

Rafael, K., “The Metal Objects,” in J. Patrich (ed.), *Archaeological Excavations at Caesarea Maritima: Areas CC, KK and NN: Final Reports: Vol. 1: The Objects* (Jerusalem: Israel Exploration Society, 2008) 433-69.

Rasmussen, K.L. et al., “Cleaning and Radiocarbon Dating of Material from Khirbet Qumran,” in J. Gunneweg, C. Greenblatt, and A. Adriaens (ed.), *Bio- and Material Cultures at Qumran: Papers from a COST Action G8 Working Group Meeting Held in Jerusalem, Israel on 22-23 May 2005* (Stuttgart: Fraunhofer IRB, 2005) 139-64.

Reed, S.A., *The Dead Sea Scrolls Catalogue: Documents, Photographs and Museum Inventory Numbers* (SBL RBS 32; ed. and rev. M.J. Lundberg with the collaboration of M.B. Phelps; Atlanta: Scholars, 1994).

Rees, S., “Agriculture,” in L. Allason-Jones (ed.), *Artefacts in Roman Britain: Their Purpose and Use* (Cambridge: Cambridge University Press, 2011) 89-113.

Reimer, P.J. et al., “IntCal13 and Marine13 Radiocarbon Age Calibration Curves 0-50,000 Years cal BP,” *Radiocarbon* 55/4 (2013) 1869-87.

Rosenthal-Heginbotham, R., “‘A Man Must Not Go Out with a Nail-Studded Sandal’: Footwear in Jewish Sources and from Archaeological Remains,” in A. De Moor, C. Fluck, and P. Linscheid (ed.), *Drawing the Threads Together: Textiles and Footwear of the 1st Millennium AD from Egypt* (Tielt, Lannoo Publishers, 2013) 268-75.

Russell, K.W., “The Earthquake Chronology of Palestine and Northwest Arabia from the 2nd through the Mid-8th Century A.D.,” *BASOR* 260 (1985) 37-59.

Sanders, J.A., “The Scroll of Psalms (11QPss) from Cave 11: A Preliminary Report,” *BASOR* 165 (1962) 11-5.

Sanders, J.A., *The Psalms Scroll of Qumrân Cave 11 (11QPs^a)* (DJD 4; Oxford: Clarendon, 1965).

Sanders. J.A., *The Dead Sea Psalms Scroll* (Ithaca, NY: Cornell University Press, 1967).

Sanders, J.A., "The Modern History of the Qumran Psalms Scroll and Canonical Criticism," in S.M. Paul et al. (ed.), *Emanuel: Studies in Hebrew Bible, Septuagint, and Dead Sea Scrolls in Honor of Emanuel Tov* (VTSup 94; Leiden: Brill, 2003) 393-411.

Schick, T., "The Early Basketry and Textiles from Cave in the Northern Judean Desert," *'Atiqot* 41 (2002) 223-39.

Schøyen, M., "Acquisition and Ownership History: A Personal Reflection," in T. Elgvin, K. Davis, and M. Langlois (ed.), *Gleanings from the Caves: Dead Sea Scrolls and Artefacts from the Schøyen Collection* (LSTS 71; London: Bloomsbury T&T Clark, 2016) 25-31.

Shah, I., *Oriental Magic* (London: Octagon, 1956).

Shamir, O., "Textiles, Basketry, and Cordage from 'En Rahel," *'Atiqot* 38 (1999) 91-123.

Shamir, O., "Textiles, Basketry, Cordage and Whorls from Mo'a (Moje Awad)," *'Atiqot* 50 (2005) 99-152.

Shamir, O., *Textile in the Land of Israel from the Roman Period till the Early Islamic Period in the Light of the Archaeological Find* (PhD. diss., Hebrew University, 2006).

Shamir, O., "Textiles, Basketry, Cordage and Fruits from 'En Tamar: Preliminary Report," in P. Bienkowski and K. Galor, *Crossing the Rift: Resources, Settlements, Patterns and Interaction in the Wadi Arabah* (LSS 3; Oxford: Oxbow, 2006) 191-4.

Shamir, O., "Organic Materials," in D. Ariel (ed.), *The Dead Sea Scrolls* (Exhibition Catalogue; Jerusalem: Israel Antiquities Authority, 2008) 116-33.

Shamir, O., "Textiles from the Chalcolithic Period, Early and Middle Bronze Age in the Southern Levant - The Continuation of Splicing," *ATR* 57 (2015) 12-25.

Shamir, O., "A Burial Textile from the First Century CE in Jerusalem Compared to Roman Textiles in the Land of Israel and the Turin Shroud," *SHS Web of Conferences* 15 (2015).

Shamir, O., "Egyptian and Nubian Textiles from Qasr el-Yahud, 9th century AD," in A. De Moor, C. Fluck, and P. Linscheid (ed.), *Textiles, Tools and Techniques of the 1st millennium AD from Egypt and Neighbouring Countries: Proceedings of the 8th Conference of the Research Group "Textiles from the Nile Valley", Antwerp, 4-6 October 2013* (Tielt: Lannoo, 2015) 48-60.

Shamir, O., "Textile Trade to Palestine in the Roman Period," in K. Droß-Krüpe and M.-L. Nosch (ed.), *Textiles, Trade and Theories from the Ancient Near East to the Mediterranean* (Münster: Ugarit-Verlag, 2016) 231-45.

Shamir, O. and A. Baginski, "The Later Textiles, Basketry and Cordage from Caves in the Judean Desert," *'Atiqot* 14 (1993) 241-55.

Shamir, O. and A. Baginski, "Textile Hoard from Jericho Cave 38 in the Qarantal Cliff," in O. Guri-Rimon (ed.), *Hoards and Genizot as Chapters in History* (Haifa: Hecht Museum, University of Haifa, 2013) 76*-77*.

Shamir, O. and A. Baginski, "The Earliest Cotton Ikat Textiles from Naḥal 'Omer Israel 650-810 CE," in M.-L. Nosch, Z. Feng, and L. Varadarajan (ed.), *Global Textile Encounters* (ATS 20; Oxford: Oxbow, 2014) 65-73.

Shamir, O. and S.A. Rosen, "Early Bronze Age Textiles from the Ramon I Rock Shelter in the Central Negev," *IEJ* 65 (2015) 129-39.

Shamir, O. and T. Schick "Chalcolithic to Medieval Textiles from the Judean Desert Caves Survey," in O. Peleg-Barkat et al. (ed.), *Between Sea and Desert: On Kings, Nomads, Cities and Monks: Essays in Honor of Joseph Patrich* (Tzemach: Kinneret Institute for Galilean Archaeology, forthcoming).

Shamir, O. and N. Sukenik, "The Christmas Cave Textiles Compared to Qumran Textiles," *ATN* 51 (2010) 26-30.

Shamir, O. and N. Sukenik, "Qumran Textiles and the Garments of Qumran's Inhabitants," *DSD* 18 (2011) 206-25.

Sheffer, A. and H. Granger-Taylor, "Textiles from Masada: A Preliminary Selection," in J. Aviram, G. Foerster, and E. Netzer (ed.), *Masada IV: The Yigael Yadin Excavations 1963-1965: Final Reports* (Jerusalem: Israel Exploration Society/Hebrew University, 1994) 149-256.

Sheffer, A. and A. Tidhar, "The Textiles from 'En-Boqeq Excavation in Israel," *Textile History* 22/1 (1991) 3-46.

Shor, P. et al., "The Leon Levy Dead Sea Scrolls Digital Library: The Digitization Project of the Dead Sea Scrolls," *JEMAHS* 2/2 (2014) 71-89.

Siegel, J.P., "The Employment of Palaeo-Hebrew Characters for the Divine Names at Qumran in the Light of Tannaitic Sources," *HUCA* 42 (1971) 159-72.

Skehan, P.W., E. Ulrich, and P.W Flint, "86. 4QPs^{d}," in E. Ulrich et al., *Qumran Cave 4. XI: Psalms to Chronicles* (DJD 16; Oxford: Clarendon, 2000) 63-71.

Soriga, E., "A Diachronic View on Fulling Technology in the Mediterranean and the Ancient Near East: Tools, Raw Materials and Natural Resources for the Finishing of Textiles," in S. Gaspa, C. Michel, and M.-L. Nosch (ed.), *Textile Terminologies from the Orient to the Mediterranean and Europe, 1000 BC to 1000 AD* (Lincoln, NE: Zea, 2017) 24-46.

Stegemann, H., *The Library of Qumran: On the Essenes, Qumran, John the Baptist, and Jesus* (Grand Rapids, MI: Eerdmans, 1998).

Stökl Ben Ezra, D., "Old Caves and Young Caves: A Statistical Reevaluation of a Qumran Consensus," *DSD* 14 (2007) 313-33.

Stökl Ben Ezra, D., "Further Reflections on Caves 1 and 11: A Response to Florentino García Martínez," in C. Hempel (ed.), *The Dead Sea Scrolls: Texts and Context* (STDJ 90; Leiden: Brill, 2010) 211-23.

Sukenik, N., *Dyes in Textiles from the Early Roman Period Found in the Judean Desert Caves: Chemical, Historical and Archaeological Aspects* (PhD diss.; Ramat Gan: Bar-Ilan University, 2013) (Hebrew).

Sukenik, N., "The Temple Scroll Wrapper from Cave 11: MS 5095/2, MS 5095/4, MS 5095/1," in T. Elgvin, K. Davis, and M. Langlois (ed.), *Gleanings from the Caves: Dead Sea Scrolls and Artefacts from the Schøyen Collection* (LSTS 71; London: Bloomsbury T&T Clark, 2016) 339-50.

Sukenik, N. et al., "Chemical Analysis of Murex-Dyed Textiles from Wadi Murabba'at, Israel," *JASR* 3 (2015) 565-70.

Sukenik, N. et al., "A Re-Evaluation of the Textile Dyes in the Cave of Letters," in J. Ortiz et al., *Textiles, Basketry and Dyes in the Ancient Mediterranean World: Proceedings of the Vth International Symposium on Textiles and Dyes in the Ancient Mediterranean World (Montserrat, 19-22 March, 2014)* (Purpureae Vestes V: Textiles and Dyes in Antiquity; Valencia: Universitat de València, 2016) 263-73.

Sukenik, N. et al., "Early Evidence (Late 2nd millennium BCE) of Plant-Based Dyeing of Textiles from Timna, Israel," *PLOS ONE* 12/6 (2017).

Sukenik, N. et al., "New Evidence of the Purple-Dye Industry at Tel Shiqmona, Israel," *Archaeometry* 59/4 (2017) 775-85.

Taylor, J.E., *The Essenes, the Scrolls and the Dead Sea* (Oxford: Oxford University Press, 2012).

Taylor, J.E., "Buried Manuscripts and Empty Tombs: The Qumran *Genizah* Theory Revisited," in A.M. Maeir, J. Magness, and L.H. Schiffman (ed.), *"Go Out and Study the Land" (Judges 18:2): Archaeological, Historical and Textual Studies in Honor of Hanan Eshel* (JSJSup 148; Leiden: Brill, 2012) 269-315.

Taylor, J.E., "The Qumran Caves in Their Regional Context: A Chronological Review with a Focus on Bar Kokhba Assemblages," in M. Fidanzio (ed.), *The Caves of Qumran: Proceedings of the International Conference, Lugano 2014* (STDJ 118; Leiden: Brill, 2016) 9-33.

Taylor, J.E. and J. van der Plicht, "Radiocarbon Dating of the Temple Scroll Wrapper and Cave 11Q," in T. Elgvin, K. Davis, and M. Langlois (ed.), *Gleanings from the Caves: Dead Sea Scrolls and Artefacts from the Schøyen Collection* (LSTS 71; London: Bloomsbury T&T Clark, 2016) 351-6.

Taylor, J.E. et al., "Qumran Textiles in the Palestine Exploration Fund, London: Radiocarbon Dating Results," *PEQ* 137 (2005) 159-67.

Tigchelaar, E.J.C., "Some More Small 11Q1 Fragments," *RdQ* 18/70 (1997) 325-30.

Tigchelaar, E.J.C., "Assessing Emanuel Tov's 'Qumran Scribal Practice'," in S. Metso, H. Najman, and E. Schuller (ed.), *The Dead Sea Scrolls: Transmission of Traditions and Production of Texts* (STDJ 92; Leiden: Brill, 2010) 173-207.

Tigchelaar, E.J.C., "Notes on the Three Qumran-Type Yadin Fragments Leading to a Discussion of Identification, Attribution, Provenance, and Names," *DSD* 19 (2012) 198-214.

Tigchelaar, E.J.C., "A Provisional List of Unprovenanced, Twenty-First Century, Dead Sea Scrolls-like Fragments," *DSD* 24 (2017) 173-88.

Tigchelaar, E.J.C., "The Yadin Qumran Fragment XQ5b (XQText B) Identified as a Fragment of 4Q285 (4QSefer ha-Milḥamah)," *RdQ* 29/110 (2017) 281-6.

Tov, E., "Lists of the Texts from the Judaean Desert," in Id. (ed.), *The Texts from the Judaean Desert: Indices and an Introduction to the Discoveries in the Judaean Desert Series* (DJD 39; Oxford: Clarendon, 2002) 27-114.

Tov, E., *Scribal Practices and Approaches Reflected in the Texts Found in the Judean Desert* (STDJ 54; Leiden: Brill, 2004).

Tov, E., "The Special Character of the Texts Found in Qumran Cave 11," in E. Chazon, D. Satran, and R. Clements (ed.), *Things Revealed: Studies in Early Jewish and Christian Literature in Honor of Michael E. Stone* (JSJSup 89; Leiden: Brill, 2004) 187-96.

Tov, E., *Revised Lists of the Texts from the Judaean Desert* (Leiden: Brill, 2010).

Trachtenberg, J., *Jewish Magic and Superstition: A Study in Folk Religion* (New York: Behrman's Jewish Book House, 1939).

Ulrich, E., "Identification of a Scribe Active at Qumran: 1QPs^{b}-4QIsa^{c}-11QM," *Meghillot* 5-6 (2008) *201-*10.

Ulrich, E., *The Biblical Qumran Scrolls: Transcriptions and Textual Variants* (VTSup 134; Leiden: Brill, 2010).

Ulrich, R.B., *Roman Woodworking* (New Haven: Yale University Press, 2007).

van der Plicht, J., "Radiocarbon Dating and the Dead Sea Scrolls: A Comment on 'Redating'," *DSD* 14 (2007) 77-89.

van der Plicht, J. and K.L. Rasmussen, "Radiocarbon Dating and Qumran," in J. Gunneweg, A. Adriaens, and J. Dik (ed.), *Holistic Qumran: Trans-Disciplinary Research of Qumran and the Dead Sea Scrolls: Proceedings of the NIAS-Lorentz Center Qumran Workshop 21-25 April 2008* (STDJ 87; Leiden: Brill, 2010) 99-121.

van der Plicht, J. et al., "Status Report: The Groningen AMS facility," *NIM B* 172 (2000) 58-65.

van der Ploeg, J.P.M., "L'édition des manuscrits de la Grotte XI de Qumrân par l'Académie Royale des Sciences des Pays-Bas," in P.W. Pestman (ed.), *Acta Orientalia Neerlandica: Proceedings of the Congress of the Dutch Oriental Society Held in Leiden on the Occasion of its 50th Anniversary, 8th-9th May 1970* (Leiden: Brill, 1971) 43-5.

van der Ploeg, J.P.M., "Une halakha inédite de Qumrân," in M. Delcor (ed.), *Qumran, sa piété, sa théologie et son milieu* (BETL 46; Paris-Gembloux/Leuven: Duculot/Leuven University Press, 1978) 107-13.

van der Ploeg, J.P.M., "Les manuscrits de la Grotte XI de Qumrân," *RdQ* 12/45 (1985) 3-15.

van der Ploeg, J.P.M., "Fragments de Psaumes de Qumrân," in Z.J. Kapera (ed.), *Intertestamental Essays in Honour of Józef Tadeusz Milik* (Qumranica Mogilanensia 6; Kraków: Enigma, 1992) 233-7.

van Styrdonck, M. et al., "What's in a ^{14}C Date?," in J. Evin (ed.), *Actes du 3ème Congrès International ^{14}C et Archéologie, Lyon, 6-10 avril 1998* (Paris: Société Préhistorique Française, 1999) 433-48.

VanderKam, J.C., *The Book of Jubilees* (CSCO 510-511/Scriptores Æthiopici 87-88; Leuven: Peeters, 1989).

de Vaux, R., "Fouilles de Khirbet Qumrân: rapport préliminaire sur les 3ᵉ, 4ᵉ, et 5ᵉ campagnes," *RB* 63 (1956) 533-77.

de Vaux, R., "Une hachette essénienne?," *VT* 9 (1959) 399-407.

de Vaux, R., "Archéologie," in P. Benoit, J.T. Milik, and R. de Vaux, *Les Grottes de Murabba'ât* (DJD 2; Oxford: Clarendon, 1961) 3-50.

de Vaux, R., "Préface," in M. Baillet, J.T. Milik, and R. de Vaux, *Les 'petites grottes' de Qumrân: Exploration de la falaise. Les grottes 2Q, 3Q, 5Q, 6Q, 7Q à 10Q. Le rouleau de cuivre* (DJD 3; Oxford: Clarendon, 1962) v.

de Vaux, R., "Archéologie," in M. Baillet, J.T. Milik, and R. de Vaux, *Les 'petites grottes' de Qumrân: Exploration de la falaise. Les grottes 2Q, 3Q, 5Q, 6Q, 7Q à 10Q. Le rouleau de cuivre* (DJD 3; Oxford: Clarendon, 1962) 3-36.

de Vaux, R., *Archaeology and the Dead Sea Scrolls* (The Schweich Lectures 1959; London: Oxford University Press for the British Academy, 1973).

Wagemakers, B. and J.E. Taylor, "New Photographs of the Qumran Excavations from 1954 and Interpretations of L.77 and L.86," *PEQ* 143 (2011) 134-56.

Wampler, J.C., "Three Cistern Groups from Tell el-Naṣbeh," *BASOR* 92 (1941) 25-43.

White, K.D., *Agricultural Implements of the Roman World* (Cambridge: Cambridge University Press, 1967).

White Crawford, S., "Qumran: Caves, Scrolls, and Buildings," in E.F. Mason (ed.), *A Teacher for All Generations: Essays in Honor of James C. VanderKam* (JSJSup 153; Leiden: Brill, 2011) 253-73.

White Crawford, S., "The Qumran Collection as a Scribal Library," in S. White Crawford and C. Wassen (ed.), *The Dead Sea Scrolls at Qumran and the Concept of a Library* (STDJ 116; Leiden: Brill, 2016) 109-31.

Wild, J.P., *Textile Manufacture in the Northern Roman Provinces* (Cambridge: Cambridge University Press, 1970).

Wild, J.P., *Textiles in Archaeology* (Princes Risborough/Aylesbury/Bucks, UK: Shire, 1988).

Wild, J.P. and F. Wild, "Berenike and Textile Trade on the Indian Ocean," in K. Droß-Krüpe (ed.), *Textile Trade and Distribution in Antiquity / Textilhandel Und -Distribution in Der Antike* (Wiesbaden: Harrassowitz, 2014) 91-110.

Wolfe, L.M. et al., "Psalm 11:1-4 (Inv. MOTB.SCR.000121)," in E. Tov, K. Davis, and R. Duke (ed.), *Dead Sea Scrolls Fragments in the Museum Collection* (PMB 1; Leiden: Brill, 2016) 190-9.

Woods, C.S., "The Conservation of Parchment," in M. Kite and R. Thomson (ed.), *Conservation of Leather and Related Materials* (Oxford: Elsevier, 2006) 200-24.

Wouters, J., "High Performance Liquid Chromatography of Anthraquinones: Analysis of Plant and Insect Extracts and Dyed Textiles," *Studies in Conservation* 30 (1985) 119-28.

Xia, N., *Ancient Egyptian Beads* (Heidelberg: Springer, 2014).

Yadin, Y., *The Finds from the Bar Kokhba Period in the Cave of Letters* (Jerusalem: Israel Exploration Society, 1963).

Yadin, Y., "Another Fragment (E) of the Psalms Scroll from Qumran Cave 11 (11QPs[a])," *Textus* 5 (1966) 1-10, Pls 1-5.

Yadin, Y., מגלת המקדש - *The Temple Scroll: Vols 1-3 and Suppl.* (Jerusalem : Israel Exploration Society, 1977 [Hebrew] / 1983 [English]).

Yahalom-Mack, N. and A. Mazar, "Various Finds from the Iron Age II Strata in Areas P and S," in A. Mazar (ed.), *Excavations at Tel Beth-Shean 1989-1996: Vol. 1: From the Late Bronze Age IIB to the Medieval Period* (Jerusalem: Israel Exploration Society/Hebrew University, 2006) 468-504.

Yaniv, B., "From Spain to the Balkans: Textile Torah Scroll Accessories in the Sephardi Communities of the Balkans," *Sefarad* 66/2 (2006) 407-42.

Yardeni, A., "A Note on a Qumran Scribe," in M. Lubetski (ed.), *New Seals and Inscriptions, Hebrew, Idumean and Cuneiform* (HBM 8; Sheffield: Phoenix, 2007) 287-98.

Yezerski, I., "Pottery of Stratum V," in E. Stern, *En-Gedi Excavations I: Final Report (1961-1965)* (Jerusalem: Hebrew University, 2007) 86-129.

Zimhoni, O., "The Pottery," in V. Fritz and A. Kempinski, *Ergebnisse der Ausgrabungen auf der Hirbet el-Msas (Tel Masos) 1972-1975* (Wiesbaden: Harrassowitz, 1983) 127-30.

Zimhoni, O., "The Pottery of Levels III and II," in D. Ussishkin (ed.), *The Renewed Archaeological Excavations at Lachish (1973-1994): Vol. 4* (MSSMNIA 22; Tel Aviv: Emery and Claire Yass Publications in Archaeology, 2004) 1789-899.

Zohary, D., M. Hopf, and E. Weiss, *Domestication of Plants in the Old World* (Oxford: Oxford University Press, [4]2013).

Zuckerman, B. and S.A. Reed, "A Fragment of an Unstudied Column of 11QtgJob: A Preliminary Report," *CAL News* 10 (1993) 1-7.

Index of Materials from Cave 11Q

Manuscript Fragments

11Q1 paleoLev[a] 10, 179, 180, 209, 210, 227, 228, 229, 238, 249, 250, 254
11Q2 Lev[b] 210, 211, 212, 216, 219, 229, 231, 238, 239, 246, 249
11Q3 Deut 241, 246, 249
11Q4 Ezek 178, 216, 229, 235, 249, 250, 254
11Q5 Ps[a] 121, 179, 180, 208, 220, 240, 242, 243, 246, 247, 249, 250, 251, 253, 254, 255
11Q6 Ps[b] 216, 222, 229, 231, 249, 253, 254, 255
11Q7 Ps[c] 182, 184, 213, 222, 229, 249, 252, 254, 255
11Q8 Ps[d] 216, 217, 219, 220, 221, 229, 231, 236, 245, 249, 251, 253, 254, 260
11Q9 Ps[e]? 207, 249
11Q10 tgJob 179, 181, 221, 249, 250, 251, 252, 255
11Q11 apocrPs 179, 181, 214, 220, 221, 231, 237, 245, 249, 250, 251, 255
11Q12 Jub 214, 241, 246, 249, 251, 252
11Q13 Melch 182, 184, 188, 231, 249, 255, 258
11Q14 Sefer ha-Milhamah 182, 212, 229, 249, 258
11Q15 Hymns[a] 249, 255, 258
11Q16 Hymns[b] 216, 249, 251
11Q17 ShirShabb 179, 181, 182, 185, 229, 231, 237, 239, 246, 249, 250, 255
11Q18 NJ ar 181, 182, 185, 186, 217, 218, 229, 239, 249, 250, 255, 258
11Q19 T[a] x, 115, 147, 152, 153, 156, 179, 180, 213, 215, 216, 217, 218, 219, 221, 229, 235, 240, 242, 246, 249, 250, 252, 253, 254, 257, 259, 261
11Q20 T[b] 182, 183, 214, 215, 217, 218, 219, 221, 229, 231, 235, 242, 246, 249, 251, 255, 257, 261
11Q21 T[c]? 235, 242, 246, 249, 257
11Q22 paleoUnidentified Text 1x, 88, 205, 206, 207, 208, 229, 231, 237, 238, 245, 249, 251, 253, 255
11Q23 cryptA Unidentified Text 222, 223, 224, 229, 249
11Q24 Unidentified Text ar 185, 224, 229, 249, 255, 258
11Q25 Unidentified Text A 229, 231, 249
11Q26 Unidentified Text B 229, 249
11Q27 Unidentified Text C 229, 249, 258
11Q28 papUnidentified Text D 226, 227, 228, 229, 249
11Q29 Fragment Related to Serekh ha-Yahad 229, 249, 257, 258
11Q30 Unclassified frags 190, 209, 229, 231, 249
11Q31 Unidentified wads 229, 249

Pottery

Gr11Q1 10, 22, 35, 88, 94
Gr 11Q5 35, 90, 95, 136
Gr11Q7 35, 91, 95, 136
Gr11Q8 90, 95, 136
Gr11Q13 91, 96, 173

Gr11Q14 90, 95
Gr11Q15 89, 90, 95
Gr11Q16 91, 96
Gr11Q17 92, 96
Gr11Q18 92, 96
Gr11Q38 92, 96
Gr11Q42 90, 95
Gr11Q49 91, 96
P11Q1 88, 94
P11Q2 92, 96
Jar Kando 393 8, 60, 63, 87, 88, 93
Lid Kando 8, 63, 88, 93

Metals
Gr11Q2 35, 158, 159, 160, 161, 163
Gr11Q3 161, 162, 163, 171, 176
Gr11Q4 35, 163, 164, 165
Gr11Q6 34, 157, 158, 160, 161, 165, 166, 167, 168, 169, 175
Gr11Q10 35, 136, 169, 170, 171, 173
Gr11Q11 35, 136, 160, 161, 165, 168, 169, 171, 172, 173, 175, 176

Stone objects
Gr11Q12 35, 136, 171, 173, 174

Textiles
Gr11Q25 (= 864394 = D027) 112, 127, 131
Gr11Q26 (= D028) 101, 102, 103, 106, 116
Gr11Q27 (= D029) 106
Gr11Q28 (= D030) 106
Gr11Q29 (= D031) 99, 100, 103, 106
Gr11Q30 (= D032) 112
Gr11Q31a (= D033a) 102, 103, 104, 106, 115, 123
Gr11Q31b (= D033b) 104, 106, 115, 155
Gr11Q32 (= D034) 103, 105, 106, 112
Gr11Q33 (= D035) 99, 100, 106
Gr11Q34 (= D038) 106
Gr11Q35 (= D037) 112, 155
Gr11Q36a (= D036a) 99, 100, 102, 103, 106, 115
Gr11Q36b (= D036b) 99, 100, 102,106
Gr11Q36c (= D036c) 99, 100, 102, 103, 106
Gr11Q37 (= D039) 106
Gr11Q39 (= D041) 101, 106
Gr11Q40a (= D042a) 106
Gr11Q40b (= D042b) 106
Gr11Q41 (= D043) 101, 106, 155
Gr11Q43 (= D045) 112
Gr11Q44 (= D046) 106
Gr11Q45 (= D066) 106
Gr11Q46a (= D079a) 106
Gr11Q46b (= D079b) 105, 107, 116
Gr11Q47/a (= D080a1) 112
Gr11Q47b (= D080a2) 107
Gr11Q48 (= D081) 107
Gr11Q50 (= D084) 99, 100, 107
Gr11Q51 (= D086) 107
Gr11Q52 (= D087) 107
Gr11Q53 (= D088) 107
Gr11Q54 (= D089) 107
Gr11Q55 (= D090) 107
Gr11Q56 (= D091) 107
Gr11Q57 (= D092) 112
Gr11Q58a (= D093a) 102, 107
Gr11Q58b (= D093b) 102, 107
Gr11Q59a1 (= D094A) 107
Gr11Q59a2 (= D094a2) 112
Gr11Q59b (= D094B) 99, 107, 119
Gr11Q60 (= D095) 107
Gr11Q61 (= D096) 107
Gr11Q62 (= D097) 112
Gr11Q63 (= D098) 102, 107
Gr11Q64a (= D114a) 107
Gr11Q64b (= D114b) 112
Gr11Q65 (= D115) 112
Gr11Q66a (= D116A) 105, 112
Gr11Q66b (= D116B) 112
Gr11Q66c (= D116C) 112
Gr11Q66d (= D116D) 112
Gr11Q66e (= D116E) 112
Gr11Q66f (= D116F) 112
Gr11Q66g (= D116G) 112
Gr11Q66h (= D116H) 112
Gr11Q66i (= D116I) 112
Gr11Q66j (= D116J) 112
Gr11Q66k (= D116K) 112
Gr11Q66l (= D116L) 112
Gr11Q67 (= D117) 107
Gr11Q68 (= D119) 102, 107
Gr11Q69 (= D120) 112
Gr11Q70 (= D121) 107
Gr11Q71 (= D122) 107
Gr11Q72 (= D123) 107
Gr11Q73 (= D124) 107
Gr11Q74 (= D125) 101, 107
Gr11Q75 (= D053) 9, 101, 102, 104, 105, 108, 112, 114, 115, 116, 119, 120, 121, 122

Gr11Q76 (= 577220) 99, 100, 108, 148, 151, 152, 155
Gr11Q77 (= 577221) 108
Gr11Q78 (= 577222) 101, 108
Gr11Q79 (= 577223) 108
Gr11Q80 (= 577224) 99, 100, 108
Gr11Q81 (= 577225) 102, 108
Gr11Q82 (= 577226) 108
Gr11Q83 (= 577227) 108
Gr11Q84 (= 577228) 108
Gr11Q85 (= 577229) 102, 108
Gr11Q86 (= 577230) 108
Gr11Q87 (= 577231) 108
Gr11Q88 (= 577232) 108
Gr11Q89 (= 577233) 108
Gr11Q90 (= 577234) 108
Gr11Q91 (= 577235) 108
Gr11Q92 (= 577236) 108
Gr11Q93 (= 577237) 108
Gr11Q94 (= 577238) 108
Gr11Q95 (= 577239) 101, 108
Gr11Q96 (= 577240) 108
Gr11Q97 (= 577241) 108
Gr11Q98 (= 577242) 108
Gr11Q99 (= 577243) 108
Gr11Q100 (= 577244) 108
Gr11Q101 (= 577245) 101, 108, 148, 151, 152, 155
Gr11Q102 (= 577246) 102, 108
Gr11Q103 (= 577247) 108
Gr11Q104 (= 577248) 109
Gr11Q105 (= 577249) 109
Gr11Q106 (= 577251) 109
Gr11Q107 (= 577252) 103, 104, 109, 148, 151, 152, 155
Gr11Q108 (= 577253) 109
Gr11Q109 (= 577254) 109
Gr11Q110 (= 577255) 109
Gr11Q111 (= 577256) 109
Gr11Q112 (= 577257) 109
Gr11Q113 (= 577258) 102, 109
Gr11Q114 (= 577259) 102, 109
Gr11Q115 (= 577260) 109
Gr11Q116 (= 577261) 109
Gr11Q117 (= 577262) 109
Gr11Q118 (= 577263) 109
Gr11Q119 (= 577264) 109, 148, 151, 152, 155
Gr11Q120 (= 577265) 109
Gr11Q121 (= 577280) 101, 109
Gr11Q122 (= 577281) 109
Gr11Q123 (= 577282) 109
Gr11Q124 (= 577284) 103, 109
Gr11Q125 (= 577285) 109
Gr11Q126 (= 577286) 103, 109
Gr11Q127 (= 577287) 109
Gr11Q128 (= 577288) 109
Gr11Q129 (= 577289) 109
Gr11Q130 (= 577290) 109
Gr11Q131 (= 577291) 110
Gr11Q132 (= 577293) 102, 103, 110, 113, 147, 148, 151, 152, 155
Gr11Q133 (= 814794) 110
Gr11Q134 (= 814795) 110
Gr11Q135 (= 814796) 110
Gr11Q136 (= 814798) 110
Gr11Q137 (= 814800) 110
Gr11Q138 (= 814801) 110
Gr11Q139 (= 814802) 110
Gr11Q140 (= 814805) 110
Gr11Q141 (= 814806) 110
Gr11Q142 (= 814808) 110
Gr11Q143 (= 814809) 110
Gr11Q144 (= 814811) 110
Gr11Q145 (= 814812) 110
Gr11Q146 (= 814813) 110
Gr11Q147 (= 814814) 110
Gr11Q148 (= 814815) 110
Gr11Q149 (= 814816) 110
Gr11Q150 (= 814817) 110
Gr11Q151 (= 814818) 110
Gr11Q152 (= 814819) 110
Gr11Q153 (= 814820) 110
Gr11Q154 (= 814821) 110
Gr11Q155 (= 814822) 110
Gr11Q156 (= 814823) 110
Gr11Q157 (= 814824) 110
Gr11Q158 (= 814825) 110
Gr11Q159 (= 814826) 110
Gr11Q160 (= 814828) 110
Gr11Q161 (= 814829) 110
Gr11Q162 (= 814830) 110
Gr11Q163 (= 814836) 110
Gr11Q164 (= 814841) 110
Gr11Q165 (= 814842) 110
Gr11Q166 (= 814843) 110
Gr11Q167 (= 814844) 110
Gr11Q168 (= 814845) 110
Gr11Q169 (= 814846) 110
Gr11Q170 (= 814847) 110
Gr11Q171 (= 814848) 111
Gr11Q172 (= 814849) 111
Gr11Q173 (= 814850) 111
Gr11Q174 (= 814851) 111
Gr11Q175 (= 814853) 111

Gr11Q176 (= 814854)	111
Gr11Q177 (= 814856)	111
Gr11Q178 (= 814858)	111
Gr11Q179 (= 814859)	104, 105, 111, 112, 116
Gr11Q180 (= 816288)	111
Gr11Q181 (= 55)	111
Gr11Q182 (= 567)	111
Gr11Q183 (= 988)	111
Gr11Q184 (= 1030A1)	111
Gr11Q185 (= 1030A2)	111
Gr11Q186 (= 1030A5)	111
Gr11Q187 (= 1030A6)	111
Gr11Q188 (= 1032A-2)	111
Gr11Q189 (= 1034A)	99, 111, 119
Gr11Q190 (= 577292)	112
Gr11Q191 (= 814827)	112
Gr11Q192 (= 814807)	112
Gr11Q195 (= D054)	111
Gr11Q196 (= D083)	111
Gr11Q197 (= 814852)	112
Gr11Q198 (= 577250)	112, 148, 150, 151, 155
Gr11Q199 (= 864407)	104, 112, 116
P11Q3 (= B2 no. 1)	111
P11Q4 (= B2 no. 2)	111
P11Q5 (= B2 no. 3)	111
P11Q6 (= B2 no. 4)	111
P11Q7 (= B2 no. 5)	111
P11Q8 (= B2 no. 6)	111
P11Q9 (= B2 no. 7)	111
P11Q10 (= B1 no. 1)	111
P11Q11 (= B1 no. 2)	112
FB11Q1 (= B201.F1)	78, 94, 111
FB11Q2 (= B201.F23)	78, 111
MS 5095/2, MS 5095/4, MS 5095/1(*Temple Scroll Wrapper*)	x, 7, 9, 97, 102, 104, 116, 119, 122, 126, 148, 151, 152, 153, 155, 156

Organic materials

Gr11Q9/1 (= 464628)	127, 131, 135, 136, 137, 138, 139, 140, 141, 143, 144, 145, 148, 150, 151, 155
Gr11Q9/2 (= 464629)	127, 131, 135, 136, 138, 139, 140, 141, 143, 144, 145, 148, 150, 151, 155
Gr11Q20a (= 864398)	125, 130
Gr11Q20b (= 864398)	125, 130
Gr11Q20c (= 864398)	125, 130
Gr11Q21a (= 864363)	126, 130
Gr11Q21b (= 864362)	126, 130
Gr11Q21c (= 870772)	130
Gr11Q21d (= 870782)	126, 131
Gr11Q22a (= 864395 = D024)	128, 133, 154
Gr11Q22b (= 864397 = D024)	128, 132
Gr11Q22c (= 864396 = D024)	128, 132, 154
Gr11Q200 (= 870781)	125, 130
Gr11Q201 (= 477617)	131
Gr11Q202 (= 351300)	127, 131
Gr11Q203 (= 351301)	127, 132
Gr11Q204 (= 864358)	127, 132
Gr11Q205 (= 864357)	127, 132
Gr11Q206 (= 864359)	127, 132
Gr11Q207 (= 447618)	128, 133
Gr11Q208 (= 848775)	128, 133
Gr11Q209 (= 848771)	129, 133
FB11Q3	78, 128, 133
FB11Q4	78, 129, 133
FB11Q5 (= B201.F2)	78, 128, 133
FB11Q6 (= B201.F21)	78

Index of Modern Authors

A

Ableman, Oren x, 179, 185, 201, 202, 203, 229, 231, 245, 253
Allegro, John M. 12, 19, 43, 44, 191, 192

B

Bahat, Dan ix, 3, 7, 9, 10, 71, 113, 128
Bélis, Mireille x, 7, 10, 97, 128, 147, 199, 251
Brooke, George 4, 7

C

Chambon, Alain 158, 163, 169
de Contenson, Henry 5, 71
Cotton, Hannah 201, 231
Couäsnon, Charles 12, 19
Cross, Frank M. 251, 255, 256, 257, 258
Crowfoot, Grace M. 22, 97, 99, 104, 105, 114, 115, 116, 119, 122

D

Dahmen, Ulrich 253
Davis, Kipp 252
De Pietri, Marco 16, 71
Delprat, Georges 3, 12, 38, 41
Dubovsky, Peter 7
Dudna, Gregory 153

E

Elgvin, Torleif 252
Eshel, Hanan 251, 252, 253
Eshel, Esther 252

F

Fidanzio, Marcello ix, x, 7, 9, 10, 16, 71, 98, 113, 128, 141, 147, 157, 158, 191
Fitzmyer, Joseph A. 24, 191
Freedman, David N. 254

G

Gandz, Solomon 140
García Martínez, Florentino 4, 206, 207, 254, 256, 257
Garofalo, Salvatore 251
Gross, Andrew 254, 255

H

Hayes, Gemma 258
Hanson, Richard S. 254
Harding, Gerald L. 1, 3, 12, 16, 18, 23, 199, 250
Herbert, Edward D. 254
Humbert, Jean-Baptiste ix, 4, 7, 10, 16, 71, 147
Hunzinger,Claus-Hunno 191, 196

L

Lacerenza, Giancarlo x
Lapp, Paul W. 5
Lemaire, André 251, 252
Levi, Gabriel 1
Libman, Lena 185, 239
Lidor, Gilad 71
Lukaszewski, Albert L. 255

M

Magness, Jodi 7
Maifredi, Alessandro 71, 85
Massonnat, Gérard 57
Mathews, Kenneth A. 254
McLean, Mark D. 254
Milik, Józef T. 191, 208, 222, 258
Mizzi, Dennis 7, 147, 191

P

Palleschi, Vincenzo 173
Patrich, Joseph ix, x, 1, 4, 7, 9, 10, 12, 24, 46, 57, 62, 63, 78, 82, 87, 98, 113

Perrot, Antony 255, 258
Pfann, Stephen 16, 223, 256
Plenderleith, Harold J. 178, 182
van der Plicht, Johannes 139, 147
van der Ploeg, Johannes 254, 255, 257
Popović, Mladen 257
Puech, Émile x, 201, 202, 235, 237, 240, 241, 243, 251, 252, 254, 255, 256, 258
Pusterla, Francesco 71

Q
Qimron, Elisha 186, 254, 255, 259, 261

R
Rabin, Ira 259
Rasmussen, Kaare Lund 147
Reed, Stephen 201, 231, 253
Richelle, Matthieu 258
Rottoli, Mauro x, 201, 202, 203, 253
Rousée, Jourdain-Marie 3, 12, 19, 38, 39, 41, 42, 200
Roux, Georges 88, 209, 251, 254

S
Sanders, James A. 179, 253
Schenker, Adrian 4
Schiffman, Lawrence 254
Schick, Alexander 191, 196
Schimdt, Francis 4
Shamir, Orit 7, 127, 147, 153
Shor, Pnina 4
Skehan, Patrick 19, 23
Skory, Giorgio 39
Stegemann, Hartmut 256
Spijkerman, Augustus 22
Starcky, Jean 38, 41
Stökl Ben Ezra, Daniel 156, 256, 258
Strugnell, John 186, 191
Sukenik, Naama 7, 9, 97, 135, 147, 153

T
de Tarragon, Jean-Michel 16
Taylor, Joan 7, 17, 147, 191, 256
Tigchelaar, Eibert x, 185, 201, 206, 207, 231
Tov, Emanuel 4, 188, 249, 251, 252, 256
Tractenberg, Joshua 140

U
Ulrich, Eugene 253, 254, 258

V
de Vaux, Roland ix, x, 1, 3, 4, 5, 6, 7, 8, 9, 10, 11, 12, 19, 22, 23, 24, 25, 26, 27, 28, 38, 41, 42, 43, 45, 46, 48, 51, 52, 55, 57, 59, 60, 61, 62, 63, 64, 65, 73, 78, 79, 82, 87, 98, 113, 125, 128, 135, 136, 156, 157, 158, 160, 161, 163, 165, 169, 171, 173, 175, 199, 200, 203, 209, 229, 250, 251, 253
Viniski, Raia 148, 149

W
Weiss, Sabine 19, 38, 39, 60
White Crawford, Sidnie 256, 257
van der Woude, Adam S. 206, 207, 254

Y
Yadin, Yigael x, 104, 179, 250, 251, 252, 253, 254, 255, 259, 260, 261
Yardeni, Ada 258
Yom-Tov, Yoram 129

Z
Zangenberg, Jürgen 4, 7, 10, 175

Index of Sites and Place Names

A

'Ain Feshkha 5, 17, 18, 19, 23, 65
'Ain Qudeirât *see* Kadesh-Barnea
Amman 11
Anafa, Tel 160
Arad, Tel 90, 91
Arbel 113

B

Beersheva 90, 91
Berenike 103
Beth-Shean 113
Beth She'an Valley 113
Bethlehem 8, 88

C

Cave of Horror 126
Cave of the Letters 99, 126, 127, 160, 171
Cave of the Pool 90
Cave of the Spear 126
Caesarea Marittima 160
Christmas Cave 148, 153

D

Dead Sea 44, 52, 67, 89, 125, 126, 127, 128, 154
Deragot, Nahal 115
Drogarati caves 155

E

Ein Feshkha *see* 'Ain Feshkha
Ein Rachel *see* 'En Rahel
Ein Tamar *see* 'En Tamar
El Deir 103
El Masaia cave 115
'En Boqeq 98
'En Rahel 104, 114, 127
'En Tamar 114, 128

F

Ful, Tell el- 89, 90

G

Galilee 113
Gezer, Tel 89
Ghassul, Tuleilat el- 91
Groningen 150, 258

H

Herculaneum 176
Ḥever, Naḥal 160, 171, 176

I

'Ira, Tell 90

J

Jericho 12, 155
Jerusalem ix, 5, 11, 19, 38, 89, 90, 150, 168, 229
Jordan Valley 113
Judaea 90, 105, 113, 147, 256
Judaean Desert 4, 9, 99, 119, 125, 126, 127, 169, 175
Jurn, Tell el- (Tel Goren) 89, 90

K

Kadesh-Barnea 90, 91
Kalhia 16, 18
Kephalonia 155
Krokodilopolis 103

L

Lachish 91
Lisan (lake) 67

M

Mafjar, Khirbet el 155

Manching 161, 163
Masada 99, 102, 103, 122, 127, 128, 147
Mashash *see* Tel Masos
Masos, Tel 89, 90, 91
Mediterranean 103, 114, 123, 163, 168
Megiddo, Tel 89
Mo'a 99, 114, 127
Mons Claudianus 103
Murabba'at, Wadi 3, 22, 127, 171

N
Naṣbeh, Tell en- 89, 90
Nein 171
Nessana 98
Nir Gallim 171

O
Odense 150

P
Pelusium 113
Pompeii 114, 176

Q
Qarantal 128
Qasr el-Yahud 128, 129

Qumran ix, x, 1, 3, 4, 5, 7, 8, 9, 12, 16, 17, 18, 19, 22, 23, 24, 25, 38, 45, 46, 47, 51, 52, 59, 60, 61, 62, 63, 64, 65, 67, 71, 73, 89, 91, 97, 99, 102, 103, 104, 105, 113, 115, 116, 117, 119, 122, 125, 126, 128, 135, 136, 149, 153, 154, 156, 158, 160, 163, 169, 171, 173, 175, 177, 178, 190, 200, 207, 231, 235, 237, 238, 242, 249, 252, 253, 254, 256, 257, 258
Khirbeh / Settlement 1, 2, 4, 8, 12, 17, 18, 19, 22, 23, 24, 46, 89, 90, 99, 156, 158, 256

Caves
1Q 1, 2, 3, 4, 5, 5n, 8n, 22, 23, 24, 46, 71, 97, 98, 99, 101, 103, 104, 105, 106, 115, 116, 117, 119, 120, 122, 124, 125, 148, 149, 175, 179, 185, 256, 257, 258
2Q 4, 5, 23, 46, 71, 126, 256
3Q 4, 5, 22, 23, 24, 46, 71, 73, 256
4Q 3, 4, 5n, 6, 10, 104, 125, 126, 179, 191, 252, 253, 256, 257, 258
5Q 4, 5, 6, 10, 23, 256
6Q 4, 10, 23, 24, 256
7Q 4, 5, 10, 23
8Q 4, 5, 10, 23, 125
9Q 4, 5, 10, 23, 65
10Q 1, 4, 10, 23
11Q ix, x, 1, 2, 3, 4, 5n, 7, 8, 9, 10, 11, 12, 13, 14, 15, 16, 17, 18, 19, 22, 23, 24, 25, 29, 30, 31, 32, 33, 35, 36, 37, 39, 40, 41, 42, 43, 44, 45, 46, 47, 48, 52, 57, 59, 60, 62, 63, 64, 65, 67, 68, 71, 72, 73, 75, 76, 79, 82, 87, 88, 89, 90, 94, 95, 96, 97, 98, 99, 101, 103, 104, 105, 106, 112, 113, 115, 116, 117, 119, 125, 127, 128, 129, 130, 135, 140, 141, 147, 148, 149, 151, 153, 154, 155, 156, 157, 158, 160, 161, 163, 168, 169, 175, 176, 177, 179, 180, 182, 185, 188, 190, 191, 192, 196, 199, 201, 202, 203, 216, 217, 226, 227, 228, 231, 235, 236, 240, 242, 243, 245, 249, 250, 251, 252, 253, 254, 256, 257, 258
GQ12 9, 30
GQ 39 90
A 46
B 46
P24 46, 63

R
Ramat Rahel 89, 91
Rhine 175
Rogem Żafir 98

S
Samaria 229
Scythopolis *see* Beth-Shean

T
Timnah (Tel Batash) 91
Tiberias 113

U
Umm Qatafa 91

V
Vesuvius 176

W
Wadi en-Nar (*Kidron Valley*) 148